Beyond Totalitarianism

In essays written jointly by specialists on Soviet and German history, the contributors to this book rethink and rework the nature of Stalinism and Nazism and establish a new methodology for viewing their histories that goes well beyond the now-outdated twentieth-century models of totalitarianism, ideology, and personality. Doing the labor of comparison gives us the means to ascertain the historicity of the two extraordinary regimes and the wreckage they have left. With the end of the Cold War and the collapse of the Soviet Union, scholars of Europe are no longer burdened with the political baggage that constricted research and conditioned interpretation and have access to hitherto closed archives. The time is right for a fresh look at the two gigantic dictatorships of the twentieth century and for a return to the original intent of thought on totalitarian regimes – understanding the intertwined trajectories of socialism and nationalism in European and global history.

Michael Geyer, Samuel N. Harper Professor of German and European History and director of the Human Rights Program at the University of Chicago, has a PhD from the Albert Ludwigs Universität Freiburg and was a Postdoctoral Fellow at the University of Oxford. He taught at the University of Michigan and as visiting professor in Bochum and Leipzig. He most recently wrote (with Konrad Jarausch) *Shattered Past: Reconstructing German History* and edited (with Lucian Hölscher) *Die Gegenwart Gottes in der modernen Gesellschaft* (2006). He has published extensively on the German military, war, and genocide as well as on resistance, terror, and religion. His current work focuses on defeat, nationalism, and self-destruction. He has been a Fellow at the American Academy in Berlin and the recipient of a Guggenheim Fellowship and a Humboldt Forschungspreis.

Sheila Fitzpatrick, the Bernadotte E. Schmitt Distinguished Service Professor in Modern Russian History at the University of Chicago, is the author of many books on Soviet social, cultural, and political history, including *The Russian Revolution*, *Stalin's Peasants*, *Everyday Stalinism*, and, most recently, *Tear Off the Masks! Identity and Imposture in Twentieth-Century Russia* (2005). With Robert Gellately, she edited *Accusatory Practices: Denunciation in Modern European History, 1789–1989*. A past president of the American Association for the Advancement of Slavic Studies (AAASS), she is a member of the American Academy of Arts and Sciences and the Australian Academy of the Humanities, as well as a regular contributor to the *London Review of Books*. Her current research topics include displaced persons in Europe after the Second World War. In 2008–9, she is a Fellow at the Wissenschaftskolleg in Berlin.

Beyond Totalitarianism

Stalinism and Nazism Compared

MICHAEL GEYER
University of Chicago

SHEILA FITZPATRICK
University of Chicago

CAMBRIDGE UNIVERSITY PRESS
Cambridge, New York, Melbourne, Madrid, Cape Town, Singapore,
São Paulo, Delhi, Dubai, Tokyo

Cambridge University Press
32 Avenue of the Americas, New York, NY 10013-2473, USA

www.cambridge.org
Information on this title: www.cambridge.org/9780521897969

First published 2009

A catalog record for this publication is available from the British Library

Library of Congress Cataloging in Publication data

Geyer, Michael, 1947–
Beyond totalitarianism: Stalinism and Nazism compared / Michael Geyer, Sheila Fitzpatrick.
 p. cm.
Includes bibliographical references and index.
ISBN 978-0-521-89796-9 (hardback) – ISBN 978-0-521-72397-8 (pbk.)
1. Totalitarianism.   2. Soviet Union – Politics and government.   3. Germany – Politics and
government – 1933–1945.   I. Fitzpatrick, Sheila.   II. Title.
JC480.G49   2009
320.53′2–dc22   2008013031

ISBN 978-0-521-89796-9 Hardback
ISBN 978-0-521-72397-8 Paperback

Transferred to digital printing 2010

Contents

Contributors

Jörg Baberowski is Professor of Eastern European History at the Humboldt-University Berlin. He is currently working on a book project, *Stalin: Karriere eines Gewalttäters*.

Christopher R. Browning is the Frank Porter Graham Professor of History at the University of North Carolina at Chapel Hill. Among his recent publications is *The Origins of the Final Solution: The Evolution of Nazi Jewish Policy, September 1939–March 1942* (2004).

Katerina Clark is Professor of Comparative Literature and of Slavic Languages and Literatures. She is working on a book tentatively titled *Moscow: The Fourth Rome*.

Anselm Doering-Manteuffel is Professor of Contemporary History, University of Tübingen. He is working on a book with the title *Deutsche Geschichte des 20. Jahrhunderts*.

Mark Edele is Senior Lecturer in History at the University of Western Australia. His book on Soviet Second World War veterans is due to appear from Oxford University Press.

Sheila Fitzpatrick is Bernadotte E. Schmitt Distinguished Service Professor in Modern Russian History at the University of Chicago. Her recent publications include *Tear Off the Masks! Identity and Imposture in Twentieth-Century Russia*, and she is currently working on a project on displaced persons in Germany after the Second World War.

Peter Fritzsche is Professor of History at the University of Illinois. He has just published *Life and Death in the Third Reich* (2008).

Christian Gerlach is Associate Professor of History at the University of Pittsburgh and in transition to the Professur für Zeitgeschichte at the University of Bern. His current research projects include "Extremely Violent Societies: Mass

Violence in the Twentieth Century" and "Making the Village Global: The Change of International Development Policies during the World Food Crisis, 1972–1975."

Michael Geyer is Samuel N. Harper Professor of German and European History at the University of Chicago. He is completing a book titled *Catastrophic Nationalism: Defeat and Self-destruction in Germany, 1918 and 1945.*

Yoram Gorlizki is Professor of Politics at the University of Manchester. He is currently completing two monographs, one on the Soviet justice system from 1948 to 1964 and the other, with Oleg Khlevniuk, on Soviet regional politics from 1945 to 1970.

Jochen Hellbeck is Associate Professor of History at Rutgers University. He is currently working on a study of the battle of Stalingrad as it was experienced on the ground level on both sides of the front.

David L. Hoffmann is Professor of History at The Ohio State University. He is currently completing a monograph entitled *Cultivating the Masses: Soviet Social Interventionism in Its International Context, 1914–1939.*

Alf Lüdtke is Professor of Historical Anthropology at the University of Erfurt and Research Fellow of the Max-Planck-Institute for the Study of Religious and Ethnical Diversity in Göttingen. He is currently completing a book project titled *Work: Production and Destruction. Vignettes on the 20th Century.*

Hans Mommsen is Professor Emeritus of Modern History at the Ruhr-University Bochum. His numerous publications on the Weimar Republic, the Third Reich, and Democratic Socialism include *The Rise and Fall of the Weimar Democracy, Alternatives to Hitler,* and *From Weimar to Auschwitz.*

Karl Schlögel is Professor of East European History at the Europa Universität Viadrina in Frankfurt/Oder. Among his recent publications are the edited volumes *Sankt Petersburg: Schauplätze eine Stadtgeschichte* and *Oder-Odra: Blicke auf einen europäischen Strom* and the paperback edition of *Berlin Ostbahnhof Europas: Russen und Deutsche in ihrem Jahrhundert* (all 2007).

Lewis H. Siegelbaum is Professor of History at Michigan State University. His most recent publication is *Cars for Comrades: The Life of the Soviet Automobile.*

Annette F. Timm is Assistant Professor of History at the University of Calgary, Alberta, Canada. She is in the process of publishing a monograph tentatively entitled *The Politics of Fertility in Twentieth-Century Berlin: Sexual Citizenship in Marriage Counseling and Venereal Disease Control.*

Nicolas Werth is Directeur de recherche at the CNRS (Centre National de la Recherche Scientifique) in Paris, at the Institut d'Histoire du Temps Présent. He is author of *Cannibal Island: Death in a Siberian Gulag, La Terreur et le Désarroi: Staline et son système,* and *Les Années Staline.*

Acknowledgments

This project was originally conceived as a joint undertaking by the two editors and Terry Martin (co-organizer 2002–3). Our plan was to gather two sets of experts, one on German history and the other on Soviet history, and pair them in the study of particular aspects of the Nazi-Stalinist comparison. Papers were to be jointly written and presented to the whole group at workshops and conferences to be held over a period of several years. The first two meetings were held in Cambridge on May 3–5, 2002, and May 2–4, 2003, and the third and fourth in Chicago on April 30–May 2, 2004, and May 20–21, 2005. The core group of participants, authors of the studies published in this volume, attended all four meetings. Other attendees at single meetings were Robert Gellately, Julie Hessler, Peter Holquist, Oleg Khlevniuk, Cornelia Rauh-Kühne, and Ronald Grigor Suny. Mark Edele joined the project as Michael Geyer's coauthor in 2007.

The project was made possible by generous support from the Davis Center for Russian Studies at Harvard, the University of Chicago, and the Andrew W. Mellon Foundation, through its 2002 Distinguished Achievement Award to Sheila Fitzpatrick. Warm thanks for organizational and practical support are due to Helen Grigoriev and Ann Sjostedt of the Davis Center and Emma Gilligan at the University of Chicago.

The editors thank the Modern European History Workshop of the University of Chicago and the Midwest Russian Historians' Workshop, held at De Paul University in October 2004, for helpful discussion of earlier drafts of the Introduction. We would also like to acknowledge the research assistance of Leah Goldberg and Barry Haneberg in translating and editing parts of the manuscript. Kimba Tichenor did invaluable work as the main editorial and research assistant during the last stages of the project. We are particularly grateful for the comments of the two anonymous readers for Cambridge University Press and for the support of two dedicated editors at the Press, Eric Crahan and Lewis Bateman.

Beyond Totalitarianism

I

Introduction

After Totalitarianism – Stalinism and Nazism Compared

Michael Geyer with assistance from Sheila Fitzpatrick

The idea of comparing Nazi Germany with the Soviet Union under Stalin is not a novel one. Notwithstanding some impressive efforts of late, however, the endeavor has achieved only limited success.[1] Where comparisons have been made, the two histories seem to pass each other like trains in the night. That is, while there is some sense that they cross paths and, hence, share a time and place – if, indeed, it is not argued that they mimic each other in a deleterious war[2] – little else seems to fit. And this is quite apart from those approaches which, on principle, deny any similarity because they consider Nazism and Stalinism to be at opposite ends of the political spectrum. Yet, despite the very real difficulties inherent in comparing the two regimes and an irreducible political resistance against such comparison, attempts to establish their commonalities have never ceased – not least as a result of the inclination to place both regimes in opposition to Western, "liberal" traditions. More often than not, comparison of Stalinism and Nazism worked by way of implicating a third party – the United States.[3] Whatever the differences between them, they appeared small in comparison with the chasm that separated them from liberal-constitutional states and free societies. Since a three-way comparison

---

[1] Alan Bullock, *Hitler and Stalin: Parallel Lives* (London: HarperCollins, 1991); Ian Kershaw and Moshe Lewin, eds., *Stalinism and Nazism: Dictatorships in Comparison* (Cambridge: Cambridge University Press, 1977); Henry Rousso, ed., *Stalinisme et nazisme: Histoire et mémoire comparées* (Paris: Éditions Complexe, 1999); English translation by Lucy Golvan et al., *Stalinism and Nazism* (Lincoln: University of Nebraska Press, 2004); Richard J. Overy, *The Dictators: Hitler's Germany and Stalin's Russia* (New York: W. W. Norton, 2004); Robert Gellately, *Lenin, Stalin, and Hitler: The Age of Social Catastrophe* (New York: Alfred A. Knopf, 2007).

[2] Klaus Jochen Arnold, *Die Wehrmacht und die Besatzungspolitik in den besetzten Gebieten der Sowjetunion: Kriegführung und Radikalisierung im "Unternehmen Barbarossa"* (Berlin: Duncker & Humblot, 2004).

[3] François Furet and Ernst Nolte, *"Feindliche Nähe": Kommunismus und Faschismus im 20. Jahrhundert* (Munich: F. A. Herbig, 1998).

I

might entail associating liberal democracy with its opposite, if only by bridging the chasm between them through the act of comparison, this procedure was commonly shunned – or deliberately used to suggest that, despite it all, the three regimes were not so far apart.[4]

This state of affairs is not good, especially considering that the material conditions for the comparative enterprise have markedly changed. For the first time historians are able to approach Nazism and Stalinism on a relatively level playing field. One may legitimately argue that historians did not take part in the first round of comparisons, a round dominated by philosophers, social scientists, and public intellectuals.[5] Since that time, however, we have accumulated sufficient primary and secondary source materials to merit a serious comparison of the two regimes. Moreover, the historiography on both regimes has grown quite large – massive and overwhelming for Nazi Germany and growing prodigiously for the Soviet Union – and is generally accessible to researchers. Comparison is now a matter of doing it – and doing it intelligently and productively.

It turns out that this is easier said than done. For one thing, thought on totalitarianism always seems to intrude, regardless of what the editors think about the concept's usefulness (on which matter they disagree). It intrudes because the concept is so deeply embedded in how historians grapple with and understand the two regimes.[6] Second, comparison proves to be a remarkably obstreperous exercise.[7] While it is easy enough to identify common turf, such as the political regime or everyday practices, it is far more difficult to make the comparison happen in actual fact. As a result, the attempt of understanding Nazi Germany and the Stalinist Soviet Union as distinct regimes is often sidetracked into an effort to better understand each other's histories. Of course, familiarity with each other's national history is a bonus. If anything, it helps to penetrate the idiosyncrasies of national historiographies.[8] But comparative history ought to add more value for the exertion of doing it, if it is to matter.

---

[4] Johan Galtung, *Hitlerismus, Stalinismus, Reaganismus: Drei Variationen zu einem Thema von Orwell* (Baden-Baden: Nomos, 1987).

[5] Alfons Söllner, Ralf Walkenhaus, and Karin Wieland, eds., *Totalitarismus, eine Ideengeschichte des 20. Jahrhunderts* (Berlin: Akademie Verlag, 1997); Hans J. Lietzmann, *Politikwissenschaft im "Zeitalter der Diktaturen": Die Entwicklung der Totalitarismustheorie Carl Joachim Friedrichs* (Opladen: Westdeutscher Verlag, 1999); Mike Schmeitzner, ed., *Totalitarismuskritik von Links: Deutsche Diskurse im 20. Jahrhundert* (Göttingen: Vandenhoeck & Ruprecht, 2007).

[6] As far as Germany is concerned, every historian of stature dealt with the issue at one point or another. Manfred Funke, ed., *Totalitarismus: Ein Studien-Reader zur Herrschaftsanalyse moderner Diktaturen* (Düsseldorf: Droste, 1978); Eckhard Jesse, Christiane Schroeder, and Thomas Grosse-Gehling, eds., *Totalitarismus im 20. Jahrhundert: eine Bilanz der internationalen Forschung*, 2nd enlarged ed. (Baden-Baden: Nomos, 1999).

[7] Deborah Cohen and Maura O'Connor, eds., *Comparison and History: Europe in Cross-National Perspective* (New York: Routledge, 2004).

[8] Jürgen Kocka, "Asymmetrical Historical Comparison: The Case of the German Sonderweg," *History and Theory* 38, no. 1 (1999): 40–50.

Compared to the grander projects of, say, "thinking the twentieth century," this is down-to-earth stuff.[9] But it is of consequence. For in wrestling with Nazism and Stalinism in joint Russian-German essays, the contributors to this book have laid bare what does and does not work. In a progression of labors and discussions in the manner of a *pilotage à vue*, they defined the nature of the two regimes and the two societies more clearly, such that, after a first round of totalitarian theorizing, we can now begin to think historically about Stalinism and Nazism.[10] Moreover, the contributors identify the difficulties inherent in a comparison that is more than the assemblage of like parts and, thus, provided insight into the epochal nature of the two regimes by way of indirection. We might want to see in this a return to the original intent of thought on totalitarian regimes – understanding the intertwined trajectories of socialism and nationalism.[11] More assuredly, doing the labor of comparison gives us the means to ascertain the historicity of the two extraordinary regimes and the wreckage they have left. The latter has become an ever more important challenge as Europe and the United States are making efforts to leave behind the twentieth century.[12]

THE WAYS OF "TOTALITARIANISM"

The terms "totalitarian" and "totalitarianism" entered political debate in the 1920s, primarily in reference to Italian fascism.[13] They moved into academic

[9] François Furet, *Le passé d'une illusion: Essai sur l'idée communiste au XXe siècle* (Paris: R. Laffont: Calmann-Lévy, 1995); Eric J. Hobsbawm, *The Age of Extremes: A History of the World, 1914–1991* (New York: Pantheon Books, 1994); Mark Mazower, *Dark Continent: Europe's Twentieth Century* (New York: Random House, 1999); Moishe Postone and Eric L. Santner, eds., *Catastrophe and Meaning: The Holocaust and the Twentieth Century* (Chicago: University of Chicago Press, 2003); Dan Diner, *Das Jahrhundert verstehen: Eine universalhistorische Deutung* (Munich: Luchterhand, 1999); Bernard Wasserstein, *Barbarism and Civilization: A History of Europe in Our Time* (Oxford and New York: Oxford University Press, 2007).

[10] Wacław Długoborski, "Das Problem des Vergleichs von Nationalsozialismus und Stalinismus," in *Lager, Zwangsarbeit, Vertreibung und Deportation: Dimensionen der Massenverbrechen in der Sowjetunion und in Deutschland 1933 bis 1945*, eds. Dittmar Dahlmann and Gerhard Hirschfeld (Essen: Klartext, 1999), 19–29; Dietrich Beyrau, "Nationalsozialistisches Regime und Stalin System: Ein riskanter Vergleich," *Osteuropa: Zeitschrift für Gegenwartsfragen des Ostens* 50, no. 6 (2000): 709–20.

[11] Roman Szporluk, *Communism and Nationalism: Karl Marx versus Friedrich List* (New York: Oxford University Press, 1988).

[12] Ira Katznelson, *Desolation and Enlightenment: Political Knowledge after Total War, Totalitarianism, and the Holocaust* (New York: Columbia University Press, 2003).

[13] Michael Halberstam, *Totalitarianism and the Modern Conception of Politics* (New Haven, CT: Yale University Press, 1999); Wolfgang Wippermann, *Totalitarismustheorien: Die Entwicklung der Diskussion von den Anfängen bis heute* (Darmstadt: Primus Verlag, 1997); Karl Schlögel, "Archäologie totaler Herrschaft," in *Deutschland und die Russische Revolution, 1917–1924*, eds. Gerd Koenen and Lew Kopelew (Munich: W. Fink Verlag, 1998), 780–804. On left totalitarianism: William David Jones, *The Lost Debate: German Socialist Intellectuals and Totalitarianism* (Urbana: University of Illinois Press, 1999); Uli Schöler, "Frühe totalitarismustheoretische

debate in the late 1940s and 1950s with a distinct focus on Germany. They gained popular and academic currency during the Cold War, mostly in reference to the Soviet Union.[14] Concurrently, they became a staple of secondary and postsecondary teaching and of media debate with works like Arthur Koestler's *Darkness at Noon* and, more prominently, George Orwell's *1984*, which made the image of the ideologically driven, mind-altering police state pervasive.[15] In popular parlance, totalitarianism lumped together the two most prominent European dictatorships of the 1930s and 1940s, Nazi Germany and the Stalinist Soviet Union, as expressions of absolute evil rather than any particular form of rule.[16] The two regimes were juxtaposed with the "righteous" path of liberal democracy, both as a way of life and as a form of governance.

As a polemical term in political debate and in academic controversy, we may also recall that "totalitarianism" stood in sharp opposition to "fascism." The latter initially served as a self-description for Italian fascists and their European imitators (including some early National Socialists). But left-wing intellectuals appropriated the term in the 1930s. Unlike the concept of totalitarianism, which linked together the dictatorships of the left and right during the first half of the twentieth century, the notion of fascism set them apart. Fascism referred exclusively to right-radical, ultranationalist movements and states. Fascism briefly dominated academic debate in the 1960s and 1970s. The academic notion of fascism, however, collapsed under the combined weight of left-wing political dogmatism and the pervasive discrediting of leftist thought during the last quarter of the twentieth century and is only just now resurfacing.[17]

Initially, historians – and, especially, German historians – showed considerable enthusiasm for the ideas of totalitarianism and, to a lesser degree, fascism. They generally held the first-generation master thinkers of totalitarianism, like Hannah Arendt or Carl Friedrich, in high regard.[18] They certainly had Carl

Ansätze der Menschewiki im Exil," *Beiträge zur Geschichte der Arbeiterbewegung* 38, no. 2 (1996): 32–47.

[14] Abbott Gleason, *Totalitarianism: The Inner History of the Cold War* (New York and Oxford: Oxford University Press, 1995).

[15] Arthur Koestler, *Darkness at Noon* (New York: Random House, 1941); George Orwell, *1984: A Novel* (London: Secker & Warburg, 1949).

[16] Dieter Nelles, "Jan Valtins 'Tagebuch der Hölle': Legende und Wirklichkeit eines Schlüsselromans der Totalitarismustheorie," *1999: Zeitschrift für Sozialgeschichte des 20. und 21. Jahrhunderts* 9, no. 1 (1994): 11–45.

[17] Wolfgang Wippermann, *Faschismustheorien: Zum Stand der gegenwärtigen Diskussion*, 5th rev. ed. (Darmstadt: Wissenschaftliche Buchgesellschaft, 1976); Sven Reichardt, "Was mit dem Faschismus passiert ist: Ein Literaturbericht zur internationalen Faschismusforschung seit 1990, Teil I," *Neue politische Literatur* 49, no. 3 (2004): 385–406; Sven Reichardt and Armin Nolzen, eds., *Faschismus in Italien und Deutschland: Studien zu Transfer und Vergleich* (Göttingen: Wallstein Verlag, 2005); Roger Griffin, Werner Loh, and Andreas Umland, eds., *Fascism Past and Present, West and East: An International Debate on Concepts and Cases in the Comparative Study of the Extrreme Right* (Stuttgart: Ibidem-Verlag, 2006).

[18] Hannah Arendt, *The Origins of Totalitarianism*, new ed. (New York: Harcourt, Brace, and World, 1966); Carl J. Friedrich and Zbigniew Brzezinski, *Totalitarian Dictatorship and Autocracy* (Cambridge, MA: Harvard University Press, 1956).

Schmidt to contend with.[19] In hindsight, it also appears that, wittingly or unwittingly, some of the best early works of historians originated out of their struggles with "theory." Karl-Dietrich Bracher's monumental studies on the Third Reich worked through Friedrich's legacy and were picked up by others, like Eberhard Jäckel, who highlighted the ideological motivation of the Nazi regime.[20] Martin Broszat's and Hans Mommsen's structural-functional interpretation of the Nazi regime's radicalizing trajectory represented a creative adaptation and transformation of Arendt's complex reading of totalitarianism that hinged on the inherent instability and the (self-perceived) lack of legitimacy of these regimes.[21] Timothy Mason's widely admired attempts to escape the strictures of a dead-end German debate that pitted intentionalists (Bracher) against structuralists (Broszat) were deeply influenced by his struggles with Marxist-Leninist orthodoxy and his attempt to resuscitate nonorthodox theories of fascism.[22]

One of the more curious reasons for the difficulty in evaluating the specific impact of theories of totalitarianism on German historiography was that thought on totalitarianism – or really on National Socialism – was so diverse. Those who found Arendt too flamboyantly intellectual and Friedrich too rigidly social scientific always had the option of choosing as their point of reference Fraenkel's *Dual State,* with its emphasis on the law, or Neumann's *Behemoth,* with its interest in monopoly capitalism, not to mention the further reaches of Critical Theory and the studies in prejudice that produced the "authoritarian

---

[19] Carl Schmitt, *Die Diktatur: Von den Anfängen des modernen Souveränitätsgedankens bis zum proletarischen Klassenkampf,* 2nd ed. (Munich and Leipzig: Duncker & Humblot, 1928); Jan-Werner Müller, *A Dangerous Mind: Carl Schmitt in Post-War European Thought* (New Haven, CT: Yale University Press, 2003).

[20] Karl Dietrich Bracher, *The German Dictatorship: The Origins, Structure, and Effects of National Socialism* (New York: Praeger, 1970); Karl Dietrich Bracher, *Zeitgeschichtliche Kontroversen: Um Faschismus, Totalitarismus, Demokratie* (Munich: Piper, 1976); Karl Dietrich Bracher, *The Age of Ideologies: A History of Political Thought in the Twentieth Century* (New York: St. Martin's Press, 1984); Eberhard Jäckel, *Hitler's Weltanschauung: A Blueprint for Power* (Middletown, CT: Wesleyan University Press, 1972).

[21] Martin Broszat, *Der Nationalsozialismus; Weltanschauung, Programm und Wirklichkeit* (Stuttgart: Deutsche Verlags-Anstalt, 1960); Martin Broszat, *Der Staat Hitlers; Grundlegung und Entwicklung seiner inneren Verfassung* (Munich: Deutscher Taschenbuch Verlag, 1969); Martin Broszat, *The Hitler State: The Foundation and Development of the Internal Structure of the Third Reich,* trans. John W. Hiden (London and New York: Longman, 1981); Hans Mommsen. "[Introduction] Hannah Arendt und der Prozeß gegen Adolf Eichmann," *Eichmann in Jerusalem: Ein Bericht von der Banalität des Bösen,* ed. Hannah Arendt (Munich and Zürich: Piper, 1986), I–XXXVII; Hans Mommsen, "The Concept of Totalitarian Dictatorship vs. the Comparative Theory of Fascism: The Case of National Socialism," in *Totalitarianism Reconsidered,* ed. Ernest A. Menze (Port Washington, NY: Kennikat Press, 1981), 146–66.

[22] Timothy Mason, "Intention and Explanation: A Current Controversy about the Interpretation of National Socialism," in *Der "Führerstaat," Mythos und Realität: Studien zur Struktur und Politik des Dritten Reiches = The "Führer State," Myth and Reality: Studies on the Structure and Politics of the Third Reich,* eds. Lothar Kettenacker and Gerhard Hirschfeld (Stuttgart: Klett-Cotta, 1981), 23–72.

personality."[23] Moreover, there were always those who traced their lineage back to theories of political religion, for whom Voegelin's 1939 treatise on *Die politischen Religionen,* Raymond Aron's less well remembered piece on the "Arrival of Secular Religions" in 1944, and Guardini's little book on the *Heilbringer* of 1946 offered useful points of departure.[24] More recently, Karl Popper seems to be making a comeback.[25] The point is that German historiography evolved out of contemporary thought on National Socialism, which itself derived from older, competing intellectual traditions; it was, for the most part, mediated by émigré intellectuals.[26] Their knowledge of the Soviet Union and its historiography was virtually nonexistent. German thought on totalitarianism was single-mindedly national despite interwar entendres[27] – an ironic move further exacerbated by the fact that the only thing that all totalitarian theorists agreed upon (and this separated their theories from ordinary or "vulgar" Marxist theories of fascism) was that National Socialism formed in one way or another an exceptional regime.

Compared to the "theoretical" excitement and the universalizing intellectual horizon of the German debate, Soviet studies was more indebted to politics and to political-science formalism, mechanically reproducing Friedrich's and Zbigniew Brzezinki's infamous six characteristics of totalitarianism.[28] The latter focused research on party structure, "levers of control," ideology, propaganda, and the leadership cult, as well as on police and labor camps, and imposed, at least in the view of its detractors, an insufferable straitjacket on Soviet studies in the first postwar decades. In actuality, however, there was a significant amount of interdisciplinary work, most notably the big Harvard Project

---

[23] Ernst Fraenkel et al., *The Dual State: A Contribution to the Theory of Dictatorship* (New York and London: Oxford University Press, 1941). Among the other authors of the above text was Edward Shils. Franz L. Neumann, *Behemoth: The Structure and Practice of National Socialism* (Toronto and New York: Oxford University Press, 1942); Theodor W. Adorno et al., *The Authoritarian Personality,* 1st ed. (New York: Harper & Row, 1950).

[24] Eric Voegelin, *Die politischen Religionen* (Stockholm: Bermann-Fischer Verlag, 1939); Eric Voegelin et al., eds., *Politische Religion? Politik, Religion und Anthropologie im Werk von Eric Voegelin* (Munich: Fink, 2003); Leo Strauss and Eric Voegelin, *Faith and Political Philosophy: The Correspondence between Leo Strauss and Eric Voegelin, 1934–1964,* trans. Peter Emberley and Barry Cooper (University Park: Pennsylvania State University Press, 1993); Raymond Aron, "L'avenir des religions séculières [1944]," *Commentaire* 8, no. 28–9 (1985): 369–83; Romano Guardini, *Der Heilbringer in Mythos, Offenbarung und Politik: Eine theologisch-politische Besinnung* (Stuttgart: Deutsche Verlags-Anstalt, 1946).

[25] Karl Raimund Popper, *The Open Society and Its Enemies,* 2 vols. (London: G. Routledge & Sons, 1945); Marc-Pierre Möll, *Gesellschaft und totalitäre Ordnung: Eine theoriegeschichtliche Auseinandersetzung mit dem Totalitarismus* (Baden-Baden: Nomos, 1998); I. C. Jarvie and Sandra Pralong, eds., *Popper's Open Society after Fifty Years: The Continuing Relevance of Karl Popper* (London; New York: Routledge, 1999).

[26] Anson Rabinbach, "Moments of Totalitarianism," *History & Theory* 45 (2006): 72–100.

[27] Karl Eimermacher, Astrid Volpert, and Gennadij A. Bordiugov, *Stürmische Aufbrüche und enttäuschte Hoffnungen: Russen und Deutsche in der Zwischenkriegszeit* (Munich: W. Fink, 2006).

[28] Friedrich and Brzezinski, *Totalitarian Dictatorship and Autocracy.*

headed by Alex Inkeles, Raymond A. Bauer, and Clyde Kluckhohn that combined political scientists with sociologists, anthropologists, and even psychologists.[29] The contributors to the Harvard Project were interested in the totalitarian model as a way of understanding political structures and processes as, for example, in *How the Soviet System Works*.[30] However, they were equally interested in everyday life, seen through the prism of modernization theory. Indeed, modernization theory was highly influential in the development of U.S. Sovietology. Thus, in *The Soviet Citizen: Daily Life in a Totalitarian Society*, Inkeles and his collaborators implicitly compared the Soviet Union both with other modernizing states, like Japan and Turkey, and with states that had already modernized, like Britain and Germany.[31] If you learned your Sovietology in the 1960s, you were almost as likely to develop an interest in modernization theory as in totalitarianism, given that Barrington Moore held more sway over first-generation totalitarian theorists than either Friedrich or Brzezinski.

In the 1970s, the challenge to the totalitarian model by political scientists like Jerry Hough placed the early Soviet experience (from the Revolution at least up to the Second World War) firmly in the context of modernization and eschewed the Nazi-Soviet comparison because of its Cold War politicization. From the 1960s to the 1980s, another comparison, deeply unsettling to many, lurked on the fringes of political scientists' discussion of the Soviet political system – the comparison with the United States. For some, this comparison was based on ideas of gradual but inexorable convergence of the two systems as the Soviet Union modernized.[32] For others, the point of the comparison was to find out how well Western social-science categories, like "interest groups" and "participation" (usually derived from U.S. experience, but claiming universal applicability), applied to the Soviet situation.[33] For a third group from the New Left, it was to convey an understanding that the United States was, in its own way, "totalitarian."[34]

---

[29] For a description of the project, see Alex Inkeles and Raymond Bauer, *The Soviet Citizen: Daily Life in a Totalitarian Society* (Cambridge, MA: Harvard University Press, 1959), 3–20.

[30] Raymond A. Bauer, Alex Inkeles, and Clyde Kluckhohn, *How the Soviet System Works: Cultural, Psychological, and Social Themes* (Cambridge, MA: Harvard University Press, 1956).

[31] Inkeles and Bauer, *The Soviet Citizen*.

[32] "Convergence" of Soviet and Western systems was much discussed, first by economists and then by political scientists; most Sovietologists, especially those in political science, took a critical stance. See the exchange of opinions in the Congress for Cultural Freedom journal *Survey* no. 47 (April 1963), 36–42; Alfred G. Meyer, "Theories of Convergence" in *Change in Communist Systems*, ed. Chalmers Johnson (Stanford, CA: Stanford University Press, 1970), 36–42; Daniel Nelson, "Political Convergence: An Empirical Assessment," *World Politics* 30, no. 3 (1978), 411–32.

[33] Jerry F. Hough, *The Soviet Union and Social Science Theory* (Cambridge, MA: Harvard University Press, 1977).

[34] Herbert Marcuse, *One Dimensional Man: Studies in the Ideology of Advanced Society* (Boston: Beacon Press, 1964) and id., "Repressive Tolerance," in Robert Paul Wolff, Barrington Moore Jr., and Herbert Marcuse, *A Critique of Pure Tolerance* (Boston: Beacon Press, 1965), 95–137.

All of this happened not so long ago; yet these debates sound as if they occurred on a different planet. The intensity of the debate and the vitriol expended and, not least, the blinders that some academics wore have now become subjects of a history in their own right. These academics produced distinctive histories and theories, all written within the penumbra of World War II and the Cold War and ineluctably marked by these wars.[35] Their import at the time is perhaps as striking as their ephemeral nature today. The debates on fascism and on totalitarianism were part and parcel of a receding world of the twentieth century, which in hindsight appears as tantalizing as it is remote.

If historians were divided about the merits of theories of totalitarianism, they have been even less enthusiastic about using totalitarianism as an analytical tool.[36] They found that the totalitarian model – with its claim of a monolithic, efficient state and of a dogmatically held, mind-altering ideology – did not describe, much less explain, historic reality. It appeared as an overly mechanistic model foisted upon them by political scientists. Time and again, historians have come away disenchanted from the concept because it proved unhelpful in articulating new research questions and in organizing empirical findings. Moreover, with the deescalation of the Cold War in the context of East-West détente, the time seemed right to leave behind concepts and ideas that had a distinctly polemical, if not outright ideological, quality. Empirical historians, in particular, came to consider terms and concepts like totalitarianism contaminated by their Cold War exploitation.[37]

Therefore, the demobilization of militant and militarized European politics during the last quarter of the twentieth century provided an unusual opening for empirical historians. Whatever grander ambitions may have driven them, they have since had their way for thirty-odd years, free from all manner of ideological and theoretical entanglements. German historians were much better off, as they had open access to archives and have systematically used them since the 1970s. Soviet historians, by contrast, have had and continue to have more difficulties, but they have made tremendous strides in the past decade and a half. Historians now know a great deal more about Nazism and Stalinism than was ever known before and most of their findings have been tested repeatedly against an ever broader stream of sources. This research-oriented, scholarly community remains, for the most part, in a posttheoretical and posttotalitarian mode.

---

[35] Abbott Gleason, *Totalitarianism: The Inner History of the Cold War* (New York and Oxford: Oxford University Press, 1995).

[36] Typically Ian Kershaw, "Totalitarianism Revisited: Nazism and Stalinism in Comparative Perspective," *Tel Aviver Jahrbuch für deutsche Geschichte* 33 (1994): 23–40; Ian Kershaw, *The Nazi Dictatorship: Problems and Perspectives of Interpretation* (London and New York: Arnold, 2000).

[37] Institut für Zeitgeschichte, ed., *Totalitarismus und Faschismus: Eine wissenschaftliche und politische Begriffskontroverse: Kolloquium im Institut für Zeitgeschichte am 24. November 1978* (Munich and Vienna: Oldenbourg, 1980).

There is much disagreement, even between the editors, whether or not this is a good state of affairs. But in the end, the tempers and bents of historians are neither here nor there. For whether coming from a more theoretical or a more empirical end, all historians have rediscovered the immensity of the mountain that they set out to scale. Whatever else may be said about Nazi Germany and the Stalinist Soviet Union, they were two immensely powerful, threatening, and contagious dictatorships that for a long moment in a short century threatened to turn the world upside down. Empirical historians mainly worked over and disposed of older concepts and ideas of totalitarianism (and, for that matter, of fascism), but their own research only made the two regimes stand out even more clearly. Hence, making sense of the Stalinist Soviet Union and Nazi Germany, with the much expanded empirical work at hand, has become of paramount importance. These two regimes may be the grand losers of twentieth-century history, but they exerted tremendous power over the century nonetheless – and continue to do so long after their defeat and collapse, respectively.

Telling metaphors were coined for this condition – Europe was a *Dark Continent* in an *Age of Extremes*.[38] But despite a tremendous wealth of research, neither of the two historiographies ever managed to sustain such encompassing metaphors, let alone employ them productively. History has for the most part remained national – and devoid of grand narratives or grand explanations. Unfortunately, this leaves us with an empirical history that is, by and large, parochial despite its broader ambitions. There is a price to pay for this self-limitation. With few exceptions, Soviet and German historians have not studied each other's work, although they have eyed each other from a distance, never quite losing the sense and sensibility that in a better and more transparent world, in which everyone knew each other's history, they might actually learn from one another – and in learning from one another might possibly achieve a better understanding of the tremendous fear and awe that both the Stalinist and the Nazi regimes elicited in their time.[39] Although historians have grown tired of the shackles imposed on their work by the concept of totalitarianism and the political debates over fascism and totalitarianism, they have also increasingly realized that the two national historiographies have to move toward each other, because, for one, antagonists as the two regimes were, they were quite literally on each other's throat and, for another, they shook the world in their antagonism. This may not be enough to make them of the same kind,[40] but it is surely enough to see them in tandem and in interaction – and to explore what they might have in common.

---

[38] See ftn 9.

[39] Tony Judt, *Past Imperfect: French Intellectuals, 1944–1956* (Berkeley: University of California Press, 1992); Julian Bourg, *After the Deluge: New Perspectives on the Intellectual and Cultural History of Postwar France* (Lanham, MD: Lexington Books, 2004); Jan-Werner Müller, *German Ideologies since 1945: Studies in the Political Thought and Culture of the Bonn Republic* (New York: Palgrave Macmillan, 2003).

[40] Leonid Luks, "Bolschewismus, Faschismus, Nationalsozialismus – Verwandte Gegner," *Geschichte und Gesellschaft* 14, no. 1 (1988): 96–115.

The project of seeing the two regimes together – its scope and its method, as well as its thematic framework – has yet to be determined. In fact, despite a number of recent studies, the very nature of the challenge remains undefined. For what is at stake is not, as it may appear at first glance, the validity of the old debates, but an effort to make historical sense of the twentieth century; and, one of the crucial touchstones of this endeavor is making sense of Nazi Germany and the Soviet Union, a task yet to be accomplished, in history, as well as of the contemporary intellectual controversies they elicited.[41]

The scholarly enterprise of historians, however, is one thing; historical trends are quite another. Whether historians like it or not, reflections on totalitarianism have been rekindled in recent years. Initially, the revival of totalitarianism could be seen primarily as a French (liberal, pro-Western) preoccupation with exorcizing the specter of late Marxism among its intellectuals and as a German as well as British (conservative) effort to provide an antidote to a dominant, social-scientific understanding of Nazism and Stalinism.[42] It has, perhaps more importantly, been encouraged by the rise of "people's power" – democracy – as a European and global phenomenon.[43] The collapse of the Soviet Union, in turn, has led to intriguing conversions – and has created some strange bedfellows.[44] Last but not least, the link between religious fundamentalism and

[41] Michael Rowe, *Collaboration and Resistance in Napoleonic Europe: State Formation in an Age of Upheaval, c. 1800–1815* (Basingstoke and New York: Palgrave Macmillan, 2003).

[42] Guy Hermet, Pierre Hassner, and Jacques Rupnik, eds., *Totalitarismes* (Paris: Economica, 1984); Léon Poliakov and Jean-Pierre Cabestan, *Les totalitarismes du XXe siècle: Un phénomène historique dépassé?* (Paris: Fayard, 1987); Stéphane Courtois, ed., *Une si longue nuit: L'apogé des régimes totalitaires en Europe, 1935–1953* (Monaco: Rocher, 2003); Michael Scott Christofferson, *French Intellectuals against the Left: The Antitotalitarian Moment of the 1970's* (New York: Berghahn Books, 2004); Uwe Backes and Eckhard Jesse, eds., *Totalitarismus, Extremismus, Terrorismus: Ein Literaturführer und Wegweiser zur Extremismusforschung in der Bundesrepublik Deutschland*, 2nd rev. ed. (Opladen: Leske + Budrich, 1985); Uwe Backes, Eckhard Jesse, and Rainer Zitelmann, eds., *Die Schatten der Vergangenheit: Impulse zur Historisierung des Nationalsozialismus* (Frankfurt am Main: Propyläen, 1990); Hermann Lübbe, and Wladyslaw Bartosyewski, eds., *Heilserwartung und Terror: Politische Religionen im 20. Jahrhundert* (Düsseldorf: Patmos, 1995); Horst Möller, ed., *Der rote Holocaust und die Deutschen: Die Debatte um das "Schwarzbuch des Kommunismus"* (Munich and Zurich: Piper, 1999); Michael Burleigh, *The Third Reich: A New History* (New York: Hill & Wang, 2000).

[43] Guillermo A. O'Donnell, Philippe C. Schmitter, and Laurence Whitehead, eds., *Transitions from Authoritarian Rule: Comparative Perspectives* (Baltimore: Johns Hopkins University Press, 1986); Juan J. Linz and Alfred C. Stepan, eds., *Problems of Democratic Transition and Consolidation: Southern Europe, South America, and Post-Communist Europe* (Baltimore: Johns Hopkins University Press, 1996); Achim Siegel, ed., *Totalitarismustheorien nach dem Ende des Kommunismus* (Cologne: Böhlau, 1998).

[44] Ferenc Fehér and Agnes Heller, *Eastern Left, Western Left: Totalitarianism, Freedom, and Democracy* (Atlantic Highlands, NJ: Humanities Press International, 1987); Wolfgang Kraushaar, *Linke Geisterfahrer: Denkanstösse für eine antitotalitäre Linke* [with an introduction by Daniel Cohn-Bendit] (Frankfurt am Main: Verlag neue Kritik, 2001); Slavoj Žižek, *Did Somebody Say Totalitarianism?* (London; New York: Verso, 2001).

terror has added buzz to the old formula.[45] Again, we note the heterogeneity of initiatives that insist on the need for a new round of thinking on totalitarianism.

In the German context, the initial impetus – often under the rubric of the comparative study of dictatorships – originated out of the attempt to integrate the East German regime into German history.[46] The notion of two dictatorships, a National Socialist and a Communist one, counterbalancing the relentless and ultimately successful Westernization and democratization of (West) Germany seemed plausible.[47] The latter meant de-exceptionalizing and, in a way, normalizing the Third Reich, even if only fringe groups doubted the extreme character of Nazism.[48] This internal German debate on the two dictatorships is particularly intriguing, as it quickly came to define the most salient effort to revitalize thought on totalitarianism. This effort is best known for rediscovering and highlighting "ideology" as a key component of Nazism (and Stalinism).[49] The novel interest in ideology led to a debate on political religion or religious politics and, more generally, various gestures in the direction of political theology.[50] The return to "ideology" developed in tandem with an approach that emphasized extreme forms of violence and terror, motivated less by interest than by principle and, hence, by reference to some higher law – be it extreme nationalism or a religious kind of belief or any other fundamentalism.[51]

The extreme violence of totalitarianism is also what exercised American scholars, public intellectuals, and pundits. The most productive area of engagement has been the field of genocide studies.[52] But the main push came from

---

[45] Michael Burleigh, *Sacred Causes: The Clash of Religion and Politics, from the Great War to the War on Terror*, 1st U.S. ed. (New York: HarperCollins, 2007).

[46] Günther Heydemann and Eckhard Jesse, eds., *Diktaturvergleich als Herausforderung: Theorie und Praxis* (Berlin: Duncker & Humblot, 1998).

[47] Hans Wilhelm Vahlefeld, *Deutschlands totalitäre Tradition: Nationalsozialismus und SED-Sozialismus als politische Religionen* (Stuttgart: Klett-Cotta, 2002).

[48] Backes et al., *Schatten der Vergangenheit*, ftn 31.

[49] Alfons Söllner, "Totalitarismus: Eine notwendige Denkfigur des 20. Jahrhunderts," *Mittelweg* 36, no. 2 (1993): 83–8.

[50] Hans Maier, *Politische Religionen: Die totalitären Regime und das Christentum* (Freiburg: Herder Verlag, 1995); Hans Maier, ed., *Totalitarismus und politische Religionen: Konzepte des Diktaturvergleichs* (Munich: F. Schoeningh Verlag, 1996); Hermann Lübbe and Wladyslaw Bartosyewski, eds., *Heilserwartung und Terror: Politische Religionen im 20. Jahrhundert* (Düsseldorf: Patmos, 1995).

[51] Robert Gellately and Ben Kiernan, eds., *The Specter of Genocide: Mass Murder in Historical Perspective* (New York: Cambridge University Press, 2003); Bernd Weisbrod, "Fundamentalist Violence: Political Violence and Political Religion in Modern Conflict," *International Social Science Journal* 174 (2002): 499–508; Christian Gerlach, "Extremely Violent Societies: An Alternative to the Concept of Genocide," *Journal of Genocide Research* 8, no. 4 (2006): 455–71. For the terror of the German Left and the debate it elicited, see Gerrit-Jan Berendse, *Schreiben im Terrordrom: Gewaltcodierung, kulturelle Erinnerung und das Bedingungsverhältnis zwischen Literatur und Raf-Terrorismus* (Munich: Edition text + kritik, 2005).

[52] Robert Gellately and Ben Kiernan, eds., *The Specter of Genocide*.

a popular- or populist-political response to the real and perceived threats to the security of the homeland, such that the debate is quite literally carried into the halls of academia.[53] American historians of Germany and the Soviet Union had each begun to reconsider the issue of Stalinism and Nazism (highlighting on the German end the ideological nature of the regime's violence and on the Soviet end the everyday micro-mechanisms of a violent regime),[54] but now they were overwhelmed by the public glamour surrounding the globalization of extreme violence, which, rightly or wrongly, turned an essentially European phenomenon into a global calamity.[55]

In Soviet times, "totalitarianism" and the Stalinist-Nazi comparison were taboo subjects, although Aesopian hints that the two regimes were comparable at times surfaced, as in Mikhail Romm's much-admired film *Obyknovennyi fashizm* (1965). The floodgates opened during perestroika: a 1989 edited volume, *Totalitarianism as a Historical Phenomenon*, reported that the term was already "intensively used" and "ever more clearly claims the status of chief explanatory model of our recent past."[56] The problem, as the editors pointed out, was that nobody knew what the term meant: a danger existed that it would become merely an empty "linguistic cliché" like "cult of personality" or "period of stagnation."[57] Orwell's *1984*, which appeared in translation in the popular monthly *Novyi mir* at the beginning of 1989,[58] was clearly a major influence. Arendt's work on totalitarianism had yet to be translated.[59] While an all-powerful party with a pervasively propagated ideology and a charismatic leader were usually part of the definitions of totalitarianism offered to Russian readers, it was the state's invasion of privacy that seemed to resonate the most: "Totalitarianism is the socio-political system (*stroi*) characterized by an all-embracing despotic interference of the state in all manifestations of the life of the social organism and the life of individuals," according to the 1991

[53] Paul Berman, *Terror and Liberalism* (New York and London: W. W. Norton, 2003); Pierre Clermont, *De Lénine à Ben Laden: La grande révolte antimoderniste du XXe siècle: Démocratie ou totalitarisme* (Monaco: Rocher, 2004); Benjamin Barber, *Fear's Empire: War, Terrorism, and Democracy* (New York and London: W. W. Norton, 2003).

[54] Peter Fritzsche, *Life and Death in the Third Reich* (Cambridge, MA: The Belknap Press of Harvard University Press, 2008); Sheila Fitzpatrick, *Stalinism: New Directions* (London and New York: Routledge, 2000).

[55] Mark Juergensmeyer, ed., *Violence and the Sacred in the Modern World* (London: Frank Cass, 1991); E. Ann Kaplan, *Trauma Culture: The Politics of Terror and Loss in Media and Literature* (New Brunswick, NJ: Rutgers University Press, 2005).

[56] A. A. Kara-Murza and A. K. Voskresenskii, eds., *Totalitarizm kak istoricheskii fenomen* (Moscow: Filosofskoe obshchestvo SSSR, 1989), 5 (preface by Kara-Murza).

[57] Ibid.

[58] *Novyi mir*, 1989, nos. 2, 3, and 4 (translation by V. Golyshev). Orwell's *Animal Farm* appeared in Russian translation a little earlier, but in a journal with small circulation, *Rodnik* (Riga), 1988, nos. 3–7 (Russian title: *Skotnyi dvor*).

[59] Kara-Murza and A. K. Voskresenskii, in *Totalitarizm*, 6. It was finally published in Russian translation as *Istoki totalitarizma* in 1995.

Philosophical Dictionary.[60] The Nazi-Stalinist comparison was sometimes invoked – most memorably in Tenghiz Abuladze's film *Repentance* (1987) – but it did not generally seem to be as interesting to Russians in the late 1980s and 1990s as it had been in the 1960s.[61]

It might well appear that, intellectually and historiographically, this is the moment at which a quarter-century of empirical scholarship is yet again being transcended. During the heyday of totalitarianism theory, historians could rightly claim that theory and ideology had been imposed upon them and that they had not engaged in the first round of comparison since they had not yet even begun seriously to study either of the societies or regimes. But now they have done their work, and it is for them to respond to the new challenges and to develop a new scholarship of integration – be it of the narrative, interpretative, or explanatory variety.

WHAT IS TO BE DONE?

There is quite a bit of movement within academia today that suggests a growing unease with the proliferation of and the disconnect in so much of current academic work, which, as the saying goes, knows more and more about less and less. For obvious reasons, this applies more to the German case than the Soviet one, where huge gaps in and intense controversies over empirical knowledge still exist. But the problem is a general one and is met with a growing readiness, if not to "theorize,"[62] then to move on to a conceptual plain where the contours of German and Russian or, for that matter, European or global history are recast. While there is a return to theory, the concern with what traditionally has been called political theology being among the dominant lineages of thought, the main departure is best described as a revived "scholarship of integration." New books, such as Ferguson's *War of the World* or Wasserstein's *Barbarism and Civilization*, but also Service's *History of World Communism*, Griffin's *Modernism and Fascism*, or Rosanvallon's *Democracy*,

[60] I. T. Frolov and A. V. Ado, eds., *Filosofskii slovar'*, 6th ed., revised and expanded (Moscow: Izdatel'stvo politicheskoi literatury, 1991).

[61] In major works on totalitarianism, scholars of the period offered very little discussion of the Nazi-Stalinist analogy. In the Kara-Murza volume, the philosopher L. V. Poliakov notes that "for me, these [the Nazi and the Stalinist] are two worlds that are different in principle" (29). The historian B. S. Orlov was more interested in the comparison – which had first struck him as a 15-year-old looking at German stamps showing the same muscular workers and happy peasant women as in official Soviet art, and later been reinforced by the Romm film – but emphasized contrast in social, demographic, and geographical circumstances as well ("Germaniia i SSSR v 30-e gody: skhodstva i razlichiia," *Totalitarizm kak istoricheskii fenomen*, 97–107). Like other Russian scholars who invoke the comparison, Orlov sees Nazism, like Stalinism, as a distorted form of socialism.

[62] Achim Siegel, *The Totalitarian Paradigm after the End of Communism: Towards a Theoretical Reassessment* (Amsterdam; Atlanta: Rodopi, 1998).

are indications of the general trend.[63] In the slightly more delimited field at hand, the history of Stalinism and Nazism, it is a scholarship on one hand that seeks out the everydayness of the regime and, quite commonly, links this agenda to an exploration of extreme violence in both societies.[64] By the same token, there is also a heightened concern for a scholarship that aims to place these regimes in their European and global contexts.[65]

The current situation leaves us with a number of openings, some of which we did not take up but that deserve mention because they have attracted considerable attention and represent viable approaches.

One important strand of scholarship is concerned with resuscitating the concept of totalitarianism. In fact, the notion of totalitarianism has resurfaced as something of a free agent and is now used to flag a rather contrary set of departures, three of which are of import. First, while it is not everyone's preferred way of tackling the problem, it is reasonable to argue that empirical historians failed fully to appreciate the depth of thought invested in the idea. For even if contemporary thinkers frequently got it wrong (Hannah Arendt may serve as the prime example), good ideas are hard to come by and should be salvaged from simplification and propagandistic misuse.[66] Overall, Soviet historians seem much more unforgiving in this regard than their German counterparts, but as much as Hannah Arendt will not go away, neither will Alexandr Solzhenitsyn or, for that matter, the group of Eastern European intellectuals who are in the equally privileged and unenviable situation of having faced both regimes.[67] Whether or not they shed light on each other's cases – Solzhenitsyn on Germany, Arendt on the Soviet Union, and Havel on both – their essays in

---

[63] Niall Ferguson, *The War of the World: History's Age of Hatred* (London and New York: Allen Lane, 2006); Bernard; Robert Service, *Comrades!: A History of World Communism* (Cambridge, MA: Harvard University Press, 2007); Roger Griffin, *Modernism and Fascism: The Sense of a Beginning under Mussolini and Hitler* (Basingstoke and New York: Palgrave Macmillan, 2007); Pierre Rosanvallon, *Democracy: Past and Future*, ed. Samuel Moyn (New York: Columbia University Press, 2006).

[64] Karl Eimermacher and Astrid Volpert, eds., *Verführungen der Gewalt: Russen und Deutsche im Ersten und Zweiten Weltkrieg* (Munich: Fink, 2005).

[65] Erwin Oberländer and Rolf Ahmann, *Autoritäre Regime in Ostmittel- und Südosteuropa 1919–1944* (Paderborn: Schöningh, 2001); Jerzy W. Borejsza, Klaus Ziemer, and Magdalena Hulas, eds., *Totalitarian and Authoritarian Regimes in Europe: Legacies and Lessons from the Twentieth Century* (New York: Berghahn Books in association with the Institute of the Polish Academy of Sciences and the German Historical Institute Warsaw, 2006).

[66] A typical case is Arendt's *Eichmann in Jerusalem* (Hannah Arendt, *Eichmann in Jerusalem: A Report on the Banality of Evil*, rev. and enlarged ed. [New York: Viking Press, 1965]). This book gets things patently wrong, as far as empirical work is concerned (David Cesarani, *Eichmann: His Life, Crime, and Legacy* [London: Heinemann, 2003]). And yet it remains important for the disquisition on the ordinariness of evil. Steven Aschheim, ed., *Hannah Arendt in Jerusalem* (Berkeley and Los Angeles: University of California Press, 2001). By the same token, historians have still a way to go to appreciate the complexity and depth of thought in Hannah Arendt, *The Origins of Totalitarianism*.

[67] Aleksandr Isaevich Solzhenitsyn, Edward E. Ericson, and Daniel J. Mahoney, *The Solzhenitsyn Reader: New and Essential Writings, 1947–2005* (Wilmington, DE: ISI Books, 2006); Václav

understanding still help us grapple with our ever-increasing wealth of empirical evidence. And perhaps, it is worth repeating, there is also a Left and, for that matter, a Communist and Socialist intellectual history to be recovered.[68]

That is to say, these and other thinkers are not only subjects for an intellectual history in its own right nor, for that matter, for a more reflexive history of the German and the Russian regimes (that is, a history that makes the self-understanding and the perception of these regimes part of its analysis) – although this kind of high intellectual history deserves more attention.[69] Rather, they yet again have much to contribute to the ongoing debate on the understanding of the two regimes, a debate, frankly, that has not been graced by a surplus of ideas. The prerequisite is to take them off their pedestal (or, for that matter, take them out of the closet) and engage them for what they have to say in a second or third reading today. That Eastern and Western theories of fascism should reenter this contest, as well, only fits the spirit of open-ended inquiry into those elements of twentieth-century thought that might inform a scholarship of integration.

We did not select the above approach, however, mainly because we think that at this point the proof is in the pudding. We believe it instead necessary to reassess the ingredients and recipes at hand before we can once again approach the gestalt as a whole. Therefore, we chose to capitalize on what empirical historians have done best over the past quarter-century: we put the two historiographies side by side, hoping that an intertwined look at their respective arrangements will encourage a new round of comparative and integrative work.

The second opening that we did not take is altogether more prominently represented. It starts from the quite astute observation that empirical research over the last quarter-century, in both the German and Soviet cases, had its own respective biases. German historians, for example, were for a very long time hesitant to engage in an in-depth analysis of ideology or, more properly, the political, moral, and emotional culture of the regime, but this has changed radically.[70] Nor did they take into consideration the emotional, quasi-religious investment in the regime or the attachments the regime was able to generate – in

---

Havel, *The Power of the Powerless: Citizens against the State in Central-Eastern Europe* (London: Hutchinson, 1985); Adam Michnik and Zinaïda Erard, *Penser La Pologne: Morale et politique de la résistance* (Paris: Découverte/Maspero, 1983).

[68] Fehér and Heller, *Eastern Left, Western Left: Totalitarianism, Freedom, and Democracy.*

[69] Anson Rabinbach, *In the Shadow of Catastrophe: German Intellectuals between Apocalypse and Enlightenment* (Berkeley and Los Angeles: University of California Press, 1997).

[70] For three intriguing and very different examples, see Deborah Dwork and Robert Jan van Pelt, *Auschwitz 1270 to the Present* (New York: W. W. Norton, 1996); Frank-Lothar Kroll, "Endzeitvorstellungen im Kommunismus und im Nationalsozialismus," in *Der Engel und die siebte Posaune... Endzeitvorstellungen in Geschichte und Literatur*, eds. Stefan Krimm and Ursula Triller (Munich: Bayerischer Schulbuch Verlag, 2000), 186–204; Dagmar Herzog, *Sex after Fascism: Memory and Morality in Twentieth-Century Germany* (Princeton, NJ and Oxford: Princeton University Press, 2005).

terms of values and norms, as well as of tastes and behaviors.[71] Under a variety of names and with diverse programmatic intents, this topic has captivated a younger generation of historians, who have made it their goal to explore the emotive and mental structures of a genocidal regime. While initially this interest focused on the mass enthusiasm for National Socialism, the main concern has shifted to exploring German society at war.[72] The Russian case is perhaps even more striking. For here the rush to the archives after 1991 was linked to what one might call, if somewhat tongue-in-cheek, the mass appropriation of Foucault, who, as a strongly anti-Communist ex-Leftist saw the Soviet Union through a totalitarian prism. This approach entailed a new round of research on issues of repression, propaganda, and popular pressure to conform, but also on the subjective and intimate remaking of personhood under Stalinism – indeed the making of a civilization.[73] Only the blind can overlook the parallelism in the two historiographical trajectories, trajectories that were kept apart by language acquisition and, one is inclined to say, the subject positions of the respective national historians.

Whether or not this approach, or rather series of approaches, that essays the civilizational or moral dimension of Nazi and Stalinist society can stand in for the whole; whether or not there is such a thing as Nazi or Soviet society (which might well be the case for the latter but applies to the former only if we also consider the wreckage the Nazi regime caused); what the relationship might be between savagery and civil society[74] – this seemed to us a largely unresolved issue on which we also disagreed. In any case, rather than turning this book into a reflection on civilization and barbarism or into another controversy over the ideological or, respectively, religious nature of the regimes,[75] we shied away from grand pronouncements and asked more specifically about the nature and the facets of the social project that emerged from these two regimes. Therefore, rather than worrying about the Weberian-type "charismatic leadership,"[76] we were rather concerned with "man and society in the age of social reconstruction," although Karl Mannheim's own thought on this

---

[71] If we think of the legacy of anti-Semitism, Claudia Koonz, *The Nazi Conscience* (Cambridge, MA: Belknap Press of Harvard University Press, 2003); Jeffrey Herf, *The Jewish Enemy: Nazi Propaganda During World War II and the Holocaust* (Cambridge, MA: Belknap Press of Harvard University Press, 2006).

[72] Militärgeschichtliches Forschungsamt, ed., *Das Deutsche Reich und der Zweite Weltkrieg*, Vol. 9/1–2: *Die deutsche Kriegsgesellschaft 1939 bis 1945* (Munich: Deutsche Verlagsanstalt, 2004).

[73] Jochen Hellbeck, *Revolution on My Mind: Writing a Diary under Stalin* (Cambridge, MA: Harvard University Press, 2006); Stephen Kotkin, *Magnetic Mountain: Stalinism as a Civilization* (Berkeley: University of California Press, 1997).

[74] Samuel Moyn, "Of Savagery and Civil Society: Pierre Clastres and the Transformation of French Political Thought," *Modern Intellectual History* 1, no. 1 (2004): 55–80.

[75] Hans Maier, *Totalitarianism and Political Religions: Concepts for the Comparison of Dictatorships*, trans. Jodi Bruhn (London and New York: Routledge, 2004).

[76] A good example is Hans-Ulrich Wehler, *Deutsche Gesellschaftsgeschichte*, Vol. 4: *Vom Beginn des Ersten Weltkrieges bis zur Gründung der beiden deutschen Staaten* (Munich: C. H. Beck, 2003).

matter, complicated by the transition into exile in Great Britain, was typically not a presence.[77]

Of course, there is yet a third trend that is prevalent in the social sciences proper but has won some ground in history as well.[78] This direction of research emphasizes the role of the state and the peculiar statism of the interwar years. In this context, a few adventurous studies have broken new ground: for example, the study of labor services in Germany and the United States or of the three new deals in Italy, Germany, and the United States.[79] But despite the pioneering theoretical work of Claude Lefort, there has been little follow-up in this tradition.[80] Carl Schmitt has had more of a following, but the impact of this scholarship on understanding the actual state Schmitt hoped to shape is strikingly limited.[81] This is changing, but for the time being most of the innovative work comes from Soviet historiography concerning Stalinism as a political regime.[82] As mentioned, there is also a growing literature that explores the rush to authoritarian and tyrannical regimes in the interwar years and the nature of modern tyrannies. While Eastern Europe figures prominently in this context, however, very few have worked the Soviet Union into the grander European and, for that matter, Eurasian picture.[83]

Overall, it makes sense to put this issue to the test and see what the new departures will yield in terms of a scholarship of integration. Hence, rather than affirming or debunking the latest wave of inquiries, we thought that we

[77] Karl Mannheim, *Man and Society in the Age of Reconstruction: Studies in Modern Social Structure* (London: Routledge and Kegan Paul, 1940).

[78] The intellectual tradition of thinking about dictatorship and tyranny is eminent and deserves separate treatment. Dieter Groh, "Cäsarismus, Napoleonismus, Bonapartismus. Führer, Chef, Imperialismus," in *Geschichtliche Grundbegriffe*, vol. 1, eds. Otto Brunner, Werner Conze, and Reinhart Koselleck (Stuttgart: Ernst Klett, 1972), 726–71; Hella Mandt, "Cäsarismus, Napoleonismus, Bonapartismus. Führer, Chef, Imperialismus," in *Geschichtliche Grundbegriffe*, vol. 6, eds. Otto Brunner, Werner Conze, and Reinhart Koselleck (Stuttgart: Ernst Klett, 1990), 651–706; Peter Baehr, and Melvin Richter, eds., *Dictatorships in History and Theory: Bonapartism, Caesarism, and Totalitarianism* (Cambridge and New York: Cambridge University Press and German Historical Institute, Washington, DC, 2004).

[79] Kiran Klaus Patel, *"Soldaten der Arbeit": Arbeitsdienste in Deutschland und den USA 1933–1945* (Göttingen: Vandenhoeck & Ruprecht, 2003); Wolfgang Schivelbusch, *Three New Deals: Reflections on Roosevelt's America, Mussolini's Italy, and Hitler's Germany, 1933–1939* (New York: Metropolitan Books, 2006).

[80] Claude Lefort, *The Political Forms of Modern Society: Bureaucracy, Democracy, Totalitarianism* (Cambridge, MA: MIT Press, 1986).

[81] But see Dan Diner, "Rassistisches Völkerrecht: Elemente der nationalsozialistischen Weltordnung," *Vierteljahrshefte für Zeitgeschichte* 37 (1989): 23–56; Friedrich Balke, *Der Staat nach seinem Ende: Die Versuchung Carl Schmitts* (Munich: Wilhelm Fink Verlag, 1996).

[82] As overviews: David L. Hoffman, ed., *Stalinism: The Essential Readings* (Oxford: Blackwell, 2003); Fitzpatrick, *Stalinism: New Directions*.

[83] Erwin Oberländer, and Rolf Ahmann, *Autoritäre Regime in Ostmittel- und Südosteuropa 1919–1944* (Paderborn: Schöningh, 2001); Gerd Koenen, "Alte Reiche, neue Reiche: Der Maoismus auf der Folie des Stalinismus – Eine Gedankenskizze," in *Moderne Zeiten?: Krieg, Revolution und Gewalt im 20. Jahrhundert*, ed. Jörg Baberowski (Göttingen: Vandenhoeck & Ruprecht, 2006), 174–201.

should take this approach for what it does best and see how far we can go with it. We added the most compelling elements of inquiry (for example, on subjectivity, on emotions and beliefs, on governance, on violence) to our own exploration of the subject, while remaining agnostic about the claim that any one of these pieces provides the capstone for an overarching interpretation of Nazism and Stalinism or, for that matter, of modern tyrannical regimes.

The overall challenge of this particular volume – and of the historiography on Nazi Germany and Stalinist Russia – should be evident by now. It is to work toward a comprehensive assessment of the two regimes and their comparability. The basic questions that we are asking are simple ones: Where does a quarter-century or, in any case, more than a decade of research leave us in our understanding of Nazi Germany and Stalinist Russia? Were the two regimes in some important way similar, as so many have thought? Were they, as others have argued, profoundly different? And what would either of these variants entail for our understanding of twentieth-century Europe? Was there a significant relationship, or even mutual dependency, between these two quintessential rogue states of twentieth-century Europe, despite their professed enmity and the monstrous life-and-death struggle in which they engaged? Or were they largely blind to each other, driven forward by their own splendid isolations and cocooned in their respective worldviews, as is suggested by the notion of "Socialism in one country" and the supremacy of Nazi racial views? And if neither holds, what might capture their rise to world-shattering prominence?

If we put these questions into more analytical language, we may want to differentiate three levels of analysis. In the first instance, any reassessment of the two regimes will have an internal dimension, which for some historians may be the only one that matters. Here the main task is to draw up a compelling account of the working of these regimes in all their parts and as a whole. With much empirical work having been done, this now requires a great deal of prudent judgment – more than is normally expended – in assessing the relative weight of research domains – proper social scientists would speak of variables – such as the political sphere, ideology, economy and issues such as surveillance, entertainment, welfare, and warfare.

On a second level, a reconsideration of the entire issue of the (synchronic) comparability of the two regimes is at issue. We will return to this point below because the question of comparison, and of comparative history, has gained a new salience among historians. But the specific challenge here is worth noting. Having escaped the epistemic prison of the totalitarian sameness of the two regimes and having indulged in the particularities of each regime for the last quarter-century, we need to ask what difference "difference" makes in understanding the two regimes. This is not merely a question as to what, if anything, comparison achieves. Rather it involves explaining how and why two regimes did so many similar things in such different ways. What we ultimately aim to produce is a better appreciation of the problems and issues that moved the two regimes and of the strategies they employed to solve them. This, in turn, could lead to a new round of informed discussions on the nature of twentieth-century tyrannical rule in Europe (and in the world) and how it differs from other forms of rule. For if the totalitarian presumption of sameness is gone, the phenomenon of twentieth-century tyrannical rule is as urgent as ever – but, unfortunately, in knowing more about each regime, it turns out that we know altogether less about the nature of their rule.

On a third level, questions of historical or diachronic context surfaced prominently, although the editors did their best to hold the contributors to a rather narrow focus on the thirties and forties – and, thus, to button down this level of analysis as far as possible. But our decision does not invalidate the line of inquiry itself, a line that is concerned with strategies of "embedding" the two regimes in their history, in their mutual relationships, and in the transactions, engagements, and disengagements that made up the world of which they were part. Here, the challenge is twofold. First, it consists in embedding each regime in its respective national history – and, not least, in acknowledging the sheer durability of the Soviet Union as a twentieth-century phenomenon and the short-lived, explosive nature of the National Socialist regime. Second, the challenge is to make sense of the rash of dictatorships that covered Europe and the world in the first half of the twentieth century, of which Stalinist Russia and Nazi Germany were by all counts the most prominent, most hard-headed, and most violent. While we have already discounted the intrinsic sameness of these regimes, the simultaneity of their occurrence requires attention as a problem of European and global history.

TOWARD A COMPARATIVE HISTORY OF STALINISM AND NAZISM

Comparison seems the right way to proceed. For it is only now that the primary and secondary sources exist for a historical comparison of the two regimes. The vast and growing historiography entraps historians in their own specialties and national histories. Therefore, whatever larger benefits there may be, the most immediate one is to get out of nationally confined historical thought. The experiment is to do on an empirical level what political scientists and philosophers have done at the theoretical level half a century ago – and, if all goes well, revise, amend, improve, or overthrow what they argued in due course. But why would anyone want to step into the same river fifty years downstream as it were? Would it not be better to consign the entire concept and framework of totalitarianism to history much as the regimes that totalitarianism tried to understand? What is there to be gained from a comparison specifically of Stalinism and Nazism? In short, does comparison really add value to what we already know?

A first line of argument in favor of a comparative history of Stalinism and Nazism points to a stunningly understudied area of research. Whatever else these two regimes may have that makes them comparable, the shock and awe they elicited in their own time – and in the Nazi case long after defeat – make these two regimes, more than any other combination, a worthwhile subject for

study. If the theorists of totalitarianism lumped Nazism and Stalinism together –
and they often did so as exiles on the far shore of the Atlantic – they were
motivated by an immediate sense of awe and fear of the two regimes. Whether
that fear was real or imagined – as, for example, in the Cold War – was (and
is) not easy to gauge, but we cannot forget or underestimate the immediacy of
the terror for many participants in the debate. Understanding the two regimes
always also meant assessing their future potentialities and their current course
of action. Sovietology is the prime example of this kind of enterprise.[84] The
study of National Socialism, in turn, aimed to determine whether these regimes,
once defeated, would reemerge and what it would take to prevent that from
occurring. Arendt, the members of the Frankfurt School, much as a conservative
historian such as Hans Rothfels were deeply troubled by this possibility.[85]
Further, these regimes simply did not act as classical political theory predicted
even tyrannies to act, or so it seemed (more so to Hannah Arendt than, say, to
Carl Friedrich). They appeared unprecedented and unpredictable in their utter
ruthlessness. Hence their novelty had to be accounted for, if only to provide
a frame of reference for understanding.[86] The difficulty in conceptualizing
totalitarian regimes is immediately apparent in even the most formalistic of
endeavors, the one by Friedrich and Brzezinski.[87] The struggle with the sheer
novelty of these regimes is perhaps clearest in the French endeavors of the time,
as, for example, in the journal *Socialisme ou Barbarie*, which by way of Claude
Lefort and Cornelius Castoriadis made it into the American debate.[88] Arendt,
Friedrich, and Castoriadis/Lefort are worlds apart analytically and politically.
However, putting the Nazi and the Soviet regime together seemed to all of
them the intelligent thing to do, because these regimes appeared to them both
frightening and unprecedented – and while we may no longer experience that
fear or, for that matter, the puzzlement, the historicity of the experience reflects
on the subject matter.

   However, even if we take past experience as a starting point, comparative
treatments quickly become caught in an epistemic crisis. The latter is less evident
in grand synthetic efforts,[89] but it is the bane of more hard-nosed, one-on-one

---

[84] Vladimir Shlapentokh, "American Sovietology from 1917–1991: An Attempt at Diagnosis,"
Russian History 22, no. 4 (1995): 406–32; Richard Pipes, *Vixi: Memoirs of a Non-Belonger*
(New Haven, CT: Yale University Press, 2003).

[85] Rabinbach, "Moments of Totalitarianism"; Elisabeth Young-Bruehl, *Hannah Arendt: For Love
of the World* (New Haven, CT: Yale University Press, 1982).

[86] Hannah Arendt, "Understanding and Politics (the Difficulties of Understanding)," in *Essays in
Understanding 1930–1954*, ed. Hannah Arendt (New York: Harcourt, Brace, 1994), 307–27.

[87] Carl J. Friedrich and Zbigniew Brzezinski, *Totalitarian Dictatorship and Autocracy.*

[88] Marcel van der Linden, "Socialisme ou Barbarie: A French Revolutionary Group (1949–65),"
Left History 5, no. 1 (1997): 7–37; Cornelius Castoriadis, *The Castoriadis Reader* (Oxford and
Malden, MA: Blackwell, 1997); Claude Lefort, *Complications: Communism and the Dilemmas
of Democracy* (New York: Columbia University Press, 2007).

[89] Richard J. Overy, *The Dictators: Hitler's Germany and Stalin's Russia* (New York: W. W.
Norton, 2004); Gellately, *Lenin, Stalin, and Hitler: The Age of Social Catastrophe.*

comparative work.[90] On one hand, the two regimes, despite their mutual and implacable ideological enmity, appear so incredibly similar that it seems only a matter of putting the two sides together to establish their commonality. Yes, their worldviews were inimical. But the fact that they both were "ideology"-driven joins them together, or so it is argued. (What ideology entails is another issue.) Their techniques of rule were quite similar, others opine, but even when and where they differed they shared a common enmity to bourgeois society and governance and to democracy. Hence, it seems only natural to explore the play of similarity and difference between the two regimes. On the other hand, when it comes to matching up the pieces, say in terms of governance or ideology, all similarities break down radically and the sheer play of differences loses meaning. When it comes to one-on-one comparison, the two societies and regimes may as well have hailed from different worlds. For better or worse, comparison, as opposed to synthesis, reveals a total mismatch. Although the two regimes seem to have a great deal in common, surely eyed each other relentlessly, were indebted to each other and borrowed from each other despite themselves, and were imbricated in each other both in war and in peace, they do not match up. Even when observing the same things or processes, historians face a basic and, some authors in our group argue, irreconcilable asymmetry.

The truly puzzling thing then is how two regimes that in many ways look so similar can be so fundamentally different. Ironically, it takes comparison to find out.

First, the acknowledgment even of irreconcilable asymmetries may lead to comparisons in a minor key. The approach should not be disparaged, all the more since no less a historian than Marc Bloch elevated this kind of minor comparison to an art form.[91] Historians tend to look over each other's shoulders – and while, in the past, it has usually been the Russian historians who canvassed German scholarship, the state of Russian scholarship today is such that German historians are well advised to do the same. If systematic comparison does not work, good kibitzing – an attitude more than an approach – has its rewards. Since, at the most elemental level, all national historiographies are shaped by arbitrary and contingent factors, it is useful for historians working in one national context to take note of what questions are being asked, what sources are being consulted, and what approaches are being used by historians working in a different one, especially if it is related. For instance, German historians of "everyday life" have for a long time focused on resistance, while the emerging Soviet historiography concentrates much more on social practices and survival strategies. A "show-and-tell" comparison thus yields new

---

[90] Ian Kershaw and Moshe Lewin, *Stalinism and Nazism: Dictatorships in Comparison* (Cambridge and New York: Cambridge University Press, 1997); Henry Rousso and Richard Joseph Golsan, eds., *Stalinism and Nazism: History and Memory Compared* (Lincoln: University of Nebraska Press, 2004).

[91] Marc Bloch, "Toward a Comparative History of European Societies," in *Enterprise and Secular Change: Readings in Economic History*, eds. Frederic C. Lane and Jelle C. Riemersma (Homewood, IL: R. D. Irwin, 1953), 494–521.

approaches and an altogether more reflexive attitude. It forces historians out of their parochial, expository, and interpretative conventions. The insights gained from such kibitzing may then well turn into a new appreciation of the subject matter at hand. Dietrich Beyrau has done this kind of comparison, looking at professional classes in both regimes.[92] With such down-to-earth comparison even the formalistic catalogue of parameters of totalitarian regimes becomes intriguing again. For we might now begin to wonder why these two regimes were so fundamentally concerned with a very few issues, like leadership, even if they settled them differently.

Second, comparison can also be used as an explanatory strategy. A simple example: if one believes that the practice of identifying entire population categories for arrest and execution is a product of Communist class-based ideology, then the same practice inspired by a race-based ideology in Nazi Germany complicates that argument. But this is, perhaps, too simple – because the stakes here are very high indeed. Comparison as a means of elucidating cause and effect has been the most contentious issue in understanding totalitarianism and fascism, ever since Ernst Nolte turned Arendt's and Friedrich's "structural" or "classical" theories of totalitarianism into a "historical-genetic" one.[93] Nolte claimed that genocidal violence was a Bolshevik invention that had to be dated back to the Russian Civil War. The Nazis picked up their genocidal idée fixe from the Bolsheviks, which is to say that the Holocaust is a derivative act and, *post hoc ergo propter hoc,* a Russian deed. By extension the Nazi war of extermination against the Soviet Union was but a boomerang that hit the originators in what amounted to a European, if not global civil war.[94] This argument was the backdrop for the German historians' debate in the eighties, which roundly rejected Nolte's argument as "ressentiment" or plainly "wrong judgment."[95]

There are other and better ways of historicizing comparison. Nolte's outrageous position has led to the unfortunate result that any form of "genealogical" research is suspect in German historiography. Reprieve comes from World

---

[92] Dietrich Beyrau, ed., *Im Dschungel der Macht: Intellektuelle Professionen unter Stalin und Hitler* (Göttingen: Vandenhoeck & Ruprecht, 2000).

[93] Ernst Nolte, "Die historisch-genetische Version der Totalitarismustheorie: Ärgernis oder Einsicht?," *Zeitschrift für Politik* 43, no. 2 (1996): 111–22.

[94] Ernst Nolte, *Der europäische Bürgerkrieg, 1917–1945: Nationalsozialismus und Bolschewismus,* 5th ed. (Munich: Herbig, 1997); Ernst Nolte, *Marxism, Fascism, Cold War* (Atlantic Highlands, NJ: Humanities Press, 1982); Francois Furet and Ernst Nolte, *"Feindliche Nähe": Kommunismus und Faschismus im 20. Jahrhundert* (Munich: F. A. Herbig, 1998); Richard Shorten, "Europe's Twentieth Century in Retrospect? A Cautious Note on the Furet/Nolte Debate," *European Legacy* 9, no. 3 (2004): 285–304.

[95] Hans Mommsen, "Das Ressentiment als Wissenschaft: Anmerkungen zu Ernst Noltes 'Der Europäische Bürgerkrieg,'" *Geschichte und Gesellschaft* 14, no. 4 (1988): 495–512; Wolfgang Schieder, "Der Nationalsozialismus im Fehlurteil philosophischer Geschichtsschreibung: Zur Methode von Ernst Noltes 'Europäischem Bürgerkrieg,'" *Geschichte und Gesellschaft* 15, no. 1 (1989): 89–114; Schmeitzner, ed., *Totalitarismuskritik von Links: Deutsche Diskurse im 20. Jahrhundert,* 519–60.

War I and Holocaust historians who consider the Great War to be the ur-catastrophe of twentieth-century European history and, therefore, the source of Bolshevism, National Socialism, and Fascism, although the Russian end of this history remained largely underdeveloped (mainly because there still is relatively little work on the "eastern front" in World War I).[96] But it was Michael Mann with his *Dark Side of Democracy* who developed a both historically and analytically preferable answer to Nolte's challenge.[97] If World War I historians had emphasized the multiple effects of a single historical event, Mann made the case that, for one, the conundrum of mass politics and popular sovereignty was at the core of the problem and that, for another, there were many solutions to the common European and, indeed, global problematique of popular sovereignty. Therefore, rather than looking at a single, historical event as origin of a given regime, we have to look at contingency and politics in the making of such regimes. This is certainly one of the more productive solutions for the conundrum of understanding how it is that these two regimes, so fundamentally different from one another, nonetheless appear so similar on the surface.

There is a third way of engaging comparison that is rather underdeveloped in the current project, although it is the rage among European historians: a comparison that focuses on transfers and mutual influences – not necessarily in the entangled sense, but in the concrete sense that symbols, practices, actions, and ways of doing things are spread, and have a way of spreading mimetically, throughout Europe.[98] Architecture and cinema are among the best examples. Propaganda techniques too are said to have circulated quickly. But what about the politics of surveillance or state violence? What about the more hard-knuckled transfers in which Bolshevik politics shaped national communist affairs and in which German politics shaped Ukrainian and other ethnic auxiliaries in the Soviet Union? And, last but not least, what about anti-Semitism?[99] The point is that there is a history of transfers and overlays, of mimesis, that must be part and parcel of any comparative history of Nazism and Stalinism.

---

[96] Ernst Schulin, "Der Erste Weltkrieg und das Ende des alten Europas," in *Jahrhundertwende: Der Aufbruch in die Moderne 1880–1930*, eds. August Nitschke et al. (Reinbek: Rowohlt, 1990), 369–403; Omer Bartov, *Mirrors of Destruction: War, Genocide, and Modern Identity* (Oxford and New York: Oxford University Press, 2000); Dietrich Beyrau, "Der Erste Weltkrieg als Bewährungsprobe: Bolschewistische Lernprozesse aus dem 'imperialistischen' Krieg," *Journal of Modern European History* 1, no. 1 (2003): 96–124; Peter Holquist, *Making War, Forging Revolution: Russia's Continuum of Crisis, 1914–1921* (Cambridge, MA: Harvard University Press, 2002).

[97] Michael Mann, *The Dark Side of Democracy: Explaining Ethnic Cleansing* (Cambridge and New York: Cambridge University Press, 2005).

[98] Michel Espagne, *Russie, France, Allemagne, Italie: Transferts quadrangulaires du néoclassicisme aux avant-gardes* (Tusson: Du Lérot, 2005); Catherine Evtuhov and Stephen Kotkin, *The Cultural Gradient: The Transmission of Ideas in Europe, 1789–1991* (Lanham, MD: Rowman & Littlefield, 2003); Matthias Middell, "Kulturtransfer und historische Komparatistik – Thesen zur ihren Verhältnis," *Comparativ* 10 (2000): 7–41.

[99] Amir Weiner, *Making Sense of War: The Second World War and the Fate of the Bolshevik Revolution* (Princeton, NJ: Princeton University Press, 2001).

The difficulty with this kind of comparison is evident. The two regimes or rather their imaginations (and their historiographies) were built on the presumed opposition between Nazism and Stalinism, and, therefore, the twain can neither meet nor borrow from each other. If an interactive or mimetic history is largely missing, it is neither an oversight nor a historiographical predisposition. Rather, the problem is that in crucial arenas of Stalinist and National Socialist affairs, the two regimes never acknowledged, or so it seems on the surface, an even subterraneous influence on each other. But this only suggests that the matter of transfers and influences is a complicated one. It obviously involves a great deal of politics that opens and closes access. It also involves more complex cultural phenomena such as mutual prejudices and stereotypes. And, not least, it depends on the relative mobility of information and people. That having been said, it would be surprising if, of all nations and of all regimes, Stalinist Russia and Nazi Germany did not connect. If indeed this were the case, their insulation would have to be treated as a grand and deliberately manufactured autism. There would still be witting or unwitting transfers to be considered (and the arenas of such transfers would have to be identified). But we might well come to the conclusion that a politics of insulation is one of the hallmarks of the two regimes – and, inasmuch as that is the case, it will be all the more important to identify the strategies of insulation employed by the two regimes – and the areas where they did not work.

These three variations of a comparative history of Nazism and Stalinism are at various degrees of distance from the first generation of theories of totalitarianism. They reject by and large the formalism of "high" social science theory, especially of the Friedrich variety, for being too inflexible in accommodating or making sense of the empirical knowledge historians have accumulated over the years. They are certainly more open to a historical-genetic approach, but look with a rather jaundiced eye on grand philosophical schemes, even if they come from François Furet or Arno Mayer, because they aim to demonstrate genetic origins, be they in the French Revolution or World War I, when historians rather find circuitous roads.[100] They surely have not taken to Ernst Nolte's monocausal explanation of the Bolshevik revolution as the source of all evil in the world, although this argument has considerable traction in the overall revival of the notion of totalitarianism in recent years.[101] It is intriguing that Hannah Arendt's work, not least because her work is so extraordinarily rich

[100] François Furet, *The Passing of an Illusion: The Idea of Communism in the Twentieth Century* (Chicago: University of Chicago Press, 1999); François Furet and Ernst Nolte, *Fascism and Communism* (Lincoln: University of Nebraska Press, 2001); Daniel Schönpflug, "Histoires Croisées: François Furet, Ernst Nolte and a Comparative History of Totalitarian Movements," *European History Quarterly* 37, no. 2 (2007): 265–90; Arno J. Mayer, *The Furies: Violence and Terror in the French and Russian Revolutions* (Princeton, NJ: Princeton University Press, 2000).

[101] Stéphane Courtois, ed., *Quand tombe la nuit: Origines et l'idée des régimes totalitaires en Europe* (Lausanne, Switzerland: L'Age d'Homme, 2001); Stéphane Courtois, ed., *Une si longue nuit: L'apogée des régimes totalitaires en Europe, 1935–1953* (Monaco: Rocher, 2003).

and irritating, has fared best, although this is more the case for Nazism than for Stalinism – and possibly even more for Imperialism than for Nazism.[102] But what she has to offer above all is what historians have rediscovered on both the Soviet and the German ends. The two regimes and the two societies went, or, rather, the two regimes and their respective self-selected elites pushed societies through processes of extraordinary, violent acceleration – a "dynamic" that some interpret as heroic "reconstruction" whereas others see, as Arendt did, the potential of self-destruction.[103]

For historians to make one or the other version of comparison happen, they will have to (re)discover what had been torn asunder by World War II and by the Cold War: the two regimes are part of a common history. Henri Pirenne made a similar point shortly after World War I when he scolded his German colleagues for withdrawing into the prison of the nation rather than thinking of the common European history they shared.[104] He believed that there were common European events, such as the effects of war and revolution, that percolate through each nation. Although Pirenne was more interested in identifying the Europeanness of these events, he was keenly aware that a key to twentieth-century comparison lay in tracing the percolation process in each nation and region. War and defeat placed societies and states in similar predicaments and could serve as starting points for comparison. Needless to say, the solutions to these common predicaments vastly differed (and one nation's solution might well have affected another's), but the point was to establish a controlled range of difference – and the way to do so consisted in historicizing the comparison. Pirenne's grand intervention entailed insisting that the *tertium comparationis* is never beyond (an ideal type like the classical notion of totalitarianism), but always in history and, as such, is conditioned by it. Comparison succeeds inasmuch as it defines its levers historically.

And then some: for it would be quite unproductive to think of "common history" in the way some of the more recent megaprojects on European history have done – providing a wide berth for everyone and everything. In history, much as in war, nothing is ever fair. The two regimes did not coexist in a common history but saw in each other potentially deadly competitors and considered the rest of the world and, especially, the dominant "first world" of capitalists or Jewish plutocrats, respectively, as equally, if not more hostile. Both set out to reshape and remake their respective nations – with extreme, genocidal violence – in order to challenge and defeat their rivals. Neither was

---

[102] Margaret Canovan, *Hannah Arendt: A Reinterpretation of Political Thought* (New York and Cambridge: Cambridge University Press, 1992); Jean-Michel Chaumont, *Autour d'Auschwitz: De la critique de la modernité à l'assomption de la responsabilité historique: Une lecture de Hannah Arendt* (Brussels: Academie Royale des sciences, des lettres et des beaux-arts, 1991).

[103] David D. Roberts, *The Totalitarian Experiment in Twentieth-Century Europe: Understanding the Poverty of Great Politics* (New York and London: Routledge, 2006), 412–52.

[104] Peter Schöttler, "Henri Pirennes Kritik an der deutschen Geschichtswissenschaft und seine Neubegründung des Komparatismus im Ersten Weltkrieg," *SozialGeschichte* 19, no. 2 (2004): 53–81.

able to escape the pushes and pulls of European and global interaction, notwithstanding their efforts to shelter themselves. Peter Gourevich refers to this phenomenon as "the second image reversed: the international sources of domestic politics."[105] The theory behind this phenomenon – historians call it "entangled history" or *histoire croisée* – need not overly concern us.[106] The main point is that we selected Russia and Germany not only because they were entangled with each other, but because their entanglement and its outcome shaped much of the twentieth century – and, lest we forget, left deep scars that shaped both nations and the rest of Europe.

In rehearsing basic strategies of comparison, we have in a circuitous way answered the initial question, why *this* comparison, the comparison of Stalinist Russia and national Socialist Germany, matters. The reason is that in understanding and making sense of the two, we gain a crucial vista into twentieth-century history that on their own neither of the two national histories can produce. Both regimes set out to transform and overcome history and pursued what, on the surface, appear to be parallel strategies. In exploring this perceived parallelism, however, we discover profound differences – differences where thought on totalitarianism once presumed sameness. It is this puzzle of acute-difference-in-manifest-similarity that leads us to believe that comparison will not only help us understand the two nations and regimes better, but will also bring new insight to the question of what made these regimes such quintessential forces in twentieth-century history.

BEYOND TOTALITARIANISM

The decision to write joint essays imposed a genuine handicap. For in the standard one-on-one comparison, scholars peddle their respective national wares and essentially engage in a "show and tell." The result is a bit like parading one's Sunday best and, not uncommonly, the most typical national costume. Two-part, nation-on-nation comparisons have the odd effect of indigenizing and typecasting or neatly categorizing their respective subjects. The current volume is not entirely exempt from this tendency. Furthermore, "head-on comparisons," in which two authors struggle with a single theme or issue, must contend with an additional set of problems: namely, when two nations are brought into such intimate proximity in one essay, historians must confront difference before they can explore mutuality. In short, authorial cohabitation reveals a number of problems inherent in the Russian-German comparison – and in the Nazism-Stalinism comparison, in particular; problems that cast

[105] Peter Gourevitch, "The Second Image Reversed: The International Sources of Domestic Politics," *International Organization* 32 (1978): 881–912.

[106] Bénédicte Zimmermann, Claude Didry, and Peter Wagner, eds., *Le travail et la nation: Histoire croisée de la France et de l'Allemagne* (Paris: Maison des sciences de l'homme, 1999); Sebastian Conrad, *Globalisierung und Nation im deutschen Kaiserreich* (Munich: Beck, 2006).

serious doubt on the value of the hard-nosed, model-oriented social scientific approach that characterized older notions of totalitarianism. But two authors working together on a common project encourages the exercise of prudent judgment that comes with the recognition of the other.

First, comparison is always case and theme sensitive. Our enterprise started with no shared, a priori position on the value of this comparison or on the balance of similarities and differences between Stalinism and Nazism. Generally speaking, the cultural historians were more likely to be interested in similarities and to appreciate totalitarian theory than the social and economic historians, who were more prone to be struck by the differences between the two societies and, hence, were less interested in the totalitarian project. The more politically oriented historians occupied the middle ground in that they shared areas of great commonality but quickly came to be impressed by the tangible differences in commonality.[107] Because of these idiosyncrasies, the ease of comparison materially depended on the subject matter at hand: where domains shared a common universe, comparison flowed easily; where they were held together only by a shared negativity (for example, dictatorship as a contrast to democracy), it did not.

Second, space mattered more than anyone could have predicted.[108] In fact, it occasionally felt as if the old categories of territory and climate might destroy the project. Needless to say the Soviet Union inherited the problem of governing a multiethnic empire, whereas Nazi Germany created one through exclusion and war. More surprising, however, was the extent to which more "classic" conditions, like size and habitability, interfered. With size came problems of multiethnicity; and, with habitability came problems of standards of living. Taken together, they impacted the issues of regime mobilization, the pursuit of violence, and, had we chosen the subject, the modes and spaces of resistance. Size determines very different degrees of permeability – in both the ability of a regime to organize a given social territory and in how that task is structured. For some participants, the "gardening metaphor" captures quite neatly the peculiarly "modern" nature of the Stalinist and Nazi regimes – but then the task is to discern specifically what gardening entailed in Russia and Germany, respectively.[109]

Third, periodization is of consequence. The editors focused on the 1930s and 1940s because that period seemed best suited for illuminating the quintessential features of Nazism and Stalinism. While most participants clamored for the temporal parameters to be moved back to at least World War I (and, in

---

[107] This phenomenon is demonstrated nicely in Overy, *The Dictators: Hitler's Germany and Stalin's Russia*.

[108] Jürgen Osterhammel, "Die Wiederkehr des Raumes: Geopolitik, Geohistorie und historische Geographie," *Neue Politische Literatur* 43 (1998): 374–97; Karl Schlögel, *Im Raume lesen wir die Zeit: Über Zivilisationsgeschichte und Geopolitik* (Munich: Carl Hanser Verlag, 2003).

[109] Zygmunt Bauman, *Modernity and the Holocaust* (Ithaca; NY: Cornell University Press, 1989); Amir Weiner, ed., *Landscaping the Human Garden: 20th-Century Population Management in a Comparative Framework* (Stanford, CA: Stanford University Press, 2003).

rare cases, forward to the Cold War), the extended comparison proved problematic because, for the most part, the national historiographies would not accommodate the long-term comparison, although there is an illustrious history of Russian-German (cultural) exchanges that ranges from the eighteenth to the twentieth centuries.[110] If the editors extended the time frame beyond the period of Nazism and Stalinism, what then was the subject of comparison? Was it democracy versus dictatorship, capitalism versus failing economies, West versus East? Why even limit the comparison to the twentieth century? Ultimately, the debate was not so much about periodization as it was about the proper subject of comparison. An even more pressing problem was how to characterize and define the period in question. If contemporaries agreed that it was a time of exceptional and exceptionally violent regimes, the resultant bias of participants was to think in terms of thirty years of war and revolution that climaxed in Stalinism and Nazism.

Fourth, the project of comparison is never neutral. As discussed above, comparison has been used time and again to justify the other regimes' actions or a third-party (American) intervention. The noxious popular and historiographical (mis)use of the other(s) as self-exculpation was on everyone's mind, although it rarely entered the debate. It is one thing, however, to avoid the invocation of the other as apology; it is quite another when this hesitation prevents one from exploring the actual imbrications of the two regimes and their ideologies.[111] What we know is that the two regimes were keenly aware of each other, observed each other, and, in several crucial cases, misjudged each other. We also know, at least in the German case (for example, the mobilization of female labor), that "the other" often acted as shorthand for what was impermissible. What we do not know is when and how the two regimes mobilized this discrete knowledge and how factual observation and fiction intertwined.

The emphasis on the intensity and aggressiveness of action that characterized the peculiar historicity of the two regimes suggested that we study practice. We were particularly interested in the act of governing, the act of using violence, the act of making society, and the act of the two regimes engaging and imagining each other. We failed, however, to reach any agreement on the role of ideology and what constituted its practice. Thus, education and architecture as sites of ideological practice fell by the wayside, as did distinct acts of believing (secular and religious). Of course, the point can be made that ideology was not a discrete domain, but an element in grounding and projecting action, without which governance, violent action, and socialization were impossible. And, hence, one may argue that ideology acted as an integral element in all practice.[112] Despite

---

[110] Karl Schlögel, *Berlin Ostbahnhof Europas: Russen und Deutsche in ihrem Jahrhundert* (Berlin: Siedler, 1998); Klaus Zernack, *Polen und Russland: Zwei Wege in der europäischen Geschichte* (Berlin: Propyläen Verlag, 1994).

[111] Wolfgang Kraushaar, "Sich aufs Eis wagen: Plädoyer für eine Auseinandersetzung mit der Totalitarismustheorie," *Mittelweg 36*, no. 2 (1993): 6–29.

[112] Lewis H. Siegelbaum, and Lewis H. Siegelbaum, eds., *Stalinism as a Way of Life: A Narrative in Documents* (New Haven, CT: Yale University Press, 2000).

some misgivings, the participants settled on this latter approach rather than breaking out ideology into a separate domain of research.[113]

GOVERNANCE. No one disputed the centrality of governance and the proximity, as opposed to separation, of state and society, although the latter was not always explicitly addressed. However, gone are ideas about the monolithic character of the political system, of obedience enforced by terror, of society as a receptor of leadership initiatives and, hence, also the concern with "levers of power" and the role of ideology. The discussion has shifted and with it the stakes in the comparative enterprise. The relevant question now is who controls the act of governing, how effective it is (and why), and what, if any, its limits are. A large and growing literature on the subject exists and we need not rehearse it at this point. Suffice it to say that by generating renewed interest in the question of legitimacy and the popularity of the regimes, social and cultural history has enhanced rather than detracted from the centrality of politics in both regimes.

Yoram Gorlizki's and Hans Mommsen's respective positions on the nature of the Stalinist and the Nazi regimes need no rehearsal here. Suffice it to say that Mommsen is well known for his structuralist approach to the Nazi regime that highlights its self-destructive social dynamics. Gorlizki pursues a reading of Stalinism that depicts the autocratic and centralized control of the Party in a symbiotic relationship with the state. Needless to say, their search for a common vantage point from which to argue their respective cases while maintaining a comparative perspective was intriguing. The resultant product, however, is an essay whose importance goes well beyond its stated focus on the state and party bureaucracy, the role of the leader, and the development (and legitimacy) of the two regimes. The added value derives from the authors' exploration into what distinguishes the two regimes: namely, that the Stalinist regime stabilized governance (with, rather than in spite of, terror and mass mobilization), whereas Nazism sought to revolutionize the state and used the war as a means of projecting a highly personalized and amorphous regime of authority on the state. The relative longevity of Stalinism and brevity and self-destructiveness of Nazism, the authors suggest, was not mere happenstance; it emerged out of the politics of the two regimes. Whether these divergent trajectories were the products of the founding moments of the two regimes, different levels of socioeconomic development, or other intervening factors, however, remains to be seen.

David Hoffmann and Annette Timm's contribution, "The Politics of Reproduction," approaches issues of governance from the societal end, revisiting the highly contested sphere of biopolitics. First, the two authors seek to establish the politics of reproduction as a site of governance in Stalinism and Nazism. While both regimes were pronatalist, neither regime succeeded in attaining the

---

[113] Igal Halfin, ed., *Language and Revolution: Making Modern Political Identities* (London and Portland, OR: F. Cass, 2002).

goal of increasing the birthrate. This observation establishes the authors' over-all position vis-à-vis their respective historiographies. In terms of comparison, the more intriguing observation is that "politics of reproduction" was an inter-national and, indeed, transnational phenomenon – and, hence, anything but homegrown. And yet, because their ideological foundations differed, Stalinist and Nazi approaches to reproductive policy could not have been further apart. In fact, the two shared more in common with third parties – Nazism with Scandinavia, Stalinism with Catholic countries! – than with each other. This, of course, raises the question, What was the goal of the two regimes' respective politics of reproduction? Was it to "make babies" (unsuccessfully, as the case was), or was it to articulate and reinforce a family ideal and, hence, to establish a politics of national cohesion? Hoffmann's and Timm's essay can also be read as a complement to and corrective of Fritzsche's and Hellbeck's essay on "The New Man."

The takeaway here is not that while the regimes shared certain features, they remained fundamentally different – that is only stating the obvious. Rather, the key point is that governance was central for both regimes and that both sought to overthrow older forms of governing. In view of the literature on totalitarianism it seemed important to highlight the rise of new policy areas in both regimes. For the canon of what constitutes politics was radically changed and expanded in both cases. This is also where the real questions begin. How does the act of governance actually work in these dictatorships and what does it take, in each case, to make it work – political patronage, a managerial outlook, bureaucratic procedures, working toward the Führer? What are the domains of an expanding political sphere that, at times, seems all-encompassing and, yet, clearly is not? What are the limits of centralized power and where are they – between center and periphery, at the seams of personalized rule? The most important issue, though, emerges from the observation that Stalinism was able to make and stabilize a political system with an overwhelmingly new elite, whereas the Nazis, with the support of the traditional elite, were not. If anything, this suggests that Nazism represents a failed revolution of the state and of the political system. The emphasis on statebuilding in the Soviet Union (at the expense of intermediate managerial structures) on one hand and the destruction of the bureaucratic state (and the rise of intermediate command authorities) in Nazi Germany on the other, together with the wholesale shift in policy-areas, are among the most important findings.

VIOLENCE. Focusing on politics, however, violates one of the first principles of the totalitarian model, which tends to subordinate politics to violence. State violence and terror, or so the argument goes, were essential elements in the totalitarian formula of rule.[114] Moreover, the phenomenon of the Gulag as a manifestation of Soviet state violence and the Holocaust as the central site of Nazi terror convey the unmistakable message that the two regimes were bent

---

[114] See, for example, Zbigniew Brzezinski, *The Permanent Purge: Politics in Soviet Totalitarianism* (Cambridge, MA: Harvard University Press, 1956).

on genocide. But was the turn to crushing force a reflection of the weakness of power as Hannah Arendt would suggest? Did terror – or, at least, certain kinds of terror – enjoy popular support, was it self-vindication, a means of social mobilization and ideological identification? Could the regime count on popular participation? If we take the Gulag Archipelago and the Holocaust as key – but by no means exchangeable – sites of terror, how do they compare to other sites of terror – or should they be treated entirely separately (as has been argued for the Holocaust)? Is there an overarching schema of violence in each regime that would allow discerning family resemblances? Not least, we have the nightmare of comparison – the question of which of the two evils was worse and how to measure the relative depravity of the two regimes.[115] In light of all these debates, the two contributions addressing regime violence had their work cut out for them. In the end, they staked out two quite different positions – one emphasizing the social embeddedness of extreme violence, the other highlighting the ideological imperative to order multiethnic empire. If we add Edele and Geyer's essay to this set of reflections, we quickly discover that the most important area of debate is less the differences between the regimes (which emerge very clearly) than the nature and the purpose of extreme violence which both regimes exercised and in which both societies participated.

Gerlach and Werth stepped back from the overheated debate regarding the comparison of Nazi and Soviet terror and closed the door on older debates concerning ideology versus economy, intentionalism versus structuralism, and similar dichotomies. They plead instead for the multicausality and multidimensionality of the violence of the two regimes – from systematic starvation to outright mass murder – and, consequently, for a broadening of the field of inquiry. Furthermore, they highlight the need for proper contextualization and historicization, so as avoid the impression that violence emerges out of the arbitrary rule of dictatorship. It is, after all, revealing that much of Soviet violence turned internal violence outward, while Nazi terror served first and foremost expansion. The authors also address the recent (primarily Germanist) concern with the study of perpetrators. Again, the "thick" comparison reveals important differences between the two nations' regimes of terror – rather than a planet Auschwitz or Gulag, we see two distinct universes developing along independent trajectories. Exemplary of this difference is the degree of underplanning and overfulfillment and overplanning and underfulfillment of goals in the Stalinist and Nazi regimes, respectively. But the key proposition is that

[115] It should be recalled that this was the subject of one of the most arduous postwar German controversies, the so-called *Historikerstreit*, which was centrally focused on the provocation of Ernst Nolte, who insisted that Nazi genocide and the Holocaust were derivative of and reacted to Bolshevik barbarism in the (Russian) Civil War. Ernst Nolte, "Marxismus und Nationalsozialismus," *Vierteljahrhefte für Zeitgeschichte* 31 (1983): 389–417; Rudolf Augstein, ed., *"Historikerstreit": Die Dokumentation der Kontroverse um die Einzigartigkeit der nationalsozialistischen Judenvernichtung* (Munich: R. Piper, 1987); *Forever in the Shadow of Hitler? Original Documents of the Historikerstreit, the Controversy Concerning the Singularity of the Holocaust* (Atlantic Highlands, NJ: Humanities Press, 1993).

violence, while mostly state driven, was deeply embedded in the respective societies. This raises not only the question of the nature of social violence, but also how and why this massive propensity for violence developed within the two societies.

In their contribution on Stalinism and Nazism as expansionist regimes, Baberowski and Doering-Manteuffel offer something of an antidote. While they surely would subscribe to most of the features highlighted by Gerlach and Werth, they are more impressed by the use of terror and violence as tools in the (re)construction of society and its ultimately counterproductive results. Building on Baumann's gardening metaphor, they emphasize the quest for and the imposition of order through violence. They further note that the extreme violence of the regimes, lethal as it was, not only failed in its pernicious goals, but left a legacy of destruction and a haunted politics of memory that have produced chaos in both the short and the long run. Lastly, they contend that Nazi and Stalinist violence is only conceivable in imperial space and in the peculiar drive to order that space. This proposition fits in well with the German debate on the subject but may well raise eyebrows in the Soviet context. In any case, Baberowski and Doering-Manteuffel have placed imperial planification as a source of extreme violence on the map.

In working through the research of the past thirty years these findings not only identify new areas of research, they rephrase some of the initial questions raised by contemporaries facing the extraordinary violence of Nazism and Stalinism. There are gains and losses to record here. The immediate contemporaries by necessity all started with the shock of recognition of unheard-of atrocities and worked their way toward a phenomenology of extreme violence, which they placed within or just beyond the boundaries of available thought. It took a long while before the experience of violence itself gained a voice. Nowadays we can observe the reverse: historians work their way from the world of actors – societies, regimes, and ideologies – toward the violence they perpetrated. The shock of extreme violence is diffused in numbers, the pervasiveness of terror, and the minute description of how it happened. To be sure, this is all necessary work, which national history cannot and should not escape. But in this situation, comparison works like Occam's razor and compels judgment. What, if anything, is captured by the notion of extreme violence? How do we distinguish killing from murder, Soviet from Nazi terror, and the latter from the violence of other belligerents in the thirties and forties? And not least, what is to be gained from historicizing violence? The answers may differ for Stalinism and Nazism, Germany and Russia; but much can be gained if we can make sense of both histories – and comparative history is a discriminating interlocutor, especially when it comes to violence, as the two essays on the subject suggest.[116] Of course, a history of violence and terror is only complete if war becomes an integral aspect of this. But the latter moves us from a comparative to an entangled

---

[116] A good start is Robert Gellately and Ben Kiernan, eds., *The Specter of Genocide: Mass Murder in Historical Perspective* (Cambridge and New York: Cambridge University Press, 2003).

history, in which the present and future of one regime are implicated in those of the other. Especially if we add Edele's and Geyer's essay, the conclusion is that, although we know a great deal, the question of extreme violence is still very far from resolved.

THE MAKING OF SOCIETY (*VERGESELLSCHAFTUNG*). While totalitarian models overwhelmingly focused on the state, the "regime," or the "system," the study of society became a subject of study early on – and here, Sovietologists took the lead. Working with refugees in Europe and North America, they investigated social stratification and mobility, the attitudes of various groups to the political system, and even informal social connections.[117] The difference between this early work and what came later is, perhaps, best characterized by the adherence of the earlier work to basic class categories – workers, peasants, and so forth – whereas more recent work is more fascinated with the capacity of social classification to generate social realities rather than simply reflect them.[118] "Ascribing class" is, of course, only one dimension of this process; ascribing nation – ethnic, racial, or otherwise – and generating a sense of nationness in fractured (German) and quicksand (Soviet) societies is another one.

Browning and Siegelbaum position themselves squarely in the "ascribing class" and "ascribing nation" paradigm and produce a beautiful example of comparative history that pinpoints the similarity of regime strategies – vis-à-vis the legitimization of new identities and the repression of old ones – and the very different trajectories that ultimately resulted. They are keenly aware of the violence involved in the act of ascription as well as in the ideological underpinnings of discursive regimes that, much as they are pushed from above, are regenerated from below. They also tentatively point to the transnational quality of these ascriptive categories and note their intrinsic differences. Class, after all, is a universal category, whereas race is categorically not. They are, however, skeptical of the more far-reaching claims of a categorical confusion (in which each regime takes over attributes of the other) and, instead, emphasize the effectiveness of the nation remade in war to create distinct postwar national identities. The double irony is that not only was it war and sacrifice that ultimately ascribed identity, but that the more exclusive German-völkish identity mutated into a cosmopolitan transnationalism after defeat, while the universal ideals of class disappeared into Soviet nationalism and, as far as Eastern Europe was concerned, imperialism.

In their article, Fitzpatrick and Lüdtke eschewed many of the standard issues of everyday scholarship, including the common concern with resistance, in order to retest a "classic" thesis, first introduced by Hannah Arendt and

---

[117] Alex Inkeles and Raymond Augustine Bauer, *The Soviet Citizen: Daily Life in a Totalitarian Society* (Cambridge, MA: Harvard University Press, 1959).

[118] Sheila Fitzpatrick, "Ascribing Class: The Construction of Social Identity in Soviet Russia," *Journal of Modern History* 65, no. 4 (1993): 745–70; idem, *Tear off the Masks! Identity and Imposture in Twentieth-Century Russia* (Princeton: Princeton University Press, 2005).

Barrington Moore, that emphasized the ability of the regimes to create a sense
of belonging in what 1950s scholarship called an atomized society, a society
in which social bonds were torn asunder either in the grand processes of modernization, industrialization, and urbanization or in the terrifying processes of
war, mobilization, and civil war. The results of their investigation are puzzling.
For as much as evidence points to societal bonds fracturing or, at a minimum, to conditions (war, inflation, and mobility) suggesting they would, there
is contrary evidence intimating that bonds of family and friendship actually
strengthened, as did workplace bonds. All this suggests that the regenerative
powers of society cannot be underestimated. However, we do not yet fully
understand the nature of this capability or the impetus that leads some of these
labors of togetherness to identify with the state and others to turn against it.

The third essay on shaping the social body by Fritzsche and Hellbeck might
be considered in opposition to the previous one, because it is so distinctly
ideology driven. They argue that the two regimes intended to create a new
collective subject, an entirely modern, illiberal, and self-fashioned personage.
They point to the long intellectual tradition of imagining this kind of subject,
the initiatives to create such personalities, and, in an exemplary fashion, the
kind of striking conversion experience that real persons underwent in becoming
not just dedicated Nazis and Stalinists, but new "men." While these labors of
self-transformation in Nazi Germany and Soviet Russia differed in significant
respects, the point of this essay is to highlight the ways in which Nazism and
Stalinism were literally embodied in the lives of people. That discipline was
central in both projects is noteworthy, not least because it suggests a site where
ascribing class, creating bonds of belonging, and transforming the self intersect
in a telling fashion. Overall, this line of inquiry – one of the key contributions
of a new Soviet history that explores – opens up a wide arena of study that
might, indeed, compare the rage for the "self-made" and "self-help man" and
may well link it to a hitherto unexplored politics of intimacy.[119]

All three of these studies on societalization depart from the older literature
that spoke of society "under" Nazism or Stalinism and, quite compellingly,
explore the extent to which the two regimes left deep and lasting imprints
on the social makeup of these nations and on social and individual self-
understanding – because ascription was transmuted into self-definition and
identification. This is the grand wager of a new social history of the two
regimes. What has been demonstrated conclusively is that the ascription of
class and nation not only occurred, but that it was perniciously effective. We
do not know with the same clarity and the same conviction how this project of
ascription worked, what social and individual needs and desires it articulated,

[119] Moritz Föllmer, "[Einleitung] Interpersonelle Kommunikation und Moderne in Deutschland."
   in *Sehnsucht nach Nähe: Interpersonelle Kommunikation in Deutschland seit dem 19. Jahrhundert* (Stuttgart: Franz Steiner Verlag, 2004), 9–44; Marie-Anne Matard-Bonucci and Pierre
   Milza, eds., *L'homme nouveau dans L'Europe fasciste, 1922–1945: Entre dictature et totalitarisme* (Paris: Fayard, 2004).

and what it really amounted to in the self-fashioning of individual identities. Nor do we have a strong sense of timing – that is, whether or not Stalinism and Nazism were particularly "pregnant" times for shaping German and Russian society. Finally, we do not know how to evaluate exigencies – the role of scarcities, life-and-death situations – or, equally important, the penchant of people to not get involved in anything at all, let alone in such arduous schemes as self-fashioning. It seems evident, though, that social groups, rather than merely being a site of regime action, are actors in their own right, actors whose practices, as, for example, the strategies of societalization (*Vergesellschaftung*), we need to fully understand before we can begin to fathom the legacies of Stalinism and Nazism. Just on the horizon of this kind of history we also discover that, much as the local and particular dominates, these social actors partake in a wider world that is partly made up of fantasies and projections, but partly also the product of transnational practices.

ENTANGLEMENTS. To move this project of revisiting Stalinism and Nazism beyond totalitarianism requires one more essential step: to explore not only the two regimes' image of each other, but the interactive processes and imaginary transaction that made Stalinism and Nazism what they were. There is, of course, a long tradition of studies that either focus on all manner of, but especially cultural exchanges between Russia and Germany or, alternatively, on war with Germany and Russia as allies, neutrals, and mortal enemies.[120] But despite various initiatives to the contrary, war and culture (and the never to be forgotten economy) retain separate trajectories and all of them hit a wall when it comes to Nazism and Stalinism. To be sure, the image of the other is by now rather well explored, but the monstrous imbrications and entanglements of Nazism and Stalinism have yet to be fully recognized. For however we turn them, the past, present, and future of both regimes and what came of them are inseparable from their *histoire croisée*.[121]

In their essay, "States of Exception," Edele and Geyer start from the proposition that in order for the notion of extreme violence to be productive it has to both enable a better understanding of the historical place of the Soviet-German war and account for the relationship between war and genocide as well as genocide and the Holocaust. The Soviet-German war was the pivotal war of twentieth-century Europe and, arguably, the twentieth-century world. It was also the climax of more than twenty years of war, revolution, and violence. The war that these two regimes fought is often called a "total war," but, the authors argue, the totality of it makes sense only if we understand it – in both practical and ideological terms – as a life and death struggle. In this context,

---

[120] Karl Schlögel, *Jenseits des großen Oktober: Das Laboratorium der Moderne, Petersburg 1909–1921* (Berlin: Siedler, 1988).

[121] Bernhard Chiari, "Geschichte als Gewalttat: Weißrußland als Kind zweier Weltkriege," in *Wehrmacht, Verbrechen, Widerstand: Vier Beiträge zum nationalsozilistischen Weltanschauungskrieg*, ed. Clemens Vollnhals (Dresden: Hannah Arendt Institut für Totalitarismusforschung, 2003), 27–44.

the question of genocide and how to place it in a history of war – and of Russo-German and Nazi-Soviet war at that – is still largely unresolved. The immediate question concerns the Holocaust, the Nazi murder of any and all Jews, in an environment of ethnic cleansing.[122] But the general question concerns the nature of war, which in the eastern parts of Europe was rarely ever contained in military battle and guided by politics. Again, the issue of comparison arises with considerable urgency, for, in their enmity, the two societies seem to have converged rather than moved apart. Thus, it can be argued, as Amir Weiner has done for the Soviet side (and Nolte for the German side), that one side acquired traits of the other – although we need to be careful in identifying what those traits were.[123] The authors suggest an altogether more entangled approach. The comparative and genetic impetus gives way to an interactive approach in which enmity shapes a peculiarly warped exchange that leaves a legacy beyond victory and defeat.

In the final essay, Clark and Schlögel analyze the process of mutual image making, a process that gained particular valence as a result of the competition and conflict between the two regimes. That the Soviet image machine fared relatively well with its split imagination as the preserver of (German) culture in a barbaric war and as the relentless resistor against imperial aggression, whereas the German image machine proved so relentlessly and violently racist, points again to the utopian dimension of one ideology and the dystopian dimension of the other. But even on the Nazi side, multiple and conflicting images coexisted. Even if we want to think of this phenomenon as an Orientalism and an Occidentalism, we still have to deal with the simultaneous importance of the phenomenon, its slippery instability, and its extremely violent realization. Overall, it is surprising how little we actually know about how the two nations understood and imagined each other.

There are two additional observations regarding an interactive German-Russian, Nazi-Soviet comparison that lead to a more general observation on the nature of comparison. The first concerns the very presence of the other side, wanted or unwanted, in each regime – Russian émigrés in Germany and occupied Europe, former Soviet subjects in German military and police units, and, conversely, Germans in Russian ones, German propaganda against the Nazi war effort, and, not least, the German origins of Marxism and the Bolshevik presence in German Communism. All of this demonstrates how porous and permeable national boundaries have proven for people and ideas. This phenomenon points not only to interpenetration, but also to a shared culture or discourse of modernity. Rather than expelling Stalinism and Nazism from this

---

[122] Norman M. Naimark, *Fires of Hatred: Ethnic Cleansing in Twentieth-Century Europe* (Cambridge, MA: Harvard University Press, 2001). See also the contributions of Gerlach and Werth as well as Baberowski and Doering-Manteuffel.

[123] Weiner, *Making Sense of War: The Second World War and the Fate of the Bolshevik Revolution.*

common culture, Clark and Schlögel strongly suggest that we must reintegrate them in order to gain a better understanding of both.

As we lift some of the dichotomizing weight off the comparison of Nazism and Stalinism, we notice that the comparison is burdened by other factors, as well. For we discover that, on the macro level, national imaginaries, contradictory and open-ended as they may be, are never innocent – and neither is their comparison. A sense of superiority is deeply invested in these imaginaries – and so too is a sense of inferiority. That is to say, comparison has its own practice. It is not something that scholars do (and do objectively), but something that nations and people experience as a simultaneous sense of empowerment and emasculation. The most concrete expressions of this phenomenon were the racist supremacy of German soldiers, on one hand, and mass rape as an act of humiliation, on the other. We might also discover it in the hidden agenda of so much totalitarian comparison that sets these two dictatorships against the third, unspoken alternative of (American) liberal capitalism and the bristling feeling of the illegitimacy of comparison that accompanies the statements of even avowed antitotalitarians in Russia and Germany. Comparison, we discover, is an emotional and, indeed, moral business.

PART I

GOVERNANCE

2

The Political (Dis)Orders of Stalinism and National Socialism

Yoram Gorlizki and Hans Mommsen

The onset of perestroika and the collapse of the Soviet system promised to redress a long-standing imbalance in the study of Stalinism and Nazism. Previous restrictions on archival access and on the openness of official Soviet discourse had meant that the corpus of credible academic research on Stalinism had lagged behind the equivalent scholarship on the Nazi system.[1] The opening of the archives and the emergence of a meticulous and even-handed post-Soviet historical scholarship have done much to set this imbalance to rights.[2] Among the most striking revelations of the last fifteen years has been the unearthing

[1] As late as 2000, in the fourth edition of his textbook, *The Nazi Dictatorship*, Ian Kershaw wrote: "Research into Stalinist government and society has reached nowhere near the level of penetration of that into the Nazi regime, and comparisons are in fact often highly superficial." See Ian Kershaw, *The Nazi Dictatorship: Problems and Perspectives of Interpretation*, 4th ed. (London: Arnold, 2000), 35.

[2] Two of the most important published archival sources on the political history of Stalinism are the series "Dokumenty sovetskoi istorii" published by ROSSPEN under the general editorship of Andrea Graziosi and Oleg Khlevniuk, and the series "Rossiia. XX vek. Dokumenty" published by Mezhdunarodnyi Fond "Demokratiia" under the general editorship of A. N. Yakovlev. The first series, which commenced in 1995, is now in its twelfth substantial volume while the second, which began in 1997 and which includes books outside the Stalin period, has now yielded over twenty volumes. An example of the excellent new Russian scholarship on the political history of Stalinism is O. V. Khlevniuk, *Politbiuro: Mekhanizmy politicheskoi vlasti v 1930-e gody* (Moscow: ROSSPEN, 1996), now available in English as *Master of the House: Stalin and His Inner Circle*, trans. Nora Seligman Favorov (New Haven, CT: Yale University Press, 2008).

We owe a special debt to Michael Geyer for his encouragement and sage advice. Thanks are also due to the participants at the Harvard and Chicago workshops and, in particular, to Sheila Fitzpatrick, Peter Fritzsche, Terry Martin, Lewis Siegelbaum, Ron Suny, and Nicolas Werth for valuable suggestions. A later version of the essay was presented at the CREES History Seminar at the University of Birmingham. Although we are unlikely to have convinced him, we are grateful to the discussant, Richard Overy, for his trenchant criticisms and to the other participants, especially John Barber, Don Filtzer, and Melanie Ilic, for theirs. The essay has further benefited from readings and comments by Oleg Khlevniuk, Vera Tolz, Mark Harrison, Peter Gatrell, and Bob Davies. Yoram Gorlizki also thanks Boaz Evron for stimulating conversations on this theme.

of a large body of evidence incriminating the Stalinist leadership in successive waves of violence against their own population. Detailed revelations on Stalinist "ethnic cleansing," on the elaborate network of slave labor camps across the country, and on Stalin's own blood-stained involvement in the running of a fiercely coercive state have tended to accentuate the strong family resemblances that bound the two systems and set them apart from the other personal dictatorships of interwar Europe. While other regimes may have had dictators and one-party states geared toward mass mobilization, none "repressed, enslaved, and then killed millions of their subjects," as Hitler's Germany and Stalin's Soviet Union did. "The two regimes belong together," the sociologist Michael Mann was to write in the mid-1990s. "It is only a question of finding the right family name."[3]

While attention has unsurprisingly turned to the new, fine-grained, and often gruesome accounts we now have of individual tragedies, and to the leaderships' culpability in the deliberate and calculated murder of hundreds of thousands of victims, that is not our purpose here.[4] Instead, our intention is to start by looking specifically at the internal political dynamics of the two regimes. Incorporating some of the empirical findings of the last fifteen years, especially from the Soviet archives, we shall argue that while Stalin's Soviet Union and Nazi Germany both had tyrants and ruling parties, the attitude and behavior of their rulers, the internal organization of their parties, and the interaction between the two were markedly different, leading to divergent patterns of development. While the higher degree of party-based institutionalization in the Soviet case enabled the leadership over the long term to keep the dynamics of political mobilization in check, in Nazi Germany the greater reliance on the institutionally amorphous cult of the Führer, on the free-floating retinue structures around him, and on a relentlessly expansionist ideology led the dynamics of political mobilization to spill out of control.

We argue that one of the reasons for this divergence was that the two dictatorships emerged in response to crises within societies at differing moments of

---

[3] Michael Mann, "The Contradictions of Continuous Revolution," in *Stalinism and Nazism: Dictatorships in Comparison*, eds. Ian Kershaw and Moshe Lewin (Cambridge: Cambridge University Press, 1997), 135. Richard Overy's recent volume, while empirically much richer, is similar in its stress on the camps and on the scale of violence as the key distinguishing feature that unites the two regimes. "The camps," Overy writes, "are what make the Hitler and Stalin dictatorships appear so distinctive from other forms of modern authoritarianism." Later, he goes on: "The two dictatorships did not just crush lives in their prisons and camps; one or the other, they destroyed entire ancient communities, exterminated millions, deported millions from their homelands.... The mere reiteration of these unimaginable statistics sets the two dictatorships apart from anything else in the modern age." See Richard Overy, *The Dictators: Hitler's Germany, Stalin's Russia* (London: Penguin Books, 2005), 594, 644–5.

[4] For a fine microstudy which traces the effects of Soviet repressive policies to the local level, see Nicolas Werth, *Cannibal Island: Death in a Siberian Gulag*, trans. Steven Rendall (Princeton, NJ: Princeton University Press, 2007). The subject of state violence is also tackled in greater detail in the chapter in this volume by Christian Gerlach and Nicolas Werth.

socioeconomic development and national integration. The Stalinist regime, as with the October Revolution before it, must be interpreted against the background of Russia's historical backwardness. It was this backwardness – defined in no small measure vis-à-vis Germany – which had induced Lenin to push for a "committee of professional revolutionaries" which could both operate in a hostile political environment and provide the unity and leadership needed to haul Russia into the orbit of the advanced Western states. In the absence of the large industrial working-class class base and the civil freedoms enjoyed by the German Social Democrats, Lenin had laid great stress on proper organization and inner party discipline. "Take the Germans. It will not be denied, I hope . . . that the working class movement there has learned to walk," he had noted in 1903. "But what takes place very largely automatically in a politically free country must in Russia be done deliberately and systematically by our organizations."[5]

After the October Revolution, backed by a growing central apparatus the party assumed a leading role in the first phase of Bolshevik state-building which lasted from 1919 to 1923. Russia's "backwardness" – again, coincidentally, vis-à-vis Germany – would also provide the background to the second phase of Bolshevik state-building from 1930 to 1934. The crash course industrialization of those years, designed to defend Russia from its more economically advanced adversaries, was accompanied by the introduction of a panoply of steering organizations, most notably in the economy. The establishment of a full-blown Stalinist state in the mid-1930s was matched by a radical social transformation. By the end of the decade Stalin's "revolution from above" had transformed the prerevolutionary class structure and created a completely new political and economic elite, which, in contrast to Nazi Germany, had sundered all ties to the prerevolutionary ruling order.

The Nazi regime emerged in a relatively advanced industrial economy where the relation of party to society was in many respects the mirror image of Russia. Whereas the Bolshevik party strove toward centralism, the Nazi party was poorly integrated and owed most of what coherence it had to the unifying force of its leader. Where the Bolsheviks seized power against the backdrop of a highly unsettled and fluid class structure marked by fast-changing party allegiances, the Nazis, as with other European fascist movements, were latecomers

[5] V. I. Lenin, "What Is to Be Done?" in Lenin, *The Years of Reaction and of the New Revival (1908–1914)*, vol. 1, ed. J. Fineberg (London: Lawrence and Wishart, 1936), 135, 147. This vision of the Bolsheviks as a tightly knit unit was of course a far cry from the fractious, fragmented, and fast-growing party of 1917. Nevertheless, impelled by the military and economic emergencies of the Civil War, the Bolsheviks did take up a centralized interventionist approach, especially from 1919, to marshaling the country's troops and economic resources. The need for centralization was an abiding theme of Lenin's throughout this period. See, for example, his "Can the Bolsheviks Retain State Power?", the second edition of which was published after the October Revolution but before the Civil War, in V. I. Lenin, *Collected Works*, vol. 26 (London: Lawrence and Wishart, 1964), 116–17.

on a political scene in which social cleavages had hardened and in which a nascent party system had already taken shape.[6] Having made their prerevolutionary pitch to an embryonic Russian proletariat – in Bolshevik parlance, the future "winners" of industrialization – the Communist Party leadership of the late 1920s went on to seek a social base for the coming Socialist Offensive in the fast-growing urban working class. In Germany although the National Socialists in the late 1920s did increasingly turn their attention to the sizable German working class, the political loyalty of much of this group had already been courted by the Nazis' opponents, the Communists and Social Democrats. Instead, the National Socialists relied on a highly heterogeneous mix of supporters, many of whom, as former nonvoters, came from social groups that were the least integrated into the relatively mature class and party structures of German society.[7]

Historical circumstances affected not only the tactics but the revolutionary potential of the Nazi and Bolshevik movements. Despite the recession and the economic crisis of the 1920s, the German class structure was not pulverized as Russia's had been by the events of 1914 to 1921. In Germany, the forces of the establishment remained sufficiently sturdy to prevent a full revolutionary takeover and to force a number of compromises on the Nazis. Whereas the Bolsheviks completely broke with established economic interests, offering only a partial and temporary reprieve during NEP, the Nazis coopted industrial and national-conservative groups, making them key players in their regime. While the Nazi regime did undergo a radical overhaul toward the end of the 1930s, this was fueled by the regime's expansionist ambitions and was, accordingly, directed outward. At no point did the Nazis commit themselves, as the party leadership under Stalin certainly did, to a coordinated program for the wholesale restructuring of domestic state and society.[8]

---

[6] Juan Linz, "Some Notes toward a Comparative Study of Fascism in Sociological Historical Perspective," in *Fascism: A Reader's Guide*, ed. Walter Laqueur (Harmondsworth: Penguin, 1979), 14–15, 26.

[7] For more on the role of former nonvoters in the Nazis' rise to power, see Jürgen W. Falter, *Hitlers Wähler* (Munich: Beck, 1991), esp. 369–70.

[8] Here our emphasis differs from that of those who see the emergence of a "racial state" in Germany in the 1930s. We suggest that the impact of the "racial state," which sought the purification of state and society on racial lines, was far more limited than Stalin's "revolution from above," which led to an unprecedented internal transformation of Soviet society. None of the consequences of the "racial state" for German state and society can compare with the effects of forced collectivization, the mass migration to the cities, the transformation of the country's occupational structure, and the Great Purges, on the USSR in the 1930s. As we shall see later, Leninist ideology also had a much greater impact on the *internal design* of the Soviet state than did the ideology of the "racial state" on German political institutions. For more on the "racial state" see, in particular, Michael Burleigh and Wolfgang Wipperman, *The Racial State: Germany 1933–1945* (Cambridge: Cambridge University Press, 1991). Other, more recent works which lay emphasis on the role of racial ideology in German society include Claudia Koonz, *The Nazi Conscience* (Cambridge, MA: Belknap Press of Harvard University Press, 2003); Jeffrey Herf, *The Jewish Enemy: Nazi Propaganda during World War II and the Holocaust* (Cambridge,

In concentrating on the role of political institutions, we do not aim to demean the importance of personal political values or of collective political identities, themes which are covered in some detail elsewhere in this volume.[9] It would nonetheless be folly to ignore the fact that in the 1930s Germany and the Soviet Union both had identifiable political institutions such as ruling parties, state bureaucracies, and leadership structures, which, as well as commanding considerable human resources, served as motors for their social and economic systems as a whole. "Stalinism" and "Nazism" may have existed as specific "subjectivities,"[10] but they also existed as distinct political systems as well. Fixing on two directly comparable and empirically concrete aspects of these systems – the roles of their leaders and ruling parties – will also allow us to trace two distinct lines of development and to show how the two political orders were moving, as it were, at different speeds and in different directions. Close scrutiny of the inner dynamics of the political order will, we go on to argue, reveal a variety of contrasts between the two social orders which other large-scale comparisons have tended to disregard or ignore.[11]

We accept that the relationship between political structures and the social undercurrents that swirled beneath them was often far from straightforward. In the Soviet case, Lenin's, and subsequently Stalin's, "relentless insistence on the centrality of political power, order, and systematic building" and technocratic vision of "the party as a vast office or factory" were often superimposed on an extremely fluid social reality.[12] If anything, the insistence on "plan," "discipline," and "organization" was repeated so often – especially in the first phase of Stalinist state-building – precisely in order to make up for an external social reality that was quite the reverse; where the leadership did try to narrow the gap between their own political goals and this reality they often ended up

---

MA: Belknap Press of Harvard University Press, 2006); and Christopher R. Browning, "Ideology, Culture, Situation, and Disposition: Holocaust Perpetrators and the Group Dynamic of Mass Killing," *NS-Gewaltherrschaft: Beiträge zur historischen Forschung und juristischen Aufarbeitung*, eds. Alfred Gottwaldt, Norbert Kampe, and Peter Klein (Berlin: Edition Hentrich, 2005), 66–76.

[9] Chapters 6, 7 and 8, by Siegelbaum and Browning, Fitzpatrick and Lüdtke, and Fritzsche and Hellbeck in this volume.

[10] See chapter 8 by Peter Fritzsche and Jochen Hellbeck in this volume.

[11] Richard Overy's impressive work *The Dictators* is a case in point. It is invariably in its efforts to press the homologies between the two systems that its arguments become most forced and its empirical errors – especially on the Soviet side – most glaring. Few specialists, for example, would accept the statement that "Kirov seems to have had little fear of Stalin" (thereby enhancing the parallels between the effects of Kirov's assassination and those of Ernest's Röhm's murder, both in 1934), the argument that Stalin had at his disposal a "secret state" centered on the Special Sector (thereby downplaying the importance of the ordinary central party apparatus in the USSR), or the assertion that the party as an institution somehow declined in the late 1930s (thereby bringing our notion of the Soviet political system into line with common interpretations of the role of the NSDAP). Cf. Overy, *The Dictators*, 52, 66–8, 70, 169–70.

[12] See Richard Stites, *Revolutionary Dreams: Utopian Vision and Experimental Life in the Russian Revolution* (Oxford: Oxford University Press, 1989), 44–5.

only in widening it.[13] Some scholars have generalized from instances of this kind to argue that it was the huge disparity between the lofty political goals of the regimes and the often brutal realities on the ground that, in some sense, helps us to define these systems.[14] In order to chart the political evolution of these states we nonetheless contend that it is vital to take the stated ambitions and institutional strategies of their leaders seriously. It was, in the first instance, their distinctive leadership strategies that set the National Socialist and Bolshevik movements apart from their wider political habitats. In 1926 it had been the reorganization of the National Socialists around an unconditional allegiance to Hitler that set the NSDAP apart from the host of tiny nationalist splinter groups that populated the German political scene;[15] in Russia, similarly, it had been the fact that it ran against the grain of traditional modes of Russian social organization that made Leninism as a creed and ideology so distinct.[16] As we shall see, once they had come to power the distinctive leadership strategies of the two movements would also have a palpable impact on their regimes by determining the shape and structure of their states and internal bureaucracies.

The Nazi and Bolshevik regimes shared many features in common. Both were autocratic police states which within months of coming to power had cracked down on opposition groups and imposed severe restrictions on civil liberties. In both the state made far-reaching demands on its citizens and placed severe limits on the private sphere. Further, the two states were both "movement regimes" marked by a continuous tension between an authority-building position, aimed at strengthening the economy and consolidating the state, and a dynamic mobilizational element aimed at transforming attitudes and preventing stagnation.[17] The balance struck between these two tendencies would, however, be very different. Over the longer term the Stalinist state showed that it could contain the dynamic element of the party and subordinate it to the longer-term goals of state-building. In the Nazi regime, however, it was the mobilizational element which took over, with highly destructive consequences. We shall argue that the divergent paths followed by the two dictatorships were

---

[13] This point, often made of the early 1930s, is a major theme of Moshe Lewin's "The Disappearance of Planning in the Plan," reproduced as chapter 5 of his *Russia/USSR/Russia: The Drive and Drift of a Superstate* (New York: New Press, 1995), 95–113.

[14] "Each dictatorship," writes Overy, "exposed a wide gulf between the stated goal and the social reality. Bridging the gulf was a process that lay at the heart of dictatorship as it distorted reality and terribly abused those who objected." Overy, *The Dictators*, xi.

[15] See in particular Joseph Nyomarkay, *Charisma and Factionalism in the Nazi Party* (Minneapolis: University of Minnesota Press, 1967), 70.

[16] To cite Ken Jowitt: "In a society where personal attachments were an integral part of social organization, *Lenin's detachment was culturally revolutionary*" (italics ours). See his *New World Disorder: The Leninist Extinction* (Berkeley: University of California Press, 1992), 7.

[17] This was a theme of Hannah Arendt's, *The Origins of Totalitarianism*, 1st ed. (New York: Harcourt, Brace, 1951), esp. 389–91. The term "mass-movement regime" was coined by Robert C. Tucker, *The Soviet Political Mind: Stalinism and Post-Stalin Change* (New York: Norton, 1971), 7–13.

not a matter of chance, but were dictated by institutional factors which were built into the two systems: namely, the contrasting roles of party and leader in their respective societies.

STATE AND PARTY STRUCTURES

The Nazis and Bolsheviks faced diverse historical challenges with differing resources, facts which shaped their approach to the organization of the state. Amidst the devastation of revolution and civil war, the main task confronting the Bolsheviks was to construct unified and continuous political authority, predicated on a new and "revolutionary" form of legitimacy, across the country's territories. This was achieved by vesting authority in a new centralized Bolshevik apparatus. To this end, the core of the party was gradually transformed, from a mere propaganda appendage to the state, to a powerful bureaucracy, with new leading committees (the Politburo and Orgburo), a fast-growing staff, and the emergence of a national system of party-controlled appointments.[18] The tasks confronting the Nazis were markedly different. When the Nazis came to power the authority of the central state was firmly established. At the same time, the Nazi leadership had formally operated within the bounds of legality and, with the legitimacy earned from the March 1933 elections, had little need to anchor their authority in alternative "revolutionary" structures. In taking over a well-functioning central state administration Hitler had less need to embark on a wholesale program of state-building or to erect central party-based decision-making structures with their attendant bureaucracies.[19]

One of the key differences between the two regimes concerned the role of the party in managing the state and in overseeing the economy. In the Stalinist system the party and state became progressively intertwined. This process was spread out over two phases. The first, which lasted from 1919 to 1923, saw the emergence of central party authority and the construction of a hierarchy of party committees across the country. Without a central administration as such or even properly constituted committees in many regions, the Bolshevik party in the first months of the Civil War was in dire need of effective organization.[20]

---

[18] The number of staff at the Central Committee rose twentyfold from March 1919 to March 1921. See T. H. Rigby, *Political Elites in the USSR: Central Leaders and Local Cadres from Lenin to Gorbachev* (Aldershot: Elgar, 1990), 76.

[19] This is not to say that there were no efforts toward centralization on Hitler's accession. In 1933 and early 1934 the autonomy of the *Länder* assemblies was destroyed. At the same time the Ministry of Interior under Wilhelm Frick tried to get the Nazified state governments under its control, for example, through the installment of central plenipotentiaries, the Reich Statthalter. However, the Reichsreform pursued by Frick failed. One reason for this was that Hitler was unwilling to submit the Gauleiter, who by now operated with some independence as minister presidents or *Oberpräsidenten*, to governmental control.

[20] This is a point made forcefully by Robert Service, *The Bolshevik Party in Revolution, 1917–1923* (Basingstoke: Macmillan, 1979), 51–2, 54–5, 57–8, 61, 72–5.

At the VIII Party Congress in March 1919 two executive bodies, the Politburo and the Orgburo, were established and a major expansion of the Central
Committee's staff authorized. Over the following year, two departments, the
organization and instruction department and the record and assignment department, were created. In order to stamp the central party's authority on regional
party organizations, the Bolshevik leadership pressed on two fronts. First, to
ensure that their policies accorded with those of the Central Committee, a
Moscow-based apparatus was erected to monitor the regional and republican
tiers of the party. In some areas, most notably in Ukraine and Samara, republican and regional committees were entirely disbanded and replaced, while in
others, for example in Siberia, where party representation was thin on the
ground, scores of party functionaries were conscripted from the center to shore
up the authority of the regional party committee.[21] Working through periodic
inspections, personal reports from regional secretaries, and occasional visits
from high-ranking central plenipotentiaries, the organization and instruction
department under Lazar Kaganovich sought to ensure that regional and republican committees complied with the central party line.[22] Secondly, the Central
Committee built up an official system of patronage. The lapsing of elective
procedures, evident in 1920, when many officials were already either co-opted
or directly selected by plenipotentiaries, had by 1923 been widened and formalized into a general system for the selection and appointment of officials.
In April 1923, at the XII Party Congress, Stalin announced that "we need to
choose functionaries who are able to implement the party line... who are able
to accept the [party's] directives as their own and are able to bring them to
life."[23] Shortly afterward, as part of Stalin's efforts to improve the efficiency of
the party-based patronage system, a resolution "On appointments" of 12 June
1923 laid down procedures for the selection and transfer of senior officials who
were now formally grouped in two lists (*nomenklatury*), the first consisting of
posts which could change hands on a resolution of the Central Committee and
the second consisting of posts to be cleared with the newly created organization and assignment department (*orgraspred*).[24] The importance to Stalin of

---

[21] Robert V. Daniels, "The Secretariat and the Local Organizations in the Russian Communist
Party, 1921–1923," *American Slavic and East European Review*, 16, no. 1 (1957): 41–2, 46–7.

[22] Daniels, 37–40. Even Moshe Lewin, who tends to emphasize the fluidity of party organizations
during the Revolution and the early Civil War, accepts that by its end, "the party was well on its
way toward becoming an administrative machine dominated by its top leaders and, increasingly,
by its *apparaty*, with little or no say left for the rank and file." Lewin, "The Civil War: Dynamics
and Legacy," in *Party, State and Society: Explorations in Social History*, eds. Diane Koenker,
William G. Rosenberg, and Ronald Grigor Suny (Bloomington: Indiana University Press, 1989),
417.

[23] Joseph Stalin, *Sochineniia*, vol. 5 (Moscow: Gos. izd-vo polit. lit-ry, 1946), 210, cited in Aleksandr Livshin and Igor' Orlov, *Vlast' i obshchestvo: dialog v pis'makh* (Moscow: ROSSPEN,
2002), 64.

[24] Stalin's efforts at rationalizing the appointments system relied on reducing the number of
decisions made in Moscow, so that Central Committee departments could concentrate their
resources on the most important cases. As a result, the number of cadres assigned from Moscow

gaining central party control of regional party committees was underscored by his appointment in the mid-1920s of a variety of trusted officials, most of whom had served under him at the Central Committee in Moscow, as secretaries of strategic regional committees. This process would include the transfer of Lazar Kaganovich to Ukraine in 1925; of Sergei Kirov, Sergei Syrtsov, and Iosif Vareikis, respectively, to Leningrad, Saratov, and Siberia in 1926; and of Andrei Andreev to the North Caucasus in 1927.[25]

Recent research suggests that the assertion of central party controls in the 1920s was highly uneven and often quite superficial. This was particularly true of some of the outlying regions of the country, where, in the wake of the Civil War, local populations continued to view the Red Army and the Bolsheviks as an occupying force. To bolster the party's presence in these areas thousands of Communists were often drafted in, sometimes from relatively far-off regions.[26] For many regions it may also be premature to accept conventional chronologies which date the end of the Civil War in 1921. In some areas partisan wars flared up for much of the 1920s and continued, albeit on a lower key, until the violent uprisings of the collectivization period.[27] As important in these areas as the imposition of party controls were the presence of Red Army detachments and the arrival of secret police units, many of which played a key role in overseeing the collection of the "tax in kind" from famine-stricken peasants in the early 1920s.[28] In some outlying provinces the establishment of party rule was thus a joint operation in which the authority of the party, often acting on the ground through proxy agencies, was propped up through quasi-military techniques. In

---

was reduced from approximately 22,500 between March 1921 and April 1922 to 6,000 from April 1923 to May 1924. By 1926, however, the number of nomenklatura posts had expanded again by a half. See James Harris, "Stalin as General Secretary: The Appointments Process and the Nature of Stalin's Power," in *Stalin: A New History*, eds. Sarah Davies and James Harris (Cambridge: Cambridge University Press, 2005), 69–70; and Oleg Khlevniuk, "Sistema tsentr-regiony v 1930–1950e gody: Predposylki politizatsii 'nomenklatury,'" *Cahiers du Monde russe* 44, no. 2–3 (2003): 255.

[25] James Hughes, "Patrimonialism and the Stalinist System: The Case of S. I. Syrtsov," *Europe-Asia Studies* 48, no. 4 (1996): 551–68. On Kirov's arrival in Leningrad, see A. V. Kvashonkin et al., eds., *Bol'shevistskoe rukovodstvo: Perepiska: 1912–1927* (Moscow: ROSSPEN, 1996), 323; and 314–15, 318.

[26] Thus, for example, three-quarters of the 4,606 communists of the Podolya region in Ukraine in 1924 had been conscripted from other regions. See Valery Vasil'ev, "Vinnitsa Oblast," in *Centre-Local Relations in the Stalinist State, 1928–1941*, ed. E. A. Rees (Basingstoke: Palgrave, 2002), 168.

[27] The argument that the "war" continued after 1921, even though it did not assume a "front-line" form, is made in S. A. Pavliuchenkov, "Ekonomicheskii liberalizm v predelakh politicheskogo monopolizma," in *Rossiia nepovskaia* (Moscow: Novyi khronograf, 2002), 15. In Podolya the partisan war against Soviet power continued until 1925, only to be followed, shortly afterward in the autumn of 1927, by the application of "harsh repressive measures" in the region's grain procurement campaign and by the onset, in the first three months of 1930s, of violent peasant resistance. Vasil'ev, "Vinnitsa," 168–9, 171. On long-running conflicts in the border regions, also see Terry Martin, *The Affirmative Action Empire: Nations and Nationalism in the Soviet Union, 1923–1939* (Ithaca, NY: Cornell University Press, 2001), 313–14.

[28] Vasil'ev, 168; Pavliuchenkov, 38–9.

addition, the controls afforded the center by its manipulation of appointments were often less substantial than they seemed. Some of the fiercest opposition to Stalin in the late 1920s would come from those, such as Uglanov, Syrtsov, and Bauman, who had earlier been hand-picked at the Central Committee apparatus to bring provincial party organizations into line.[29] Despite the many efforts to subordinate regional party organizations, it was in the 1920s that the relative autonomy of provincial party committees, many of which were courted by the contending power factions in Moscow, reached its peak.[30]

The second stage of Stalinist state-building began in the late 1920s. Much of it centered on the goal, heralded by the First Five-Year Plan, of centralizing authority over the economy, as republican and regional tiers of administration surrendered important prerogatives, such as the right to allocate resources, to set targets, and to manage large- and medium-scale heavy industrial enterprises, to their new all-union superiors.[31] Ever concerned that the central directives emanating from Moscow existed only "on paper," Stalin attached particular importance to the apparatus for the "verification of implementation."[32] The forces of centralization seized not only the economy, but also the political sphere proper. The restructuring of party committees at all levels according to the branch system at the XVII Party Congress in 1934 was designed to bring all lines of command under the central party apparatus in Moscow. Furthermore, the formation of a department of leading party organs, also in 1934, and the widening of the Central Committee's nomenklatura a year later, were designed to beef up the Central Committee's oversight over provincial, city, and district committees.[33] In other fields as well, such as education, the arts, the security police, the armed forces, and the criminal justice system, newly established Moscow-based all-union authorities usurped administrative powers previously held by republican and regional bodies.[34] The creation of these new centralized hierarchies was accompanied, in the mid-1930s, by a finely differentiated and quite traditional system of ranks and titles which would not have been out of place in the Tsarist era. As Terry Martin rightly observes, however, while the cultural and social sectors may have taken a "traditionalist" turn after 1933, in

---

[29] E. A. Rees, "The Changing Nature of Centre-Local Relations in the USSR, 1928–1936," in *Centre-Local Relations in the Stalinist State, 1928–1941,* ed. E. A. Rees (Basingstoke: Palgrave, 2002), 15.

[30] On the widespread lack of control by the center of regional authorities, see Livshin and Orlov, 66, 82; on the degradation at the lower levels of administration, as reflected in high levels of drunkenness and corruption, see ibid, 76–9.

[31] A. V. Venediktov, *Organizatsiia gosudarstvennoi promyshlennosti v SSSR,* 2: 1921–1934 (Leningrad: Izdat. Leningrad. Univ., 1961), 540, 582–6.

[32] See O. V. Khlevniuk et al., eds., *Stalinskoe politbiuro v 30-e gody* (Moscow: ROSSPEN, 1995), 82–6.

[33] Khlevniuk, "First Generation of Stalinist 'Party Generals,'" in *Centre-Local Relations in the Stalinist State 1928–1941,* ed. E. A. Rees 48–9.

[34] See, for example, I. B. Berkhin, "K istorii razrabotki konstitutsii SSSR v 1936 g." in *Stroitel'stvo sovetskogo gosudarstva: Sbornik Statei: K 70–letiiu doktora istoricheskikh nauk, prof E. B. Genkinoi,* ed. Iuri Aleksandrovich Poliakov (Moscow: "Nauka," 1972), 67.

the political and economic fields these years witnessed an entrenchment, rather than a repudiation, of the main thrust of Stalin's "socialist offensive," one of the most important prongs of which was the assertion of a centralized political dictatorship.[35]

Centralization was accompanied by steps to fuse the country's party and state structures, especially at the summit of the political system. Stalin had long been frustrated by the estrangement of the Politburo from matters of economic administration.[36] He also appears to have been perturbed by the ability of the Council of People's Commissars (Sovnarkom) under Rykov to obstruct the Central Committee apparatus.[37] In September 1930 Stalin instructed Molotov to take over from Rykov as head of Sovnarkom:

> Vyacheslav, 1) It seems to me that the issue of the top government hierarchy should be finally resolved by the fall. This will also provide the solution to the matter of leadership in general, *because the party and soviet authorities are closely interwoven and inseparable from each other.* My opinion on that score is as follows . . . b) You'll have to take over Rykov's place as chairman of the Council of People's Commissars and Labor Defense Council. This is necessary. Otherwise, there will be a split between the soviet and the party leadership. *With such a setup, we'll have complete unity between soviet and party leaders, and this will unquestionably double our strength.*[38]

Six weeks later, on 4 November 1930, Stalin elaborated: "The chair of Sovnarkom exists so that in his everyday work he may carry out the directives of the party."[39]

The centralization of controls and the interlocking of party and state committees at the apex of the political system did not mean that regional political authorities voluntarily caved in to the will of the center. Although many regional party secretaries had been enthusiastic partisans of collectivization in 1930, the center encountered questioning and resistance from them during the famine and industrial disturbances of 1932.[40] In some areas, the center would continue to face obstruction from regional party authorities well into the 1930s. At the same time, an institutionally consolidated apparatus connecting the Central Committee with regional party authorities now existed. Long

---

[35] See Martin, 415.

[36] "The Politburo," Stalin had complained to Molotov in July 1925, "is in an awkward position because it has been torn away from economic affairs. . . . Take a look at *Ekonomicheskaia zhizn'* and you'll see that our funds are being allocated by Smilga and by Strumilin plus Groman, while the Politburo . . . is changing from a directing body into a court of appeals, into something like 'a council of elders.'" Lars T. Lih et al., eds., *Stalin's Letters to Molotov 1925–1936*, trans. Catherine A. Fitzpatrick (New Haven, CT: Yale University Press, 1995), 89.

[37] O. V. Khlevniuk, *Politbiuro: Mekhanizmy politicheskoi vlasti v 1930-e gody* (Moscow: ROSSPEN, 1996), 25.

[38] (Italics ours). Lars T. Lih et al, eds., 217.

[39] Khlevniuk, *Politbiuro*, 49–50.

[40] Khlevniuk, "The First Generation of Stalinist 'Party Generals,'" 42–5.

sinews stretching from the central party apparatus in Moscow relayed pressures to regional and district party committees on issues ranging from internal party control to the battle to increase industrial and agricultural production. For their part, most regional party bureaucracies were well staffed and enjoyed a wide range of responsibilities which included the appointment of regional-level executives in state and economic organizations. As for the regional soviets (that is, the formal agencies of the state), most were under the thumb of their equivalent party committee: thus the staff of their executive committees were often recommended, their policies approved, and even the dates of their meetings set by the party apparatus. By the mid-late 1930s in most provinces the seasonal and monthly rhythms of the party and state apparatus had become closely synchronized.[41]

Following two intensive phases of state-building in the early 1920s and 1930s the party apparatus of the mid-1930s consisted of a hierarchy of secretariats with wide responsibilities. In exercising patronage and in determining policy, the leading party committees and their bureaucracies had become inseparable from the activities of the state. By contrast, in Hitler's Germany the party's engagement with and control of the state apparatus were far more circumscribed. In opposition the NSDAP had never existed as a hierarchic committee-based body. Being deeply decentralized it spawned, as did other fascist movements, a variety of auxiliary organizations including, most significantly, its paramilitary combat organization the SA, which, in many areas, played a more important galvanizing role than did the party organization itself.[42] Conceived as a vehicle for political mobilization, the party had little in the way of institutionalized internal decision-making structures.[43] The party's rules of association, dating from June 1926, confirmed that Hitler could lead the party independently of the majority decisions of the party's managing board and ruling committees. The National Socialists' Reich directorate, consisting

---

[41] An old yet still valuable archive-based account is Merle Fainsod, *Smolensk under Soviet Rule* (Cambridge, MA: Harvard University Press, 1958), 62–7, 69–74, 93. For a more recent archival work, this time based on the Nizhnii Novgorod archives, which makes much the same points, see S. V. Ustinkin, "Apparat vlasti i mekhanizm upravleniia obschestva," in *Obshchestvo i vlast': Rossiiskaia provintsiia: 1930 g-iun'1941 g*, vol. 2, eds. Andrei Nikolaevich Sakharov et al. (Moscow: Institut rossiiskoi istorii RAN, 2002), 15–17. While the degree of party control clearly varied across the country, even in some of the more remote regions, such as West Siberia, where, according to Shearer, "the institutions of Soviet power were [still] poorly established" in the early to mid-1930s, by the end of the decade, following administrative redistricting, the reorganization of the colonies, and an influx of new settlers, "life in the western parts of Siberia... looked increasingly like life in the European parts of the country." See David R. Shearer, "Modernity and Backwardness on the Soviet Frontier: Western Siberia in the 1930s," in Donald J. Raleigh, *Provincial Landscapes: Local Dimensions of Soviet Power, 1917–1953* (Pittsburgh: University of Pittsburgh Press, 2001), 208, 213–16.

[42] Peter Longerich, *Die braunen Bataillone: Geschichte der SA* (Munich: Beck, 1989), 152–64.

[43] On the abortive attempts to set up a leadership council or a Senate, and on the completely impotent conferences of party potentates and the postrally conferences of party officials, see Hans Mommsen, "Hitler's Position in the Nazi System," *From Weimar to Auschwitz*, trans. Philip O'Connor (Cambridge: Polity, 1991), 164.

of six committees, was "in practice illusory," according to one commentator. Equally its small leadership bureaucracy was confined, by sharp contrast with the Bolsheviks, to maintenance of a central membership roll and the party treasury.[44] One reason for this was Hitler's own aversion to a central party organization. Despite Strasser's efforts in creating the Reichorganisationsleitung I and in adding to it a planning agency, the Reichorganisationsleitung II,[45] Hitler deliberately dissolved both, returning to the Gauleiter their independence and thereby effectively splitting the party into thirty-six quasi-independent organizations. The Political Central Commission created in their place was in no position to substitute for the apparatus built by Strasser and tended to avoid bureaucratic structures as such.[46] After coming to power, the main central party organization that would, from around 1935–6, achieve genuine institutional authority was the Staff of the Führer's Deputy, based in Munich under the leadership of Martin Bormann.[47] However the institutional leverage even of this increasingly formidable apparatus was checked by independent power bases which derived their authority directly from Hitler. The greatest obstacle was the Staff's inability to encroach on the powers and prerogatives of the Gauleiter, whose standing and autonomy were regularly vouchsafed by Hitler himself.[48] Somewhat paradoxically, it was a measure of the limits to the independent institutional authority of the office that, with its rather esoteric origins, the Staff of the Führer's Deputy was so heavily dependent for its rise on the personality and entrepreneurial skills of its head, Martin Bormann, who in effect became Hitler's private secretary from around 1936.[49] Without its own source of legitimacy, the Staff would never match the near-mythic position of the Central Committee apparatus in the Leninist system.

---

[44] Broszat, *The Hitler State: The Foundation and Development of the Internal Structure of the Third Reich*, trans. John W. Hiden (London and New York: Longman, 1981), 43–4.

[45] Strasser was himself an effective manager who played a key coordinating role in the crucial election campaigns from September 1930 to July 1932. See Peter D. Stachura, "'Der Fall Strasser': Gregor Strasser, Hitler and National Socialism," in *The Shaping of the Nazi State*, ed. Peter D. Stachura (London: Croom Helm, 1978), 88–130.

[46] Peter Longerich, *Hitlers Stellvertreter: Führung der Partei und Kontrolle des Staatsapparats durch den Stab Hess und die Partei-Kanzlei Bormann* (Munich: K. G. Saur, 1992), 178–83.

[47] The activities of the two main departments of this office, Department II, for Internal Party Affairs, led by Hellmuth Friedrichs, and Department III, for the Affairs of State, headed by Walter Sommer, are well described in Jeremy Noakes and Geoffrey Pridham, eds., *Nazism: A Documentary Reader: State, Economy and Society, 1933–1939*, rev. ed., vol. 2 (Exeter: Exeter University Press, 2000), 46–51.

[48] Hitler's relationship with the Gauleiter is discussed in greater detail in the section on "retinue structures" in this essay.

[49] In this respect Overy's representation of Bormann as "Hitler's Poskrebyshev" is misguided in that his access to Hitler allowed Bormann to become a formidable political actor and power broker in his own right. In this sense Bormann and the Staff of the Führer's Deputy (later, from 1941, the Party Chancellery) resembled the "leader-retinue structures" which are discussed in greater detail in the next section of this essay. Although Poskrebyshev was known on occasion to taunt Stalin's colleagues, he was strictly forbidden by Stalin to build up his own power base. Cf. Overy, *The Dictators*, 72.

Underlining the collaborative and coalitional nature of the first Hitler government, formal party representation in government and the civil service were far more limited than in the Soviet Union. Within six months of the October Revolution *all* portfolios in the Sovnarkom had been held by Bolsheviks; six months into Hitler's dictatorship Darre had become only the fourth NSDAP minister; of the twelve departmental chiefs in the government in 1935, over two years after coming to power, seven, including those with the most powerful portfolios, were non-NSDAP conservatives. At lower levels there were also limits to the governing role of the party, as many of the party's general political officers complained of being passed over in favor of the traditional civil service.[50] Further, despite the party's right, under the 1935 municipal code, to participate in the appointment of senior civil servants, there were too few long-serving party members (i.e., those who had joined before 30 January 1933) with sufficient qualifications to fill these positions.[51] For their part, most state secretaries to Reich Ministers were either men who had joined the party late or, more often still, not party professionals. Even personnel heads within the ministries were often themselves not party members. In the ongoing struggle between officials from the state administration and the more radical party leaders, it was, at least until 1937, normally the former, with the support of the Minister of Interior Frick, who prevailed.[52]

Although one of the NSDAP's favored slogans, based on Hitler's speech at the Nuremberg rally of 8 September 1934, was that "the party commands the state," this proved something of an illusion.[53] In September 1934, the party was in no position to guide or monitor the state. In the more intimate environment of an address to the party Gauleiter on 2 February 1934 Hitler confessed that the party's main role was to make the "people receptive to projected government measures," "to help carry out the measures which have been ordered by the Government," and "to support the Government in every way."[54] Indeed, immediately after the September proclamation the Reich Minister of the Interior, Frick, stepped in and issued a clarification, that "Party offices have no authority whatever to issue instructions to agencies of the State. These agencies receive their instructions solely from their superiors within the State apparatus."[55] To the extent that there were efforts to "integrate" the activities of party and state, the famous Law for Ensuring the Unity of Party and State of 1 December 1933 had been largely designed not so much to bring the state

---

[50] Mommsen, "Hitler's Position in the Nazi System," 169; Noakes and Pridham, *Nazism*, vol. 2, 33–4.

[51] Horst Matzerath, *Nationalsozialismus und kommunale Selbstverwaltung* (Stuttgart [u.a.]: Kohlhammer, 1970).

[52] Günther Neliba, *Wilhelm Frick: Der Legalist des Unrechtsstaates: Eine politische Biographie* (Paderborn: Schöningh, 1992), 125–6; and Broszat, *The Hitler State*, 243–4, 251–3.

[53] Cited in Peter Diehl-Thiele, *Partei und Staat im Dritten Reich: Untersuchungen zum Verhältnis von NSDAP und allgemeiner innerer Staatsvwerwaltung 1933–1945* (Munich: Beck, 1969), 28.

[54] Noakes and Pridham, *Nazism*, vol. 2, 40.

[55] Ibid, 42.

apparatus under party tutelage as to ensure the subordination of the party to a Ministry of Interior under Frick's command.[56] In fact, a somewhat uneasy relationship between party and state may well have suited Hitler, for it kept at bay any institutional constraints on his own freedom of movement. It was probably for this reason that Hitler pointedly reserved for himself the right to "issue the regulations required for the execution and augmentation" of the Law.[57]

In the Soviet Union it was the party which lent unity to state structures. By contrast, Nazi Germany lacked any specific integrative institutions as such.[58] The cabinet lost its importance and, save for public rituals, ceased to meet altogether after 1938.[59] The party leadership in turn lacked a leading body which could replace the cabinet; attempts by Frick, Rosenberg, and others to establish a leadership election council were all blocked by Hitler. Instead the Nazi regime was heavily reliant for what coherence it had on Hitler's charismatic authority. In the early stages, the regime was extremely dependent on Hitler's pull as a charismatic leader for its high levels of social support. Thus it was Hitler's image as Führer rather than the reputation or activities of party organizations which helped convert millions of former nonvoters to the party's cause on 5 March 1933. When voters were presented with one prearranged list in the Reichstag elections of 12 November 1933 this was, typically, not an NSDAP list but "The Führer's list."[60] Once Hitler was in power, his importance to the unity of the system was made plain by the Reich Minister of the Interior, Frick, when he informed civil servants that the Hitler salute was "to be used generally as the German greeting... now that the party system has finished and the entire government of the German Reich is under the control of Reich Chancellor Adolf Hitler."[61] Hitler's centrality to the political order was constitutionally reinforced, on the death of President von Hindenburg, by

[56] This program too, however, was aborted as a result of the determined opposition of party functionaries. At the same time, in some areas the party's functions were absorbed by the state. Thus, for example, its propaganda duties, one of the main functions of the party, were taken over by the Reich's Propaganda Ministry, which assumed direct control over the NSDAP propaganda sections. See Neliba, 86–96.

[57] See clause 8 of the law reproduced in Noakes and Pridham, *Nazism*, vol. 2, 40. "[Hitler's] whole aim," Hans Frank would later recall in his memoirs, "was to transfer the independent position he had in the NSDAP and its inner structure to the State. On 30 January 1933 he brought this aim with him." Cited in ibid, 7.

[58] For a fuller discussion, see Hans Mommsen, "Hitler's Position in the Nazi System," 163–88.

[59] The demise of the cabinet, which met only four times in 1936, seven times in 1937, and for the last time on 5 February 1938, is eloquently described in Noakes and Pridham, *Nazism*, vol. 2, 18–21. For a fuller account, see Lothar Gruchmann, "Die 'Reichsregierung' im Führerstaat: Stellung und Funktion des Kabinetts im nationalsozialistischen Herrschaftssystem," in *Klassenjustiz und Pluralismus: Festschrift für Ernst Fraenkel zum 75. Geburtstag*, eds. Günther Doeker and Winfried Stefani (Hamburg: Hoffmann und Camp, 1973), 187–223.

[60] Karl Dietrich Bracher, Wolfgang Sauer, and Gerhard Schulz, *Die nationalsozialistische Machtergreifung: Studien zur Errichtung des totalitären Herrschaftsstems in Deutschland 1933/34* (Cologne and Opladen: Westdeutscher Verlag, 1960), 35–6.

[61] Cited in Broszat, 91.

the Law on the Head of State of the German Reich of 1 August 1934, which amalgamated the offices of Reich President and Reich Chancellor in a new post of "Führer and Reich Chancellor," later shortened to "Führer," thus making the notion of Führer official and endowing Hitler with a supreme constitutional role that Stalin would never possess.[62] Not long after this, on 20 August 1934, a personal statement of loyalty to Hitler as "Führer of the German nation and People" was inserted into the Beamteneid, the oath that was recited by all civil servants.[63] Rather than relying on an institutional framework, it was on the strength of Hitler's leadership cult that the "Gleichschaltung" was achieved.

In the Soviet Union the Communist Party apparatus of the 1930s had turned into a hierarchy of bureaucracies with its own institutional identity. For all of Lenin's ambitions of building a well-oiled party machine, it would nonetheless be an error to overemphasize the "formal" or "impersonal" aspects of the party apparatus. For much of the 1930s official hierarchies were ridden with informal networks. Where they had a strong vertical dimension and where they appeared to be particularly durable, Stalin's usual inclination was to take decisive action to break down these networks.[64] By contrast, Nazi Germany witnessed the proliferation of personalized network-based agencies – so-called "leader-retinue structures" – which were not only tolerated but generated by Hitler himself.[65] The spread of agencies of this kind, which embraced functions which were not only dear to Hitler but of central strategic importance to the state, reflected a deep-seated willingness on Hitler's part to give his deputies a free hand in running their own briefs and in building up their operations on a relatively informal basis. As General Inspector for the German Road System, Fritz Todt derived his authority not from a normal departmental or ministerial office, but from his direct line to the Führer, which would, eventually, provide

---

[62] Jeremy Noakes and Geoffrey Pridham, *Nazism 1919–1945: The Rise to Power 1919–1934*, rev. ed., vol. 1 (Exeter: Exeter University Press, 2000), 185; and idem, *Nazism*, vol. 2, 4–6. Stalin's appointment as Chair of Sovnarkom in March 1941 (in addition to his existing position as General Secretary of the Central Committee) was of little constitutional consequence. Its significance lay, by contrast, in the fact that it allowed Stalin to position himself vis-à-vis the Leninist tradition, since Lenin himself had been head of Sovnarkom but never General Secretary.

[63] Sigrun Mühl-Benninghaus, *Das Beamtentum in der NS-Diktatur bis zum Ausbruch des Zweiten Weltkrieges* (Düsseldorf: Droste), 1996, 109–10.

[64] Stalin was not wary of all networks. As various commentators have noted, where medium-term patron-client relations tied Stalin himself to clients in the regions these networks may have facilitated the creation of a centralized party-based hierarchy by enabling Stalin to utilize clientelist norms and practices to bind regional party organizations to the center. What Stalin appears to have been extremely wary of were long-standing "lateral" networks at the regional level which appeared to be obstructing his policies or "vertical" networks which were tied to Moscow-based leaders over whom he had little day-to-day control. See, for example, T. H. Rigby, "Was Stalin a Disloyal Patron?" in *Political Elites in the USSR: Central Leaders and Local Cadres from Lenin to Gorbachev* (Aldershot: Edward Elgar, 1990), 127; and John Willerton, *Patronage and Politics in the USSR* (Cambridge: Cambridge University Press, 1992), 29–32.

[65] The term is from Broszat, 276. Much of the following paragraphs on "retinue structures" is derived from ibid., 265–6, 297–9, 300–1.

cover for the creation of an independent "Organization Todt" (OT).[66] Lacking credentials as a party functionary or as a career diplomat, Joachim von Ribbentrop held a political position that was "derived exclusively from the personal services which [he], the wine and spirits importer, had been able to render the Führer before the takeover of power in Berlin." From this position he created a "bureau" to which he attracted over sixty subordinates, including many of his own associates.[67] Similarly, with the formation of the General Council for the Four Year-Plan under Herman Göring in 1938, a key former ministry, the Reich Ministry of Economics, was downgraded to the "Executive Organ of the Commissioner for the Four-Year Plan" under Göring, while former ministers, such as Darré and Seldte, were displaced by state secretaries whose primary ties were also to Göring.[68]

The most significant of the personalized structures of administration were the territorial Gau organizations and the SS. The strictly personal conception of politics was exemplified by Hitler's relationship with the Gauleiter.[69] Answerable only to the Führer, the Gauleiter were treated as Hitler's personal followers. In marked contrast with the continually hectored regional party leaders in Stalin's USSR, the Gauleiter were allowed to carve out their own spheres of influence, which were virtually impervious to control by higher party authorities or by the Reich Ministry of Interior. As we saw earlier, as much as anything else it was the existence of the Gauleiter, with their special connection to Hitler, which prevented the emergence of a centralized hierarchy within the party.[70] The Gauleiter drew their personal power from their direct

[66] For a thorough discussion of the Todt apparatus, see Dieter Rebentisch, *Führerstaat und Verwaltung im Zweiten Weltkrieg: Verfassungsentwicklung und Verwaltungspolitik, 1939–1945* (Stuttgart: F. Steiner Verlag, 1989), 347–8.

[67] On his accession as Foreign Minister, many of his plenipotentiaries and special aides remained physically and institutionally removed from the rest of the ministry. On Ribbentrop's role as foreign policy adviser to Hitler and his private diplomacy prior to 1938, see Wolfgang Michalka, *Ribbentrop und die deutsche Weltpolitik 1933–1940* (Munich: W. Fink, 1980), 39–49; and J. Henke, *England in Hitlers politischem Kalkül, 1935–1939* (Boppard am Rhein: , 1973), 304–5.

[68] Dietmar Petzina, *Autarkiepolitik im Dritten Reich: Der nationalsozialistische Vierjahresplan* (Stuttgart: Deutsche Verlagsanstalt, 1968), 67–78. No less important was the role of the German Labor Front (DAF), which usurped the assets of the former trade unions and comprised white- and blue-collar workers in a centralized organization claiming to represent the interests of labor, albeit without acquiring the status of a Reich ministry. Ronald Smelser, *Robert Ley: Hitlers Mann an der "Arbeitsfront": Eine Biographie*, trans. Karl Nicolai and Heidi Nicolai (Paderborn: Ferdinand Schöningh, 1989).

[69] "The Gauleiter," Hitler would later confide to Goebbels in mid-August 1942, "[are] my most loyal and reliable colleagues. If I lost trust in them I wouldn't know whom to trust." Meetings with the Gauleiter were the only forum where Hitler regularly convened with other party leaders. There were twenty-seven of these meetings between 1933 and 1939 and a further nineteen during the war. See Ian Kershaw, *Hitler, 1936–1945: Nemesis* (Harmondworth: Allen Lane, 2001), 536; and Overy, *The Dictators*, 166.

[70] Also see Hans Mommsen, "National Socialism: Continuity and Change," in Mommsen, *From Weimar to Auschwitz*, 155, 157; idem, "Hitler's Position in the Nazi System," 169; Dietrich Orlow, *The History of the Nazi Party: 1933–1945*, vol. 2 (Pittsburgh: University of Pittsburgh Press, 1973), 8.

relation to Hitler, but also from the fact that the great majority of them had
acquired positions within the *state* system, be it as Oberpräsidenten in Prussia, as Landshauptleute, or as ministers within those Land governments which
had survived Frick's centralizing ambitions. In general what formal political
authority they had did not derive from their position within the party but from
their usurpation of state offices.[71]

Although unique, the role of the SS was indicative of a wider principle of
organization within the Nazi regime. A leader-retinue structure par excellence,
the SS was exclusively answerable to the Reich SS leader, Heinrich Himmler,
and, through him, to the Führer. First usurping the functions of the political
police in the individual Länder (federal states), Himmler extended his powers by including the ordinary police force in the growing SS empire. The SS
administration was centralized with the establishment in 1939 of the Reich
Security Main Office (RSHA), which became a powerful nerve center for the
regime, forming in some respects a "state within a state." While the ordinary
SS lost much of its importance during the war as its membership fell, its military arm, the so-called "Weapons SS," grew to such an extent that, in terms
of the number of soldiers at its disposal and the quality of its equipment, it
became a serious rival to the Wehrmacht. Like the National Socialist system
as a whole, through a process of cell division the Reich SS Leader's area of
command presented in miniature the picture of a progressive growth of subsidiary offices, ancillary organizations, and leader authorities. Yet although
it was engaged in myriad activities, the SS retained a certain organizational
coherence, and it remained, with Hitler's blessing, and despite its enormous
power, under the continuous control of one individual, Heinrich Himmler.[72]
Rather than being knitted together by the party, as was the case in the Soviet
Union, in Hitler's Germany the state depended for whatever overall coherence
it had on the gelling effect of the "Hitler cult," and, at a lower level, on the
dictator's own, deliberately cultivated "retinue structures."

The presence of the NSDAP in German society certainly went well beyond
the intimate relationships Hitler had with his confidants, while the party's
activities extended far beyond the simple projection of the Hitler cult. After
the NSDAP came to power, its membership rose dramatically, so that it
quickly overtook the Soviet Communist Party in size. Its membership leapt
from 849,000 in 1933 to almost 2.5 million in 1935, making the party half
as large again as the Soviet Communist Party; by 1939 its membership had
soared to 4,985,000, so that it was well over three times the size of the Bolshevik party, and that in an overall population that was under half that of the
Soviet Union's.[73] These membership figures are indicative of the quite different

[71] Peter Hüttenberger, *Die Gauleiter: Studie zum Wandel des Machtgefüges in der NSDAP*
(Stuttgart: Deutsche Verlag-Anstalt, 1969) 75–137.

[72] Robert L. Koehl, *The Black Corps: The Structure and Power Struggles of the Nazi SS* (Madison:
University of Wisconsin., 1983); Heinz Höhne, *Der Orden unter dem Totenkopf: Geschichte
der SS*, 3rd ed. (Munich: C. Bertelsmann, 1983).

[73] For the most convenient comparative tables see Overy, *The Dictators*, 138–40. The overall
population of the USSR in the 1930s ranged from approximately 161 million to 170 million

roles of the parties in the two societies. The grassroots organization of the NSDAP around residential and domestic "cells" and "blocks" which "brought the party into every household" underscored the intrusive role of the party as a propaganda agency which aimed to mobilize "every inhabitant, members or not . . . into a vast all-inclusive national movement."[74] By contrast, the requirement that Communist Party cells be based not at the place of residence but at the workplace and that they achieve production targets and fulfill policies laid down by the party's Central Committee underlined the important economic and managerial responsibilities of the party in the administration of the party-state. In Germany, even at the local and district levels, where the party's administrative presence was at its greatest, relations between party and state were marked by a continual tension which appears, according to Noakes and Pridham, to have been "built into the system."[75] By contrast, the activities of the local party organization in the USSR, which included administering the official patronage system, the nomenklatura, were closely harmonized with those of the local state. The Communist Party's relative smallness underlined its self-identification as an elite force whose membership were entrusted with, in effect, running the Soviet state.[76]

The contrasting roles of the party in state-building also found expression in two quite different ideologies. In the Soviet case the state embraced a programmatic class-based ideology, which, by means of a variety of structures of class-based discrimination, had quite tangible implications for the ways in which its own population was treated. Although there was a disjuncture between the ideological underpinnings of Leninism – which had argued that capitalism had fostered a clear class structure in Russia – and a reality in which, after years of social upheaval, the country's already frail class structure came close to disintegration, the class issue continued to be taken seriously and was a thorn in the leadership's side until well into the 1930s.[77] Further, Leninist ideology – unlike traditional Marxism – attributed a key role to the vanguard party in leading the "dictatorship of the proletariat." As its custodian, the party apparatus was to play the pivotal part in disseminating the official ideology and in realizing its stated ambitions. Even later, "under Stalin," according to one eminent neo-Weberian theorist, "the emphasis on the leader . . . always remained subordinate to the Party as the agent capable of formulating a correct line, a program

---

while that of Germany, prior to the annexation of Bohemia-Moravia, ranged from about 66 million to 80 million.

[74] Overy, *The Dictators*, 146–7, 155. Overy cites the work of C. W. Reibel, *Das Fundament der Diktatur: Die NSDAP-Ortsgruppen 1932–1945* (Paderborn, 2002); and D. Schmiechen-Ackermann, "Der 'Blockwart,'" *Vierteljahrshefte für Zeitgeschichte* 48 (2000): 575–602.

[75] Noakes and Pridham, *Nazism*, vol. 2, 61–4, quote from 64.

[76] For the very high party saturation in 1933 of the local state apparatus and of the management of local industry and agriculture, see T. H. Rigby, *Communist Party Membership in the U.S.S.R., 1917–1967* (Princeton, NJ: Princeton University Press, 1968), 200, 418, 420, 427–8.

[77] For a useful discussion of these issues and of how class was eventually incorporated into a "soslovie model," see Sheila Fitzpatrick, "Ascribing Class: The Construction of Social Identity in Soviet Russia," *Journal of Modern History* 65, no. 4 (1993): 745–68.

separate from the personal insight of the leader."[78] The Nazis' ruling ideology was altogether different. Fiercely exclusive and ultranationalist, it was in its early stages inseparable from the utterances of its leader. Never grounded in a canonical text and defying theoretical systematization, the "abstract, utopian and vague National Socialist ideology," writes Broszat, "only achieved what reality and certainty it had through the medium of Hitler."[79] For this reason the "ideology" of the regime merged, to a far greater degree than did its equivalents in the USSR, with the Hitler cult which enveloped the state's propaganda machine.[80] To the extent that a secondary programmatic ideology that was relatively independent of Hitler did emerge in the 1930s – that of the "racial state" – it found no core institutional expression of the kind achieved by the Communist Party as the embodiment of Leninism in the Soviet Union.[81]

The Nazi and Stalinist states operated along very different lines. The Stalinist state was built on a Leninist foundation which involved the construction of a highly centralized party with a well-staffed bureaucracy. In exercising patronage, formulating policy, and discharging other statelike responsibilities, the party became fully intertwined with the state. The Leninist legacy also included the institutional means of conflict resolution in the form of a hierarchy of committees, including the Central Committee and the Politburo, at which ideological and policy differences could be thrashed out. However removed its actions were from its utopian aims, the regime sought to justify its policies in terms of a Marxist-Leninist system of ideas which attached particular importance to the notions of class and ruling party. The Nazi regime by contrast had its origins in the decentralized and amorphous NSDAP movement of the 1920s in which central headquarters had relatively little authority over either regional party bodies or the party's auxiliary combat organizations.[82] In the absence of clear decision-making structures or of an integrated programmatic ideology the movement, both in its time of struggle and immediately after assuming power, was held together almost entirely by its leader and his cult. Rather than becoming systematically fused with the state, as was the case in the Soviet Union, the Nazi party, despite its many public duties, did not, as an institution, mesh smoothly with the cogs of the German state.[83] While regional party leaders, as

---

[78] Jowitt, *New World Disorder*, 9–10. Earlier Jowitt writes: "It is not in the appreciation of heroism that Leninism differs from Nazism; it is in the designation of the heroic agent. For Lenin, the Party is hero – not the individual leader." See 6–7.

[79] Broszat, 18, 29.

[80] Ian Kershaw, *Der Hitler-Mythos: Volksmeinung und Propaganda im Dritten Reich* (Stuttgart: Deutsche Verlags-Anstalt, 1980), 46–71.

[81] Here our emphasis differs from that of Michael Burleigh and Wolfgang Wipperman, who attach priority to the quest for racial purification as an independent unifying principle of the Nazi regime. See their *The Racial State, Germany 1933–1945* (Cambridge: Cambridge University Press, 1991).

[82] The main exception were the financial controls exercised by the Munich organization under Franz Xaver Schwarz, who supervised party finances at all levels.

[83] Even at the municipal level, where the party was able to monopolize staffing policy, its prerogatives were partly neutralized by the intensification of supervision by the Lander governments.

individuals, may have filled leading positions in the state, their authority did not stem from their party offices, and their policies were rarely coordinated with those of the wider state system.

Despite their very different origins the Nazi and Soviet regimes did, in some respects, converge during the 1930s, the era of full-blown Stalinism. It was at the beginning of this decade that Stalin, like Hitler, assumed the powers of a full-scale dictator and began to brush aside the institutions of conflict resolution and decision making that had existed within the party and to lean toward more informal modes of policy formation. It was at this stage too that the Stalin cult gathered pace and that an increasingly malleable Marxist-Leninist ideology took on a Stalinist coloring and, with it, conservative and nationalist overtones.[84] In terms of their structure and dynamics, however, the Nazi and Soviet states never fully converged. One reason was that even at the height of Stalin's dictatorship the party retained the characteristics of an integrated bureaucracy and continued to discharge a large variety of statelike functions. A second key difference, however, concerned the leaders themselves. Stalin and Hitler were linchpins of their respective states. Although the states over which they presided were dictatorships defined, in large part, by the nature of their dictator's rule, they were dictatorships of a different sort. The fact that Stalin and Hitler had different personalities and behavioral patterns would have major implications for the organization of their respective states. It is to these implications that we now turn.

LEADERS

As man and ruler, Stalin differed markedly from Hitler. This is important for our understanding of the political system, since Stalin's success as a politician corresponded closely with the institutional and political environment in which he had risen and prospered. From his prerevolutionary days Stalin had been a

---

[84] Albeit less so than Jowitt, our approach shares a certain amount in common with the work of Joseph Nyomarkay (*Charisma and Factionalism in the Nazi Party* [Minneapolis: University of Minnesota Press, 1967]), who distinguishes the Nazi form of "charismatic totalitarianism" from its Soviet "ideological" counterpart. According to Nyomarkay, the Nazi Party was little more than a "charismatic group" whose organization was based on organic rather than bureaucratic lines and whose primary function was to "generate, maintain and enhance Hitler's charismatic personality" (26, 33, 151). However, to the extent that Nyomarkay's is a study of the "political movement primarily in its pre-power stage" rather than as an "established political order," his comparison of the Nazi and Soviet systems becomes somewhat blurred for the mid-1930s (10 and fn. 1, 147). One difference between our approach and his relates to the role Nyomarkay assigns to Marxist "ideology" as the source of authority in communist systems. "Communist leaders," Nyomarkay wrote, "always justify themselves by claiming to be the correct interpreters of the Marxist ideology, and on this basis they claim the loyalty of their followers" (149). This, however, seems inappropriate for the Soviet Union in the 1930s. We suggest that in the USSR in this period authority was equally grounded not only in Stalin's leadership but in the conventions and institutional continuities of the party itself, which often had little or nothing to do with Marxist ideology as such.

committee man and party functionary, who had built a reputation for administrative effectiveness. In the early phase of the Bolshevik regime Stalin had not only sat on and chaired the overlapping administrative committees of the party, such as the Orgburo and Secretariat, but had, with the help of allies such as Molotov and Kaganovich, in effect designed these institutions by setting out new roles and responsibilities for them. In doing so, Stalin also built up a small army of party functionaries. "Koba is training me magnificently," the head of the bureau to the Secretariat, A. M. Nazaretian, wrote to Ordzhonikidze in the summer of 1922:

> He is turning me into an absolute clerk and overseer of the decisions of the Politburo, the Orgburo and the Secretariat. . . . Il'ich [i.e. Lenin] has in him a most reliable Cerberus, intrepidly standing at the gates of the TsK [Central Committee]. What we found here was indescribably bad, but now the work of the TsK has visibly changed . . . now everything has been shaken up. Come in the autumn and you will see.

"The latest fashionable phrase in Moscow," he went on, "relates to those employed by the TsK who have not yet received assignments, who are hanging as it were, in mid-air. About them we say: '[They are] under Stalin.'"[85]

Over the course of the 1920s Stalin, along with Molotov, devoted considerable attention to management of the Central Committee apparatus, allowing himself to be drawn into lengthy discussions on appointments and on the division of responsibilities among Secretaries and between departments.[86] By the end of the decade Stalin had consolidated his reputation as an institution builder. Over the next few years his horizons would broaden. The expansion and reconfiguration of the state apparatus in the late 1920s and early 1930s entailed a complex process in which Stalin would play a key role. At the same time, in this period Stalin strongly consolidated his position as the country's undisputed leader. The relationship between these processes is not incidental, for it shows how Stalin's own authority was grounded in the internal institutional structures and ideological conventions of the Leninist party-state.

By the end of the 1920s Stalin had firmly established his position as the effective head of the Politburo.[87] He was not yet, however, a dictator; nor did he have things all his own way.[88] Stalin's defeat of the "Right Opposition" demonstrated both his command of internal organizational issues and his

[85] Kvashonkin et al., eds., *Bol'shevistskoe rukovodstvo*, 262–3.

[86] See, for example, Khlevniuk et al., eds., *Stalinskoe politbiuro v 30-e gody*, 113; and Lih et al., eds., 88.

[87] Referring to Lenin's comments in his "Testament" of 1922 that Stalin had, as General Secretary, "concentrated immense power in his hands," Bukharin, Rykov, and Tomskii, in their declaration of 9 February 1929, asserted that "since these words were written, this 'immense power' has become even more 'immense.'" V. P. Danilov et al., eds., *Kak lomali NEP: Stenogrammy plenumov TsK VKP(b) 1928–1929 gg.*, vol. 4 (Moscow: MFD, 2000), 614–15.

[88] For a recent assessment, see Yoram Gorlizki and Oleg Khlevniuk, "Stalin and His Circle," in *The Cambridge History of Russia*, vol. 3, ed. Ronal Grigor Suny (Cambridge: Cambridge University Press, 2006), 246–8. For specific examples, also see A. V. Kvashonkin et al., eds.,

astute manipulation of the party's ideological conventions. More than merely controlling appointments, Stalin, together with Molotov, used organizational measures, such as calling ad hoc meetings of Secretaries, briefing against opponents at regional bureaus, and organizing lower-level resolutions, to foster an atmosphere of ideological orthodoxy ahead of the crucial April 1929 plenum of the Central Committee. "Without notifying the Politburo," Bukharin, Rykov, and Tomskii claimed in their statement of 9 February 1929, "the Secretariat has summoned a large number of gubkom Secretaries and created an atmosphere in which anyone holding a particular opinion is ipso facto *an opponent of the Central Committee.*"[89] At the same time, one reason that Stalin was able to deploy these procedural mechanisms to such effect was that he had a better grasp of the salience of ideological conventions at the party's lower ranks. Thus a key thrust of the charges laid at Bukharin, Rykov, and Tomskii by Stalin's allies was that the triumvirate had neglected the unfolding "class struggle" in the countryside.[90]

Even after the defeat of the "right-deviation," in the early 1930s Stalin still had to contend with those powerful members of the Politburo, such as Ordzhonikidze, who headed important departments, and who, especially where the interests of their department came under threat, were known to take issue with him.[91] The way that Stalin dealt with resistance of this kind again reveals something about the nature of his power in this period. In the numerous confrontations over resource allocation which marked the latter stages of the First Five-Year Plan, Stalin routinely displayed an impressive command of the details of economic organization and policy. To this end he was often drawn into matters, usually quite technical, of policymaking, especially those involving the setting of industrial plans and the attainment of procurement targets.[92]

Sovetskoe rukovodstvo: Perepiska, 1928–1941 (Moscow: ROSSPEN, 1999), 8, 22–2, 58–9; Lih et al., eds., 149; and Khlevniuk, *Politbiuro*, 37–40, 46.

[89] (Italics ours) Danilov et al. , 613. Molotov also arranged resolutions from the provinces critical of the triumvirate to be passed and subsequently deployed at the April plenum. At the plenum itself Yaroslavsky, in the opening speech, alluded to highly critical resolutions from regional party organizations in Ukraine, the Urals, and the Far East, against the triumvirate. Danilov et al, eds., 42–3.

[90] Danilov et al., eds., 236–42, 295–6, 299–300, 445–7. For a work that persuasively highlights Stalin's distinctive and popular presentation to the party's rank and file of the industrialization drive as a form of "class war," see Hiroaki Kuromiya, *Stalin's Industrial Revolution* (Cambridge: Cambridge University Press, 1988), esp. 109–13.

[91] For more on this see Gorlizki and Khlevniuk, "Stalin and His Circle," 249–51; and, more generally, Oleg Khlevniuk, *In Stalin's Shadow: The Career of 'Sergo' Ordzhonikidze*, edited with an introduction by Donald J. Raleigh, trans. David J. Nordlander (Armonk, NY: M. E. Sharpe, 1995).

[92] Khlevniuk et al., eds., *Stalinskoe politbiuro v 30-e gody*, 133; Lih et al., eds., 168–9, 203, 205; O. V. Khlevniuk et al., eds., *Stalin i Kaganovich* (Moscow: ROSSPEN, 2001), 460, 592–3, 601. Rees suggests that Stalin maintained a particular interest in procurements, in part because it was easier for him to exercise authority over these targets than over industrial targets, which involved more complex issues in reconciling figures for different branches of the economy. Rees, "Changing Nature," 30.

Rather than merely delegating policy documents to specialists, he often liked
to see papers and to edit them, especially where he felt that a document had
wider political ramifications. It was in this often quite technical idiom that
Stalin aimed to resolve the numerous battles over economic and organizational
issues which were a typical feature of leadership battles in the early 1930s.[93]

Stalin's power was grounded in the administrative structures of party and
state. Just as he had learned how to "work" party procedures in the 1920s he
had, now, learned how to operate the new institutions of the centrally managed
economy. By launching seemingly innocuous inquiries, referring issues to commissions, or casting doubt on the minutiae of an economic policy, Stalin could
put colleagues and whole bureaucracies under intense psychological pressure.
The intimate knowledge of the political and economic system he had helped to
fashion would prove invaluable when it came to keeping his colleagues in line.
The contrast with Hitler and with the new political order in Germany was a
sharp one. Whereas Stalin's rise had rested to a great extent on his control of
the party and state apparatus, Hitler's chief political weapons were his talent
and reputation as a public speaker and demagogue.[94] His virtuoso skills as
propagandist were key to the rise of the NSDAP in the 1920s and to the ability
of the party to set itself apart from other right-wing groups. In the early 1930s
it was Hitler's capacity to exploit the propaganda opportunities afforded by
election campaigns which helped propel the party forward. It was chiefly the
attraction of Hitler's personality as Führer rather than that of the NSDAP
which tipped the balance in the elections of March 1933. In much the same
way that Stalin's power matched the bureaucratic strength of the Communist
Party, so did Hitler's strengths correspond to the standing of the NSDAP as an
agitational mass movement.

Hitler's qualities as leader were not only central to the rise of the Nazis
in opposition. They would also help define the kind of state and administration over which he presided. Hitler ruled in many respects as a public
speaker. Almost all of his most important policy decisions were accompanied
by major speeches. Such articulations of the "Führer's will" replaced any institutional decision making, systematic policy consultations, or regular contact
with members of his government. The contrast with Stalin was again strong.
Stalin worked ceaselessly on the machinery of government, putting in sixteen-
hour days attending committees, overseeing personnel assignments, and editing
mounds of policy documents and bureaucratic directives. By the time an ailing
Hindenburg had retired to East Prussia at the end of 1933, "that" recalls his

---

[93] It was also characteristic of Stalin's leadership in this period that, having played a part in the
design of the country's new economic institutions, he was often keen to seek specifically organizational or administrative solutions to the problems which then emerged. See, for example,
Khlevniuk et al., eds., *Stalinskoe politbiuro v 30-e gody*, 123–4, and Khlevniuk et al., eds.,
Stalin i Kaganovich, 19, 232–3, 262.

[94] From 1924 to 1928 Hitler had to accept a ban on public presentations, as a consequence
of which he concentrated his propaganda activities on writing lead articles for *Voelkische
Beobachter* and on writing *Mein Kampf*. He only resumed his role as public speaker in 1929.

press officer, Otto Dietrich, "was the end of Hitler's hard-working schedule. He once more reverted to his habit of rising at noon and during the day entered his office only for important receptions."[95] Hitler avoided going into the Reich chancellery to study documents, preferring oral reports from Lammers and a multitude of changing advisers. His interventions in the affairs of government tended to be accidental, frequently on account of misleading press reports or private information. One of his adjutants from the mid-1930s recalled: "He disliked reading files. I got decisions out of him, even on very important matters, without him ever asking me for the relevant papers. He took the view that many things sorted themselves out if they were left alone."[96] He had, concludes one biographer, "neither aptitude nor ability for organizational matters. Organization he could leave to others; propaganda – mobilization of the masses – was what he was good at, and what he wanted to do."[97]

Neither Hitler nor Stalin could have attained the position he did without enormous reserves of political energy. Their energies would, however, find quite different outlets. Whereas Stalin was an interventionist, hands-on manager of everyday governmental affairs, Hitler liked to maintain a fair distance from the nuts and bolts of government. This contrast in the preferences of the leaders was reflected in different approaches to subordinate bureaucracies and to those who headed them. Hitler was ordinarily quite content to delegate affairs of state to his deputies and to the leader-retinue structures which they commanded. He also preferred administration with the minimum of conflict or controversy. Thus he insisted that individual ministers agree on common positions among themselves before presenting them to the cabinet for ratification. The appointment of Hess as Deputy to the Führer was designed precisely to spare Hitler "unwelcome direct confrontations."[98] This would have two consequences for the structure of government. First, Hitler was content to have his deputies cultivate their own power bases. Thus, as we saw earlier, as Hitler's "special confidant," Göring was allowed to build up a portfolio of departments, including the office of Prussian Minister President, Reich Commissioner of Aviation, Reich Forestry Commissioner, Head of the General Council of the Four-Year Plan, and special aide on foreign affairs. Much like Himmler and the heads of the other retinue structures around Hitler, Göring was allowed to carve out a personal empire for himself.[99] Secondly, Hitler was unwilling to confront senior figures and was extremely reluctant to have those who had served the movement either publicly humiliated or executed. Eschewing a divide and rule strategy, he even avoided manipulating the rivalries which rapidly emerged between his deputies after the seizure of power. So long as his own personal

---

[95] Otto Dietrich, *12 Jahre mit Hitler* (Munich: Isar Verlag, 1955), 249.
[96] Fritz Wiedemann, *Der Mann, der Feldherr werden wollte: Erlebnisse und Erfahrungen des Vorgesetzten Hitlers im 1. Weltkrieg und seines späteren persönlichen Adjutanten* (Velbert: Kettwig, 1964), 68–9 and 80–108.
[97] Ian Kershaw, *Hitler, 1889–1936: Hubris* (Harmondsworth: Penguin, 1998), 156.
[98] Broszat, 202.
[99] Ibid, 278–80, 300–1, 308.

prestige was unaffected, Hitler's socio-Darwinist obsessions led him to believe that personal and institutional rivalries should be allowed to follow their own course. Although this approach could in the short term be highly effective and quite compatible with a utilitarian emphasis on "achievement," it did little for the overall coherence of the state apparatus. Hitler's conflict-averse stance and his associated unwillingness to deal head-on with decisions of fundamental importance often meant that problems were dealt with anemically, normally by setting up yet more administrative units to cope with them. Hence bureaucracies tended to multiply, undermining the administrative unity of the state.

Stalin's treatment of his colleagues was quite the reverse. As in the Hitler leadership, disputes were likely to arise among Stalin's immediate deputies, normally over resources or personnel. Yet far from shunning or ignoring them, or having them resolved behind closed doors, as was Hitler's wont, Stalin seized on policy conflicts of this kind as a valuable source of information on the policy positions of his colleagues and of the bureaucracies they headed. "I cannot know everything," Stalin once told the Minister of Communications, I. V. Kovalev; "that is why I pay particular attention to disagreements, objections, I look into why they started, to find out what is going on."[100] This attitude to conflict was consistent with Stalin's wider attitude to the management of his colleagues. Rather than pursuing a laissez-faire approach and leaving his deputies to their own devices, Stalin kept his entourage on a short leash. Even when Stalin was in the south, spending months near the Black Sea in the summer, he insisted on a daily exchange of policy documents of all kinds with his Politburo colleagues in Moscow. "As before we receive from the boss a steady stream of directives," Kaganovich wrote in 1932.[101] Rather than merely casting his eye over documents, Stalin usually read them thoroughly, either editing them for style or, on occasion, dismissing draft resolutions *tout court*. Rejections of this kind could put members of the entourage under immense pressure. It was entirely consistent with the nature of Stalin's authority that in the more extreme confrontations of this kind he could accuse offenders of "violating the position of the Central Committee" or, even, of being "anti-Party."[102]

In terms of their approach to work and to their entourages Hitler and Stalin were at polar ends of an imaginary dictatorial leadership spectrum. Hitler was a leader who cared little for organizational work and who channeled most of his energy into the worlds of propaganda and public oratory. Stalin, by contrast, was a hard-working machine politician who thrived in the world

---

[100] Cited in Konstantin Simonov, *Glazami cheloveka moego pokoleniia: Razmyshleniia o I. V. Staline* (Moscow: Novosti, 1989), 160–1.

[101] *Politbiuro v 30-e gody*, 126.

[102] In one of the better known episodes Stalin characterized the decision of the Politburo, initiated by Ordzhonikidze, to censure the deputy procurator general Andrey Vyshinsky in August 1933 as an "outrage." "The conduct of Sergo [Ordzhonikidze!]" he wrote to Molotov shortly afterward, "cannot be characterized as anything other than anti-Party." Lih et al, eds., 234; Khlevniuk, *Politburo*, 92–3; Khlevniuk et al, eds., *Stalin i Kaganovich*, 303–4.

of committees, personnel assignments, and internal directives. Where Hitler left his subordinates and the bureaucracies they managed to fight out their conflicts among themselves, Stalin did his best to rein them in, monitoring and micromanaging their behavior. The contrast, however, was by no means merely one of personality. The two leaders answered the needs and matched the peculiarities of the systems they headed. As supreme propagandist Hitler the orator spearheaded a mass-agitational party movement whose relationship to the state was never properly fixed or institutionalized. As master bureaucrat and organizer, Stalin headed a massive all-embracing hierarchy in which a well-staffed party bureaucracy – to a great extent molded by him – came to assume a pivotal role.

The behavior of the two leaders and the mechanics of the political systems they headed were by no means constant or unchanging. Both systems were marked by dynamic characteristics which were rooted in large part in the extraordinary ambitions of their leaders. These ambitions would push both political systems into major upheavals in the late 1930s. Yet these upheavals took on very different forms. In order to trace the complex and fast-changing trajectories of the regimes in this period we pay particular attention to the interaction of the key structural components – parties and leaders – that were the subject of the first two parts of the essay.

PATTERNS OF DEVELOPMENT

The task Stalin faced in controlling the party-state bureaucracy was of a different order from Hitler's. One reason was that the overall remit of the Soviet party-state, which included the micromanagement of most aspects of the economy, was considerably wider. In the Soviet case the authority and overall effectiveness of the state also rested to a far greater degree on a large party apparatus. But the party apparatus was itself dogged by long-standing concerns over the quality of its staff. In the early 1930s this would combine with Stalin's relentless need to manage and control, as well as a growing suspiciousness on his part toward certain sections of the party bureaucracy, to mean that the vanguard party's apparatus was itself subjected to a period of intensive scrutiny. Somewhat fortunately for Stalin, and unlike in National Socialist Germany, the Bolsheviks had in the party "purge" a relatively institutionalized mechanism for carrying out an operation of this kind. Party purges, which had taken the form either of *chistki* (cleanings) or *proverki* (verifications), had, since 1919, been applied nationally at intervals of around two to three years and become a recurrent feature of Communist Party life. But whereas purges had up until this point principally been applied to the rank and file in the form of "membership screening exercises," from around 1933 the purge mechanism was turned against the party apparatus itself.

The reasons behind this turn of events, and as to why the purge of the party apparatus became extremely violent, forming one of the principal strands of the Great Terror of 1937–8, are complex. Following recent research one may

identify three major contributory elements.[103] First, a series of purges, beginning with the *chistka* of summer 1933, revealed severe problems in the party's
records and membership-accounting procedures and suggested that the concentration of the party on economic tasks during the industrial transformation
had been at the expense of the more traditional areas of party work, such as the
political training of cadres. In the rush to acquire new personnel, "alien" and
"nonparty" elements had reportedly wormed their way into the party organization. The relative ineffectiveness of the 1933 purge which followed and of
the subsequent "verification of documents" of 1935 was attributed by the central authorities to the fact that these processes were effectively in the hands of
regional party leaders, who were determined to protect their own networks.[104]

In addition, however, there were two other, relatively independent, factors
which fed into the widening vortex of coercion which would culminate in the
Great Terror. The first of these was the Stalinist regime's tendency, evident
for much of the 1930s, to resort to relatively arbitrary and coercive measures,
such as searches, mass arrests, and deportations, to deal with a whole host of
socioeconomic problems. After 1933, in particular, the Soviet police shifted
their attention away from class war in the countryside to cleanse the country's
major cities as well as other strategic locations of "socially harmful elements"
(*sotsvrediteli*). "Mass operations" of this kind, launched against *sotsvrediteli*
and national minorities by a decree of 9 May 1935, were deemed so successful
that they were extended to other social problems.[105] These two factors would
combine, in 1937, with a third, the imperative, as the Soviet leadership saw it,
in the face of deepening international tensions and the growing threat of war,
to ensure the "moral-political unity" of Soviet society. Following the events in
Spain, the authorities became anxious that a German invasion, which appeared
increasingly likely, would be the signal for armed uprisings by disaffected
groups, most notably members of diaspora nationalities who had contacts
with conationals abroad, and the million or so class-alien kulaks who, half
a decade after collectivization, were released, in theory at least, from their
original conditions of exile. Noting the sudden change in language in mid-
1937, as Soviet leaders began to talk of a threat of a "fifth column," David
Shearer suggests that it "was the threat of war which introduced a national

---

[103] The approach here draws on David Shearer, "Social Disorder, Mass Repression and the NKVD
during the 1930s," in *Stalin's Terror: High Politics and Mass Repression in the Soviet Union,*
eds. Barry McLoughlin and Kevin McDermott (London and New York: Palgrave Macmillan,
2003), 85–117. One may note that, as with recent accounts of the Holocaust, which tend now
to emphasize the confluence of a variety of factors such as racial anti-Semitism, the unexpected
conditions of rule in German-occupied Europe, and the conflictual nature of the German state,
most accounts of the Great Terror now tend to eschew monocausal explanations.

[104] See J. Arch Getty and Oleg V. Naumov, *The Road to Terror: Stalin and the Self-Destruction
of the Bolsheviks, 1932–1939* (New Haven, CT: Yale University Press, 1999), 125–7, 197–8,
222.

[105] See David Shearer, "Social Disorder," 86, 97–8, 100, 111; Paul Hagenloh, "'Socially Harmful
Elements' and the Great Terror," in Sheila Fitzpatrick, ed., *Stalinism: New Directions* (London:
Routledge, 2000), 290–4, 297–300.

and ethnic element into Soviet policies of repression and gave those policies a sense of urgency."[106]

These concerns over political resistance, social disorder, and national contamination coalesced in 1937–8, as over one and a half million people were arrested on political charges, of whom approximately 681,000 were executed, in a chaotic frenzy of bloodletting and denunciations which came to be known as the Great Terror. The political purpose of the terror – and even if there was such a thing – is a matter over which historians continue to disagree. It does appear, however, that, at first at least, the purges were initiated by a small central leadership under Stalin.[107] The degree of centralization of the terror is underlined by the fact that in July 1937, prior to the mass repression, the Politburo provisionally agreed and subsequently confirmed "targets" for the number of executions that were to take place in each region.[108] In subsequent months, the Politburo monitored the implementation of this order very closely.[109] Equally, underlying the first phase of the terror, in the second half of 1937, was a strong impetus to continue the centralizing trends which had begun earlier in the decade, by penetrating and finally breaking down regional political networks. The attack on "family circles" and "local cliques" had indeed been one of the main themes of Stalin's speech at the February–March 1937 Central Committee plenum which effectively set the stage for the Great Terror. In the second half of 1937 nearly all of the eighty regional party leaders, as well as party leaders in the republics, were arrested and most were executed. In most cases this process was centrally orchestrated, with Stalin dispatching plenipotentiaries to the regions to oversee the purge

[106] Shearer, "Social Disorder," 111; and in general, 104–5, 111–13. Shearer's argument draws on the seminal article by Oleg Khlevniuk, "Objectives of the Great Terror, 1937–1938," in *Soviet History, 1917–53: Essays in Honour of R. W. Davies*, eds. Julian Cooper, Maureen Perrie, and E. A. Rees (Basingstoke: Macmillan, 1995), esp. 152, 168–9, 173; Oleg Khlevniuk, "The Reasons for the Great Terror: The Foreign Political Aspect," in *Russia in the Age of Wars, 1914–1945*, eds. Silvio Pons and Andrea Romano (Milan: Feltrinelli 1998), 163–5. A recent article which also stresses the importance of the oncoming war to the instigation of the 1937–8 purges is Hiroaki Kuromiya, "Accounting for the Great Terror," *Jahrbücher für Geschichte Osteuropas* 53, no. 1 (2005): 86–101, esp. 88–93.

[107] Ahead of the purges, on the eve of the February 1937 plenum, the head of the leading party organs sector of the Central Committee, Georgii Malenkov, prepared an inventory of those officials, most of whom were later to be arrested, who had, at one stage or another, deviated from the "party line." See Khlevniuk, "Objectives of the Great Terror, 1937–1938," 159, 160, 162, 165.

[108] See the infamous NKVD Order no. 00447 of 30 July 1937, "On Operations to Repress Former Kulaks, Criminals, and Other Anti-Soviet Elements," which approved an overall target of 269,000 sentences, and which in turn was rubber-stamped by a Politburo resolution the following day, reproduced in V. N. Khaustov, V. Naumov, and N. S. Plotnikova, eds., *Lubianka: Stalin i glavnoe upravlenie gosbezopasnosti NKVD 1937–1938: Dokumenty* (Moscow: Mezhdunarodnyi fond "Demokratiia," 2004), 273–82.

[109] On this see, in particular, Barry McLoughlin, "Mass Operations of the NKVD: A Survey," in *Stalin's Terror*, eds. Barry McLoughlin and Kevin McDermott (New York: Palgrave Macmillan, 2003), 129–32.

process.[110] Unlike the "mass operations," which affected the vast majority
of victims and which were held in secret and usually lacked any semblance of
procedure, the Central Committee went to some length to ensure that trials of
regional potentates were held in public; that they followed the rules, elementary as they were, for military tribunals; and that the arrests themselves were
preceded by highly publicized regional party plena.[111]

When the Great Terror was eventually brought to a halt in the autumn
of 1938, the process was closely managed by the center and, in particular,
by the Party's Central Committee. Two directives, of 20 September and 14
November, accorded the department of leading party organs of the Central
Committee the right to screen, and to confirm the appointments of, all NKVD
executives down to the local level, while a third, of 15 November 1938, signed
by Stalin and Molotov instructed: "We order in the strongest possible terms:
Until further notice, a halt as of 16 November to examination of all cases by
the *troiki* and military tribunals." A Politburo resolution, two days later, on
17 November 1938, strictly prohibited any further "mass operations" by the
NKVD, liquidated the "*troiki*," and reintroduced strong qualitative controls
on authorizations for arrests.[112] The relative suddenness with which these
procedures were implemented has indeed led some commentators to suggest
that Stalin succeeded in "turning off the mass terror."[113]

The purges paradoxically fostered a new, more stable and centralized leadership system. The central government, the military, the regional and republican
leaderships, and the economic infrastructure had all been chastened. At the
very summit of the system, the immediate prewar years may be regarded as
the highwater mark of Stalin's dictatorship.[114] Having had five members of
the Politburo arrested and executed, Stalin put in their place a new generation of young leaders, all known for their work qualities, who had played no
role during the revolution and who owed their rise entirely to him. At the
top level, Stalin also constituted around himself an informal "ruling group"
centered on the Politburo and the newly created executive committee of the
Sovnarkom. Similarly, in the regions, Old Bolsheviks were replaced by a new
generation of young, proletarian, Soviet-educated incumbents. "Stalin," writes
Oleg Khlevniuk, "considered the promotion of young leaders [in the regions]

---

[110] E. A. Rees, "The Great Purges and the XVIII Party Congress of 1939," in *Centre-Local Relations in the Stalinist State 1928–1941* (Basingstoke: Palgrave), 192. For persuasive evidence of
central coordination of this process through Stalin's plenipotentiaries, see *Sovetskoe rukovodstvo*, 364–5, 393–7.

[111] McLoughlin, "Mass Operations of the NKVD," 144.

[112] The full text of the first two directives is in Khaustov, Naumov, and Plotnikova, eds., 550–2,
604–6. The latter two are reproduced in ibid., 606–11, and, in English, in Getty and Naumov,
Road to Terror, 531–7.

[113] Peter H. Solomon, *Soviet Criminal Justice under Stalin* (New York: Cambridge University
Press, 1996), 264.

[114] For a fuller discussion, see Gorlizki and Khlevniuk, "Stalin and his Circle," 252–4; and
Khlevniuk, *Politbiuro*, 246–7, 248–9, 256.

to be the best means of strengthening the regime. They were better-educated, healthy, energetic and free from the routine of former 'revolutionary service' and bureaucratic family circles."[115]

The ending of the purges witnessed a variety of moves to consolidate and stabilize the political order. A recent survey of the NKVD in the city of Nizhnii Novgorod detected a clear pattern in early 1939 of "normalization – affecting everything from newspaper publications to rules of dress and hygiene."[116] The restoration of governmental authority was also augmented by a largely successful effort to stamp out the chorus of appeals against the actions of the NKVD.[117] Stalin's infamous telegraphic text of 10 January 1939 clarifying that the "application of methods of physical pressure in NKVD practice [had been] made permissible in 1937 in accordance with the Central Committee" was, as Khlevniuk convincingly argues, intended less to justify future secret police abuses, as Khrushchev would later claim, than to close ranks and halt social criticism of the Commissariat.[118] More generally, the ending of the purges saw the Communist Party resume its position at the heart of the political system. The prepurge equilibrium between the Party and the NKVD, which in many areas had been broken with the First Moscow Show Trial in August 1936, as NKVD officials took charge of party elections, assumed party positions, and arrested leading party functionaries, was quickly restored in the immediate aftermath of the terror.[119] The Central Committee was quick to stamp its authority on lower levels of the party and state apparatus, as its nomenklatura was formalized and extended and a new huge cadre administration was set up under Georgii Malenkov.[120] In order to placate officials, at the XVIII Party Congress in March 1939, Stalin claimed that though the purge of 1937–8 had been unavoidable, there would be no repetition, while Zhdanov assured delegates that the party's method of mass purging would not be used in the future.

---

[115] Khlevniuk, "First Generation of Stalinist 'Party Generals,'" 58–60.

[116] Cynthia Hooper, "Shifting Stalinism: The 'Normalization' of Repression, 1939–41," in *BASEES Annual Conference* (Cambridge, 2004), 3–4, cited with permission. Also see Cynthia Hooper, "Terror from Within: Participation and Coercion in Soviet Power, 1924–1964" (Ph.D. diss., Princeton University, 2003), 255–61.

[117] Hooper writes, for example, of how over a period of a few months the regime managed to "shut down" the wave of criticism and "to raise a cross over the past." See Hooper, "Shifting Stalinism," 13; Hooper, "Terror of Intimacy: Family Politics in the 1930s Soviet Union," in *Everyday Life in Early Soviet Russia: Taking the Revolution Inside*, eds. Christina Kiaer and Eric Naiman (Bloomington: University of Indiana Press, 2005), 82; and more generally, Hooper, "Terror from Within," 292–7, 301–2.

[118] Khlevniuk, "Party and NKVD: Power Relationships in the Years of the Great Terror," in *Stalin's Terror*, eds. Barry McLoughlin and Kevin McDermott (New York: Palgrave Macmillan, 2003), 31.

[119] Khlevniuk, "Party and NKVD," 30, cf. 22–6.

[120] See "Postanovlenie Politbiuro ob uchete, proverke i utverzhdenii v TsK VKP(b) otvetstvennykh rabotnikov..." of 20 September 1938 in Khlevniuk et al., eds., *Stalinskoe politbiuro v 30-e gody*, 42–4; and Khlevniuk, *Politbiuro*, 248.

As with Stalin's Soviet Union the German political system under Hitler experienced a tension between the party in its "movement phase," which relates to the period until January 1933, and the "regime phase," when the emphasis was on consolidating the authority of the state.[121] That tension, however, would play itself out in a different way. The first stages after the seizure of power in Germany were signified by efforts to tame the radical ambitions of the party and, especially, of the SA Stormtroopers, leading to an open conflict between Hitler, Göring, the army, and the SS on the one side, and Ernst Röhm on the other, which culminated in the murders of 30 June 1934. On account of the military weakness of the Reich, Hitler steered a rather moderate course up to 1937, except for the anti-Jewish legislation which started in April 1933. During this phase, the party found itself in a relatively passive governmental role. The progressive radicalization of the Hitler regime after this point was not merely a function of the contingent pressures placed on Hitler and on his system by a disastrous war. It was also the result of an uncontrollably expansionist ideology and the institutional disarray, marked by a complete absence of institutions for reconciling interests or achieving compromise, which lay at the heart of the Nazi regime.

It would be wrong to deny that the Nazi regime entirely lacked a capacity for order and self-containment. Following the first, frenzied wave of insurgency from below from March 1933, when the NSDAP, with the help of its armed combat wing, the SA, staged mass meetings in Land capitals across the country, parading troops, hoisting flags, ransacking police stations, and getting even with long-term political adversaries, in the summer of 1933, with the NSDAP monopoly of power now secure, Hitler was able to proclaim an end to the "National Socialist revolution" and move to restore the authority of the Reich ministries. "The stream of revolution once released," he famously announced in a speech of 6 July 1933, "must be guided into the secure bed of evolution."[122] Over the next year, until the establishment of the absolute supremacy of the Führer in the summer of 1934, there was continual oscillation between the opposing tendencies to make revolution and to halt it. From then on, however, until 1937/8 an equilibrium was established between the stabilizing factors of an authoritarian state and the dynamic forces of the National Socialist movement. With all its contradictions and contrary tendencies, the distribution of power within the German state remained relatively fixed. For much of this period, the substance of Nazi policies was also kept broadly within the bounds of traditional, German nationalist and national-conservative ideas and aims.

That Hitler was able to contain the "revolutionary" elements of his new regime was due in large part to the fact that he had not presided over a

---

[121] These categories are derived from Arendt's discussion of the tension between the party as "movement" and the party "in government." Hannah Arendt, *The Origins of Totalitarianism*, 1st ed. (New York: Harcourt, Brace, 1951), 389–92.

[122] Max Domarus, *Hitler: Reden und Proklationen*, vol. 1 (Munich: Domarus [self-published], 1963), 286.

revolution as such. Basing his accession to power on an alliance with national-conservative forces, Hitler continued to maintain a coexistence in government with nonparty elements well into the late 1930s. Rather than sweeping away existing interest groups, Hitler's government reached a modus vivendi with key elements of the German economic establishment. Thus, for example, the appointment of Schacht, a nonparty man, as president of the Reich Bank on 17 March 1933, served to placate leading business interests.[123] It was largely out of a wish not to alienate big business and the banks and, in particular, not to bring about major shortages, that soon after coming to power Hitler's administration also retreated from its hard line on the department stores.[124] Least affected by the party's political "coordination" were the captains of industry (Krupp, Thyssen, and Siemens), who, by means of their own special standing with Hitler, as well as their direct support from the likes of Schacht, Hugenberg, and Göring, were able to deflect with ease any encroachments by party officials. It was a measure of Hitler's sensitivity to industrial interests that, on 29 May 1933, he summoned fifty leading industrialists and bank directors to listen to their advice on job creation.[125] Far from damaging the interests of big business, the Hitler government enhanced business's bargaining power by, in effect, dismantling the system of worker rights erected under Weimar with a Law for the Ordering of National Labor which was promulgated on 20 January 1934.[126]

Rather than refashioning society there was a loose fit between the goals of the Nazi regime and the preexisting social order. For this reason the purge mechanism was poorly institutionalized and only haltingly implemented. The National Socialist commissioners appointed in March and April 1933 in most Reich and Land ministries to cleanse these bodies of "undesirable elements" were used mainly on a one-off basis. In order to prevent the personnel policy of the state from being taken over by the party, the law of 7 April 1933 on the Restoration of the Professional Civil Service subjected the purging of the civil service apparatus to clear legal conditions and, crucially, placed the process in the hands of the state apparatus. In the event, the purges were quite limited, with only 1 to 2 percent of the country's one and a half million civil servants being retired or dismissed without pension on political or racial

---

[123] On Hitler's economic policy, see Avraham Barkai, *Das Wirtschaftssystem des Nationalsozialismus: Ideologie, Theorie, Politik, 1933–1945*, 2nd ed. (Frankfurt am Main: Fischer Taschenbuch, 1988); Richard R. Overy, *The Nazi Economic Recovery 1933–1938* (London [u.a.]: Macmillan, 1984).

[124] See Heinrich Uhlig, *Die Warenhäuser im Dritten Reich* (Cologne: Westdeutscher Verlag, 1956), 115–19; Helmut Genschel, *Die Verdrängung der Juden aus der Wirtschaft im Dritten Reich* (Gottingen: Musterschmidt Verlag, 1966), 79–80.

[125] It was on the basis of this discussion that in mid-July 1933 a permanent General Council of the Economy was set up.

[126] See Tilla Siegel, *Leistung und Lohn in der nationalsozialistischen Ordnung der Arbeit* (Opladen: Westdeutscher Verlag, 1989); cf. Rüdiger Hachtman, *Industriearbeit im "Dritten Reich": Untersuchungen zu den Lohn – und Arbeitsbedingungen in Deutschland 1933–1945* (Gottingen: Vandenhoeck & Ruprecht, 1989).

grounds.[127] The fear that the party would itself become contaminated was also milder than in the Soviet Union. Although, in order to guard against "March converts" a bar on new members was imposed on 1 May 1933 and an obligatory two-year probationary period was introduced on 26 June, there were no membership screenings or mass "verification" programs, the threat of which almost permanently hung over the Bolshevik party.[128] The link between the purge apparatus, such as it was, and the security services was also far looser than in the Soviet Union. One reason for this was that Hitler himself was willing to maintain a safe distance from the security apparatus, delegating control over its affairs to Himmler, and was far less inclined than was Stalin to use it against his own party. Perhaps the best example of this was Hitler's relative reluctance to strike against the high SA leadership in the summer of 1934. The "Night of the Long Knives" was carried out only after Hitler had come under considerable pressure from Himmler, Göring, and the Wehrmacht to act, especially following von Papen's Marburg speech. The attack, which also targeted civilians and potential opponents, such as General von Schleicher, claimed eighty-eight victims and was – in comparison with the Stalinist purges – limited in scope, as were the ensuing dismissals of party members and other alleged followers of Röhm. Rather than underlining the revolutionary impulse of the regime, the attack on the SA was meant to bring to an end the party "revolution from below."[129]

It was in 1938 that the regime broke free of these self-imposed ordinances. That year saw the expulsion of conservatives from the army (Blomberg, Fritsch), the Foreign Ministry (von Neurath), and the economic administration (Schacht), all of whom had been pillars of moderation and bulwarks against excessive party influence, and their replacement by Hitler's partisans.[130] In setting up civilian administration in the newly annexed areas of Austria and the Sudenten territories in 1938, Hitler brought in members of the party's old guard and sought to strengthen the party's role. By deliberately bypassing the ministerial bureaucracies in Berlin the Austrian Gaue presaged the new "model Gaue" of the annexed territories to the east, which "reflected the

---

[127] See Jane Caplan, *Government without Administration: State and Civil Service in Weimar and Nazi Germany* (Oxford: Clarendon Press, 1988), 139–88; Sigrun Mühl-Benninghaus, *Das Beamtentum in der NS-Diktatur bis zum Ausbruch des Zweiten Weltkrieges* (Düsseldorf: Droste, 1996) 60–83; Broszat, 196, 198, 245.

[128] Cf. Michael H. Kater, *The Nazi Party: A Social Profile of Members and Leaders, 1919–1945* (Cambridge, MA: Harvard University Press, 1983), 72–115; Dietrich Orlow, *The History of the Nazi Party, 1933–1945*, vol. 2 (Pittsburgh: University of Pittsburgh Press, 1973), 49–50.

[129] See Heinz Höhne, *Mordsache Röhm: Hitlers Durchbruch zur Alleinherrschaft, 1933–1934* (Hamburg: Rowohlt, 1984), 286–96; and Broszat, 213. Although there was a relatively high turnover of party officials from 1933 to 1935, the movement of the vast majority of them had relatively little to do with the Röhm purge or with any institutionalized purge mechanism as such. See Kater, *The Nazi Party*, 190–1; cf. Overy, *The Dictators*, 141.

[130] See Karl-Heinz Janssen and Fritz Tobias, *Der Sturz der Generäle: Hitler und die Blomberg-Fritsch-Krise 1938* (Munich: Beck, 1994), 148–9, 154–5.

structure of the Hitler movement more than they did that of the authoritarian state."[131]

The policy shift of 1938 and, in particular, the start of the war the following year marked a turn toward a new radical phase of the Nazi regime from which it would never fully recover. With it, the precarious balance between the authoritarian forces of order and the transforming impulses coming from the party was finally broken. Although this switch happened quite abruptly, it was not incidental to the development of the state. In fact, it was driven by features of the National Socialist regime which distinguished it quite markedly from its Soviet counterpart. The first of these was the territorial expansionism of the Nazi regime. Nazi thinking had been characterized by a dynamic impulse toward territorial growth which had been evident even before the NSDAP accession in 1933. Many of the Nazis' early economic and demographic prescriptions had been based on establishing German "living space" in Eastern Europe.[132] Hitler's revelation of radical foreign policy plans and a will to war at the end of 1937, as well as his annexation of Austria and the Sudetenland the following year, were fully in keeping with the regime's long-term strategic ambitions. Secondly, the structures of the Reich government became increasingly disrupted through the proliferation of direct special powers from Hitler, the accumulation of authority in the hands of individual party satraps, and the establishment of yet more central organs.[133] Above all, the growing SS apparatus, culminating in the establishment of a Reich Main Security Office, the incorporation of the ordinary police force, and Himmler's installment as Minister of Interior (and, later, as chief of the Home Army), would create a sufficiently independent power base such that, after 1941, it also controlled occupied territories in East and West and became the main executive arm for the annihilation of European Jewry.[134]

---

[131] Broszat, 123–4, 128, 254. In the annexation of Austria in 1938 Hitler set up Gaue, headed by members of the party's old guard, which united state and territorial administrative units and were directly subordinate to the leader's office. S. John A. Bernbaum, "The New Elite: Nazi Leadership in Austria, 1938–1945," in *Austrian History Yearbook*, 14 (1978), 145–60; Emmerich Tálos, Ernst Hanisch, and Wolfgang Neugebauer, *NS–Herrschaft in Österreich 1938–1945* (Vienna: Verlag für Gesellschaftskritik, 1988); Dieter Rebentisch, *Führerstaat und Verwaltung in Zweiten Weltkrieg: Verfassungsentwicklung und Verwaltungspolitik 1939–1945* (Stuttgart: F. Steiner Verlag, 1989), 170–1.

[132] Cf. Klaus Hildebrand, "Die Geschichte der deutschen Außenpolitik (1933–1945) im Urteil der neueren Forschung," in *Deutsche Außenpolitik 1933–1945: Kalkül oder Dogma*, 4th ed. (Stuttgart [u.a.]: Kohlhammer, 1980), 188–9; Gerhard Weinberg, *The Foreign Policy of Hitler's Germany: Diplomatic Revolution in Europe 1933–1936* (Chicago: University of Chicago Press, 1970), 14–24; and Hans-Adolf Jacobsen, "Zur Struktur der NS–Außenpolitik 1933–1945," in Manfred Funke, ed., *Hitler, Deutschland und die Mächte* (Düsseldorf: Droste, 1978), 169–75.

[133] Rebentisch, *Führerstaat und Verwaltung*, 293–4 and 331–69.

[134] Forming something of a "state within a state," Himmler did not, however, gain control over the Gauleiter or the party Chancellery under Martin Borman, while Albert Speer, the minister for armaments and ammunition, had his own line of communication to Hitler. The best analysis of the structure of the SS apparatus is still Hans Buchheim, "Die SS – das Herrschaftsimperium," in

As a social revolutionary state the Soviet regime had, in the purge, an instrument for refining its party membership and apparatus. In the late 1930s this instrument was adapted to rein in and liquidate regional party leaders and to crush any residue of opposition within the top leadership. As well as centralizing and disciplining the party-state, the terror opened career avenues for a new generation of young and recently socialized Soviet cadres. The consolidation of the Stalinist regime was based on a combination of industrial transformation, social revolution, and an extensive and well-organized party bureaucracy which had fully penetrated the state. In the Nazi case the sequence was quite different. The relative stability of the early Nazi regime was reliant almost entirely on norms and state structures inherited from the preexisting German state and from a power-sharing agreement with national-conservative allies. When these stabilizing forces were stripped away in the late 1930s the expansionist dynamic of the state was laid bare and an array of free-floating leadership-retinue structures, with no grounding in the constitution, were let loose.

THE WAR

Arguably more than any other period, the war years present particular problems of comparison. Not only were the Soviet and National Socialist political systems highly fluid in these years, but throughout the war the fortunes of one were inversely related to those of the other. For much of the first phase of the war, Germany fought a war of aggression, while the Soviet Union was engaged in a struggle for survival. As Soviet forces retreated and much of the country's territory was occupied, the Soviet government was relocated and some traditional decision-making structures were either dissolved or transformed. For its part, Germany expanded, annexing some territories and setting up a variety of new political arrangements in others.[135] In the second half of the war, the fortunes of the two belligerents were reversed, with major political

---

Anatomie des SS-Staates, 7th ed., eds. Hans Buchheim et al. (Munich: Deutschen Taschenbuch Verlag, 1999), 30–40.

[135] There were five categories of territory incorporated into German administration: first were the areas which were formally annexed (e.g., Danzig-West Prussia, Warthegau); second were those areas which were not formally incorporated but effectively treated as part of the Reich (e.g., Alsace-Lorraine, Luxembourg); third were populations which were treated as Germanic and placed under civilian administration, but slated for future integration into the Greater German Empire (e.g., Norway, Holland, Flemish parts of Belgium); fourth were areas which were designated for future German colonization (Protectorate of Bohemia, General Gouvernmnent in Poland, Reich Commissariat for Ostland); and last occupied areas of continuing military significance which were placed under military administration (e.g., areas to the immediate rear of the zones of operation in the USSR). For a good description, see Jürgen Förster, "From 'Blitzkrieg' to 'Total War': Germany's War in Europe," in *A World at Total War: Global Conflict and the Politics of Destruction, 1937–1945*, eds. Roger Chickering, Stig Förster, Bernd Greiner (Washington, DC, and Cambridge: German Historical Institute and Cambridge University Press, 2005), 94.

consequences, as the Soviet political order restabilized while the structures of National Socialist government and administration became ever more fractured and disarticulated.

On the eve of the war, as we have seen, patterns of high-level decision making in the two countries had followed different paths. In the Soviet Union, after the purges, leading members of the Politburo had continued to meet collectively on a near-daily basis within the framework of Stalin's "ruling group." Below the cabinet, the party existed as a hierarchic organization and committee meetings of its core bureaucratic directorates, the Orgburo and Secretariat, were held on a regular basis, normally with the attendance of at least one Politburo member. By contrast, there was no equivalent collective cabinetlike body in the German system. Hitler's ingrained secretiveness and his preference for one-on-one meetings had eroded formal patterns of government and administration. Unlike in the USSR, neither a clear-cut party-based hierarchic structure of command nor a collective body for determining party policy was ever instituted. Even the Council of Ministers for Reich Defense, formed on the eve of the war, which could have played a useful role in coordinating civilian industrial and military requirements, was disbanded after only six meetings as its chairman, Göring, did not want to challenge the Führer's political prerogatives.[136]

For much of the first phase of the war, until the victory at Stalingrad, the Soviet political system embraced "informal" or "extraordinary" principles of decision making and resource allocation.[137] When the new war cabinet, the State Defense Committee (GKO), was set up on 30 June 1941, members of the committee were assigned their own teams and granted virtually unlimited authority to settle issues within their jurisdictions.[138] Similarly, the one hundred or so GKO plenipotentiaries who were appointed in the first six months of the war were endowed with the supreme authority of the GKO to override the objections of local leaders and committees, even where the latter formally occupied more senior positions. In fact, these near-total mandates of authority to individuals to deal with particular policies or issues were somewhat reminiscent of the "leader-retinue" structures which had existed in the Nazi system since the mid-1930s. In addition, traditional party structures were undermined in the early phase of the war, as many party cells were deserted or dissolved, thousands of party officials were conscripted to the front, and the party was deployed in a more openly "mobilizational" role as Central Committee *partorgs* were set up in large enterprises, military commissars reestablished

---

[136] Jürgen Förster, "From 'Blitzkrieg' to 'Total War,'" 92.

[137] John Barber and Mark Harrison, *The Soviet Home Front 1941–1945: A Social and Economic History of the USSR in World War II* (London and New York: Longman, 1991), 198; Sanford R. Lieberman, "Crisis Management in the USSR: Wartime System of Administration and Control," in *The Impact of World War II on the Soviet Union*, ed. Susan Linz (Totowa, NJ: Rowman & Allanhead, 1985), 65–6.

[138] On the "working groups" see Iurii Gor'kov, *Gosudarstvennyi Komitet Oborony postanovliaet: 1941–1945: Tsifry i dokumenty* (Moscow: Olma-Press, 2002), 55, 72.

at the front, and political departments resurrected at the Machine Tractor Stations.[139]

Although the state defense committee was an extraordinary body, with variable attendance and no agendas or minutes, it was nonetheless in many respects a continuation of the "ruling group" which had existed before the war. As with that body, the GKO was a collective entity, consisting of political leaders, which discharged a range of cabinetlike functions.[140] In fact, all its members were full or candidate members of the Politburo.[141] Nor should one exaggerate the formlessness of its proceedings. Over a half of the GKO's 9,971 decrees were passed by means of a vote.[142] Following a resolution of February 1942, there was also a relatively clear division of labor among its members.[143] With only a small staff of its own, the GKO relied heavily on the bureaucracies of the party and state and most of its business was implemented through regular party and state channels.[144] Similarly at a local level GKO plenipotentiaries tended to rely on local party committees to implement decisions.[145]

Not only was the GKO a fully functioning cabinet, but its leader took an active part in its affairs. Almost a quarter (2,256 out of 9,971) of all GKO resolutions were signed by Stalin, and many of these were either completely written, dictated, or substantially amended by him.[146] In fact, much as in the early 1930s, and to a far greater degree than Hitler, Stalin was drawn into the finer details of managing the war economy through the GKO. Following the loss of production during the evacuation and occupation of Soviet territory in the summer of 1941, for example, Stalin dictated a telegram to the Gor'kii obkom and to directors of tank-producing factories in the region on the need to raise

---

[139] Altogether in the war, 13,850 leading party officials, including leading party secretaries and Central Committee staff, were mobilized to serve in the armed forces. See Iu. P. Petrov, "KPSS – Organizator i rukovoditel' pobedy sovetskogo naroda v velikoi otechestvennoi voine," *Voprosy istorii*, no. 5 (1970): 16

[140] The cabinet-like functions of the GKO are emphasized in A. A. Pechenkin, "Gosudarstvennyi Komitet Oborony v 1941 godu," *Otechestvennaia istoriia*, 4–5 (1994): 140.

[141] With the exception of Bulganin, who joined the GKO in November 1944 and was made a candidate member of the Politburo in March 1946, all the other eight full members of the GKO were members of the Politburo. The notion that the prewar Politburo continued to operate, albeit under the auspices of the GKO, can be found in Iu. A. Gor'kov ["K istorii sozdaniia goskomiteta oborony," *Novaia i noveishaia istoriia*, no. 4 (1999): 32], who writes, "Resolutions of the GKO were, in effect, resolutions of the Politburo of the Central Committee."

[142] Gor'kov, *Gosudarstvennyi Komitet Oborony postanovliaet*, 69.

[143] "O raspredelenii obiazannostei mezhdu chlenami GKO" in Gor'kov, *Gosudarstvennyi Komitet*, 70–1.

[144] A. A. Pechenkin, "Gosudarstvennyi Komitet Oborony v 1941 godu," 131; the Central Committee also had its own plenipotentiaries, who focused on nonmilitary issues such as the procurements of fuel. Politburo resolution of 23 July 1942, "Ob upolnomochennom TsK VKP(b) i SNK SSSR po obespecheniiu zagotovok mestnykh vidov topliva" RGASPI f. 17 op. 3 d. 1045 ll. 23–4.

[145] Petrov, "KPSS – Organizator i rukovoditel,'" 13.

[146] Gor'kov, *Gosudarstvennyi Komitet*, 80–1.

production from three tanks to four to five tanks a day.[147] On another occasion, having ordered that the Ministry of Defense and Gosplan provide him and the rest of the GKO every month with a schedule for the daily production of antitank ammunition, Stalin went on to dictate a draft resolution that directed that the secretaries of the six most proximate regional party committees take day-to-day control of the production of 45 mm anti-tank and 76 mm division guns and that they report to Stalin personally on the fulfillment of this program every day.[148]

By contrast, on the eve of the war, the upper reaches of the German state had dissolved into a series of one-to-one relationships between Hitler and a variety of favored individuals. As the war progressed, without a cabinet or a collective agency, such as the de facto Politburo or the GKO, to provide a regularized forum for interaction and discussion, the processes by which policies were initiated and decisions reached became ever more disjointed and fragmentary.[149] Unlike the USSR, where all leading directives were formally issued under the authority of the institutions of the party-state, most often the GKO, but sometimes as resolutions of the Central Committee or Sovnarkom, the majority of key wartime edicts and resolutions in Germany were received as "Hitler" directives.[150] Further, some of the fiercest policy conflicts of the early phase of the war, such as on how to resolve the competing claims between the army and the war industries for manpower, were resolved, outside the framework of a collective decision-making body, by Hitler alone, in this case in favor of the latter. Once these procedures for relatively unstructured one-person decision making had been established, they became self-reinforcing. Thus, for example, after Hitler had in effect stripped the leadership of the armed forces of any capacity for collective action on the eve of the war, it was army leaders such as von Fritsch, Beck, and Halder who, in their desire to preserve their own influence over policy, opposed the creation of an agency to oversee all the German armed forces. "As a result, no institution such as a war cabinet, joint chiefs of staff or a combined services committee existed in Nazi Germany; the threads came together only in the hands of Hitler."[151]

The fact that there had not been a deep-seated transformation of the social structure in Germany under the Nazis also had an impact on the kinds of societal pressures which impinged on the political and economic system during the war. Without the Soviet state's economic and coercive instruments,

---

[147] Pechenkin, 132–3. On 3 March 1942 Stalin authored a Politburo resolution obliging the director of factory no. 26, V. P. Balandin, to produce 800 M-105P aircraft motors in March, with a view to producing 30 a day by the end of March and 40 a day in April. RGASPI, f. 17 op. 162 d. 37 l. 32.

[148] Gor'kov, *Gosudarstvennyi Komitet*, 74; Pechenkin, 133–4.

[149] This is discussed in Kershaw, *Hitler, 1936–45*, 186, 311–13.

[150] According to Overy, of the 650 major legislative acts promulgated during the war years, only 72 were formal laws, while 241 were Führer decrees and 173 Führer orders. See Overy, *The Dictators*, 71.

[151] Jürgen Förster, "From 'Blitzkrieg' to 'Total War,'" 92, 100–1.

the German state found it harder to depress social demands. Unlike the Soviet case, where the social structure and social expectations had been refashioned to limit, as far as possible, constraints on the state's economic and military priorities, the German state's capabilities were circumscribed by powerful social pressures, especially in the consumer sector. Further, to the extent that the Hitler state co-opted existing social interests, it was also contained by them. Having allied itself to established corporate interests, the state found that its economic structures and policies had, in certain respects, become "privatized"; thus, the unreconstituted nature of German society was mirrored in the structure of social and economic interests within the state. With the outbreak of war, a variety of political-economic alliances, each headed by a powerful state department but supported by major business interests, participated in the relatively unstructured competition for resources. At the highest levels these state departments included Walter Funk's Ministry of Economics, the War Economy Office headed by General Georg Thomas at Supreme Headquarters, and Göring's FYP organization; below them another twenty-seven national offices played their part in the planning anarchy.[152]

The fact that a relatively underdeveloped economy such as the Soviet Union's did not collapse on being invaded, as did many other countries in a similar position, and that the Soviet Union was able to mobilize so rapidly in the face of calamitous military defeats is relevant to our theme, for it points to two distinctive features of the Soviet political system. One key to this success was not so much the fact that the Soviet Union had detailed economic controls, as that it was able to maintain economic integration under intense stress. Before the war, the Soviet economy had taken significant steps toward overcoming the strategic disadvantage of a low developmental level through the establishment of a centralized, integrated system for allocating industrial and agricultural products. Soviet leaders had deployed a "superior institutional capacity for integration and coordination" which matched or exceeded that of much more highly developed economies so that, despite a relatively poor economy, the USSR could commit a very high proportion of national resources to the war effort.[153] A second factor, given the relative balance of resources in the first phase of the war, which helps account for the Soviet Union's ability to stave off collapse, was the extraordinarily coercive approach of Stalin not only to his own troops, but to civilians as well. The infamous orders on surrender and on retreat (no. 270 of 16 August 1941 "On Capture" and order no. 227

---

[152] Werner Abelshauser, "Germany: Guns, Butter and Economic Miracles," in Mark Harrison, ed, *The Economics of World War II: Six Great Powers in International Comparison* (Cambridge: Cambridge University Press, 1998), 145, 155–6.

[153] Mark Harrison, "The Economics of World War II: An Overview," in *The Economics of World War II: Six Great Powers in International Comparison*, ed. Mark Harrison (Cambridge and New York: Cambridge University Press, 1998), 20, 24; and Mark Harrison, "The Soviet Union: The Defeated Victor," in *The Economics of World War II: Six Great Powers in International Comparison*, ed. Mark Harrison (Cambridge and New York: Cambridge University Press, 1998), 270–2.

"Not a Step Back" of 28 July 1941), which were designed to threaten any "collaboration" with death, were complemented by mass deportations of the Soviet Union's own ethnic groups, and extraordinarily severe punishments not only for various food crimes and looting, but also for lateness, absenteeism, and illegal quitting at work. It was this form of leadership which allowed Stalin, in Mark Harrison's words, to "close off the options of honorable surrender."[154]

The Soviet Union's victory at Stalingrad considerably shifted the military balance in its favor, a fact which soon brought on a stabilization in decision-making structures. At this stage a variety of collective bodies designed to facilitate political and economic integration were reestablished. Thus a new operational bureau of the GKO consisting of four senior politicians, Molotov, Beria, Malenkov, and Mikoian, was set up on 8 December 1942.[155] For the rest of the war, the bureau passed 2,256 resolutions on military affairs and as many again on defense production.[156] With the upturn in the military situation, there was also a reemergence of traditional party structures at the center, in the regions, and in the newly occupied territories. So as to "bring organizational order" to the work of regional party committees and to "raise the account-ability" of regional party secretaries, on 6 August 1943 the work of regional party secretaries was rationalized and a clear authority structure subordinat-ing regional party organizations to the Central Committee was reinstated.[157] Attention was also paid to establishing embryonic party-based bodies in the newly occupied territories and subordinating these directly to the All-Union Central Committee.[158]

In Nazi Germany, the Party also played an increasing role as the war pro-gressed, but its position in the wider political landscape was very different and tended to undermine political integration rather than reinforce it. In the

---

[154] The use of coercion as part of Stalin's strategy is discussed at length in Mark Harrison, "The USSR and Total War: Why Didn't the Soviet Economy Collapse in 1942?" in Chickering et al., *A World at Total War*, eds. Roger Chickering, Stig Förster, and Bernd Greiner (Washington, DC, and Cambridge: German Historical Institute and Cambridge University Press, 2005), 153–5.

[155] The full text of the resolution (no. 2615) can be found in Gor'kov, *Gosudarstvennyi Komitet*, 521–2. The activities of the GKO bureau, which were further extended on 18 May 1944, were similar to those of the Bureau of Sovnarkom, which had first been set up on the eve of the war. See Gorlizki and Khlevniuk, "Stalin and His Circle," 256; and Gor'kov, 532–3.

[156] Gor'kov, *Gosudarstvennyi Komitet*, 31.

[157] One of the resolutions of 6 August entrusted the senior Central Committee Secretary and Politburo member Georgii Malenkov with day to day supervision of regional party committees and gave him the right "to summon and to hear reports at the Secretariat and the Orgburo, of first secretaries of obkoms, kraikoms, and the Central Committees of the union republic parties, and to carry out through the Secretariat and Orgburo necessary decisions and practical measures for correcting shortcomings and improving the work of local party organizations in accordance with the results of these checks." RGASPI f. 17 op. 3 d. 1048 l. 37.

[158] Sanford Lieberman, "The Re-Sovietization of Formerly Occupied Areas of the USSR during WWII," in *The Soviet Empire Reconsidered: Essays in Honor of Adam B. Ulam*, eds. Sanford Lieberman et al. (Boulder, CO: Westview Press, 1994), 51–2; and RGASPI f. 17 op. 3 d. 1048 ll. 36–7.

economic sphere, rationalization of the war economy, which finally enabled
mass production of armaments, did lead to a dramatic increase in labor productivity in the armaments sector.[159] However, in the political sphere, authority became if anything even more fragmented than it had been before. At the
very highest level there continued to be no central administrative authority to
coordinate the war effort. The new "Committee of Three," which consisted of
the heads of the chancelleries for administration, party affairs, and the armed
forces (Lammers, Bormann, and Keitel) and which had been set up during
the Stalingrad crisis to allocate manpower, met only eleven times. Attempts to
regenerate the Reich Defense Council also came to naught. Rather, it was the
orders issued under Hitler's authority, the so-called "Hitler orders," that prescribed aggregate levels of arms production, allocated labor between industry
and the military, and initiated operational planning.[160] In July 1944 Goebbels's
efforts to create a more effective central government, despite formally gaining
Hitler's grudging approval, did not lead to a fundamental reform of the leadership structure, largely as a result of Hitler's continuing fears that measures of
this kind would run into opposition among lower-level leaders and therefore
affect his prestige.[161]

At lower levels too whatever unity had existed in the government dissolved
as the party began, in an increasingly haphazard and uncoordinated fashion, to
grab more and more powers. Leaders such as Goebbels, Bormann, and Robert
Ley responded to the growing sense of crisis with the notion that only the
party was able to achieve a turnaround in German history. Through repeated
references to the "*Kampfzeit*" of the early 1920s, and in particular to the provisional defeat of 9 November 1923, they argued that only the party could
reverse the various setbacks which had afflicted the country. Although much of
this assumed a propagandistic aspect, as membership assemblies, propaganda
marches, and public rallies were convened, the process of "partification" also
impacted on the already fragmentary structure of the state.[162] Thus Gauleiter
doubled up as Reich Defense Commissioners and a growing number of them
became chiefs of civilian administration. The party also offered its services as
an auxiliary to the security police and the Gestapo and assumed oversight and

---

[159] Stimulated by the adoption of mass production and the greater planning integration afforded
by the new Ministry of Armaments and Munitions, labor productivity grew by 60 percent in
the armaments sector between 1939 and 1944, considerably outstripping productivity in the
other branches of German heavy industry. Yet despite Hitler's initially promising to give Speer
full control, deriving from his own authority as Führer, over the economy, Speer's Ministry of
Armaments and Munitions had limited authority over labor allocation and aircraft production
and had a fraught relationship with the army, whose generals had difficulty deferring to a
civilian institution led by an architect with little military experience. By summer 1944 Speer
in any case appears to have lost Hitler's confidence. See Abelshauser, "Guns, Butter," 156–7;
and Overy, *The Dictators*, 506–8.

[160] Forster, "From Blitzkrieg," 93.

[161] Hans Mommsen, "The Dissolution of the Third Reich: Crisis, Management and Collapse,
1943–1945," *Bulletin of the German Historical Institute*, no. 27 (Fall 2001): 11.

[162] The term "partification" was first introduced in Orlow, *History of the Nazi Party II.*

motivational functions in the military.[163] The mushrooming of institutions, special powers, and specific legal arrangements disrupted the unified bureaucratic state and speeded up the process of radicalization just as much as any ideological extremism.[164]

As much as it may have accorded with the propaganda and ideological dictates of the Nazi leadership, this sudden widening of the party's jurisdiction could occur precisely because relations between party and state were so unstable. The internal infighting between party and state officials drained the energies not only of subalterns, but also of senior party leaders. Efforts to circumvent these damaging struggles by broadening the authority of top party officials yielded few tangible benefits. The replacement of Frick by Himmler as Reich interior minister, for example, did little to reduce the administrative infighting at the heart of the state. The effects of partification were, in a sense, self-perpetuating, for in addition to prolonging the war by implanting the notion that new resources could be unearthed through strength of will, partification also helped destroy the last institutional legacies from the old order which could have provided a platform for either resistance or dissent. After the failed attempt on Hitler's life, the military leadership was led by fanatical generals supported by roving field courts while the nearly omnipotent Gauleiter and Reich Defense Commissioners unleashed waves of terror by setting up summary courts in each Gau and turning the Labor Educational Centers into virtual concentration camps.[165]

Soviet administrative and political institutions were structurally better adjusted to the goals of wartime mobilization than were their German equivalents. In the German case, it was only in the second half of the war that Hitler reluctantly agreed to pursue a strategy of "total mobilization." However, although this mobilization was fueled by war aims which were virtually free of restraint, it lacked a clear administrative or institutional basis. After Stalingrad the main political expression of "total mobilization" was a process of "partification" which rested to a large degree on calls to complete the Nazi "revolution" of 1933 and to establish unrestricted party rule in all relevant political realms. By the very end of the war, after July 1944, "total partification" had undercut the last unified, institutional bases of the Nazi political order, including the military leadership. The continuing and ultimately self-destructive mobilization of people and resources, not least the relentless exploitation of forced labor, occurred decentrally and varied according to local conditions, institutional capacities, and fanatical commitment to the Nazi cause. Overall, it is this

---

[163] In December 1943 "National Socialist Leadership Officers" were assigned down to the divisional level in order to aid commanders in instructing soldiers in the principles of National Socialism. Selected and trained by the party, these political officers were attached to every military unit in order to ensure that commanders were toeing the party line, much as the commissars had done in the Red Army.

[164] Mommsen, "Dissolution of the Third Reich," 14–16, 18; and see Kershaw, *Hitler, 1936–45,* 314–16.

[165] Hans Mommsen, "The Dissolution of the Third Reich," 11, 12, 19–20.

infrastructure of mid-level power in the military, the state bureaucracy (as, for example, food distribution), the economy, and the SS that kept Nazi Germany in the war. By contrast, the war confirmed the high mobilizational capacity of the Soviet economic system for military as well as peacetime goals; and it showed that the Soviet Union's mobilizational capacities, tried out before the war on the campaigns to "build socialism," could be used just as effectively for military purposes.[166] The combination of a more coercive economy and an institutionally more clearly delineated political order made for a system which was better adapted to the needs of war.

In the postwar period, there is no longer a benchmark for comparing the two systems. Certainly, we must beware of ascribing the continuation of the one order and the ending of the other to the nature of their political systems, since this had far more to do with other factors, most notably the fortunes of their military campaigns. Nonetheless, the subsequent evolution of the Soviet system in the early postwar period was marked by a continuation of some features whose origins can be traced to the war and prewar periods. First, there continued to be growing institutional stabilization at the summit of the system, where a ruling collective carried on meeting on a regular basis to decide issues of national importance.[167] This had not been the case in Nazi Germany since the mid-1930s. Secondly, the party and, in particular the party apparatus, not only continued to function, but provided the backbone of the political system, while the system of party-based patronage, the nomenklatura, which was consolidated in the postwar period, helped to reinforce and bind together the centralized hierarchies of the state.[168]

CONCLUSION

The Soviet political order was never a smoothly functioning "machine" as it has been portrayed in some versions of the "totalitarian" model. The Soviet system was, however, able to remain politically and economically integrated, even under the most severe external shock of World War II. This high degree of integration may be attributed to a number of factors. One, certainly, was the extreme coercion displayed by Stalin against his own population not only during the Great Terror, but also during the war. Another important factor was the role of the centrally managed economy, which allowed the state to mobilize resources very quickly and, through the system of food procurement erected in the early 1930s, to ensure that farmers could not deny food to the towns.[169] From the political perspective, however, the most important factor in holding

---

[166] Mark Harrison, "The Soviet Union: The Defeated Victor," 297; Barber and Harrison, 20.

[167] Yoram Gorlizki, "Ordinary Stalinism: The Council of Ministers and the Soviet Neo-Patrimonial State, 1945–1953," *Journal of Modern History* 74, no. 4 (2002): 699–736.

[168] Yoram Gorlizki and Oleg Khlevniuk, *Cold Peace: Stalin and the Soviet Ruling Circle, 1945–53* (New York: Oxford University Press, 2004), chapter 2, "State Building Stalin Style," 45–68; and Oleg Khlevniuk, "Sistema tsentr-regiony v 1930–1950e gody: Predposylki politizatsii 'nomenklatury'," 253–68.

[169] Harrison, "Economics of World War II: An Overview," 24.

the political system together was the role of a centralized and institutionally integrated party, which formed the core of the party-state. Even at the height of Stalinism, the party existed as an entity independent of the leader. The fact that the party existed as a continuous, integrated hierarchy, which was institutionally and ideologically embedded in the system, meant that it always existed as a resource for correcting and reining in the regime's more extreme policies. The institutional continuity of the party provided the basis for self-containment which the Soviet system had and the National Socialist system lacked.

To the extent that theirs was a conception of politics as mobilization, the main transformation which the Nazis brought about was one of subjective consciousness.[170] The Nazis, however, did not bring about a revolution in the sense of a deep-seated social transformation or the forging of a new state.[171] The political and administrative system of National Socialism was too disjointed for it to be characterized as a "Nazi state" as such. At its summit there was no collective cabinet. The key bureaucracies were headed by free-floating "retinue-structures" that developed considerable mobilizational energy especially in the latter phases of the war. The party's role in the system was far hazier, as was its relationship to the ordinary institutions of government. Instead, the state and ideology relied to a far greater extent for what coherence they had on the cult of the Führer. This combination of a flimsy institutional basis, when allied to an expansionist ideology, led to a highly divided and fragmentary political order.

The divergent paths of the Stalinist and Nazi regimes corresponded to the strengths and attributes of their leaders. Stalin was very much a *praktik*, a machine politician and state-builder who earned a reputation for getting things done. His ambition was to turn the Soviet Union into a great power by means of a new type of party-state. Hitler, by contrast, had very little interest in state-building per se. His conception of politics, by contrast, was largely one of "agitation" and "propaganda." Mobilization mattered, not institutions. "The consistency," wrote Martin Broszat some years ago, "which the National Socialist 'revolution' showed in destroying the existing constitutional order was largely absent when it came to constructive organization and to the centralized exercise of power."[172]

---

[170] This point is made in Kershaw's textbook, *The Nazi Dictatorship*, 173–4.
[171] Although we do not accept that there was a fundamental transformation of the class structure in Germany of the kind that occurred in the USSR in the 1920s and 1930s, our position is quite compatible with recent research that has identified relatively high levels of social mobility among a group of educated National Socialists who had internalized the ideology of race in the 1920s and who would rise to prominence as ruthless technocrats in the leaderships of the SS, the police and security agencies, and also in the new ideological apparatus of the state. See, in particular, Ulrich Herbert, *Best: Biographische Studien über Radikalismus, Weltanshauung und Vernunft, 1903–1989* (Bonn: J. H. W. Dietz, 1996); and Michael Wildt, *Generation des Unbedingten: Das Führungskorps des Reichssicherheitshauptamtes* (Hamburg: Hamburger Edition, 2002).
[172] Broszat, 133.

At an informal meeting after the party rally of 1938 Hitler is reported to have told his companions that if he ever came to the conclusion that the party was unnecessary for the historical task posed for him, he would not hesitate to destroy it.[173] Such a statement would have been inconceivable for Stalin. At no point during Stalin's tenure was there the faintest prospect that the party as an integrated institutional entity would be marginalized, let alone destroyed. After Stalin's death, at the Central Committee plenum of July 1953, former colleagues, such as Kaganovich, Molotov, and Voroshilov, not only vaunted the party, but praised its leading organ, the Central Committee, as, in Kaganovich's words, the "holy of holies," in a way that no National Socialist could have spoken of a leading Nazi committee. The only leader who considered downgrading the role of the party, Beria, not only was peremptorily removed, but earned a stinging rebuke from Khrushchev: "Beria denies the ruling role of the party, he limits its role to cadres (and that only at first) and propaganda. But is this really a Marxist-Leninist approach to the party? Is this how Lenin and Stalin taught us how to approach the party? Beria's views on the party are *no different from Hitler's*."[174] Notwithstanding Stalin's own "teachings" on the party, the powerful party-based institutional continuity that spanned his tenure rested on "an ideal basis of Leninist party organization, membership definition, and policy organization" that were, in Jowitt's words, "independent from [Stalin's own] personal insight."[175] This not only meant that there was potentially within the Leninist party a legitimate basis for Khrushchev to go on and attack Stalin's "cult of personality," but that, unlike Hitler's Germany, there was a basis for the Soviet political order to retain its identity, in the longer term, without the dictator. Under Stalin the Soviet dictatorship had achieved not only a social revolution but the conditions of a stable political order. The seeds of this order, which were sown in the late 1930s and in the early postwar period, would then come to fruition with Stalin's death.[176]

---

[173] Cited from Frank, 1953, 235–6, in Nyomarkay, *Charisma and Factionalism*, 27.

[174] V. Naumov and Iu. Sigachev, eds., *Lavrentii Beriia, 1953: Stenogramma iul'skogo plenuma TsK KPSS i drugie dokumenty* (Moscow: MFD, 1999), 233 (italics ours).

[175] Jowitt, *New World Disorder*, 8.

[176] For what remains one of the best analyses of this process, see Peter Hauslohner, "Politics before Gorbachev: Destalinization and the Roots of Reform," in Seweryn Bialer, ed, *Politics, Society, and Nationality inside Gorbachev's Russia* (Boulder, CO: Westview Press, 1989), 41–90.

3

Utopian Biopolitics

Reproductive Policies, Gender Roles, and Sexuality in Nazi Germany and the Soviet Union

David L. Hoffmann and Annette F. Timm

Reproduction was a matter of extreme importance to Nazi and Soviet leaders, and for this reason alone their reproductive policies merit close scholarly attention. But Nazi and Soviet attempts to manage reproduction are also significant in what they reveal about their leaders' respective visions of how to transform populations and shape societies. As was true of governments throughout interwar Europe, the Nazi and Soviet regimes assumed that the state could and should regulate reproduction. Particularly given the need for a large population in an age of mass warfare, virtually every country in Europe enacted pronatalist policies. But within this common rubric of state management of reproduction, Nazi Germany and the Soviet Union pursued very different reproductive policies – policies that reflected stark ideological, structural, and disciplinary differences between the two countries. Each regime sought to transform society, reshape social bonds, and rewrite the social contract along fundamentally illiberal yet modernist lines. Individual liberties were rejected in favor of two quite different collectivist projects: the establishment of a racially defined *Volksgemeinschaft* to provide social support for the hegemony of the "Aryan" master race over Europe and the world and the much more universalist project of creating a classless, socialist society to serve as the model for the emancipation of humanity as a whole. Both of these agendas called for individual citizens to view reproductive and sexual choices in terms of service to the state. Yet the divergence of goals – the Nazi exaltation of the "Aryan" race above and against all others versus the Soviet development of a universal sociopolitical model for the entire human race – combined with immense differences in economic and social structure to produce quite different policies toward reproduction.

The differences in how reproduction was managed in the Soviet Union and Nazi Germany can serve as a reminder of the weaknesses of the concept of totalitarianism in comparing the two regimes. On the one hand, a significant superficial similarity in how motherhood was glorified and the fact that both strongly supported the basic idea that state welfare should take precedence over individual welfare could lead one to conclude that both displayed a total-itarian tendency to integrate the private sphere into state projects. While this similarity should not be discounted and in fact provides the foundation of the comparison to follow, the differences far outweighed the similarities, high-lighting the necessity of exploring ideological, social, and cultural differences and actual policy implementation in each case.[1] Methodologically, the sheer complexity of reproduction as a social, cultural, and political issue requires an approach that crosses previously sacrosanct historiographical boundaries that have often served to keep actually quite related themes in isolated boxes. Historians have too often unquestioningly replicated contemporary prejudices or the disciplinary specialties of their historical subjects, methodologically sep-arating, for example, sexuality from reproduction, the history of women or gender from the history of society and politics more generally, or the history of demography from the history of war. A comparison of reproductive poli-tics in two totalitarian regimes emphasizes the artificiality of these divisions, because it points to the interconnectedness of these spheres; only by including these various perspectives can the differences in what are superficially similar totalitarian projects be explained.

Population policy is a particularly amenable topic to international com-parison, since the very idea of controlling birthrates arose out of concerns about international competition. The combination of similarities and differ-ences between the Nazi and Soviet cases will emphasize not only the usefulness of the comparison, but also the degree to which reproductive policies were intertwined with the larger ideological goals of each state. Population policy in the mid-twentieth century was, after all, a zero sum game. Fear of the other was the motivating factor in encouraging a higher birthrate at home. This was always explicit in German rhetoric about the danger of falling birthrates, par-ticularly during the interwar period. Although the Soviets explicitly rejected the link between the birthrate and military might, the specter of international com-petition always loomed large, and actual experiences in World War II encour-aged a rethinking of the relationship between war and babies. The degree to which each of these societies viewed themselves as being engaged in a life-and-death struggle for survival also had a profound effect on gender roles and associated social, family, and health policies. Both the looming presence and the real experience of war infused social policies with a tone of urgency that intensified tendencies toward social classification and the hardening of norms common to all modernizing states. Normative gender ideals were enshrined into government policy in both states, providing, for instance, clear ideologi-cal pronouncements and policies about the roles of mothers and fathers. The threat of death (taken by both societies to mean social or national rather than

---

[1] One might add that the totalitarian model also obscures the fact that both Soviet and Nazi welfare policies had precedents and counterparts in nontotalitarian states. See Edward Ross Dickinson, "Biopolitics, Fascism, Democracy: Some Reflections on Our Discourse about 'Modernity,'" *Central European History* 37, no. 1 (2004): 1–48.

individual death) made calls for gender conformity seem all the more vital. In both regimes, homosexuality was viewed as a threat to the survival of the nation, since it was presumed to weaken fighting strength. In Nazi Germany (and to some extent in the Soviet Union) motherhood was extolled as a nationalistic provision of the state with soldiers. These rhetorical responses to human sexuality and reproduction did result in policies that actively curtailed individual choice in the reproductive and sexual sphere. Women were prevented from becoming full public actors in Nazi Germany, and in both countries homosexuals were persecuted, while able-bodied men were forced to understand their roles as citizens to be intimately intertwined with their duties as soldiers.[2] But these elements of social control belied the energizing effects of many policies oriented toward reproduction in the two regimes. Far from simply controlling sexual desire, the regimes tended to awaken it through promises of a utopian future and the creation of enthusiasm for new roles for the individual within the state. Totalitarian biopolitics promised to reward individuals for their physical risks and their willingness to direct sexual desire toward nationalistic or ideological goals.

To compare these processes in Nazi and Soviet society, three fundamental differences will be emphasized (though not discretely separated) below. First of all, differences in the material circumstances of the two societies must provide the background for any comparison of social policy.[3] We must not lose sight of the fact that the Nazis appropriated bureaucratic and political structures in what was a relatively stable, industrially advanced society, while the Soviets sought to remake the Russian social and political system fundamentally by replacing existing structures and forcibly accelerating processes of industrialization and urbanization.[4] A second and quite obvious difference is the striking dissimilarity in approaches to eugenics. In contrast to eugenicists in Nazi Germany (and many other Western nations), Soviet eugenicists failed to reconcile their science with the ruling ideology; the Soviet government ultimately denounced eugenics as a "fascist science," with decisive consequences for reproductive policy. A final stark contrast between the Soviet and Nazi regimes are their assumptions about gender. Although superficially similar (in terms of glorifying motherhood and condemning homosexuality, for instance),

---

[2] This is a theme that deserves its own extended treatment and comparison but can only be lightly touched on here. Important recent literature includes: Joshua A. Sanborn, *Drafting the Russian Nation: Military Conscription, Total War, and Mass Politics, 1905–1925* (DeKalb: Northern Illinois University Press, 2003); Ute Frevert, *Die kasernierte Nation: Militärdienst und Zivilgesellschaft in Deutschland* (Munich: C. H. Beck, 2001); Thomas Kühne, "Zwischen Männerbund und Volksgemeinschaft: Hitlers Soldaten und der Mythos der Kameradschaft," *Archiv für Sozialgeschichte* 38 (1998): 165–89.

[3] Susan Gross Solomon makes this point convincingly for abortion policy: "The Soviet Legalization of Abortion in German Medical Discourse: A Study of the Use of Selective Perceptions in Cross-Cultural Scientific Relations." *Social Studies of Science* 22 (1992): 455–85, esp. 469.

[4] This comment was inspired by Karl Schlögel's contributions to the discussion about state violence at the first meeting of the authors of this volume.

policymakers in the two regimes fundamentally disagreed about the relationship between the family and paid labor – the single-breadwinner family in Nazi ideology contrasts with the dual-wageearner model of Soviet households.

STATE MANAGEMENT OF REPRODUCTION

The conceptual and structural preconditions for state attempts to manage reproduction were not created by totalitarian states. The roots of such intervention lay in the early modern period, when rulers became increasingly interested in the population and its productive capacity. In particular, cameralist thinkers in the sixteenth and seventeenth centuries systematically analyzed the relationship between the state's economic and military power and the size and productivity of its population. During the eighteenth century, Enlightenment thinkers developed ideas about the rational reordering of human society, and these notions further heightened the ambitions of political leaders to use state power to reshape the population. But it was only in the nineteenth century, with the emergence of new professional disciplines, that government officials and reformers began thinking about "social" problems. This trend would contribute to state welfare programs and state attempts to manage reproduction.

Reproduction had previously been considered a natural phenomenon – something that lay beyond state control or scientific management. Even seventeenth-century cameralist thinkers who viewed a large population as a source of cheap labor and national wealth had only vague conceptions of how one might manage reproduction to control the quantity and quality of children born.[5] But when social scientists and government officials began to think of society as an object to be studied, sculpted, and improved, reproduction emerged as an important sphere of state interference. Throughout the eighteenth century, demography and associated fields developed as disciplines, and their practitioners began to study birthrates. In the nineteenth century officials began to compile regular censuses, which made it possible to study long-term population trends and to aspire to influence them.

The most prominent founder of the new science of demography, Thomas Malthus, had warned of overpopulation in his 1803 *Essay on the Principle of Population*. Declines in mortality rates had indeed allowed populations to rise rapidly in the eighteenth century, as England's population jumped from 5.6 to 8.7 million between 1741 and 1801.[6] By the late nineteenth century, however, fertility had declined, and warnings about overpopulation shifted to

---

[5] For a philosophically oriented overview of early modern population policy see Martin Furhmann, *Volksvermehrung als Staatsaufgabe? Bevölkerungs- und Ehepolitik in der deutschen politischen und ökonomischen Theorie des 18. und 19. Jahrhunderts* (Paderborn: Ferdinand Schöningh, 2002). A more convincing and historically contextualized account that emphasizes the history of sexuality is Isabel V. Hull, *Sexuality, State, and Civil Society in Germany, 1700–1815* (Ithaca, NY: Cornell University Press, 1996).

[6] Maria Sophia Quine, *Population Politics in Twentieth-Century Europe: Fascist Dictatorships and Liberal Democracies* (New York: Routledge, 1996), 1–2.

fears of underpopulation. In France, the first country to experience a decline in fertility, a census in 1854–5 revealed that the total number of deaths exceeded the total number of births. Worries about depopulation proliferated following defeat in the Franco-Prussian War, when French leaders began to fear that their population was too small to compete militarily with Germany. By 1900 an extra-parliamentary commission on depopulation was created; it reported that the "development, prosperity and grandeur of France" depended upon raising the birthrate. In other European countries falling fertility by the end of the nineteenth century also prompted warnings of national decline and demographic extinction. In Germany, the annual birthrate of 42.6 per thousand in 1876 had dropped to 28.2 by 1912, and the 1912 census provoked national alarm about "race suicide."[7]

In the wake of the First World War, political leaders across Europe sought to manage and increase their populations as never before. Mass warfare required huge numbers of troops and made clear the link between population size and military power. Moreover, the horrendous casualties of the war prompted fears in many countries about their populations' capacities to sustain military action in the future. Political leaders came to see the size of the population as a critical resource, necessary for national defense, and they focused on reproduction as central to sustaining the population. As a member of the British government declared in 1915: "In the competition and conflict of civilizations it is the mass of the nations that tells.... The ideals for which Britain stands can only prevail as long as they are backed by sufficient numbers.... Under existing conditions we waste before birth and in infancy a large part of our population."[8] Similarly the German General Staff, in a 1917 memorandum on the German population and army, stated that the falling birthrate was "worse than the losses through the war" in causing population decrease.[9]

When fighting ceased, the major combatants were faced not only with the frightful human cost of the war, but with a demographic catastrophe. France lost 1,393,515 soldiers, Britain 765,400, and Italy 680,070. One German statistician calculated that in addition to its 2 million soldiers killed in action, Germany lost 750,000 civilian victims of the Allied blockade, 100,000 people to the 1918 influenza epidemic, up to 3.5 million never born because of the war, and 6.5 million people no longer in Germany because of territorial losses, for a total deficit of nearly 13 million.[10] The loss of young men across Europe

---

[7] Quine, 52–65, 100–1.

[8] Pat Thane, "Visions of Gender in the Making of the British Welfare State: The Case of Women in the British Labour Party and Social Policy, 1906–1945," in *Maternity and Gender Policies: Women and the Rise of the European Welfare States 1880s–1950s*, eds. Gisela Bock and Pat Thane (London: Routledge, 1991), 105.

[9] General Ludendorff, *The General Staff and Its Problems: The History of the Relations between the High Command and the German Imperial Government as Revealed by Official Documents*, vol. 1, trans. F. A. Holt (New York: E. P. Dutton, 1920), 202.

[10] Quine, 17–18; Cornelia Usborne, *The Politics of the Body in Weimar Germany: Women's Reproductive Rights and Duties* (London: Macmillan, 1992), 31.

reduced the number of potential fathers so sharply that Britain's birthrate fell by roughly 40 percent between 1914 and 1930, prompting one member of parliament to declare that population decline constituted "a danger to the maintenance of the British Empire."[11] One German social hygienist warned that Germany in 1924 had a birthrate of only 20.4 per thousand people, barely high enough to maintain the population at current levels, and he concluded, "we must...make possible to every married couple by means of economic insurance of parenthood that they shall fulfill their reproductive duties."[12] German social hygienists also warned about the disastrous demographic consequences of the spread of fertility-threatening venereal diseases caused by the separation of families and the supposed loosening of sexual morality during the war.[13] The VD crisis (real or perceived) thus prompted policymakers to link reproduction with sexual behavior explicitly in a way that had not been socially acceptable before the war.[14] The crucial goal of preserving the fertility rates, they argued, justified unsavory references to individual sexual choices.

In Russia, unlike in some countries of Western Europe, fertility remained high throughout the nineteenth century. But Russian casualties in the First World War proved as severe as those in Western Europe and, when added to deaths during the Civil War and ensuing famine, totaled 16 million.[15] This demographic cataclysm provoked concern among Soviet leaders and scholars and prompted intensified attention to population statistics. The Central Statistical Administration compiled detailed monthly statistics on Civil War casualties for every province and district of the country.[16] It also established a commission to study the effect of First World War casualties and noted that these losses severely diminished the labor as well as the military capacity of the population.

---

[11] Quine, 17–18; PRO MH 58/311. The number of births per thousand people in England and Wales fell from 25.5 in 1920 to 14.4 in 1933. See Thane, "Visions," 99–100.

[12] Alfred Grotjahn, "Differential Birth Rate in Germany," in *Proceedings of the World Population Conference held at the Salle Centrale, Geneva, August 29th to September 3rd, 1927*, ed. Margaret Sanger (London: E. Arnold: 1927), 154; Soloway, 277. On Canada, see Cynthia R. Comacchio, "'The Infant Soldier': Early Child Welfare Efforts in Ontario," in *Women and Children First: International Maternal and Infant Welfare, 1870–1945*, eds. Valerie Fildes et al. (New York: Routledge, 1993), 106.

[13] Historians dispute the actual numbers. Richard Bessel argues, for instance, that venereal diseases did not substantially increase as a consequence of the war. See *Germany after the First World War* (Don Mills: Oxford University Press, 1993), 238.

[14] Doctors, educators, health activists, and government officials generally began their speeches and pamphlets on the subject with an apology for the unpleasant and embarrassing subject they would be addressing. See Annette F. Timm, "The Politics of Fertility: Population Politics and Health Care in Berlin, 1919–1972" (Ph.D. diss., University of Chicago, 1999), 83–4.

[15] Ansley Coale, Barbara Anderson, and Erna Harm, *Human Fertility in Russia since the Nineteenth Century* (Princeton, NJ: Princeton University Press, 1979), 16; Frank Lorimer, *The Population of the Soviet Union* (Geneva, 1946), 40–1.

[16] RGAE f. 1562, op. 21, d. 3552, ll. 1–20; see also Vl. Avaramov, "Zhertvy imperialisticheskoi voiny v Rossii," *Izvestiia narodnogo komissariata zdravookhraneniia* 3, no. 1–2 (1920): 39–42; Serge Bagotzky, "Les pertes de la Russie pendant la guerre mondiale (1914–1917)," *Revue internationale de la Croix Rouge* 61 (1924): 16–21.

It called "the depreciation of the labor productivity of millions of the most able-bodied elements of the population," a matter in urgent need of statistical study.[17] One Soviet professor declared that the Russian empire's prewar population of 172 million had fallen to 90 million as a result of wars, famine, and territorial losses. He equated a large population with national security and warned that some Western European countries, notably Germany, were threatening to overtake the population of the Soviet Union.[18]

Despite horrendous wartime losses, the Soviet Union faced less of a decline in the postwar birthrate than did the countries of Western Europe. Because Soviet society was still largely a peasant population in the 1920s, its birthrate remained high despite the loss of young men during World War I and the Civil War. Nonetheless, Soviet officials and demographers continued to monitor population trends closely and were alarmed by the precipitous drop in fertility that accompanied industrialization, collectivization, and the 1932–3 famine. The Central Statistical Administration tabulated annual fertility and mortality rates for every administrative district in the country, so Soviet officials knew, for example, that there were nearly ten times as many deaths as births reported in Khar'kov district in 1933, as a result of the famine in Ukraine.[19] An extensive demographic study in 1934 revealed that the Soviet birthrate overall had fallen from 42.2 births per thousand people in 1928 to 31.0 in 1932. Moreover, S. G. Strumilin, the author of the study and one of the country's leading statisticians, demonstrated that the drop in fertility correlated with urbanization and the entrance of women into the industrial workforce – trends that had to continue if industrialization were to move ahead.[20]

Strumilin's other major finding was that among groups in the population, those with higher wages had lower fertility. Not only did workers have lower fertility than peasants, but urbanized workers had lower fertility than peasant in-migrants to the city, and white-collar employees had the lowest fertility of all. This discovery contradicted previous research that had identified economic hardship as the primary cause of low fertility.[21] Soviet officials now had to revise their assumption that the birthrate would rise as material conditions improved. Increasingly they saw low fertility as the result of women's choices to have abortions – choices made by women who, in their view, could afford

[17] RGAE f. 1562, op. 21, d. 25, l. 17; also Trudy komissii po obsledivaniiu sanitarnykh posledstvii voiny 1914–1920 (Moscow: Gosizdat, 1923).
[18] Prof. K. K. Skrobanskii, "Abort i protivozachatochnye sredstva," *Zhurnal akusherstva i zhenskikh boleznei* 35 no. 1 (1924), as cited in Janet Hyer, "Managing the Female Organism: Doctors and the Medicalization of Women's Paid Work in Soviet Russia during the 1920s," in *Women in Russia and Ukraine*, ed. Rosalind Marsh (New York: Cambridge University Press, 1996), 117.
[19] RGAE f. 1562 s. ch., op. 329, d. 21, ll. 125–7. According to official statistics, the totals for all Ukraine in 1933 were 449,877 births and 1,908,907 deaths; l. 109.
[20] S. G. Strumilin, "K probleme rozhdaemosti v rabochei srede," *Problemy ekonomiki truda* (Moscow: Gos. Izd-vo polit. Lit-ry, 1957), 194–8.
[21] Strumilin, 201–4; V. Z. Drobizhev, *U istokov sovetskoi demografii* (Moscow: "Mysl'", 1987), 22.

to have children but chose not to out of personal preference. One other factor that exacerbated the decline in fertility and Soviet officials' concern was the abnormally small population cohort that entered its childbearing years in the mid-1930s. The First World War had not only decimated a generation of young men, but had greatly reduced the number of children born between 1915 and 1920. It was this reduced cohort that reached childbearing age in the mid-1930s, even further depressing the birthrate.[22] Consequently Soviet officials became as obsessed with declining birthrates as did their counterparts in Western Europe.

In addition to its demographic repercussions, World War I also reinforced social Darwinist ideas about the competition of nations, and the struggle of races to survive and propagate. Mussolini articulated these ideas most explicitly when he declared, "Fertile people have a right to an Empire, those with the will to propagate their race on the face of the earth."[23] Leaders throughout Europe linked falling birthrates in the 1930s to a decline in national power. One Spanish demographer warned that without more children, "Spain will be reduced, she will shrink, the national economy will be without producers and consumers; the State, without soldiers; the Nation, without blood."[24] Franco had the goal of increasing the Spanish population to 40 million within a few decades and saw this as a means to recapture Spain's faded glory and world prominence.[25] The Swedish government appointed a population commission in 1935 following the publication of a best-selling book by Alva and Gunnar Myrdal which described the falling birthrate as a slow, national suicide.[26] And a range of political leaders and scholars in interwar Romania also believed that the country's strength and survival rested on its birthrate and "biological capital."[27] Population policy and even the motivation to improve reproductive health care were thus never purely domestic concerns. They always depended upon international comparisons, and, particularly in totalitarian regimes, concerns about strengthening the birthrate were linked to processes of national self-definition.

Even before the rise of the Nazis, social Darwinian concerns about the need to strengthen the health of the population in preparation for international competition were arguably stronger in Germany than in any other European

[22] E. A. Sadvokasova, *Sotsial'no-gigienicheskie aspekty regulirovaniia razmerov sem'i* (Moscow: Meditsina, 1969), 28–9.

[23] David G. Horn, *Social Bodies: Science, Reproduction, and Italian Modernity* (Princeton, NJ: Princeton University Press, 1994), 59. See also Quine, 34; Carl Ipsen, *Dictating Demography: The Problem of Population in Fascist Italy* (New York: Cambridge University Press, 1996), 65–8.

[24] Mary Nash, "Pronatalism and Motherhood in Franco's Spain," in Bock and Thane, eds., 163.

[25] Quine, 88.

[26] Karin Johannisson, "The People's Health: Public Health Policies in Sweden," *The History of Public Health and the Modern State*, ed. Dorothy Porter (Amsterdam: Editions Rodopi B. V., 1994), 178.

[27] Maria Bucur, *Eugenics and Modernization in Interwar Romania* (Pittsburgh: University of Pittsburgh Press, 2002).

country. But several different types of social Darwinian and eugenic thinking were prevalent in the Weimar period. There can be no convincing argument made about a direct line of continuity between the radically elitist and eugenically interventionist Darwinian thinking of, say, Alfred Ploetz at the turn of the century and the racial ideology of the Third Reich. Between these two temporal signposts one finds a diversity of eugenic thought, including a numerically strong and politically influential contingent of socialist eugenicists, who espoused socially progressive and class-sensitive social policies while nationalistically insisting on the need to direct vast government resources to the threat of population decline.[28] Soon after World War I, progressive doctors who were often affiliated with the Social Democratic Party were instrumental in creating the new hybrid field of social hygiene, with its emphasis on prevention of national decline and its insistence that medicine and welfare programs had to attack both problems, declining quantity and quality in the population. By the time the Nazis came to power, they could build on widespread fears of the national consequences of a declining birthrate, fears that had been fanned by an extremely wide diversity of social and scientific "experts" of all political persuasions. Even socialist reformers like Alfred Grotjahn (the first director of the department of social hygiene in the medical faculty at the University of Berlin) whose explicit concern was the improvement of the lot of working-class citizens insisted on the higher national purpose of their efforts and the need to avert impending national decline.[29]

Nevertheless, social hygienists and eugenicists of leftist persuasions were pushed to the side or actively repressed under the Nazis (not least because many of them were of Jewish heritage),[30] and eugenics and population policy in Germany took on a fiercely racist tone. In *Mein Kampf*, Adolf Hitler stressed the racial ideology that would underlie all National Socialist efforts in the sphere of reproductive health:

> That which today all sides have neglected in this area, the *völkische* state must make up for. It must place race at the center of everyday life. It must guarantee [racial] purity. It must declare the child to be the most valuable product of any *Volk*. It must see to it that only those who are healthy produce children; that only one sin really exists: to bring a child into the world despite one's own illnesses or

---

[28] See Michael Schwartz, *Sozialististische Eugenik: Eugenische Sozialtechnologien in Debatten und Politik der deutschen Sozialdemokratie, 1890–1933* (Bonn: J. H. W. Dietz Nachfolger, 1995).

[29] On Grotjahn see Karl-Heinz Roth, "Scheinalternativen im Gesundheitswesen: Alfred Grotjahn (1869–1931) – Integrationsfigur etablierter Sozialmedizin und nationalsozialistischer Rassenhygiene" in *Erfassung zur Vernichtung: Von der Sozialhygiene zum "Gesetz zur Sterbehilfe,"* ed. Karl-Heinz Roth (Berlin: Verlagsgesellschaft Gesundheit, 1984), 31–56.

[30] In Berlin in 1933, 3,423 of the total of 6,558 doctors were "non-Aryan," amounting to 52.2 percent. The percentage of Jewish doctors in insurance practice was even higher: 59.7 percent. See Stephan Leibfried and Florian Tennstedt, "Health-Insurance Policy and Berufsverbote in the Nazi Takeover," in *Political Values and Health Care: The German Experience*, ed. Donald W. Light and Alexander Schuller (Cambridge, MA: MIT Press, 1986), 163–84.

one's own inferiorities, while there is one highest honor: to forgo it. On the other hand it must also stand as reprehensible to withhold healthy children from the nation.[31]

All individual reproductive decisions, Hitler argued, must be directed toward the goal of strengthening the nation and subordinating individual concerns to the good of the *Volk*. Here, as in other statements from Nazi leaders, the implication was that without this kind of attention to the connection between individual reproductive decisions and the survival of the race, the very survival of the nation was threatened.

Soviet leaders also envisioned reproductive competition between countries, but they conceived of this competition in ideological rather than biological or racial terms. The Central Statistical Administration compiled annual charts on fertility, which showed in 1935, for example, that Soviet fertility was higher than that of all "the capitalist countries" (listing all the other countries of Europe).[32] I. A. Kraval', the head of the statistics division of Gosplan, argued that the Soviet Union's higher fertility proved the superiority of socialism over capitalism.[33] And in 1935 Stalin boasted that because of workers' improved material conditions, "the population has begun to multiply much more quickly than in previous times.... Now each year our population increases by around three million people. This means that each year we receive an increase equivalent to the whole of Finland."[34] Such thinking interpreted high fertility as a sign of superiority, though in the Soviet case the competition was conceived as between political systems rather than between races.

Soviet leaders' sense of reproductive competition differed from that of other European leaders, because they had a different conception of their population. The Soviet Union was a multinational federation, in which all national and ethnic groups were supposed to be equal partners. According to Marxist ideology, national differences both within the Soviet Union and between other countries were to disappear over time, as all national and ethnic groups became merged under socialism.[35] Given this ideological orientation, competition between nations to propagate and dominate other peoples or races made no sense. Instead a high birthrate among all nationalities in the Soviet Union would demonstrate the superiority of socialism and help it spread to other countries.

[31] My translation of a quote from *Mein Kampf*, cited in "Grundthemen der weltanschaulichen Schulung: Bevölkerungspolitik des Dritten Reiches und ihre Träger" n.d. (an internal educational pamphlet for health administrators), BAB/NS 22/521.

[32] RGAE f. 1562, s. ch., op. 329, d. 83, l. 1. The report also listed the fertility rates of republics within the Soviet Union. Armenia had the highest fertility, followed by the Russian Federation, Turkmenistan, Belorussia, Azerbaijan, Ukraine, and Tajikistan.

[33] *Pravda*, January 1, 1936, 8.

[34] Quoted in "Zabota o zdorov'e detei," *Gigiena i zdorov'e*, no. 9 (1938): 1.

[35] In practice, the Soviet government actually fostered national particularism. See Yuri Slezkine, "The USSR as a Communal Apartment, or How a Socialist State Promoted Ethnic Particularism," *Slavic Review* 51, no. 1 (1992): 414–52; Terry Martin, *The Affirmative Action Empire: Nations and Nationalism in the Soviet Union, 1923–1939* (Ithaca, NY: Cornell University Press, 2001).

Reproductive policies in both the Soviet Union and Nazi Germany were largely administered through their respective health care systems, and for that reason it is helpful to consider briefly the formation and structure of these systems. As a largely rural, underdeveloped society, prerevolutionary Russia had neither adequate medical facilities nor a centralized state health care system. Medical care was primarily provided by locally based *zemstvo* physicians, who, despite their lack of resources, aspired to provide free, universal health care to Russia's overwhelmingly peasant population. Following the October Revolution, the Soviet government placed all medical care under centralized state control. It founded the Commissariat of Health on July 11, 1918, emphasizing the need for coordinated state action to fight epidemics, purify drinking water, improve sanitation, and provide health care for "the broad mass of the population." While *zemstvo* doctors were initially hostile toward the Soviet state, most came to see the Bolsheviks as allies in their efforts to establish free and universal health care (and abolish private medicine), to prevent epidemics, and to promote sanitary education. Some of them even joined the Bolshevik Party and played a leading role building the Soviet health care system.[36] The structure of the Soviet health care system, then, reflected a number of currents in the new Soviet state: the anticapitalism and statism of Bolshevik ideology, the centralizing prerogative in the fight against epidemics raging in the country, and *zemstvo* physicians' belief in social medicine, with an emphasis on free universal health care, preventive medicine, sanitation, and hygiene.[37]

Despite the initial ambition of Soviet health officials and doctors to provide free, universal health care, they lacked the resources to fulfill their goals. Under the New Economic Policy of the 1920s, existing state clinics and hospitals remained badly underfunded and plans to broaden health care went unrealized. During the early 1930s, the Commissariat of Health expanded health care in factories and prioritized the well-being of industrial workers, largely neglecting the rest of the population. At the end of the 1930s, Soviet officials increased allocations for the health care of the general population, and in particular emphasized maternity care and the construction of children's hospitals. These priorities signaled a weakening of the productivist emphasis in state health care and also reflected the pronatalist campaign in the period leading up to the Second World War.[38] Even given the considerable expansion of the Soviet health care system during the Stalinist period, medical services overall continued to be inadequate. Notwithstanding health officials' objective of providing comprehensive health care to the population, they were unable to overcome the country's prerevolutionary legacy of underdevelopment. During the

[36] John F. Hutchinson, "Who Killed Cock Robin?: An Inquiry into the Death of Zemstvo Medicine," in *Health and Society in Revolutionary Russia*, eds. Susan Gross Solomon and John F. Hutchinson (Bloomington: Indiana University Press, 1990), 4, 20.

[37] Hutchinson concludes that the Commissariat of Health "owed much more to Russian precedent and tradition than to Bolshevik ideology." John F. Hutchinson, *Politics and Public Health in Revolutionary Russia, 1890–1918* (Baltimore: Johns Hopkins University Press, 1990), 202.

[38] Chris Burton, "Medical Welfare during Late Stalinism: A Study of Doctors and the Soviet Health System, 1945–1953" (Ph.D. diss., University of Chicago, 2000), 33–9.

industrialization drive and the Second World War, the Soviet government chan-neled most available resources to building steel mills and expanding military production, while shortages of qualified medical personnel and facilities con-tinued. As we will discuss below, these deficiencies hampered official efforts to entice women to have more children by providing maternity services and to use medical personnel in a policing role to prevent women from having abortions.

Like the Soviets, Nazi politicians and propagandists considered health care a key pillar of the new society. Unlike their Soviet counterparts, however, the Nazis did not have to create entirely new structures of health care provision but could impose their theories upon an already comprehensive and highly bureau-cratized system. Beginning with the 1883 Bismarckian law on compulsory sick-ness insurance for workers, which established the world's first national health care program, the scope of medical involvement in society had already been dramatically increased.[39] German citizens were the beneficiaries of the most comprehensive and accessible health care system in the world. Indeed, one could argue that by exposing doctors to the working classes for the first time, univer-sal health insurance inspired medical ideas about influencing health outcomes on a mass scale. This almost universal system of health care was a structural prerequisite for National Socialism's intervention into reproductive health care, though not without a substantial ideological and structural reorganization.

Soon after coming to power in 1933, the National Socialists set out to rad-ically transform the system of health insurance funds.[40] Capitalizing on the discontent that had grown during the economically unstable Weimar years, the Nazis set out to restructure the administration of health care entirely with the goal of redirecting it toward "the healthy, enthusiastic, productive, military fit, racially valuable German man of the future."[41] Personal needs, the right to life, and individual bodily integrity were subordinated to the quest for "perfect human material," and all forms of self-government within insurance funds were quashed.[42] Soon after, extensive and ultimately fruitless efforts to integrate and restructure Germany's regionally diverse health care system began under the auspices of the the Law for the Standardization of the Health Care System (Gesetz über die Vereinheitlichung des Gesundheitswesens) of July 3, 1934, which sought to create a centralized health care administration while replacing voluntary and government welfare agencies with new organizations devoted

---

[39] For a synopsis, see Donald W. Light, "State, Profession, and Political Values," in *Political Values and Health Care: The German Experience*, ed. Donald W. Light and Alexander Schuller (Cambridge, MA, and London: MIT Press, 1986), 3.

[40] Extensive doctors' strikes in the 1920s, declining medical benefits during the inflationary period and the depression, and infighting among the administration (accused of mismanagement), business circles, and doctors groups all contributed to a negative public attitude toward the existing system.

[41] A 1939 quote from the Nazi Minister of Labor, Seldte, cited in Peter Rosenberg, "The Origin and the Development of Compulsory Health Insurance in Germany," in *Political Values and Health Care: The German Experience*, eds. Donald W. Light and Alexander Schuller (Cambridge, MA, and London: MIT University Press, 1986), 119.

[42] Ibid.

to racial hygiene and the National Socialist *Weltanschauung*.[43] This effort at *Gleichschaltung* (synchronization) in the medical sphere created a new system of state-run health bureaus and state-appointed medical administrators to facilitate standardization across the Reich. A new focus on "genetic and racial counseling" was to replace the Weimar tradition of linking health care to economic productivity. The public health system was now to become the "executive organ of National Socialist genetic health policy."[44]

Complete federal unity in health care was never achieved, and battles between state and communal medical administrations raged throughout the Third Reich.[45] Nevertheless, Arthur Gütt, Ministerial Director of the *Volksgesundheit* (people's health) department of the Reich Ministry of the Interior, continually praised the achievements of standardization and argued that it had helped improve Germany's genetic health (*Erbgesundheit*) while weeding out those with genetic illnesses and inferiorities (*Minderwertigkeiten*).[46] To counteract the decline in genetic value (*Erbwerte*), Gütt created 742 regional health offices (*Gesundheitsämter*) across the country.[47] But federal authorities never had the resources to take control of the health offices in large cities, who continued to depend upon local administrative practices. Nevertheless, Nazi medical reorganization imposed an administrative structure that aided in the dissemination of racial ideas and created a bureaucracy for the elimination of racially and genetically "inferior" individuals. Institutions that had originally been set up in the Weimar Republic to help the chronically sick to improve their standard of living and become reintegrated into society were now converted to the purpose of weeding these undesirables out of the ranks of those deserving government assistance.

EUGENICS

The emphasis on the collective good and on racial health is an indication of the centrality of eugenics in Nazi health care. Under the Nazis, eugenics became

[43] The standard account of the struggles surrounding this law is: Alfons Labisch and Florian Tennstedt, *Der Weg zum "Gesetz über die Vereinheitlichung des Gesundheitswesens," vom 3. Juli 1934: Entwicklungslinien und -momente des staatlichen und kommunalen Gesundheitswesens in Deutschland* (Düsseldorf: Akademie für öffentliches Gesundheitswesen, 1985). See also Norbert Frei, ed., *Medizin und Gesundheitspolitik in der NS-Zeit* (Munich: Oldenbourg, 1991).

[44] Winfried Süß, "Gesundheitspolitik," in *Drei Wege deutscher Sozialstaatlichkeit: NS-Diktatur, Bundesrepublik und DDR im Vergleich*, ed. Hans Günter Hockerts (Munich: Oldenbourg, 1998), 63.

[45] Ursula Grell, "'Gesundheit ist Pflicht' – Das öffentliche Gesundheitswesen Berlins 1933–1939," in *Totgeschwiegen 1933–1945: zur Geschichte der Wittenauer Heilstätten; seit 1957 Karl-Bonhoeffer-Nervenklinik*, 2nd ed., ed. Arbeitsgruppe zur Erforschung der Geschichte der Karl-Bonhoeffer-Nervenklinik (Berlin: Hentrich, 1989), 52.

[46] See for example, Ursula Grell, "Aufgaben der Gesundheitsämter im dritten Reich," *Archiv für Bevölkerungswissenschaft (Volkskunde) und Bevölkerungspolitik* 1 (1935): 280–1; and Arthur Gütt, *Der Aufbau des Gesundheitswesens im Dritten Reich*, 4th rev. ed. (Berlin: Junker and Dünnhaupt, 1938), 12.

[47] Arthur Gütt, *Die Rassenpflege im Dritten Reich* (Hamburg: Hanseatische Verlagsanstalt, 1940), 14.

the guiding principle of medical practice, not just in the field of reproduction, but in almost every medical specialty. Unlike socialist schools of thought on eugenics, which had often stressed the need to prevent illnesses for humane reasons, the guiding principle of Nazi eugenics was racial hygiene. Advocates of Nazi racial hygiene (*Rassenhygiene*) were guided by the pessimistic assumption that doctors had to be guardians of racial purity, turning their attention to both internal (genetic) and external (racial) threats, if an almost inevitable degeneration of the German *Volk* was to be avoided. Hereditary illnesses were defined more broadly and more ideologically than ever before.[48] Nazis like Arthur Gütt insisted, for instance, that racial hygiene and eugenics should target not only physical features and deficits but also "mental and spiritual qualities and with them character." The purview of genetics was thus widened and the links among eugenics, racism, and population policy were made explicit. "Whoever recognizes genetic science," Gütt insisted, "must necessarily embrace not only the concept of race itself, but also the necessity of population and racial policy."[49] It should also be noted that while National Socialist eugenics, like Weimar eugenics, was mostly practiced in a Mendelian mode with an emphasis on the immutability of genetic traits, Lamarckism and the idea that environment might affect the germplasm crept in when it was ideologically convenient.[50] Discussions about the need to protect men against venereal disease, for instance, included the argument that these diseases might damage the male germ cell (*Keimzelle*), and distinctions between congenital and genetic defects were often fuzzy.[51]

It should not be surprising, of course, that Nazi eugenics did not maintain strict scientific standards. Race was generally defined in genetic and biological but also in spiritual terms. According to Gütt, racial purity, and society itself, could be damaged through cultural mechanisms that destroy both the psychological and physical reproductive energies of the *Volk*. Gütt argued that only

[48] For an overview see: Sheila Faith Weiss, "The Race Hygiene Movement in Germany 1904–1945," in *The Wellborn Science: Eugenics in Germany, France, Brazil and Russia*, ed. Mark B. Adams (New York: Oxford University Press, 1990), 3–68.

[49] Arthur Gütt, *Bevölkerungs- und Rassenpolitik* (Berlin: Industrieverlag Spaeth & Linde, 1936), 20.

[50] Mendelian genetics, inspired by the mid-nineteenth-century writings of the monk Gregor Mendel, holds that individuals inherit a set of *unchanged* units (now called genes) from both parents. For any given pair of inherited units, only one will emerge as a trait in an individual. (There will not, in other words, be a blending of traits.) But the parental trait that is not manifested in the individual can still be passed on to that individual's offspring. Mendel's basic tenets still form the foundation for our understanding of genetic transmission. Lamarckian genetics, on the other hand, derived from the thinking of the French biologist Jean-Baptiste Lamarck (1744–1824), hold that the environment can affect the genetic traits of an individual and that these *acquired* traits can then be passed on to the next generation.

[51] See the discussion of *Keimschädigung* in Heinz Woltereck, ed., *Erbkunde, Rassenpflege, Bevölkerungspolitik: Schicksalsfragen des deutschen Volkes* (Leipzig: Quelle & Meyer, 1935), 102–7. By 1935 the idea that VD could cause a *Keimschädigung* had been discounted. See Bodo Spiethoff, *Die Geschlechtskrankheiten im Lichte der Bevölkerungspolitik, Erbgesundheits- und Rassenpflege* (Berlin, [1934]), 13.

an active fight against these cultural forces and the degenerate races that produce them could bring about national renewal. Social policy, he argued, must contain both "eliminationist" (*ausmerzenden*) and "supportive" (*fördernden*) policies so that the inferior (*Minderwertigen*) and weak no longer drained away resources from the important task of fortifying genetically healthy and valuable (*lebenswerten*) Germans.[52] From the beginning, then, demands for eugenic measures were phrased in terms of a life-or-death struggle that could only be won on Darwinian terms. In the Nazi interpretation this meant weeding out all weak links and insisting that the German *Volk* was an organic, racial unity.

The Nazis were single-minded in their desire to eliminate all types of disability from German society, and they relied on a racialized definition of the *Volk* to justify the separation, segregation, and eventual sterilization or elimination of both unfit Germans (mentally retarded, congenitally diseased, homosexuals, political dissidents) and otherwise genetically healthy non-Germans (Jews, Gypsies, and Slavs).[53] Too much has been written about the consequences of this ideology even to summarize here, and the harshest resulting measures (euthanasia and racial genocide) fall outside the purview of this essay.[54] For our purposes it must suffice to highlight the culturally pessimistic and ultimately militaristic language of Nazi eugenics, since this contrasts dramatically with the medical language in Stalinist Russia. Adolf Hitler was particularly likely to link reproduction and militaristic goals. In a speech in Nuremberg on September 13, 1935, he said: "I would be ashamed to be a German man if in the case of war a woman ever had to go to the front. Woman has her own battlefield: With every child she bears for the nation, she fights her battle for the nation."[55]

This militaristic language contrasts with the Soviet perspective on eugenics, particularly in the Stalinist era. In the 1920s, German and Soviet eugenicists had actually engaged in a lively exchange of ideas, though the compatibility of their perspectives was, even then, often superficially exaggerated by their shared

---

[52] He uses these terms in ibid., 8.

[53] See Gisela Bock, *Zwangssterilisation im Nationalsozialismus: Studien zur Rassenpolitik und Frauenpolitik* (Opladen: Westdeutscher Verlag, 1986). It is now becoming commonplace to think of euthanasia as the first stage of the Holocaust. See: Michael Burleigh, *Death and Deliverance: "Euthanasia" in Germany c. 1900–1945* (Cambridge: Cambridge University Press, 1994); and especially Henry Friedlander, *The Origins of Nazi Genocide: From Euthanasia to the Final Solution* (Chapel Hill: University of North Carolina Press, 1995).

[54] Leaving aside works that specifically set out to describe and explain the Holocaust, the most oft-cited general accounts of Nazi racial hygiene and eugenics are: Paul Weindling, *Health, Race, and German Politics Between National Unification and Nazism, 1870–1945* (Cambridge and New York: Cambridge University Press, 1989); Michael Burleigh and Wolfgang Wippermann, *The Racial State: Germany, 1933–1945* (Cambridge and New York: Cambridge University Press, 1991); Robert N. Proctor, *Racial Hygiene: Medicine under the Nazis* (Cambridge, MA: Harvard University Press, 1988); and Peter Weingart, Jürgen Kroll, and Kurt Bayertz, *Rasse, Blut und Gene: Geschichte der Eugenik und Rassenhygiene in Deutschland* (Frankfurt am Main: Suhrkamp, 1988).

[55] "Grundthemen der weltanschaulichen Schulung," in BAB/NS 22/521.

position as international outcasts (the Germans as the initiators of World War I, and the Soviets as the creators of a hated Communist regime).[56] Scientists and health experts in each country, Susan Gross Solomon informs us, also often used each other's demographic statistics in disingenuous ways to support political causes at home.[57] Close cooperation ended, however, even before the rise of the Nazis, as we shall soon see, and the respective ideological frameworks of the Stalinist and Nazi regimes had a decisive impact on scientific thought in each country. Soviet policymakers, some of whom were initially convinced that eugenics was compatible with the Bolshevik dream of revolutionary transformation, came to believe that Mendelian genetics was incompatible with the project to create new Soviet citizens. The pessimism and militarism of German-style eugenics were rejected in favor of a more positively oriented faith in the need to concentrate on improving the social environment.

The Soviet government initially embraced eugenics and in 1920 created the Russian Eugenics Society (under the Commissariat of Health). The following year the Soviet Academy of Sciences founded its Bureau of Eugenics. These official organizations helped Russian eugenicists keep up their contacts with eugenicists abroad, as the Russian Eugenics Society selected a representative to the International Commission of Eugenics; established contacts with eugenic societies in the United States, England, and Germany; and sent its president to the 1924 International Congress of Eugenics in Milan.[58] The society's journal, *Russian Eugenics Journal*, reviewed a large number of foreign books on eugenics and published the programs of foreign eugenic societies. It also published articles analyzing the impact of the war on the populations of Europe and advocating registration and control of marriage for eugenic reasons.[59]

Because Marxism emphasized the role of the environment in shaping the individual, official ideology favored Lamarckian over Mendelian eugenics. Accordingly most Soviet eugenicists maintained a Lamarckian orientation. Despite this orientation, however, the Soviet eugenics movement eventually ran afoul of official ideology. In 1930, at a time when a Marxist orthodoxy was imposed on all social sciences, the Soviet government disbanded the Russian Eugenics Society. And in keeping with the fervor of the industrialization drive,

[56] Loren R. Graham, "Science and Values: The Eugenics Movement in Germany and Russia in the 1920s." *American Historical Review* 82, no. 5 (1977): 1148.

[57] Susan Gross Solomon, "The Soviet Legalization of Abortion in German Medical Discourse: A Study of the Use of Selective Perceptions in Cross-Cultural Scientific Relations." *Social Studies of Science* 22 (1992): 455–85.

[58] Mark Adams, "Eugenics as Social Medicine in Revolutionary Russia: Prophets, Patrons, and the Dialectics of Discipline-Building in *Health and Society in Revolutionary Russia*, eds. Susan Gross Solomon and John Hutchinson (Bloomington: Indiana University Press, 1990), 204–7; Loren Graham, *Between Science and Values* (New York: Columbia University Press, 1981), 232–5.

[59] A. V. Gorbunov, "Vliianie mirovoi voiny na dvizhenie naseleniia Evropy," *Russkii evgenicheskii zhurnal*, no. 1 (1922); Prof. P. I. Liublinskii, "Brak i evgenika" *Russkii evgenicheskii zhurnal*, no. 2 (1927). The Commissariat of Health's Department of Foreign Information also reported on eugenic ideas promoted in other countries; GARF f. A-482, op. 35, d. 144, ll. 306–12.

Russian eugenicists were forced to concede that the development of natural resources was more important and practical than the eugenic development of the population.[60] Nevertheless, the formal termination of the eugenics movement did not mean the end of eugenic thinking among Soviet scientists and policymakers. Many eugenicists moved over to the Gorky Research Institute of Medical Genetics, where they continued to discuss human genetics without using the term *eugenics*.[61]

The final demise of Soviet eugenics occurred in 1936–7, when the work of geneticists at the Gorky Institute became associated with fascist eugenics. Trofim D. Lysenko and his followers were eager to attack hereditary genetics in order to buttress their own Lamarckian genetics, and they denounced a number of leading medical geneticists who were subsequently arrested and shot during the purges.[62] The fact that eugenics was ultimately condemned as a fascist science demonstrates not only the influence of ideology, in particular Marxism's emphasis on environmental over genetic determinants of social behavior, but also Soviet leaders' desire to highlight ideological distinctions by differentiating socialist from fascist reproductive policies. Contrary to Soviet officials' claim, eugenics was not exclusively a fascist science, because it was practiced widely in nonfascist countries such as the United States. But with rising ideological and international tensions of the 1930s, the Soviet Union rejected eugenics more firmly than ever, not only because it contradicted Soviet nurturist and universalist thought, but because they associated it with fascism.

Eugenics is perhaps the clearest example of state and expert attempts to effect a biosocial transformation through control of reproduction. The appeal of eugenics lay in its promise to improve the human species through technocratic means. In an age when population management seemed not only possible but necessary, it is not surprising that so many political leaders and social reformers turned to eugenics. But equally interesting is the way that eugenics assumed such different forms depending upon political ideologies, social conditions, and the ethnic mix of populations. The ultimate demise of eugenics in the Soviet Union illustrates that even the government most committed to social transformation could reject a science of human biological transformation for ideological reasons. The rejection of eugenics, however, did not lead to a rejection of efforts to encourage a higher birthrate. In fact, the Stalinist case in particular demonstrates the necessity of keeping the various categories (eugenics, population policy, reproductive politics, racial hygiene) separate. Although many historical case studies demonstrate how interrelated these fields often were, the practical implementation often looked quite different, and the different ideological strands must be kept separate in any international comparison.

---

[60] Adams in Solomon, ed., 219.

[61] Mark B. Adams, "Eugenics in Russia, 1900–1940," in *The Wellborn Science: Eugenics in Germany, France, Brazil, and Russia*, ed. Mark B. Adams (Oxford: Oxford University Press, 1989), 188–9.

[62] Adams, "Eugenics in Russia," 196.

A comparative examination of the implementation of reproductive policies in the Third Reich and Stalinist Russia makes this clear.

THE IMPLEMENTATION OF REPRODUCTIVE POLICIES: COERCION AND INCENTIVE

Political leaders' consternation with population trends led them to contemplate ways to increase the birthrate. Once populations could be represented statistically, and fertility trends explained on the basis of demographic studies, it became possible to conceive of state and expert control of fertility. Contraception, abortion, and reproductive health became a focus for state intervention. Governments across Europe also began to provide material support for mothers. A wide range of people, from state officials and health experts, to members of women's organizations and religious groups, agitated for increased government aid to mothers. While the politics of maternalist welfare, and the policies adopted, varied from one country to another, the overall trend was toward extensive state intervention and propaganda designed to promote motherhood. There are significant differences in the forms that the "rationalization" of motherhood took in each case, and the Nazi and Soviet regimes ascribed very different roles to the genders. Yet both formulated policies toward reproduction and sexuality that intertwined elements of coercion and incentive in the effort to instrumentalize private spheres of life in the interests of larger ideological goals. Coercion often went hand in hand with state-legitimizing incentives for compliant or supportive citizens.[63] An outline of the implementation of population policy in each regime will demonstrate that the categories of pronatalism and antinatalism should be employed only with due consideration of the fact that policies in either category could serve to coerce citizens into acting against their wishes or – sometimes simultaneously – reward them in the interests of propaganda and state legitimation. The rubric of totalitarianism does not account for this ambiguity and fails to highlight the complexity, internal inconsistency, and mixed results of social policy, in terms of both political goals and the impact on individuals.

National Socialist coercive pronatalism began soon after the *Machtergreifung* (seizure of power). The Nazis were very explicit about their intentions to confine woman to her "smaller" role of house, home, and family and reserve the public sphere for men. Speaking to the National Socialist Women's Organization in September 1934, Hitler argued:

> If the man's world is said to be the State, his struggle, his readiness to devote his powers to the service of the community, then it may perhaps be said that the woman's is a smaller world. For her world is her husband, her family, her children, and her home. But what would become of the greater world if there

---

[63] For a pioneering study of how the valorization of motherhood helped bolster the goals of the Nazi regime, see Claudia Koonz, *Mothers in the Fatherland: Woman, the Family, and Nazi Politics* (New York: St. Martin's Press, 1981).

were no one to tend and care for the smaller one?...The two worlds are not antagonistic. They complement each other, they belong together just as man and woman belong together. We do not consider it correct for the woman to interfere in the world of the man, in his main sphere. We consider it natural if these two worlds remain distinct. To the one belongs the strength of feeling, the strength of the soul. To the other belongs the strength of vision, of toughness, of decision, and of the willingness to act. In the one case this strength demands the willingness of the woman to risk her life to preserve this important cell and to multiply it, and in the other case it demands from the man the readiness to safeguard life. The sacrifices which the man makes in the struggle of his nation, the woman makes in the preservation of that nation in individual cases. What the man gives in courage on the battlefield, the woman gives in eternal self-sacrifice, in eternal pain and suffering. Every child that a woman brings into the world is a battle, a battle waged for the existence of her people.[64]

Unlike the Soviets, who at least in theory envisioned an equal role for women in the economy and public sphere, women in the Third Reich were explicitly informed that their natures and duties were primarily maternal. The first indication that the Nazis would make good on these ideological claims about women's role through coercive measures was the speed with which they shut down the birth control clinics that had proliferated in the Weimar Republic.[65] Authorities initially relied on anti-Communist legislation to shut down the clinics, since many were run by the KPD or by Communist doctors.[66] Despite these early measures, birth control practices were widely disseminated in the Third Reich.[67] Contraceptives only came under a comprehensive ban in January 1941, when Heinrich Himmler issued a Police Ordinance banning their production and distribution.[68] It is significant that Himmler's ban excluded

---

[64] Jeremy Noakes and Geoffrey Pridham, ed., *Nazism, 1919–1945: A Documentary Reader*, vol. 1 (Exeter: University of Exeter Press, 1997), 449.

[65] Grossmann, *Reforming Sex*, 136–49; and Gabriele Czarnowski, "Frauen – Staat – Medizin: Aspekte der Körperpolitik im Nationalsozialismus," *Beiträge zur feministischen Theorie und Praxis* 8 (1985): 84–5.

[66] Lisa Pine, *Nazi Family Policy, 1933–1945* (Oxford and New York: Berg, 1997), 19.

[67] Historians have not yet achieved consensus on the availability of birth control in the Third Reich. This is perhaps a problem of definition. The fact that condoms were excluded from laws outlawing birth control in the Third Reich meant that they were officially classified as prophylactics (against venereal disease), despite the fact that they could also be used for birth control. Historians (not to mention their historical sources) have not always been specific enough about what they mean when they write about birth control. When, for instance, Robert G. Waite argues that that even teenagers were "well acquainted with contraceptives" in the early 1940s and that teenage girls in Lüneburg used birth control regularly, he does not say what kind of devices or practices they were actually using (see Robert G. Waite, "Teenage Sexuality in Nazi Germany," *Journal of the History of Sexuality* 8, no. 3 [1998]: 434–76). It is necessary, in other words, to distinguish between prophylactic birth control (condoms), nonprophylactic birth control (which can include, of course, various forms of continence and "natural" methods), and nonprophylactic contraceptive devices.

[68] Discussions about making birth control illegal, supported by Adolf Hitler, began much earlier. See the minutes of meeting of Sachverständigenbeirat für Bevölkerungs- und Rassenpolitik, 3 August 1933, in BA-B, R43 II/720a, Bl. 120–6.

condoms. Concerns about venereal disease and the view of many Nazi leaders (particularly Himmler) that male workers and soldiers required sexual outlets to be effective and productive persuaded them that condoms had to remain available to men seeking the services of prostitutes. While women's sexuality was conceived exclusively in terms of the relationship to reproduction, men were expected (even encouraged) to stray, in the interests of improving fighting morale and worker productivity.[69]

Pointing out this encouragement of male extramarital sexual activity should not be taken as an argument that the Nazi ideal of supporting the family weakened or conflicted with actual practice; Nazi leaders like Himmler simply assumed that even family men would be promiscuous. But these policies do point to the need to relativize our focus on "family policy" by putting it in context with other Nazi views on sexual behavior.[70] The Nazi emphasis on the family was accompanied by a coercive attitude toward nonmarital sexual activity, but not in the sense that the antifascist sexual revolutionaries of the 1960s claimed.[71] Contrary to some stereotypes, the Third Reich was not a particularly sexually repressive society, since individuals were encouraged to engage in sexual activity outside marriage as long as it resulted in the birth of more "Aryan" babies or invigorated men for productive work in industry and soldiering. Whereas Soviet policymakers raged against the "Red Don Juans" who abandoned their families, the Nazis accepted promiscuity and virtually insatiable sexual appetites as central to male nature. Himmler, in fact, assumed that these urges would be racially valuable, since they would prompt truly patriotic Germans to produce "Aryan" children both within and outside traditional marriages. The best soldiers, he insisted – those most likely to require prostitutes for sexual relief on the front because of their strongly masculine energies – would also, for the same reasons, be the most prolific of citizens once they returned to their wives.[72]

---

[69] The result of this mentality was state support for prostitution. See Annette F. Timm, "Sex with a Purpose: Prostitution, Venereal Disease and Militarized Masculinity in the Third Reich." *Journal of the History of Sexuality* 11, no. 1–2 (2002): 223–55.

[70] See, for example, Pine; Irmgard Weyrather, *Muttertag und Mutterkreuz: Der Kult um die "deutsche Mutter" im Nationalsozialismus* (Frankfurt am Main: Fischer Taschenbuch Verlag, 1993); and Gabriele Czarnowski, *Das kontrollierte Paar: Ehe- und Sexualpolitik im National-sozialismus* (Weinheim: Deutsche Studien Verlag, 1991).

[71] Dagmar Herzog, "'Pleasure, Sex and Politics Belong Together': Post-Holocaust Memory and the Sexual Revolution in West Germany," *Critical Inquiry* 24, no. 2 (1998): 393–444. Herzog exposes the ideological and historically inaccurate nature of the New Leftist claim "that it was sexual repression that engendered the Nazi capacity for cruelty and mass murder" (397).

[72] See his famous October 1939 speech, in which he called upon all racially "valuable" and patriotic Germans to produce children, even if they were illegitimate, to feed the nation's need for soldiers. This was a very controversial stance, even within the party. See George L. Mosse, *Nationalism and Sexuality: Respectability and Abnormal Sexuality in Modern Europe* (New York: H. Fertig, 1985), 166–7. The impact of the speech on actual practice has been vastly overblown, particularly by those who have used it to make the inaccurate claim that Himmler's *Lebensborn* maternity homes were "breeding farms" where SS soldiers impregnated fertile Aryan women. The most authoritative book on the *Lebensborn* is Georg Lilienthal, *Der "Lebensborn e. V.": Ein Instrument nationalsozialistischer Rassenpolitik* (Stuttgart: Fischer

The comparison to Soviet policies is instructive. Soviet young people, Sheila Fitzpatrick informs us, received conflicting messages about sexual freedom. Soviet propaganda about the emancipation of women and explicit arguments by party members like Aleksandra Kollontai gave them the impression that "sexual and political liberation went together."[73] This ran counter to the views of Lenin and other Old Bolsheviks, who expected sexual restraint and viewed sexual freedom as a distraction from the task of building a new society. An anti-decadence propaganda campaign was accordingly directed at Komsomol members in 1926–7.[74] While sexual norms continued to be debated throughout the 1920s, by the 1930s, with the end of NEP and small-scale capitalism, the danger of bourgeois influences within the family receded in the minds of Soviet leaders, and they more actively promoted stable families and sexual propriety. At the same time, they never adopted the strict division of gender roles characteristic of the Nazis, and indeed they recruited women into the industrial workforce.[75] The absence in the Soviet Union of the kind of racial ideology that prompted Nazi policymakers to view the family as the "germ cell" of the nation and illegitimate children as a "gift" to the Führer (as long as they were racially "desirable") meant that despite revolutionary rhetoric, official Soviet policy on sexuality was much *less* radical than that of key National Socialists. While Himmler and others advocated a kind of repressive desublimation, as Herbert Marcuse once described it,[76] Soviet officials sought to sublimate sexual energies to the tasks of socialist construction. No generalization about

---

1985). Actual practice in *Lebensborn* homes must be distinguished from the fantasies of some Nazi leaders (particularly Himmler) about policies to be introduced in the future. See Hans Peter Bleuel, *Sex and Society in Nazi Germany*, ed. and with introduction by Heinrich Fraenkel, trans. J. Maxwell Brownjohn (Philadelphia: Lippincott, 1973), 169.

[73] Sheila Fitzpatrick, *The Cultural Front: Power and Culture in Revolutionary Russia* (Ithaca, NY: Cornell University Press, 1992), 68. See also Eric Naiman, *Sex in Public: The Incarnation of Early Soviet Ideology* (Princeton, NJ: Princeton University Press, 1997).

[74] Ibid., 69.

[75] For further discussion, see Wendy Z. Goldman, *Women at the Gates: Gender and Industry in Stalin's Russia* (Cambridge and New York: Cambridge University Press, 2002); Elizabeth Wood, *The Baba and the Comrade: Gender and Politics in Revolutionary Russia* (Bloomington: Indiana University Press, 1997); Melanie Ilic, *Women Workers in the Soviet Interwar Economy: From "Protection" to "Equality"* (New York: St. Martin's Press in association with Centre for Russian and East European Studies, University of Birmingham, 1999).

[76] In late 1941, Marcuse wrote an unpublished analysis in which he argued that the Nazis had lifted sexual taboos for repressive purposes. (See "Über soziale und politische Aspekte des Nationalsozialismus," in Herbert Marcuse, *Feindanalysen: Über die Deutschen*, ed. Peter-Erwin Jansen and Detlev Claussen [Lüneburg: zu Klampen Verlag, 1998], 91–117, available in translation as *Technology, War and Fascism*.) He argued here that the sexual activity in Nazi youth camps, the sexual excesses of the "racial elites," and anti-Semitic pornography were all part and parcel of Nazi population policy. They were ways of rewarding and/or encouraging the extra labor power required from the population to achieve the aggressive racist aims of the state. By lifting sexual taboos, Marcuse argued, the Nazis made sex into a political domain. Hitherto repressed sexual energies were now socialized and put to work for the regime. The individual was taught to understand his/her sexual satisfaction as a patriotic duty. In the process the last bastion of the individual – the last area in which private wishes and desires could be addressed and fulfilled – was torn down.

attitudes toward sexuality could thus encompass practice in these two regimes (either internally or in comparison). Seemingly sacrosanct ideological values (such as the centrality of the family in Nazi social policy, or ideas about sexual liberation in the Soviet Union) were regularly compromised in the interests of what were considered more pressing practical exigencies.

The degree of support for bourgeois family values among Nazi policymakers depended upon their perceived value for the militaristic goals of the regime. While prostitution was tolerated and even planned (though not publicly valorized) as a reward for hard-fighting soldiers, and extramarital sex was encouraged if it produced more "Aryan" babies, unorthodox forms of sexual expression thought to diminish fighting strength were actively repressed. Himmler's argument for prostitution rested on his belief that the close comradeship of the fighting unit (the *Männerbund*) created a breeding ground for homosexual urges that needed to be counteracted through punishment and the creation of possibilities for heterosexual sex.[77] Aside from making prostitutes available, he ordered that soldiers engaged in the invasion of Poland in 1939 would be released "from otherwise necessary bourgeois [*bürgerlicher*] laws and habits" so that children could be conceived "even outside of marriage with German women and girls of good blood." Bourgeois values were to take a backseat to the "victory of the child" as a necessary corollary to the "victory of the sword."[78] Hitler, though less vocal on the subject, agreed, insisting, "Our uprising has nothing to do with bourgeois virtues. We are an uprising born of our nation's strength – the strength of its loins as well, if you like."[79] Sexual prowess, reproduction, and fighting strength were all combined in this worldview, and homosexuality, particularly in military ranks, thus represented not just a moral, but a military threat. This view prevailed against the more libertine arguments of Ernst Röhm, who argued against all forms of bourgeois prudishness in sexual matters, particularly with reference to homosexuality.[80]

[77] Justifying his tolerance for military prostitution, Himmler argued: "In this area we will be as generous as we can possibly be, since one cannot on the one hand want to prevent that the whole male youth wanders off towards homosexuality and on the other hand leave them no way out." Quoted in Christa Paul, *Zwangsprostitution: Staatlich errichtete Bordelle im Nationalsozialismus* (Berlin: Edition Hentrich, 1994), 12. On the *Männerbund* and militarized masculinity in the Third Reich, see George L. Mosse, *Nationalism and Sexuality: Respectability and Abnormal Sexuality in Modern Europe* (New York: H. Fertig, 1985); and Thomas Kühne, "'Aus diesem Krieg werden nicht nur harte Männer heimkehren': Kriegskameradschaft und Männlichkeit im 20. Jahrhundert," in *Männergeschichte – Geschlechtergeschichte: Männlichkeit im Wandel der Moderne, Reihe Geschichte und Geschlechter*, ed. Thomas Kühne (Frankfurt am Main [u.a.]: Campus, 1996).

[78] "SS-Befehl für die gesamte SS und Polizei" 28 Oct. 1939, in Bundesarchiv (Berlin) – hereafter BA-B – NS19/3973.

[79] Quoted in Hans Peter Bleuel, *Sex and Society in Nazi Germany* (New York: Dorset Press, 1996), 3.

[80] Ernst Röhm openly rejected bourgeois sexuality and its hypocrisies in his 1928 autobiography, *Die Geschichte eines Hochverräters* (Munich, 1928). But, as Eleanor Hancock has argued, this position was always an uncomfortable one in the Nazi Party and "came into conflict with the more usual National Socialist view of sexuality, which saw its main purpose as reproduc-

The militarization of masculinity in the Third Reich ultimately won the day on issues of sexual propriety. In cases where sexual energies could be harnessed to military campaigns, they were encouraged. When sexual activity was thought to threaten fighting strength, as did homosexuality, it was harshly repressed.[81]

But the emphasis on uniting military and reproductive energies also affected those who conformed to the Nazi masculine ideal. Married men in SS units were often given short leaves to visit with their wives in hotels near the front, in the hope that they would conceive a child.[82] Himmler expected SS members to be exemplary fathers of large families (with at least four children), and he expected infertile SS couples to adopt. SS officers were compelled under a 1936 order to become supporting members of Lebensborn e.V., an organization dedicated to helping racially valuable families with many children and unwed mothers about to give birth to racially valuable children.[83] Fatherhood and soldiering were linked in Himmler's ideology. He even considered requesting funding for *Lebensborn* directly from the military budget of Generalfeldmarschall Keitel.[84] While this never happened, Himmler did find ways of using the victories in the East to help create his racial utopias, in terms of not only annihilating racial enemies, but also adding to the racial stock of the *Volksgemeinschaft*. In March 1939, he had mused

> that every nordic person that we take from other peoples will be a loss of leadership-capable blood for them and a benefit for us. Through every successful action, we gain two people, one that our opponent loses and who will no longer be standing against us as an enemy, and one that will now be standing with us and finding for us.[85]

Later in the war, this theoretical zero sum game became a reality, and *Lebensborn* officials began kidnapping Aryan-looking Polish children and adopting

---

tion." See Eleanor Hancock, "'Only the Real, the True, the Masculine Held Its Value': Ernst Röhm, Masculinity, and Male Homosexuality," *Journal of the History of Sexuality* 8, no. 4 (1998): 623–4.

[81] Space constraints preclude a detailed discussion of the persecution of homosexuals in the Third Reich. This subject has received detailed attention in recent years. For brief overviews see: Geoffrey Giles, "The Denial of Homosexuality: Same-Sex Incidents in Himmler's SS and Police," *Journal of the History of Sexuality* 11, no. 1–2 (2002): 256–90; Geoffrey Giles, "'The Most Unkindest Cut of All': Castration, Homosexuality, and Nazi Justice," *Journal of Contemporary History* 27, no. 1 (1992): 41–61; and Erwin J. Haeberle, "Swastika, Pink Triangle, and Yellow Star: The Destruction of Sexology and the Persecution of Homosexuals in Nazi Germany," in *Hidden from History: Reclaiming the Gay and Lesbian Past*, ed. Martin Duberman et al. (New York: New American Library, 1989), 365–79.

[82] For an examples Himmler's orders to this effect, see BAB/NS19/2769 and BA-B – NS19/3594.

[83] An excerpt from this order is reprinted in BA-B – /NS19/3973, Bl. 9–10.

[84] A 1940 draft letter (that was never sent) argues that properly funding *Lebensborn* could prevent six hundred thousand abortions yearly, thus providing an extra two hundred regiments of soldiers within eighteen or twenty years. See letter dated July 1940 in BA-B – NS19/1082, Bl. 6–7.

[85] Himmler to Reichsminister Lammers, 11 March 1939, BA-B – NS2/55, 1939), Bl. 139–40.

them out to German families, many of whom were unaware of the exact circumstances of the children's departure from their homes.[86] This program is
perhaps the best example of how Nazi conceptions of family were explicitly
linked to violence and to primitive understandings of the connection between
physical (in this case military) strength and the right to fatherhood.

The Soviet attitude toward fatherhood had an entirely different focus. In
tandem with its pronatalist campaign, the Soviet government sought to enforce
paternal obligations. A 1933 decree that required all births to be registered
within one month included provisions for a mother to name the father of her
child regardless of whether they were married or even whether he was present.
Men who did not acknowledge paternity of a child would still be registered
as the father if a mother named him as such and provided any evidence of
cohabitation.[87] In 1936 the same law that outlawed abortion and made divorce
more difficult also tightened regulations on child support. It set minimal levels
of child support as one-fourth of the unmarried or divorced father's salary for
one child, one-third for two children, and one-half for three or more children.
It also increased the penalty for nonpayment of child support to two years
in prison.[88] In subsequent years the Soviet government proved serious about
paternal responsibility and took numerous steps to track down delinquent
fathers.[89] Soviet propaganda also stressed the importance of paternity; a lead
article in *Pravda* entitled "Father" stated that "a father is a social educator. He
must prepare good Soviet citizens." Another article stated, "A poor husband
and father cannot be a good citizen. People who abuse the freedom of divorce
should be punished."[90]

It was just prior to the campaign to strengthen the family that the Soviet
government recriminalized male homosexuality. In December 1933 the head
of the Soviet secret police, Genrikh Iagoda, sent Stalin a draft decree outlawing sodomy and justified it by citing "associations of pederasts" engaged in
"the recruitment and corruption of completely healthy young people." The
Politburo approved the ban on male homosexuality, which was issued as
law in March 1934.[91] Dan Healey notes that the Soviet recriminalization of
sodomy was preceded by Hitler's accession to power and a virulent propaganda war between fascism and communism which included mutual accusations of homosexuality. In this atmosphere, homosexuality became associated
with fascism in the eyes of Soviet officials, and in fact Maxim Gorky justified

---

[86] See Gitta Sereny, *The German Trauma: Experiences and Reflections, 1938–2001* (London:
Penguin Books, 2000).

[87] *Gosudarstvennoe upravlenie: Kodifitsirovannyi sbornik zakonodatel'stva RSFSR na 1 ianvariia
1934 goda* (Moscow, 1934), 49.

[88] *Sobranie zakonov i rasporiazhenii*, no. 34 (21 July 1936): 515–16.

[89] GARF f. 9492 s.ch., op. 1, d. 2, l. 183; TsMAM f. 819, op. 1, d. 3, l. 1; f. 2429, op. 7, d. 200,
l. 34; d. 220, l. 4.

[90] *Pravda* 9 June 1936, 1; *Ogonek* 10 January 1936, 4; Timasheff, 197.

[91] *Istochnik*, no. 5–6 (1993): 164–5.

the antisodomy law with the slogan "Destroy the homosexuals – fascism will disappear."[92]

Healey also points out that attacks on homosexuality coincided with the Soviet government's mid-1930s drives to cleanse cities of "social anomalies" and to promote the (heterosexual) family. In 1936 the Commissar of Justice Nikolai Krylenko linked homosexuality with bourgeois decadence and counterrevolution and stated that it had no place in a socialist society founded on healthy principles. He called homosexuals "declassed rabble, either from the dregs of society or from the remnants of the exploiting classes." Krylenko declared that homosexuals were not needed "in the environment of workers taking the point of view of normal relations between the sexes, who are building their society on healthy principles."[93] Emphasis on the family should thus be seen as part of a larger effort by the Soviet government to make heterosexuality and procreation compulsory in the interests of the state and larger society.[94]

In addition to enforcing heteronormative behavior and paternal obligations among men, the Soviet government sought to rationalize and maximize reproduction through a range of studies and measures to safeguard women's reproductive capacities. Soviet medical specialists in the 1920s used the language of industrial production to describe reproduction, including the term "productive capacity" to describe women's ability to become pregnant and bear healthy babies.[95] A. S. Gofshtein, in his article "The Rationalization of Maternity," described mothers as "producers" and wrote that pregnancy could be "productive" or "unproductive," depending on whether it ended with the birth of a healthy child or with miscarriage, abortion, or infant mortality. Gofshtein studied the histories of pregnant women and calculated that women would optimize their productivity by having three children, all four years apart. He noted that more frequent pregnancies weakened "the female organism," produced sickly children, and diminished women's value in the workforce.[96] Other Soviet doctors studied reproductive capacity by combining obstetrics and gynecology with anthropometry (for example, measuring women's pelvises). One

[92] Dan Healey, *Homosexual Desire in Revolutionary Russia: The Regulation of Sexual and Gender Dissent* (Chicago: University of Chicago Press, 2001), 182–90. See also Laura Engelstein, "Soviet Policy toward Male Homosexuality: Its Origins and Historical Roots," *Journal of Homosexuality* 29, no. 2–3 (1994): 155–78.

[93] N. V. Krylenko, "Ob izmeneniiakh i dopolneniiakh kodeksov RSFSR," *Sovetskaia iustitsiia*, no. 7 (1936), as cited in Healey, 196. See also James Riordan, "Sexual Minorities: The Status of Gays and Lesbians in Russian-Soviet-Russian Society," *Women in Russia and Ukraine*, ed. Rosalind Marsh (Cambridge, UK: Cambridge University Press, 1996), 160; Igor Kon, "Sexual Minorities," in *Sex and Russian Society*, eds. I. Kon and James Riordan (Bloomington: Indiana University Press, 1993), 92.

[94] On the prosecution of sodomy cases after 1933, see Healey, chapter 8, 207–28.

[95] Hyer, 113.

[96] A. S. Gofshtein, "Ratsionalizatsiia materinstva," *Vrachebnoe delo* , no. 19 (1927), as cited in Hyer, 113–18.

researcher warned that women who worked in factories had narrower (and hence inferior) pelvises than women who did not.[97]

Because women in the Soviet system were expected to serve as both mothers and workers, specialists showed particular concern with the effects of industrial labor on women's reproductive abilities. They conducted studies on the effect of heavy lifting and concluded that it could damage pelvic organs and cause problems with pregnancy. In 1921 and again in 1927 the Soviet government established employment guidelines to ensure that women were not in jobs that required heavy lifting, for fear that such work would harm their reproductive organs.[98] Health officials also promoted physical examinations and education as means to protect women's reproductive capacities. Delegates to the Third All-Union Conference on the Protection of Maternity and Infancy in 1926 stressed that young women from the beginning of their sexual maturity should have regular medical consultations, initially arranged through schools. They also noted that these consultations would give doctors the opportunity to educate them about the dangers of abortion and diseases. Throughout the 1920s specialists on women's hygiene and sexual enlightenment carried on studies and educational efforts, most of which emphasized the social importance of women's reproductive health and childbearing.[99]

The legislative centerpiece of the Soviet government's campaign to raise the birthrate was the decree of June 27, 1936, which outlawed abortion, except for medical reasons. Politburo discussion of the decree prior to its promulgation emphasized the importance of achieving the maximal possible birthrate.[100] The Politburo subsequently decided "to limit as much as possible the list of medical reasons" for permitting an abortion, and this decision was promulgated later in a November 1936 decree that limited the medical reasons for permitting an abortion to cases in which hereditary diseases were likely or in which a woman's life was endangered. The decree stated, "Abortion is not only harmful for a woman's health, but is also a serious social evil, the battle with which is the duty of every conscious citizen, most of all medical personnel."[101]

The ban on abortion was preceded by a huge publicity campaign and public discussion of a draft of the decree, and it was followed by further propaganda on the new law's validity and importance. Numerous articles stressed the harm

---

[97] Hyer, 115.

[98] Hyer, 116–17; Thomas Schrand, "Industrialization and the Stalinist Gender System: Women Workers in the Soviet Economy, 1928–1941" (Ph.D. diss., University of Michigan, 1994), 159–60. Similar policies regulating work for pregnant women were instituted in Weimar Germany. See Patricia R. Stokes, "Contested Conceptions: Experiences and Discourses of Pregnancy and Childbirth in Germany, 1914–1933" (Ph.D. diss., Cornell University, 2003).

[99] *Resoliutsii III Vsesoiuznogo soveshchaniia po okhrane materinstva i mladenchestva* (1926), 17–18; Malinovskii and Shvartsman, 5. For discussion of Soviet sexual enlightenment programs, see Frances Lee Bernstein, *The Dictatorship of Sex: Lifestyle Advice for the Soviet Masses* (DeKalb: Northern Illinois University Press, 2007).

[100] *Sobranie zakonov i rasporiazhenii*, no. 34 (21 July 1936): 510–11; RGASPI f. 17, op. 3, d. 976, l. 4.

[101] RGASPI f. 17, op. 3, d. 980, l. 1; d. 982, ll. 126–30.

that abortions did to women's physical and mental health.[102] (No mention was made of the extreme danger posed to the health of women who in the wake of this law sought illegal abortions.) One article asserted that the "single goal" of the decree was "the protection of the health of the Soviet mother."[103] Commissar Semashko warned that abortion could not only cause infertility, but also have an adverse effect on a woman's other organs and nervous system. But he also justified the ban on abortion as crucial to "the state task of increasing the population of the Soviet Union." He went on to compare the fertility rate of the Soviet Union with those of other industrialized countries and argued that the abortion ban would allow the country to maintain or even increase its superior birthrate.[104] Here again it is noteworthy that Semashko referred to increasing the population as a "state task." Rather than conceptualize population issues in terms of "national superiority" or "race suicide," he and other Soviet leaders espoused a nonracial approach that sought to boost the birthrate to build socialism and prove its ideological ascendance.

This, of course, contrasts sharply with the racialized reproductive policies in the Third Reich. Nazi racial hygienists went beyond arguments about proving the superiority of their political and health care system through higher birthrates and conceived of even the domestic population in highly competitive terms. An ideological division was made between those who were and those who were not considered racially and genetically desirable. The former were to have no access to abortion, since the children they might produce were considered too valuable to the nation. Differential access to abortion based on racial criteria can thus be viewed as a form of coercive pronatalism.[105] Those of "lesser value" (*Minderwertigen*), while also not given reproductive choice, were certainly provided access to or sometimes forced into an abortion. Abortion laws, which had been liberalized somewhat in the Weimar Republic, were tightened in May 1933.[106] Thereafter a woman who procured or induced an abortion for herself or the practitioners of abortion were subject to between one-day and five-year detentions, or up to fifteen years if money had changed

---

[102] *Rabotnitsa i krest'ianka*, no. 11 (1936): 6; *Rabotnitsa i krest'ianka*, no. 12 (1936): 1. See also *Izvestiia*, 5 June 1935.

[103] *Pravda*, 5 September 1936, 4.

[104] N. A. Semashko, "Zamechatel'nyi zakon (o zapreshchenii aborta)," *Front nauki i tekhniki*, no. 7 (1936): 38. For further discussion, see Susan Gross Solomon, "The Demographic Argument in Soviet Debates over the Legalization of Abortion in the 1920s," *Cahiers du Monde russe et sovietique* 33 (1992): 59–82.

[105] Atina Grossman also makes this argument. See her chapter "The Debate That Will Not End: The Politics of Abortion in Germany from Weimar to National Socialism and the Postwar Period," in *Medicine and Modernity: Public Health and Medical Care in Nineteenth- and Twentieth-Century Germany*, eds. Manfred Berg and Geoffrey Cocks (Washington, DC, and Cambridge: German Historical Institute and Cambridge University Press, 1997), 195–6. This runs counter to Gisela Bock's argument (in *Zwangssterilisation im Nationalsozialismus*) that Nazi reproductive policies can be characterized as primarily antinatalist.

[106] Paragraphs 219 and 220, which had been eliminated from the Penal Code in Weimar era reforms, were reintroduced, once again prohibiting education about abortion or abortifacients.

hands.[107] Then in June 1935, the policies on abortion were linked explicitly to eugenic sterilization measures when an amendment to the July 14, 1933, sterilization law (the Law for the Prevention of Hereditarily Diseased Offspring, which had called for the mandatory surgical sterilization of all people with "hereditary" diseases)[108] declared even very late-term abortions legal if they were certified eugenically necessary by a medical commission. Thereafter, eugenic abortions were followed by sterilization. That Nazi medical authorities envisioned abortion primarily as a eugenic measure was further emphasized in the Reichsärztekammer's 1936 "Guidelines for Interruption of Pregnancy and Sterilization on Health Grounds," which narrowed the possibilities for therapeutic abortions (that is, abortions made necessary by threats to the woman's health) to only very severe cases.[109]

Nazi abortion policy must be understood as a continuation of the spirit of the 1933 sterilization law, not least because the two policies were eventually linked. The first sterilization law had been followed by an extensive propaganda campaign that used terms like "differential decreases in the birthrate," "quantity versus quality," and "constitution of the genetic makeup of our *Volk*" to argue that sterilization of the unfit was a necessary countermeasure against racial degeneration.[110] Despite the antinatalist tone of the policies on sterilization and abortion, they were formulated with the understanding that such measures were a necessary step toward eventually increasing the number of desirable births. The desire to prevent the hereditarily sick from reproducing must be understood in the context of the twisted Darwinian logic of Nazi lawmakers: they assumed that an ever-increasing number of diseased individuals would overwhelm societal resources and eventually lead to *both* a qualitative and a numerical decline in the German population. Pronatalist and antinatalist tendencies in the Third Reich are thus not easily separated, and a lack of voluntary access to abortion and birth control coexisted with forced sterilization and abortion for those declared racially and eugenically "of lesser value."[111] Banning abortion in the Third Reich, as in the Soviet Union, was a form of coercive pronatalism for the portion of the population considered racially desirable, even while it must also be considered a eugenic and antinatalist measure

---

[107] Pine, 20.

[108] The official English translation of the law described these in the following terms: innate mental deficiency, schizophrenia, manic-depressive-insanity, hereditary epilepsy, hereditary (Huntington's) chorea, hereditary blindness, hereditary deafness, severe hereditary physical deformity. See "The Law for the Prevention of Hereditary Disease in Posterity," clipping in Freie Universität Berlin, Sammlung Rott (hereafter FUB, Slg Rott), C5b, 9101, Box 8. For an official text and explanation of the law see: Arthur Gütt, *Gesetz zur Verhütung erbkranken Nachwuchses vom 14. Juli 1933, mit Auszug aus dem Gesetz gegen gefährliche Gewohnheitsverbrecher und über Massregeln der Sicherung und Besserung vom 24. Nov. 1933* (Munich: J. F. Lehmann, 1934).

[109] Grossmann, "The Debate That Will Not End," 196.

[110] Cited in Bock, *Zwangssterilisation im Nationalsozialismus*, 90.

[111] Gabriele Czarnowski, *Das kontrollierte Paar*, 15.

for others. A similar mixture of pronatalist and antinatalist objectives was apparent in marriage policy.

In this context, we must also mention the Nuremberg Laws of 1935, the most infamous of which was the "Law for the Protection of German Blood and German Honor," or the Blutschutzgesetz, which outlawed marriages between Jews and gentiles and classified Jews according to degree of racial mixing. Soon after, on October 18, 1935, the Ehegesundheitsgesetz (marital health law, officially called the Gesetz zum Schutze der Erbgesundheit des deutschen Volkes) was proclaimed. This law definitively transformed marriage counseling from the Weimar model (which although professing eugenic considerations "mostly provided contraceptives and sex advice") to a system of government sponsored *Bevölkerungspolitik* – large, "fit" families became the exclusive goal of marital health regulations.[112] The law prohibited marriages between partners likely to produce "undesirable" offspring or between an infertile, sterilized, or otherwise unfit partner and a racially desirable one.[113] Additional decrees to the marital health law stipulated that health certificates (*Ehetauglichkeitszeugnisse*),[114] which had been certified by newly created counseling centers for genetic and racial health (Beratungsstellen für Erbgesundheit und Rassenpflege), had to be exchanged before marriage. A circular clarifying the application of the law emphasized the eugenic considerations that should be applied, stating that "careful evaluation of all circumstances speaking for and against the marriage must be undertaken, primarily with reference to genetic and health considerations."[115] Despite the link between the Ehegesundheitsgesetz and the Blutschutzgesetz, then, the emphasis of the former remained on eugenic health rather than racial considerations. The Ehegesundheitsgesetz was clearly directed at the majority population and meant to strengthen the core society for nationalistic purposes. An increasing number of exceptions made during the application of the law demonstrates the degree to which policymakers saw this aspect of their racial policy as a legitimizing feature of the regime. The aim was to sell the Ehegesundheitsgesetz to the German public as an instrument of personal protection.[116]

It is clear, then, that neither Nazi nor Soviet reproductive health policy confined itself to coercive measures and that even some apparently coercive policies were formulated so as to encourage compliance on the part of citizens. We will now turn to policies that provided even more explicit incentives for

---

[112] Grossmann, *Reforming Sex*, 141.

[113] The law also only applied to German citizens, or in cases of German men who married foreign women. If a German woman married a foreign man, their future children were not considered Germans and the woman lost her citizenship.

[114] Note the change in terminology from Weimar usage, which had called marital health certificates *Ehegesundheitszeugnissen*. It is no longer simply health, but "fitness" for marriage that is being certified.

[115] Reichsminister des Innern to Landesregierungen etc., 18 Feb. 1939 in Landesarchiv Berlin (hereafter LAB), Rep. 12, Acc. 1641, Nr. 239.

[116] For further clarification see Timm, "The Politics of Fertility," 289–300.

citizens who were either racially desirable (in the Nazi case) or politically compliant, demonstrating that population policy was not only an instrument of social control but also a means of legitimizing state projects. It was a crucial component of the respective projects to remake society.

Alongside coercive measures to raise the birthrate, the Soviet government offered financial inducements for women to have many children. The same decree that outlawed abortion granted women a 2,000-ruble annual bonus for each child they had over six children and a 5,000-ruble bonus for each child over ten children. These bonuses drew an immediate response from women with seven or more children. Local officials were deluged by requests from (primarily peasant) women who qualified for these bonuses.[117]

In addition to bonuses paid to individuals, the Soviet government encouraged motherhood by providing maternity facilities and services. Within months of coming to power, the Soviet government founded a large number of maternity homes, nurseries, milk kitchens, and pediatric clinics. With the pronatalist push of the mid-1930s, funding for maternity wards and nurseries increased even more, though not nearly enough to meet the needs of the millions of women in the workforce. Given that the Soviet government channeled virtually all resources into rapid industrialization, it lacked the money for adequate child care facilities. But in principle, the Soviet government committed itself to complete care for mothers and children.[118] The Soviet government also sought to ensure that women did not avoid pregnancy for fear of losing their jobs or wages. As early as 1921 the government decreed that pregnant women who were unable to work were entitled to receive their full salary from workers' insurance funds. By 1927 Soviet law guaranteed women eight weeks of paid leave both before and after giving birth.[119]

As part of its pronatalist campaign of the mid-1930s, the Soviet government also celebrated motherhood and portrayed having children as a natural and fulfilling part of a woman's life. Articles in the Soviet press stressed the happiness that children brought to women's lives. One testimonial from a woman with five children described how much her children loved her, while another article claimed that children took care of each other, so that having many children was an advantage rather than a burden.[120]

While Soviet efforts to glorify motherhood resembled pronatalist propaganda in other countries, they were distinguished in one crucial way. The Soviet government encouraged and expected women to continue working while

---

[117] *Sobranie zakonov i rasporiazhenii*, no. 34 (July 21, 1936), p. 511; GARF f. 5446, op. 18a, d. 2753, l. 4. The Soviet government had to allot 35 million rubles in 1936 alone to pay such bonuses; GARF f. 5446, op. 18a, d. 2753, l. 31.

[118] Drobizhev, 109, 122; GARF f. 5446, op. 18a, d. 2754, l. 45. See, for example, the draft of a pamphlet by Elena Stasova, "For Women in the USSR All Paths Are Open," in which she stresses the concern and material aid provided by the Soviet government to mothers. RGASPI f. 17, op. 120, d. 202, l. 11.

[119] GARF f. 4085, op. 12, d. 320, l. 16; Molkov, ed. (1927), 318.

[120] *Martenovka*, 1 May 1936, 5; *Rabotnitsa i krest'ianka*, no. 15 (1936): 5; *Rabotnitsa i krest'ianka*, no. 2 (1936): 20. See also *Gigiena i zdorov'e*, no. 4 (1938): 6.

pregnant and after giving birth. To ensure that pregnant women could find or maintain jobs outside the home, the Politburo approved a decree in October 1936 that made it a criminal offense to refuse to hire or to lower the pay of women during pregnancy.[121] Soviet leaders, then, constructed gender in a way that stressed women's roles as both workers and mothers, and they insisted there was no contradiction between the two. In contrast, many officials and social commentators in Western Europe blamed feminism and women's employment outside the home for the weakening of traditional female roles and the decline in the birthrate.[122]

As we have already seen, the Nazis emphasized that woman's place was in the home, and most of the positive financial incentives they offered to encourage women to have more children were predicated on the assumption of a single-earner family. Differing markedly from Soviet policy, the Nazis offered some of their financial incentives for births only to women who gave up paid employment. The policy of providing marriage loans to genetically "fit" couples began as a labor policy – as a measure to decrease unemployment by removing women from the workforce. Enshrined in section five (Promotion of the Marriage Rate) of the Law to Decrease Unemployment of June 1, 1933,[123] the law on marriage decreed that eligible couples could apply to receive loans of up to one thousand Reichsmarks to buy goods needed to establish a household. Eligibility was limited to engaged or recently married couples when the wife or female partner was employed but promised to give up her job upon marriage. The exact stipulations of length of employment were gradually loosened, so that by the end of August, even women who had only worked for a period of six months sometime between 1928 and 1933 were eligible. Gabriele Czarnowski has argued that the policy was not simply a reactionary effort to redomesticate women, but rather a very modern attempt to manipulate female labor. The initial goal of expanding job opportunities for men by removing married women from the labor market was abandoned in the changed economic circumstances after 1936. After the boom in armaments industries and the resulting shortage of labor, women no longer had to give up their jobs to receive the loans.[124] As one contemporary commentator put it, the "population political goal [of the law] remained the same as it had been in 1933,"[125] but it now served to encourage rather than discourage female employment, since the requirement of previous employment remained.

Nevertheless, after 1936, the primary effect of the law was to place an ever-expanding percentage of married couples under eugenic surveillance, since racial and eugenic criteria were stipulations for eligibility. By 1937, Czarnowski

---

[121] RGASPI f. 17, op. 3, d. 981, l. 69.

[122] See Offen, 138.

[123] A copy of the law, along with the various revisions and decrees, can be found in Reichsfinanzministerium, *Ehestandsdarlehen* (Berlin, 1935).

[124] The changes to the marriage loan policy in 1937 were not simply cosmetic. A separate law, "The Law for the Promotion of Marriage Rates," was promulgated.

[125] Cited in Czarnowski, *Das kontrollierte Paar*, 105; Erich Berlitz, *Ehestandsdarlehen* (Berlin and Vienna: Spaeth & Linde, 1940), 39.

argues, the racial hygienic criteria were dominant, and "the public health examinations for marriage loans proved themselves to be one of the most important turning points between 'supportive' and 'eliminationist' reproductive politics."[126] In other words, this apparently "positive" eugenic measure provided public health doctors with a wealth of genetic and social information about prospective marriage candidates that could be used for negative eugenic purposes. Ever more stringent and bureaucratically organized eugenic testing for marriage loans led to a decrease in the number of couples applying for them. New forms in January 1934 were likely partly responsible for this decrease, since patients had only to look at the long list of illnesses and the blank spaces for information on family members to begin to fear that there might be information they had better hide from medical officials.[127]

All the same, the policy must be interpreted as an attempt to legitimize the health plans of the regime. For the most part, marriage loans were provided as a benefit and accepted by the public as a right of citizenship. A demonstration of this can be found in a letter of complaint from a Berlin man whose fiancée had just undergone a health examination for a marriage loan application in May 1936. After complaining about general bureaucratic delays and annoyances, the author described his outrage at the conditions under which his fiancée was examined:

> One has to report...to room 35, *am Urban*, for a blood examination. On this door hangs a large enamel sign "Clinic for the Venereally Diseased."
>
> Any commentary about this would actually be superfluous, but in the hopes of emphatically awakening the bureaus that will perhaps receive this letter, and which are apparently somewhat obtuse, I would like to say, that...every delicately sensitive female heart is extremely offended and shamed to sit next to the painted flowers [*Pflänzchen*], whose source of income is too obviously visible in their appearances, [not to mention the fear] *of then being denounced by the mouth of some casual acquaintance as belonging to the contaminated.* Apparently the head of this clinic has more understanding than the administration of the district of Kreuzberg, because he saw us together upon our request and added the phrase "...for a marriage loan" when he called our names.[128]

The tone is clearly that of an outraged citizen who feels that he has not been treated with due respect. There is a sense of entitlement, and his goal, he claims, is to improve conditions so that others will not have to suffer through the same. The complainant's outrage is not imaginable outside a context of considerable consensus about the state's right to be involved in marriage. It is not the policy itself that the man decries, but the disrespectful way that it was carried out. The complaint is therefore evidence that marriage loans were part of the

---

[126] Ibid., 109.
[127] Ibid., 133.
[128] The letter, dated 26 May 1936, was typed out (it is unclear whether the emphasis is from the original author or whether it was added by the typist) and forwarded to the Oberbürgermeister in the HGA through the Stadtmedizinalrat. The matter was taken seriously, and immediate changes were recommended. LAB, Rep. 12, Acc. 1641, Nr. 246.

construction of consensus in the Nazi state – they proved to many citizens that all the talk about hearth and home had some substance.[129] While ultimately unsuccessful in actually raising the birthrate, these measures prompted a considerable degree of voluntary public involvement in state welfare measures.

A similar policy, that has received more attention from historians, was the practice of rewarding mothers of many children with service crosses and small gifts.[130] Beginning in 1939, crosses were awarded to mothers with four or more children (in bronze for four or five children, silver for six or seven, and gold for eight or more) on Mother's Day – now on August 12, Hitler's mother's birthday. Like the marriage loans, these crosses also awakened a sense of entitlement in the population and were meant to integrate their recipients into the ideological and social structure of the Nazi state. Irmgard Weyrather has argued that the crosses functioned "as a binding agent to the regime and as content of the political religion of National Socialism."[131] Reactions to the medal ceremonies were generally positive. Government informers, who collected data on public opinion about the medals, noted that the most significant complaints arose when mothers considered to be "asocial" (that ill-defined term that could encompass anything from having a child who had stolen something, to obvious social dysfunction, criminality, or mental illness) were granted motherhood service crosses.[132] In general, though, propaganda efforts paid off with large numbers of applications for the crosses. In the first few years of the program, for example, the Berlin district health offices were flooded with applications and begged for extra personnel to process them, particularly once the war began in 1939.[133] Award ceremonies and propaganda made explicit connections between the war effort and the mothers who had provided the Reich with sons and soldiers.

COMPARING PRONATALIST STATE INTERVENTION

While leaders in all European countries shared pronatalist goals, the policies they adopted varied considerably from one country to another. Nazi officials sought to control the "quality," the "racial fitness," and the quantity of children born, and they enacted antinatalist as well as pronatalist measures. The Soviet Union, on the other hand, promoted reproduction among all citizens,

[129] Robert Moeller, *Protecting Motherhood: Women and Family in the Politics of Postwar Germany* (Berkeley: University of California Press, 1993), 17.

[130] See especially Weyrather, *Muttertag und Mutterkreuz*.

[131] Ibid., 151. For a copy of the official policy see "Das Ehrenkreuz der Deutschen Mutter," *AGfV Mitteilungen*, no. 2 (16 January 1939): 1–2.

[132] Ibid., 147.

[133] See, for example, the letter from the district of Treptow to the Oberbürgermeister, 6 May 1939, in LAB, Rep. 12, Acc. 1641, Nr. 247. In October 1939, the Reich Ministry of the Interior issued a directive to all regions to clear up the backlog of applications immediately and make every effort to ensure that at least all those women over 50 years of age had their crosses in hand before Christmas. Letter describing RMI memo from Oberbürgermeister Berlin, 30 Oct. 1939, in ibid.

without regard to race, nationality, or mental and physical abilities. The particular reproductive policies adopted by the Soviet government were a result not only of socialist ideology, but also of the nurturist orientation of Russian disciplinary culture – itself a product of Russian political and social conditions. While Soviet policies, then, were part of an international trend toward state management of reproduction, they reflected a particular disciplinary and ideological orientation, as well as a distinct conception of the population. By placing in comparative context Nazi and Soviet reproductive policies, from abortion legislation and the promotion of motherhood to eugenic policies and child-raising programs, it is possible to demonstrate how the broader shift toward state interventionism assumed particular forms in Nazi Germany and the Soviet Union.

In the Third Reich, reproductive policy and the biological determinism that was its foundation were one component of what one might think of, following Detlev Peukert, as an attempt to transcend death through nonreligious means. In his article "The Genesis of the 'Final Solution' from the Spirit of Science," Peukert describes a process through which, over the course of the century, the early successes of biomedicine and improved hygiene and welfare methods in cities, schools, and social programs inspired experts in the natural and social sciences, especially medical professionals, to ever-increasing optimism for the future perfectability of society.[134] The Nazi state radicalized the already overly optimistic goals of the early social hygienists. Since the very concept of *Volksgemeinschaft* was vague and difficult to define in the positive, Peukert argues, the National Socialist movement "drifted onto an increasingly radical negative concentration on the eradication of a world of enemies."[135] Without religion to explain death, and faced with evidence that scientific optimism about the perfectability of society and the eradication of illness had been premature or entirely misguided, National Socialism sought ever more radical solutions to social problems.[136] An irrational search for new means of avoiding death was the consequence:

> A "logodicy" of the human sciences accordingly drives the sciences into irrationality. It inevitably becomes fixated on the utopian dream of the gradual elimination of death, even while this dream is unfailingly confuted in the life of each particular individual. One obvious escape from the dilemma is to split the target of scientific

---

[134] Peukert's argument follows in the tradition of early philosophical reactions to the Holocaust, like Theodor Adorno and Max Horkheimer, *Dialectic of Enlightenment: Philosophical Fragments*, trans. John Cumming (New York: Continuum Books, 2002). Others have in turn followed in Peukert's footsteps in analyzing the history of social policy from the perspective of the Enlightenment goal of human perfectability. See, for example, Manfred Kappeler, *Der schreckliche Traum vom vollkommenen Menschen: Rassenhygiene und Eugenik in der Sozialen Arbeit* (Marburg: Schüren Presseverlag, 2000).

[135] Detlev J. K. Peukert, "The Genesis of the 'Final Solution' from the Spirit of Science," in *Reevaluating the Third Reich*, eds. Thomas Childers and Jane Caplan (New York and London: Holmes & Meier 1993), 236.

[136] Ibid., 238.

endeavor into the merely ephemeral body of the individual, and the potentially immortal body of the *Volk* or race. Only the latter – specifically, its undying material substratum in the form of the genetic code – can guarantee the undying victory of science itself.[137]

The obstacle of the individual body and its unwillingness to conform to utopian ideals could now be pushed aside with a simple decision: individuals could be determined fit to enter the "ideal *Volkskörper*" or they could be cast aside and eventually eliminated. The collective body was thus preserved, purified, and made eternal. This attempt at transcending the limits of earthly existence was also linked to the broader ideological goal of creating the "thousand-year Reich," since increasing the quality and quantity of births was always tied to goals of an aggressive military policy. The apparent contradiction between the search for *Lebensraum* and claiming that birthrates were plunging to dangerous levels can only be reconciled with reference to this larger goal.

In the Soviet Union, Marxist ideology militated against the biological determinism that served as the basis for the strange and semimystical mixture of pro- and antinatalism in the Third Reich, stressing instead environmental and socioeconomic determinants of people's consciousness and behavior. Even prior to the October Revolution and the establishment of Marxism as state ideology, Russian social scientists and physicians tended to reject biologistic explanations in favor of environmental and social ones. As members of the Russian intelligentsia, they blamed the downtrodden condition of Russian peasants and workers on the despotic tsarist autocracy, and the impoverished circumstances in which the population lived. Seeing the masses as an ally in their struggle against the autocracy, they believed in the people's innate goodness and sought to educate, uplift, and liberate them. Indeed to the extent that many members of the Russian intelligentsia saw the uplifting of the masses as their mission, they gravitated toward medicine and social science that rejected biological determinism. Russian disciplinary culture, then, like Marxism, strongly favored nurturist over hereditarian explanations and programs.[138]

Accordingly, the Soviet government encouraged reproduction among all members of the population, without distinction by ethnicity or class. Soviet health officials stressed the need to increase postnatal care among national minorities in order to raise their birthrates.[139] When the Soviet government began granting women a 2,000-ruble annual bonus for each child they had over six children, it specified that mothers with seven or more children should receive bonuses regardless of their social origins, and even regardless of whether their husbands had been arrested for counterrevolutionary activity.[140] Thus the

[137] Ibid., 241.
[138] Prerevolutionary Russian social thinkers' rejection of Malthusian ideas was also shaped by social and political conditions. See Daniel P. Todes, *Darwin without Malthus: The Struggle for Existence in Russian Evolutionary Thought* (New York: Oxford University Press, 1989).
[139] *Resoliutsii III Vses. Soveshchaniia po okhrane materinstva i mladenchestva* (1926), 2, 10.
[140] GARF f. 5446, op. 18a, d. 2754, l. 32.

Soviet government promoted reproduction even among those it considered class or ideological enemies, in contrast to the Nazi government, which limited the reproduction of those it considered racial enemies.

Soviet pronatalism can thus be distinguished from its Nazi counterpart by quite a different purpose for increasing the birthrate. While Nazi population policy was intimately connected to plans for racial and political dominance over Europe and the world, the Soviets explicitly rejected arguments linking the goal of higher birthrates to increases in military strength. Already in May 1918, with memories of the carnage of the First World War still fresh, Soviet delegates to a congress on social welfare resolved that infant mortality be reduced and children's lives preserved "not for a new slaughter, but as builders of a new, beautiful, working life, as spiritually and physically strong citizens, fighters for the ideals of socialism and humankind." The resolution went on to reiterate that children not be raised to be slaughtered in wars caused by "the criminal negligence of a capitalist state," but rather to provide productive labor to build the new society.[141] The Soviet purpose for increasing the population, then, was to produce laborers rather than soldiers. Of course Soviet leaders also had military concerns, particularly with the rising international tensions of the late 1930s, but such concern was a defensive one.

While there were considerable differences between the theoretical goals of Nazi and Soviet pronatalism, we must also note a striking similarity in how the two regimes viewed reproductive politics as a politically (and perhaps psychologically) mobilizing sphere of government action. In both cases the regimes attempted to construct a new imaginary for the guidance of personal sexual and reproductive decisions. Through a wide spectrum of social policies, both the Nazis and the Soviets attempted to reconcile the apparent contradiction between individual sexual and reproductive desires and the needs of a collectivist state. They created an entirely new form of enthusiasm for the creation of life, a motivation to reproduce that was now to be tied to larger state ideological goals. Individuals were expected to make personal sacrifices; materialistic and sexual desires were to be controlled or subordinated to higher-order causes: the creation of a racialized *Volksgemeinschaft* or a socialist utopia. Both the creation of life and the risk of death (on the battlefield or in childbirth) were framed in collectivist terms. In itself, this was not a huge departure from the symbolic meaning given to life and death in modern states since at least the French Revolution. But in return for individual submission to varying forms of mass mobilization, the two dictatorships offered much more specific promises for new beginnings. Individuals were told exactly how they would be participating in idealized societies with their own intrinsic (not God-given) purposes, giving their individual private choices new meaning. Valorization and reward (in the form of health and welfare benefits) encouraged emotional responses to a new configuration of social reproduction. This was less a process of social control

---

[141] As cited in Drobizhev, 110.

than it was an energization of the symbolic meaning of citizenship and individual participation in the state. While the goals of Nazi and Soviet reproductive policies diverged sharply, the utopian impulse and the motivation to employ reproductive policies to integrate individual actions into a state-collectivist project were similar.

Also similar was the ultimate ineffectiveness of pronatalist policies in both states. We can summarize the situation for the Third Reich by stating that no sustained increase in the birthrate was achieved.[142] Even where small increases are apparent, we must keep in mind that statistical analyses of the birthrate actually tell us very little about the success of Nazi pronatalism. The brief rise in the birthrate between 1933 and 1938 (up to 1,349,000 per year from 971,000) can just as easily be attributed to the effects of natural business cycles that were also prevalent in other European countries as to the success of Nazi population policy. The birthrate had, after all, been at a low point in 1933 and would presumably have risen regardless of social policy.[143]

The social impact of these policies, while even more difficult to measure, was certainly more significant. The initial announcement of the marriage loans policy was greeted with enormous public enthusiasm. Applications in the first few months far surpassed expectations. By the spring of 1934, 194,485 loans had been granted across the Reich.[144] In Berlin, the newspapers reported an increased enthusiasm for marriage and credited it to the availability of marriage loans. Both the *Vossische Zeitung* and the *Völkischer Beobachter* proclaimed Berlin an example to the rest of the country, citing 10,251 applications for marriage loans by November 1933.[145] The flood continued into January 1934, with the *Berliner Tageblatt* claiming that twelve thousand couples had applied for loans in the last three months.[146] As we have seen, this enthusiasm waned as the eugenic testing involved became more stringent and known to the general public. Nevertheless, the numbers of voluntary participants cannot be discounted. The enthusiastic public reception of both marriage loans and motherhood crosses certainly helped create feelings of inclusion for those who benefited.[147] As in other times and places, it will always be impossible to make generalized arguments about the population's motivations for having children. But there is certainly enough evidence to suggest that the population

---

[142] Czarnowski, "Frauen – Staat – Medizin," 81.

[143] See Bock, *Zwangssterilisation im Nationalsozialismus*, 142–53

[144] Ibid., 112.

[145] "Ehestandstandsdarlehen in Berlin: Bisher 5000 Anträge bewilligt," *Vossische Zeitung*, 22 November 1933, clipping in FUB Slg Rott, C6(4), Box 10; and "Die heiratsfreudige . . . : Bisher über 10 000 Anträge auf Ehestandsdarlehen," *Völkischer Beobachter*, 22 November 1933, in ibid.

[146] Keine Bedenken beim Ehestandskandidaten . . . ": Heiratslustige vor dem Richterstuhl des Arztes," *Berliner Tageblatt*, 5 January 1934, clipping in ibid.

[147] Weyrather makes this argument about motherhood crosses, and I find it much more convincing than Gisela Bock's insistence (*Zwangssterilisation im Nationalsozialismus*, 142–53) that the crosses had nothing to do with pronatalist policies. Weyrather explicitly takes Bock to task on this point. See *Muttertag und Mutterkreuz*, 151.

was willing to accept the marriage loans and motherhood crosses as a bonus of belonging to the national *Volksgemeinschaft* and as a public reward even when most still continued to think of reproduction as a private act. This valorization of motherhood bore no direct relationship to effective welfare support for families; nor did it likely increase the number of children that a given family was likely to have. But it may well have encouraged some to have children earlier than they had originally planned, and, even more importantly, it likely coaxed them into understanding this act as an expression of national duty.

A similarly lively response followed the implementation of the new marriage laws. The public reception of the Nazi attempt to legitimate social policy through a redefinition of marriage was not, as has occasionally been asserted or implied, universally negative. The collection of private petitions to federal, state, and city governments reveals that many citizens saw the new laws as a means of manipulating social policy for their own ends. Citizens wrote to government demanding that official calls for more healthy German children be supported with improved access to medical care, decreased rents, and better economic conditions.[148] There were also personal appeals to the Führer, asking him to introduce laws that would allow them to better control the marital choices of their children. The tone of these letters, even from the hands of relatively uneducated citizens, proves that Nazi propaganda about the declining birthrate and the need to implement population political laws had reached public consciousness even during the early days of the Third Reich.

What was the popular response to the Soviet pronatalist campaign? Government reports indicated that the population received the decree banning abortion "enthusiastically." Some women who received birth bonuses did write letters to thank Stalin and promised to continue having children.[149] Yet in practice the response of most Soviet women was far from enthusiastic. The ban on abortion led to a huge number of illegal abortions. Commissariat of Health reports in October and November 1936 cited thousands of cases of women hospitalized after poorly performed illegal abortions. Of the 356,200 abortions performed in hospitals in 1937, and 417,600 in 1938, only 10 percent had been authorized, and the rest were incomplete illegal abortions.[150] In response the Soviet government stepped up efforts to identify those who performed illegal abortions and in 1937 arrested and convicted 4,133 abortionists. As the law dictated, those found guilty of performing abortions were sentenced to a minimum of two years in prison.[151] But despite considerable efforts, Soviet

---

[148] See, for example, the letters in BA-B – RMI 1501/26231, Bl., 44–6, 61–3, 70, 77–80, 198.

[149] GARF f. 5446, op. 18a, d. 2753, ll. 15, 22, 26, 35.

[150] GARF f. 5446, op. 18a, d. 2753, l. 85; RGAE f. 1562 s.ch., op. 329, d. 407, ll. 22–5. Another 1937 report noted that the figure of 323,438 cases of incomplete abortions that had to be completed in hospitals in the RSFSR was clear evidence of a mass of underground abortions; GARF f. A-482, op. 29, d. 5, l. 9.

[151] *Sovetskaia iustitsiia*, no. 34 (1936 34), 16; RGAE f. 1562 s.ch., op. 329, d. 407, l. 25; TsMAM f. 819, op. 2, d. 27, ll. 12–15. Those who had performed multiple abortions often received four years' imprisonment or more.

authorities found it difficult to catch underground abortionists, because women who entered hospitals after botched abortions rarely cooperated with police.[152]

The ban on abortion did result in a rise in the birthrate, but this rise was limited and temporary. The birthrate per thousand people rose from 30.1 in 1935, to 33.6 in 1936, to 39.6 in 1937. But in 1938 the birthrate began to decline again, and by 1940, marital fertility for European Russians was below the 1936 level.[153] The enormous social disruption of the purges and mobilization for war in part accounted for the decline of the birthrate beginning in 1938. But even before these disruptions the birthrate had not even approached preindustrialization levels, and evidence on illegal abortions indicates that Soviet women as a whole did not abide by the government's abortion ban. As Soviet authorities had noted in 1920, but then chose to ignore in 1936, the outlawing of abortion only drove women to seek illegal abortions. Repression proved ineffective at raising the birthrate in the long term.

The Second World War produced catastrophic casualties and further depressed fertility, so it is not surprising that during the war and postwar period the Soviet government made renewed efforts to prevent abortions and raise the birthrate. In July 1944 it issued a new family edict that retained the 1936 ban on abortion and made divorce even more difficult and expensive. The new law also ended single mothers' right to sue fathers for child support and in its place granted them state financial assistance.[154] But many women continued to terminate their pregnancies, and in 1945 the Soviet government expressed alarm at the extremely high rate of underground abortions.[155] The Ministry of Health reported that in 1949, 93,597 women had been granted legal abortions for medical reasons, but it estimated that this figure accounted for only 10.4 percent of all abortions – meaning that over eight hundred thousand underground abortions had taken place that year.[156] The Ministry recommended that doctors closely monitor pregnant women (including visiting their homes and forcibly hospitalizing those women suspected of wanting an abortion) as the best way to prevent abortions, but doctors by and large did not engage in this type of policing. Understaffed hospitals and clinics lacked the personnel for home visits and lacked the beds to hospitalize pregnant women. Nor

---

[152] From 1938 to 1940, prosecutions for abortion declined, and despite a rise in convictions in 1941, the criminalization of abortion overall proved to be, in the words of one leading scholar, "a particularly ineffective extension of the criminal law." Peter Solomon, 220–1.

[153] Lorimer, 134; Coale, 16. Fertility in the first quarter of 1938 was substantially below the 1937 level; RGAE f. 1562 s.ch., op. 329, d. 186, l. 5. For further discussion, see Wendy Z. Goldman, *Women, the State, and Revolution: Soviet Family Policy and Social Life, 1917–1936* (New York: Cambridge University Press, 1993), 294–5.

[154] See Greta Louise Bucher, "The Impact of World War II on Moscow Women: Gender Consciousness and Relationships in the Immediate Postwar Period, 1945–1953" (Ph.D. diss., Ohio State University, 1995), 9.

[155] Burton, 281.

[156] Bucher, 236. Oral history interviews conducted by Bucher in Moscow in the early 1990s revealed that most women knew of underground abortionists and that the practice was widespread; 251.

is it clear that doctors would have policed women's pregnancies even if they were able. Some doctors warned that pregnant women would avoid clinics if medical personnel played a policing role, and others even performed illegal abortions themselves.[157] Birth bonuses and the glorification of motherhood also proved ineffective in the fight to prevent abortions and raise the birthrate. The women who received the bonuses were primarily peasant women who already had many children prior to the introduction of monetary incentives. The resources allotted to expand maternity wards and child care were insufficient to improve markedly the lives of mothers. Government priorities continued to focus on heavy industry, while child care systems and communal dining facilities remained woefully underfunded. And given the equally underfunded consumer sector, women had enormous difficulty simply obtaining basic necessities for their children.

One other crucial consideration is women's place in the workforce. As mentioned above, women had been recruited in large numbers into industry during the 1930s, and the official emphasis on motherhood was in no way intended to free women from their obligation to perform "socially useful labor" outside the home. Indeed the Second World War further accelerated women's entrance into industry – women constituted 92 percent of all new workers recruited between 1941 and 1950 – and postwar propaganda continued to stress women's roles as both workers and mothers.[158] Soviet law did allow women up to two months of maternity leave – a fact Stalin took care to stress publicly – but this was only another small inducement for women to have children.[159] The realities of Soviet life saddled women with the double burden of full-time work and uncompensated domestic chores. Soviet leaders wished to exploit both the labor and the childbearing capabilities of the female population, and they proved unwilling, official rhetoric notwithstanding, to assume state responsibility for domestic chores and child raising.[160]

While the war served to advance the goals that Soviet population policy had originally set out to achieve (the integration of mothers into the workforce) it greatly complicated some, though not all aspects of Nazi population policy. It is certainly true that the war provided a cover for genocidal crimes in the East and the maltreatment of slave laborers and others on German soil, drastically increasing the intensity of the regime's violence toward certain groups of clearly defined enemies. This aspect of Nazi population policy has been explored in detail elsewhere and is not the primary focus of the present essay. Keeping this in mind, however, we can also argue that the war limited the reach and decreased the power of various other bureaucracies involved in population

---

[157] Bucher, 238–42; Burton, 289–90.
[158] Bucher, 7, 23.
[159] See Stalin's statement for the resolutions of the 1935 congress of collective farm shock workers, RGASPI f. 17, op. 120, d. 138, l. 85.
[160] For further discussion, see David L. Hoffmann, *Stalinist Values: The Cultural Norms of Soviet Modernity* (Ithaca, NY: Cornell University Press, 2003), chapter 3, 88–117.

management. Leaving aside the obvious fact that wars tend to separate potential fathers from potential mothers, manipulation of individual decision making became more difficult under conditions of extreme understaffing and general social turmoil as the war progressed. Decisions about genetic "value" now tended to be made on a rather ad hoc basis. Local health administrators even began to believe that stringent definitions of genetic fitness previously stipulated for marital health examinations, marriage loans, and other population policies were being relaxed. Although they were admonished by officials from the Reich Ministry of the Interior,[161] it is clear that work in local marital health clinics no longer proceeded entirely according to plan during the war. For one thing, the war drastically increased the daily workload in the genetic health clinics (as a result of a flood of marriage loan applications from soldiers about to leave for the front, and an increase in political pressure to process applications for motherhood service medals) while halving the available personnel, now regularly called into military service or seconded to other duties.[162] Under these conditions, local health offices in Berlin reported that they only had time to track down the most pressing sterilization cases and that the monitoring of "asocials" was now all but impossible.[163] Needless to say, Allied bombing raids in the major cities also destroyed the files necessary to implement these various policies.

These factors clearly limited the scope and breadth of Nazi population policy during the war. Given the increased latitude of local officials to decide which cases were truly "pressing" and which were not, and given the absence of supporting documents, it is likely that the enforcement of strict provisions for positive eugenic measures and the selection of individuals for negative eugenic measures became even more random and less predictable. As the war dragged on and Germany's military position weakened, the façade of a comprehensive system of eugenic controls began to crumble. In September 1944, the Reich Ministry of the Interior informed the chancellery that total war conditions required further restrictions to the sterilization law. Most genetic health courts were shut down as of October 1, 1944, with only one lower court remaining

---

[161] The RMI's Linden wrote to Berlin's genetic health court on 5 Dec. 1939 complaining that too many health offices were taking the August directive as a sign that sterilization policy and the implementation of the marriage law were to all but cease during the war. He instructed Berlin authorities that "the laws should be carried out within the boundaries of the possible." See Linden to Erbgesundheitsgericht, Berlin, 5 Dec. 1939, in LAB, Rep. 12, Acc. 1641, Nr. 246.

[162] See Chef der Sippenamt im RuS. Hauptamt SS, 26 Oct. 1939, in ibid. and Sütterlin "an die Gesundheitsämter," 21 Dec. 1939, in LAB, Rep. 12, Acc. 1641, Nr. 247. See also "Vierteljahres-Bericht April–Juni–Juli–Sept. 1939" signed by Reinhardt, 15 Nov. 1939, in ibid. By 1940, several districts reported that motherhood service medal applications were taking precedence over genetic data collection and other duties. See, for example, the reports from Tempelhof dated 6 September 1940, in ibid.

[163] Ibid.: Kreuzberg, 6 Sept. 1940; Schöneberg, 13 Sept. 1940; and Lichtenberg, 10 Sept. 1940. The Berlin district Horst Wessel, for instance, faced 1,600 unprocessed sterilization cases going back as far as 1934. See Bezirksbürgermeister in Horst Wessel to Oberbürgermeister, 9 May 1939, in ibid.

for each state. Pending cases were to be dropped unless they were "particularly urgent and straight forward."[164]

To sum up, it seems clear that taken as a whole and leaving the case of the Holocaust aside, World War II had quite different effects on the politics of reproduction in Nazi Germany and the Soviet Union. In the Soviet case, the war reinforced the original motivations and goals of these policies, highlighting the increasingly important integration of women into the workforce. In the Third Reich, the most striking effect of the war was to make it increasingly difficult actually to implement the coercive population policies directed at the general population (as opposed to more easily identifiable enemy groups). In neither case did policies geared toward increasing the birthrate actually work.

CONCLUSION

All this leaves us with the puzzling question of whether Nazi and Stalinist regimes had more in common with each other in the sphere of reproductive policies than one or the other of them shared with nontotalitarian regimes. The question cannot be fully answered here, but it must remain in the back of our minds as we attempt to draw conclusions from this comparative analysis. One cannot argue, for instance, that totalitarian systems of government necessarily lead to an intense concern with population policy and/or reproductive policy. While the Nazi case would seem to bear out a connection with totalitarian/utopian ideology and intensified concern with issues of reproduction, closer examination reveals that the concern with marriage and reproduction and the increasingly genocidal nature of Nazi population policy had more to do with the specific racial ideology of the regime than with any peculiarly totalitarian feature. The comparison with the Soviet Union bears out the problems with totalitarianism as an explanatory model in this particular case. It is also only with attention to racial policy that we can understand the seeming contradictions between antinatalist and pronatalist tendencies in Nazi reproductive politics.

In the Soviet case, we find that reproductive policies had much in common with other contemporary examples. Like governments throughout Europe in the interwar period, the Soviet government utilized a combination of propaganda, incentives, and (beginning in 1936) a ban on abortion to try to raise the birthrate. While the rhetoric of Soviet leaders also – as in the Nazi case – depicted reproduction as a matter of each citizen's duty to the state, actual policies remained rather innocuous in comparison with their Nazi counterparts. The Soviet government in no way sought to limit the reproduction of any of its citizens and rejected the eugenic sterilizations practiced not only in Nazi Germany but in Scandinavian countries and the United States. Soviet reproductive policies more closely resembled those of the Catholic countries

---

[164] BA-B – R43 II/722, Bl. 206–9. See order in *Ministerialblatt des Reichs und Preussischen Ministerium des Innern*, Ausgabe B, Nr. 37, 6 Sept. 1944.

of Western Europe – France, Italy, Spain, and Portugal – which also sought to raise the birthrate without limiting the reproduction of those members of society deemed "unfit."

Our conclusions on the issue of the uniqueness of these two cases and the degree to which this particular national comparison is useful are at an admittedly very preliminary stage, but our account certainly suggests the importance of the differences in ideology in shaping reproductive policies in each case. Different ideological goals crucially influenced policy implementation in each case. It mattered, in other words, that Nazis were envisioning a semimystical, racially pure, and eternal *Volkskörper* when they set out to transform how individuals made reproductive and sexual decisions, while the Soviets were chiefly concerned with increasing labor power for the task of socialist construction.

Finally, one might add that much more thought must be given to the comparison of how the respective populations responded to reproductive policies. We have hinted here that both regimes made an effort to depict these policies (even some of the more coercive measures) as positive, legitimizing policies of national cohesion. Coercion was often counteracted or ameliorated through various financial or symbolic rewards, and, at least in the German case, coercive measures directed toward clearly defined "outsiders" served to highlight the insider status of those not affected. But we need to think more about how successful this integrative aspect of reproductive policy was in each case. The Third Reich, despite economic constraints, had more money to give to these programs. On the other hand, the Soviets' acceptance of women's dual function as mothers and workers was at least a realistic appraisal of actual social circumstances and avoided the kind of contradiction between the ideology of feminine domesticity and the reality of widespread female employment faced by Nazi policymakers. Since neither of these regimes succeeded in substantially influencing birthrates, we must go beyond the statistical analyses of traditional demographic history and integrate sociohistorical and sociocultural perspectives to begin to find answers to such questions.

PART II

VIOLENCE

4

State Violence – Violent Societies

Christian Gerlach and Nicolas Werth

COMPARING MASS VIOLENCE – APPROACH AND QUESTIONS

The academic book market certainly does not lack scholarly analyses comparing Nazism and Stalinism, and, many of these analyses address the issue of mass violence, the topic of this essay.[1] The particularly sensitive nature of our topic and the controversial outcomes of past attempts to compare German and Soviet violence require some specific methodological reflections. On this basis, we try to contribute to a new and perhaps more conciliatory approach to the comparative history of violence.

Most existing studies on mass violence focus on the Soviet and German camp systems, usually reducing the great variety of camps to a select "representative" few on each side – namely, the concentration camps and the Gulag.[2] Operated by the SS and the NKVD, respectively, these camp systems appear ideally suited for characterizing – even imagining – the "totalitarian" state. The focus of these studies is primarily on the methods of violence (again, reduced to a select few examples), the intensity or level of violence,[3] the role of the state machinery in such violence, and the ideology upon which each respective state was based.

---

[1] Ian Kershaw and Moshe Lewin, eds., *Stalinism and Nazism: Dictatorships in Comparison* (Cambridge: Cambridge University Press, 1997); Henry Rousso and Nicolas Werth, eds., *Stalinisme et Nazisme: Histoire et Memoires comparees* (Brussels: Complexe, 1999); Dittmar Dahlmann and Gerhard Hirschfeld, eds., *Lager, Zwangsarbeit, Deportation und Verfolgung: Dimensionen der Massenverbrechen in der Sowjetunion und in Deutschland 1933 bis 1945* (Essen: Klartext, 1999).

[2] Gerhard Armanski, *Maschinen des Terrors: Das Lager (KZ und GULAG) in der Moderne* (Münster: Westfälisches Dampfboot, 1993).

[3] Among the more recent approaches Stephen Wheatcroft, "Ausmaß und Wesen der deutschen und sowjetischen Massentötungen und Repressionen," in *Lager, Zwangsarbeit, Deportation und Verfolgung: Dimensionen der Massenverbrechen in der Sowjetunion und in Deutschland 1933 bis 1945*, eds. Ditmar Dahlmann and Gerhard Hirschfeld (Essen: Klartext, 1999), 67–109.

We are grateful to Ulrike Goeken-Haidl, Peter Klein, and Dieter Pohl for their suggestions and support in searching material for this contribution.

For a long time, little scholarly attention was paid to responsible perpetrators and functionaries. As many Soviet archival records have only recently become available, research on German perpetrators is somewhat more fully developed. Yet, even here, our concrete knowledge about perpetrator groups and individuals is sketchy, fragmentary, unbalanced, and still without a solid, agreed-upon theoretical framework.[4] Furthermore, certain subject areas have been woefully neglected: little research has been conducted on German mass exterminations *outside* the Jewish Holocaust and the reasonably well-explored "euthanasia" program, and an overall analysis of the different German policies of extermination within one framework remains to be undertaken.

Recent research into Nazi crimes, however, suggests a potentially profitable alternative approach to the comparison of German and Soviet violence. Four features are particularly characteristic of this research: a focus upon (1) the detailed course of events in specific regions, (2) the political context of events, (3) the ideas and motives of perpetrators, and (4) the utilization of new empirical bases and greater amounts of documentation. Stressing these aspects has resulted in an enhanced understanding of and emphasis upon the realization of violence, rather than upon plans and intentions. In turn, this has provided us with a more nuanced understanding of the balance of power and agency between periphery and center. Indeed, it appears that initiatives from mid- and low-level functionaries and from institutions other than the SS and the police played significantly larger roles in the policies of extermination than previously assumed, whether civil administrations, the ministerial bureaucracy, the military, or the academic intelligentsia. What is particularly stunning is not the dominance or importance of any one specific group, but the diversity of backgrounds, experiences, education, and age groups involved.

Among the topics receiving the most attention are concentration camps, occupation policy, the German military, and the expropriation and so-called aryanization of Jewish property. While a variety of approaches have been utilized, it is noteworthy that these studies generally tend to be complementary rather than contradictory. Gone are the heated controversies of old. Historians have sought to argue "beyond [the theoretical schools of] intentionalism and functionalism," to quote Christopher Browning.[5] The new research is not about discerning the one "true" explanation; it is about elements of explanation. Rather than intellectual confusion, it reflects a new sense of complexity

---

[4] Gerhard Paul, ed., *Die Täter der Shoah: Fanatische Nationalsozialisten oder ganz normale Deutsche*, Dachauer Symposien zur Zeitgeschichte (Göttingen: Wallstein, 2002); Christian Gerlach, ed., *Durchschnittstäter: Handeln und Motivation* (Berlin: Verlag der Buchläden, 2000). To mention just one stunning fact: a scholarly biography of Reinhard Heydrich does not yet exist.

[5] Christopher Browning, "Beyond Intentionalism and Functionalism: The Decision for the Final Solution Reconsidered," in his *The Path to Genocide: Essays on Launching the Final Solution* (Cambridge and New York: Cambridge University Press, 1992), 86–121.

in our understanding of these events. With many non-Nazis among the perse-cutors, the earlier assumed contradiction between ideologues and pragmatists in Nazi Germany appears out of date; instead, differences appear to have been only gradual, and cooperation between authorities more decisive than conflict. An increasing number of scholars further accept that ideology and economy were often mutually reinforcing, rather than opposing, forces. As a result, Ger-man extermination policies can only be regarded as multicausal. Recognizing that a complex of alternatively reinforcing and competing factors and argu-ments resulted in the dynamics of destruction, the long-pursued search for the prioritarian factor appears unnecessary, even counterproductive. The interplay among political, economic, military, and other "pragmatic" motives further questions the distinction often made between "ideological" and "utilitarian" mass extermination in genocide studies.[6] Having begun with an investigation into the Nazi system, historians of Nazi Germany are on their way to under-standing an extremely violent society.

The same can be said of historians investigating Stalinism, although an enor-mous deficit of research on perpetrators, supporters, and bystanders remains. Since the "archival revolution," Soviet historians have gained a solid under-standing of the categories, methods, and magnitude of Soviet violence. No longer is the overall scope or scale of repression debated.[7] This factual basis has produced a more nuanced understanding of Stalinist repression. It now appears not to have been a single phenomenon, not one uniform policy fueled exclusively by ideology, but rather a number of interrelated repressive lines and policies, divergent in scope, character, and intensity; implemented through legal and extralegal means; and aimed at different categories of "enemies." The event historians of Stalinism label "The Great Terror" of 1937–8, for example, is now best understood as the convergence of several phenomena: the outcome of tensions among the Stalinist elite and in center-periphery relations, the culmination of a decade-long radicalization of policies against marginal and "socially harmful" elements, and the result of a growing and specifically "Soviet xenophobia" targeting "diaspora nationalities."[8]

---

[6] This is, for example, acknowledged by Roger Smith, "Pluralismus und Humanismus in der Genozidforschung," in *Genozid und Modern: Strukturen kollektiver Gewalt im 20. Jahrhundert*, eds. Mihran Dabag and Kristin Platt (Opladen: Leske + Budrich, 1998), 309–19, here 310–11 and 313–14, and various contributions in Hans-Lukas Kieser and Dominik J. Schaller, eds., *Der Völkermord an den Armeniern und die Shoah = The Armenian Genocide and the Shoah* (Zurich: Chronos, 2002). But see earlier attempts at typologies like Roger Smith, "Human Destructiveness and Politics: The Twentieth Century as an Age of Genocide," in *Genocide and the Modern Age: Etiology and Case Studies of Mass Death*, eds. Isidor Wallimann and Michael N. Dobkowski (New York: Greenwood Press, 1987), 21–41; also Frank Chalk and Kurt Jonassohn, *The History and Sociology of Genocide: Analyses and Case Studies* (New Haven, CT: Yale University Press, 1990), 12–32.

[7] Let us remember how important this topic, both particularly vulnerable to political passion and unamenable to solution, was just a few years ago.

[8] Sheila Fitzpatrick, ed., *Stalinism: New Directions* (New York: Routledge, 2000).

An empirical and more in-depth approach combined with the necessary – and now possible – contextualization of events will lead historians exploring the repressive and violent dimensions of the Stalinist state and society toward questions that have already been explored by their colleagues working in the field of Nazi Germany, specifically, questions concerning

- Decision-making processes (discussed without the proper documentary basis in the 1970s and 1980s);
- Implementation processes, including the complex interaction between central and local levels; "excesses" and foot dragging, if not overt resistance; and planned operations and improvisation (the example of dekulakization illustrates this point vividly);[9] and
- The public and the secret in the development of repressive policies and mass violence. On the public side, the instrumentalization of social and ethnic tensions, "mobilization techniques," "political theater," public scapegoating campaigns, and social participation. On the secret side, police operations and "hidden transcripts" (for example, transcripts relating to the secret NKVD operations of 1937–8, not designed for circulation or even discussion among midrank Party officials).

Comparative analyses allow us to locate parallel and/or contradictory developments in analogous situations, to explain similarities, and to establish broader historical patterns or identify alternatives. In so doing, historians attempt to avoid overspecialization; they seek to widen their horizons in order to facilitate generalization. Yet, despite the many calls for historical comparison, there remains a gap between the great ambitions driving such scholarship and the resultant work product, a gap often exacerbated by a lack of conceptual reflection. In general, comparative studies tend to focus on a select few variables and factors, to strive toward "macrocausal" explanations, to ask "why" instead of "how," to establish limited contexts, and to seek the effective paradox.[10] It is precisely complexity, multicausal thinking, and broad contextualization which are for structural reasons not the strong points of historical comparisons. In other words, in a comparison, the very achievements of research in

---

[9] See the important collections of documents recently published, *Tragediia sovetskoi derevni (1927–1939)*, eds. V. P. Danilov and L. Viola, 5 vols. (Moscow: ROSSPEN, 1998–2003); *Sovetskaia derevnia glazami VCK, OGPU, NKVD, 1918–1939*, eds. V. P. Danilov and A. Berelowitch (Moscow: ROSSPEN, 1998–2004).

[10] Cf. Deborah Cohen, "Comparative History: Buyer Beware," *Bulletin of the German Historical Institute Washington* 29 (2001): 23–33; the critical reflections of Thomas Welskopp, "Stolpersteine auf dem Königsweg: Methodenkritische Anmerkungen zum internationalen Vergleich in der Gesellschaftsgeschichte," *Archiv für Sozialgeschichte* 35 (1995): 339–67, esp. 341 and 348; and for the state of the art, see Heinz-Gerhard Haupt and Jürgen Kocka, "Historischer Vergleich: Methoden, Aufgaben, Probleme," in *Geschichte und Vergleich: Ansätze und Ergebnisse international vergleichender Geschichtsschreibung*, eds. Haupt and Kocka (Frankfurt, New York: Campus, 1996), 9–45.

our respective fields are in danger of being lost. The problem of working with limited space, of potentially losing empirical ground, or overabstraction and oversimplification suggests that we refrain from an overall comparison of Nazi and Soviet violence and concentrate on case studies instead, however condensed they have to be. Given the described complexities, the model of totalitarianism provides no useful framework to us.

Given the extent of popular participation in the persecution of various victim groups – whether related to plunder, denunciation, professional advancement, or the use of forced labor – it does not seem useful to limit our analysis here to that of "state violence." Recent studies demonstrate, for example, that most Germans who organized or actively participated in mass violence not only were members of various state and parastatal agencies, but actually considered themselves to be functionaries of the state.[11] On the other hand, officials were deliberately given considerable autonomy in the Nazi system. Hence, truly to understand why so many Germans participated in violence we need to go beyond the structure of the state, just as we need to go beyond an exclusive focus on the manifestation of violence.

Rather, we seek to understand Nazi Germany and the Soviet Union as extremely violent societies.[12] They stand as the extreme cases within a group that includes not a few modern and colonial societies: the late Ottoman Empire (1908–23), a number of Eastern European countries within the Nazi-German sphere of influence,[13] Cambodia in the 1970s, Indonesia since 1965,[14] Colombia throughout much of the twentieth century, and the United States of America during the nineteenth century. While the overall levels of violence may have been high in each case, they are in many respects dissimilar. Yet, in each case we can discern that rather than a solitary, uniform system of persecution and

---

[11] For example, this was different from the German violence against the Herero and Nama, 1904 to 1907, in what is today Namibia, where many German nonofficials played important roles. See Jürgen Zimmerer, "Holocaust und Kolonialismus: Beitrag zu einer Archäologie des genozidalen Gedankens," *Zeitschrift für Geschichtswissenschaft* 51, no. 12 (2003): 1098–1119.

[12] Cf. Christian Gerlach, "Extremely Violent Societies: An Alternative to the Concept of Genocide," *Journal of Genocide Research* 8, no. 4 (2006): 455–71.

[13] For instance, in Croatia, mass exterminations were aimed especially at Serbs, Jews, and Gypsies from 1941 to 1945; in "Greater Hungary," aside from Jews, violence, deprivation of rights, oppression, and huge resettlement plans targeted Romanians, Serbs, and Gypsies.

[14] With regard to Cambodia, recent research shows (despite some controversy) that aside from certain social groups ethnic distinctions were very important in the definition of target groups. Cf. Ben Kiernan, *The Pol Pot Regime: Race, Power and Genocide in Cambodia under the Khmer Rouge, 1975–1979* (New Haven, CT: Yale University Press, 1996); for Indonesia, one can point to the anticommunist persecution and pogroms of 1965, the occupation of East Timor (1975–99), collective resettlement from the densely to lesser populated islands, and the violent struggle over autonomy in regions like Aceh and West Papua (Irian Jaya). Researchers have identified a long and deep-rooted tradition of violence. See Freek Colombijn and Thomas J. Lindblad, eds. *Roots of Violence in Indonesia* (Leiden: KILTV, 2002).

violence, a variety of policies and forms of mass violence were utilized against victim groups. Class-related civil war and, often, external conflict were intimately entwined with ethnic strife and selective social policies.

All of this prompts us to ask the question of social participation. Our focus here is on identifying policies enacted against common victim groups within both the German and Soviet systems and the often substantial differences in the type and intensity of the violence inflicted upon the groups in question. It is hoped that such an analysis will help us understand how both political systems and societies generated violence.

Our main questions for each participatory group are, Which interests and attitudes led to violence? Which institutional structures were involved? Which methods of violence were employed and to what extent? What role did public participation, consent, or dissent play? How important was "initiative from below" or impetus from the regions? And, finally, considering the above questions, how can the role of the state best be characterized? In attempting to answer these questions, we compare mass violence against the following groups: so-called "asocials," victims of ethnic resettlement, and prisoners of war during and after the Second World War.

As our analysis focuses upon groups that were subjected to varying types and levels of violence, "comparative genocide research" does not provide a useful conceptual framework. Nor, for that matter, would the creation of a typology or the application of a singular sociological, psychological, or political model appear promising as a starting point. In most of the cases discussed here, the term "genocide" has rarely, if ever, been applied – whether this relates to the mass death of POWs, forced ethnic resettlement, or the persecution of "asocials." Broadly speaking, a common, agreed-upon scholarly definition of "genocide" does not exist – and this arbitrariness is unsurprising, considering that "genocide" is an inherently instrumental term, created and utilized for political purposes and oriented toward the unanimous moral condemnation, prevention if possible, military intervention, and juridical prosecution after a transition of power. Moreover, the concept of "genocide" (for which intentions are central) implies that on a state level long-intended, carefully prepared master plans for destruction exist – a concept that appears too simple, though not entirely wrong, in light of recent research into the dynamics of state-organized mass violence.[15] Often, a comparison of "genocides" leads to endless debates about definitions, about the inclusion and exclusion of cases, and to a race for the more intentional, more original, or more total case. The understanding of "mass violence" applied here is more open and includes forced resettlement, deliberately inadequate supplies, sterilization, forced labor, and excessive imprisonment.

---

[15] For more detail, see Christian Gerlach, "Nationsbildung im Krieg: Wirtschaftliche Faktoren bei der Vernichtung der Armenier und beim Mord an den ungarischen Juden," in *The Armenian Genocide and the Shoah*, eds. Kieser and Schaller (Zürich: Chronos, 2002), 347–422, here 348–52.

CASE STUDIES

"Socially Harmful Elements" in the Soviet Union; "Asocials" in Nazi Germany

The categorization of "socially dangerous" and "socially harmful" elements emerged in the Soviet Union during the early 1930s in the context of forced industrialization, collectivization, and dekulakization. At the time, authorities were particularly concerned with (a) cleansing strategic urban centers, inundated with peasants fleeing collectivization, of "unreliable" and "parasitic" elements; (b) strengthening the state's control over population flows; and (c) reestablishing "order" in a disorderly, "quicksand society." In late 1932, a set of decrees introduced the "passportization"[16] of the urban population. A separate, secret instruction from January 14, 1933,[17] specified the categories of persons to be denied a passport and registration and, thus, to be deprived of the right to live in major Soviet towns: persons "not involved in production or the work of institutions or schools, and that are not engaged in any other form of socially useful work"; kulaks or de-kulakized peasants who had fled the countryside or the "special settlements" to which they had been deported; the rural unemployed who had entered cities without a formal work invitation; "obvious labor shirkers or disorganizers of production"; *lishentsy* (disenfranchised persons);[18] persons with a criminal record; and all family members of persons falling into one of these categories. All of these people were to be expelled from cities subject to the passport regime ("regime cities"). Evidently, they were *not yet* systematically labeled as "socially dangerous." In the following years, however, police authorities tended to use the newly created passport system to carry out increasingly repressive extrajudicial campaigns against an ever-broader range of "expellees." These expellees were no longer subjected solely to a prohibition on living in "regime cities" but, increasingly, were banished to "special settlements" and punished with camp sentences. The social cleansing of major towns and the radicalization of policing practices against such marginal elements – described by the police as *sotsvrednye,* or "socially harmful" – opened the way for even more extreme measures, such as the secret execution quotas introduced during the "Great Terror" of 1937–8. These more extreme measures targeted de-kulakized peasants who had fled their "special

[16] In the following two years, police authorities issued over 12 million passports to residents of so-called "regime locations" (major cities like Moscow, Leningrad, Kharkov, along with border zones and internal areas of strategic importance), in addition to approximately 15 million passports for other urban "nonregime" areas.

[17] GARF, f. 5446, op. 15a, d. 1096, ll. 67–75; Gijs Kessler, "The Passport System and State Control over Population Flows in the Soviet Union, 1932–1940," *Cahiers du Monde russe* 42, no. 2–4 (2001): 477–504.

[18] According to the 1918 Constitution of the RSFSR, seven categories of people were disenfranchised. These categories included "ex-landowners," "ex-nobles," "ex-tsarist high-ranking civil servants," "ex-tsarist policemen," and persons living on private income (traders, shopkeepers, craftsmen). In 1929, there were approximately 3.7 million *lishentsy.*

settlements," ex-convicts, criminals, vagrants, and disenfranchised and other "declassed elements."

In fact, however, the categorization of "socially dangerous" elements appeared long before the political and social upheavals of the 1930s. It was explicitly mentioned, for example, in a March 24, 1924, secret resolution of the USSR Central Executive Committee (TsIK). According to this document, the OGPU "Special Board" was given the right to banish, exile, or expel from the USSR or send to a concentration camp[19] for up to three years several categories of "socially dangerous individuals": people guilty of "state crimes," bandits, counterfeiters, drug dealers, "malicious speculators," as well as "individuals considered socially dangerous in light of past activities, in particular those having two or more past sentences or four arrests for suspicions of crime."[20]

The implication of this text remained limited during the 1920s, despite a number of spectacular police raids in Moscow and Leningrad that were directed against "speculators" and "recidivist thieves."[21] In 1927, for example, only 11,000 "socially dangerous elements" served extrajudicial sentences of banishment, while several thousand more were incarcerated in the Solovki concentration camp.[22]

The situation fundamentally changed after 1930. Between 1930 and 1932, an unprecedented wave of repression and exclusion descended upon alleged "social enemies" in the Soviet Union, especially in the countryside. Over 2 million "kulaks" were deported to Siberia, the Far North, the Urals, and other "inhospitable parts" of the country. Not all acquiesced to their fate, however, and by 1936, over 600,000 "kulaks" had fled the "special settlements" to which they had been assigned. Governmental authorities considered these insubordinate masses of socially marginal elements to be a major breeding ground for crime and deviance.

Forced collectivization and dekulakization, in conjunction with the economic devastation wrought by the 1932–3 famine, only served to swell further the ranks of those considered socially marginal. Poverty, starvation, and death produced armies of vagrants and beggars, abandoned children, and orphans that thronged toward the Soviet Union's major cities. With few options available, they often joined street gangs and engaged in acts of petty theft and

---

[19] In the 1920s, the term "concentration camp" was used for the camps run by the OGPU (the Solovki camps and the Suzdal' special camp). The term "corrective labor camp" would be used only after 1929–30.

[20] A. I. Kokurin and N. V. Petrov, *Lubianka, 1917–1960. Spravochnik* (Moscow: Iz. Mezhdunarodnyi Fond Demokratiia, 1997), 179–81.

[21] On May 4, 1926, F. Dzherzhinskii sent to G. Iagoda an ambitious program aimed at "cleansing Moscow from all its speculators, thieves, parasites." These people were to be sent to "inhospitable parts" of the USSR (RGASPI, 76/3/390/3–4).

[22] Paul M. Hagenloh, "'Socially Harmful Elements' and the Great Terror," in *Stalinism: New Directions*, ed. Sheila Fitzpatrick (London and New York: Routledge, 2000), 289; S. A. Krasil'nikov, *Na izlomakh sotsial'noi struktury: Marginaly v postrevoliutsionnom rossiiskom obshchestve* (Novosibirsk: Novosibirskii gos. universitet, 1998), 49.

criminality in order to survive. The "anticapitalist" revolution of 1929–30, a revolution that aimed to eradicate private trade and enterprise, ironically served to exacerbate the problem of social marginalization, as well. After all, former traders and businessmen knew little else than to "speculate" (that is, to buy and resell scarce consumer goods), and this activity too would soon be considered "socially harmful" and subject to legal prosecution.

In 1933, the regime responded to what it considered social chaos in the cities and countryside by ordering vast police sweeps and large-scale operations against targeted groups that resulted in the immediate expulsion of problematic and marginal elements. In April 1933, police in Moscow and Leningrad arrested over 6,000 "socially harmful elements" and deported them to Tomsk. Upon arrival in Tomsk, they were transferred to barges and unloaded, without food or tools, on a desert island situated at the junction of the Ob and Nazina Rivers. Within a few weeks over 4,000 had died of hunger and exhaustion.[23] In July 1933, police raids in Moscow led to the arrest of over 5,000 Gypsies and their deportation to "special settlements" in Western Siberia.[24] In December of the same year, the Politburo instructed the OGPU to deport "beggars and declassed elements" to "special settlements" and labor camps.[25] Several months later, the Politburo launched a campaign against "speculators" and the "unemployed gathering in markets," resulting in the arrest, deportation, or expulsion of over 113,000 persons in 1934 alone.[26] Large-scale operations against "speculators" would continue over the following years. Indeed, directives signed by top officials (Stalin or Molotov) provided guidance figures for the number of "speculators" to be arrested and processed via extrajudicial procedures.[27] From 1935 on, hooligans too were identified as "socially harmful elements" and were subject to extrajudicial sentencing through special police *troika*, three-man boards set up specifically to address *sotsvrednye*. In 1935, police operations rounded up 160,000 homeless and juvenile delinquents, many of whom were sent to NKVD youth labor colonies.[28] By the mid-1930s, many of these "socially harmful elements" had received sentences of up to five years' confinement in the camp system. Police *troiki* sentenced 120,000 "socially harmful elements" in 1935 and 140,000 in 1936. In 1939, *sotsvrednye* formed the second largest group among Gulag inmates (285,000,

---

[23] S. Krasil'nikov and V. P. Danilov, eds., *Spetspereselentsy v Zapadnoi Sibiri, 1933–1938*, vol. 3 (Novosibirsk: "EKOR", 1994), 89–99.

[24] GARF, f. 9479. op. 1, d. 19, l. 7. This operation seems to have been better organized, the deported being settled upon arrival in barracks and given some tools and food to start "working in the fields."

[25] RGASPI, f. 17, op. 162, d 15, l. 161. In 1934, over 13,000 "professional beggars" were deported from Moscow.

[26] Hagenloh, 294.

[27] See, for example, the joint government-Party directive of July 19, 1936, ordering the arrest of 5,000 "socially harmful speculators" in Moscow, Leningrad, Kiev, and Minsk; David Shearer, "Social Disorder, Mass Repression and the NKVD during the 1930s," *Cahiers du Monde russe* 42, no. 2–4 (2001): 526.

[28] Ibid.

or approximately 22 percent of the total inmate population), second only to "counterrevolutionaries" (445,000, or approximately 35 percent).[29]

As a result of the regime's efforts to restore order to its major cities, a permanent stratum of social outcasts and expellees emerged. Yet, even under the watchful eye of the police, NKVD officials lamented that only a small portion of these "socially harmful" elements were "properly isolated"; the majority of them, those temporarily expelled or deported, remained ongoing causes of public disorder. Accordingly, by 1937, formerly "socially harmful" individuals were reclassified as potentially dangerous elements on the basis of allegations that they harbored "anti-Soviet" and "counter-revolutionary" sentiments and that they were the source of "all sorts of diversionary crimes." The "mass operations" of the summer of 1937, launched in accordance with NKVD Order 00447 ("Concerning the Punishment of Former Kulaks, Criminals and Other Anti-Soviet Elements"), served as the final and most radical stage in the campaign against "socially harmful elements." Significantly, several of the regions specifically targeted by Order 00447 – that is, those with the highest "quotas in the first or second categories,"[30] such as Western Siberia, the Southern Urals, the Far East, and the Azov-Black Sea Territory – were precisely those regions that possessed the largest concentration of deportees, expellees and social outcasts previously driven out of the "passportized areas."

At the present state of research our knowledge of the 767,000 persons repressed in the course of the 00447 operations[31] (of which half were executed) remains quite fragmentary. Who exactly were these "socially harmful elements," targeted and marginalized, catalogued by the police when denied a passport and often simply arrested in markets and at railway stations as local NKVD authorities sought to fulfill – and overfulfill – their quotas?[32] The first and largest group included so-called "ex-kulaks" "who [had] returned home, [had] escaped labor settlements, [and] who [carried] out anti-soviet activities." A second group comprised "criminals – bandits, robbers, recidivist thieves, professional contraband smugglers, [and] cattle thieves – who [carried out] illegal activities or who [were] associated with the criminal underworld." A third group included a wide range of social and political outcasts, such as "members of anti-Soviet parties, former Whites, former tsarist

[29] J. A. Getty, G. T. Rittersporn, and V. Zemskov, "Les victimes de la répression pénale dans l'URSS d'avant-guerre," *Revue des Etudes Slaves* 65/IV (1993): 631–43.

[30] People in the "first category" were to be "immediately arrested and, after consideration of their case by troiki, shot." People ascribed to the "second category" were "subject to arrest and to confinement in camps for a term ranging from 8 to 10 years." Numbers of "former kulaks" and "criminals" to be shot or sent to camps were presented by regional party and NKVD authorities and approved by the Politburo. Order 00447 was first published in *Trud*, no. 88, June 4, 1992. English translation in J. Arch Getty and Oleg V. Naumov, eds., *The Road to Terror* (London and New Haven, CT: Yale University Press, 2000), 473–80.

[31] Lasting from August 1937 to November 1938, the 00447 operations were the largest of the dozen or so secret "mass operations" of the "Great Terror."

[32] P. Hagenloh, op. cit.; D. Shearer, op. cit.; N. Werth, "Repenser la Grande Terreur en URSS, 1937–1938," *Le Débat*, no. 122 (November/December, 2002): 118–39.

policemen and functionaries, re-émigrés, sectarian activists, church officials and others ... who [were] hiding from punishment or [had] escaped from places of confinement and continue[d] to carry out anti-soviet activities." Regional and local studies, which have only just begun to emerge on the topic of NKVD Order 00447, confirm that most victims belonged to the categories of social outcasts.[33]

Subsequent to the burst of radicalization under Order 00447, repression against social outcasts and marginals continued, but at more moderate levels. Yet, even during the war, large-scale police sweeps were occasionally launched in major towns. Police reports note, however, that the task of extracting "socially harmful elements" was becoming increasingly difficult, as marginals and social outcasts mixed with and merged into the masses of deportees and evacuees.[34]

During the immediate postwar years, police authorities, alarmed by the high level of social disorder and petty criminality, once again systematically purged the principal "regime cities" of "antisocial and parasitic elements" (these terms had, by then, replaced the label "socially harmful"). Exploiting the widespread sense of insecurity and the general desire for "order," police authorities increasingly relied upon night patrols that comprised demobilized soldiers, networks of voluntary "police assistance groups," and superintendents and doorkeepers to round up "violators of the passport regime," vagrants, beggars, the homeless, and other marginals. By the end of 1946, the "passport departments" of the regular police claimed to have received the "assistance" of over 560,000 voluntary and auxiliary persons. The participation of such auxiliaries, however, was broadly considered to be "ineffective" and "unprofessional." In 1946, they accounted for less than 15 percent of all alleged "passport violators" (all the same, 15 percent represents 230,000 alleged violators).[35] During 1947, as poverty and famine spread over much of the postwar country, the number of vagrants, beggars, homeless, and other marginal individuals skyrocketed.[36] During that year, over 500,000 "violators of the passport regime" were expelled from "regime cities;" and over 50,000 were sentenced to forced labor as "malicious violators of the passport regime," "antisocial elements," "parasites," and "persons not engaged in any form of socially useful work."[37]

---

[33] See, for example, for Smolensk, R. Manning, "Massovaia operatsiia protiv kulakov i prestupnykh elementov," in *Stalinizm v rossiiskoi provintsii: Smolenskie arkhivnye dokumenty v prochtenii zarubezhnykh istorikov*, ed. E. V. Kodin (Smolensk: SGPU 1999), 230–54; for Tatarskaia ASSR, see A. Stepanov, "Provedenie kulatskoï operatsii v Tatarii," in *Kak Terror stal "Bolshim,"* eds. Marc Junge and Rolf Binner (Moscow: Airo-XX, 2003), 260–321.

[34] See, for example, NKVD Order no. 001693 (December 17, 1941), "On the Cleansing of the City of Kuibyshev of Its Socially Harmful Elements."

[35] GARF, f. 9415, op. 3, d. 1419.

[36] According to police sources, there were over 2 million beggars in 1947. See V. F. Zima, *Golod v SSSR 1946–1947 godov: Proiskhozhdenie/ Posledstviia* (Moscow: In-t rossiiskoi istorii, 1996), 217.

[37] GARF, f. 9415, op. 3, d. 1429.

The highest state authorities actively promoted this policy: in February 1947, a secret government resolution "authorized" the MVD in Moscow to arrest 5,000 "antisocial elements" within a two-month period. Processed via extra-judicial procedures, they were sentenced to exile or sent to camps. In 1948, 1949, and 1951, an array of secret governmental resolutions ordered the fur-ther intensification of police measures against beggars and vagrants, many of whom were war invalids.[38]

In Germany, too, a rather vaguely defined set of social subgroups was accused of deviant behavior and persecuted as "asocials." After 1939, they were categorized as *Gemeinschaftsfremde* and *Gemeinschaftsunfähige*, "alien to the community" and "socially unfit," respectively. Experts with the regime, however, criticized the lack of a common definition for "asocial." In order to differentiate between those "alien" to society and those only temporarily "alienated" from it as a result of adverse conditions, they defined "asocial-ness" as a biologically determined condition. Yet, the term remained quite arbitrary: among those groups included under the label "asocial" were beg-gars, tramps, and vagabonds; the homeless; "idlers;" people who lived off public welfare for long periods; the "work-shy," those who refused to work, and, during the Second World War, persons with records of poor work perfor-mance; alcoholics unable to work; persistent criminal offenders; "roughnecks;" "grousers;" "psychopaths"; prostitutes, pimps, and persons with unconven-tional sexual tendencies; hard-nosed traffic offenders; men who failed to pay alimony or child support; persons unable to maintain a respectable household or to educate their children; and *asoziale Großfamilien* (large families from the lower strata of society).[39]

There was often little definitional distinction between "asocials" and other persecuted groups, such as Gypsies, criminals, homosexuals, and the mentally disabled. Moreover, the term "asocial" was often simply used as a reinforcing epithet for groups already targeted for other reasons. For example, one might find reference to an "asocial Gypsy" or an "asocial Jew" – a somewhat prob-lematic description in that it makes it virtually impossible to determine whether or not a person was persecuted or killed as an "asocial" or as a member of some other category. This remains the case despite the fact that, in concentra-tion camps, "asocials" were forced to wear a distinctive black triangle on their

---

[38] A large proportion (over 40 percent) of the "beggars" arrested in 1951–2 were war invalids (V. Zima, 220–2).

[39] Wolfgang Ayaß, *"Asoziale" im Nationalsozialismus* (Stuttgart: Klett-Cotta, 1995), 105–6, 106–13; Lisa Pine, *Nazi Family Policy, 1933–1945* (Oxford and New York: Berg, 1997), 117–23; Ayaß, "'Asoziale': die verachteten Verfolgten" in *Verfolgung als Gruppenschicksal*, eds. Wolfgang Benz and Barbara Distel (Dachau: Verlag Dachauer Hefte, 1998), 50–66, here 51–3; Martin Broszat, "Konzentrationslager," in *Anatomie des SS-Staates*, vol. 2, 4th ed., ed. Hans Bocheim (Munich: Deutscher Taschenbuch Verlag, 1984), 9–135, here 70–1 and 76–7; Ernst Klee, ed., *"Euthanasie" im NS-Staat: die "Vernichtung lebensunwerten Lebens"* (Frankfurt am Main: Fischer, 1986), 356–7; Klaus Scherer, *"Asozial" im Dritten Reich: die vergessenen Verfolgten* (Münster: VOTUM Verlag, 1990), 48–56.

uniform to differentiate them from criminals (who donned green triangles), homosexuals (pink), Gypsies (brown or, often, also black), and Jews (marked with an additional yellow triangle). Within the camps, there was little group solidarity between the socially diverse "asocials," and they enjoyed little respect from other groups of prisoners.[40]

Interestingly, pressure for more rigorous policies against the above-mentioned groups, including policies of internment sterilization, long preceded the Nazi assumption of power in 1933. The historical record amply demonstrates that welfare officials, medical doctors, and political parties had been discussing precisely such repressive policies and regulations well back into the nineteenth century; and, after the First World War, the German state actively began to extend its influence over labor markets by trading welfare provisions for increased control.[41] In this light, new steps, such as a September 1933 police raid on beggars that netted more than 10,000 individuals, only continued and radicalized previous tendencies. Yet, throughout much of the 1930s, everyday measures against "asocials" remained relatively mild and were generally confined to threats, registration, compulsory work, exclusion from welfare payments, communally organized interment in labor houses (*Arbeitshäuser*), camps for compulsory work (*Pflichtarbeitslager*), or homes for vagabonds (*Wanderhöfe*).[42]

From 1938 on, however, these relatively mild forms of internment were replaced by mass imprisonment in concentration camps. "Operation Work-Shy in the Reich," which specifically targeted unemployed men considered fit for work and resulted in the arrest of over 12,000 people, was one of the initial steps in the radicalization of policy toward "asocials." The restructuring of the concentration camp system (until early 1940, "asocials" constituted the largest group of prisoners) and the related recruitment of forced labor in the camps for construction projects were major factors in the radicalization of policy, especially considering that full employment in the economy had been reached.

While many sick and disabled were in fact arrested, it was, perhaps, the intimidation of those spared that represented the key objective – and not only

---

[40] Ayaß, *Asoziale*, 169.

[41] Horst Kahrs, "Die ordnende Hand der Arbeitsämter: Zur deutschen Arbeitsverwaltung 1933 bis 1939," in *Arbeitsmarkt und Sondererlaß: Menschenverwertung, Rassenpolitik und Arbeitsamt*, ed. Wolf Grüner (Berlin: Rotbuch Verlag, 1990), 9–61, in particular 11–19, 41–3; Klee, 29–33, 36–43; Patrick Wagner, *Volksgemeinschaft ohne Verbrecher: Konzeption und Praxis der Kriminalpolizei in der Zeit der Weimarer Republik und des Nationalsozialismus* (Hamburg: Christians, 1996), 19–189; Claudia Brunner, *Frauenarbeit im Männerstaat: Wohlfahrtspflegerinnen im Spannungsfeld kommunaler Sozialpolitik in München 1918–1938* (Pfaffenweiler: Centaurus, 1994).

[42] Ayaß, *Asoziale*, 20–32, 41–104, 118–23. In Bavaria alone, 16,000 people had been interned in the *Wanderhöfe* at different times by 1940. See also Götz Aly and Karl Heinz Roth, *Die restlose Erfassung: Volkszählen, Identifizieren, Aussondern im Nationalsozialismus* (Berlin: Rotbuch Verlag, 1984), especially 105–9.

of this particular operation.[43] This claim is supported by the following parallel developments. As the Nazi labor administration centralized its organization in 1935–6,[44] employment offices simultaneously intensified the registration of and restrictions placed on the unemployed; similarly, when the Nazi welfare agency, Winterhilfswerk, became a permanent organization in 1937–8, it curtailed its services and raised its definitional hurdle for vulnerability – this, despite the fact that funding for the organization actually increased. No longer was it the agency's *sole* objective to ameliorate the sufferings of all citizens impacted by the Great Depression. Biology mattered, as well. Indeed, starting in 1933, individuals could receive support only with an acceptable genetic certificate.[45]

Between 1935 and 1938, a new approach gained favor with the police – an approach based upon the racist belief that certain individuals and families were biologically degenerate and, thus, predetermined to exhibit deviant behavior, including shying away from work. In accordance with this perspective, police work shifted from the "fight against enemies" to that of "racial control" (*generelle Rassenprävention*).[46] "Asocials," however, continued to be arrested. In 1942 and 1943, large operations led to the transfer of 12,000 "asocial" prisoners from German jails to concentration camps and the arrest of "asocial" Poles residing in the General Government.[47] Not only did "asocials" suffer from the camp system's already high mortality rates, but they were further targeted in the course of the 1941 "Operation 14f13" (euthanasia) killings, which resulted in the murder of sick camp prisoners, and in the general euthanasia killing program. Still others met their fate in the mass murder of Gypsies

---

[43] Wolfgang Ayaß, "Ein Gebot der nationalen Arbeitsdisziplin: Die Aktion 'Arbeitsscheu Reich' 1938," in *Feinderklärung und Prävention: Kriminalbiologie, Zigeunerforschung und Asozialenpolitik* (Berlin: Rotbuch, 1988), especially 63, 67–70; idem, *Asoziale*, 139–65; Wagner, *Volksgemeinschaft*, 279–92; Karin Orth, *Das System der nationalsozialistischen Konzentrationslager* (Hamburg: Hamburger, 1999), 48–53; Broszat, "Nationalsozialistische Konzentrationslager," 77–78, 93; cf. Timothy Mason, *Social Policy in the Third Reich: The Working Class and the "National Community,"* trans. John Broadwin (Providence, RI: Berg, 1993), 185–95.

[44] Kahrs, "Die ordnende Hand," esp. 36–7; Andreas Kranig, *Lockung und Zwang: Zur Arbeitsverfassung im Dritten Reich* (Stuttgart: Deutsch Verlags-Anstalt, 1983), 153–7.

[45] Herwart Vorländer, *Die NSV: Darstellung und Dokumentation einer nationalsozialistischen Organisation* (Boppard am Rhein: H. Boldt, 1988), 54, 60–1; Peter Hammerschmidt, *Die Wohlfahrtsverbände im NS-Staat: Die NSV und die konfessionellen Verbände (Caritas und Innere Mission) im Gefüge der Wohlfahrtspflege des Nationalsozialismus* (Opladen: Leske + Budrich, 1999), 397–407.

[46] Ulrich Herbert, "Von der Gegnerbekämpfung zur rassischen Generalprävention': 'Schutzhaft' und Konzentrationslager in der Konzeption der Gestapo-Führung 1933–1939," in *Die nationalsozialistischen Konzentrationslager: Entwicklung und Struktur*, eds. Ulrich Herbert, Karin Orth, and Christoph Dieckmann (Göttingen: Wallstein, 1998), 60–86; Wagner, *Volksgemeinschaft*, 254–98.

[47] Broszat, "Konzentrationslager," 125; Helmut Krausnick, "Judenverfolgung," in *Anatomie des SS-Staates* (Munich: Deutscher Taschenbuch Verlag, 1999), 233–366, here 320 and 358; Klee, 358–63.

and criminals.[48] It must be noted, however, that gaping holes remain in our knowledge of the practices of repression between 1940 and 1945.

In 1940, an additional category of camp emerged in Germany: "labor education camps." In total, two hundred such Gestapo-run camps were built, with a capacity for approximately 40,000 inmates. It was in these camps that many "work-shy" and those with substandard work performance served their time. Internment lasted up to eight weeks (although inmates were often subsequently sent to concentration camps) and aimed to shock prisoners with brutal work and living conditions. Employers, meanwhile, knew that there was a strong likelihood that their employees would return after only a relatively short period of absence. While these camps complemented the campaigns against deviants, their main target was industrial workers already employed, not the outcasts, homeless, or unemployed. The primary responsibility for addressing the latter remained with the criminal police – at least officially.[49]

In reality, actions targeting "asocials" were hardly confined to the police; rather, violence against "asocials" in Nazi Germany was very much shaped by the networking between public and private welfare institutions, labor officials, medical doctors, the criminal police, and the Gestapo. Despite the fact that principal authority lay with the criminal police, for example, the Gestapo often interfered in police operations. Officials in welfare bureaus and *Wanderer (vagrant)* welfare houses submitted their own recommendations and proposals regarding the arrest of certain individuals and groups and, not infrequently, recommended concentration camp imprisonment and sterilization. Some labor offices and welfare bureaus went so far as to maintain their own card indices and operate their own internment camps. The National Socialist People's Welfare Organization (NSV) denounced individuals as well. At the local level, communal authorities invested tremendous energy in the cleansing of their cities of "asocials."[50] Indeed, the impetus for ever-more radical measures against "asocials" resulted primarily from local and regional pressures. Without all of these competing pressures, individual arrests and mass raids by the police would most certainly have yielded smaller results. At this

---

[48] See the dispute about how many "asocials" were targeted in "operation 14f13" between Walter Grode, *Die Sonderbehandlung 14f13' in den Konzentrationslagern des Dritten Reiches* (Frankfurt am Main: P. Lang, 1987), especially 87, and Orth, *System*, 114–21; cf. Götz Aly, "Medizin gegen Unbrauchbare," in *Aussonderung und Tod: Die klinische Hinrichtung der Unbrauchbaren* (Berlin: Rotbuch, 1987), 9–74, here 34–56.

[49] Gabriele Lotfi, *KZ der Gestapo: Arbeitserziehungslager im Dritten Reich* (Stuttgart: Deutsche Verlags-Anstalt, 2000), in particular 89, 117 and 216; Ayaß, *Asoziale*, 177–9.

[50] Ayaß, "Gebot," 45, 49–51, 62–3, 65; Ayaß, *Asoziale*, 57–104 (for communally run camps, 100–2, 123–37); Pine, *Nazi Family Policy*, 128–46; for officials from different levels within the Welfare Bureau in Munich, Claudia Brunner, "'Fürsorgeempfänger wurden ausgemerzt': Die Sozialpolitik des Münchner Wohlfahrtsamtes am Ende der Weimarer Republik und in der frühen NS-Zeit," in *Durchschnittstäter*, ed. Christian Gerlach (Berlin: Verlag der Büchladen, 2000), 53–72; Kahrs, "Die ordnende Hand," 31; many telling examples in Klee, 30–3, 54–6, 345–56; cf. Wagner, *Volksgemeinschaft ohne Verbrecher*.

time, however, there is not yet sufficient evidence to determine adequately the
extent to which the German public, broadly considered, consented to such
violence. Current research seems to indicate that the majority of denunciations
originated from official rather than private channels.

Because of the rather nebulous definition of the term, it is impossible to
determine precisely how many people were arrested or murdered as "asocials"
and how many of them were released from concentration camps.[51] The most
convincing estimate to date is that 63,000 to 82,000 "criminals" or "asocials" were imprisoned in concentration camps between 1933 and 1945. Of
these, 26,000 to 34,000 did not survive the war. Included in these figures
were an estimated two-thirds of approximately 20,000 "criminals" interned
in concentration camps who did not return alive. Relatively few Gypsies, it
appears, were marked as "asocials."[52] These figures, however, do not reflect
other forms of persecution. Accordingly, it seems reasonable to approximate
that some 100,000 "asocials" and criminals were imprisoned in camps or sentenced to death, and that 50,000 of them did not survive the Nazi era. The
majority of the latter fell victim to the euthanasia program, perished in the
concentration camps, or died in the Gestapo's "labor education camps."

That having been said, the overall degree of violence inflicted against "asocials" in Nazi Germany was much lower than that in the Soviet Union. In fact,
abundant evidence suggests that, in Germany, intimidation and deterrence were
as instrumental as the arrests themselves. And, it was precisely the shifting definition of "asocials" that proved so useful in increasing public pressure for
conformity. Often, police measures against the "asocial" were publicized in
the German press. The criminal police published novels and tracts, some of
which were widely circulated, articulating the eugenic view that their officers
were "doctors for the social body."[53] If the absolute level of violence required
to restore social order in the wake of the Great Depression and to construct
the new Nazi social order is considered substantial, but relatively low compared to Soviet standards, this is a consequence of the Nazi logic of integration
and exclusion. Experts and official surveys suggested that only relatively few
people could not be reintegrated productively in society. Note that most of

---

[51] See for releases Ayaß, "Gebot," 61–6.

[52] Wagner, *Volksgemeinschaft*, 9, 333, 343 (according to a speech of Himmler in October 1943,
70,000 of 110,000 German non-Jews arrested at different times in concentration camps were
"asocials" and criminals, the rest of the 40,000 political opponents). Cf. Nikolaus Wachsmann,
"'Annihilation through Labor': The Killing of State Prisoners in the Third Reich," in *Journal of
Modern History* 71, no. 3 (1999): 624–59, here 649–50. Michael Zimmermann, *Rassenutopie
und Genozid: Die nationalsozialistische "Lösung der Zigeunerfrag"* (Hamburg: Christians,
1996), 118–19, suggests that 10 percent or less of the "asocials" in concentration camps were
Gypsies. For foreign forced workers inside the Reich and inhabitants of the German-occupied
areas, no data are available even for an educated guess.

[53] Ayaß, *Asoziale*, 30, 10; Ayaß, "Gebot," 51; Kahrs, "Die ordnende Hand," 51; Robert Gellately,
Hingeschaut und weggesehen: Hitler und sein Volk, trans. Holger Fliessbach (Stuttgart and
Munich: Deutsche Verlags-Anstalt, 2002), 60, 108, 132–8; for press reports see ibid., 94–8,
114–15; for the novels Wagner, *Volksgemeinschaft*, 9 and 409, note 5.

the 10 million who lived off public welfare in 1933 were reintegrated into the labor market after some months or years without personal repression. The labor offices and the Reich Labor Service became involved only when they felt the need to reeducate people or to get them accustomed to hard work. Only a minor portion of tramps in 1933 were actually considered "asocial," and, in 1937, of 215,000 persons with limited fitness for use in the labor market, only 6.6 percent were classified as having "flaws in personality" and only 2.4 percent were categorized as "work-shy."[54]

The fact that years of efforts to pass a "law against those alien to the community" (*Gemeinschaftsfremdengesetz*) met with no success indicates that the regime was careful to limit who was to be persecuted as "asocial." The law would have resulted in the regulation of policy against "asocials" and the legalization and expansion of measures already taken by the police. According to the law, the criminal police would have been able to determine whether "asocials" should be placed in concentration camps. Many would undoubtedly have been sterilized. Plans were even included for regular executions of persistent offenders. In essence, the objections made (at different times) by the Reich Ministries of Justice and of Agriculture, the head of the Nazi Party's Justice Bureau, Hans Frank, Propaganda Minister Goebbels, and Hitler centered on the sense of lawlessness, the fear that political worries would spread among the German population, and that too much power would be accorded the SS and police in the arena of social policy.[55] Earlier attempts to introduce a Custody Law (*Bewahrungsgesetz*), demanded by welfare experts since the 1920s, that would intern persons selected by public welfare authorities were equally futile. While the rules envisioned by advocates of the law were ultimately surpassed by the reality of post-1938 Nazi Germany,[56] it can be assumed that the "law against those alien to the community" would have resulted in more than just the legalization of existing practice, for legal authorization may very well have led to new dynamics of violence.[57]

In a way, the persecution of "asocials" in Nazi Germany can be viewed as another example of the vast gap between intention and reality that accompanied Nazi violence, particularly if one takes into account estimates of police and other experts that there were 1.0 to 1.6 million "asocials" in Germany.[58] It appears that many politicians considered the actual level of repression and the extant apparatus and legal framework to be sufficient, at least during the war – this, despite their ideological conviction that being "asocial" was

---

[54] Brunner, "'Fürsorgeempfänger,'" 55–6; Klee, 39; Kahrs, "Die ordnende Hand," 43–6, 49; Kiran Patel, *Soldaten der Arbeit: Arbeitsdienste in Deutschland und in den USA, 1933 bis 1945* (Göttingen: Vandenhoeck & Ruprecht, 2003).

[55] Wagner, "Gesetz," 75–99; Ayaß, *Asoziale*, 202–9; Gellately, *Hingeschaut*, 148.

[56] Ayaß, *Asoziale*, 14–18, 88–100.

[57] This point is discussed in ibid., 208, and Ralph Giordano, *Wenn Hitler den Krieg gewonnen hätte: Die Pläne der Nazis nach dem Endsieg* (Hamburg: Rasch & Röhring, 1989), 200–13.

[58] Wagner, *Volksgemeinschaft*, 375; quote: Heinrich Wilhelm Kranz, Professor of Race Cultivation at the University of Gießen, in a statement of 1940, Klee, 177.

a racial-biological condition.[59] Another interpretation, of course, is that for some – for example, criminalists – a society purged of "genetically determined criminal and deviant German citizens" remained a "vision for the future."[60] In any case, an official overall plan for the persecution of "asocials" was never adopted.[61] The centralization of repressive machinery that occurred around 1938 remained limited, and only in some regions – regions with particularly "eager" authorities – were card indices of "asocial" persons expanded.[62]

Perhaps more than in the Soviet case, German violence against "asocials" aimed at establishing social discipline and was based on a diverse spectrum of societal values regarding labor, crime, family, and sexuality.[63] Control over the labor market was also a critical factor in Germany, especially when one considers mass raids on persons deemed "asocial." Many "asocials" were arrested for labor-related "offenses." Yet, the main Nazi objective, at least domestically, was not to mobilize labor by throwing as many "asocials" as possible into camps. Rather, it was to enhance labor discipline among "free" German workers through the pressure to conform. The same, of course, did not apply to foreigners, who were forced to work one way or another. Radically violent responses to "labor contract offenses" (there were 30,000 such offenses in each month of 1943) included internment in concentration and labor education camps.

The key difference that emerges when comparing the cases of persecution between "asocials" and "socially harmful elements" is the magnitude of violence, which, in turn, suggests that violence served different purposes. Both political systems responded to extreme socioeconomic crisis with intense repression. In the Soviet Union, social discipline was restored by employing the most violent of methods: repressing the uprooted, declassed, and the marginalized. This holds in Germany, as well – although, here, property offenses increased much less markedly after 1929 than Nazi (and public) perception suggests.[64] Many of the groups persecuted in both countries were also identical: the homeless, criminals, prostitutes, and so on. The registration of such groups also played an important role in both states. In Germany, too, there were quotas for the arrest of "asocials," at least in some instances.[65] Forced labor was also a common means of punishment. And, at some point, "asocials" or "socially harmful elements" represented a major, if not the largest, segment of inmates within the concentration camp and Gulag systems (for example, in 1938–9).

---

[59] For the latter point, Herbert, "Von der Gegnerbekämpfung," 74.

[60] Wagner, *Volksgemeinschaft*, 375.

[61] Ayaß, *Asoziale*, 219–20.

[62] Ibid., 110–12 and 224–5.

[63] This argument has already been stressed by Detlev Peukert, *Volksgenossen und Gemeinschaftsfremde: Anpassung, Ausmerze und Aufbegehren unter dem Nationalsozialismus* (Cologne: Bund-Verlag, 1982).

[64] Wagner, *Volksgemeinschaft*, 30–8 and 214–19.

[65] Gellately, *Hingeschaut*, 142, for "operation work-shy in the Reich."

In both cases, violence against "asocials" was related to both restoring social order *and* creating a new social order. But, while the latter aspect was of minor importance in Nazi Germany, change was central to Soviet society. It was less the capacity of the Nazi state to implement social policy measures than the ability of an already industrial society to reintegrate itself that marked the decisive difference with the Soviet Union, hence the lower levels of actual violence. The USSR, a developing economy undergoing rapid, forced industrialization and confronted with mass internal migration, proved incapable of integrating its millions of uprooted and impoverished other than by extreme violence. Given that the persecution of "socially harmful elements" represented a significant proportion of internal Soviet violence (unlike in Germany), it seems justified to label this sort of mass violence "developmental" violence.

Ethnicity-Based Resettlements

The establishment of a new ethnic order in Eastern Europe was central to Nazi ideology. In *Mein Kampf*, Hitler adamantly refused to recognize the validity of the reestablished pre-1919 borders in Eastern Europe, especially as they related to the territory of the Soviet Union. He envisioned a German empire in the East, as it was only there that sufficient "living space" could be found. Conquering this space and resettling it with Germans, mainly farmers, would allow for racial, social, and moral improvement, all of which were necessary for Germany to prevail in the ethnic "struggle for survival."[66] Of course, a major expansion of German territory into the East (and the subjugation of Eastern Europe to German economic interests) was also one of the key German war aims during the First World War, a policy supported by many influential figures. During the Second World War, though, the principal objective of virtually every German ethnicity-based resettlement project – with the notable exception of those relating to Jews[67] – was to settle Germans in the place of non-Germans.

In the early years of the Third Reich, settlement policy was dominated by the Reich Ministry for Food and Agriculture and a number of related parastatal organizations, such as the State Peasant Organizations and the Reichsstelle für Raumordnung (Reich Office for Area Planning). These institutions sought to combat overcrowding and poverty in the countryside and to arrest rural out-migration. The military, on the other hand, wanted to actively settle veterans, including war disabled, in the German countryside.[68] Between 1938 and 1941,

---

[66] Hitler, *Mein Kampf*, 641–67.

[67] Another exception was a population exchange with the Soviet Union in 1939, when 35,000 Ukrainians and Byelorussians chose to move to the USSR, whereas 15,000 Poles moved from there to German-occupied Poland. In addition, 40,000 to 60,000 Ukrainians moved from the German-annexed parts of western Poland eastward to the German-occupied General Government of Poland. Czeslaw Madajczyk and Berthold Puchert, *Die Okkupationspolitik Nazideutschlands in Polen 1939–1945* (Cologne: Pahl-Rugenstein, 1988), 244.

[68] For the first fact see Michael G. Esch, *"Gesunde Verhältnisse": Deutsche und polnische Bevölkerungspolitik in Ostmitteleuropa 1939–1950* (Marburg: Herder-Institut, 1998), 88–92

the SS assumed responsibility for most settlement-related policies. Rather than expanding the old SS's Head Office for Race and Settlement, though, entirely new bodies and agencies were erected, agencies like the Reichskommissar für die Festigung deutschen Volkstums (Reich Commissioner for the Strengthening of Germandom [RKF]) and the Umwandererzentralstelle as well as the Einwandererzentralstelle (the Central Bureaus for Emigration and Immigration, respectively). Preexisting agencies dealing with settlement policy, such as the Volksdeutsche Mittelstelle, which dealt with ethnic Germans from abroad, were placed under SS authority.[69] However, the suborganizations of the SS still had to cooperate with – and often struggle against – regional authorities.

From 1939 to 1942, plans for settlement and resettlement became increasingly radical – a tendency that culminated between the summer of 1941 and late 1942 with the drafting of the Generalplan Ost (General Plan for the East) and a Generalsiedlungsplan (General Plan for Settlement) for large parts of Poland and portions of the Soviet Union. The Generalsiedlungsplan also encompassed Slovenia, Bohemia and Moravia, Alsace, Lorraine, and Luxembourg. The plans submitted by the RKF – which concentrated on Poland – and the Reichssicherheitshauptamt (Head Office of Reich Security) envisioned the settlement of 12.4 million Germans in these regions over a thirty-year period. In order to create space for these settlers, it was estimated that between 31 and 51 million people, chiefly Slavs and explicitly excluding Jews, would need to be resettled, most likely to inner Russia and Siberia.[70] In what was the most extensive of all known Nazi settlement plans, the Arbeitswissenschaftliches Institut (the Institute for Labor Science of the German Labor Front) anticipated that 100 million Germans would be needed to settle the East over the next hundred years. At the conclusion of the century, according to this plan's vision, the only people

(Esch provides an interesting comparison of German and Polish policies of restructuring and resettlement); the role of the army is stressed by Rolf-Dieter Müller, *Hitlers Ostkrieg und die deutsche Siedlungspolitik* (Frankfurt am Main: Fischer Taschenbuch Verlag, 1991), esp. 25–39.

[69] With a different view, emphasizing the importance of the Head Office of Race and Settlement, see Isabel Heinemann, *Rasse, Siedlung, deutsches Blut: Das Rasse- und Siedlungshauptamt der SS und die rassenpolitische Neuordnung Europas* (Göttingen: Wallstein, 2003). For the RKF, see Robert L. Koehl, *R.K.F.D.V.: German Resettlement and Population Policy 1939–1945* (Cambridge, MA: Harvard University Press, 1957).

[70] "Dispositionen und Berechnungsgrundlagen für einen Generalsiedlungsplan," 29 October and 23 December 1942, in Mechtild Rössler and Sabine Schjleiermacher, eds., *Der "Generalplan Ost: Hauptlinien der nationalsozialistischen Planungs- und Vernichtungspolitik* (Berlin: Akademie Verlag, 1993), 96–117; Czesław Madajczyk, ed., "Generalplan Ost," *Polish Western Affairs* 3, no. 2 (1962): 391–442; Helmut Heiber, "Der Generalplan Ost," *Vierteljahrshefte für Zeitgeschichte* 6 (1958): 281–325; Czesław Madajczyk and Stanislaw Biernacki, *Vom Generalplan Ost zum Generalsiedlungsplan* (Munich: Saur, 1994). The most comprehensive overview, though sometimes with questionable conclusions, is Karl Heinz Roth, "'Generalplan Ost' – 'Gesamtplan Ost': Forschungsstand, Quellenprobleme, neue Ergebnisse," in *Der "Generalplan Ost,": Hauptlinien der nationalsozialistischen Planungs- und Vernichtungspolitik*, eds. Mechtild Rössler, Sabine Schleiermacher, and Cordula Tollmein (Berlin: Akademie Verlag, 1993), 25–95.

residing in all of Eastern Europe, right up to the Ural Mountains, would be German.[71] Plans to settle 1 to 3 million Dutch in the Soviet Union (mainly in the Pripet marshes) never materialized.[72] But, again, this lack of correlation between plan and reality was nothing unusual in settlement policy. Indeed, actual resettlements were only loosely based on plans laid out by the RKF, the main settlement planning authority. The reason: regional settlements and settlement policies were heavily influenced by the interests of powerful regional administrators; thus actual settlements only partially adhered to central plans.

There was a further gap between plan and reality. Plainly stated, fulfilling the settlement plans as proposed would have required more Germans than actually existed. Planners responded by increasing the numbers of those able to be "germanized" (*Eindeutschungsfähige*) by "discovering" millions of Poles, Czechs, and others of allegedly "German blood." In November 1939, Hitler prohibited the RKF from resettling Germans from the Greater German Reich (Reichsdeutsche) in the eastern territories during the war, so as not to distract German soldiers from their immediate objectives.[73] The only group allowed to act as settlers were ethnic Germans from abroad, virtually all of them from Eastern and Southeastern Europe. Processing and relocating hundreds of thousands of ethnic Germans from abroad, however, proved too large and complex a task for the bureaucratic apparatuses of the SS, the Volksdeutsche Mittelstelle, and local administrations to organize in a wartime environment.

Between October 1939 and the end of 1942, 629,000 ethnic Germans were moved into German occupied territories – the majority (465,000) prior to December 1940. In accordance with a series of German-Soviet treaties, most of the 629,000 (429,000) were from territories annexed by the USSR in 1939–40 (eastern Poland, northern Romania, the Baltic republics); the rest were from southern Tyrol (Italy; 79,000), Romania (77,000), and Yugoslavia (34,000). Yet, by late 1942, fewer than 445,000 had actually been "resettled" in the East: 332,000 in the annexed parts of western Poland, 70,000 in the "Old Reich" (pre-1937 German territory) and Austria, and 13,500 in the annexed areas of Slovenia. Many of these settlers, furthermore, had received only provisional homes.[74] Given that this was a state-organized and highly bureaucratic process, hundreds of thousands were mired – for years on end – in temporary camps of the Volksdeutsche Mittelstelle, where they were discontent, disillusioned,

---

[71] Michael Hepp, "'Die Durchdringung des Ostens in Rohstoff- und Landwirtschaft': Vorschläge des Arbeitswissenschaftlichen Instituts der Deutschen Arbeitsfront zur Ausbeutung der UdSSR aus dem Jahre 1941," *Sozial Geschichte* 2, no. 4 (1987): 96–134.

[72] Koos Bosma, "Verbindungen zwischen Ost- und Westkolonisation," in *Der "Generalplan Ost,"* eds. Mechtild Rössler, Sabine Schleiermacher and Cordula Tollmien (Berlin: Akademie Verlag, 1993), 198–214. About 1,000 Dutch were taken to the German-occupied Soviet territories and served there as managers on model farms, agents of trade companies, fishermen, and artisans in Byelorussia and Ukraine.

[73] Müller, *Hitlers Ostkrieg und die deutsche Siedlungspolitik*, 87.

[74] Figures in this paragraph are taken from "Einleitung," in Peter Witte, ed., *Der Dienstkalender Heinrich Himmlers 1941–1942* (Hamburg: Christians, 1999), 13–98, here 81–2.

and angry.[75] There they were categorized into four different groups, based upon the "German People's List," and screened according to political and cultural criteria. Most also received a "racial screening" by the SS, where they were classified as "Z-cases" (to be resettled in the new territories), "A-cases" (suitable for the Old Reich only), or "S-cases" ("special cases," many of whom were deported to concentration camps).

The situation in these camps put significant pressure on regional authorities to make room for settlers. By the end of 1942, 365,000 Poles and Jews had been deported from their homes in annexed western Poland and moved into the General Government. From the incorporated territories of Alsace, Lorraine, and Luxembourg, 100,000 persons were relocated either to France or to Germany. With the annexation of Slovenia, 54,000 Slovenians were forcibly deported to Serbia or Croatia or placed in forced labor camps. Hundreds of thousands of Poles, beyond the figures mentioned above, shared the fate of the latter or were displaced (*verdrängt*) within their region to make room for ethnic Germans – more than 194,000 were displaced in the *Wartheland* in western Poland alone.[76]

By and large, the final settlement of ethnic Germans was confined to former Polish, French, Yugoslavian, and, in a few cases, Czechoslovakian territories annexed by Germany. In three notable exceptions, ethnic Germans settlers were destined for other occupied areas. (1) Some 20,000 ethnic Germans were resettled in the counties of Zamosc and Lublin in the General Government, for which 108,000 Poles were deported (of an estimated 400,000 required to allow the complete resettlement of the region). In what was considered a model operation, the latter were categorized into three groups: one went to Germany as forced labor; another was transferred to other areas of the General Government; and, a final group was destined for Auschwitz concentration camp. Of the 30,000 children deported from the Zamosc region in the course of this operation, 10,000 died. (2) Roughly 20,000 ethnic Germans, who had been resettled from Lithuania in 1939–40, were resettled back into Lithuania in 1942 and 1943. And (3) of the 200,000 Soviet Germans, whom the German Army found in the conquered parts of the Ukraine and southern Russia, at least 43,000 were locally resettled in new, though preliminary, villages in the northern Ukraine in late 1942.[77] An estimated 50,000 to 70,000 Ukrainians

[75] Pathbreaking on this is Götz Aly, *'Final Solution': Nazi Population Policy and the Murder of European Jews*, trans. Belinda Cooper and Allison Brown (London and New York: Oxford University Press, 1999).

[76] Witte, ed., *Dienstkalender*, 82; Madajczyk, *Okkupationspolitik*, 405–21; Report Stapoleitstelle Litzmannstadt [Lodz] for October 1944, 1 November 1944, in Czeslaw Luczak, ed., *Polozenie ludnosci Polskiej w tzw. Kraju Warty w okresie Hitlerowskiej okupacji* (Poznan: Instytyt Zachodni, 1990), 158–60.

[77] See Bruno Wasser, *Himmlers Raumplanung im Osten: Der Generalplan Ost in Polen 1940–1944* (Basel and Boston: Birkhäuser, 1993); Czeslaw Madajczyk and Franciszek Cieselak, *Zamojszczyzna – Sonderlaboratorium SS* (Warsaw: Ludowa Spółdzielnia Wydawnicza, DSP, 1977); Christoph Dieckmann, "Deutsche Besatzungspolitik und Massenverbrechen in Litauen

had to make room for them. It was, however, perhaps the first time that foreign peasants were themselves resettled in new, though modest, farms in the southern Ukraine.[78]

The bulk of the German racial resettlement program took place in the annexed areas of western Poland. The region where the majority of incoming ethnic Germans were to settle – the Reichsgau Wartheland around Poznan and Lodz – may serve as an example here.[79] In neighboring areas like Danzig-West Prussia and the district of Bialystok, conflict often erupted between the SS and local civil administrators under Gauleiters Forster and Koch, and, generally speaking, the latter won. For example, Forster's staff, despite the SS, simply declared large portions of the local populace to be German without much bureaucratic ado or slow, methodological racial screening. In contrast, Gauleiter Greiser of the Wartheland worked in close cooperation with SS. Practically, this meant that a number of civil and SS institutions would work together with the Volksdeutsche Mittelstelle and coordinate their resettlement efforts with the needs and interests of Nazi Party welfare, women's and youth agencies, and private business.[80] Direct violence – including the beating and murder of transportees – was primarily meted out by local police and German militias. The Volksdeutsche Selbstschutz, for example, totaled over 100,000 members and was responsible for several mass executions in 1939 and 1940.[81] Ethnic German settlers too were involved in violent confrontations with those they were to replace.

Such conflict is unsurprising, given that Poles were initially allowed only twenty minutes' to one hour's advance notice of their deportation and were permitted to take only ten to thirty kilograms of personal belongings and 20 to 200 zlotys with them. They had to leave behind the bulk of their personal and professional possessions. In most cases, Poles were driven from their farms late at night or in the early morning. Ethnic German settlers replaced them within

1941–1944: Täter, Zuschauer, Opfer" (Ph.D. thesis, University of Freiburg, 2003), chapter D 3; Wendy Lower, *Nazi Empire-Building and the Holocaust in Ukraine* (Chapel Hill: University of North Carolina Press, 2005); for Lublin, figures up to 50,000 German settlers have been mentioned. The number of 400,000 Poles to be resettled was mentioned in a letter by the SS and Police Leader of Lublin, Globocnik, on 15 August 1942; see Esch, 357.

[78] Christian Gerlach, "Die deutsche Agrarreform in den besetzten sowjetischen Gebieten," in *Besatzung und Bündnis: Deutsche Herrschaftsstrategien in Ost- und Südosteuropa* (Berlin: Verlag der Buchläden, 1995), 9–60, here 35.

[79] The following description is mainly based on Madajczyk, *Okkupationspolitik*, 405–21, and *Biuletyn Glownej Komisji Badania zbrodni Hitlerowskich w Polsce*, vol. 21 (Warsaw: Ministerstwa Sprawiedliwosci, 1970), 24–43. Cf. also Dieter Schenk, *Hitlers Mann in Danzig: Albert Forster und die NS-Verbrechen in Danzig-Westpreußen* (Bonn: J. H. W. Dietz, 2000); Sybille Steinbacher, *"Musterstadt" Auschwitz: Germanisierungspolitik und Judenmord in Ostoberschlesien* (Munich: K. G. Saur, 2000); Waclaw Dlugoborski, ed., *Polozenie ludnosci Polskiej w rejencji Katowickiej w latach 1939–1945* (Poznan: Instytut Zachodni, 1983).

[80] The best description of these practices is Wasser, *Himmlers Raumplanung*, 72–132.

[81] See Christian Jansen and Arno Weißbecker, *Der "Volksdeutsche Selbstschutz" in Polen 1939/40* (Munich: Oldenbourg, 1992).

hours – after all, the abandoned livestock required care. The logistical complexity of such actions, however, ruled out short-term, large-scale resettlements and, instead, resulted in a patchwork, stuttering process that facilitated the development of passive resistance on the part of the Polish citizenry. Indeed, it was not unusual for half or more of those persons earmarked for deportation to go into hiding. And, later, it was not uncommon for ethnic German settlers – whether it was because they desired to exploit cheap labor or because they feared reprisals – to use such illegals as farmhands, rather than reporting them to the authorities.[82]

Nazi settlement policy concerned more than simply depositing ethnic German settlers in new surroundings. A small army of planners, functionaries, and social service officials existed to assist and supervise the settlers. They intended fundamentally to restructure entire regions, to abolish the problem of "overpopulation" by distributing the population in a "healthy" and modern manner, and to create new social and economic infrastructures. Wherever possible, Germans farms were to be larger than those that Poles possessed. Even the architecture and landscapes of villages, towns, and cities were to be "germanized." In the process of "germanization," all local ethnic Germans and many Poles were subjected to racial screenings. In total, 4 million people throughout all of Europe, the majority of whom were ethnic Germans, underwent such screenings.[83]

Originally, Poles (peasants as well as so-called elites) and Jews affected by the resettlement programs were directly and collectively deported from the *Wartheland* to the General Government. From late 1940 on, however, Poles were no longer deported directly into the General Government; they were first taken to resettlement camps. There they were categorized into different groups: skilled workers to be used for forced labor, those capable of becoming "germanized," and those to be deported. Some camps later became work camps, where refugees were held for long periods. Living conditions in these camps were harsh, with up to 1,000 deaths reported per camp. With the exception of those selected for forced labor, little is known about the fate of those deported. They were quartered in the homes of fellow Polish citizens or, if possible, put up with relatives in the General Government. Many became dependent upon the meager welfare services available there. Ultimately, it was at the behest of the German administration in the General Government that the further deportation of Poles and Jews into that territory was stopped in 1941. The administration argued that the overpopulation of the territory was causing economic and social unrest and fostered the development of Polish resistance.

---

[82] See Madajczyk, *Okkupationspolitik*, 405–21; Esch, 341–42; and Czeslaw Luczak, eds., *Wysiedlenia ludnosci Polskiej na tzw. ziemiach wsielomych do Rzeszy 1939–1945* (Poznan: Instytut Zachodni, 1969), and Luczak, ed., *Polozenie* vol. XIII, 17–18, 63–4, 105–60.

[83] See various chapters in Rössler, Schleiermacher, and Tollmien, *Der "Generalplan Ost"*; Götz Aly and Susanne Heim, *Vordenker der Vernichtung: Auschwitz und die Pläne für eine neue europäische Ordnung* (Hamburg: Hoffmann und Campe, 1991); Esch, 79–102 and 128–65. For the racial screenings see Heinemann, *Rasse*.

While this might have been tolerated (or dealt with violently) when the principal aim of German policy in the region was subjugation and plunder, it was not conducive to later German policies that emphasized the systematic exploitation of labor and resources, policies that required a docile and controllable population.

The ultimate realization that it would be impossible to deport certain population groups fully played a critical role in the development of Nazi extermination policies. For without deportation as a viable long-term option, the political pressure to make room for ethnic Germans in annexed western Poland soon led to ever more radical alternatives, including mass murder. When hospitals were needed for incoming ethnic Germans and for the German army between 1939 and 1941, for example, some 20,000 residents in homes for the disabled in the annexed Polish territories were simply killed. Also note that the first German extermination camp was located in Chelmno, Wartheland, and became operational on December 8, 1941; Auschwitz, located in incorporated eastern Upper Silesia, became an extermination camp in early 1942.[84]

At the same time, not all resettlements were ethnic resettlements. In many regions, the German administration imposed extreme geographic mobility on the population – whether related to the deportation of forced labor, the ghettoization of Jews, the forced evacuation of populations during military retreat, the resettlement of populations in the course of antipartisan warfare, the setting up of military training areas, the evacuation of populations from towns and cities to ease the food and housing situation, or the billeting of the German military.[85] Much of this was an extremely violent version of the geographic mobility in war – and for the war economy – related to conditions that other European societies like Britons and Soviets faced.[86]

As recent research based on new archival evidence has shown,[87] ethnic deportations were a major component of Stalinist repressive policies. Over a twenty-year period, from the 1930s to the early 1950s, approximately

---

[84] Aly, *Final Solution*, 70–6; Volker Rieß, *Die Anfänge der Vernichtung "lebensunwerten Lebens" in den Reichsgauen Danzig-Westpreußen und Wartheland 1939/40* (Frankfurt am Main and New York: Lang, 1995); Esch, 324–65; for connections between German settlement policy and the history of Auschwitz, see Steinbacher, *"Musterstadt" Auschwitz*; Robert Jan van Pelt and Deborak Dwork, *Auschwitz: 1270 to the Present* (New York and London: Norton, 1996).

[85] In occupied Byelorussia, 2 million out of 9 million inhabitants became victims of such enforced mobility; see Christian Gerlach, "Umsiedlungen und gelenkte Bevölkerungsbewegung in Weißrußland 1941–1944," in Dahlmann and Hirschfeld eds., *Lager*, 553–65; Christian Gerlach, *Kalkulierte Morde: Die deutsche Wirtschafts- und Vernichtungspolititik in Weißrußland 1941–1944* (Hamburg: Hamburger Edition, 1999), 1160–1.

[86] For this mobility, see Mark Mazower, *Dark Continent: Europe's Twentieth Century* (New York: Vintage Books, 2000), 185.

[87] Among numerous recent studies on the subject, Terry Martin, *The Affirmative Action Empire* (Ithaca, NY, and London: Cornell University Press, 2001); idem, "Origins of Soviet Ethnic Cleansing," *Journal of Modern History*, 70 (1998): 813–61; N. F. Bugai, *L. Beriia – I. Stalinu: Soglasno vashemu ukazaniiu* (Moscow: AIRO XX, 1995); N. F. Bugai and A. M. Gonov, *Kavkaz–Narody v eshelonakh* (Moscow: INSAN, 1998).

3 million Soviet citizens were subjected to ethnic-based resettlement. The scope, implementation, context, and reasons for these deportations, however, varied considerably.

As Terry Martin has convincingly shown, the December 1932–January 1933 deportation of some 60,000 Kuban' Cossacks – collectively charged not only with resistance to socialism but with Ukrainian nationalism – marked "the transition from class-based deportations, which predominated prior to 1933, to the ethnic deportations that predominated from 1933 to 1953."[88] The first ethnic deportations (1935–6) were directed against diaspora nationalities, stigmatized as "hostile" on the basis of alleged ties to their ethnic compatriots living beyond Soviet borders – Soviet citizens of Polish and German origin living in western districts of the Ukraine and Soviet citizens of Finnish origins residing in the Leningrad border region. These partial deportations, which affected tens of thousands of families,[89] reflected a particular type of "Soviet xenophobia":[90] an ideological rather than ethnic concept, characterized by fear of foreign capitalist influence and resurgent Russian nationalism.

The deportation of the Korean minority from the Far Eastern region (September–October 1937) marked another major shift in resettlement policy: for the first time, an entire ethnically defined group was deported en masse ("administratively resettled"), under the pretext that the Korean community was "rich soil for the Japanese to till."[91] In contrast to the class-based deportation of "kulaks" six or seven years earlier, during which deportees were often abandoned in the middle of nowhere, the relocation of over 170,000 Koreans to remote parts of Central Asia and Kazakhstan appears to have been carried out in a relatively "efficient" manner and with limited violence.[92] Deportees were even provided with their own collective farms and cultural institutions, despite the fact that every single Korean had been declared a potential spy and traitor!

The next large-scale deportations to target entire ethnic groups took place during the "Great Patriotic War." The first series of deportations, logically enough, targeted Soviet Germans.[93] Between September 1941 and February 1942, over 900,000 persons – that is, over 70 percent of the entire Soviet German community – were deported to various parts of Kazakhstan and Siberia

---

[88] Terry Martin, 847.

[89] Approximately 30,000 Soviet Finns deported from the Leningrad border region to Kazakhstan (1935); 80,000 Soviet citizens of Polish and German origin from western districts of the Ukraine to Kazakhstan and Uzbekistan in 1935 and 1936.

[90] In the words of Terry Martin.

[91] Terry Martin, 334. In fact, there were strong ethnic tensions between Russians and Koreans around Vladivostok. A plan to deport 10,000 Koreans had been prepared in 1930 but had not been implemented.

[92] See previous discussion of "socially harmful elements."

[93] This perception lay partly in the Third Reich claim that it was entitled to intervene in the affairs of "ethnic Germans" in the Soviet Union; see Francine Hirsch, "Race without the Practice of Racial Politics," *Slavic Review* 61, no. 1 (2002): 37.

in a series of mass police operations that mobilized tens of thousands of NKVD special troops. This first wave of deportations was followed by a second one: between November 1943 and May 1944, six ethnic groups (the Karachai, the Kalmyks, the Chechens, the Ingush, the Balkars, and the Crimean Tatars) were deported in toto – altogether some 900,000 persons[94] – on the pretext that they had "collaborated with the Nazi occupiers." In addition to these total deportations, the ethnic cleansing of diaspora minorities with suspected cross-border ethnic loyalties continued – both during and after the war. In these smaller operations, tens of thousands of Greeks, Crimean Bulgarians, Meskhetian Turks, Kurds, Iranians, and Khemshils were deported from the Black Sea and Transcaucasian border regions.

Unlike diaspora minorities suspected of possible connections to foreign nation states, the Chechens and Ingush fell into a unique category, a category of those that did not quite fit into the Soviet whole, a category of nationalities that resisted Soviet efforts to remake their traditions and to reform their culture and ways of life.[95] In 1926, 1930, and 1932, heavily armed punitive expeditions sought, in vain, to eradicate Chechen "banditism" from the unstable and unassimilated borderland regions of the Caucasus (a problem inherited from the Tsarist period). Frustrated by these failures, Soviet authorities in 1944 sought "once and forever" to solve the "Chechen problem" and relieve the Russian minorities (30 percent of the population) living in the Chechen-Ingush ASSR by conducting a massive ethnic cleansing operation.

The preparation for this grand operation took over four months. The initial plans were modified numerous times, as regional Party authorities in the Novosibirsk, Krasnoiarsk, Omsk, and Altai regions each refused to accept new waves of deportees – especially Chechens! In the end, Kirgizstan and Kazakhstan had no choice but to accommodate them. It took several more months for the police to identify physically those to be deported, as individuals often lived in scattered communities outside the Chechen-Ingush Republic or were serving as officers and soldiers in the Soviet army.[96] Logistical preparations were meticulously planned and personally overseen by Lavrentii Beria and his two deputies, Ivan Serov and Bogdan Kobulov, the three of whom traveled to Groznyi to supervise the operation. Note that several key features of this operation – "a hierarchy in the structure of command, a confined theater of operations, and a culture of impunity"[97] – are common to other twentieth-century ethnic cleansings, as well.

---

[94] Among numerous recent studies on wartime ethnic deportations in the Soviet Union, see N. F. Bugai and A. M. Gonov, *Kavkaz–Narody v eshelonakh*; P. Polian, *Ne po svoei vole* (Moscow: Memorial, 2001); Norman M. Naimark, *Fires of Hatred: Ethnic Cleansing in Twentieth-century Europe* (Cambridge, MA: Harvard University Press, 2001), esp. 85–107.

[95] Hirsch, 38.

[96] P. Polian, 122–4.

[97] J. Semelin, "Analysis of a Mass Crime: Ethnic Cleansing in the Former Yugoslavia, 1991–1999," in *The Specters of Genocide: Mass Murder in Historical Perspective*, eds. Ben Kiernan and Robert Gellately (Cambridge: Cambridge University Press, 2003), 353–73.

Finally, over the course of six days in 1944 (February 23–8), 119,000 soldiers and officers of the NKVD arrested over 500,000 men, women, and children[98] and forcibly removed them from their ancestral homelands. Deportees had an hour or so to gather their belongings (100 kilograms per family) before being herded onto trucks and sealed in unheated freight cars. Because of poor weather conditions in the mountainous and isolated regions of Chechnya, a number of NKVD squads were temporarily stranded with their victims; thousands were outright massacred.[99] After a three- to four-week journey, during the course of which many died from hunger and exhaustion, the deportees arrived in Kazakhstan or Central Asia and were dispatched to kolkhozes and factories. Uprooted from their homes, they not only suffered from appalling living conditions, but faced enormous difficulties in adapting to a totally new, and generally very hard, social and working environment. Following this deportation, the Chechen-Ingush ASSR was suppressed from the collective memory, as well: its place-names were changed, its buildings destroyed, its cemeteries bulldozed, and Chechen national figures were removed from the *Great Soviet Encyclopedia*. In October 1948, a report of the Administration for Special Resettlements calculated that of the people deported from the Caucasus and Crimea in 1943 and 1944, nearly one in four, or 200,000, had died by mid-1948.[100]

On November 26, 1948, a decree from the Presidium of the Supreme Soviet of the USSR declared that all those deported between 1941 and 1945 would retain that status "in perpetuity," thus implying that the offending characteristics of the "punished people" were "necessarily transmitted to the next generation."[101] Considering this specific aspect of Stalinist ethnic cleansing, can one argue that "racial logic was at work," that "traces of racial politics crept into Soviet nationalities policies"?[102] In a recent debate over these issues,[103] Francine Hirsch reminded us that the Soviet regime did not persecute nationalities because of suspected "biological weaknesses," that it did not aspire to eliminate races, genotypes, or racial traits. Its aim was to control and eradicate all forms of national particularism that did not accord with the global project of the Soviet empire of nations or delayed the realization of the Communist utopia. Based on the conviction that nationalities, like classes, were sociohistorical groups with a shared consciousness, rather than racial-biological groups,

---

[98] N. F. Bugai, 153–8.

[99] P. Polian, 123.

[100] N. Werth, "A State against Its People: Violence, Repression and Terror in the Soviet Union," in *The Black Book of Communism*, eds. Stéphane Courtois et al. (Cambridge, MA: Harvard University Press, 1999), 223.

[101] Eric D. Weitz, "Racial Politics without the Concept of Race," *Slavic Review* 61, no. 1 (2002): 18. Discussing this point, F. Hirsch noted that female deportees who married men of other nationalities in the region of resettlement and cast off their old national cultures could be reinstated as Soviet citizens. Hirsch, 41.

[102] Weitz, 3.

[103] Weitz, 1–29; Hirsch, 30–43; Amir Weiner, "Nothing by Certainty," *Slavic Review* 61, no. 1 (2002): 44–53; Alaina Lemon, "Without a 'Concept'?: Race as Discursive Practice," *Slavic Review* 61, no. 1 (2002): 54–61.

the Soviet regime's treatment of targeted nationalities may best be understood as "a form of ethno-historical excision."[104] Rather than the physical existence of each and every member of the targeted community, it was the national, cultural, and historical identities that the regime sought to eradicate. This might explain why a regime that had the capacity to launch and implement genocidal campaigns did not operate death camps and exterminate entire ethnic groups.

It would seem that Soviet and German ethnicity-based resettlements were of different types: German policies concerned settling Germans; Soviet policies concerned deporting minorities from strategically important areas. One could indeed say that Nazi Germany and the Soviet Union represent two types of nation-building: one, an expanding homogeneous nation-state; the other, a multinational state attempting to discipline brutally its ethnic minorities.[105]

The Soviet Union pursued a policy in which security considerations, reeducation, and assimilation were critical elements in the resettling of domestic minorities. Entire ethnic communities came under the suspicion of being potential spies, agents, supporters of foreign powers, or obstacles to progress and socialism. If not outright racism, nationalism and ethnic stereotypes seem to have played a significant role, especially in the treatment of the people of the Caucasus and the Crimean Tatars. In contrast, German forced resettlements were intimately linked to imperial expansion, and those based on ethnicity were largely confined to those territories it annexed. Such measures aimed to incorporate, develop, and homogenize more efficiently the territories concerned. Even those Soviet political persecutions that most closely resembled German policies – such as the treatment of the annexed territories (for example, the Baltic republics or eastern Poland) and policies that targeted political, economic, and intellectual elites – were not based on similar intentions. That is, Soviet intentions never included the wholesale removal and replacement of native populations in the longer run. Yet, both Germany and the Soviet Union fought and suppressed native nationalisms in annexed areas, especially in Poland. In the end, political, individual, and armed resistance limited Germany's ability to carry out its resettlement plans. Instead, military failure forced it to evacuate hundreds of thousands of ethnic Germans from Eastern and Southeastern Europe.

Prisoners of War

Even prior to the invasion of the Soviet Union, the German civilian and military leadership made provisions to separate and kill selected categories of Soviet POWs and to provide the remainder with grossly insufficient provisions and supplies. While this policy would undergo a number of modifications over

---

[104] Hirsch, 40.
[105] This difference tends to get lost if both cases of enforced resettlements are subsumed under the term "ethnic cleansing." Norman M. Naimark, *Fires of Hatred: Ethnic Cleansing in Twentieth-Century Europe* (Cambridge, MA, and London, 2001), 104–6.

time, it was never completely revised. In the end, of the 3.3 million Red Army soldiers captured before the end of 1941, nearly 2 million died in German custody. Of the 5.7 million Soviet troops captured over the course of the entire war, between 2.5 million and 3.3 million perished.[106] By 1945, mass graves for Soviet POWs littered Europe's war-ravaged landscape; mass graves were found in Norway and France, in Germany and Poland – although most Soviet POW victims died while still on Soviet soil.

Plans to undersupply Soviet POWs systematically initially arose in the framework of a general policy of starvation directed at those populations living in Soviet territories occupied by the German army, designed in early 1941. These plans, intended both to ameliorate the critical supply situation on the Eastern Front and to buttress Germany's own limited food supplies, primarily targeted populations living in northern and central Russia, Byelorussia, and urban environments.[107] It was, of course, tremendously naïve to imagine that these populations would peacefully starve to death. With only skeletal occupation forces policing these areas, it was virtually impossible to prevent Soviet citizens from "illegally" procuring food (with the notable exception of besieged Leningrad, where approximately 600,000 civilians died). In the end, it was pressure from regional occupation authorities – who required a pliable urban workforce and a functioning infrastructure and who wished to avoid epidemics and public unrest – that led to the abandonment of the original starvation scheme. Given the enormous and growing supply needs of the German military on the Eastern Front, however, policy was not fully reversed in practice. Supplies allocated to the civilian populations remained grossly insufficient. It was in this context that from September 1941 on, a policy of *selective* extermination emerged. The largest group affected were prisoners of war. Soviet POWs viewed as "unfit for work" were, quite simply, left to die of starvation: they were physically separated from other POWs and placed on greatly reduced diets. Largely unable to attain food outside their rations, they had little chance of survival. The death rate among prisoners quickly skyrocketed; and, from October 1941 on, larger POW camps witnessed up to four hundred prisoners' deaths per day – a rate

---

[106] Still the most persuasive calculations of victim figures are from Streit (higher) and Streim (lower); Christian Streit, *Keine Kameraden: Die Wehrmacht und die sowjetischen Kriegsgefangenen 1941–1945*, 4th ed. (Bonn: Verlag J. H. W. Dietz Nachf., 1991); Alfred Streim, *Die Behandlung sowjetischer Kriegsgefangener im Fall Barbarossa* (Heidelberg and Karlsruhe: Müller, 1981). The discovery of new sources in Russia and Germany (many of the German personal files of Soviet POWs were located) allows the conclusion that the death toll was lower than assumed in camps inside the German Reich. See Reinhard Otto, "Sowjetische Kriegsgefangene: Neue Quellen und Erkenntnisse," in *"Wir sind die Herren dieses Landes": Ursachen, Verlauf und Folgen des deutschen Überfalls auf die Sowjetunion*, ed. Babette Quinkert (Hamburg: VSA Verlag, 2002), 124–35; Rolf Keller and Reinhard Otto, "Das Massensterben der sowjetischen Kriegsgefangenen und die Wehrmachtbürokratie: Unterlagen zur Registrierung der sowjetischen Kriegsgefangenen 1941–1945 in deutschen und russischen Institutionen," *Militärgeschichtliche Mitteilungen* 57 (1998): 49–80. It is still uncertain whether general estimates of victim numbers will have to be revised downward, too.

[107] Aly and Heim, *Vordenker*, 365–93; Gerlach, *Kalkulierte Morde*, 46–76.

nearly as high as those achieved by the individual *Einsatzgruppen* during this same period. Between September and December 1941, an average of 15,000 Soviet POWs lost their lives each and every day – according to numerous reports, malnutrition was the leading culprit; disease was a distant second.[108] Only in the spring of 1942, which brought an increased urgency to the utilization of forced labor, did the situation ease somewhat. Yet, even then, Soviet POWs did not receive adequate nutrition.

Only a minor portion of all Soviet POWs killed died in large-scale executions. According to the secret "Commissar Order" of June 6, 1941, political officers among Red Army POWs were to be murdered. Practically, such special treatment meant that political officers either were shot by the troops who captured them, were killed by POW camp guards, or were handed over to police authorities, who either shot them themselves or sent them to concentration camps. The concentration camp, itself, was virtually equivalent to a death sentence: most perished within a few months under particularly harsh conditions reserved for political POWs or were outright murdered in gas chambers or gas vans or through other methods. It is estimated that 120,000 Soviet POWs were handed over to the SS and police during the course of the Second World War.[109] Because the data are highly fragmentary, however, no reliable estimates exist for the total number of political officers murdered. In addition to political officers, there were also attempts to single out and murder Jewish and, until September 1941, "Asian" Soviet POWs. At varying times and in varying regions, other select POW groups also became the target of exterminatory policies: most notably, Red Army officers and female Red Army soldiers.[110]

Whereas the "Commissar Order" was largely abandoned by May 1942, as it inadvertently strengthened military resistance whenever Red Army soldiers were aware of such policies, other killings of Soviet POWs continued unabated: up to several hundred thousand Soviet POWs were shot by German guards during exhausting forced marches, while filing through the streets of occupied Soviet cities, or while being loaded and unloaded at railway stations. In these cases, the perpetrators were regular German soldiers, often on orders from low- or mid-ranking officers. On a typical forced march, for which insufficient provisions of food, beverage, and carts were provided, only a handful of officers and rank-and-file guards were allocated to accompany the prisoners. As senior officers usually planned these marches, the relatively junior officers and rank-and-file guards assigned to them were placed in a rather unenviable position. With a demanding schedule and vastly inadequate supplies, it was inevitable that many POWs would be unable to finish the journey, and, with so few

[108] Streit, *Keine Kameraden*, 128–90.
[109] Streim, *Behandlung*, 244; cf. Reinhard Otto, *Wehrmacht, Gestapo und sowjetische Kriegsgefangene im deutschen Reichsgebiet 1941/42* (Munich: Oldenbourg, 1998). The estimate of 580,000 to 600,000 given by Streit, *Keine Kameraden*, 354, seems by far exaggerated.
[110] For women, see Gerlach, *Kalkulierte Morde*, 777–8; an oral history compilation about the 800,000 female Red Army soldiers is Swetlana Alexijewitsch, *Der Krieg hat kein weibliches Gesicht* (Berlin: Henschelverl. Kunst u. Gesellschaft, 1987).

guards, some would try to flee. In any event, a situation developed in which guards often chose to execute POWs unable to continue along the route – a strategy perhaps designed both to motivate the marchers onward and to forestall possible resistance. In occupied Ukraine, there were even army-level orders to shoot POWs who could not continue.[111] Taking this practice into consideration, we must conclude that the German military was responsible for the direct murder of most Soviet POWs, not the SS or the police.

While it is broadly accepted that there existed a high-level extermination policy against certain groups of Soviet POWs in German captivity,[112] it is important to remember that those who died were not the victims of some anonymous force or faceless system. High-level political orders coincided with the ground-level actions of German army officers and soldiers. Especially during the early days of the conflict, German troops regularly exhibited a tendency toward excessive violence by adhering to "no prisoner" policies, on orders originating everywhere from army corps to platoon level. On occasion, officers' orders *not* to shoot weak and injured Soviet prisoners during forced marches to the rear were willfully ignored by the troops assigned to them – usually Sicherungsdivisionen or Landesschützenbataillone, units that primarily comprised older reservists. Once in camp, from October 1941, Soviet prisoners were separated into two groups: a group categorized as "fit for labor" – and, thus, selected for survival – and a group categorized as "unfit for work" – and, thus, slated for death. While those deemed "fit for labor" were spatially separated from their less fortunate comrades, they nonetheless remained subject to overly heavy labor demands and indiscriminately cruel treatment – in the camps as well as at the workplace – suggesting that different German troops were involved in the violence. As a result, the death rate among those "fit for work" remained extraordinarily high. Even after senior civilian and military authorities introduced a policy in the spring of 1942 that sought to keep workers alive, Soviet POWs continued to be overworked, underfed, and brutally treated, resulting in continued elevated mortality rates.[113] It seems that the mentalities of many guards and lower-level commanders proved too inflexible for such rapid policy shifts. From a source perspective, it has been the personal statements and testaments of surviving Soviet POWs – a source base until recently neglected by Western researchers as "biased," despite their simultaneous reliance upon oral testimony in researching the fate of German POWs – that most fully demonstrate the intensity and unpredictability of the violence inflicted by German troops upon Soviet prisoners. At the same time,

---

[111] Streit, *Keine Kameraden*, 162–71.

[112] For opposite statements that seem unpersuasive, see Streim, *Sowjetische Kriegsgefangene in Hitlers Vernichtungskrieg* (Heidelberg: Müller, 1982), 14 (who tried to put the blame chiefly on the SS), and Christian Hartmann, "Massensterben oder Massenvernichtung?Sowjetische Kriegsgefangene im 'Unternehmen Barbarossa' – Aus dem Tagebuch eines Lagerkommandanten," *Vierteljahrshefte für Zeitgeschichte* 49 (2001): 97–158.

[113] Streit, *Keine Kameraden*; Gerlach, *Kalkulierte Morde*, 796–829.

it should be remembered that many guards did *not* participate in beatings, torture, or killings.[114]

A number of factors influenced the violence inflicted upon Soviet POWs. In part, it was the product of a racist ideology deeply entrenched within the German military, an ideology that produced a sense of absolute superiority. Interestingly, with the exception of ethnic Germans and Jews, relatively little distinction was made between different ethnic groups among POWs.[115] Anti-Communism represented another factor in the maltreatment of Soviet prisoners. Given the flight and evacuation of Soviet officials from territories conquered by the Germans, Soviet POWs were, by and large, the only representatives of the Soviet state ever to fall into German hands. Accordingly, the German military tended to treat them as if they were responsible for all Soviet "crimes."[116] This mentality may have contributed to the fact that the death rate among Soviet POWs remained significantly higher than that of the 2 million Soviet civilians deported to Germany as forced labor from 1942. The combination of racist and anti-Bolshevik sentiments resulted in the assignment of particularly exhausting and dangerous work to Soviet POWs, such as quarry mining. Finally, local emergencies, whether concerning German troop supplies and transportation or the fear of civil revolt and resistance, often led regional occupation authorities to undernourish and undersupply Soviet POWs further, a policy that only elevated their already high death rates. The death rate in the General Government of Poland and in areas under the control of Army Group Center in late 1941, for example, exceeded 30 percent per month. The recurrence of such local emergencies helps to account for the substantial discrepancies in mortality rates in different regions at any given time.[117]

While economic, military, and political considerations were not fully independent of ideological motives, they played critical roles in the ongoing crescendo of violence against Soviet POWs. Indeed, it was precisely the combination of virulent racism, anti-Communism, and key moments in a deadly military conflict that produced conditions under which extreme political and military measures appeared justified and mass death seemed inevitable.

And yet, contrary to Soviet policy toward German POWs,[118] up to 1 million Soviet POWs served with the German armed forces, whether as (voluntary

---

[114] The last point is emphasized by Jens Nagel and Jörg Osterloh, "Wachmannschaften in Lagern für sowjetischen Kriegsgefangene: Eine Annäherung," in *Durchschnittstäter*, ed. Christian Gerlach (Berlin: Verlag der Buchläden, 2000), 73–93.

[115] However, most of the 269,000 Soviet POWs released by the end of 1941 were Ukrainians. See OKH/GenStdH/GenQu, Abt.K.Verw. (Qu4/Kgf), "Kriegsgefangenenlage im Operationsgebiet," 1 January 1942, BA-MA RH 3/v.150, 4.

[116] Memo Canaris to Keitel, 15 September 1941, in *Anatomie des SS-Staates*, 208–10.

[117] Christian Gerlach, *Krieg, Ernährung, Völkermord: Forschungen zur deutschen Vernichtungspolitik im Zweiten Weltkrieg* (Hamburg: Hamburger Edition, 1998), 45–6.

[118] But see for Soviet efforts for political reeducation of German POWs Andreas Hilger, *Deutsche Kriegsgefangene in der Sowjetunion: Kriegsfangenenpolitik, Lageralltag und Erinnerung* (Essen: Klartext, 2000), 220–54; Gert Robel, *Die deutschen Kriegsgefangenen in der Sowjetunion: Antifa* (Munich and BielefeldMunich: Giesekind, 1974).

and coerced) laborers (*Hilfswillige* or *Hiwis*) or, as in the case of Muslims and
Ukrainians, in armed auxiliary units of the German army and the Waffen-SS.
Here, the military's attitude toward Soviet POWs was a product of militant
German anti-Communism, an uncompromising desire to emerge victorious
against the USSR, and a wish to "save German blood."[119] Interestingly, the
German military used Soviet POWs despite Hitler's strong and constant resis-
tance to the idea. A history of the *Hiwis*, of foreign labor within the armed
forces, remains to be written.

Whereas the German leadership had at least made vague plans regarding
the treatment of Soviet POWs prior to the invasion of the USSR, the Soviet
government had made no particular provisions for German POWs in the event
of a German-Soviet War. In accordance with its refusal to ratify the 1929
Geneva Convention, the Soviet government disregarded international rules in
the treatment of Polish and Finnish POWs captured during the campaigns
of 1939 and 1940. Not only did the Soviet government refuse to supply the
International Red Cross with details concerning the fate of these POWs, Stalin
and Beria planned and implemented, in total secrecy, the execution of over
25,000 Polish prisoners – officers, officials, and members of the social and
political elite – during March and April 1940.[120]

A few weeks after the German invasion, amid the crumbling of the Soviet
Union's defensive fronts and the surrender of hundreds of thousands of Soviet
troops, the Soviet government sent a note to Berlin (via the Swedish embassy)
stating that the USSR was ready – on the basis of reciprocity – to apply the
provisions of the 1907 Hague Convention to German POWs.[121] The German
government, of course, refused to consider this "Bolshevik propaganda." Until
the end of 1942, very few Germans were prisoners of the Red Army; indeed, in
November 1942, fewer than 20,000 German POWs had been registered in the
NKVD's UPVI camps for prisoners of war and internees.[122] Obviously, many
more had been captured than these registers suggest. A number of documents
from Soviet military sources suggest that the summary execution ("liquida-
tion") of prisoners on the battlefield was not an infrequent practice, especially during the early stages of the war.[123] In late August 1941, for example,

[119] George H. Stein, *The Waffen-SS: Hitler's Elite Guard at War, 1939–1945* (Ithaca, NY: Cornell
University Press, 1966); Bernd Wegner, *Hitlers politische Soldaten: Die Waffen-SS 1933–
1945*, 4th ed. (Paderborn: F. Schöningh, 1990); Hans-Werner Neulen, *An deutscher Seite:
Internationale Freiwillige von Wehrmacht und Waffen-SS* (Munich: Universitas, 1985).

[120] On the "Katyn Affair," the most recent and complete study is R. G. Pikhoia and V. P. Kozlov,
eds., *Katyn'* (Moscow: Mezhdunarodnyi Fond Demokratia, 1997).

[121] On this episode, V. B. Konasov, *Sud'by nemetskikh voennoplennykh v SSSR* (Volodga: Izd-
vo Vologodskogo In-ta povysheniia kvalifikatsii i perepodgotovki pedagogicheskikh kadrov,
1996), 27–36.

[122] Klaus-Dieter Müller, Konstantin Nikischkin, and Günther Wagenlehner, eds., *Die Tragödie
der Gefangenschaft in Deutschland und in der Sowjetunion 1941–1956* (Köln: Böhlau, 1998).

[123] V. B. Konasov, 26; A. S. Iakushevskii, "Rasstrel v klevernom pole," *Novoe vremia* 25 (1993):
40–2, here 42; M. M. Zagorul'ko, ed., *Voennoplennye v SSSR, 1939–1956* (Moscow: Logos,
2000), 16–17.

the commandant of several army corps issued orders condemning the "practice, contrary to international rules, of executing prisoners" and threatening to court martial officers and soldiers engaged in the summary execution of POWs.[124]

With the capitulation of the German Sixth Army at Stalingrad, however, Soviet military commanders and the NKVD were, for the first time, confronted with the problem of managing large numbers of German POWs, many of whom were in a poor physical state – starved, sick, and frozen. Many died of hunger, exhaustion, or battle wounds between the time of their capture and their registration in a number of hastily organized camps; many others, unable to continue marching, were simply shot by guards en route. Of the 110,000 POWs transferred, in accordance with NKVD Order 00398 (March 1, 1943), from holding camps in front areas to camps in the rear, fewer than 35,000 arrived alive. All others died.[125] The little information that exists on POW transfer convoys and POW camps suggests that 20 to 25 percent of all POWs evacuated to rear camps died during the course of their transfer; another 30 to 50 percent died within two months of their transfer.[126] In the two-and-a-half month period from February until mid-April 1943 alone, 100,000 German POWs died. Of the 291,856 German POWs registered over the course of the war to that point, 171,774 (or 59 percent) perished.[127]

As the flow of German prisoners steadily increased, mirroring the reversal in military fortunes, the UPVI system was reorganized in order to "put to work and more efficiently exploit POW manpower." During the summer of 1943, daily food rations were raised, albeit only slightly, and a network of special hospitals for wounded and sick POWs was established.[128] Nonetheless, mortality rates remained high throughout 1943. A number of NKVD and military orders condemning the "arbitrary stripping of essential personal possessions from POWs, such as clothing and shoes"[129] or the "excessive and indiscriminate cruelty against POWs"[130] shed light on the everyday physical violence exerted "from below" on German prisoners of war. This violence, though, was apparently based neither on racist ideology nor on political anti-Nazism. It was simply considered legitimate retribution for the cruelty of an enemy that had not respected the laws of war. At the 1943 Teheran Conference, Stalin outlined to Churchill the Soviet Union's postwar policy toward German POWs and civilian internees: up to 4 million Germans would be kept for several

---

[124] V. B. Konasov, 26.

[125] M. M. Zagorul'ko, 30.

[126] Examples in Zagorul'ko, 31–32. In over 90 percent of the cases, death was caused by "distrophia."

[127] Ibid.

[128] Zagorul'ko, 33.

[129] Stefan Karner, "GUPVI: The Soviet Main Administration for Prisoners of War and Internees during World War II," *Bulletin du Comité international d'Histoire de la deuxième guerre mondiale* no. 27/28 (1995): 183; V. B. Konasov, 57.

[130] V. B. Konasov, 58.

years after the war's end in order to help rebuild what the Wehrmacht had destroyed.[131]

The rapid advance of Soviet forces in 1944 added to the UPVI camps hundreds of thousands of additional POWs. The system, undersupplied in almost every category, was not prepared to cope with such an influx. Nevertheless, the UPVI administration claimed that, during the summer of 1944, 80 percent of all POWs were put to work (50 percent in the winter).[132] But the largest influx of detainees – both prisoners of war and civilians (mostly German men between the ages of seventeen and fifty)[133] – occurred during the final months of the war. Between January and early May 1945, the number of POWs registered in GUPVI camps increased from seven hundred to over 2 million.[134] Following the surrender of the German armed forces, Soviet front line camps took in an additional 1.3 million POWs. Registering so many prisoners and transferring them to permanent camps in the rear were an enormous task that took over half a year to complete, during which period many thousands died of hunger, exhaustion, and disease. Soviet authorities, however, were obsessed with one concern: "rationally" exploiting all available POW manpower for reconstruction needs and repatriating all POWs unable to work (principally, invalids and sick POWs).[135] According to two projects submitted by Beria to Stalin (on June 4 and August 10, 1945, respectively), over 930,000 POWs of varying nationalities (among them over 600,000 Germans) were to be repatriated before October 15, 1945,[136] and, according to GUPVI sources, over 1 million POWs of various nationalities were repatriated during all of 1945. The great majority of these repatriation cases were invalids.[137]

By early 1946, after the first wave of repatriations had been completed, nearly 2 million POWs (including 0.5 million Japanese and over 1.2 million Germans) were, quite literally, forced to participate in the reconstruction of the Soviet Union, whether in GUPVI camps or as part of "isolated labor battalions" under the control of the Ministry of Armed Forces. In 1946, approximately 49 percent of POWs worked in the construction sector and in

---

[131] W. Churchill, *The Second World War*, vol. 2 (London:Cassell, 1949), 187. Stalin added that 50,000 officers should be simply shot. Only after Churchill's negative reaction to this statement did Stalin reluctantly admit that he "was joking."

[132] S. Karner and B. Marx, "World War II Prisoners of War in the Soviet Union Economy," *Bulletin du Comité international d'histoire de la deuxième guerre mondiale* no. 27–28 (1995): 194.

[133] But also valid for women between the ages of 18 and 30. According to Soviet sources, in January–April 1945, over 208,000 German adults (157,000 men and 51,000 women) from Eastern Prussia and Silesia were transferred to the Soviet Union and sent to "reconstruction battalions" (M. M. Zagorul'ko, 33–4).

[134] Report of L. Beria to Stalin, May, 11, 1945 (GARF, f. 9401. op. 2, d. 96, ll. 10–11); V. B. Konasov, 126.

[135] See the numerous GKO and NKVD orders of June–August 1945 on these questions (V. B. Konasov, 125–6).

[136] V. B. Konasov, ibid ; M. M. Zagorul'ko, 36–7.

[137] V. B. Konasov, 128–9.

construction-related industries. Another 22 percent were occupied in the energy sector.[138] In contrast, Soviet POWs in German hands worked, above all, for the German military (as "personal slaves for the troops," as one report put it) at or near the front, although some also worked in the mining, construction, and agriculture industries.[139]

The fate of German POWs in the postwar Soviet Union was certainly a harsh one, but was it any harsher than that of Gulag inmates? Both were subject to the same Soviet system of norms, "a system where quantity counted more than quality, illusion more than reality."[140] Similarly, food and, thus, survival depended upon the fulfillment of work quotas, which varied considerably according to local conditions. An inspection of one of the "isolated labor battalions" in October 1945, for example, discovered that orders and rules were willfully ignored. Prisoners worked fourteen hours per day with minimal rations. As a result, no more than 27 percent of inmates were able to work at any given time.

Often, POWs actually worked side by side with Gulag inmates, Soviet repatriates, and former Soviet POWs assigned to "labor battalions." According to a number of interviewees,[141] this shared experience, combined with increased contact with Soviet citizens, helped to correct the biased ideological image they had been fed of their former enemy.

Apart from the harsh conditions of everyday life, the main frustration for German POWs was the continuous delay in repatriation. According to official Soviet data from 1956, at the end of 1945, 1,448,654 German POWs remained in captivity. At the end of 1947, 833,449 German POWs remained in the Soviet Union; 495,855 at the end of 1948. Most prisoners were released only in 1949, at the end of which the number of German POWs in Soviet custody fell to 83,260. By 1950, that number had been further whittled to 28,711, the majority of whom were held as "convicts" until 1955. Thus, there appear to have been two major waves of releases: one in late 1945 (primarily of invalids) and a second one lasting from the second half of 1948 through 1949.

These figures and, in particular, the official death toll of 356,687 German POWs (excluding Austrians), however, are highly controversial. V. B. Konasov and others have shown that especially in the postwar period Soviet authorities constantly manipulated and corrected the number of POWs detained, repatriated, disappeared, killed, and/or deceased. In 1947, the Sovinformbiuro

---

[138] Hilger, *Deutsche Kriegsgefangene*, 173–219; Stefan Karner, *Im Archipel GUPVI: Kriegsgefangenschaft und Internierung in der Sowjetunion 1941–1956* (Vienna and Munich: R. Oldenbourg, 1995), 136–59, esp. 142; Werner Ratza, *Die deutschen Kriegsgefangenen in der Sowjetunion: Der Faktor Arbeit, zur Geschichte der deutschen Kriegsgefangenen des Zweiten Weltkrieges*, vol. 4 (Munich and Bielefeld: Giesekind, 1973).

[139] Streit, *Keine Kameraden*, 268–88; the quote is from "Wirtschaftsinspektion Mitte, Aktenvermerk über die Dienstbesprechung am 31.5.1943 bei Heeresgruppe Mitte, O.Qu," Bundesarchiv (Militärisches Zwischenarchiv) Potsdam, F 42859: 1071.

[140] S. Karner and B. Marx, 198.

[141] See the Archive of the Ludwig Boltzmann Institute for Research on War Consequences.

reported 3.15 million German POWs[142] – a vast and, perhaps, unbridgeable discrepancy with the figure of 833,449 POWs listed above. Another factor supporting a critical assessment of these figures is the number of unaccounted deaths among Soviet and German soldiers captured, but not registered – incalculable for Soviet POWs and perhaps as high as 275,000 to 550,000 for German POWs.[143] In any case, whereas Soviet POWs sustained by far the highest mortality rates among all prisoners in German captivity, the official death rate for German POWs in Soviet hands (15 percent) was actually significantly below that of Italian (57 percent) and Romanian (29 percent) POWs.[144]

The "war over figures" (begun long ago by German historians contesting official Soviet data)[145] is not yet over. In the foreword to the recent and largest-ever published volume of documents on Second World War POWs in the Soviet Union,[146] a volume that amply illustrates the point made by V. B. Konasov, one reads: "In the USSR, 15 percent [approximately 357,000] of all POWs died; in Germany, 57 percent [approximately 3 million]. This difference mathematically demonstrates the fundamental differences between the two systems and shows on whose side justice and the law resided."[147] Were the values of law and justice ever really operative on either side, especially as concerned prisoners of war?

There are a number of parallels between the treatment of POWs in the Soviet Union and in Nazi Germany.[148] Hunger, forced labor, noncompliance with international law, and violence led to high mortality rates among both groups of

---

[142] See Karner, *Archipel GUPVI*, 204, and the extensive statistical annex in Hilger, *Deutsche Kriegsgefangene*, 380–428.

[143] Gerlach, *Kalkulierte Morde*, 774–9; Hilger, *Deutsche Kriegsgefangene*, 56–62, 371–2, 389; Karner, *Im Archipel GUPVI*, 14, 58, 178. Karner estimates that between 500,000 and 1 million POWs in Soviet hands died before registration, with 55 percent of all prisoners being Germans and 3 percent Austrians. For the experience of the violence in the first days of captivity, see, for example, accounts of German POWs Kurt Tappert, Heinrich Merck, and Karl Zacharias in *Kriegsgefangene im Osten: Briefe, Bilder, Berichte*, ed. Eva Berthold (Königstein/Ts: Athenäum, 1981), 34–9, 51–60, and 154–7.

[144] Karner, *Archipel GUPVI*, 79. Yet one has to keep in mind that most Italian military fell into Soviet captivity in the winter of 1942–3, when death rates of POWs were generally at their peak.

[145] See Kurt Böhme, *Die deutschen Kriegsgefangenen in Sowjetischer Hand: Eine Bilanz* (Bielefeld: E. und W. Giesekind, 1966), 3–50 and 106–26; Arthur L. Smith, *"Die vermißte Million": Zum Schicksal der deutschen Kriegsgefangenen nach dem Zweiten Weltkrieg* (Munich, 1992), esp. 75–81, 87.

[146] M. M. Zagorul'ko, ed., *Voennoplennye v SSSR, 1939–1956: Dokumenty i materialy* (Moscow: Logos, 2000).

[147] Ibid, 11.

[148] Stefan Karner's attempt at a comparison seems rather sketchy; Stefan Karner, "Konzentrations- und Kriegsgefangenenlager in Deutschland und in der Sowjetunion: Ansätze zu einem Vergleich von Lagern in totalitäten Regimen," in *In der Hand des Feindes: Kriegsgefangenschaft von der Antike bis zum Zweiten Weltkrieg*, ed. Rüdiger Overmans (Cologne: Böhlau, 1999), 387–411. See also Christian Streit, "Deutsche und sowjetische Kriegsgefangene," in *Kriegsverbrechen im 20. Jahrhundert*, eds. Wolfram Wette and Gerd R. Ueberschär (Darmstadt: Wissenschaft Buchgesellschaft, 2001), 178–92.

prisoners. On both sides, POW supplies were inadequate and disorganized; on both sides, corruption and embezzlement further reduced that which actually reached POWs. Trends in mortality rates were also similar: from very high levels in the early stages of the war, death rates generally diminished over the course of captivity. Also, in both the German and Soviet cases, it is evident that grassroots initiatives played an important role in the escalation of violence and the killing of prisoners. It is difficult to imagine an environment in which citizens in either country could have been under less political control in the wielding of violence. The mass rape of women in eastern Germany, Austria, and Hungary demonstrates the low level of discipline among Soviet troops and their readiness to inflict physical violence.[149]

The main difference in the two cases, vis-à-vis the treatment of POWs, lies in the role played by political and military leaders. Only in the German case were there a high-level intention to kill large numbers of Soviet POWs and a program to realize it. At the level of policy, Soviet authorities more often sought to improve the camp system and to ameliorate prisoners' living conditions through organizational change and the punishment of Soviet soldiers who had violated their duties. Orders prohibiting abuse, which existed on the German side as well, seem to have been more frequent on the Soviet side. Let us also not forget that hunger for Soviet and German POWs had a different significance than hunger in Germany. The starvation of prisoners in German hands served to maintain comfortable levels of food consumption for Germans, whereas in the Soviet Union, as a result of the German invasion and occupation of large swaths of territory, food was scarce for both civilians and the military, a situation that shifted to famine in 1942 and 1946–7.[150]

CONCLUSION

Given the complexity of each individual case, it is difficult to draw overall conclusions or make generalizations about a subset of mass crimes, let alone about all of them together. We shall, therefore, confine ourselves to making a few key observations, rather than attempting to provide a general comparative explanatory framework for German and Soviet violence.

---

[149] Gerhard Keiderling, "'Als Befreier unsere Herzen brachen': Zu den Übergriffen der Sowjetarmee in Berlin 1945," *Deutschland Archiv* 28 (1995): 234–43; Andrea Petö, "Stimmen des Schweigens: Erinnerungen an Vergewaltigungen in den Hauptstädten des 'ersten Opfers' (Wien) und des 'letzten Verbündeten Hitlers' (Budapest) 1945," *Zeitschrift für Geschichtswissenschaft* 47 (1999): 892–913. See also Norman Naimark, *The Russians in Germany: A History of the Soviet Zone of Occupation 1945–1949* (Cambridge, MA: Belknap Press of Harvard University Press, 1995).

[150] See for this context Erich Maschke, "Einleitung," in *Die deutschen Kriegsgefangenen in der Sowjetunion: Der Faktor Hunger*, ed. Hedwig Fleischhacker (Munich: Kommission für deutsche Kriegsgefangenen Geschichte, 1965), vii–xxxviii; for the wartime period see William Moskoff, *The Bread of Affliction: The Food Supply in the USSR during World War II* (Cambridge and New York: Cambridge University Press, 1990).

Mass violence is not simply a matter of police or other repressive state organs. From the victim group case studies presented here ("asocials," victims of ethnic resettlement projects, and prisoners of war), it would seem that "initiative from below" and public participation or support were important factors in the genesis of such violence. However, other factors were involved, as well, such as what could be called a given polity's "overall acclimation to violence," a factor related to that polity's recent experiences of war, revolution, and counterrevolution. In both cases, we selected relatively understudied and underrecognized victim groups, groups that have been shown little remorse by German or Soviet society, let alone by their erstwhile perpetrators. We selected groups that have not stood in the limelight of intense historical interest. This subject choice is also reflected in the relatively deficient state of research about them. These groups remain marginal to, if they are at all reflected in, the collective memory of the war, and they receive little empathy from the public or professional historians. More such groups could have been discussed, such as the more than 5 million civilians forced to work in Nazi Germany and the several hundred thousand foreign workers brought into the Soviet Union.

To begin with, this analysis questions the assertion that secrecy hid mass violence from the broader public – a finding corroborated by recent research on the Holocaust and on political oppression in both countries. First and foremost, participation in violence and mass murder was much broader than previously thought. Secondly, we need to reconsider our understanding of the places where violence occurred – where Jews were shot; where POWs were starved, beaten, and forced to work; and so forth. Working on construction sites and in mines and factories, victim groups often remained in close contact with the native population. In the Soviet Union, "special settlers" lived and worked together with "ordinary" citizens. Third, there was an internal debate regarding such policies. Fourth, there were many who profited from repression and violence: citizens claiming Jewish property; soldiers robbing POWs; individuals taking over attractive jobs from people arrested, deported, or killed; workers professionally benefiting from the arrest, deportation, or murder of their colleagues; families residing in the apartments and homes of those deported. Fifth, there were many different arguments used to demand violence against the above-mentioned groups. However, every argument – whether that of military necessity, national security, labor, food, poverty, or criminality – was couched in language that aroused genuine public fears and concerns. Contextualizing the arguments in this manner made violence appear almost as an imperative. It should be added that, in combination with racial ideology and more traditional forms of anti-Semitism, many of these arguments were also used in justifying the extermination of European Jews.

Investigating the fate of Soviet and German prisoners of war reveals much about the grassroots nature of the abuse, neglect, and killing of victims. Even the direct orders of superiors to halt such violence – something that happened far more frequently on the Soviet side – utterly failed. The existence of such orders, however, clearly demonstrates that the violence meted out to German

POWs was not merely the result of orders descending from a centralized, state-organized system. The mass rape of German women and girls in 1945 reinforces this notion. As to the persecution of "asocials" and "socially harmful elements," a small army of police and municipal authorities, public welfare officials, labor authorities, social scientists, pedagogues, and journalists supported the regime's policies: mass arrests; reeducation programs, labor camps, restrictive labor legislation, and various policies addressing undesired migration, the "exploitation" of welfare services, and criminality. Such participation provided a breeding ground for violence and facilitated what often appears to have been a rather fluid transition from repression to mass death. Among the cases discussed here, the Soviet Union's wartime deportation of entire ethnic communities least fits the pattern of public participation; yet, very little is known about those who took advantage of the situation.[151] Certainly, our knowledge of the mass deportation of Poles and other nationalities by Nazi Germany and the subsequent settlement of ethnic Germans in their place – a process that resulted in many thousands of deaths – supports the notion that a multitude of groups within the state bureaucracy and among ordinary citizens supported these policies.

As arguments encouraging the separation, imprisonment, or removal, in one form or another, of victim groups often emerged from below, we presume that the broader population possessed a fair amount of knowledge regarding such persecutions. However, it is one thing to condone the separation, imprisonment, or removal of population groups and quite another to support mass murder. And, with regard to the latter, it has been much more difficult to establish precisely how much ordinary citizens knew about the mass murder of victims or the methods applied. In such highly organized and bureaucratic societies, the act of killing itself remained a matter for officials and state, party, and police functionaries. In both systems, there was at least a partial attempt to shield the broader population from knowledge about mass killings. No death figures were ever published by the contemporary media. Various speeches by Reichsführer-SS Himmler to killing units in German-occupied Soviet territories in 1941 and one notorious speech to SS leaders at a meeting in Poznan in 1943 indicate that the work of killing – and, in particular, that of mass shootings – was viewed as "hard," dirty, and mentally distressing work, nothing to talk about or of which to boast. Himmler told his listeners that "decent" men had the "obligation" and "moral right" to take on themselves the task of carrying out these cruel, but necessary acts in order to save the next generation of Germans from having to do it.[152] Indeed, the utilization of gas chambers

---

[151] See the suppositions in Naimark, *Fires of Hatred*, 106.

[152] For 1941, see Witte et al., *Dienstkalender*, 195 and 225; quotes from Himmler's Poznan speech, 4 October 1943, *The Trial of the Major War Criminals before the International Military Tribunal*, vol. 29 (Nuremberg, 1948), 145–6. For a recording excerpt, http://www.nationalsozialismus.de/dokumente/tondokumente/heinrich-himmler-posener-rede-vom-04101943-auszug-5-min-mp3, accessed 7 September 2007.

aimed, in part, to reduce the stress murder placed upon the conscience of perpetrators.

In the Soviet Union, there was a similarly strong tendency to "professionalize" violence. The instrumentalization of social tensions among the various strata of peasants and the use of violence from below during the process of "dekulakization" (1930–2) were, in hindsight, considered "counterproductive." This experience, however, allowed the Party leadership and the political police to draw a major lesson: it was more efficient to rely on police records than on denunciations or the haphazard initiatives of "activists." Henceforth, large-scale arrests and deportations were not to be publicized and were to be organized by "professionals." As for mass executions, 700,000–800,000 of which were carried out during the "Great Terror," they were to be implemented in an "efficient manner" and in total secrecy by NKVD staff. However, as a number of later investigations into so-called "abuses" and "excesses" of the *ezhovshchina* revealed, the seeming arbitrariness of the "execution quotas" allotted to regional NKVD organizations created an environment that stimulated the use of violence among rank-and-file police – prisoners were tortured, beaten to death, drowned, and decapitated.[153]

One dimension that deserves further scholarly examination is the role played by petitions, complaints, and "public accusations." Research to date has largely been limited to political denunciations, especially in the case of Nazi Germany.[154] However, it has been shown that "Soviet denunciations were not addressed exclusively or even mainly to the secret police (NKVD)." Such accusations were sent to a number of agencies within the Communist Party and the government: to the People's Commissariat of Workers' and Peasants' Inspection, to high-level politicians, to the public prosecutor's office, and, importantly, to newspapers. The extent to which such "signals from below" contributed to Soviet policymaking needs to be more fully analyzed. Even in "denunciations" sent directly to the NKVD or KGB, the dominant themes were not political opposition, but abuse of power, neglect of duties, financial

---

[153] GARF, f. 8131, op. 37, d. 145, l. 184; Nicolas Werth, "Repenser la Grande Terreur," *Le Débat* 122 (November/December 2002): 116–43.

[154] See Robert Gellately, "Denunciations in Twentieth-Century Germany: Aspects of Self-Policing in the Third Reich and in the German Democratic Republic," in *Accusatory Practices: Denunciation in Modern European History, 1789–1989*, eds. Sheila Fitzpatrick and Robert Gellately (Chicago and London: University of Chicago Press, 1997), 185–221; idem, *The Gestapo and German Society: Enforcing Racial Policy 1933–1945* (Oxford: Clarendon Press, 1990), 129–58; Gisela Diewald-Kerkmann, *Politische Denunziation im NS-Regime oder Die kleine Macht der "Volksgenossen"* (Bonn: Dietz, 1995); Bernward Dörner, *"Heimtücke": Das Gesetz als Waffe. Kontrolle, Abschreckung und Verfolgung in Deutschland 1933–1945* (Paderborn: Schöningh, 1998); Katrin Dördelmann, *Die Macht der Worte: Denunziation im nationalsozialistischen Köln* (Cologne: Emons Verlag, 1997); Rita Wolters, *Verrat für die Volksgemeinschaft: Denunziantinnen im Dritten Reich* (Pfaffenweiler: Centaurus, 1996); Vandana Joshi, *Gender and Power in the Third Reich: Female Denouncers and the Gestapo, 1933–45* (Basingstoke: Macmillan Palgrave, 2003).

misdemeanors, corruption, and "moral breakdown."[155] If denunciations, generally speaking, were indeed commonplace and if political accusations, in particular, were embedded within the same culture of petitioning and complaint, this suggests that popular political participation and the violence that emerged were closely intertwined, that they were not mutually exclusive categories, even while the state remained the principal agent for the organization and carrying out of violence.

In the strategic use of the most intense forms of persecution and violence, however, the two regimes greatly differed. In Nazi Germany, for example, "asocials" were heavily persecuted domestically, but the number of camp arrests and related deaths never approached the magnitude attained in the Soviet Union. The same is true for the regime's political opponents. Despite the brutal discipline of and the very real violence inflicted by the Nazi regime, their domestic approach was less confrontational and more integrative than the Soviet one. If one includes "asocials," criminals, political opponents, Jews, Gypsies, the "terminally ill," and, toward the end of the war, deserters, then the Nazi regime killed some 500,00 to 600,000 of its own citizens (0.6 to 0.8 percent of the total population). Yet, in areas occupied by the German army, exclusion rather than inclusion applied. Especially in Eastern Europe, German violence was extreme. Roughly speaking, some 12 to 14 million noncombatants were killed in occupied Europe during the war (5 to 6 percent of those under German occupation).[156] The largest groups to suffer were European Jews, Soviet POWs, peasants caught up in antipartisan operations in Eastern and Southern Europe, and forced laborers deported to Germany. The nature of these categories underscores the fact that 96 percent of all victims of Nazi violence were non-German.

In contrast, Soviet mass violence was directed more internally than externally. In part, it could be argued that Soviet violence was "developmental," as Mark Levene argues for "genocide" in general;[157] in the USSR it had to do with collectivization and industrialization. Certainly, there were massive deportations from territories annexed by the Soviet Union – first of elites (1939–41) and later of hundreds of thousands of forced workers (toward the end of the

---

[155] See Sheila Fitzpatrick, "Signals from Below: Soviet Letters of Denunciation of the 1930s," and Vladimir A. Kozlov, "Denunciation and its Functions in Soviet Governance: A Study of Denunciations and their Bureaucratic Handling from Soviet Police Archives, 1944–1953," in Fitzpatrick and Gellately, *Accusatory Practices*, 85–120 and 121–52 (quotes on 88 and 125).

[156] A similar estimate on slightly different assumptions is given by Dieter Pohl, *Verfolgung und Massenmord in der NS-Zeit 1933–1945* (Darmstadt: Wissenschaftliche Buchgesellschaft, 2003), 153.

[157] "Modern genocide, in conclusion, is developmental." Mark Levene, "Creating a Modern 'Zone of Genocide': The Impact of Nation- and State Formation on Eastern Anatolia, 1878–1923," *Holocaust and Genocide Studies* 12, no. 3 (1998): 393–433, here 419–20. It could be argued that Nazi German violence, too, had a "developmental" aspect: much of it occurred in relation to the attempt to transform occupied countries into more productive or surplus-generating areas.

Second World War). Many of those deported perished or were executed, especially during the first wave of deportations. However, the violence reserved for "non-Soviets" was no harsher than that which was reserved for Soviet citizens. And it occurred on a much smaller scale. Between the early 1930s and 1953, it is estimated that 1.0 to 1.2 million Soviet citizens were executed, most of them on the basis of extrajudicial sentences (75 percent of these executions were carried out in the eighteen months between July 1937 and the end of 1938). Of the over 6 million Soviet citizens deported, approximately 1.5 million experienced an untimely death. Between 16 and 17 million Soviet citizens were subject to imprisonment or forced labor; 10 percent of them died in the camps.[158] Only a minority of them, some 3 million in total, were ever convicted of alleged "counterrevolutionary" activities. The great majority of those sent to camp – nearly 80 percent – were products of the general criminalization of small offenses and social insubordination that resulted from the regime's attempts to "restore order" to an unsettled, undisciplined, and disorderly "quicksand society." The largest contingents of prisoners were accused of petty theft, "speculation," "work desertion," "hooliganism," and other forms of "socially dangerous behavior." Finally, one should not forget to mention one particularly extreme form of mass violence, that which was directed against large parts of the collectivized *kolkhoz* peasantry in 1932 and 1933. The consequence of this violence was the last great peacetime European famine and millions of starved victims.

German and Soviet violence differed in another fundamental way, as well: in all of the cases referenced above, as well as in many others, plans existed in Germany – plans that were often widely distributed and shared – for a scale of violence that far exceeded anything that actually transpired. While some 50,000 "asocials" may have been killed in Nazi Germany, experts estimated that 1.0 to 1.6 million "asocials" would ultimately need to be eliminated. Similarly, while more than 1 million people were resettled in the early stages of germanizing Eastern Europe and other German-annexed territories, plans required that at least 30 million more be resettled. Again: 3 million Soviet POWs died in German captivity, but there were plans to allow tens of millions of Soviet citizens, including POWs, to starve to death within a year following the German attack on the USSR. And, these are not the only cases: 11 million Jews were targeted for death in the Holocaust (6 million were killed); millions of additional foreign workers would have been deported to Germany, if conditions allowed; and, utopian military plans would only have spread the violence further. The planned magnitude of absolute violence – beyond the dimension of violence and death actually inflicted upon Europe – made Nazi Germany a unique threat.

---

[158] Iu.A Poliakov and V.B. Zhiromskaia, *Naselenie Rossii v XX veke*, Part 1, 320; Part 2, 195 (Moscow: ROSSPEN, 2000, 2001).

This is not to suggest that Nazi violence was solely the product of a set of detailed, long-term plans directly related to the establishment of an Aryan utopia. The very fact that a number of the Nazis' more ambitious plans for murder did not develop far beyond the stage of theory demonstrates that obstacles and/or opposition to their realization existed. Secondly, it needs to be remembered that violence was often diverted into unexpected directions – or, at least, into directions not implicit in Nazi ideology. The passive resistance of Soviet citizens and their spirited determination to survive, for example, foiled Nazi Germany's original plans to starve large segments of that population to death. This popular resistance, in turn, led to a series of ad hoc and hastily planned efforts to starve – or otherwise kill – selected vulnerable population groups, above all Soviet POWs "unfit for work." "Short-term plans" (*Nahpläne*) to settle ethnic Germans in western Poland and to resettle over a million evicted Poles in the General Government also largely failed. The blocking of such limited resettlements, of course, was an inauspicious omen for the longer-term implementation of Generalplan Ost. These failures substantially contributed to the genesis of the mass murder of Jews and disabled hospital inmates in these regions. It was also only the failure of the campaign in the East that led to a labor policy completely in contradiction with the tenets of Nazi racism: the utilization of millions of foreign workers in the Reich, the bulk of whom were Poles and Soviet citizens.

In other words, in Nazi Germany, too, internal and external resistance limited the regime's ability to realize its murderous plans. Sometimes, the threat of potential resistance alone was sufficient to curtail violence, as was the case with the "euthanasia" program and with actions taken against so-called "half-Jews" and "quarter-Jews." Until recently, researchers have downplayed such dissent and resistance; however, it is likely to become a more prominent feature in future research efforts, once the factual and analytical bases for Nazi violence have been established. Some German policies of extermination were delayed or limited because of the war situation, while others were aggravated.

In the Soviet Union, too, authorities penned plenty of plans relating to the arrest, deportation, or execution of "kulaks," "socially harmful elements," "anti-Soviet elements," and people belonging to "enemy nations." OGPU Order number 44/21 (February 2, 1930), for example, provided each individual region with round-number quotas for the number of kulaks of the first category to be arrested and sent to camps and of kulaks of the second category to be deported. The increased quotas provided in NKVD Order 00447 (July 30, 1937)[159] are characteristic of the "figure mania" that permeated every sector of Soviet economic, political, and social life during the 1930s. These figures reflect both the illusion of planning and the Soviet obsession with social engineering.

From its inception, the "planification" of mass violence revealed its limitations. For example, far from being a "planned" operation based on "firm

[159] Cf. ftn. 10.

quotas," as OGPU leaders had hoped, "dekulakization" descended into a chaotic and largely uncontrolled process. Deportation operations were completely uncoordinated between source and destination, often resulting in the unprecedented and deadly phenomenon known as "abandonment in deportation."[160] Over a year passed before a special commission, directly attached to the Politburo, ordered a "stop [to] the dreadful mess in the deportation of manpower." By that point, initial dekulakization quotas had been overfulfilled threefold and authorities were forced to deal with over 1.5 million deportees. The emergence of an internal dynamic that repeatedly resulted in the "overfulfillment of quotas" is among the more remarkable features of "planned" repressive operations, such as dekulakization and the campaigns to eradicate "socially harmful elements." With regard to the latter, recently declassified correspondence between the Politburo and local authorities reveals, in chilling bureaucratic detail, the dynamics and mechanics of this mass crime. Centralized planning combined with bureaucratic reflexes spurred local officials, many of whom had only recently been promoted, to anticipate and surpass directives from Moscow in an effort to please their superiors. "Planned" to be finished within four months, the 1937 campaign to eradicate "socially harmful elements" lasted fifteen months. The number of people "in the first category" (to be shot) was surpassed by 325 percent and in "the second category" (to be sent to camps), by 140 percent.[161]

Superficially, this tendency resembles a much-noted characteristic of the Nazi regime: that is, the penchant of officials and functionaries, often left without detailed instructions, both to anticipate and to shape German policies on the ground. However, the phrase typically associated with such a mentality, "working toward the Führer" (based on Ian Kershaw's famous citation of German State Secretary Werner Willikens),[162] does not adequately convey the complexity of the system. It provides a sense of the self-confidence of German functionaries, but it does not reflect the internal dynamics of the system, the interagency rivalry in a world with multiple power centers, and the constant negotiation and coordination required to get anything done.

In both cases – Nazi Germany and Stalinist Soviet Union – mass violence went far beyond the implementation of detailed, long-term plans. In Nazi Germany, utopian plans generally exceeded the actual extent of violence; whereas, in the Soviet Union, plans for violence – violence directed primarily at Soviet citizens – were, as a rule, *overfulfilled*. The ostensible aim of social violence also differed in both cases, as did the chronology of violent events. In German society, mass violence – directed primarily against external "enemies" and, as

---

[160] Nicolas Werth, "Déplacés spéciaux et colons de travail dans la société stalinienne," *XXème Siècle. Revue d'Histoire*, 54 (1997): 34–50.

[161] Rolf Binner & Marc Junge, "'Wie der Terror gross wurde': Massenmord und Lagerhaft nach Befehl 00447," *Cahiers du Monde russe* 42, no. 2–4 (2001): 557–614; N. Werth, "Repenser la Grande Terreur."

[162] Quoted several times in Ian Kershaw, *Hitler*, 2 vols. (London: W. W. Norton, 1998 and 2000).

such, a form of "imperialist" violence – not only reached its peak during the war, but fundamentally changed in nature and scope. Soviet mass violence – which can partly be characterized as "developmental" violence – culminated during the tremendous social upheavals of the 1930s, long before the outbreak of war with Germany.

5

The Quest for Order and the Pursuit of Terror

*National Socialist Germany and the Stalinist
Soviet Union as Multiethnic Empires*

Jörg Baberowski and Anselm Doering-Manteuffel
Translation by Barry Haneberg

National Socialism and Stalinism both sought systematically to structure and classify a seemingly chaotic modern world. Classification here, however, should not be understood solely as the act of categorizing in order to grasp reality, for it is also an act of inclusion and exclusion. It is a violent act that forces others to submit to its ascriptions. And yet, while classification seeks to produce order from chaos, it ironically produces the very anarchy and ambiguity that it seeks to overcome.

The quest for order is a human necessity – everywhere and at all times. What characterizes the modern variant, however, is its demand for unambiguity and exclusivity – and, by extension, the ability to differentiate between legitimate and illegitimate order. What is excluded from ordered society loses any claim to equality; the excluded must either remove itself (for example, via assimilation, emigration, and so forth) or be forcibly removed. In this manner, the modern search for order not only produces ambivalence, it produces the very categories of humanity that it must then eliminate. This is how Zygmunt Bauman judged the character of modern dictatorship.[1] One could further argue that terror and genocide were the flip sides of these efforts to construct a better world, a world cleansed of the excluded.[2]

Empire emerged as the site in which utopian purity fantasies were implemented and, as necessary, redefined. The Soviet Union was already a multinational empire when the Bolsheviks began to reorder it according to their own ideas – an empire that defied central control and, thus, had to be destroyed through internal conquest. National Socialist Germany, by contrast, was a

---

[1] Zygmunt Bauman, *Moderne und Ambivalenz: Das Ende der Eindeutigkeit* (Frankfurt am Main: Fischer, 1995), 29–30.
[2] Ibid., 61; Omer Bartov, "Utopie und Gewalt: Neugeburt und Vernichtung des Menschen," in *Wege in die Gewalt: Die modernen politischen Religionen*, eds. Bronislaw Baczko and Hans Maier (Frankfurt am Main: Fischer, 2000), 92–120. See also David L. Hoffmann, *Stalinist Values: The Cultural Norms of Soviet Modernity 1917–1941* (Ithaca, NY: Cornell University Press, 2003).

nation-state that became a multinational empire through military expansion and, in the process, acquired a level of ethnic and cultural diversity that its political leaders found intolerable. In the end, both regimes exacerbated the very chaos that they sought to eliminate. As a result, the world outside their familiar, enclosed orders – a world that they were often complicit in creating – came to be viewed as one of potentially threatening counterorders.[3]

How is it, though, that National Socialists and Bolsheviks both came to understand difference as a threat, and why did they pursue extermination campaigns to eradicate such difference? Most importantly, they actually believed it possible to eliminate forever what they perceived to be a disorienting and disturbing diversity of cultures and communities. This belief itself derived from an eschatological ideology of redemption, an ideology that represented future life as a permanent order of social, national, and racial homogeneity. In order to realize such an order, "enemies" embodied within social, national, or racial collectives had to be destroyed. This ideology, of course, did not simply appear; it developed within a specific cultural context and it radicalized whenever conditions appeared to slip out of control. In a sense, utopias are the product of "self-hallucination" (Karl Schlögel), and through it, National Socialists and Bolsheviks alike were able to survive emergency situations that they themselves had created. They needed chaos and an enemy representing such chaos in order to protect themselves and to justify the necessity of permanent cleansing.[4]

Friend-enemy categorization was not the only way that theoreticians and practitioners of ordering strategies envisioned overcoming ambiguity in social

---

[3] Eric Weitz, *A Century of Genocide: Utopias of Race and Nation* (Princeton, NJ: Princeton University Press, 2003), 8–15, 53–101; Peter Holquist, "To Count, to Extract, and to Exterminate: Population Statistics and Population Politics in Late Imperial and Soviet Russia" in *A State of Nations: Empire and Nation-Making in the Age of Lenin and Stalin*, eds. Ronald Suny and Terry Martin (New York and Oxford: Oxford University Press, 2001), 111–44; Jörg Baberowski, *Der Feind ist überall: Stalinismus im Kaukasus* (Munich: Deutsche Verlags-Anstalt, 2003); Philippe Burrin, "Totalitäre Gewalt als historische Möglichkeit," in *Utopie und Gewalt*, eds. Baczko and Maier, 83–201; Christopher Browning, *Die Entfesselung der "Endlösung" Nationalsozialistische Judenpolitik 1939–1942*, trans. Klaus-Dieter Schmidt (Berlin: Propyläen, 2003), 604–17.

[4] Karl Schlögel, "Utopie als Notstandsdenken – einige Überlegungen zur Diskussion über Utopie und Sowjetkommunismus," in *Utopie und politische Herrschaft im Europa der Zwischenkriegszeit*, ed. Wolfgang Hardtwig (Munich: Oldenbourg, 2003), 77–96; Michail K. Ryklin, *Räume des Jubels: Totalitarismus und Differenz* (Frankfurt am Main: Suhrkamp, 2003), 19; Eric Weitz, "Racial Politics without the Concept of Race: Reevaluating Soviet Ethnic and National Purges," *Slavic Review* 61 (2002), 1–29; Gerd Koenen, *Utopie der Säuberung: Was war der Kommunismus?* (Berlin: Fest-Verlag, 1998); Jörg Baberowski, *Der rote Terror: Die Geschichte des Stalinismus*, 2nd ed. (Munich: Deutsche Verlags-Anstalt, 2004); Ian Kershaw, "Adolf Hitler und die Realisierung der nationalsozialistischen Rassenutopie," in *Utopie und politische Herrschaft*, 133–44; Götz Aly, "'Judenumsiedlung': Überlegungen zur politischen Vorgeschichte des Holocaust," *Nationalsozialistische Vernichtungspolitik 1939–1945: Neue Forschungen und Kontroversen*, 4th ed., ed. Ulrich Herbert (Frankfurt am Main: Fischer, 2001), 67–97; Christoph Dieckmann, "Der Krieg und die Ermordung der litauischen Juden," in *Nationalsozialistische Vernichtungspolitik*, 329; Ludolf Herbst, *Das nationalsozialistische Deutschland 1933–1945: Die Entfesselung der Gewalt: Rassismus und Krieg* (Frankfurt am Main: Suhrkamp, 1996), 374–88.

relations. National Socialists, like the Bolsheviks, experienced the First World War and the subsequent civil war as conflicts produced within multiethnic, extremely violent contexts. While the one envisioned "barbarians" and "sub-humans," the other discovered "traitors" and "enemies" – all of whom were embodied in races or ethnicities. Not only did these experiences precede their respective ordering programs, they served to constitute them. Wherever military forces, colonial officials, ethnologists, and anthropologists worked to realize clearly defined orders, multiethnicity was viewed as an evil that had to be eradicated. And it was as a result of the experiences of German and Russian officers during the First World War and of Freikorps soldiers and Bolshevik functionaries during the subsequent civil wars that ethnic conflicts were always also the most brutal of conflicts. That purification fantasies ultimately became reality can only be explained in reference to this "foreknowledge" with which the perpetrators marched into battle.[5]

NATIONAL SOCIALIST GERMANY

Among the necessary preconditions for National Socialist expansion were certain cultural traditions and ideological beliefs that long predated the war in the East. These traditions and ideologies were integral to the emergence of the ethnic-racial concept of "Lebensraum." The origins of this concept lay in the experience of the First World War, when German soldiers were confronted with unfamiliar people living in relatively "primitive" conditions in a foreign, seemingly endless land. The war in the East forced a confrontation with this other cultural reality – a reality that the army and occupation administration perceived as "uncultured."[6]

From the very beginning, German occupation authorities in Poland and in the Baltic territories pursued policies aimed not only at establishing economic and political control, but at remodeling the structure of local societies in accordance with German concepts of "culture" and "order." This amounted to a forcible transformation of social realities along German administrative lines. Over the course of the war, practical experiences in these matters mixed with older, more traditional Prussian prejudices, producing an image of "the East" that would dominate the ethnic-racial discourse of the interwar period.

---

[5] Vejas Gabriel Liulevicius, *War Land on the Eastern Front: Culture, National Identity, and German Occupation in World War I* (Cambridge: Cambridge University Press, 2000); Paul J. Weindling, *Epidemics and Genocide in Eastern Europe: 1890–1945* (Oxford: Oxford University Press, 2000); Eric Lohr, "The Russian Army and the Jews: Mass Deportations, Hostages, and Violence during World War I," *Russian Review* 60 (2001): 404–19; Peter Holquist, *Making War, Forging Revolution: Russia's Continuum of Crisis, 1914–1921* (Cambridge, MA: Harvard University Press, 2002); Joshua A. Sanborn, *Drafting the Russian Nation: Military Conscription, Total War, and Mass Politics 1905–1925* (DeKalb: Northern Illinois University Press, 2003), 74–94.

[6] Liulevicius, 151–75.

Economic exploitation disrupted the socioeconomic equilibrium in occupied areas, exacerbating the impression of mass poverty and encouraging the spread of disease. Of course, this only reified the perception of an "unclean" people in the East and increased demands to "cleanse" the region. The military administration reacted with a spate of bureaucratic regulatory measures aimed at both improving and monitoring hygienic conditions. These measures included the registration, counting, and photographing of local populations. With regulation, however, control and subjugation came to be bureaucratically practiced. As a consequence, cleanliness and social discipline assumed a causal relationship, a relationship constructed by the German bureaucracy and its understanding of "order."[7]

The lack of ethnic homogeneity among "subject" populations in German-occupied Poland and in the "Ober Ost" military administration in the Baltic[8] further influenced German views, as occupational bureaucracies found such complexity difficult to order.[9] Attempts to "Germanize" population groups ultimately led to the reactive formation of ethnic blocs. In the process of differentiating themselves from and against enemy Germans, however, these blocs simultaneously and consciously differentiated and divided themselves from and against one another.[10]

As a result of their experiences with ethnic diversity, disorder, filth, and poor hygiene, German conceptions of the East radically changed over the course of the war. While terms such as "land" and "people," each with its own concrete characteristics, dominated at the onset of occupation, by 1915/16 a shift to the abstract and collective concepts of "space" (*Raum*) and "race" (*Volk*) had occurred.[11] These modified concepts enabled Germans to transcend semantically the political-geographical and ethnic complexity of the region.[12] Territories and populations were considered in relation to one another; and, as a result, the concepts of foreign lands and foreign peoples were much easier to comprehend. The antithetical perspectives of "Germany" and "Germans" here, and of "space" and "race" there soon developed. In this manner, Central Europe was reconceptualized. Academic scholars followed with attempts to define political-geographic "space" clearly, to map its diversity, to locate

---

[7] Ibid., 54–88.

[8] "Ober Ost" was the abbreviation for "Oberbefehlshaber der gesamten deutschen Streitkräfte im Osten" (Supreme Command of all German Combat Forces in the East), a territory encompassing Estonia, Latvia, Lithuania, and parts of White Russia. See Abba Strazhas, *Deutsche Ostpolitik im Ersten Weltkrieg: Der Fall Ober Ost, 1915–1917* (Wiesbaden: Harrassowitz, 1993).

[9] See Oberbefehlshaber Ost, ed., *Völker-Verteilung in West-Rußland* (Hamburg: L. Friederichsen, 1917).

[10] Liulevicius, 118–29.

[11] Cf. ibid., 106–7.

[12] Werner Köster, *Die Rede über den "Raum": Zur semantischen Karriere eines deutschen Konzepts* (Heidelberg: Synchron, 2002); Stefan Breuer, *Ordnungen der Ungleichheit: Die deutsche Rechte im Widerstreit ihrer Ideen 1871–1945* (Darmstadt: Wissenschaftliche Buchgesellschaft, 2001), 77–104; Uwe Puschner, *Die völkische Bewegung im wilhelminischen Kaiserreich: Sprache – Rasse – Religion* (Darmstadt: Wissenschaftliche Buchgesellschaft, 2001).

German "ethnic groups" and "language islands," with the ultimate goal of establishing "order," producing ethnic homogeneity, and ascertaining attractive areas for German settlement.[13] The very concept of "ethnic cleansing" was contained in this semantic shift from "Land and People" to "Space and Race."[14]

Nonetheless, German occupational authorities during the First World War acted within a legal framework. As dictatorial as individual measures may have been, they maintained a sense of legitimacy and produced an effective legal space. German occupation was structured according to German administrative law, and, importantly, its stipulations applied to native Germans, as well. This is one manner in which German occupation during World War I differed from the occupational terror under the National Socialists.[15]

It must also be recalled that German soldiers on the Eastern Front never directly experienced military defeat; in fact, Germany forced a punitive peace treaty upon the revolutionary Bolshevik government in March 1918. While imperial Germany began to collapse soon thereafter, and in November 1918 physically capitulated, these facts were simply not recognized in the East. The situation among Russia, the Baltic countries, and Germany remained uncertain. This uncertainty, combined with the incursion of Soviet troops into the Baltic territories, led to the formation of volunteer units – units that were originally intended solely to support the withdrawal of regular German troops.[16]

These voluntary formations, the Freikorps, represent a critical link between the realities of the First World War on the Eastern Front and the National Socialist politics of conquest in Central and Eastern Europe after 1939.[17]

---

[13] Guntram Henrik Herb, *Under the Map of Germany: Nationalism and Propaganda, 1918–1945* (London: Routledge, 1997).

[14] The Chairman of the Alldeutschen Verband (All German Union), Heinrich Claß, utilized this term as well as the concept of "nationaler Flurbereinigung" (the redistribution/cleansing of territory and people) in his propaganda for an annexationist foreign policy during the First World War. For him, the concepts of "Nation" and "Volk" were interchangeable. Rainer Hering, *Konstruierte Nation: Der Alldeutsche Verband 1890 bis 1939* (Hamburg: Christians, 2003), 135. Cf. Hans Mommsen, "Der 'Ostraum' in Ideologie und Praxis des Nationalsozialismus und der Holocaust," in *Von Weimar nach Auschwitz: Zur Geschichte Deutschlands in der Weltkriegsepoche* (Stuttgart: Deutsche Verlags-Anstalt, 1999), 283–94, 285. The idea of a new war and of an ethnic "Flurbereinigung" was formulated programmatically by Ewald Banse in *Raum und Volk im Weltkriege: Gedanken über eine nationale Wehrlehre* (Oldenburg: Gerhard Stalling, 1932), 15–178, 401–3. The significance of expulsion and mass murder in the act of "ethnic cleansing" is a topic developed further by Norman M. Naimark in *Fires of Hatred: Ethnic Cleansing in Twentieth Century Europe* (Cambridge, MA: Harvard University Press, 2001).

[15] Werner Basler, *Deutschlands Annexionspolitik in Polen und im Baltikum 1914–1918* (Berlin [East]: Rütten & Loening, 1962). Hans Fenske, "Die Verwaltung im Ersten Weltkrieg. §7: Die Verwaltung der besetzten Gebiete," in *Deutsche Verwaltungsgeschichte*, vol. 3, eds. Kurt G. A. Jeserich, et. al. (Stuttgart: Deutsche Verlags-Anstalt, 1984), 902–4.

[16] Hagen Schulze, *Freikorps und Republik 1918–1920* (Boppard am Rhein: Harald Boldt, 1969).

[17] Robert G. L. Waite, *Vanguard of Nazism: The Free Corps Movement in Post War Germany, 1918–1923* (Cambridge, MA: Harvard University Press, 1952).

Established as anti-Bolshevik fighting units, they had the tasks of both obstructing the further penetration of the Bolsheviks into the Baltic territories and preventing the escalation of social revolution in Germany. But while Freikorps troops in Germany worked with the revolutionary government, the *Volksbeauftragte*, and helped to stabilize the government formed by the National (constitutional) Assembly and thus ensured that a new, democratic order could be established, Freikorps troops in the East served no discernible constructive purpose. Military struggle was of the essence, without consideration for any potential political ordering system and without any connection to an objective legality. Freikorps in the East became extremely brutal and violence-prone civil-military units, driven by expectations that, at the end of the struggle, they would receive territory of their own.[18] The association of fighting with settlement determined their orientation. They utilized the concepts of "space" and "race" in order to maximize their interests. They did not act according to the political-social norms of the world from which they came; indeed, they abandoned them. This attitude fundamentally distinguished their actions from those of the imperial military and civil administration and foreshadowed SS practices during the Second World War.[19]

Freikorps generally served as reservoir for militant individuals who thought of their group experience as warriors, the *Kampfgemeinschaft*, as a model of social ordering and supported the leadership principle (*Führerherrschaft*). Thus, they typically acted as point of reference for all those who opposed the democratic and civil-society order of the Weimar Republic. The formation of Freikorp units between the end of the First World War and 1920 also served as the "socializing moment" for a cohort of youth that was unable to experience combat during the war. The majority of these youth did not serve in Freikorps units stationed in the East, in the Baltics, or in Silesia, but rather in units operating within Germany proper. As such, their experiences provided them with no practical knowledge of the people inhabiting Eastern Europe. They were not personally familiar with Lithuanians, Letts, Poles, or White Russians. They knew just as little about Jews in the East, many of whom had served in the German military administration since 1915.[20] Their experiences did, however, provide them with a propensity for violence and a diminished respect for law and legality.

In lieu of actual, concrete experiences with the cultural realities of Eastern Europe, young Freikorps members adopted the ideological image of "the East" wholesale. Only from the description of older Freikorps soldiers, those who had served in the army, did they learn of the backward civilization that peddled

---

[18] Liulevicius, 238–40.

[19] Michael Wildt, *Generation des Unbedingten: Das Führungskorps des Reichssicherheitshauptamts* (Hamburg: Hamburger Edition, 2002), 601–6.

[20] Steven E. Aschheim, *Brothers and Strangers: The East European Jew in German and German Jewish Consciousness, 1800–1923* (Madison: University of Wisconsin Press, 1982), 139–214; Liulevicius, 117–20, 180–2.

on in the wide expanses of the East. They heard of "disorder," which referred both to the confusing ethnic diversity of the East and to an everyday life whose cultural norms the Germans could simply not decode. This image of "disorder" was laced with tales of poor hygiene and of "filth." On top of this were descriptions of Bolshevik Commissars, who were often Jewish. Out of this mélange of ideas and observations, the Freikorps developed an aggressive, ideologically based ethnic-racist, anti-Semitic, and anti-Bolshevik posture – a posture that merged with that of National Socialism in the early 1920s.

The experience of war in the East and the resultant collective imagining of "the East" significantly influenced German society, especially the academic elite, during the interwar period. They built upon the ideological concepts of the racial nation (*Volkstum*) and living space (*Lebensraum*) and legitimized the proliferation of such ideas in the educational sphere.[21] Indeed, the academic discourse on race in the 1920s played an important role in the acceptance of National Socialism by middle-class intellectuals.[22]

This environment was especially important for the development of two trends. The first produced German "Eastern Studies" (*Ostforschung*) and the ethnic-racial "Native Peoples and Cultures Research" field (*Volks- und Kulturbodenforschung*). These initiatives emerged out of the impulse virtually to reconquer the East after Germany had lost large swaths of conquered territory and was forced to relinquish its own territory in the East as a result of the peace treaty.[23] Secondly, this environment was formative for the mental and intellectual development of young men, of students, who would later become the core actors in National Socialist imperialism.[24] Within this latter group, a considerable number of Freikorps fighters from the years 1918/19 were to be found.

The first trend resulted from the experiences of imperial expansion under the peace of Brest-Litovsk, of military-political collapse with significant loss of territory and the development of a resultant sense of national humiliation. Public and academic debates in this milieu unleashed compensatory energies that aimed to establish certain Eastern Central European territories as German territories.[25] This sentiment produced the academic discipline of *Ostforschung* and the field of *Volks- und Kulturbodenforschung*.

---

[21] Woodruff D. Smith, *Politics and the Sciences of Culture in Germany 1840–1920* (Oxford: Oxford University Press, 1991).

[22] Ulrich Herbert, "'Generation der Sachlichkeit': Die völkische Studentenbewegung der frühen zwanziger Jahre in Deutschland," in *Zivilisation und Barbarei: Die widersprüchlichen Potentiale der Moderne*, eds. Frank Bajohr et al. (Hamburg: Christians 1991), 115–44.

[23] Michael Burleigh, *Germany Turns Eastwards: A Study of Ostforschung in the Third Reich* (Cambridge: Cambridge University Press, 1988); Ingo Haar and Michael Fahlbusch, eds. *German Scholars and Ethnic Cleansing, 1919–1945* (New York: Berghahn Books, 2005); Michael Fahlbusch, "*Wo der deutsche...ist, ist Deutschland!*": Die Stiftung für deutsche Volks- und Kulturbodenforschung in Leipzig 1920–1933 (Bochum: Brockmeyer, 1994).

[24] Herbert, "Generation"; Idem, *Best: Biographische Studien über Radikalismus, Weltanschauung und Vernunft, 1903–1989* (Bonn: Dietz, 1996), 42–130; Wildt, 72–142.

[25] Andreas Hillgruber, "'Revisionismus': Kontinuität und Wandel in der Außenpolitik der Weimarer Republik," *Historische Zeitschrift* 237 (1983): 597–621; Daniel T. Murphy, *The*

Ostforschung was based on the ideological premise that not only did inter-connected settlements of Germanic populations exist throughout Eastern Central Europe, but that German remained the spoken language in these locales – "linguistic islands," as the research jargon called them. Broad swaths of territory encompassing these settlements were deemed German "cultural territory" and served as the ideological justification for the penetration of the East.[26] But it was National Socialism itself that produced the practical conditions for Eastern expansion: an aggressive war that not only was planned but, from the very beginning, incorporated the goals of "ethnic cleansing." This represents the one developmental trend that led directly from the experience of war in the East to the realities of the National Socialist system.

The second trend influenced the mentality and academic qualifications of those who would later become the key implementers of National Socialist imperialism. This group was primarily composed of the war generation, born around 1890, and the so-called war children, born after 1900.[27] These two groups differed in that the older members were shaped by their participation in war and the experience of the front, while the younger members knew only the home front. They were not able to experience front life and, instead, compensated for its absence through participation in the Freikorps. What united both groups was their fixation upon the end of the war, a fixation that strongly influenced their perceptions of the present and their imaginings of the future. They understood the First World War as a fundamental rupture of their sense of self and civilizations. The worldviews and structural norms of late-nineteenth-century Germany were no longer valid. Society had fundamentally changed as a result of the disintegration of class boundaries and mass impoverishment; social stability had simply collapsed. The question of one's place in society and the meaning of one's own existence presented itself anew with unexpected sharpness. Accordingly, a cultural orientation with changed perceptions of reality emerged in the postwar years. Tradition and cultural legacy no longer constituted the defining categories of this orientation; rather, it formed around the desire for a new order with long-term sustainability.[28] Where the future was constructed, the old, the past, would have no meaning. "Space" (*Raum*) and "people" (*Volk*) could be understood as eternal concepts without epoch-specific meaning, as could "soil," "race," and "art." The idea that one could construct an entirely new order from this basis enabled the fiction that a future without the ballast of the past could be made possible. This world picture

Heroic Earth: Geopolitical Thought in Weimar Germany, 1918–1933 (Kent, OH: Kent State University Press, 1997).

[26] Herb, 49–94, 95.

[27] Detlev Peukert, *Die Weimarer Republik: Krisenjahre der Klassischen Moderne* (Frankfurt am Main: Suhrkamp, 1987), 91–111.

[28] Lutz Raphael, "Sozialexperten in Deutschland zwischen konservativem Ordnungsdenken und rassistischer Utopie (1918–1945)," in *Utopie als Notstandsdenken*, 327–46; Birgit Kletzin, *Europa aus Rasse und Raum: Die nationalsozialistische Idee der neuen Ordnung* (Münster: LIT, 2002), 54–109.

emerged from the cultural destruction of the war and had a lasting influence on the spiritual climate of the 1920s. It was especially influential in universities, where it was absorbed by the war youth, those students born after 1900.[29] Those students arriving from Freikorps duty present an interesting example. They already thought in the categories of *Volk*, "space," and "race" and they integrated these categories into their concept of an overarching new order. After the National Socialist assumption of power, many of them joined the political police and the SS.[30] The destruction of the German *Rechtstaat* and of public morals through the NS system, combined with Hitler's will to war, created tremendous freedom of action for these individuals. After 1939, this freedom enabled them to implement everything from "ethnic cleansing" to the genocide of European Jewry. Their position in the system of NS control, their relation to the Wehrmacht, and the principles behind their actions defined the war of conquest in Eastern Europe.

Together, the experiences of the First World War and the Treaty of Versailles, ethnic-racial ideologies, and emergent generational perspectives formed the ideological preconditions for the National Socialists' policies of conquest. Material preconditions were created after the assumption of power in 1933. Foremost among these were the army's acceptance of the regime's political goals and its subordination to Hitler, thus making it dependent on his political will. Only under such conditions could a war of conquest, such as the one Hitler planned, be conducted as a war for the "Germanization"[31] of much of Eastern Europe. These conditions were realized in 1938.

The disempowerment of the army was both calculated and consequential. Hitler assumed nominal control over the Reichswehr upon the death of Reichspresident Paul von Hindenburg in August 1934. He achieved effective control over the army in 1938 with the removal of General Werner von Fritsch, head of OKH.[32] Prior to both these events, in June 1934, the SA leadership was murdered, as this organization was no longer instrumental once the NSDAP consolidated state power. The military leadership accepted this act of terror in the expectation that, henceforth, the army would remain the only armed force in the NS state.[33] Yet already in September 1934, Hitler instructed the Reich Minister

---

[29] Anselm Doering-Manteuffel, "Mensch, Maschine, Zeit: Fortschrittsbewußtsein und Kulturkritik im ersten Drittel des 20. Jahrhunderts," in *Jahrbuch des Historischen Kollegs 2003* (Munich: Oldenbourg, 2004), 91–119.

[30] Jens Banach, *Heydrichs Elite: Das Führerkorps der Sicherheitspolizei und des SD 1936–1945* (Paderborn: Schöningh, 1998), 35–86.

[31] On the topic of "Germanization" and its use by Hitler see, among others, Andreas Wirsching, "'Man kann nur Boden germanisieren': Eine neue Quelle zu Hitlers Rede vor den Spitzen der Reichswehr am 3. Februar 1933," *Vierteljahrshefte für Zeitgeschichte* 49 (2001): 517–50.

[32] Klaus-Jürgen Müller, *Das Heer und Hitler: Armee und nationalsozialistisches Regime 1933–1940* (Stuttgart: Deutsche Verlags-Anstalt, 1969).

[33] Klaus-Jürgen Müller, *Armee und Drittes Reich 1933–1939: Darstellung und Dokumentation* (Paderborn: Schöningh, 1987).

for War to increase the number of SS military units (*Verfügungstruppe*) and, therewith, began the construction of what would become the Waffen-SS.[34] The Waffen-SS acted as a National Socialist political army, while the Wehrmacht sought to maintain its traditional role as the army of the nation-state.[35] The political army formed the instrument for conducting an ideologically moti- vated, racial war of conquest as a war of ethnic destruction. In contrast, the traditional army was, in its own self-understanding, an instrument for politi- cal struggle between states and, as such, was not suited for a policy of ethnic cleansing in conquered territories. Until 1939, the Waffen-SS acted alone as the political army. Subordinated to Hitler's political will, however, the Wehr- macht quickly recognized that it too would have to assume certain functions of a political army. As a result, intense conflicts developed between the German High Command, on the one side, and Hitler and the leadership of the Waffen- SS, on the other. While it is true that NS political officers were integrated into the Wehrmacht only after the assassination attempt of 20 July 1944, the re-formation of the Wehrmacht into a National Socialist army, with requisite political tasks, began in the fall of 1939.

Within weeks of the invasion of Poland, many military commanders – though certainly not all – had accepted the fact that this war would not be limited to the front lines, but rather would extend into the interior and include the mass murder of civilian populations through Einsatzgruppen of the Secu- rity Police and the Security Service (SD).[36] Thus, already in 1939, Wehrmacht generals were prepared to accept ideologically justified violence against civilian populations as a characteristic of *this* war.

The invasion of Poland began as a traditional military struggle between nation-states. Behind the army, however, stood units of the Security Police and the Security Service, ready for deployment under orders from Reichsführers SS und Chef der deutschen Polizei Heinrich Himmler. These units operated according to the tenets of National Socialist racial selection. They escalated what began as a traditional war of conquest over another state into a racial war, a war of ethnic-racial expulsion, destruction, and "Germanization." Their task, according to guidelines from July 1939, was to "fight all elements hostile to the Reich and to Germans" in Poland.[37] From the very beginning, they operated independent of the military's administrative and police order. On 17 October 1939, Hitler dissolved the military administration of occupied Poland, justifying the act by noting that the Wehrmacht would no longer have to deal with population policy. He simultaneously decreed that members of Waffen- SS, SS-Totenkopfverbände, and German police units on "special duty" were

---

[34] Ibid., 71–8, 209–10; Bernd Wegner, *Hitlers Politische Soldaten: Die Waffen-SS 1933– 1945: Leitbild, Struktur und Funktion einer nationalsozialistischen Elite*, 5th ed. (Paderborn: Schöningh, 1997), 84–95.

[35] Robert J. O'Neill, *The German Army and the Nazi Party, 1933–1939* (New York: James H. Heineman, 1966), 62–83.

[36] Müller, *Heer*, 422–70.

[37] Wildt, 426.

released from the prescripts of standard military law.[38] Given that Himmler ensured that the laws of the German Reich ended at the Reich border, an extralegal zone was effectively created in the conquered territories, and it was into these extralegal zones that the Einsatzkommandos of the Security Police and the SD marched, murdered Jewish populations, and set in motion the *völkische Flurbereinigung*, a massive project of ethnic cleansing, that the radical Right had had on its agenda since 1916.[39]

The Wehrmacht initially sought to dissociate itself from this endeavor, but soon enough it found itself complicit in its operation. Just as in Belgium in 1914, the military leadership viewed the conquered population as fundamentally weak.[40] Effective opposition to the German military was neither imagined nor expected. This perception was not only a reflection of traditional Prussian cultural presumptions against Poland; it also reflected the experiences of the First World War on the Eastern Front. To this was added the disparaging image of the native population as backward and "inferior." This view then fused with the ethnic-racist, overwhelmingly anti-Semitic discourse that emerged in German society during the interwar period. After 1939, these views increasingly manifested themselves in the behavioral patterns of Wehrmacht units as they worked to deprive "Polish subhumans"[41] of both the right and the ability to oppose occupation. The fact that opposition nonetheless developed, however, produced a particular nervousness and fear of "franktireurs."

Reinhard Heydrich, head of the Security Police and the SD, utilized the situation in order psychologically to link guerrilla warfare with Jewishness in the minds of German soldiers. This strategy harked back to the experiences of the First World War but in this case, ethnic confusion, cultural backwardness, and "filth" were explained exclusively via anti-Semitic argumentation, such that Jews were presented as the authoritative cause of disorder and chaos. In order to produce "order" on Polish territory, the Germans had to eliminate the Jews. Heydrich stigmatized the Jews as enemies of "order." Propaganda, in turn, disseminated these ideas through the rank and file and indoctrinated the Wehrmacht along appropriate ideological lines. Jews, according to Heydrich's office, were active participants in partisan warfare.[42] In this manner, Heydrich justified the racially and ideologically motivated persecution of the Jewish population in Poland and set in motion the mass murder of Jewry. The Wehrmacht remained silent and was increasingly drawn into complicity.

The pace of annihilation was determined by SS formations of the Reichssicherheitshauptamt (RSHA), but it was Hitler who provided them with the necessary latitude for action. Rather than providing direct orders, which

---

[38] Müller, *Heer*, 435–6; Wildt, 474–6.

[39] Hitler used the term "völkische Flurbereinigung" in his deliberations with General Brauchitsch, Senior Commander of the Army, on 7 September 1939. Herbert, *Best*, 241.

[40] John Horne and Alan Kramer, *German Atrocities, 1914: A History of Denial* (New Haven, CT: Yale University Press, 2001), 89–174.

[41] Wildt, 437.

[42] Ibid., 438.

Hitler only rarely did, he offered operational leeway and extralegal zones. This effectively negated traditional prohibitions and taboos and marginalized the defenders of state and military legality. The SS leadership immediately occupied these "free zones." They utilized operational freedom in order to act in a manner unconcerned with traditional notions of ethics, morals, and legality derived from the value systems of the nation-state and civil society.[43]

During the First World War, one could already observe this shift from cultural to structural perceptions, vis-à-vis the occupied territories, in the language of the Ober Ost occupation authorities. The tendency inherent within this shift was formative for the SS elite. It represented the abandonment of a worldview that considered social conditions historically derived structures and that understood growth and dissolution, change and progress, as characteristic of human action. Instead, the style of thought within the SS elite built upon the categories of ethnicity, race, space, and eternity. The very term "eternity," a thousand-year time span, entailed an imagined "history" based upon a mythical understanding of the past, but which contained little or no conception of actual historical developments.[44] This perspective contained revolutionary potential in that it negated history. Whoever fails to recognize the law, the state, and the nation as ordering principles between societies, and freedom and self-determination as ordering principles within society, places himself in the situation of having to create an image of an entirely different order, however utopian that may be.[45] In this manner, cultural value orientations could be redefined, in turn enabling the redefinition of human relations.

In an effort to develop a temporal schematic for the war in the East that both emphasizes the escalation of the conflict and differentiates between Wehrmacht and SS areas of operation, we have segmented the war into three periods of increasingly dynamic destruction and terror – the first and second of which particularly crassly illustrate the "ordering madness." The first phase lasted from the attack on Poland in the fall of 1939 until the invasion of the Soviet Union in June 1941. This phase – the conquest and subjugation of Poland – demonstrated the practical impossibility of effecting an ethnic reordering solely on racial grounds. On the one side stood mass murder, deportation, and the resettlement of native populations; on the other side, considerable efforts were taken to colonize territories with German or what was determined as racially German stock. From the very beginning, German rule was the rule of terror. The racist ideologies of *Volkstum* and *Lebensraum* existed without reference to real social and economic conditions; they entirely ignored the

---

[43] Ian Kershaw, *Hitler, 1936–1945*, trans. Klaus Kochmann (Stuttgart: Deutsche Verlags-Anstalt, 2000), 325–59.

[44] Wolfgang Hardtwig, "Die Krise des Geschichtsbewußtseins in Kaiserreich und Weimarer Republik und der Aufstieg des Nationalsozialismus," in *Jahrbuch des Historischen Kollegs 2001* (Munich: Oldenbourg, 2002), 47–75; Doering-Manteuffel, 115–17.

[45] Frank-Lothar Kroll, *Utopie als Ideologie: Geschichtsdenken und politisches Handeln im Dritten Reich* (Paderborn: Schöningh, 1998).

cultural intertwinement and multiethnic nature of societies, not to mention the actual working of agrarian and commercial economies. The attempted whole-sale shift of entire population groups resulted in the utter collapse of supply and production networks and produced administrative chaos in its wake. The desire to Germanize "space" in occupied Poland led to population policies that were both haphazard and without clear end goals.[46] Deportation and mass murder were intertwined from the very beginning. Even if it was not yet the intention to murder all Jews, but rather to relocate them forcibly to distant, isolated colonies, the brutal measures of implementing this new order nonethe-less hinted at the coming "Final Solution of the Jewish Question."[47] Even the plan to ship all Jews to Madagascar implied nothing other than genocide.[48] This period was a period of experimentation with genocide; the decisive radi-calization of policy occurred in the fall of 1941.

Under these conditions, the ability to conduct a purely traditional war came into doubt. The Army High Command's demand that occupied territories be placed under military administration indicates that, in general, it was only now that the true character of war in the East and the dangerous gravity of Hitler's racial hatred became clear. Indeed, there were protests against the extension of military action against civilian populations. By the end of 1939, however, the Army High Command accepted that the Wehrmacht would be responsible only for military matters.[49] The administration of Polish territory – in other words, Germanization as a program of mass murder and ethnic reconstruction – was left to the executors of the political will. Interestingly, the desire of many military commanders to avoid confrontations with the reality of this type of occupation led not to their distancing from racial war but to their acceptance of the military's politically inspired exclusion from the administration of occupied territories.[50] In this manner, racism was able to become established as the leading operational principle in occupational administration. This did not fail to have an effect, and within one and a half years, it was a broadly accepted principle.[51]

The Einsatzgruppen of the Security Police and the SD marched behind the Wehrmacht, and with them also marched the Einsatzgruppen of the SS

[46] Michael G. Esch, "'Ohne Rücksicht auf historisch Gewordenes': Raumplanung und Raumord-nung im besetzten Polen 1939–1944," *Modelle für ein deutsches Europa: Ökonomie und Herrschaft im Großwirtschaftsraum*, ed. Horst Kahrs (Berlin: Rotbuch-Verlag, 1992), 77–123.

[47] Götz Aly, *"Endlösung": Völkerverschiebung und der Mord an den europäischen Juden* (Frank-furt am Main: Fischer, 1995); Peter Longerich, *Politik der Vernichtung: Eine Gesamtdarstellung der nationalsozialistischen Judenverfolgung* (Munich: Piper, 1998), 273–92.

[48] Magnus Brechtken, *"Madagaskar für die Juden": Antisemitische Idee und politische Praxis 1885–1945* (Munich: Oldenbourg, 1997).

[49] Müller, *Heer*, 429–38.

[50] Hans Umbreit, "Auf dem Weg zur Kontinentalherrschaft," in *Das Deutsche Reich und der Zweite Weltkrieg*, vol. V/1, ed. Militärgeschichte Forschungsamt (Stuttgart: Deutsche Verlags-Anstalt, 1988), 41.

[51] Wolfram Wette, *Die Wehrmacht: Feindbilder, Vernichtungskrieg, Legenden* (Frankfurt am Main: Fischer, 2001), 95–104.

Race- and Resettlement Office (*Rasse- und Siedlungshauptamts der SS [RuS-Einsatzgruppen]*).[52] While units of the Security Police began to murder members of the political elite, union leaders, church elders, and the Polish intelligentsia – not to mention the Jewish population – the RuS-Einsatzgruppen registered and seized all useful agricultural territory. They deported the inhabitants and sought to replace them with racially German settlers. These settlers overwhelmingly were from the Baltic territories and, often enough, indicated that they did not consider themselves to be German.[53]

Hitler immediately created the organizational prerequisites for resettlement. On 7 October 1939, he named Heinrich Himmler to the position of "Reich Commissioner for the Strengthening of the German Race" (*Reichskommissar für die Festigung deutschen Volkstum" [RKF]*).[54] In this, he conferred upon Himmler decision making power over settlement policy, resettlement, land distribution, and new settlement – in other words, deportation and ethnic cleansing. In those areas destined for annexation – Danzig, West Prussia, Posen, East Upper Silesia – so-called heads of civil administration were inserted alongside the military administration. The personnel of this Civil Administration overwhelmingly came from the SS and quickly sought to amass administrative power in their own hands. Administration here consisted of confiscations, repression, and terror, vis-à-vis the Poles, and the organization of mass murder, vis-à-vis the Jews. On 12 October 1939, Hitler signed into law the establishment of the "General Government for Occupied Polish Territories." On 26 October, military administration over these territories officially ceased.

The General Government encompassed the core Polish territories, including the districts of Krakow, Radom, Warsaw, and Lublin, and served as an experimental laboratory for National Socialist population policies. It was here that the largest resettlements transpired, and it was here that genocide was centered. Until 1941, collection camps in West Galicia – the District of Lublin in the General Government – served as the destination for victims of Germanization (principally Poles, Jews, and Gypsies) in the annexed territories and the occupied portions of Poland.[55] Until the invasion of the Soviet Union, the eastern border of the Lublin District served as the demarcation line between the German and Soviet spheres of interest, in accordance with the Hitler-Stalin Pact of 23 August 1939. The Red Army occupied the eastern half of Galicia,

---

[52] Isabel Heinemann, *"Rasse, Siedlung, deutsches Blut": Das Rasse- und Siedlungshauptamt der SS und die rassenpolitische Neuordnung Europas* (Göttingen: Wallstein, 2003).

[53] Aly, *Endlösung*, 25.

[54] Robert L. Koehl, *RKFVD: German Resettlement und Population Policy 1939–194: A History of the Commission for Strengthening of Germandom* (Cambridge, MA: Harvard University Press, 1957).

[55] Jan T. Gross, *Polish Society under German Occupation: The Generalgouvernement, 1939–1944* (Princeton, NJ: Princeton University Press, 1979); Dieter Pohl, *Von der "Judenpolitik" zum Judenmord: Der Distrikt Lublin des Generalgouvernements 1939–1944* (Frankfurt am Main: Peter Lang, 1993); Aly, *Endlösung*, 29–55.

including Lemberg (L'vov) and Tarnopol, in September 1939, but by the fall of 1941, it too was fused into the General Government as the District of Galicia.

In the course of only a few weeks during the fall and winter of 1939, occupied Poland was transformed into a virtually lawless territory. The governors of the annexed regions of Danzig-West Prussia and Posen (after January 1940, the Wartheland), as well as the governor of the General Government, were not bound by German law.[56] The governors received orders directly from Hitler to Germanize their territories through the expulsion of native Poles into the General Government, the extermination of Jews, and the immigration of suitable German stock. The ideological fixation on a racially ordered utopia, centered on the concepts of *Raum* and *Volk*, ignored all rules of legality and entirely removed the constraints of traditional administrative bureaucracy.

"Blood Is Our Frontier," a slogan among SS intellectuals,[57] expressed their demand that political borders be established according to ethnic, rather than political, criteria. The war provided the physical, conceptual, and morally unconstrained space of action[58] that the SS leadership had long imagined in their ahistorical, ethnic-racial ideologies. And, in accordance with their own assessment of the problem, they now utilized mass murder in the service of "ethnic cleansing" and of extending the border of "German blood" as far as possible.

Occupational terror was practiced both by the Einsatzgruppen of the Security Police and by the RuS-Einsatzkommandos. The Einsatzgruppen of the Security Police immediately began to arrest and murder Polish elites and to deport Jewish men between the ages of fifteen and sixty, a process that often included mass murder.[59] Ghettos were established in large cities in order to coordinate better the resettlement and deportation of the Jewish population. By the end of September 1939, a decision had been made in Berlin to Germanize existing German provinces in Poland and to create a new "district for foreign-speaking populations centered in Krakow."[60] Jews from the annexed territories, along with Jews from the Reich itself, were to be deported into this no-man's-land. Simultaneous with the establishment of the RSHA as the

---

[56] Banach, 222. Helmut Krausnick, Hans-Heinrich Wilhelm, *Die Truppe des Weltanschau-ungskrieges: Die Einsatzgruppen der Sicherheitspolizei und des SD 1938–1942* (Stuttgart: Deutsche Verlags-Anstalt, 1981), 84–5; Ruth-Bettina Birn, *Die Höheren SS- und Polizeiführer: Himmlers Vertreter im Reich und in den besetzten Gebieten* (Düsseldorf: Droste, 1986), 186–206.

[57] Raimund Schnabel, "Ewig ist das Blut," *SS-Leitheft* 2, 25 March 1936, 13.

[58] On the European dimension of National Socialist imperialism see Hans Mommsen, "Umvolkungspläne und der Holocaust," in idem, *Von Weimar nach Auschwitz*, 295–308; Peter Schöttler, "Eine Art 'Generalplan West': Die Stuckart-Denkschrift vom 14. Juni 1940 und die Planungen für eine neue deutsch-französische Grenze im Zweiten Weltkrieg," *SozialGeschichte* 18 (2003): 83–131.

[59] Krausnick and Wilhelm, 41–55.

[60] Heydrich's comments to senior RSHA and Einsatzgruppen leaders on 21 September 1939. Quoted from Wildt, 457.

organizational center for racial resettlement and Jewish expulsion, its chief, Reinhard Heydrich, and Adolf Eichmann, then head of the "Central Office for Jewish Emigration" in Prague, proposed the creation of a Reich ghetto that would be situated at the border between West and East Galicia, on the demarcation line between the German and Soviet spheres of influence. Apparently, the RSHA wanted to prove that the mass deportation of Jews out of the Reich was possible and that a Jewish reservation in occupied Poland (or on the island of Madagascar) could be established. The infeasibility of this plan was already demonstrated by February 1940, however, as the German administration in the General Government was simply unable, on such short notice, logistically to accommodate hundreds of thousands of refugees in hastily established camps and to provide them with basic essentials.[61] The refugee problem continued to fester until the second phase of the war in 1941. With the "Final Solution of the Jewish Question," the occupation forces took the final, unthinkable step and initiated the industrial extermination of humanity.

Territorial control was affected by RuS-Einsatzkommandos. Toward the end of October 1939, Himmler enacted a resettlement and expulsion program in the annexed territories that was intended to Germanize these territories along racial lines. All Jews, and a significant portion of the Polish population, were to be deported in preparation for ultimate German settlement.[62] Experts from the Race and Settlement Office were asked not only to classify local populations according to racial criteria but also to categorize and confiscate all desirable land "in Polish and Jewish hands."[63] From the circle of RuS experts, land distribution offices, as well as SS settlement and SS work details, were formed in order to register and classify all potential settlement areas and to plan the redistribution of agriculturally valuable land. This registration process was completed by 1941. The confiscation of Polish and Jewish property continued until the end of 1942.

In the annexed territories of Danzig-West Prussia, Posen/Warthegau, and East Upper Silesia, more than 80 percent of the registered agricultural enterprises were confiscated. Economic property – industrial enterprises, as well as smaller-scale and family-owned businesses – was registered by an agency subordinated to Hermann Göring, Deputy for the Four-Year Plan. As a result of this division of labor between Göring's Haupttreuhandstelle Ost and Himmler's Reichs Commissary for the Strengthening of the German Race, German settlement and population policies developed an overwhelmingly agricultural and seemingly antimodern character.[64] The impression of antimodernism, however, is deceiving. The modernity of the SS lay in its mania for concrete order: an order based on population policies, as these enabled the SS clearly to design

---

[61] Longerich, 251–72.
[62] Heinemann, *Rasse*, 192–3.
[63] Ibid., 201.
[64] Cf. Rolf-Dieter Müller, *Hitlers Ostkrieg und die deutsche Siedlungspolitik: Die Zusammenarbeit von Wehrmacht, Wirtschaft und SS* (Frankfurt am Main: Fischer, 1991), 103–4.

"space," settle it with only a given type of individual, and design a typified world of "essentially" German villages and towns. The "disorder" of the native culture was to be transformed through modern rationality into a homogeneous "order," and in order to achieve this goal the native society was excised and removed. Here we can see how the National Socialist utopia was both modern and terroristic.

And here as well the character of National Socialist population policies becomes clear. National Socialism ideologically constructed the Jew as a particular type of enemy and doggedly pursued this enemy into every corner of Europe.[65] Connected with this ideology was the belief in a hierarchical value of races – a hierarchy in which Jews and Gypsies resided at the very bottom, while Slavs, scaled from Russians to Poles to Lithuanians, hovered slightly above them. The Poles' own native anti-Semitism and hostility toward Jews and Bolsheviks only seemed to confirm the validity of this hierarchy in the eyes of many National Socialists.[66] The interactions among ideological constructions of "the enemy," racial-biological hierarchies, and the confirmation of related ideological assumptions in actual foreign experiences help to explain the nature of SS population policies. While the Polish population was selectively repressed, displaced, and killed, policies regarding the Jewish population were total and without exception. With the practical experience of deportation into ghettos, the concept of a resolution to the Jewish Problem through physical annihilation soon emerged. This realization began to influence the thinking of SS settlement experts, and in 1941 the transfer of populations into the General Government was halted.

As National Socialist population policies aimed to conform *Raum* and *Volk* with a schematically conceptualized and German-dominated order, officials sought to coordinate expulsion and resettlement with one another. The expulsion of native populations and the resettlement of racially suitable Germanic stock were two sides of the same coin. During the first phase of the war, new settlers overwhelmingly arrived from the Baltics and Eastern Poland. Before their naturalization into one of the annexed territories, though, these individuals were forced to undergo an examination by SS racial experts. They were registered in a German "Volks" list and, in order to ensure accurate racial classification, were ranked according to language ability and ancestry. In the "utopia of the 'racially' pure" settler society, "race" and "Germanness" were

---

[65] On the escalation of Jewish persecution toward the goal of total annihilation – a process that began with the Jews of Eastern Europe and, after 1942, extended to include German Jews and, ultimately, all Jews of Europe – see Christian Gerlach, "Die Wannsee-Konferenz, das Schicksal der deutschen Juden und Hitlers politische Grundsatzentscheidung, alle Juden Europas zu ermorden," in *Krieg, Ernährung, Völkermord: Forschungen zur deutschen Vernichtungspolitik im Zweiten Weltkrieg* (Hamburg: Hamburger Edition, 1998), 85–166. Gerlach's argument that the Wannsee Conference represented the qualitative leap toward absolute annihilation does not contradict the "Anti-Semitism with Reason" of the *völkisch* students of the 1920s. Lethal ideas preceded lethal action.

[66] Cf. Baberowski, *Der rote Terror*.

determinant conditions of membership and ensured that conquered "space" was administered in an "orderly" manner.[67]

The second phase of conquest and expansion dated from the summer of 1941 and lasted until the summer of 1943, when the Red Army's counteroffensive destroyed any remaining possibility of long-term imperial control of territory in the East. Destruction and terror increasingly radicalized during this period. In the two years from 1941 to 1943, Himmler's SS was able to create and secure monopolistic control over racial policies in the new order of Eastern Europe and radicalized its demands for the ethnic subjugation of occupied territories. At the same time, cooperation among the SS, the Wehrmacht, and military and civil administrations in occupied White Russia and the Ukraine grew ever closer. Ultimately, the ability to distinguish between SS and other instances of occupational reality all but disappeared. Despite the outward cooperation among elements of state, army and party, however, the demand of the SS leadership unilaterally to define the nature and form of this new racial order rendered SS control exclusive.

Prior to the invasion of the Soviet Union, ministries in Berlin had developed a number of plans for the economic utilization of the conquered territories. White Russia and, in part, the Ukraine were to serve as areas of pure exploitation. Only certain "spaces" within the Ukraine were selected for Germanization; the rest of the Ukraine was to be scoured for raw materials. In May 1941, a work group concerned within the Reich Ministry for Nutrition and Agriculture proposed deliberately produced mass starvation – in effect, genocide – as a legitimate economic program.[68] This "starvation plan" was justified with the same rhetoric that supported the ahistorical new order developed in the academic discourse of the 1920s: "Under no circumstances will the conditions of the past remain; rather it is the abandonment of that past that will emerge." Moreover, this plan went beyond rhetoric – it represented quite real, material sentiments. The abandonment of the past implied the "incorporation of Russian agriculture into the European sphere."[69] For those who read this formulation with the knowledge of what later occurred, it is not difficult to recognize that this statement could only be derived from an ideological position. The "abandonment of the past" led to the annihilation of Russia; it led to the destruction of *Raum* and *Volk* as historical facts and, instead, allowed them to be rearranged without historical condition. The enormity of the notion that 30 million people might be allowed to starve corresponds with the equally

[67] Heinemann, *Rasse*, 260–82.
[68] Christian Gerlach, *Kalkulierte Morde: Die deutsche Wirtschafts- und Vernichtungspolitik in Weißrußland 1941–1944* (Hamburg: Hamburger Edition, 1999), 46–59, 47ff.; and footnote 62 on Herbert Backe (born 1896), which contains a brief generational profile of the "war children" (*Kriegsjugend*). There is, however, as Gerlach notes, no biography for him.
[69] "'Wirtschaftliche Richtlinien für Wirtschaftsorganisation Ost, Gruppe Landwirtschaft' vom 23. Mai 1941," in *Der Prozeß gegen die Hauptkriegsverbrecher vor dem Internationalen Militärgerichtshof, Nürnberg 1947–1949*, vol. 36, ed. P. A. Steiniger (Berlin: Rütten & Loening, 1960), 135–57.

horrifying concept that a country, a space with its own centuries-long historical development, could simply be wiped clean. This was indeed a deadly utopia.

Even in the Wehrmacht, few reservations were expressed regarding Hitler's intent to conduct the war against the Soviet Union as a political-ideological and racial-ideological war of destruction. The army authorized the "Kommissarbefehl," which dictated that political officers, in and out of uniform, were to be immediately shot and demonstrated therewith that there would be no further disagreements regarding the conduct of war, such as those that occurred during the Polish campaign.[70] True, individual commanders did ignore the order, but these isolated incidents failed to alter the general political consensus. Furthermore, the readiness to conduct an anti-Bolshevik crusade implied an agreement to pursue the war as a racial war against "*Jewish* Bolshevism."

Already during the winter of 1939/40, Hitler ordered settlement experts and other Ostforschung specialists to plan for the (re)construction of the Eastern territories.[71] After the invasion of the Soviet Union, planning accelerated and, between November 1941 and May 1942, resulted in the "General Plan East" (Generalplan Ost). By 1942/43, Generalplan Ost had further evolved into the "General Settlement Plan" (Generalsiedlungsplan).[72] The General Government[73] as well as the conquered territories of the Soviet Union – especially the Ukraine,[74] but also parts of White Russia[75] – were to be subject to the coming racial-political order. As we already noted in the annexed Polish territories, ethnic cleansing was closely linked to the destruction of the Jews, who were stigmatized as partisans and were pursued by both SS-Einsatzgruppen and Wehrmacht units stationed in the army rear. In the process, the Germans profited from the collaboration of locals, who assisted in locating Jews and organizing them into forced labor teams or transporting them into ghettos.[76]

---

[70] Christian Streit, *Keine Kameraden: Die Wehrmacht und die sowjetischen Kriegsgefangenen 1941–1945* ([1978], rev. ed. Bonn: Dietz, 1997); Christian Streit, "Ostkrieg, Antibolschewismus und 'Endlösung'" *Geschichte und Gesellschaft* 17 (1991): 242–55.

[71] Müller, *Ostkrieg*, 88 and 130–8.

[72] Dietrich Eichholtz, "Der 'Generalplan Ost': Über eine Ausgeburt imperialistischer Denkart und Politik," *Jahrbuch für Geschichte* 26 (1982): 217–74; Mechtild Rössler, Sabine Schleiermacher, and Cordula Tollmien, eds., *Der "Generalplan Ost": Hauptlinien der nationalsozialistischen Planungs- und Vernichtungspolitik* (Berlin: Akademie, 1993); Czeslaw Madajczyk, ed., *Vom Generalplan Ost zum Generalsiedlungsplan* (Munich: Saur, 1994).

[73] Dieter Pohl, *Nationalsozialistische Judenverfolgung in Ostgalizien 1941–1944: Organisation und Durchführung eines staatlichen Massenverbrechens,* 2nd ed. (Munich: Oldenbourg, 1997); Thomas Sandkühler, *"Endlösung" in Galizien: Der Judenmord in Ostpolen und die Rettungsinitiativen von Berthold Beitz 1941–1944* (Bonn: Dietz, 1996).

[74] Karel C. Berkhoff, *Harvest of Despair: Life and Death in Ukraine under Nazi Rule* (Cambridge, MA: Harvard University Press, 2004); Wendy Lower, "A New Ordering of Space and Race: Nazi Colonial Dreams in Zhytomir, Ukraine, 1941–1944," *German Studies Review* 25 (2002): 227–54; Wendy Lower, *Nazi Empire-Building and the Holocaust in Ukraine* (Chapel Hill: North Carolina University Press, 2005).

[75] Gerlach, *Kalkulierte Morde*; Bernhard Chiari, *Alltag hinter der Front: Besatzung, Kollaboration und Widerstand in Weißrußland 1941–1944* (Düsseldorf: Droste, 1998).

[76] Gerlach, *Kalkulierte Morde*, 503–774; Chiari, *Alltag hinter der Front*, 96–159.

The planning for Generalplan Ost was based upon the presumption that Jews would no linger have to be considered in the planning for the resettlement of the indigenous populations.[77] Regardless of the exact day in 1941 that the decision for the "Final Solution of the Jewish Problem" was made,[78] the results of the Wannsee Conference of 20 January 1942 and those measures prepared between May and July 1942[79] conformed chronologically and objectively with the racial- and ethnic-political beliefs of the SS leadership in the RHSA, the Race and Settlement Main Office, and the Reich Commissary for the Strengthening of the German Volk. The systematic murder of Jews in extermination camps, with the explicit goal of eradicating all Jewish life in Europe, began during the summer of 1942.

The absurdity and the practical ineptitude of the National Socialist settlement and Germanizing policies are demonstrated by their attempt to register "German blood" – including individuals that RuS experts classified as ethnic Germans or of German descent – and to settle them in arbitrarily defined "German" villages. SS settlement teams (*SS-Ansiedlungsstäbe*) from the RKF and village officials were primarily men, but in the spirit of National Socialist family politics, with its cult for heroic maternity, women from the NS-Frauenschaft were also included. They practiced motherhood as if they were soldiers in a racial war.[80] The despotic nature of RuS population policies proved to be quite difficult for Germanic settlers as well, as many were forced to move and create a new life for themselves in a foreign land, rather than remaining in their native home. This highhandedness against racially German settlers transpired alongside the violent expulsion of natives, and wherever resistance to resettlement was offered, violence often escalated into outright terror. All of this violence, however, was conditioned upon, indeed presumed, the complete annihilation of the Jewish population. The county of Zamosc in the district of Lublin experienced such a population transfer during the winter of 1942/3. In this instance, the brutality of the system is demonstrated by the fact that, in order to house 10,000 Volksdeutsche, 50,000 Poles were expelled from their homes. The perverse reality of these Germanization schemes is that race and settlement experts were unable to recruit sufficient Volksdeutsche, racial Germans, or otherwise suitable stock for their resettlement needs. It would not suffice that a mere 10,000 settle Zamosc; the plan intended ten times that number. Similar to and simultaneous with Zamosc, attempts were made in the fall of 1942 gradually to Germanize the Ukraine by establishing Volksdeutsch colonies. In September 1942, Himmler ordered 43,000 Volksdeutsche to be settled in the Generalkommissariat Zhitomir. This was the "Hegewald" colony – a

---

[77] Heinemann, *Rasse*, S. 382.

[78] Christopher Browning, *Fateful Months: Essays on the Emergence of the Final Solution* (New York: Holmes & Meier, 1991); Gerlach, "Die Wannsee-Konferenz."

[79] Pohl, *Judenverfolgung*, 203–5.

[80] Elizabeth Harvey, "'Die deutsche Frau im Osten': 'Rasse,' Geschlecht und öffentlicher Raum im besetzten Polen 1940–1944," *Archiv für Sozialgeschichte* 38 (1998): 191–214.

colony in which Himmler took particular interest. In contrast to Zamosc, however, it was envisioned that "Hegewald" would provide the surrounding region with protection from partisan attacks.[81] In any case, "Hegewald" was as much a disaster as Zamosc. Even though there were fewer-than-expected settlers, administrators were still unable to provide even the basics for a viable, self-sufficient farming community. To add insult to injury, they were subjected to partisan attacks by formerly expelled Ukrainians, had to flee before the onrushing Red Army in November 1943, and ultimately ended up in collection centers in the Warthegau.

Flight and chaos were important features of the third phase: the phase of retreat. But the primary feature is noteworthy in that it stood in stark contrast to chaos – namely, uninterrupted and orderly racial destruction. The period between the summer of 1943 and the winter of 1944/5, when the Red Army crossed the German border, is characterized by the industrial murder of Jews in extermination camps and the trafficking of laborers from the eastern territories for the purpose of forced labor in German agriculture and industry. From the perspective of RuS experts planning for the future of the occupied territories, 1943 was a year of uncertainty. It was abundantly clear that previous attempts to Germanize "space" in the East had failed. In Germany itself, a significant lack of industrial and agricultural labor became apparent. The dire need for labor led to the utilization of labor from the occupied territories, as a result of which standard racial-political practices of biological examinations, classification, and selection were no longer stringently applied.[82] In order to discourage sexual relations between forced laborers and German women, however, death loomed over the head of any forced laborer who transgressed these boundaries.[83] At the same time, race and settlement experts were focusing on perhaps the most despicable form of human trafficking. They quite literally stole Polish children who appeared racially suitable – on occasion, under the very eyes of their parents – in order to have them adopted by married couples in the Reich.[84]

If one considers these events in relation to long-term historical processes, the semantic shift that occurred during the First World War – the slow transition of perception from that of "Land" and "People" in their embedded cultures to the ahistorical formulations of *Volk* and *Raum* – initiated a development that ultimately resulted in race's occupying the center of a complex worldview. National Socialism combined vitalism, anti-Semitism, and anti-Bolshevism, but it was ethnic-racist anti-Semitism that fueled its most destructive tendencies.

---

[81] Lower, *Nazi Colonial Schemes*; Heinemann, *Rasse*, 453–64.

[82] Gerlach, *Kalkulierte Morde*, 1091.

[83] Heinemann, *Rasse*, 475–507, 495.

[84] Gitta Sereny, "Stolen Children" in *The German Trauma: Experiences and Reflections 1938–2000* (London: Penguin, 2000), 25–52.

THE STALINIST SOVIET UNION

National Socialist terror slid out of control as it extended beyond the borders of the German Reich and into areas which, in their mental map, were inhabited by "barbarian" races and "subhumans." The Stalinist terror, in contrast, directed itself inward and only during the latter moments of the war spilled outside the borders of the Soviet Union. Nonetheless, Stalinist terror was no less an act of conquest than the National Socialist's war in the East, as the Bolsheviks sought to force their concept of order onto all groups within their diverse empire and to eradicate the ambivalence embodied within such diversity.

The Bolsheviks were the true implementers of the modern project of homogenizing unambiguity (*Eindeutigkeit*). Its origins reach back to the early nineteenth century, when the Tsar's officials surveyed and categorized the territory and populations of his diverse empire. Its essence lay in the racialization and hierarchization of the populations that inhabited the multinational Russian Empire. In this way, Tsarist modernizers followed the European example of the nation-state. Premodern societies were agrarian, religious, estate-based, and multiethnic; modern societies were urban, secularized, and national. As officials had already classified the societies of historical epochs, they simply retooled these same hierarchies for modern usage. Accordingly, Muslims lived in the past; Christians in the present. The nation-state represented progress; multinational empire, backwardness. In this manner, "modernization" implied the overcoming of all aspects of backwardness and disorder, and Tsarist officials were accordingly charged with overcoming them. It is also the reason for the expedited pace with which they worked to level the empire.

Because modernizers within the Tsarist bureaucracy remained fixed to the idea of nationalization and homogenization, empire, with its uncomfortable diversity, became a potential danger. Ethnic differences were now perceived as threats, especially in the Caucasus and Central Asian regions, where the "barbarian" nature of life was most evident. If they failed to adopt European lifestyles or if they resisted "modernization," nomads and Muslims were termed "wild men" and "lepers."[85] Government officials in the Petersburg government saw matters no differently. Thus, the governor of the Caucasus spoke of "criminal tendencies," of "savage customs," and of "the spread of disease" when he reported to the the Interior Minister in St. Petersburg on the life of Muslims and nomads. Furthermore, these diseases were appropriated ethnic identities. As such, recalcitrant and unassimilated ethnic groups were treated and considered just as one does a virus in a sick body.[86]

---

[85] Holquist, "To Count," 111–44.

[86] Rossiiskii gosudarstvennyi istoricheskii arkhiv (RGIA), f. 932, op. 1, d. 319, l. 43; RGIA, Biblioteka (1894–1917), op. 1, d. 25, l. 75; RGIA, f 396, op. 5, d. 719, ll. 3–6; Baberowski, *Der Feind*, 42–3, 72–4.

This endeavor evolved from the colonial context, in Russia just as in Europe, and it was the colonial experts – ethnologists, legal anthropologists, orientalists, and doctors – who biologized ethnic difference.[87] With such a perspective, even Tsarist generals were able to justify ethnic cleansing, as they did during the mid-nineteenth-century Caucasus Wars, during which Tsarist troops evicted more than 500,000 Circassians and Chechens from their homes, destroyed their villages, and resettled Cossacks in their stead. Resettlement experts justified this action by placing it in a broader European context that included the expulsion of Arabs from Spain in the early-seventeenth century.[88] Only with the First World War, however, did population strategists receive the opportunity to implement their fantasies of a reordered empire. When Kazakh and Kirgiz tribes rose against colonial subjugation in 1915, for example, Russian settlers and soldiers engaged in a deliberate campaign of annihilation against the nomads in order to expel them and to transform the steppe into an ethnically homogeneous space. Several hundred thousand men and women were killed or evicted from their homeland.[89]

Although the methods of expulsion first developed within the colonial context, they were not limited to that context. In the course of the First World War, the Tsarist military created havoc in European regions of the empire. In 1915, the Tsar's Chief of the General Staff, Ianushkevich, ordered the retreating army

[87] Holquist, "To Count," 122–4; Weindling, 73–108; Andrei M. Pegushev, "Pervaia mirovaia voina i kolonial'nyi mir: Retrospektiva s uchetom etnofaktora," in *Pervaia mirovaia voina: Prolog XX veka*, ed. Viktor Mal'kov (Moscow: Nauka, 1998), 408–19; Strazhas; Gesine Krüger, *Kriegsbewältigung und Geschichtsbewußtsein: Realität, Deutung und Verarbeitung des deutschen Kolonialkrieges in Namibia 1904 bis 1907* (Göttingen: Vandenhoeck & Ruprecht, 1999); Tilman Dedering, "'A Certain Rigorous Treatment of All Parts of the Nation': The Annihilation of the Herero in German South-West Africa 1904," in *The Massacre in History*, ed. Mark Levene, Penny Roberts (New York: Berghahn, 1999), 205–22; Stephanus B. Spies, *Methods of Barbarism? Roberts and Kitchener and Civilians in the Boer Republics, January 1900–May 1902* (Cape Town: Human & Rousseau, 1977).

[88] A. P. Berzhe, "Vyselenie gortsev s Kavkaza," *Russkaia starina*, no. 1 (1882): 161–76, 337–63; M. Ia. Ol'shevskii, "Kavkaz i pokorenie vostochnoi ego chasti, 1858–1861," *Russkaia starina*, no. 9 (1894): 22–43; no. 4 (1895): 179–89; no. 6 (1895): 171–84; no. 9 (1895): 105–17; no. 10 (1895): 129–66; Dmitrii A. Miliutin, *Vospominaniia general-fel'dmarshala grafa Dmitriia Alekseevicha Miliutina 1816–1843* (Moscow: Studiia TRIT E, 1997), 306–14; "Pereselenie tuzemtsev Kubanskoi oblasti v Turtsiiu i na ukazannye im mesta v predelakh oblasti," in T. Kh. Kumykov, *Vyselenie adygov v Turtsiiu- posledstvie Kavkazskoi voiny* (Na'lchik: El'brus, 1994), 88–112; G. A. Dzagurov, ed., *Pereselenie gortsev v Turtsiiu* (Rostov on Don, 1925), 36–7; "O vyselenii Tatarov iz Kryma v 1860 godu: zapiska general-ad"iutanta E. I. Totlebena," *Russkaia starina*, no. 6 (1893): 531–50; "Pereselenie Tatarov iz Kryma v Turtsiiu; iz zapisok G. P. Levitskogo," *Vestnik Evropy*, no. 5 (1882): 596–639.

[89] Daniel R. Brower, "Kyrgyz Nomads and Russian Pioneers. Colonization and Ethnic Conflict in the Turkestan Revolt of 1916," *Jahrbücher für Geschichte Osteuropas* 44 (1996): 41–53; Edward Sokol, *The Revolt of 1916 in Russian Central Asia* (Baltimore: Johns Hopkins University Press, 1954); Kusbek Usenbaev, *Vosstanie 1916 goda v Kirgizii* (Frunze: Ilim, 1967); A. V. Piaskovskii and S. G. Agadzhanov, eds., *Vosstanie 1916 goda v srednei azii i Kazakhstana* (Moscow: Izdatel'stvo AN SSSR, 1960); G. I. Broido, "Materialy k istorii vosstaniia Kirgizov v 1916 godu," *Novyi vostok* 6 (1924): 407–34.

to lay waste to border territories, remove their populations, and outright expel any "enemy" ethnic groups. "Enemy" nations included Jews and Germans, as well as Turkish Muslims in the Caucasus. There were pogroms against the German population in Moscow and several other large cities; in many small towns and villages, Russian and Ukrainian soldiers massacred Jews and expelled thousands from their villages, deporting them into the Russian interior; in the Caucasus, Armenian soldiers openly terrorized Muslim civilians.[90] Tsarist generals considered Muslims, Poles, and Germans spies and potential traitors to the fatherland; Jews were considered politically unreliable. The war enabled the murder and deportation of these imagined enemies.

The Tsar's generals were absolutely certain that Russia's multiethnicity was its greatest weakness. Europe's modern military powers were ethnically homogeneous nation-states with national armies. Tsarist generals understood Germany's military superiority in precisely this regard.[91] Militarized nations were superior to multiethnic, fragmented societies. It appeared to be a natural law. Russia would only be able to withstand external threats when it removed "unreliable" national minorities from its border regions, when it separated ethnic groups from one another and reorganized the army according to national categories. Indeed, this occurred during the course of the First World War when the General Staff created and deployed exclusively Ukrainian and Armenian military formations.[92]

Ethnic cleansing refuted the very raison d'être of empire; it destroyed its multiethnic basis without creating the desired sense of nationhood. At a minimum, the Tsar's civilian ministers and many of his governors in the provinces recognized this dilemma, but they could do little against the fervor of the officers and nationalists who sought to translate their dreams into reality under the cover of war. The ethnic composition of Russia was not all that changed during the First World War. Millions were forced from their homes and hundreds of

---

[90] Eric Lohr, "The Russian Army," 404–19; Eric Lohr, *Nationalizing the Russian Empire: The Campaign against Enemy Aliens during World War I* (Cambridge, MA: Harvard University Press, 2003); Sanborn, 119–22; Mark von Hagen, "The Great War and the Mobilization of Ethnicity in the Russian Empire," in *Post-Soviet Political Order: Conflict and State-Building*, eds. Barnett R. Rubin and Jack Snyder (London: Routledge, 1998), 34–57; Holquist, "To Count," 124–5; S. G. Nelipovich, "Nemetskuiu pakost' uvolit', i bez nezhnostei," *Voenno-istoricheskii zhurnal* 1 (1997): 42–52; Victor Dönninghaus, *Die Deutschen in der Moskauer Gesellschaft: Symbiose und Konflikte 1494–1941* (Munich: Oldenbourg, 2002), 367–516; Baberowski, *Der Feind*, S. 84–96; Eli Weinerman, "Racism, Racial Prejudice and the Jews in Late Imperial Russia," *Ethnic and Racial Studies* 17 (1994): 442–95; A. B. Tsfasman, "Pervaia mirovaia voina i evrei Rossii 1914–1917," in *Chelovek i voina: Voina kak iavlenie kultury*, eds. Igor V. Narskii and Olga Iu. Nikonova (Moscow: AIRO-XX, 2001), 171–80; Wolfgang J. Mommsen, "Die Anfänge des Ethnic Cleansing und die Umsiedlungspolitik im Ersten Weltkrieg," in *Mentalitäten – Nationen – Spannungsfelder*, ed. Eduard Mühle (Marburg: Herder, 2001), 147–62.

[91] Among other Russian generals, General Brusilov saw it this way; see Aleksei A. Brusilov, *Moi vospominaniia* (Moscow: ROSSPEN, 2001), 73, 77.

[92] Sanborn, 74–82; von Hagen, "The Great War," 34–57.

thousands died in pogroms and ethnic cleansing actions. These pogroms and forced population transfers confronted population groups unfamiliar to one another under circumstances that inevitably made them into enemies.[93]

Deportations and interethnic conflict continued during the Revolution and the Civil War. More than 100,000 Jews died in pogroms perpetrated by revolutionary and counterrevolutionary armies. In the Caucasus and in Central Asia, the Revolution developed into a bloody conflict between Muslims and Christians, nomads and Russian settlers, locals and refugees. In the city of Baku alone, more than 10,000 inhabitants died as a result of violence between Armenians and Turks in 1918. Contact with strangers – soldiers, refugees, or migrants – now regularly ended up in violence. And where social and ethnic hierarchies mirrored one another, social conflict invited interethnic pogroms.[94] Add to this the "mass violence" of the Bolsheviks against their real and imagined enemies, such as the Cossacks in the Don region, and the encompassing nature of violence becomes glaring. The interethnic violence and psychic destruction that the Great War had wrought upon the Tsar's empire were overwhelming. Under the conditions of a multinational empire, the modern search for a homogeneous order led to absolute catastrophe.

The Bolsheviks dreamed of a comprehensive and well-defined order. Socialism understood itself as the realization of modern desires to transform ambiguity into certainty. In this sense, the multinational empire was, for Lenin and his supporters, a provocation that had to be eradicated. But the Bolsheviks wanted to do more than simply register, categorize, and control the population. They sought to change the very soul of their subjects, to transform their ways of life, and to release them from the disease of backwardness. This differentiated them from the Tsar's officials and generals. In the Bolshevik view of the world, one belonged to a class, and, thus, the Bolsheviks registered Russia's multinational population according to social categories. Individuals became members of classes – and, as Marxists believed that classes waged war against one another, they implicitly classified people as friends and enemies.[95]

However, people understand themselves in cultural contexts and they describe the conditions under which they live in differing manners and in different languages. They communicate in language and culture, not in class structures. Put differently: classes existed within nations; and whoever wished

93 Peter Gatrell, *A Whole Empire Walking: Refugees during Russia in World War I* (Bloomington: Indiana University Press, 1999), 15–32.

94 Charles Steinwedel, "To Make a Difference: The Category of Ethnicity in Late Imperial Russian Politics 1861–1917," in *Russian Modernity*, eds. David L. Hoffmann and Yanni Kotsonis (New York: St. Martin Press, 2000), 79–81; Gatrell, 128–40, 171–96; Holquist, *Making War*; B. Baikov, "Vospominaniia o Revoliutsii v Zakavkaz'e 1917–1920 gg." *Arkhiv Russkoi Revoliutsii* 9 (1923): 120–36; Baberowski, *Der Feind*, 133–6, 148–9.

95 Sheila Fitzpatrick, "Ascribing Class: The Construction of Social Identity in Soviet Russia," *Journal of Modern History* 65, no. 4 (1993): 745–68. Idem, ed., *Stalinism: New Directions* (London: Routledge, 2000), 20–46; Golfo Alexopoulos, *Stalin's Outcasts: Aliens, Citizens, and the Soviet State, 1926–1936* (Ithaca, NY: Cornell University Press, 2003), 1–11.

to transform the class structure of society had to know how to operate within the very cultures and languages that one sought to void. The act of overcoming ethnic diversity presumed its existence. Thus, socialism became an imperial project. The Bolsheviks transformed the Soviet Union into a state of nations, into a multinational community in which every nation lived independently. In each of the national reservations, national languages dominated and the local ethnicity enjoyed privileges not applicable to other and minority ethnicities. For, in the Bolshevik state there were advanced and backward, new and old nations. Backward nations were at an advantage relative to advanced nations in that their cultural autonomy was preserved. This resulted from the belief that the Bolshevik order would only prevail once it had been communicated to the backward nations in their own language and culture.[96]

Practical considerations were not alone in defining the nationalization of the Soviet Union. Lenin and his Marxist followers considered the nation-state to be an expression of modernity as it could be found in Western Europe. In contrast, multinational empires were anachronistic and the expression of backward relations. Empires arose only in order to be destroyed by the national virus in the course of history. Even those Bolsheviks who were not in favor of nationalization shared this belief in historical determinism.[97] For Stalin, Ordzhonikidze, Mikoian, Kaganovich, and those second-tier Bolsheviks who knew what it meant to belong to an ethnic minority, nations were more than just a transitional stage on the way to socialism. They considered nations to be communities of fate. People belonged to nations, just as they belonged to their class; one could not leave this community at one's own discretion.

Stalinist functionaries, in contrast to Lenin and European socialists, nurtured romantic, essentialist ideas of the nation. These ideas stemmed from their experiences with violence at the periphery of empire during the 1905 Revolution, the First World War, and the Civil War. At the empire's periphery, social conflicts were always also ethnic conflicts, and wherever nomads rose against settlers, Muslim unskilled laborers rose against skilled laborers, or Ukrainian farmers rose against Jewish artisans, class conflict disappeared in pogroms. Stalinist functionaries typically came from the periphery and learned their political craft in the empire's multiethnic zones of violence. In these zones, friends and enemies appeared as members of self-defined social and ethnic collectives. Central authorities knew that in order for these collectives to be effectively incorporated

---

[96] Yuri Slezkine, "The USSR as a Communal Appartment, or How a Socialist State Promoted Ethnic Particularism," *Slavic Review* 53 (1994): 415–52; Terry Martin, *The Affirmative Action Empire: Nations and Nationalism in the Soviet Union, 1923–1939* (Ithaca, NY: Cornell University Press, 2001); Baberowski, *Der Feind*, 184–214, 314–22.

[97] Vladimir I. Lenin, "Über das Selbstbestimmungsrecht der Nationen," in Vladimir I. Lenin, *Ausgewählte Werke*, vol. 1 (Berlin [East]: Dietz Verlag, 1978), 688; Jeremy Smith, *The Bolsheviks and the National Question, 1917–1923* (London: Macmillan, 1999), 7–28. Cf. also the debates of the Eighth Party Congress and of theTwelfth Party Congress of the RKP(B) in 1919 and 1923, respectively, *Vos'moi s"ezd RKP(B). Mart 1919. Protokoly* (Moscow, 1959); *Dvenadtsatyi s"ezd RKP(B) 17–25 aprelia 1923 goda. Stenograficheskii otchet* (Moscow, 1968).

within a meaningful order, they would have to be able to recognize themselves and their world within that order.[98]

However, self-descriptions of nationalities were often ambiguous and confusing. Consequently, none of the central authorities could actually answer the question, What was an Uzbek, a Kazakh, a Chechen, or a Mountain Jew from the Caucasus? How was one to recognize an Uzbek? By his language? On his belonging to a certain tribe? By his particular customs and manners? Nobody in the government could provide satisfying answers. For the Ukrainian National-Communist Skrypnik, all Muslims in the empire were "Turks"; Trotsky considered Uzbeks to be "Sarts"; and, when confronted with the bloody conflict in the Caucasus, Lenin had to be shown maps depicting the populations' ethnic composition.[99] For this reason, the government left it to experts to survey the Soviet Union anew: orientalists, ethnologists, linguists, and "bourgeois" scientists. Throughout the Soviet Union of the 1920s, tribes, clans, and linguistic groups were redefined as nations and accorded territories. Rural dialects were raised into the hierarchy of national languages, and wherever there was no written language, one was devised by linguists. Such demarcations were also consummated in western regions of the empire, such as when the Ukraine, White Russia, and the Russian Federation swapped territories during the 1920s. By the mid-1920s, the resurveying of the Soviet Union and the objective classification of ethnic attributes had been completed.[100] As Sergei Dimanshtein described in 1937, Soviet nationality policies transformed an "indistinct, amorphous mass" into individual nations.[101] A Turkish-speaking Muslim in the Caucasus was henceforth an Azerbaijani. He now spoke a national language, he had a homeland with a capital city, and, as a result of his "cultural backwardness," he enjoyed privileges over and above those of Christians who lived in "his" land. The Bolsheviks created a world according to their own expectations. The subjected cooperated in the construction of this world order in that they

---

[98] Anastas Mikoian, *Tak bylo* (Moscow: Vagrius, 1999); Nikita S. Khrushchev, *Khrushchev Remembers: The Glasnost Tapes* (Boston: Little, Brown and Co., 1990); Lazar M. Kaganovich, *Pamiatnye zapiski* (Moscow: Vagrius, 1997); Alfred J. Rieber, "Stalin: Man of the Borderlands," *American Historical Review* 53 (2001): 1651–91; Baberowski, *Der rote Terror*, 196–8.

[99] *Tainy natsional'noi politiki TsK RKP: Stenograficheskii otchet sekretnogo IV soveshchaniia TsK RKP 1923 goda*, ed. Ia N. Gibadulin (Moscow: INSAN, 1992), 79–80; Gosudarstvennyi arkhiv Rossiiskoi Federatsii (GARF), f. 3316, op. 509, ll. 64–69; Mikoian, 151–3; Baberowski, *Der Feind*, 237.

[100] Martin, *The Affirmative Action Empire*, 31–55; Terry Martin, "Modernization or Neo-Traditionalism? Ascribed Nationality and Soviet Primordialism," in Fitzpatrick, *Stalinism*, 348–67; Francine Hirsch, "The Soviet Union as a Work-in-Progress. Ethnographers and the Category Nationality in the 1926, 1937, and 1939 Censuses," *Slavic Review* 56 (1997): 251–78; Francine Hirsch, "Toward an Empire of Nations: Border-Making and the Formation of Soviet National Identities," *Russian Review* 59 (2000): 201–26; Francine Hirsch, "Empire of Nations: Colonial Technologies and the Making of the Soviet Union, 1917–1939" (Ph.D. diss., Princeton University), 1998; Yuri Slezkine, "N. Ia. Marr and the National Origins of Ethnogenesis," *Slavic Review* 55 (1996): 826–62.

[101] S. Dimanshtein, "Stalin – tvorets sovetskoi gosudarstvennosti narodov SSSR," *Revoliutsiia i natsional'nosti*, no. 1 (1937): 23.

behaved toward each other in a manner that leading Bolsheviks understood as an endorsement of their worldview.[102]

The "ethnicization" of the Soviet everyday carried with it national quotas that, among other things, determined which nationality was to be favored in the distribution of particular work and academic opportunities. The "indigenization" of the Party and state apparatus also awakened claims by those who had been excluded from the halls of government prior to the Revolution. The Bolsheviks nationalized backwardness; they forced their subjects to submit not only to social, but to national confessions as well.[103] Already by the end of the 1920s, subjects in all regions of the Soviet Union defined who they were in ways that accorded with the Bolsheviks' social and national categories. Even when one contested membership in a negatively viewed social or national group, the existence of the group was confirmed in the very act of denial. The status of a person in Soviet society thus depended upon how one acted in relation to ascribed social and national attributes and how one used these attributes to his or her own advantage. Turkish or Tatar workers in Baku or Kazan' preferred to be members of a "backward" nation, while Russian workers typically spoke in the language of "class" whenever they wished to demonstrate their superiority over the privileged "barbarians."[104]

Thus, nations were not only language communities. They were cultural communities, recognizable by their customs and manners. This essentialist, romantic understanding of the nation, however, contradicted the very project of social and cultural homogenization that the Bolsheviks had scribbled on their flags. For wherever social relations were indigenized, the importance and influence of nationalist Communists increased, for whom cultural autonomy and national identity meant more than the Socialism of the Bolsheviks.[105] By the mid-1920s, the GPU leadership had already warned Ukrainian nationalists, Azerbaijani Kemalists, and Tatar and Uzbek religious reformers about allegedly working to undermine the Communist Party. In March 1927, the

---

[102] Alexopoulos, 129–57; Baberowski, *Der Feind*, 314–49.

[103] Douglas Northrop, "Nationalizing Backwardness: Gender, Empire and Uzbek Identity," in *A State of Nations*, eds. Ronald G. Suny, Ronald Grigor, and Terry Martin, 191–220; Martin, *The Affirmative Action Empire*, 125–81.

[104] Baberowski, *Der Feind*, 349–68; Alexopoulos, 13–43; Martin, *The Affirmative Action Empire*, 348–67; Sarah Davies, *Popular Opinion in Stalin's Russia: Terror, Propaganda, and Dissent, 1934–1941* (Cambridge: Cambridge University Press, 1997), 82–90.

[105] Azade-Ayse Rorlich, "Sultangaliev and Islam," in *Ethnic and National Issues in Russian and Eastern European History: Select Papers from the Fifth World Congress of Eastern European Studies, Warsaw, 1995*, ed. John Morison (New York: St. Martin Press, 2000), 64–73; Adeeb Khaled, "Nationalizing the Revolution in Central Asia: The Transformation of Jadidism 1917–1920," in Suny and Martin, 145–62; Alexandre Bennigsen and Samuel E. Wimbush, *Muslim National Communism in the Soviet Union: A Revolutionary Strategy for the Colonial World* (Chicago: University of Chicago Press, 1979), 8–19; Alexandre Bennigsen and Chantal Lemercier-Quelquejay, *Les mouvements nationaux chez les musulmans de Russie: Le "Sultangalievisme" au Tatarstan* (Paris: Mouton, 1960); Baberowski, *Der Feind*, 223–41; Martin, *The Affirmative Action Empire*, 211–72.

GPU in Azerbaijan discovered a "not insignificant net of anti-Soviet elements" that had misused the Turkification of schools, universities, and the state apparatus in order to spread the nationalist program of Turkish Kemalists in the Caucasus. The First Secretary of the Azerbaijani Communist Party, Ali Heidar Karaev, proclaimed at a plenum of the local Central Committee that it was now time to lead a "merciless fight" against such nationalists. Nationalism was no path to Socialism, he argued. It was its contradiction. Wherever "bourgeois" professors and teachers indoctrinated students in the spirit of national emancipation, wherever Islamic spiritual reformers spoke of secularization but meant national self-determination, and wherever workers prioritized national privileges, Bolsheviks were silenced. This dilemma was recognized by the advocates of nationalization in the Politburo. In response, Stalin and Kaganovich authorized the GPU, in the late summer of 1926, to utilize violence against Ukrainian nationalists. A campaign against Islamic scholars, alleged Pan-Turkists, and religious officials was launched in the Asiatic regions of the Soviet Union in 1927.[106]

It was no accident that this terror grew out of the cultural revolution of the late 1920s, as Bolsheviks regarded national elites not only as representatives of their nation, but as interpreters of cultures that were contrary to the envisioned Soviet order. Thus, when the regime began to close churches and mosques, to prohibit festivals and rituals, to remove books from libraries, and to "civilize" farmers and "liberate" women, it had to eliminate these elites' competing interpretations of events. The Bolsheviks sought a place in the hearts and minds of their subjects. To this purpose, they had not only to erase their cultural memory, but to remove the interpreters of culture from their life. Therefore, class struggle in the national territories of the Soviet Union was, first and foremost, a struggle over meaning and interpretation. In arresting, deporting, and murdering national Communists, "bourgeois" nationalists, teachers and professors, priests, mullahs, shamans, and ethnic leaders, the Bolsheviks were eliminating their ideological opponents. Terror was more than a "social prophylactic": it was a cultural-revolutionary attack upon existing ways of life. Such an approach, however, contradicted the essentialist concept of the cultural nation. For how could Tatars or Uzbeks not be Muslims if their adherence to Islam constituted their nation? As a result, opposition to the central government's cultural-revolutionary campaigns developed in all regions of the Soviet Union. In virtually every town and village, opposition manifested itself in national forms; traditions, whose meaning nobody had ever questioned, became objects

---

[106] Rossiiskii gosudarstvennyi arkhiv sotsial'noi i politicheskoi istorii (RGASPI), f. 17, op. 67, d. 410, ll. 1, 45; RGASPI, f. 17, op. 17, d. 12, l. 153; RGASPI, f. 17, op. 17, d. 20, l. 80; Yuri Shapoval, "The GPU-NKVD as an Instrument of Counter-Ukrainization in the 1920s and the 1930s," in *Culture, Nation and Identity: The Ukrainian-Russian Encounter, 1600–1945*, eds. Andreas Kappeler et al. (Toronto: Canadian Institute of Ukrainian Studies Press, 2003), 329–31.

of resistance. Violence first emerged in the Soviet Union's Islamic regions during the Bolsheviks' crusade against religion and during the unveiling campaigns.[107]

At the periphery, cultural revolutionaries stood with their backs to the wall. There were simply not enough committed Bolsheviks even within national Party organizations to translate the Communist message effectively into appropriate local cultural contexts. In many regions, peasants and workers, in addition to local elites, opposed the Communists. The regime lost its ability to control several regions in the spring and summer of 1930 as in Azerbaijan and in Dagestan. In the republics of Chechnya and Ingushetia Soviet power collapsed under the resistance of armed bands of peasants. The regime fought a war against the local population in the Ukraine and the Crimea and regularly deployed military units in order to suppress rebellion.[108] In Western Ukrainian villages, peasants spread the rumor of an imminent war between Poland and the Soviet Union; similarly, Turkish or Persian troops were expected to invade the Caucasus. And, wherever living conditions were unbearable, peasants simply fled into neighboring lands: China, Iran, Turkey, or Poland. By the same token, peasants of Polish or German heritage not only fled in large numbers; they also applied for emigration papers or begged for assistance from foreign consulates.[109]

It was no longer an issue of class enemies, kulaks, and "socially foreign elements" that had to be deported or placed in camps. Events at the periphery strengthened the government's belief that the enemy was everywhere and that it was hiding in ethnic groups. Such ideas were particularly common where social stigmatizations corresponded with national attributes. In border regions of White Russia and the Ukraine, the registration of kulaks served simultaneously as a means of ethnic discrimination of minorities. German and Polish peasants not only were members of an ethnic group, but also became members of the kulak nation. The same also applied for Cossacks in the Kuban and for

---

[107] Douglas Northrop, *Veiled Empire: Gender and Power in Stalinist Central Asia* (Ithaca, NY: Cornell University Press, 2004), 69–101; Douglas Northrop, "Subaltern Dialogues. Subversion and Resistance in Stalin's Russia," in *Contending with Stalinism: Soviet Power and Popular Resistance in the 1930s*, ed. Lynne Viola (Ithaca, NY: Cornell University Press, 2002), 109–38; Baberowski, *Der Feind*, 561–86, 599–661; Marianne Ruth Kamp, "Unveiling Uzbek Women: Liberation, Representation and Discourse 1906–1929" (Ph.D. diss., University of Chicago, 1998).

[108] Victor Danilov et al., eds., *Tragediia sovetskoi derevni: Kollektivizatsiia, i raskulachivanie: Dokumenty i materialy*, Vol. 1: *noiabr' 1929–dekabr' 1930* (Moscow: ROSSPEN, 2000), 239, 240–1, 260, 430–2.

[109] *Tragediia sovetskoi derevni*, vol. 2, 236; *Tragediia sovetskoi derevni*, vol. 3, 318; Nikolai A. Ivnitskii, "Stalinskaia revoliutsiia 'sverkhu' i krest'ianstvo," in *Mentalitet i agrarnoe razvitie Rossii (XIX–XX vv.)* eds. V. P. Danilov and L. V. Milov (Moscow: ROSSPEN, 1996), 247–59; Jörg Baberowski, "Stalinismus 'von oben': Kulakendeportationen in der Sowjetunion 1929–1933," in *Jahrbücher für Geschichte Osteuropas* 46 (1998), 572–95; Baberowski, *Der Feind*, 691–721.

Chechens and Kurds, who became members of "White Guard" or "Bandit" nations – the former because they had the reputation of loyalty to the Tsar's regime, the latter as a result of their collective opposition to the cultural revolution. On numerous occasions during collectivization, it was not only "wealthy peasants" who were arrested and deported, but the entire populations of recalcitrant villages. In many regions dekulakization was nothing other than ethnic cleansing; indeed, in the Kuban, the former was used as local euphemism for the latter.[110]

Ethnic minorities in the border regions were suspected of treason and of potential allegiance to neighboring states. Until the mid-1920s, the regime still believed that by presenting itself as the defender of national minorities living on both sides of the Soviet border, it could destabilize neighboring states. In light of the mass impoverishment of the peasantry and the outright terror that resulted from Soviet policies, however, this strategy resulted in the very opposite. Nobody wanted an export of misery across the borders. As a result, Poland, Finland, the Baltic republics, Turkey, and Iran became rivals in the struggle over political order. By the end of the 1920s, there were no longer any doubts in Moscow that the Soviet Union would prevail. However, the Soviet leadership now considered itself threatened not only from within, but also from without. Its external enemies encouraged unrest and incited their "compatriots" within the Soviet Union to rebel against the central government. As such, ethnic minorities became traitor nations undermining Soviet society with the poison of separatism.[111]

At the beginning of 1930, as the regime stood at the precipice, obsessions turned into delusions. At the Tenth Party Congress of the Azerbaijani Communist Party in March 1930, Nikolai Gikalo, Stalin's governor in Azerbaijan, declared that a peasant revolt then rocking the Caucasus Republic had been incited by "Polish agents." "And, as we know, the English control Polish espionage."[112] Even in Moscow, politicians spoke of the danger of national disintegration: from Chechens and Kurdish Bandits, to Polish, German, Iranian, and Korean spies, all of whom had to be removed from the border regions. At a meeting of the district Party secretariat of the RSFSR on 21 February 1930, Stalin and Molotov warned of the dangers threatening Soviet order in the European and Asian border regions. The collectivization of agriculture and the subjugation of the population could only succeed if this danger was averted, he emphasized. For Molotov, not even the Crimea, inhabited by Muslim Tatars, was safe territory. While it may be separated from foreign territories by the

[110] *Tragediia sovetskoi derevni*, vol. 3, 146, 529–31; Abdurahman Avtorkhanov, "The Chechens and Ingush during the Soviet Period and its Antecedents," in *The North Caucasus Barrier: The Russian Advance towards the Muslim World*, eds. Marie B. Broxup and Abdurahman Avtorkhanov (New York: St. Martin's Press, 1992), 157–66; John B. Dunlop, *Russia Confronts Chechnya: Roots of a Separatist Conflict* (Cambridge: Cambridge University Press, 1998), 40–55; Martin, *The Affirmative Action Empire*, 291–308.

[111] Baberowski, *Der Feind*, 396–410; 713–18; Martin, *The Affirmative Action Empire*, 319–28.

[112] RGASPI, f. 17, op. 17, d. 190, ll. 74–5.

Black Sea, "with a good telescope and circling above . . . in an airplane, one can see Constantinople." As such, even in the Crimea "the border issue" had "to be addressed."[113]

Communist leaders isolated the Soviet Union. Nobody was to leave or enter the Soviet Union without permission. Borders were secured and closed; peasants and nomads were prohibited from crossing under the threat of military force. In the Caucasus, the regime registered all Iranian and Turkish citizens and expelled them from the Soviet Union. The regime simultaneously began to deport ethnic minorities from border areas. On 20 February 1930, the Politburo placed the border regions of the Caucasus and Central Asia under military control and ordered the removal of all "kulak families not of local nationality" from the region.[114] In March 1930, the Politburo ordered the GPU to arrest and deport "bandits" and "families of individuals condemned for banditry, espionage, active counterrevolution and professional smuggling" in the western border regions of the Soviet Union; 3,000 to 3,500 families in the border areas of White Russia and 10,000 to 15,000 families from those in the Ukraine were to be removed. Already in 1927, the central government encouraged the resettlement of Kurds from the Armenian enclave of Nakhichevan in northern Azerbaijan in order fully to separate Armenian Christians from Muslims.[115] In 1928, as violent ethnic conflicts developed among Chinese, Korean, and Russian settlers in the Far East, local Bolsheviks advocated similar solutions. All Koreans living in the strategically important region of Vladivostok were to be expelled. While this program was not implemented until ten years later, it was in 1928 that the party leadership decided that border territories had to be "cleansed" of all potentially unreliable ethnic groups.[116]

This paranoia was growing during the thirties and was influenced by developments in other countries, as well. The National Socialist rise to power in Germany; the establishment of authoritarian, Fascist regimes in East Central Europe and on the southern flank of the Soviet Union; and the Spanish Civil War proved to Soviet leaders that there were both internal and external enemies. Spy mania, fear of foreigners, and xenophobia all developed out of the conviction that foreign powers were working to destroy the Soviet Union.

Countermeasures began with the deportation of the Kuban Cossacks in 1933. On 14 December 1932, Stalin ordered the GPU to deport "all inhabitants" of the Cossack *stanitsa* of Poltava "into the northern regions of the USSR" and to resettle their homeland with "faithful Red Army collective farmers." Two weeks later, the head of the secret political division of the GPU,

---

[113] *Tragediia sovetskoi derevni*, vol. 2, 215.

[114] RGASPI, f. 17, op. 162 (osobaia papka), d. 8, l. 99; Baberowski, *Der Feind*, 715–19.

[115] Gosudarstvennyi arkhiv noveishei istorii Azerbaidzhanskoi Respubliki (GANI), f. 27, op. 1, d. 190, ll. 3–6, 42, 82, 99, 119; Martin, *The Affirmative Action Empire*, 322.

[116] Martin, *The Affirmative Action Empire*, 322–4. Cf. also Michael Gelb, "An Early Soviet Ethnic Deportation: The Far-Eastern Koreans," *Russian Review* 54 (1995): 389–411; A. Zakir, "Zemel'naia politika v kolkhoznom dvizhenii sredi koreitsev," *Revoliutsiia i natsional'nosti* 2–3 (1931): 76–81.

Georgii Molchanov, telegraphed Moscow that eighty-six Cossack families had been loaded onto railway cars and transported north. Arrests and deportations of Cossacks followed in the other cities and villages of the Kuban region shortly thereafter – in the end, more than 60,000 people were deported.[117] It is true that the Cossacks were not an ethnic minority, but rather an estate whose members had opposed collectivization and, thus, upon whom the Bolsheviks sought revenge. As Kaganovich stated, "Every one must answer for his neighbor."[118] Nonetheless, the deportation of the Kuban Cossacks acted as a model for later ethnic cleansings.

After the murder of the Leningrad Party Chief, Sergei Kirov, in December 1934, the regime sought revenge on its imagined, collective enemies. In the city and areas surrounding Leningrad, more than 22,000 Germans, Latvians, Estonians, and Finns were registered as enemies and deported into Central Asia. In the Ukrainian regions of Vinnitsa and Kiev, the GPU arrested more than 45,000 people in early 1935 as "social aliens" and "unreliable elements." Of those arrested, 57 percent were Poles and Germans. In January 1936, deportations from the Ukraine continued. During the course of this operation, more than half of all remaining Germans and Poles were expelled from their homes. The final report of the NKVD from October 1936 indicated that 69,000 people were deported from the Ukraine and resettled in Kazakhstan.[119]

Several months later, in July 1936, the regional committee for the Far East asked the Central Government for permission to liberate the border territories from Japanese spies and saboteurs. In August 1937, Stalin and Molotov submitted a plan that called for the deportation of the entire Korean population from the Far East. When this operation concluded in October 1937, more than 172,000 Koreans had fallen victim to it. At the peak of the Great Terror, the regime implemented similar policies in all border regions of the Soviet Union. Wherever it envisioned enemies, the Soviet government simply deported all members of the allegedly unreliable ethnic group, as exemplified by the deportation of all Kurds living in the border regions of Azerbaijan and Armenia.[120]

The Bolshevik government justified these deportations as acts of national self-defense. That is why potentially treasonous collectives were only deported from border regions. Germans, Finns, Estonians, Letts, Kurds, and Poles stood

[117] *Tragediia sovetskoi derevni*, vol. 3, 577, 584, 611.
[118] Martin, *The Affirmative Action Empire*, 326–7.
[119] *Tragediia sovetskoi derevni*, vol. 4, 550–1; Viktor N. Zemskov, *Spetsposelentsy v SSSR 1930–1960* (Moscow: Nauka, 2003), 78–9.
[120] Martin, *The Affirmative Action Empire*, 328–35; Nikolai F. Bugai, "Vyselenie sovetskikh koreitsev s Dal'nego vostoka," *Voprosy istorii* 5 (1994): 141–8; Zemskov, *Spetsposelentsy v SSSR*, 80–2; Gelb, "An Early Soviet Ethnic Deportation," 389–411; Michael Gelb, "Ethnicity during the Ezhovshchina: A Historiography," in Morison, 192–213; Jörg Baberowski, "Stalinismus an der Peripherie: Das Beispiel Azerbaidzhan 1920–1941," in *Stalinismus vor dem Zweiten Weltkrieg: Neue Wege der Forschung*, eds. Manfred Hildermeier and Elisabeth Müller-Luckner (Munich: Oldenbourg, 1998), 307–35.

under suspicion, but so long as they did not live in the border regions, they were not ill treated. More than anything else, this differentiated the early Bolshevik concept of ethnic cleansing from the racial paranoia of the National Socialists. This self-imposed limitation, however, disappeared in the mass terror of the summer of 1937, when Stalin and his supporters abandoned all remaining moral scruples. Enemies of the regime came to be defined by objective characteristics – characteristics that were placed upon them by the Bolsheviks and from which they could no longer escape. That is, in 1937 it was no longer relevant whether an ethnic minority lived in a border region or in the very center of the Soviet Union. Whoever was defined as an enemy of the regime became the object of violence.[121]

Why did this shift occur? The number of stigmatized and socially untouchable groups constantly increased under the Bolshevik order, as it transformed peasants into beggars, thieves, and vagrants and declared as enemies all those who did not fit into their model Socialist society. One could argue that the more defined and precise the Bolsheviks' envisioned order became, the greater the number of those that were forcibly excluded from it. The Bolshevik leadership, in essence, created a world of enemies, and ultimately there was no other solution to the threat that these imagined enemies posed than their total physical annihilation.

As far as leading Stalinist officials were concerned, mass terror against the population was nothing more than a social prophylactic. It cleansed society of spies, traitors, enemies of Soviet power, "parasites," and "socially alien elements" – all cancerous elements that destroyed society from within. Mass terror was a Soviet variant of the "final solution."[122] It left its subjects with no alternative. By 1937, nobody could any longer believe that providing "proof" of one's innocence would spare one's life. Whoever was declared a member of an enemy collective perished with that collective. This terror differentiated itself

---

[121] Amir Weiner, *Making Sense of War: The Second World War and the Fate of the Bolshevik Revolution* (Princeton, NJ: Princeton University Press, 2001), 138–49.

[122] RGASPI, f. 82, op. 2, d. 884, ll. 14–15; RGASPI, f. 82, op. 2, d. 537, ll. 96–155; RGASPI, f. 81, op. 3, d. 229, ll. 73–4; RGASPI, f. 81, op. 3, d. 228, ll. 50–2; L. P. Kosheleva, O. V. Naumov, and L. A. Rogova, eds., "Materialy fevral'sko-martovskogo plenuma TsK VKP(b) 1937 goda," *Voprosy istorii*, no. 5 (1993): 14–15; no. 6 (1993): 5–6, 21–5; David R. Shearer, "Modernity and Backwardness on the Soviet Frontier: Western Siberia in the 1930s," in *Provincial Landscapes: Local Dimensions of Soviet Power, 1917–1953*, ed. Donald J. Raleigh (Pittsburgh: University of Pittsburgh Press, 2001), 203–6; Paul Hagenloh, "'Socially Harmful Elements' and the Great Terror," in Fitzpatrick, *Stalinism*, 286–308; David R. Shearer, "Crime and Social Disorder in Stalin's Russia: A Reassessment of the Great Retreat and the Origins of Mass Repression," *Cahiers du Monde russe* 39 (1998): 119–48; John Scott, *Behind the Urals: An American Worker in Russia's City of Steel*, reprint from 1942 (Bloomington: Indiana University Press, 1989), 186–7; Sergei A. Papkov and V. A. Isupov, *Stalinskii terror v Sibiri 1928–1941* (Novosibirsk: Izdatel'stvo Sibirskogo otdeleniia Rossiiskoi Akademiia Nauk, 1997), 174; Lewis H. Siegelbaum and Andrei K. Sokolov, eds., *Stalinism as a Way of Life: A Narrative in Documents* (New Haven, CT: Yale University Press, 2001), 390; Rolf Binner and Marc Junge, "Wie der Terror 'groß' wurde: Massenmord und Lagerhaft nach Befehl 00447," *Cahiers du Monde russe* 42 (2001): 557–614, here 559.

from the National Socialist war of annihilation only in that it gave perpetrators the option of deporting their victims to Central Asia, where they were then abandoned to their fate.

Between August 1937 and November 1938, however, it was not only former kulaks, criminals, and "anti-Soviet" elements that were murdered or placed in camps. The Bolsheviks aimed at the destruction of enemy nations, at a homogenization of the ethnic landscape of the Soviet Union – a landscape in which majorities would be liberated from minorities. On 20 July 1927, Stalin authorized the People's Commissar for Internal Affairs, Nikolai Ezhov, to arrest and deport all Germans working in the Soviet armaments industry. It was entirely irrelevant whether they were citizens of the German Reich or members of the Communist Party of Germany. Any person who came under suspicion could be arrested, deported, or shot. During the "German Operation," more than 40,000 individuals were sent to death by Committees of Three (*troiki*) and by so-called album procedures, in which local lists of suspicious persons were signed off by the central leadership in Moscow. In addition to Germans, this operation netted individuals who had contact with German diplomats or former soldiers who had been prisoners of war in Germany during the First World War.[123] The NKVD proceeded similarly during the "Polish Operation" that began shortly thereafter, in August 1937. At first, Stalin and Ezhov directed this terror at members of "the Polish military organization," former Polish prisoners of war who remained in the Soviet Union, Polish emigrants, members of Polish political parties, and Polish populations in the Soviet Union's western border zones. Within weeks of its launch, however, Ezhov gave local NKVD posts the order to extend the operation to include "all Poles." "The Poles have to be completely annihilated." Whoever the NKVD identified as a Polish agent lost his freedom or his life. The terror spared nobody. Almost all members of the Polish section of the Communist International were murdered. In August 1938, the Polish Communist Party had to disband, as its members had all been arrested or murdered. More than 35,000 Poles were deported out of the Polish-Ukrainian border region.[124]

Wherever the presence of national minorities threatened the ethnic homogeneity of cities, districts, or territories, the Bolsheviks classified them as sworn enemies. Latvians, Estonians, Koreans, Finns, Kurds, Greeks, Armenians, Turks, and Bulgarians were, so long as they were living outside their "homeland," a danger to the Socialist order. Alexander Weissberg-Cybulski, an Austrian scientist who had fallen into the hands of the Khar'kov NKVD,

---

[123] Nikita Ochotin and Arseni Roginski, "Zur Geschichte der 'Deutschen Operation' des NKWD 1937–1938," in *Jahrbuch für Historische Kommunismusforschung* (2000/2001): 89–125.

[124] GULAG, 104–6; Nikita V. Petrov and Arseni B. Roginskii, "'Pol'skaia operatsiia' NKVD 1937–1938 gg.," in *Repressii protiv poliakov i pol'skikh grazhdan*, ed. A. E. Gur'ianov (Moscow: Zven'ia, 1997), 22–43; Vladimir Piatnitskii, *Zagovor protiv Stalina* (Moscow: Sovremennik, 1998), 72–3; Marc Jansen and Nikita Petrov, *Stalin's Loyal Executioner: People's Commissar Nikolai Ezhov, 1895–1940* (Stanford, CA: Hoover Institution Press, 2002), 98–9; Gelb, "Ethnicity," 192–4.

recalled how members of national minorities were imprisoned during the fall of 1937: "A rumor began to spread during September that Latvians were being arrested; then came the Armenians. We did not understand what this meant. We did not believe it possible that the GPU was using such insignificant criteria as ethnic identity [as a measure of a man's political conviction] as the justification for the repressions. We could not but recognize, however, that on one day all new prisoners were Latvians; on another day, Armenians. In both cases we are dealing with hundreds of people." Shortly thereafter, the NKVD arrested Greeks, Poles, Bulgarians, Germans, and Latvians living in the city of Khar'kov. Their clubs were closed; their newspapers shut. Even those villages formed by German colonists in the areas surrounding Khar'kov were emptied. In the Leningrad region, peasants of Estonian and Finnish descent were registered and transported out of their villages. In Siberia, the NKVD combed through Red Army divisions for Germans and Poles and arrested all soldiers and officers who belonged to these nationalities. Nowhere, however, did the terror against ethnic minorities rage more brutally than in the industrial and border regions of the Soviet Union. In the Donbass region, for example, almost all Germans, Poles, and Latvians were shot during national operations.[125]

The "national operations" of 1937 and 1938 did not unfold according to a set plan; there were not even rough numbers for NKVD organs to target. So-called two-man committees (*dvoiki*), formed by the respective head of the NKVD and the local public prosecutor, were to decide who belonged to the national contingents and, thus, who was to be sentenced to death. In many regions, the line between social and national characteristics blurred. Thousands of Polish, German, and Latvian victims died because the governmental organs had categorized them as "socially alien elements." Nomads living on the Afghan and Chinese border were registered, on Stalin's order, as "bandits" and kulaks and were subsequently deported or shot. In 1938, Stalin ordered the Party Chief of Tajikistan to arrest 30,000 nomads in the border territory and to send them to camps. In this manner, the regime meant to prevent nomads from allying with Muslim warlords operating across the border in Afghanistan.[126]

In the process, perpetrators lost their self-control. They used the opportunity to eliminate national minorities and to murder "foreigners." At no time, however, did the central government let control over national operations slip from its hands, not least due to the album procedure. In the last instance, it was Ezhov and the Chief Prosecutor of the Soviet Union, Andrei Vyshinskii, who decided how many people would be deported or killed and who signed,

[125] RGASPI, f. 558, op. 11, d. 57, ll. 1–3; Alexander Weissberg-Cybulski, *Hexensabbat* (Frankfurt am Main: Suhrkamp, 1977), 276–7, 286–7; Michael Gelb, "The Western Finnic Minorities and the Origins of the Stalinist Nationalities Deportations," *Nationalities Papers* 24 (1996): 237–68; Gelb, "Ethnicity," 196–7; Papkov, 199; Hiroaki Kuromiya, *Freedom and Terror in the Donbas: A Ukrainian-Russian Borderland, 1870s–1990s* (Cambridge: Cambridge University Press, 2002), 231–4.
[126] RGASPI, f. 558, op. 11, d. 57, l. 72; RGASPI, f. 82, op. 2, d. 671, l. 53.

often on a daily basis, the list provided by local authorities. National operations continued even as actions against Party members and "socially alien
elements" had passed their zenith. At the end of January 1938, Stalin directed
the NKVD to extend national operations until 15 April in order to eradicate
all enemy spies and saboteurs definitively. One could also say that 1937 was
the year of social cleansing; 1938, the year of ethnic cleansing. More than
350,000 fell victim to national operations, which lasted until November 1938.
During the Polish Operation alone, 144,000 were arrested. Nearly 250,000
lives were extinguished by NKVD execution squads – more than 70 percent
of which occurred during National Operations. Ethnic cleansing was not a
marginal phenomenon of Stalin's terror. Rather, it was at the core.[127] Socially
"cleansed" environments could only survive as ethnically homogeneous environments. Classes existed within nations. It lay in the logic of this kind of
thinking that people had to suffer for their ethnic heritage only when they were
a minority. Typically, Armenians were removed from Khar'kov and Odessa,
but not from the Armenian Republic. Thus, ethnic cleansings did not put an end
to "multinational" empire. Instead, they were violent homogenization strategies that deported minorities from border territories and large cities in order to
remove potential threats as well as to liberate majorities from minorities within
their territories. In the multinational empire of the Bolsheviks, the nationalities
did not live with one another, but rather next to one another.[128]

After the Great Terror, Stalinism lived off ever-new conspiracies and sought out
ever-more victims. Bolsheviks continued to stigmatize and punish collectives
into the 1940s. But now there were only "objectively" defined enemies, which
no longer required confessions. With this development, the enemy was no
longer complicit in his or her own destruction. Furthermore, Bolsheviks no
longer spoke of kulaks and "former people" when they classified people into
enemy categories; rather they spoke of "Germans," "Poles," and "asocials"
or "criminals." Asocial elements became generically alien. This fear of others
blossomed in a milieu of Soviet isolation, in which life beyond the borders of the
Soviet Union was cut off and became unimaginable.[129] What Bolshevik leaders
did not recognize as being within their own trusted milieu, they interpreted

---

[127] Barry McLoughlin, "Die Massenoperationen des NKVD. Dynamik des Terrors 1937/1938" in
Stalinscher Terror 1934–1941: Eine Forschungsbilanz, ed. Wladislaw Hedeler (Berlin: Basis-
Druck, 2002), 42; Jansen, Petrov, 99, 103. Limited, erroneous figures available in Rolf Binner
and Marc Junge, "'S etoi publikoi tseremonit'sia ne sleduet': Die Zielgruppen des Befehls Nr.
00447 und der Große Terror aus der Sicht des Befehls Nr. 00447," *Cahiers du Monde russe*
43 (2002): 207–8.

[128] Weiner, 138–49. For a discussion on the origins of the Bolshevik violence against nationalities
see Weitz, "Racial Politics," 1–29; Weitz, *A Century of Genocide*, 53–101; Francine Hirsch,
"Race without the Practice of Racial Politics," *Slavic Review* 61 (2002): 30–43.

[129] As noted by the American ambassador in Moscow, Smith, when he spoke with Stalin and his
retinue, Walter Bedell Smith, *Meine drei Jahre in Moskau*, trans. Werner G. Krug (Hamburg:
Hoffmann and Campe, 1950), 66–7.

as a threat. And because the Bolsheviks contaminated Soviet society with a poisonous "hatred of the foreigner," Soviet society only received information that conformed to its xenophobic expectations. When the Bolsheviks expanded into foreign territory after the Hitler-Stalin Pact, they exported this culture of hate and xenophobia.

Nowhere is this more apparent than in Eastern Poland, which was allocated to the Soviet Union after the Hitler-Stalin Pact of September 1939. Here the Bolsheviks pursued a merciless campaign against priests, landlords, and nobles, just as they had in the Soviet Union. This terror, however, was no longer characterized as a social prophylactic. From the start, it aimed to eliminate the Polish elite in those regions annexed by the Soviet Union. In early 1940, the Bolsheviks began to arrest representatives of the Polish state, landlords, and Polish settlers who had immigrated into the region from West Poland in the 1930s and to deport them to Kazakhstan. These deportations occurred in several waves. They began in February with shipments of Polish settlers and their families and ended in June with the deportation of more than 60,000 Jews who had fled from German-occupied Poland. The Cheka surprised their victims: in only a few days, they arrested over 10,000 people, escorted them to railway stations, and loaded them in unheated cattle cars. Nobody counted the number of victims who died from exposure and hunger on their way into exile.[130]

The Bolshevik leadership left no doubt that they were set on eliminating the Polish elite. In early March 1940, Lavrentii Beria proposed to Stalin the execution of 14,700 Polish officers and 11,000 former landlords, industrialists, and state employees who had ended up in Soviet prisoner-of-war camps and prisons. A report from Beria to Stalin claimed that Polish officers and landlords represented "sworn enemies of Soviet power, filled with hate against the Soviet order." As such, Polish officers were under no circumstances to be released from confinement. "Each and every one of them awaits release only such that they can actively participate in the fight against Soviet forces." Beria saw only one option: these "incurable enemies" had to be shot en masse. He did not forget to add that "more than 97 percent" of those incarcerated were of Polish origin.

---

[130] Jan T. Gross, *Revolution from Abroad: The Soviet Conquest of Poland's Western Ukraine and Western Belorussia*, 2nd ed. (Princeton, NJ: Princeton University Press, 2002), 187–224; S. G. Filippov, "Deiatel'nost' organov VKP(B) v zapadnykh oblastiakh Ukrainy i Belorussii v 1939–1941 gg." in Gur'ianov, 44–76; Oleg A. Gorlanov and Arsenii B. Roginskii, "Ob arestakh v zapadnykh oblastiakh Belorussii i Ukrainy v 1939–1941 gg.," in Gur'ianov, 77–113; A. E. Gur'ianov, "Masshtaby deportatsii naseleniia v glub SSSR v mae–iune 1941 g.," in Gur'ianov, 137–75; V. Parsadanov, "Deportatsiia naseleniia iz Zapadnoi Ukrainy i Zapadnoi Belorussii," *Novaia i noveishaia istoriia* 2 (1989): 26–44; Wanda K. Roman, "Die sowjetische Okkupation der polnischen Ostgebiete 1939 bis 1941," in *Die polnische Heimatarmee: Geschichte und Mythos der Armia Krajowa seit dem Zweiten Weltkrieg*, ed. Bernhard Chiari (Munich: Oldenbourg, 2003), 104–6; Keith Sword, *Deportation and Exile: Poles in the Soviet Union, 1939–1948* (London: Macmillan, 1994); Nicolas Werth, *Ein Staat gegen sein Volk: Das Schwarzbuch des Kommunismus* (Munich: Piper, 2002), 232–5; Salomon W. Slowes, *Der Weg nach Katyn: Bericht eines polnischen Offiziers* (Hamburg: Europäische Verlags-Anstalt, 2000).

Stalin immediately agreed and, on 5 March 1940, the Politburo sanctioned the execution of Polish officers and state officials. Forty-five hundred of them were murdered in the Katyn forest.[131] The deportation of families of prisoners of war and of imprisoned state officials began two weeks later – in total, more than 26,000 families.[132]

Immediately following the occupation of Poland, Soviet security forces began to remap the ethnic makeup of occupied territories. All Polish nationals living along Soviet-German occupation borders were summarily deported. In order to break the traditional power of landowners and government officials, the Bolsheviks incited Ukrainians, White Russians, and Jews against their Polish neighbors. In many regions, hate propaganda provoked Jews and White Russians to lynch former Polish officials and landowners. In October 1939, the Politburo decided to separate Jewish, Ukrainian, and White Russian prisoners of war from Polish officers and sent them home.[133] The Bolsheviks publicly depicted themselves as the defenders of Ukrainian and White Russian peasants, whom they had liberated from the yoke of oppression. From this perspective, incorporating the conquered territories into the White Russian and Ukrainian Soviet Republics was far more than a simple formality. It reflected the Bolshevik inversion of ethnic hierarchies. The idea of establishing a Polish republic was never seriously contemplated.

The situation of the Jewish population in Poland also changed as a result of occupation. For many Jews, Soviet victory symbolized, more than anything else, an end to the discrimination that they had suffered under Polish rule. They initially viewed the Bolsheviks as a protective force that would save them from the incursions of Ukrainian peasants and Polish officials. The Bolsheviks also provided "secularized" Jews with new opportunities for social mobility. In many villages, Jews actually filled the positions of expelled Polish functionaries.[134]

At the same time, however, the Bolshevik terror was in no way limited to the Polish population. Shortly after occupation, all foreign citizens, including Jews who had fled German occupation, were registered and deported to Central Asia. Indeed, nearly all Jews deported from the Soviet-occupied zone during 1940 had come from German-occupied Poland. It was of no consequence that they were fleeing Nazi terror. All "foreigners" in Soviet-controlled territory were suspected of being potential troublemakers or spies, regardless of their motivation for fleeing their native land. In the end, nearly 60,000 Jews and

---

[131] R. G. Pikhoia and Aleksandr Geishtor, eds., *Katyn': Plenniki neob"iavlennoi voiny* (Moscow: Mezhdunarodnyi Fond "Demokratiia," 1997), 384–92.

[132] Pikhoia and Geishtor, eds., *Katyn'*, 526–7.

[133] Pikhoia and Geishtor, eds., *Katyn'*, 118–19; Roman, 93; Gross, *Revolution*, 35–70, 114–22.

[134] Werner Benecke, *Die Ostgebiete der Zweiten Polnischen Republik: Staatsmacht und öffentliche Ordnung in einer Minderheitenregion 1918–1939* (Cologne: Böhlau, 1999); Gross, *Revolution*, 263, 267–8.

200,000 Poles – nearly 10 percent of the entire Polish population in Soviet-occupied Poland – fell victim to these deportations.[135]

Between May and June 1941, deportations extended into the annexed Baltic provinces, Bessarabia, and the Finnish-Soviet border region. And, once again, the Bolsheviks sought to rid the territories of intellectual elites. With the emergence of mass opposition to forced collectivization in the Western Ukraine and White Russia, elites there too were targeted. And because elites were typically members of titular nations, terror was always also a form of ethnic cleansing. Cumulatively, more than 85,000 – primarily Ukrainians, Latvians, Estonians, Lithuanians, and Romanians – were deported to Central Asia between May and June 1941.[136]

Both the Stalinist and National Socialist regimes conducted wars of annihilation against internal and external enemies – enemies that they classified in terms of class, race, and nation. Thus, when the Wehrmacht invaded the Soviet Union on 22 June 1941, it was not only armies that met on the battlefield, but also respective ideological delusions, as the murderous behavior of the one only confirmed the imagination of the other: namely, that races and nations were responsible for the destruction of order. That is why the Second World War did not result in the de-Stalinization of the Soviet Union, as the myth of the Great Patriotic War might suggest. The war only confirmed Bolshevik expectations, and it confirmed them because National Socialist occupation policies left those subject to its rule no other option than to accept those ethnic and racial categories that the National Socialists assigned them. In other words, the National Socialists inadvertently collaborated in the Stalinist objectification of the enemy.[137]

In the Ukrainian and Lithuanian-Belorussian border area, the eruption of war represented a reversal of mass terror. Already on 24 June 1941, Beria ordered NKVD operatives in the Ukraine and the Baltic to murder all imprisoned "counterrevolutionaries." Retreating soldiers of the Red Army destroyed villages and killed or deported their inhabitants. When the Chekists had extra time before the arrival of German troops, they shot prisoners. The West Ukrainian city of L'vov experienced a particularly brutal massacre: more than 12,000 people were shot or tortured to death. Many prisoners could not be evacuated before the arrival of German troops, but many others died in death marches into the interior of the Soviet Union. In the city of Lutsk, the Chekists

---

[135] GARF, f. 9479, op. 1, d. 89, l. 221; Zemskov, *Spetsposelentsy v SSSR*, 84–9.

[136] Zemskov, *Spetsposelentsy v SSSR*, 89–91; Roman, 105; Dieter Pohl, "Die Ukraine im Zweiten Weltkrieg," in Ukraine: *Geographie, ethnische Struktur, Geschichte, Sprache und Literatur, Kultur, Politik, Bildung, Wirtschaft, Recht*, ed. Peter Jordan (Frankfurt am Main: Lang, 2001), 340–2; Mikola Iwanou, "Terror, Deportation, Genozid: Demographische Veränderungen in Weißrußland im 20. Jahrhundert," in *Handbuch der Geschichte Weißrußlands*, eds. Dietrich Beyrau and Rainer Lindner (Göttingen: Vandenhoeck & Ruprecht, 2001), 433.

[137] On the meaning of ethnicities as an enemy category since the Second World War see Baberowski, *Der rote Terror*, 209–40; Weiner, 239–97.

separated Polish and Ukrainian prisoners before they murdered them. There was no longer any escape from this cycle of violence. Once the Red Army left the border areas, Ukrainians and Lithuanians unleashed their pent-up rage on local Jews, who had the reputation of being sympathetic to the Communists. Frenzied Lithuanian and Ukrainian militias organized pogroms, and now there was nobody to stand in their way. German soldiers witnessed precisely what they expected and what National Socialist propaganda had predicted. These pogroms conducted by Ukrainians, Poles, and Lithuanians against Communists and Jews during the first weeks of the war only seemed to confirm the alleged symbiosis between Communism and Judaism. For members of the SS, it justified their racial war of annihilation.[138]

National Socialists forced those under its control to adopt their system of racial categorization. They registered Jews, Russians, Poles, White Russians, Ukrainians, Latvians, and Lithuanians in a hierarchy of races. It was impossible to avoid being assigned to one or another category, for the National Socialists not only ordered their own, but also the world of the "other" according to racial criteria. Whoever wanted to survive had either to adopt or fight the predefined characteristics of his respective category, whether or not it contradicted one's own faith or identity. As a Jew, the chances of survival were slim. In the hierarchy of races, Ukrainians and Poles stood above Russians, while Latvians and Estonians stood above Ukrainians and Poles. Even within prisoner-of war camps, the world was structured according to ethnicity. Ukrainians could count on receiving better treatment than Russians and Jews. That is why captured Ukrainian soldiers were typically adamant in identifying themselves as Ukrainian. Ukrainians were even used to guard Russian prisoners. In White Russia, Latvia, Estonia, and Lithuania, German occupation forces recruited local auxiliary police forces solely from members of the respective titular nation. Thousands of Ukrainians, as well as Cossacks, Kalmyks, Crimean Tatars, Azerbaijani, and Georgian prisoners of war enlisted with the Wehrmacht, the SS, and the NS civil administration and worked toward the destruction of the Stalinist empire. Typically, during the first year of the war in the East, Germans shot Russian and Jewish hostages in retaliation for partisan attacks on German soldiers, but not Ukrainians.[139]

---

[138] Walter Kempowski, *Das Echolot: Barbarossa '41: Ein kollektives Tagebuch* (Munich: Knaus, 2002), 216; Roger D. Petersen, *Understanding Ethnic Violence: Fear, Hatred, and Resentment in Twentieth-Century Eastern Europe* (Cambridge: Cambridge University Press, 2002), 96–9; Bogdan Musial, *"Konterrevolutionäre Elemente sind zu erschießen": Die Brutalisierung des deutsch-sowjetischen Krieges im Sommer 1941* (Berlin: Propyläen, 2000), 172–99, 249–55; Frank Golczewski, "Die Ukraine im Zweiten Weltkrieg," in *Geschichte der Ukraine*, ed. *Frank Golszewski* (Göttingen: Vandenhoeck & Ruprecht, 1993), 246–52.

[139] Weiner, 156–7; Chiari, *Alltag hinter der Front*, 270–9; Martin Dean, *Collaboration in the Holocaust: Crimes of the Local Police in Belorussia and Ukraine, 1941–1944* (New York: St. Martin's Press, 2000), 21; Robert G. Waite, "Kollaboration und deutsche Besatzungspolitik in Lettland 1941 bis 1945," in *Okkupation und Kollaboration (1938–1945): Beiträge zu Konzepten und Praxis der Kollaboration in der deutschen Okkupationspolitik*, ed. Werner Röhr (Berlin: Hüthig, 1994), 217–37; Tanja Penter, "Die lokale Gesellschaft im Donbass unter

The German occupation regime was not only excessively terroristic; it also exacerbated existing interethnic tensions within occupied territories. Ukrainian partisans of the nationalistic OUN, the Polish Armia Krajowa, the Latvian and Lithuanian resistance movements, and Soviet partisans not only fought the German occupation; they fought each other. During the spring of 1944, the Polish Armia Krajowa in Volhynia destroyed a dozen Ukrainian villages and killed more than 1,000 Ukrainians – allegedly as a result of combat operations. It is estimated that between 1942 and 1944 100,000 Poles and 20,000 Ukrainians in the region were killed as a result of interethnic conflict.[140] In the Ukraine, violence against Jews continued even after German armies evacuated the region. Indeed, interethnic violence raged in the Ukraine, Eastern Poland, and the Baltic republics into the late 1940s.[141]

In this war, the concept of a person's social identity lost all meaning. All that mattered were "race" and "ethnicity." And because people came to identify themselves and others in categories provided by the German occupiers, Bolshevik leaders identified German-occupied territories as arenas of interethnic conflict. Thus, when the Red Army briefly occupied the city Rostov in December 1941, the NKVD arrested all ethnic Germans and Armenians, and when the Wehrmacht reoccupied the city in early 1942, SS-Einsatzgruppen murdered all remaining Jews.[142]

The Bolsheviks conducted war not only against an external enemy, but against internal enemies, as well: deserters, collaborators, nationalist partisans, and hostile nationalities, all of whom allegedly cooperated with the Germans in the destruction of the Soviet Union. In this war, essentialist nationalism triumphed over the social revolution that legitimated the Bolsheviks.

---

deutscher Okkupation 1941–1943," in *Kooperation und Verbrechen: Formen der "Kollaboration" im östlichen Europa 1939–1945*, eds. Christoph Dieckmann, Babette Quinkert, and Tatjana Tönsmeyer (Göttingen: Wallstein, 2003), 201; Golczewski, *Die Ukraine*, 251–60; Carl Schüddekopf, *Krieg: Erzählungen aus dem Schweigen: Deutsche Soldaten über den Zweiten Weltkrieg* (Reinbek bei Hamburg: Rowohlt, 1997), 232; Dieter Pohl, "Russian, Ukrainians, and German Occupational Policy, 1941–43," in Kappeler, *Culture, Nation and Identity*, 277–97. On the reversal of hierarchies, see Petersen, 135.

[140] Chiari, *Alltag hinter der Front*; Waldemar Bednarski, "Das Gesicht des Krieges in der Gemeinde Kotlice (Kreis Zamosc) 1939–1945," in Chiari, *Die polnische Heimatarmee*, 421–3; Frank Golczewski, "Die Heimatarmee und die Juden," in Chiari, *Die polnische Heimatarmee*, 635–76; Piotr Niwinski, "Die nationale Frage im Wilnagebiet," in Chiari, *Die polnische Heimatarmee*, 617–64; Grzegorz Motyka, "Der polnisch-ukrainische Gegensatz in Wolhynien und Ostgalizien," in Chiari, *Die polnische Heimatarmee*, 531–47; Oleg A. Zarubinsky, "The 'Red' Partisan Movement in Ukraine during World War II. A Contemporary Assessment," *Journal of Slavic Military Studies* 9 (1996): 399–416.

[141] RGASPI, Fond 82, opis' 897, ll 106–23, 135–9, 143–5; E. Laasi, "Der Untergrundkrieg in Estland, 1945–1953," in *Auch wir sind Europa: zur jüngeren Geschichte und aktuellen Entwicklung des Baltikums: baltische Pressestimmen und Dokumente*, ed. Ruth Kibelka (Berlin: Aufbau-Verlag, 1991), 70–82.

[142] Andrej Angrick, *Besatzungspolitik und Massenmord: Die Einsatzgruppe D in der südlichen Sowjetunion 1941–1943* (Hamburg: Hamburger Edition, 2003), 640–1.

As soon as German troops had invaded the Soviet Union, Bolshevik leaders took revenge on Germans residing there. In late summer 1941, the Republic of Volga Germans was dissolved. All Germans living in the republic were registered and, shortly thereafter, deported to Kazakhstan. The Supreme Soviet's decree legitimizing this act spoke of the need to eliminate "saboteurs and spies" before they had the opportunity to collaborate with the invading Germans. Between November 1943 and December 1944, when the German Wehrmacht no longer posed a significant threat to the region, Stalin and Beria deported the Crimean Tatars and the various nationalities of the Caucasus – Chechens, Ingush, Karachai, Balkars, Kalmyks, and Meskhetians – to Central Asia. Those Finns and Germans remaining in Leningrad – 60,000 people – were similarly arrested and deported to Central Asia in the spring and summer of 1942. In the second half of 1944, additional "suspicious" nations were deported: Greeks, Bulgarians, and Armenians from the Crimea; Turkish Meskhetians and Kurds from the Caucasus. More than 3 million people were evicted from their homelands in this manner, among them more than 1 million Germans and 470,000 Chechens and Ingush.[143] For the Bolsheviks, these deportations were not a side issue. Indeed, it appears that the resettlement of ethnicities was more important than victory in battle. After all, how is one to explain why the regime diverted 10,000 trucks and wagons, 100,000 NKVD soldiers, and three entire armies into the Caucasus when they were desperately needed at the front?[144]

Molotov admitted years later, in an interview with the journalist Feliks Chuev, that he and Stalin were not concerned with individual guilt or responsibility of the deported. People who belonged to an enemy nation, he maintained, represented a potential danger to the Soviet order. As such, they had to be deported. "During the war, we were confronted with mass treason. Battalions

---

[143] Jörg Ganzenmüller, "Das belagerte Leningrad 1941–1944: Eine Großstadt in den Strategien der Angreifer und der Angegriffenen" (Diss. Universität Freiburg 2003), 289–300; Viktor N. Zemskov, "Zakliuchennye, spetsposelentsy, ssyl'noposelentsy, ssyl'nye i vyslannye: Statistiko-geograficheskii aspekt," *Istoriia SSSR* 5 (1991): 151–65, esp. 162; Naimark, 85–107; Weitz, *A Century of Genocide*, 79–82; Benjamin Pinkus, "Die Deportation der deutschen Minderheit in der Sowjetunion 1941–1945," in *Zwei Wege nach Moskau: Vom Hitler-Stalin-Pakt bis zum "Unternehmen Barbarossa,"* ed. Bernd Wegner (Munich: Piper, 1991), 464–79; Nikolai F. Bugai, "K voprosu o deportatsii narody SSSR v 30–40-kh godakh," *Istoriia SSSR* 6 (1989): 135–44; Nikolai F. Bugai and Askarbi M. Gonov, *Kavkaz: narody v eshelonakh: 20–60-gody* (Moscow: INSAN, 1998), 118–222; *Nakazannyi narod: Repressii protiv rossiiskikh nemtsev* (Moscow: Zven'ja, 1999); Aleksander M. Nekrich, *Punished Peoples: The Deportation and Fate of Soviet Minorities at the End of the Second World War* (New York: Norton, 1978); Vera Tolz, "New Information about the Deportation of Ethnic Groups in the USSR during World War 2," in *World War 2 and the Soviet People*, eds. John Garrard and Carol Garrard (New York: St. Martin's Press, 1993), 161–79; "'Pogruzheny v eshelony i otpravleny k mestam poselenii...' L. Beriia – I. Stalinu," *Istoriia SSSR* 1 (1991): 143–60; Nikolai F. Bugai, *L. Beriia – I. Stalinu: "Soglasno vashemu ukazaniiu..."* (Moscow: AIRO-XX, 1995), 104–5, 128; Robert Conquest, *Stalins Völkermord: Wolgadeutsche, Krimtataren, Kaukasier* (Vienna: Europa-Verlag, 1970).

[144] Nekrich, 108–9; Nikolai F. Bugai, *Iosif Stalin – Lavrentiiu Berii: "ikh nado deportirovat'": Dokumenty, fakty, kommentarii* (Moscow: Druzba narodov, 1992), 106.

of Caucasians stood opposite us on the front lines; they were in our rear. Of course, innocents suffered, as well. But I think that the right thing was done at the time."[145] Molotov merely expressed what the Bolshevik leadership believed: namely, that the enemy surrounded them. Germans and Crimean Tatars were enemies that had to be rid from the world: the former because they belonged to the aggressor nation, the latter because many of them had served the German occupiers. Chechens, Ingush, and Balkars represented armed thieves and enemies of the kolkhoz order. From the 1920s, the regime continually waged war against rebellious populations in the Caucasus.[146] With the German invasion of the Soviet Union, the hour of revenge had struck for the potential enemies of Soviet power. An investigative commission of the NKVD, which traveled to the region in October 1943, determined that Chechens and Ingush were religious fanatics and bandits, a constant threat to Soviet order. Accordingly, Beria hammered this message into his minions in charge of the February 1944 deportations from the Caucasus: "Not a single one is to escape."[147]

Deportations of Chechens and Ingush began on 23 February 1944. Already on 29 February, Stalin received from Beria, on location in the Caucasus, the final report: 478,479 people had been "loaded onto railway wagons," 91,250 Ingush and 387,229 Chechens.[148] For victims, the action came as a surprise. Only a few weeks prior to the action, units of the Red Army and the NKVD were moved into the region. Not even the soldiers knew the purpose of their deployment to the Caucasus. The night before the deportations began, Beria informed the local head of government, Mollaev, what the next days would entail. Mollaev "broke into tears," Beria told Stalin. He then "pulled himself together" and executed all orders without any resistance. Beria then called together local Party members, Muslim notables, and Sufi sheiks and forced them, under the threat of violence, to cooperate with the NKVD. They were to ensure that deportations, beginning during the night of 22 February, ran smoothly. Nothing remained to chance. Tanks blocked side streets; soldiers occupied Chechen and Ingush villages. Before villagers were loaded onto trucks and driven to railway stations, Mullahs and local Communists disclosed to them the contents of Stalin's deportation order. And, with the final train, the mullahs and local Communists joined their compatriots in exile.[149]

Evidently there was only limited resistance to these deportations; where resistance did emerge, Beria's henchmen executed those responsible. In one village, the entire population – more than seven hundred, in total – was locked in a barn and burned alive. Of course, such events were not mentioned in Beria's

[145] Feliks I. Chuev, *Sto sorok besed s Molotovym* (Moscow: Terra, 1991), 277. In the 1960s, Kaganovich also expressed this view: S. Parfenov, "'Zheleznyi Lazar': Konets kar'ery," *Rodina*, no. 2 (1990): 74.
[146] "Vtoroe pokorenie Kavkaza: bol'sheviki i chechenskie povstantsy," *Rodina*, no. 6 (1995): 43–8; Dunlop, 44–58; Avtorkhanov, "Chechens and Ingush," 156–83; Nekrich, 43–50.
[147] GARF, f. 9401, op. 2, d. 64, l. 161; Dunlop, 62.
[148] GARF, f. 9401, op. 2, d. 64, l. 161.
[149] GARF, f. 9401, op. 2, d. 64, l. 166; GARF, f. 9479, op. 1, d. 183, l. 41.

report to Stalin. He telegraphed Moscow indicating that the deportations went as "normal," that resistance was nicked in the bud, and that more than 20,000 weapons were confiscated.[150]

Nobody stayed behind; not even the local Communists were able to avoid the terror. Absolutely nothing remained that alluded to those exiled. The autonomous republics of the Chechens and Ingush disappeared just as the republics of the Crimean Tatars and Volga Germans had. Russian immigrants moved into the homes of those deported; villages and settlements received Slavic names; Chechen signs were replaced with Russian signs. Stalin himself gave the order to destroy places of worship, monuments, and cemeteries that were reminders of the exiled. It appeared as if the Chechens, the Crimean Tatars, and Germans had never lived in their own homeland. The regime eternalized this stigmatization at the end of the 1940s when it decreed that the exiled were never to return to their former homeland. Germans, Chechens, and Crimean Tatars carried the mark of Cain; they were second-class humans and remained so for decades.[151]

Nearly a quarter of all Chechens and Ingush died between 1944 and 1948. Many of the young and the old froze to death during the trek into exile. In Kazakhstan, thousands more succumbed to hunger, cold, and typhus. Once at their final destination, there was neither housing nor care for those deported; the impoverished local population refused to include Chechens in their kolkhoz. In December 1944, the Director of the "Cherepovetsles" Trust, Ol'khovnikov, reported that exiled Chechens were not able to take on their forced labor duties. Without clothing and shoes, without sufficient nourishment, they were dying like flies. Whoever survived was too weak to work.[152] The fact that the Soviets were never able to overcome the refractoriness of the deported illustrates the absurdity of Soviet resettlement schemes. Already in July 1944, Beria reported to Stalin that unrest had broken out among Chechen "special settlers" in Kazakhstan. To bring "saboteurs, shirkers, and malingerers" to account, NKVD units were sent to the region and more than 2,000 "bandit elements" and thieves were arrested.[153]

The Bolsheviks raised xenophobia to the level of state ideology; they contaminated their own multinational empire with a poisonous hatred of foreigners and otherness. And, for this reason, ethnic cleansing did not stop with the end

---

[150] GARF, f. 9401, op. 2, d. 64, l. 161; "Krovavyi pepel Khaibakha," in *Tak eto bylo: Natsional'nye repressii v SSSR 1919–1952 gody*, vol. 2, ed. Svetlana Alieva (Moscow: Insan, 1993), 170–9; Naimark, 96–7.

[151] Bugai, "K voprosu o deportatsii," 135–44; Dunlop, 73–4; Naimark, 98–99; Wolfgang Leonhard, *Die Revolution entläßt ihre Kinder*, 3rd ed. (Cologne: Kiepenheuer und Witsch, 1981), 125–30.

[152] GARF, f. 9479, op. 1, d. 177, ll. 1–6; GARF, f. 9479, op. 1, d. 153, ll. 42–3; Dunlop, 70–1; Naimark, 97; Tolz, 165–9; Nekrich, 124–6; Viktor N. Zemskov, "Spetsposelentsy (po dokumentatsii NKVD-MVD SSSR)," *Sotsiologicheskie issledovaniia* 11 (1990), 3–17; Zemskov, "Zakliuchennye," 151–65.

[153] GARF, f. 9401, op. 2, d. 65, ll. 311–14.

of the Second World War. Interethnic wars raged in the Ukraine until the late 1940s: the Bolshevik regime incited an unprecedented hate campaign against Germans and Ukrainians. In nearly all regions Ukrainians were removed from leading state and Party apparatuses and replaced with Russians from the central government. More than 150,000 Ukrainian rebels were killed; thousands of Germans and Romanians fell victim to summary executions in the months following the war's end. In total, between 1940 and 1953, more than 0.5 million people were deported from the Ukraine.[154] In the Baltic republics, reacquired by the Soviet Union in 1944, Bolshevik leaders conducted a "campaign of destruction" against national elites.[155] In the collective memory of the Baltic nations, Stalinism is synonymous with attempted genocide.

The fact that Soviet Jews were stigmatized as "agents" of Zionism and were likewise held in captivity only corresponds to and confirms the perverse logic of Stalinist xenophobia. All that mattered for leading Bolsheviks was that the founding of the State of Israel created a homeland for Jews outside the Soviet Union. As a result, Jews inside the Soviet Union fell under suspicion, regardless of whether they recognized themselves as Jews or not. After 1947, state-sanctioned anti-Semitism assumed hysterical proportions and essentially merged with the existing anti-Jewish sentiment of many Russians and Ukrainians. By early 1953, at the latest, Stalin considered expelling all Jews from cities in the European portion of the Soviet Union. Only the death of the dictator in March 1953 spared Soviet Jews from the same fate as the Germans and Chechens.[156] Stalin's death was simultaneously the death of Stalinism. With

---

[154] RGASPI, f. 82, op. 2, d. 897, ll. 106–23, 135–9, 143–5; Frank Golczewski, "Ukraine – Bürgerkrieg und Resowjetisierung," in *Kriegsende in Europa: Vom Beginn des deutschen Machtzerfalls bis zur Stabilisierung der Nachkriegsordnung, 1944–1948*, eds. Ulrich Herbert and Axel Schildt (Essen: Klartext, 1998), 89–99; Sheila Fitzpatrick, "Postwar Soviet Society: The 'Return to Normalcy,' 1945–1953," in *The Impact of World War II on the Soviet Union*, ed. Susan J. Linz (Totowa, NJ: Rowman & Allanheld, 1985), 134; Weiner, 59, 163–90; Pohl, "Russian," 295–7.

[155] RGASPI, f. 82, op. 2, d. 897, ll. 143–5; Toivo U. Raun, *Estonia and the Estonians* (Stanford, CA: Hoover Institution Press, 1991), 181–3; Laasi, 70–82; Zemskov, *Spetsposelentsy v SSSR*, 155–6; Baberowski, *Der rote Terror*, 248.

[156] Weiner, 191–235; 287–90; RGASPI, f. 558, op. 11, d. 904, ll. 27–35, 39; RGASPI, f. 82, op. 2, d. 148, ll. 126–31; Andrej D. Sacharow, *Mein Leben* (Munich: Piper, 1991), 177–8; Shimon Redlich, *War, Holocaust and Stalinism: A Documented History of the Jewish Anti-Fascist Commitee in the USSR* (Luxembourg: Harwood Academic Publishers, 1995); Vladimir Naumov, "Die Vernichtung des Jüdischen Antifaschistischen Komitees," in *Der Spätstalinismus und die "jüdische Frage": Zur antisemitischen Wende des Kommunismus*, ed. Leonid Luks (Cologne: Böhlau, 1998), 123–6; Vladimir Naumov, ed., *Nepravednyi sud: Poslednyi stalinskii rasstrel: Stenogramma sudebnogo protsessa nad chlenami Evreiskogo Antifashistskogo Komiteta* (Moscow: Nauka, 1994); Iakov Etinger, "The Doctor's Plot: Stalin's Solution to the Jewish Question," in *Jews and Jewish Life in Russia and the Soviet Union*, ed. Ya'acov Ro'i (Ilford: Cass, 1995), 103–24; Aleksander Lokshin, "The Doctors' Plot: The Non-Jewish Response," in Ro'i, 157–67; Zhores A. Medvedev, "Stalin i 'delo vrachei': Novye materialy," *Voprosy istorii* 1 (2003): 78–103; Gennadii Kostyrchenko, *Out of the Red Shadows: Anti-Semitism in Stalin's Russia* (Amherst, NY: Prometheus Books, 1995); Arno Lustiger, *Rotbuch: Stalin und die Juden* (Berlin: Aufbau-Verlag, 1998), 108–22; Alexander Borschtschagowski,

his death so too died the utopia of permanent cleansing and the desire to annihilate all hostile collectives. Xenophobia, however, remained, and whenever
crises developed, resentment blossomed once again. By the 1960s or 1970s,
however, nobody anymore seriously considered the physical destruction of
imagined enemies.

Stalinism was an attempt to establish an order devoid of ambivalence and uncertainty. In this manner, it was similar to the racial purity utopia of the National
Socialists. The Bolsheviks, though, were not racists. They had a concept of race;
they understood that there were people with different biological characteristics;
but this insight had no practical meaning for them. Race was not destiny; Russians did not belong to a racially superior community.[157] Leading Bolsheviks
considered the attempt to breed superior humans a diversion. Indeed, Stalin
executed the Soviet Union's top geneticists in 1937 and dissolved their institute.
V. N. Starovskii, the chief statistician in the central planning agency, Gosplan,
summarized his thoughts on Nazi biological thought as follows: "If a person
who by blood is a negro was brought up in such a society and with such a
language and culture that he calls himself Russian, there is nothing incorrect
about this even if his skin color is black."[158]

According to Bolsheviks, nations were cultural communities of descent.
Whoever belonged to such a nation could not simply relinquish one's membership. One was trapped in one's own genealogy. But one could work to
overcome oneself, and, thus, one could become another. Note, for example,
that it was Lazar Kaganovich, a Jew, who had to implement the anti-Semitic
strategy of late Stalinism. The Bolshevik utopia of ethnic cleansing lived off the
idea of ethnically homogeneous territories. They wanted to isolate enemies and
to separate nations from one another. The Stalinist ordering project sought ethnic homogeneity, but it never succeeded because ethnic particularism always
creates new cultures of difference. And in this contradiction lies the origins
of Stalinist mass terror.[159] Why, though, did the Stalinist spiral of violence
never descend into industrially organized mass murder? Because the Bolsheviks
had an alternative solution. They could and did send stigmatized collectives
to Central Asia and, in this way, deliver them from the "danger zone." However, the ethnic and social "reordering" of Soviet society was only possible

---

Orden für einen Mord: Die Judenverfolgung unter Stalin (Berlin: Propyläen, 1997); Yakov
Rapoport, *The Doctors' Plot*; Jonathan Brent, Valdimir Naumov, *Stalin's Last Crime: The
Plot against the Jewish Doctors, 1948–1953* (New York: HarperCollins, 2003), 283–311.

[157] Compare with the debate initiated by Eric Weitz vis-à-vis Bolshevik "racism": Weitz, "Racial
Politics," 1–29. For a critique of Weitz: Hirsch, "Race," 30–43.

[158] Mark B. Adams, "Eugenics in Russia, 1900–1940," in *The Wellborn Science: Eugenics in
Germany, France, Brazil, and Russia*, ed. Mark B. Adams (New York: Oxford University
Press, 1990), 194–5; Hans-Walter Schmuhl, "Rassenhygiene in Deutschland – Eugenik in der
Sowjetunion: Ein Vergleich," in *Im Dschungel der Macht: Intellektuelle Professionen unter
Stalin und Hitler*, ed. Dietrich Beyrau (Göttingen: Vandenhoeck & Ruprecht, 2000), 360–77.

[159] Weiner, 138, 207. Quoted in Hirsch, "The Soviet Union," 274–5.

because those in power created new spaces of ambivalence in the Asian parts of the Soviet Union. Central Asia became a reservation of outcasts; it became a ghetto for enemy nations and "socially foreign elements." Thus could the Bolsheviks refrain from the complete physical annihilation of their imagined enemies.

The National Socialist war of annihilation and the Stalinist campaign of ethnic cleansing celebrated their greatest triumphs when and where their respective concepts of order confronted a rather more complicated reality, when unequivocal order confronted an ambiguous environment.[160] Thus, it is within empire that Stalinist and National Socialist crimes are to be located. It is only within empire that Bolsheviks and National Socialists could continually work to create and destroy ever-new collective enemies. One could also argue that empire befitted them. Had empire not existed – National Socialists and Bolsheviks would have had to invent it.

---

[160] Weitz, "Racial Politics," 26–9; Baberowski, *Der rote Terror*, 12–16, 257.

PART III

SOCIALIZATION

6

Frameworks for Social Engineering

Stalinist Schema of Identification and the Nazi Volksgemeinschaft

Christopher R. Browning and Lewis H. Siegelbaum

All modern states engage in the practices of identifying and categorizing their populations. This organizational work seems critical to the achievement and maintenance of states' authoritativeness. The power of the state as an "identifier" has been related to its possession of "the material and symbolic resources to impose the categories, classificatory schemes, and modes of social counting and accounting with which bureaucrats, judges, teachers, and doctors must work and to which non-state actors must refer."[1] So unlike in other respects, the USSR under Stalin and Nazi Germany both experienced radical recategorizations of their respective populations. In this essay we seek to clarify the nature of the relationship between the identifying practices that each state employed and its agenda for massive social engineering.

Both the Stalinist schema of identification and the Nazi ideal of *Volksgemeinschaft* were animated by the desire to transform society in the image of certain ascribed qualities. In the case of Soviet Russia, these revolved around class, later to be supplemented and even supplanted by nationality. For the Nazis, purification of the racially defined community became the paramount objective of social policy. Identification in this sense was a necessary (but not sufficient) activity in the production of new social identities that lay at the core of both the Stalinist and Nazi agendas for social change. The degree to which each realized its agenda is highly debatable, but there is little doubt that these "illiberal" regimes impinged on and legitimated new identities.[2] In what follows, we pay particular attention to the ideological underpinnings

[1] Rogers Brubaker and Frederick Cooper, "Beyond 'Identity,'" *Theory and Society* 29, no. 1 (2000): 15–17.

[2] Mabel Berezin, "Political Belonging: Emotion, Nation, and Identity in Fascist Italy," in George Steinmetz, ed., *State/Culture: State Formation after the Cultural Turn* (Ithaca, NY: Cornell University Press, 1999), 357–63; Anna Krylova, "The Tenacious Liberal Subject in Soviet Studies," *Kritika* 1, no. 1 (2000): 119–46. Within Soviet studies, the first to explore "the Stalinist soul" was Jochen Hellbeck. See his "Fashioning the Stalinist Soul: The Diary of Stepan Podlubnyi (1931–1939)," *Jahrbücher für Geschichte Osteuropas*, 44, no. 3 (1996): 344–73.

of social identification; the specific practices designed to make more legible and thereby promote the inclusion, exclusion, and marginalization of social groups;, and how "ordinary" Germans and Soviet citizens experienced these practices.

SETTING PARAMETERS

Class analysis, rooted in a Marxist understanding of the "laws" of history, was central to Bolshevik leaders' attempts to comprehend and shape the society over which they presided. The problem was that the revolution and civil war had effectively declassed Russian society.[3] The expropriation of capitalists and landowners had left the proletariat, oxymoron-like, without a class antagonist. Moreover, as a result of the breakdown of industry, recruitment into the armed forces, and flight to the countryside, the industrial proletariat had become a nearly empty shell of its former self. The peasantry, comprising the vast majority of the population, remained more or less intact (as did the pastoralists of Central Asia, the mountain societies of the Caucasus, and what would come to be referred to as the "small peoples of the North"), but peasants fit awkwardly into the Bolsheviks' notion of a proletarian dictatorship, to say nothing of the postcapitalist future envisioned for Soviet Russia.

Still, class distinctions were made for both ideological and practical reasons. The RSFSR's constitution of 1918, defining as its "principal object" "the dictatorship of the urban and rural proletariat and the poorest peasantry . . . and the complete suppression of the bourgeoisie," enshrined class in law. Whereas "the laboring masses" were granted the full rights of citizenship, "parasitic strata" were denied the right to vote or stand for elected office (hence, the popular term *lishentsy* – the disenfranchised).[4] The latter included *inter alia* persons employing hired labor for the sake of profit or living on income not derived from their own labor, private businessmen, clerics of all denominations, and members of the tsarist police, gendarmes, secret police, and ruling dynasty, who collectively were known as "former (*byvshie*) people."[5]

Class not only had legal status. During the civil war and for some time thereafter, it was tied to ration levels, housing provision, and other everyday

---

[3] See Sheila Fitzpatrick, "The Bolsheviks' Dilemma: Class, Culture and Politics in the Early Soviet Years," *Slavic Review* 47, no. 4 (1988): 599–613, reprinted in Fitzpatrick, *The Cultural Front* (Ithaca, NY: Cornell University Press, 1992), 16–36; idem, "The Problem of Class Identity in NEP Society," in *Russia in the Era of NEP: Explorations in Soviet Society and Culture*, eds. Sheila Fitzpatrick, Alexander Rabinowitch, and Richard Stites (Bloomington: Indiana University Press, 1991), 12–33, and especially idem, "Ascribing Class: The Construction of Social Identity in Soviet Russia," *Journal of Modern History* 65, no. 4 (1993): 745–68. These articles are the *vade mecum* of understanding questions of class after the 1917 Revolution.

[4] Rex Wade, ed., *The Triumph of Bolshevism, 1917–1919*. Vol. 1: *Documents of Soviet History* (Gulf Breeze, FL: Academic International Press, 1991), 192–200.

[5] See, respectively, Golfo Alexopoulos, *Stalin's Outcasts: Aliens, Citizens and the Soviet State, 1926–1936* (Ithaca, NY: Cornell University Press, 2003), and T. M. Smirnova, *"Byvshie liudi" Sovetskoi Rossii: strategii vyzhivaniia i puti integratsii, 1917–1936 gody* (Moscow: Mir istorii, 2003).

concerns. It saturated public discourse and was an inescapable part of social identities. Of available identities none was more advantageous than proletarian. Because the state that was being erected in such haste and with so much fanfare was defined as proletarian, and because its social foundations were so flimsy, proletarianness was available to a far larger proportion of the population than industrial workers. In Moshe Lewin's terms, the proletariat encompassed both "hidden" and "hiding classes."[6]

The Bolsheviks, without much controversy, identified the landless (*batraki*) and poor (*bedniaki*) among the peasantry as proletarians even if many of them did not identify themselves as such. Employees of the rapidly expanding soviet administration, commercial agents, and many in the free professions claimed proletarian status, although from time to time this was rejected by Bolshevik watchdogs who worried that such groups were "infecting" the working class with their "petty bourgeois" attitudes.[7] Finally, the Bolsheviks, consisting mainly of industrial workers, landless peasants, Red Army soldiers, and (especially in leadership positions) the intelligentsia, considered themselves the vanguard of the proletariat. As such, they projected onto themselves the proletariat's idealized (male) qualities: "hardness," the merging of the self into the collective, and a revolutionary, scientific worldview.[8]

Proletarian status proved more problematic in other cases and circumstances. It generally was denied to so-called middle peasants (*seredniaki*). Although toilers, they at best (in the Bolsheviks' estimation) wavered in their affinity to the proletarian cause and at worst succumbed to the ideological influence of their rich, kulak neighbors.[9] The intelligentsia also presented problems of class definition. While permitted, indeed encouraged, to serve the proletarian cause as "specialists," intellectuals were labeled bourgeois partly because of their predominantly nonproletarian social origins and prerevolutionary experience, but also because of what Lenin referred to as their "habits of life, conditions of work, [and] abnormal separation of mental from manual labor."[10] When it came to class consciousness (as distinct from interest or location) even workers were considered lacking, particularly when they insisted on defending

---

[6] Moshe Lewin, "Concluding Remarks," in *Making Workers Soviet: Power, Class and Identity*, eds. Lewis H. Siegelbaum and Ronald Grigor Suny (Ithaca, NY: Cornell University Press, 1994), 381–3.

[7] See Daniel T. Orlovsky, "State Building in the Civil War Era: The Role of the Lower–Middle Strata," in *Party, State, and Society in the Russian Civil War: Explorations in Social History*, eds. Diane P. Koenker, William G. Rosenberg, and Ronald Grigor Suny (Bloomington: Indiana University Press, 1989), 180–209.

[8] For a recent interpretation of Bolsheviks' self–identification before and after the October Revolution see Igal Halfin, *From Darkness to Light: Class, Consciousness, and Salvation in Revolutionary Russia* (Pittsburgh: University of Pittsburgh Press, 2000).

[9] These issues are discussed in Moshe Lewin, *Russian Peasants and Soviet Power: A Study of Collectivization*, trans. Irene Nove and John Biggart (London: Allen & Unwin, 1968); and Teodor Shanin, *The Awkward Class: Political Sociology of Peasantry in a Developing Society: Russia 1910–1925* (Oxford: Clarendon Press, 1972).

[10] V. I. Lenin, "Kak organizovat' sorevnovanie," in *Polnoe sobranie sochinenii*, 5th ed., vol. 34 (Moscow: Partizdat, 1959–65), 126.

caste privileges and skills, engaged in strikes, or otherwise disappointed the Bolsheviks by violating labor discipline.[11]

Nevertheless, as the mythologized heroes of the October Revolution and the ultimate subjects of history, workers had distinct advantages over other officially recognized groups in terms of access to material and cultural resources, as well as entry into the Communist Party itself. Candidates for party membership had their class pedigrees scrutinized on the assumption that proletarianness – or landlessness in the case of peasants – made them more reliable cadres. The more years "at the bench" (*u stanka*) the better. Service in the Red Army as a volunteer during the civil war also helped, not only with entry into the party but also, for those lacking genuinely proletarian credentials, with admittance into workers' preparatory schools (*rabfaky*) and educational advancement beyond.[12]

The same preferential principle pertained to non-Russian nationality. Beginning in 1923, the Bolsheviks established a vast and multifaceted system of positive discrimination in favor of non-Russians partly to overcome the evil of Russian "great power chauvinism," and partly to forestall the emergence of non-Russian nationalism. This "affirmative action empire," consisting of ethnoterritorial units from union and autonomous republics down to national districts and village soviets, prescribed the use of indigenous languages in education, publishing, and official correspondence; it applied national quotas for entry into educational and government institutions and otherwise promoted what Stalin in 1930 referred to as "the flowering of national culture, socialist in content and national in form."[13]

This meant that in the 1920s, Russians and Russian national culture were subjected to reverse discrimination. In the Mountain and Kazakh ASSRs, Russian settlers were expelled and the lands they had occupied were returned to indigenous peoples. Elsewhere, they were permitted, as a minority people, to form national soviets at the district and village levels, but especially in Ukraine republic authorities closely monitored them, and the "Russian Question" remained a highly sensitive issue. Within the realm of the "symbolic politics of national identity," alphabet reform, that is, the shift to the Latin script for over sixty languages (as of 1932), was animated by Russophobia as well as the association of the Cyrillic alphabet with "autocratic oppression, missionary propaganda [and] Great Russian national chauvinism."[14]

[11] See John Hatch, "Labor Conflict in Moscow, 1921–1925," and Hiroaki Kuromiya, "Workers' Artels and Soviet Production Relations," both in *Russia in the Era of NEP: Explorations in Soviet Society and Culture*, eds. Sheila Fitzpatrick, Alexander Rabinowitch, and Richard Stites (Bloomington: Indiana University Press, 1991), 58–71, 72–88; and William J. Chase, *Workers, Society and the Soviet State: Labor and Life in Moscow, 1918–1929* (Urbana and Chicago: University of Illinois Press, 1987).

[12] Sheila Fitzpatrick, *Education and Social Mobility in the Soviet Union, 1921–1934* (Cambridge: Cambridge University Press, 1979).

[13] Terry Martin, *The Affirmative Action Empire: Nations and Nationalism in the Soviet Union, 1923–1939* (Ithaca, NY: Cornell University Press, 2001). Quotation on 155.

[14] Ibid., 184, 197.

Within these parameters of privilege and stigmatization, Soviet citizens could exercise considerable latitude (or artifice) in constructing desirable social identities. Offspring of nationally or socially heterogeneous couples might choose to stress the identity of the parent that would be most advantageous; children of *lishentsy* could publicly declare that they were disowning ("breaking all ties with") their parents; *lishentsy* petitioned to have their rights reinstated, either by emphasizing a Soviet self (the performance of socially useful labor, service in the Red Army, and so forth) or by throwing themselves on the mercy of soviet authorities; peasants who had hired laborers or owned more than one draft animal could hire out their own labor or animals, transforming themselves into poor peasants; and so forth.[15]

The policing of social identities was therefore no easy task. Local soviets kept electoral registers from which social aliens were to be excluded, but this did not prevent kulaks, priests, and mullahs from voting and being elected to rural soviets in the mid-1920s.[16] As already indicated, the party was more stringent about checking the social credentials of candidate members, and the Komsomol was heavily involved in purging educational institutions of social aliens via "light cavalry raids" and other techniques. But there were no precise or universally accepted rules about how much weight to give to one's current occupation, prerevolutionary social position, or parents' social status, and thus here too it was possible to duck for cover, petition, or otherwise outwit the invigilators.

Sometimes, it was not individuals' subterfuge but genuine puzzlement about what was politically correct that caused difficulty in distinguishing between acceptable and stigmatized social identities. In Uzbekistan, the party's contradictory messages – identifying the veil (*parandzha, paranji* in Uzbek) as emblematic of nationality but also condemning it as unhygienic and a marker of backwardness – made it almost impossible for someone to be both "Uzbek" and "soviet," and still less a loyal party member.[17] During the party's "face the countryside" campaign of the mid-1920s, Bukharin could (in)famously urge peasants to "enrich yourselves" while other, particularly lower-ranking, party members continued to persecute peasants who had done just that. In the case of the Don Cossacks, the party refused to acknowledge any ethnic distinctiveness and treated the Cossack masses as indistinguishable from non-Cossack peasant

[15] Golfo Alexopoulos, "The Ritual Lament: A Narrative of Appeal in the 1920s and 1930s," *Russian History/Histoire Russe*, 24, nos. 1–2 (1997): 117–30; Sheila Fitzpatrick, *Stalin's Peasants: Resistance and Survival in the Russian Village after Collectivization* (Oxford: Oxford University Press, 1994), 28–33.

[16] E. H. Carr, *Socialism in One Country, 1924–1926*, vol. 2. (New York: Macmillan, 1960), 344–51.

[17] Douglas Northrop, "Subaltern Dialogues: Subversion and Resistance in Soviet Uzbek Family Law," *Slavic Review* 60, no. 1 (2001): 115–39; Northrop, "Nationalizing Backwardness: Gender, Empire, and Uzbek Identity," in *A State of Nations: Empire and Nation-Making in the Age of Lenin and Stalin*, eds. Ronald Grigor Suny and Terry Martin (Oxford: Oxford University Press, 2001), 191–220.

settlers (*inogorodnie*). But this was precisely what Cossacks feared most and why they overwhelmingly had opposed the Bolsheviks in the first place.

Unlike in the Soviet Union in the 1920s, social identity in Weimar Germany was primarily a matter of individual construction, not ascription by the state. And unlike in the "declassed" society of the Soviet Union that the Bolsheviks attempted to comprehend and shape according to the class-based ideology of Marxism, the Nazis emerged within a society whose all too enduring class divisions and political tensions, exacerbated by a widely shared sense of national humiliation and economic disaster, they sought to transcend through an ideology of race. A myth of transcendent unity, the ideal of *Volksgemeinschaft*, provided the common ground, by virtue of which many Germans ultimately came to identify with Adolf Hitler, the Nazi Party, and the Third Reich.

In the early years of the Weimar Republic, Germans' sense of identity derived from nation, confession, class, political party, and milieu.[18] If a sense of national identity united Germans, the other factors divided them. In the period of the Kaiserreich at least a relative coherence and stability (though certainly not without tensions) resulted from the rather consistent partial overlap of confession, class, party, and milieu. Within the Catholic milieu, confession trumped class, and Catholics of all classes tended to support the Center Party. Most of the Protestant liberal bourgeoisie identified with the National Liberals and Progressives, most Protestant national conservatives with the Conservative Party. A socialist milieu, composed primarily of urban industrial but not Catholic workers, provided the core of support for the SPD. In the Weimar period this relatively stable configuration collapsed. Only the Catholic milieu and its political counterpart, the Center Party, remained intact. Within the socialist milieu the Communists, and briefly the Independent Socialists, challenged the SPD. Diametrically opposed views toward parliamentary democracy precluded reconciliation within the milieu, while class war rhetoric, the specter of the Bolshevik Revolution, and the taint of insufficient nationalist credentials hindered the expansion of either party beyond. The middle-class liberal parties (DVP and DDP) not only failed to unite but also experienced inexorable erosion. Their combined vote share of 23 percent in 1919 dropped to 16.4 percent in 1924, 13.6 percent in 1928, 8.3 percent in 1930, and 2.2 percent in 1932.[19] The DNVP attempted to fill the void as a party of national and bourgeois unity, reaching a highpoint of 20.5 percent in 1924. But inflexibly pursuing economic policies tied to the interests of a wealthy minority, like the Center and socialist parties, it too could not break out of its self-imposed ghetto walls despite its

---

[18] For a pioneering study of the connection between social milieu and the rise of the Nazis, see Adelheid von Saldern, "Sozialmilieus und der Aufstieg des Nationalsozialismus in Norddeutschland (1930–1933)," *Norddeutschland im Nationalsozialismus*, ed. Frank Bajohjr (Hamburg: Ergebnisse Verlag, 1993), 20–53.

[19] For the collapse of the middle–class liberal parties, see Larry Eugene Jones, *German Liberalism and the Dissolution of the Weimar Party System, 1918–1933* (Chapel Hill: University of North Carolina Press, 1988).

nationalist rhetoric.[20] Frustrated agrarian and middle-class voters turned to a plethora of special interest and protest splinter parties, each equally ineffectual in protecting its constituency but counterproductively contributing to the very political instability at the national level that it was protesting. In short, by 1928 the socialist milieu was divided by internecine warfare and coherent political representation of the agrarian and middle-class milieus had all but collapsed.

Ironically, despite the introduction of suffrage for women in the new Weimar constitution and the fact that promised legal equality was far from realized in practice, gender as a factor of identity proved less divisive than class, confession, and milieu, as "women closed ranks with the men who shared their political views and avoided appeals to cooperate as women across the political spectrum."[21] Despite traditionalists' dismay and alarm, parties on the conservative end of the political spectrum benefited more from the women's vote than did those on the left.[22] And across the political spectrum, including parties on the left, "broad segments of the Weimar population" shared a "consensus" that by virtue of "natural difference" women should concentrate on their own "natural" spheres of activity.[23]

Germany was not a "quicksand" society ruled by a one-party revolutionary regime as in the Soviet Union.[24] Rather it was a modern society governed by a "quicksand" political system, in which one political alternative after another either was stuck in the mud or had disappeared into it. With the onset of the Great Depression, parliamentary governance collapsed, as no majority could be found for any consistent economic policy or even for democracy itself. In the parliamentary elections of September 1930, the Nazi vote jumped from 2.6 percent to 18.3 percent and in those of July 1932 its share of the vote rose to 37.4 percent – a significant plurality.

What were the sources of Nazi electoral success, and what does that indicate about the self-perception and identity of those who joined or voted for them? The sources of the Nazis' electoral gains were primarily threefold. They devoured almost entirely the former electorate of both the mainstream non-Catholic, nonsocialist parties – DNVP, DVP, and DDP – as well as the successor splinter parties of the conservative and liberal milieus. Second, they won a disproportionate share of the new voters, both those who previously

---

[20] Peter Fritzsche, *Germans into Nazis* (Cambridge, MA: Harvard University Press, 1998), 199–200.

[21] Claudia Koonz, *Mothers in the Fatherland: Women, the Family, and Nazi Politics* (New York: St. Martin's Press, 1987), 34.

[22] Ute Frevert, *Women in German History: From Bourgeois Emancipation to Sexual Liberation* (New York and Oxford: Berg, 1989), 172; Nancy Reagin, *A German Women's Movement: Class and Gender in Hanover, 1880–1933* (Chapel Hill: University of North Carolina Press, 1995), 205, 219.

[23] Karen Hagemann, "Men's Demonstrations and Women's Protest: Gender in Collective Action in the Urban Working-Class Milieu during the Weimar Republic," *Gender & History* 5, no. 1 (1993): 110–11.

[24] For this characterization of Soviet society, see Moshe Lewin, *The Making of the Soviet System: Essays in the Social History of Interwar Russia* (New York: Pantheon Books, 1985), 265.

abstained for lack of enthusiasm and those coming of age. And third, they won considerable numbers of ex-SPD voters. Only the Center and Communist Parties held their own against the Nazi appeal.[25] Precisely because the hard core of the Catholic and socialist milieus remained relatively immune to Nazism, Catholics and the urban proletariat were "underrepresented" among Nazi voters and party members. The Nazi Party in turn was predominantly Protestant (40 percent of whom voted Nazi as opposed to 16 percent of the Catholics) and somewhat more middle-class than working class (60–40 percent for both voters and party members).[26] The Nazi Party members tended to come more frequently from small communities under five thousand and less often from cities of over one hundred thousand, and they were more youthful than their rivals.[27]

In the past, the harsh anti-Marxist stance of the Nazis, the tendency of both the Nazis' vanquished socialist rivals then and academic analysts since to privilege class as an explanatory factor, the higher visibility of the middle-class component of Nazi members and voters in comparison to its working-class element, and the propensity to dismiss Nazi rhetoric on topics other than race and war as merely calculated, opportunistic, and without substance, have all contributed to the portrayal of the Nazis as the vehicle of middle- and lower-middle-class mobilization and triumph over a working-class challenge in a class war.[28] In place of the privileged position that class had in the historical explanation of National Socialism, however, other factors have now also been increasingly taken into consideration. Recent research has revealed the extent of the working-class component (or a diverse "lower class" to use the less ideologically and emotionally freighted terminology of Detlef Mühlenberger),[29] leading to a recharacterization of the Nazis as a *Volkspartei*[30] – a heterogeneous mass movement broadly representative of German society and held together by something other than class panic and class interest.

---

[25] Jürgen Falter, "War die NSDAP die erste deutsche Volkspartei?" *Nationalsozialismus und Modernisierung*, eds. Michael Prinz and Rainer Zittelman (Darmstadt: Wissenschaftliche Buchgesellschaft, 1994), 32–3; Jürgen Falter, "The National Socialist Mobilization of New Voters: 1928–1933," in *The Formation of the Nazi Constituency, 1919–1933*, ed. Thomas Childers (Totowa, NJ: Barnes and Noble, 1986), 217–19. Conan Fischer, *The Rise of the Nazis*, 2nd ed. (Manchester and New York: Manchester University Press and Palgrave, 2002), 100, 121.

[26] Falter, "War die NSDAP die erste Deutsche Volkspartei," 33–4, 38, 41–2, 44. Fischer, *The Rise of the Nazis*, 108–9, 118–19, 122.

[27] Jürgen Falter, "The Young Membership of the NSDAP between 1925 and 1933," in *The Rise of National Socialism and the Working Classes in Weimar Germany* ed. Conan Fischer (Providence, RI and Oxford: Berghahn Books, 1996), 81–8.

[28] The classic example of this approach on the microhistorical level is William Sheridan Allen, *The Nazi Seizure of Power: The Experience of a Single German Town, 1930–1935* (Chicago: Quadrangle, 1965; rev. ed., New York: F. Watts, 1984).

[29] Detlef Mühlberger, *Hitler's Followers: Studies in the Sociology of the Nazi Movement* (London and New York: Routledge, 1991).

[30] The many contributions of Jürgen Falter, such as "War die NSDAP die erste Deutsche Volkspartei?"

The Nazis were anti-Marxist, antiliberal, antidemocratic, anti-Semitic, and to a lesser extent, anticapitalist and anti-"reactionary." And they expertly and sensitively tailored special appeals to different constituencies and regions. But what, in broad and sweeping terms, were they for that provided the "glue" to attract and hold together their heterogeneous membership and voters? What, in short, allowed so many different Germans to identify with one political movement in a society previously characterized by intense political fragmentation and the impenetrable walls of distinct social milieus? The ideal of *Volksgemeinschaft* was key in this regard.[31] Its tremendously evocative power, sufficient to bind the Nazi movement and the German people together, must be understood in the context of two drastically contrasting experiences in recent German history.

The first was the popular memory of euphoric unity in August 1914 juxtaposed with the prewar political, social, and confessional tensions. The divisions of the Kaiserreich seemingly had been overcome in a moment of mythic transcendence. In the not so distant past, according to this popular memory, Germans had been united in their self-sacrifice, unquestioning loyalty, discipline, toughness, and martial valor. This had allowed them to conquer a vast East European empire and carried them to the brink of victory in the west as well.[32] The second contrasting popular memory was one of sudden defeat, revolution, hyperinflation, and economic collapse. National humiliation, political gridlock, economic vulnerability, and vast unemployment, moral and cultural decadence, societal breakdown, and the looming threat of Bolshevism constituted the new German condition, which could only be remedied by a return to the mythic unity of August 1914.

Central to the Nazi message was its self-representation as the vehicle of a restored *Volksgemeinschaft*.[33] This was not a fig leaf of opportunistic and insincere electoral rhetoric to cover the naked assertion of class interest, but an integral element of Nazi ideology. For Hitler and National Socialism (and in ideology it is difficult to separate the two), race was the defining element of reality and the driving force of history. The culture of the collective and the behavior of the individual were both merely reflections and epiphenomena of a racial and biological foundation. Hence class, as well as other bonds of affiliation and identity, and, above all, political parties based on economic interest were viewed as forms of "false consciousness" that threatened to divide

---

[31] For other recent studies that emphasize the centrality of *Volksgemeinschaft*, see Fritzsche, *Germans into Nazis*; Claude-Christian W. Szejnmann, *Nazism in Central Germany: The Brownshirts in 'Red' Saxony* (New York: Berghahn Books, 1999); and Fischer, *The Rise of the Nazis*.

[32] Jeffrey Verhey, *The Spirit of 1914: Militarism, Myth and Mobilization in Germany* (Cambridge: Cambridge University Press, 2000).

[33] The Nazis were considerably more successful than their rivals in appropriating the "political topos" of *Volksgemeinschaft*. Michael Wildt, "'Volksgemeinschaft' als politischer Topos in der Weimarer Republik," in *NS–Gewaltschaft: Beiträge zur historischen Forschung und juristisichen Aufarbeitung*, eds. Alfred Gottwaldt, Norbert Kampe, and Peter Klein (Berlin: Edition Hentrich, 2005), 23–39.

racial comrades and unite racial rivals in a manner inherently inimical to the well-being of the racial collective or *Volksgemeinschaft* and contrary to the law of nature.

The Nazi attack on the "party system" was as vituperative as its attack on Marxism. But in the latter regard it is important to note that in their self-understanding, the Nazis could "hate the sin" (Marxism) and still "love the sinner" (the misled German workers). They did not understand their victory as the triumph of the middle class over the working class, but rather as a victory for the unity of the German people over the divisive "party system" and divisive "Marxism." The Nazi triumph was seen as a victory not in class warfare but over class warfare. This was a victory, so understood, that many Germans of all walks of life longed for and identified with. And they considered their giving up past political loyalties and throwing in their lot with the Nazis, placing the common good above self-interest, to be an act of "idealism."

Such a conception of Nazi "idealism" and the wide resonance of the *Volksgemeinschaft* seem also to account for why the unremitting Nazi assertion of male supremacy and opposition to women's emancipation had no severe electoral repercussions, and its female vote only slightly trailed its male vote. Bourgeois women's organizations in particular had increasingly identified with opposition to Weimar parliamentary democracy and the SPD and espoused virulent nationalism. Such groups had long given up advocating general women's issues while accepting women's "natural roles," especially for restoring traditional family values in the face of Weimar's alleged "degeneracy." They were particularly vulnerable to equating their own idealized vision of *Volksgemeinschaft* with that of the Nazis.[34]

CLASS MATTERS; RACE MATTERS

The class animus to Soviet politics and ascribed social identities reached its zenith during the "socialist offensive" of the late 1920s and early 1930s. The main targets in this offensive were kulaks, NEPmen (the "new bourgeoisie" engendered by the legal revival of trade and small-scale private entrepreneurship under the New Economic Policy), and artisans who hired labor, as well as remnants of other "class-alien elements" who were to be purged from Soviet institutions. Here attention will focus mainly on dekulakization, the most massive of the operations and, since the opening of the archives, the one that is best documented.

Dekulakization was an extremely blunt instrument that was used to promote collectivization. The bluntness was inscribed into the guidelines contained in a Politburo resolution of January 30, 1930, that included "orientational" numbers (in thousands) of families from each region to be sent to "concentration camps" and deported to remote parts of the country. "The numbers in each

---

[34] Frevert, *Women in German History*, 198–99, 203–4, 207–16; Reagin, *A German Women's Movement*, 221–57.

of the three categories of liquidated kulak farms," read the resolution, "must be strictly differentiated by district, depending on the actual number of kulak farms, so long as the general number of liquidated farms in all districts con- stitutes on average approximately three to five percent." So, the OGPU (the political police), which was mandated to carry out these instructions, was to pay attention to the "actual number of kulak farms," but at the same time ensure that an "average" of between 3 and 5 percent was reached, all the while preventing expropriations from spreading to "any part of *seredniak* farms."[35] The contradictory messages contained in this one sentence are quite staggering.

The identification of kulaks in each village undergoing collectivization was the job of commissions of rural soviets in which representatives from *raion* executive committees, party organizations, poor peasants, and the OGPU par- ticipated. The commissions typically relied on lists of disenfranchised persons kept by local electoral offices. But often this was only a starting point. It appears that almost anyone was fair game for inventory taking and confisca- tion – relatives (sometimes distant) of identified kulaks, those who had taken advantage of opportunities presented by the Stolypin reforms for separating from village communes or been on the wrong side during the civil war, Red Army veterans who returned to their native villages, temporarily prosperous families, village troublemakers, outsiders such as schoolteachers, and so on.[36] This explosive combination of the party's quota-driven agenda and the working out of personal antipathies virtually guaranteed the "distortions," "excesses," and "outrages" that appeared routinely in reports from the provinces, were famously condemned by Stalin in March 1930, but persisted thereafter.[37] At the same time, a portent of what was to come later in the decade was the confla- tion of (particularly Polish and German) ethnic and class categories which led to the Stalin era's "first instance of ethnic deportation" in the western border regions.[38]

Like its urban equivalent, the bourgeoisie, *kulak* became an all-purpose term of abuse and denunciation. Collectivized peasants learned to use it without much difficulty to oust chairmen and other officials who abused them, or as a weapon against those with whom they were feuding. Schoolchildren, inspired by the cult of Pavlik Morozov, did the same even in urban areas. Officials

---

[35] V. Danilov et al., eds., *Tragediia sovetskoi derevni, Kollektivizatsiia i raskulachivanie: Doku- menty i materialy v 5 tomakh, 1927–1939*, vol. 2 (Moscow: ROSSPEN, 2000), 127.

[36] Fitzpatrick, *Stalin's Peasants*, 54–9; A. K. Sokolov, ed., *Golos naroda: Pis'ma i otkliki riadovykh sovetskikh grazhdan o sobytiiakh 1918–1932 gg.* (Moscow: ROSSPEN, 1998), 289–96. By the same token, petitions from collective farmers in the mid-1930s to have their civil rights restored suggest that it was possible to avoid dekulakization even if one did appear on a list of the disenfranchised. See T. I. Slavko, *Kulatskaia ssylka na Urale, 1930–1936* (Moscow: Mosgorarkhiv, 1995), 24–5, 37–8.

[37] Stalin's article, "Dizzy with Success," appeared in *Pravda* on March 1, 1930. For reports of excesses, see Andrea Graziosi, "Collectivisation, Révoltes paysannes et politiques gouverne- mentales à travers les rapports du GPU d'Ukraine de février–mars 1930," *Cahiers du Monde russe* 35, no. 3 (1994): 437–632; *Tragediia sovetskoi derevni*, 322–34, 333–4, 545–8.

[38] Martin, *Affirmative Action Empire*, 322.

used it as a symbol of criminality and hostility to socialism. It also assumed adjectival form, as in the case of a report by an NKVD sergeant from Rostov oblast that characterized the persecution of a kolkhoz woman by a brigade leader as a "kulak-type assault."[39]

One might imagine that the mirror image of the kulak was the collective farmer (*kolkhoznik*), but most often one finds that term used in a neutral sense. Perhaps this was because in ideological terms collective farms constituted an intermediary form of property between individual ownership (represented by *edinolichniki*, who as late as 1936 still comprised between 10 and 15 percent of all peasant households) and fully socialized – that is, state – property. Indeed, the attention that peasants lavished on their household plots at the expense of collective farm duties mocked this ideological formulation. The fact that collective farmers often were represented iconographically by women – who paradoxically bore the main burden of labor on household plots – suggests not only the perpetuation of the folkloric connection with fecundity, but also, perhaps, the party's lingering difficulty in imagining their male counterparts as fully fledged members of the socialist community.[40]

It was the proletarian who stood at the opposite end of the ideological spectrum from the kulak and the bourgeois. As already noted, this always was more of an ideological term for the Bolsheviks than one with sociological content. But one of the characteristic features of the culturally revolution- ary period of the First Five-Year Plan was the extraordinary extent to which young Communist activists in the professions adopted the proletarian mantle to distinguish themselves from and launch attacks against their "bourgeois" elders.[41] Hence, irrespective of their own class backgrounds, militant writ- ers and critics joined the Russian Association of Proletarian Writers (RAPP); similarly inclined musicians established the Russian Association of Proletarian Musicians (RAPM) while architects formed the All-Union Association of Pro- letarian Architects (VOPRA); artists in Ukraine established the All-Ukrainian Association of Proletarian Artists (VUAPKh); and the Association of Revolu- tionary Workers of Cinematography (ARRK) promoted "proletarian cinema" in its journal *Cinema and Life*, which was renamed *Proletarian Cinema* in January 1931.

The heyday of identification with the proletariat was accompanied by changes in dress, personal appearance, and forms of entertainment. Oxford

---

[39] Lewis H. Siegelbaum and Andrei Sokolov, *Stalinism as a Way of Life: A Narrative in Documents* (New Haven, CT: Yale University Press, 2000), 317–18, 325, 378; Fitzpatrick, *Stalin's Peasants*, 260.

[40] Matt F. Oja, *From Krestianka to Udarnitsa: Rural Women and the Vydvizhenie Campaign, 1933–1941* (Pittsburgh: Center for Russian and Eastern European Studies, University of Pitts- burgh, 1996); Roberta Manning, "Women in the Soviet Countryside on the Eve of World War II," in *Russian Peasant Women*, eds. Beatrice Farnsworth and Lynne Viola (New York: Oxford University Press, 1992), 206–35; Fitzpatrick, *Stalin's Peasants*, 181–2.

[41] Sheila Fitzpatrick, "Cultural Revolution as Class War," in *Cultural Revolution in Russia, 1928– 1931*, ed. Sheila Fitzpatrick (Bloomington: Indiana University Press, 1978), 8–40.

trousers and "Jim" lace-boots, which had acquired popularity among urban dwellers in the 1920s, were eclipsed late in the decade with the heightened political importance of asceticism in dress and the increasing difficulty of finding or affording new clothing of any kind. The hostility toward intellectuals during these years made even Sergei Kirov, Leningrad party boss, afraid to be seen in public wearing glasses. Such NEP era pastimes as card playing and the foxtrot were driven underground, while amateur "agitprop" theater and mass gymnastics caught on especially among urban youth.[42]

Real workers with prerevolutionary experience meanwhile were experiencing a "crisis of proletarian identity," as their living standards plummeted, their craft skills came under attack from officially promoted speed-ups, and their claims to shop floor leadership and other "labor aristocratic" tendencies were challenged by relative newcomers and party officials.[43] In these rapidly changing circumstances, the meanings of such Lenin era shibboleths as labor discipline and class consciousness became highly contested. From whom, after all, should workers have taken instruction and orders on the shop floor – engineering-technical personnel who owing to their bourgeois backgrounds could be suspected of "wrecking," trade union officials who had yet to learn to "face toward production," or recent promotees (*vydvizhentsy*) who had limited training for their new jobs?

On the assumption that work experience (*stazh*) was positively correlated to class consciousness, *Trud v SSSR*, a statistical compendium that appeared irregularly during the 1930s, applied a rough and ready guide to how many years in industry was minimally necessary: three for hereditary workers with no ties to agriculture, five for other groups not connected with agriculture, five for kolkhozniks and poor peasants, and ten for middle peasants.[44] As crude or absurd as the criterion was, it did suggest that the party had its work cut out for itself in promoting class consciousness: by 1933 according to a trade union census conducted in that year, over half the workforce had less than three years of production experience.[45]

All of this is to suggest that while class mattered a great deal in terms of access to rights and goods, it was not indelible. Numerous opportunities existed for "*byvshie liudi*," "*lishentsy*," and those who fell into other stigmatized categories to rehabilitate themselves, mostly by the performance of "socially useful labor." Rates of rehabilitation actually grew toward the mid-1930s, reaching approximately half of all petitioners. Of course, the decisions to grant or restore rights were often arbitrary, depending on connections, the whims

[42] Natalia Lebina, *Povsednevnaia zhizn' sovetskogo goroda: Normy i anomalii, 1920–1930 gody* (St. Petersburg: Zhurnal "Neva," 1999), 211–20; Lynn Mally, *Revolutionary Acts: Amateur Theater and the Soviet State, 1917–1938* (Ithaca, NY: Cornell University Press, 2000), 146–80.

[43] Hiroaki Kuromiya, "The Crisis of Proletarian Identity in the Soviet Factory, 1928–1929," *Slavic Review* 44, no. 2 (1985): 280–97.

[44] Z. L. Mindlin and S. A. Kheinman, eds., *Trud v SSSR, Ekonomiko-statisticheskii spravochnik* (Moscow: Ekonomgiz, 1932), 26.

[45] *Profsoiuznaia perepis' 1932–1933 g.* (Moscow: Profizdat, 1934), 16.

of local officials, or whether a campaign to be on guard against "simulators" was under way.[46] But that such a mechanism existed is significant in that it counteracted the divisiveness of the class basis of the political community. It clearly distinguishes the USSR from the biopolitical criteria employed in Nazi Germany.

The redemptive quality of labor was the obverse of the ascriptive association of the bourgeois class with parasitism. Hard labor coerced from prisoners, such as former bourgeois wreckers, kulak saboteurs, and other criminals assigned to the White Sea–Baltic Canal construction project, earned them the opportunity for redemption if they were fortunate enough to survive its rigors.[47] At the White Sea–Baltic canal as throughout the labor camps and colonies to which kulaks and their families had been consigned as "special settlers" (*spetspereselentsy*), it was possible to become a shock worker by participating in socialist competition, joining shock brigades, and producing results over and above one's prescribed output norm.[48] As on the "inside," so in Soviet society in general, shock worker status served as an index of class consciousness, one that immersed the trade unions, enterprise staff, and party organizers in an immensity of statistical calculation and paperwork. But because the number of shock workers also was an index of the success of agitational work by party and union activists, statistical inflation was inevitable. By 1931 over half of the industrial workforce was recorded as consisting of shock workers, necessitating the use of such modifiers as "outstanding," "best," and "noted" (*znatnye*) to distinguish the most deserving from the ordinary or pretend (*lzhe-*) shock workers.[49]

Such distinctions could be of vital importance to those so designated, especially during the years of the most intense food shortages when the regime constructed and applied to the general population a "hierarchy of consumption."[50] The hierarchy, based on a combination of ration categories and geopolitical distinctions, crudely reflected the regime's priorities according to which production workers were to receive more than those involved in services and clerical work, urban inhabitants were privileged compared to collective and state farm workers, and, among cities, Moscow and Leningrad were the most

---

[46] Alexopoulos, *Stalin's Outcasts*, 34–7, 90–4, 165–6.

[47] Maksim Gorkii, L. L. Averbakh, and S. G. Firin, eds., *Belomorsko–Baltiiskii kanal imeni Stalina, istoriia stroitel'stva* (Moscow: Gosudarstvennoe izdatel'stvo "Istoriia fabrik i zavodov," 1934).

[48] In many cases, sheer physical survival must have been at stake. On the peasants arrested as kulaks and deported as special settlers see Lynne Viola, *The Unknown Gulag: The Lost World of Stalin's Special Settlements* (Oxford and New York: Oxford University Press, 2007).

[49] Hiroaki Kuromiya, *Stalin's Industrial Revolution: Politics and Workers, 1928–1932* (Cambridge: Cambridge University Press, 1988), 319–23; Lewis H. Siegelbaum, *Stakhanovism and the Politics of Productivity in the USSR, 1935–1941* (Cambridge: Cambridge University Press, 1988), 40–5.

[50] The term was coined by Elena Osokina. See her *Ierarkhiia potrebleniia: O zhizni liudei v usloviiakh stalinskogo snabzheniia 1928–1935 gg.* (Moscow: MGOU, 1993). On preferential treatment for shock workers, see Julie Hessler, "Culture of Shortages: A Social History of Soviet Trade" (Ph.D. diss., University of Chicago, 1996), 121–6.

privileged, followed by other "regime" cities to which residence was restricted to those holding internal passports. Literally a matter of life and death, passports and ration coupons were forged and traded on an apparently massive scale, thus involving an enormous number of Soviet citizens in what amounted to identity fraud.[51]

The Nazis had come to power in no small part through their capacity to appropriate and personify the ideal of a recovered *Volksgemeinschaft* that found great resonance in German society. In so doing, the Nazis tapped into such a reservoir of wishful thinking that few fully understood or cared how the ideal was also being transformed in Nazi hands. In 1914 the term connoted the unity of the German people (as an organic national community, not an artificial society or *Gesellschaft*), in which previous political, social, and confessional divisions among Germans were transcended. The emphasis was on unity through inclusion. Under the Nazis the term came to mean quite literally a "community of race." Unity was now defined primarily by exclusion, particularly of those deemed both alien and responsible for the betrayal and fragmentation of the *Volksgemeinshcaft* at the end of World War I and the subsequent defeat and revolution but also of those deemed biologically defective.[52]

As in the Soviet Union, a dictatorial regime now set out to engineer the creation of a homogeneous, utopian society, but the defining principle was racial, not class, purification. At the center of the Nazi obsession were not the elastic concepts of kulak and NEP man but the all too precisely definable concept of Jew.[53] In Nazi ideology the Jews represented a double threat to the *Volksgemeinschaft*. First, as allegedly rootless and stateless by nature, Jews were claimed by the Nazis to be an inherently parasitical people who not only lived off their hosts but simultaneously polluted the purity of the hosts' "blood" by race mixing. The underlying assumption, of course, was that "pure blood" was a precondition of the strength, vigor, and creativity of the *Volksgemeinschaft*, while "mixed blood" spelled its doom through degeneration, sterility, and weakness. Secondly, the Jews were perceived as the carriers of those subversive ideas that most threatened to undermine the will of the *Volksgemeinschaft* to wage the unrelenting, no holds barred, struggle for *Lebensraum* against other racial communities that was essential for its own survival. These ideas represented a sequence of monstrous "Jewish conspiracies": Christianity, with its message of love thy neighbor and turn the other cheek; liberalism, with its advocacy of equality before the law, personal freedom, and the egotistical

---

[51] Elena Osokina, *Za fasadom stalinskogo izobiliia: raspredelenie i rynok v snabzhenii naseleniia v gody industrializatsii, 1927–1941* (Moscow: ROSSPEN, 1998), 141–60.

[52] For the "inclusive" and "exclusive" potential in the "ideas of 1914," see: Steffen Bruendel, *Volksgemeinschaft oder Volksstaat: Die "Ideen von 1914" und die Neuordung Deutschlands im Ersten Weltkrieg* (Berlin: Akademie Verlag, 2003).

[53] For the broader social, rather than narrow legal, process of defining Jews, see Omer Bartov, "Defining Enemies, Making Victims: Germans, Jews, and the Holocaust," *American Historical Review* 103, no. 3 (1998): 258–71.

pursuit of individual economic self-interest; and Marxism, with its primacy of international working-class solidarity above national loyalty. If the law of nature was racial struggle, then, the Jews represented in essence antinature, the never-ending, pernicious attempt to persuade mankind consciously to act unnaturally. Wayward Germans could be won back to the *Volksgemeinschaft*, but with the Jewish enemy there could be no compromise.

The Nazi regime moved quickly in 1933. The dismantling of the multi-party system and the labor unions, as well as the crushing of the leadership cadres of the SPD and KPD, were portrayed as a triumph over the key instruments of Jewish divisiveness and subversion. But the Jews were to be attacked not just symbolically but also as individuals. The regime undid Jewish emancipation based on equality before the law and promulgated discriminatory laws aimed at ending the Jews' alleged inordinate influence on German society through purging them from the civil service, the professions, and cultural life. The "civic death" of German Jewry in 1933 was followed by their "social death" in 1935. The Nuremberg Laws and subsequent implementation regulations not only defined the "full" Jew by law (anyone with three or four grandparents who was a member of the Jewish religious community, or anyone with two such grandparents who was married to a Jew), but also forbade marriage and sexual intercourse between Jews and "Aryans." The potential accusation of *Rassenschande* severed virtually all remaining social ties between Jews and other Germans. As a practical concession that tacitly acknowledged the extent of Jewish assimilation and intermarriage in German society, however, the Nazi regime permitted the existence of somewhat less-persecuted categories of so-called first- and second-degree *Mischlinge* (people with two or one Jewish grandparent, respectively) as well as "full" Jews living in mixed marriages. In the language of the regime, to be less persecuted was to be "privileged."

Political repression and legal discrimination to end purported Jewish influence within the *Volksgemeinschaft* were an initial but by no means the final goal of the Nazi regime. The very physical presence of the Jew had to cease as well – a goal that Hitler had articulated as early as 1919 when he called for the "removal of the Jews altogether" (*Entfernung der Juden überhaupt*).[54] The legal persecution of the Jews thus became a means to an end. Making Jewish life in Germany increasingly unbearable and making clear to the Jews that they had no future there were intended to coerce them to emigrate, with the ultimate vision that Germany would become *judenfrei* or "free of Jews."[55]

---

[54] Ian Kershaw, *Hitler, 1889–1936: Hubris* (New York: Norton, 1999), 125.

[55] On the evolution of Nazi persecution of Jews, see Karl Schleunes, *The Twisted Road to Auschwitz* (Urbana: University of Illinois Press, 1970); Uwe Adam, *Judenpolitik im Dritten Reich* (Düsseldorf: Droste, 1972); Michael Wildt, *Judenpolitik des SD 1935 bis 1938: Eine Dokumentation* (Munich: Oldenbourg, 1995); Saul Friedländer, *The Years of Persecution.* Vol. 1, *Nazi Germany and the Jews* (New York: HarperCollins, 1997).

But the *Volksgemeinschaft* was threatened not only from without by the presence of racially alien elements but also from within by biologically defective or "degenerate" members, whose reproduction would "dilute" and "weaken" the vitality, strength, and purity of the German racial community and thereby undermine its capacity to wage relentless and unending struggle successfully. They also constituted an economic "burden" (*Belastung*) that would drain resources from rather than contribute to the *Volksgemeinschaft*. Hence, in addition to the legal and social exclusion and envisioned expulsion of the Jews, the regime pursued quite literally the surgical exclusion of those deemed hereditarily defective through compulsory sterilization (enacted into law in July 1933).[56]

Unlike the concept of Jew, however, these Germans considered biologically/hereditarily defective could not be neatly categorized in mass by legal definition. The categories of affliction justifying compulsory sterilization included both hereditary physical defects (blindness, deafness, epilepsy) as well as nebulous mental and behavioral categories considered hereditary, such as feeblemindedness, manic-depression, schizophrenia, and severe alcoholism. "Applications" (denunciations?) for compulsory sterilization could be made by doctors, institution directors, and public health officials and were adjudicated on an individual basis by "hereditary health courts" (*Erbgesundheitsgerichte*), whose verdicts (routinely around 90 percent in favor of sterilization) were enforced by the police. Congenital feeblemindedness was both the most imprecise diagnosis and most frequently invoked justification (roughly 50 percent followed by schizophrenia at 25 percent). In the prewar years over three hundred thousand Germans were sterilized.[57] A whole battery of antinatal and pronatal measures (for example, compulsory abortion for pregnant women subjected to compulsory sterilization versus harsh penalties for abortions by persons deemed healthy) supplemented the 1933 "Law for the Prevention of Hereditarily Diseased Offspring" and, quite apart from racial anti-Semitism and the exclusion of Jews, thoroughly biologized the notion of *Volksgemeinschaft* as a racial community.[58]

While the regime drew lines that excluded small minorities of Germans from the *Volksgemeinschaft*, it also developed the rituals, symbols, and rhetoric of inclusion for the vast majority. Class-based associational life gave way to consolidated Nazi associations, stretching from local small-town singing clubs to national organizations such as the German Workers Front. A number of women's organizations were assimilated into the NS-Frauenschaft, and a separate organizational sphere was created for women, extending from youth to

[56] Gisela Bock, *Zwangssterilisation im Nationalsozialismus: Studien zur Rassenpolitik und Frauenpolitik* (Opladen: Westdeutscher Verlag, 1986).

[57] Henry Friedlander, *The Origins of Nazi Genocide* (Chapel Hill: University of North Carolina Press, 1995), 23–38.

[58] Bock, *Zwangssterilisation im Nationalsozialismus*, 94–103.

adulthood. Programs like Kraft durch Freude offered to lower-class Germans the opportunity for vacations previously reserved for the propertied. The Work Service and Land Year ensured in turn that privileged Germans would be given the duty of doing healthy and productive physical labor in the community. With the introduction of military conscription in 1935, all fit male Germans – excluding Jews of course – were once again pressed into the same uniform and the same training, invoking the patriotic "socialism of the trenches" of the Great War. Such rituals, symbols, and rhetoric would scarcely have been effective, however, if they were simply cynical manipulations of the regime imposed from above. Both Nazi and SPD sources at the time reported numerous complaints and widespread dissatisfaction on economic issues among various groups such as industrial workers and peasants, but they did not crystallize into broader disaffection much less opposition to the regime. As Ian Kershaw concluded, "Nazism painted over rather than eliminated the divisions within German society," and the credibility of the *Volksgemeinschaft* myth derived from "interpreted" rather than "objective" conditions.[59] This was possible in part because of a "readiness for consensus" (*Konsensbereitschaft*) based on a widespread longing for security and normality after traumatic crisis.[60]

Complementing the myth of the *Volksgemeinschaft* was the increasingly pervasive and effective "Hitler myth." Charismatic identification of Germans with Hitler as the personification of a German renewal transcending the mundane and petty problems and shortcomings of everyday life reinforced the belief in a *Volksgemeinschaft* transcending the divisions of German society. Just as a "readiness for consensus" underlay Germans' belief that the Third Reich had restored the *Volksgemeinschaft*, Hitler's charisma likewise reflected society's transcendental longings and hopes.[61]

If the Nazi regime was based on a blend of coercion and consent, it also constituted a blend of restoration and revolution. As long as political effectiveness and great power status were restored, unemployment eased, and economic

---

[59] Ian Kershaw, *Popular Opinion and Political Dissent in the Third Reich, Bavaria 1933–1945* (Oxford: Clarendon Press, 1983), esp. 2, 384.

[60] The term comes from Bernd Stöver, *Volksgemeinschaft im Dritten Reich: Die Konsensbereitschaft der Deutschen aus der Sicht sozialistischer Exilberichte* (Düsseldorf: Droste, 1993). For the attraction of the notion of *Volksgemeinschaft* for workers and youth, see: David Welch, "Nazi Propaganda and the *Volksgemeinschaft*: Constructing a People's Community," *Journal of Contemporary History* 39, no. 2 (2004): 213–38. Another attractive aspect of the notion of *Volksgemeinschaft* was the way in which Germans could invoke and appropriate it in their negotiations with party and state. John Connelly, "The Uses of *Volksgemeinschaft*: Letters to the NSDAP Kreisleitung Eisenach, 1939–1940," *Journal of Modern History* 68, no. 4 (1996), 899–930.

[61] Ian Kershaw, *The "Hitler Myth": Image and Reality in the Third Reich* (Oxford: Oxford University Press, 1987); Martin Broszat, "Soziale Motivation und Führerbindung des National Sozialismus," *Vierteljahrshefte für Zeitgeschichte* 18 (1970): 395–409; Stöver, *Volksgemeinschaft im Dritten Reich*, 295–306.

hope returned, the regime's racial revolution – starting cautiously and proceeding incrementally – found consent, both tacit and overt, among the vast majority, and coercion was reserved for the victims. By the mid-1930s there was little doubt that the Nazis had won the support of the "majority of the majority"[62] who had not voted for them prior to 1933. Compared to the success of the policies of inclusion, the policies of exclusion had cost the regime virtually nothing. And compared with the horrendous loss of life wrought by the Stalinist regime's collectivization drive, forced industrialization, and famine, the Nazi regime could still boast of a relatively "bloodless" revolution.

EXPANDING EXCLUSION: ENEMIES OF THE PEOPLE, ENEMY NATIONS, AND ASOCIALS

Toward the end of the First Five-Year Plan, the regime's obsession with proletarian purity noticeably diminished. A harbinger was Stalin's speech of June 23, 1931, in which he condemned "specialist baiting" and called for the reinstatement of bourgeois specialists who had proven their dedication to the cause of socialist construction.[63] Increasingly, statistical surveys and other authoritative publications lumped together new promotees and the old technical intelligentsia as "engineering-technical personnel" (ITR), and their status and privileges rose. In April 1932, most of the above-mentioned "proletarian" associations were disbanded by order of the Central Committee.[64] The proletariat, it would seem, was relieved of its mission as an agent of history; by the middle of the decade, Stalin could proclaim that it was "cadres" who decided "everything."[65]

This is not to suggest that the "commanders of production" enjoyed a free rein. One of the purposes of the Stakhanovite movement was to expose output-restrictive practices that had taken hold in both industry and agriculture and put managers on notice that they would not be tolerated. Another, of course, was to identify the most productive workers and collective farmers and reward them in a more lavish fashion than previously.[66] But though largely confined to these two groups, Stakhanovite status was articulated less in terms of class

---

[62] Sebastian Haffner, *Anmerkungen zu Hitler* (Munich: Kindler, 1978), 43. For positive memories of the 1930s that persisted even into the postwar period, see Ulrich Herbert, "Good Times, Bad Times: Memories of the Third Reich," in *Life in the Third Reich*, ed. Richard Bessel (Oxford: Oxford University Press, 1987), 97–113.

[63] I. V. Stalin, *Sochineniia*, vol. 13 (Moscow: Gos. izd–vo polit. Lit–ry, 1946–51), 69–73.

[64] "Resolution of the Central Committee on the Reconstruction of Literary-Artistic Organizations, 23 April 1932," in *KPSS v rezoliutsiiakh i resheniiakh s"ezdov, konferentsii i plenumov TsK*, 9th ed., vol. 5 (Moscow: Politizdat, 1982–89), 407–8. The more inclusive "Soviet" replaced "proletarian" as in the case of the title of ARRK's journal.

[65] I. V. Stalin, *Sochineniia*, 3 vols. (numbered 1[XIV]–3[XVI] of Stalin's *Sochineniia* published in 13 vols.), ed. Robert H. McNeal (Stanford, CA: The Hoover Institute on War Revolution and Peace, Stanford University, 1967), XIV: 56–64.

[66] Siegelbaum, *Stakhanovism*, esp. chapter 3, "Managers and Specialists in the Stakhanovite Year," 99–144 and Chapter 4, "The Making of Stakhanovites," 145–78.

than as exemplary of the emergence of the "new Soviet person," confident in his/her skills and "cultured" – or at least interested in becoming so – in other facets of daily life.[67]

Another, more broad-ranging indication of the deemphasis on class was the dismantling of legal and institutional structures of class discrimination. This process, which at first proceeded cautiously and informally with respect to former kulaks and their offspring, culminated in the 1936 Soviet Constitution's declaration of civil rights for all citizens. The logic of this step was that the former exploiting classes had been decisively routed and the USSR had become a socialist society consisting, as Stalin asserted at the Extraordinary Eighth Congress of Soviets in November 1936, "exclusively of workers, peasants, and the intelligentsia."[68] For census purposes, in both 1937 and 1939, respondents were asked to identify themselves according to one of the following "social groups" (*obshchestvennye gruppy*): workers, employees, collective farmers, independent farmers, craftsmen, people of the free professions or servants of a (religious) cult, and nontoiling elements.[69] Although the order of the categories roughly corresponded to their ideologically charged valence, none was associated with restrictions on civil rights.

The diminution in importance of class as the basis for legal discrimination – not incidentally accompanied by the abolition of rationing in 1935 – did not mean that class was of no consequence as a basis for self-identification. The use of terms such as "intelligent" or for that matter *muzhik* remained potent means of identifying with an affinitive community. Class resentments also remained palpable at the popular level. "The road has been opened for kulaks and priests," complained one collective farmer during a discussion of the draft constitution, "but nothing has changed for us." This was one of many remarks recorded in NKVD summaries of such discussions that expressed apprehension about dispossessed kulaks returning from exile to reclaim their property and the granting of voting rights to priests.[70]

At the same time, resentment against those who had ensconced themselves in comfortable positions and purportedly did no work also found expression. As another collective farmer from Azov–Black Sea *krai* wrote in connection with

---

[67] Ibid., 223–36; Vadim Volkov, "The Concept of *kul'turnost'*: Notes on the Stalinist Civilizing Process," in *Stalinism, New Directions*, ed. Sheila Fitzpatrick (London: Routledge, 2000), 226–8. Allusions to Stakhanovites tended to be organic ("Stalin's tribe") or mythohistorical ("Soviet knights" (*bogatyri*)) rather than expressed in class terms.

[68] I. V. Stalin, *O proekte konstitutsii Soiuza SSR: Doklad na VIII Vsesoiuznom chrezvychainom s"ezde sovetov* (Moscow: Partizdat, 1936), 10.

[69] V. B. Zhiromskaia, I. N. Kiselev, and Iu. A. Poliakov, *Polveka pod grifom sekretno: Vsesoiuznaia perepis' naseleniia 1937 goda* (Moscow: Nauka, 1996), 12–13. Left out were dependents (who were supposed to record the category of the person on whom they relied for support, or in the case of pensioners, the group to which they previously had belonged), and the over 2 million inmates and civilian employees of prisons, labor camps, and colonies who were counted in separate "special" censuses (104–23).

[70] Quoted in Siegelbaum and Sokolov, *Stalinism as a Way of Life*, 184. See also Fitzpatrick, *Stalin's Peasants*, 241.

the draft constitution, "A special paragraph needs to be included . . . saying that all able-bodied men and women who do absolutely no work and are not engaged in any activity for the general benefit shall be deprived of political rights. The point is that a new Soviet bourgeoisie – loafer-parasites – is taking shape." Yet another collective farmer, describing bureaucrats as "offshoots of the capitalist class," asked for the insertion of a clause that would protect working people from their exploitation; and a Red Army soldier, writing from Chita, targeted the "wives of many directors, managers, engineers and technicians" who "don't work and have a servant," which he considered "out-and-out exploitation."[71]

During the Great Purges of 1937–8 the Politburo targeted politically powerful individuals and groups for arrest and execution, affording a measure of satisfaction to many who had nursed grievances against the "higher-ups" (*verkhushki*). Subordinates and rivals, emboldened by the campaign of vigilance initiated by the February 1937 plenum of the Central Committee, meanwhile denounced smaller fry – that is, local political authorities, administrators, and bosses. In both cases, the accused usually were characterized as counterrevolutionaries, wreckers, Trotskyites, traitors, spies, vermin, and, more generically, "enemies of the people." The last of these terms appeared in article 131 of the constitution ("Persons who encroach on public or socialist property are enemies of the people"), and it can be found in correspondence with the constitutional commission.[72] Although authors of denunciations continued to include incriminating references to the alien social origins of the accused for many years afterward, "enemy of the people" essentially replaced "class enemy" in official parlance.[73] This was the logical extension of the declaration made at the Seventeenth Party Congress that the class enemy had been defeated "decisively."

Two other dimensions of the Great Purges recently have received considerable attention from scholars, and both bear directly on the state's expanding identification of enemies: the "mass operations" of the summer and autumn of 1937 and the overlapping but slightly longer-lasting "national operations." The mass operations, conducted on the basis of a Politburo resolution and the NKVD's Order No. 447, represented a recapitulation of the dekulakization campaign in terms of their modus operandi (quotas assigned to each region, categories distinguishing between "most hostile" and "less active," and corresponding punishments).[74] They also were the culmination of several years of mounting frustration over the failure of the internal passport regime, imposed in 1933, to stem the tide of illegal "parasitical" elements in the cities as well as

[71] Quoted in Siegelbaum and Sokolov, *Stalinism as a Way of Life*, 195–6.

[72] *Konstitutsiia (Osnovnoi zakon) Soiuza Sovetskikh Sotsialisticheskikh Respublik* (Moscow: Gos. iz–vo iurid. Lit–ry, 1963), 105; Siegelbaum and Sokolov, *Stalinism as a Way of Life*, 197.

[73] Vladimir A. Kozlov, "Denunciation and Its Functions in Soviet Governance: From the Archive of the Soviet Ministry of Internal Affairs, 1944–53," in *Stalinism, New Directions*, ed. Sheila Fitzpatrick (London: Routledge), 132.

[74] *Trud*, 2 June 1991.

crimes against persons and property in both urban and rural areas. Kulaks, or rather former kulaks, were again prime targets for repression, although other "socially harmful" (*sotsvrednye*) and "anti-Soviet elements" such as escaped and former convicts, former participants in anti-Soviet and bandit uprisings, recidivist criminals, political refugees, beggars, and other declassed groups were also included in the round-ups.[75] The frequent, in fact increasing, use of such terms – like that of "enemy of the people" – is itself indicative not only of the diminution of the language of class, but also of the conceptual difficulty of explaining deviant behavior in other terms.

The linguistic shifts are well illustrated in the case of rural communities in Western Siberia. Having been dekulakized and deported from their villages in European Russia, they were reclassified as special (and after 1934 labor) settlers. Many died or fled, hiding their class-alien backgrounds if they could, but others remained. In May 1934 some of their civil rights were restored, and in January 1935 they received the right to vote. The model Kolkhoz Charter of March 1935 permitted them to join or form collective farms in their new places of settlement. How many actually took advantage of this provision is unknown, but it must have been sufficient to prompt party plenipotentiaries to cease referring to residents of collective and state farms as *kolkhozniki* and *sovkhozniki* and instead to use the less approbatory moniker of "peasants."[76] As such, they, or at least substantial numbers of them, could be subjected once more to dekulakization. These individuals thus traversed the following linguistic terrain: kulak > special/labor settler > collective/state farmer > peasant > kulak.

The national operations, formally carried out against "espionage and sabotage contingents" of diaspora nationalities, were predicated on the assumption that just about anyone with cross-border ethnic ties was a spy (or at least had the potential for being so) and thus actually resulted in ethnic cleansing.[77] Even party members in good standing, Red Army veterans, and those whose ancestors had resided for centuries in the Russian empire were subjected to arrest, deportation, or execution. Nationality, it would seem, was absolutized, trumping any other identity.

The conceptual obverse of "enemy nations" was not so much the Russian nation, but rather the "friendship of the peoples," a formulation that Stalin

---

[75] See David Shearer, "Crime and Social Disorder in Stalin's Russia: A Reassessment of the Great Retreat and the Origins of Mass Repression," *Cahiers du Monde russe* 39 (1998): 119–48; idem., "To Count and Cleanse: Passportization and the Reconstruction of the Soviet Population during the 1930s," unpublished paper presented at AAASS Annual Convention, 2001; Paul Hagenloh, "'Socially Harmful Elements' and the Great Terror," in *Stalinism, New Directions*, ed. Sheila Fitzpatrick (London: Routledge, 2000), 286–308. See also the contribution by Nicholas Werth and Christian Gerlach in this volume.

[76] David Shearer, "Policing the Soviet Frontier: Social Disorder and Repression in Western Siberia during the 1930s," unpublished paper presented at AAASS Annual Convention, 1997. Shearer, citing an archival source from the Western Siberian *krai*, gives the figure of 14,886 kulaks arrested and sentenced by special NKVD courts by October 1937 (41).

[77] Terry Martin, "The Origins of Soviet Ethnic Cleansing," *Journal of Modern History*, 70 (1998): 847–51. Martin, *Affirmative Action Empire*, 328–41.

introduced in December 1935 and that remained the cornerstone of "Soviet patriotism" and "the Soviet people" (*sovetskii narod*).[78] If there was any Soviet parallel to the Nazis' vision of the *Volksgemeinschaft*, this was it: the Soviet people composed of the harmonious "socialist nations," each of which was endowed with/assigned its own territory, national language, and culture. Each represented itself to the others by performances of *völkisch* dance troupes, choirs, and musical ensembles and canonized works of "people's poets" published in translation. National stereotypes flourished within this treacly discourse: Georgians were invariably "sunny," Ukrainians were "broad spirited" and so forth. This Stalinist schema did a lot of ideological work. It helped to build nations and foster the creation of national elites. It was, as Terry Martin has quipped, "the highest form of imperialism."[79]

The imperial nature of the USSR had to do with the political subordination of constituent nations to Moscow, or, more precisely, the supranational All-Union Communist Party (Bolsheviks). Yet, from the late 1930s onward, Russians occupied the explicit role as "first among equals," the "most soviet and most revolutionary" nation, according to Stalin.[80] State authorities routinely extolled Russian culture as "the most progressive," the study of the Russian language was made mandatory in all non-Russian schools by a Central Committee resolution of March 1938, and the latinized alphabets of Central Asian languages were re-cyrillicized. The *étatism* extolled by Stalin became increasingly Russocentric.[81]

Despite essentializing tendencies, national identity was never officially equated with bioracial characteristics. From the 1920s onward, Soviet citizens were required to indicate their nationality on personnel forms (including from 1932 their internal passports) but were permitted to choose their own nationality. In April 1938, the NKVD decreed that henceforth for the purposes of passport registration, nationality would be determined on the basis of ascribed hereditary status, that is, the nationality of the parents. The decree almost certainly was prompted by concern that members of enemy nations would try to mask their "true" nationality by identifying themselves otherwise.[82] Still, the decree did not apply in the case of the 1939 census, which, like earlier censuses, relied on self-definition.[83]

As if to confirm Trotsky's "law of combined and uneven development," the sovietization of territories annexed in 1939–40 involved virtually all the

---

[78] Martin, *Affirmative Action Empire*, 451–60.
[79] Terry Martin, "Affirmative Action Empire: The Soviet Union as the Highest Form of Imperialism," in Suny and Martin, *State of Nations*, 67–90.
[80] Martin, *Affirmative Action Empire*, 453.
[81] David Brandenberger, *National Bolshevism: Stalinist Mass Culture and the Formation of Modern Russian National Identity, 1931–1956* (Cambridge, MA: Harvard University Press, 2002), esp. 43–112.
[82] Martin, *Affirmative Action Empire*, 451.
[83] Francine Hirsch, "The Soviet Union as a Work-in-Progress: Ethnographers and the Category Nationality in the 1926, 1937, and 1939 Censuses," *Slavic Review* 56, no. 2 (1997), 274; idem, "Race without the Practice of Racial Politics," *Slavic Review* 61, no. 1 (2002): 39–41.

stages through which the rest of the Soviet Union had passed during the 1930s. In what became the western parts of Ukraine and Belorussia, ethnic Poles were subjected to deportations and executions on both class (landlord, kulak) and ethnic (enemy nation) grounds. Ukrainians and Belorussians now began to be referred to as "great," a "curious episode of Stalinist semantics" that placed these peoples on a par with Russians, whose "great" status had been proclaimed in 1937.[84] In the Baltic republics, ethnic Germans were "repatriated" westward, while "fascists" and other "enemies of the people," who were overwhelmingly of Baltic ethnicity, were imprisoned, executed, or sent in the opposite direction.[85]

All these measures were driven by state security concerns, and yet the heightening of security consciousness (if such a thing were possible!) only seemed to undermine any sense of security. From Kustanai *oblast'* in Kazakhstan, it was reported in August 1940 that "kulaks and bourgeoisie exiled from the former Poland" were committing "possible acts of sabotage" and having a "demoralizing influence" on kolkhoz labor discipline. "Obviously fascist books (in Finnish), which should have been removed long ago" were discovered in January 1941 in the principal's office of a vocational school in Vyborg, while from Przemysl in western Ukraine came a denunciation of the head of the NKVD's City Department because he allegedly had issued a "permanent pass" to a merchant named Unger, "a man who is hostile to Soviet rule, had contact with the Polish police," and had intervened on behalf of Plishke, "a German intelligence agent" who had been under arrest.[86]

If the focal point of Soviet exclusionary practices in the late 1930s shifted from class enemies to "enemies of the people" and "enemy nations," Nazi exclusionary practices remained firmly grounded in race but expanded along many axes. Anti-Semitic persecution intensified with the systematic and total (as opposed to the previous informal, decentralized) confiscation of Jewish property in 1938, resulting in the "economic death" of German Jewry.[87] The hooliganistic violence, murder, arson of synagogues, and vandalism of Jewish

---

[84] Serhy Yekelchyk, "Stalinist Patriotism as Imperial Discourse: Reconciling the Ukrainian and Russian 'Heroic Pasts,' 1939–1945," unpublished paper presented at Midwest Russian History Workshop (University of Chicago, 2000), 14. See also idem, *Stalin's Empire of Memory: Russian-Ukrainian Relations in the Soviet Historical Imagination* (Toronto: University of Toronto Press, 2004), 24–32, 351–2. On repression of Poles, see Jan T. Gross, *Revolution from Abroad: The Soviet Conquest of Poland's Western Ukraine and Western Belorussia* (Princeton, NJ: Princeton University Press, 1988); and S. V. Mironenko and N. Vert [Werth], eds., *Istoriia stalinskogo GULaga: konets 1920-kh–pervaia polovina 1950-kh godov*. Vol. 1, *Massovye repressii v SSSR* (Moscow: ROSSPEN, 2004), 389–407.

[85] John Hiden and Patrick Salmon, *The Baltic Nations and Europe: Estonia, Latvia and Lithuania in the Twentieth Century*, rev. ed. (London: Longman, 1994), 114–15.

[86] Quoted in Siegelbaum and Sokolov, *Stalinism as a Way of Life*, 264–5, 279–81.

[87] Avraham Barkai, *From Boycott to Annihilation: The Economic Struggle of German Jews, 1933–1943* (Hanover, NH: University Press of New England, 1989); Frank Bajohr, *"Aryanisation" in Hamburg: The Economic Exclusion of Jews and the Confiscation of Their Property in Nazi Germany* (New York: Berghahn Books, 2002).

businesses of the November pogrom had no positive resonance among most of the German people, who were indifferent to the fate of the Jews but not to a public flouting of deeply ingrained values concerning the preservation of order, propriety, and property.[88] But the widespread sharing out of "aryanized" Jewish property meant that more Germans were beneficiaries of this state-sanctioned pillaging in 1938 than of the purge of Jews from the professions, universities, and civil service in 1933. This expanded complicity more than balanced the unease caused by the November pogrom.[89]

Compulsory sterilization, aimed at eliminating hereditary health defects from the German gene pool by preventing reproduction by those deemed hereditarily ill, was fatefully expanded in 1937. The offspring of German mothers and African fathers, who were among the French army troops from Morocco, Algeria, Tunisia, and Madagascar that took part in the postwar occupation in Germany, were pejoratively referred to as the "Rhineland bastards," and Göring ordered a census of these children as soon as the Nazis came to power. As the oldest of these African-German children approached maturity, the Nazi regime took action. In the summer of 1937, hundreds of these children were summoned before commissions of doctors and anthropologists, who certified that they were the carriers of "alien racial characteristics." Thereupon the mother (and when present the stepfather) was "persuaded" to agree to a "voluntary" sterilization that was carried out secretly without the case's being submitted to the "heredity health courts."[90] This small and stigmatized group of African-Germans could be dealt with summarily in ways that the far more numerous and socially connected Jewish *Mischlinge* could not.

Between political opponents to the regime, who could be recovered for the racial community through altering behavior by punishment, coercion, and reeducation, on the one hand, and the racially alien and biologically defective who were fated for elimination through expulsion or sterilization, on the other, was a murky borderland inhabited by people identified and stigmatized as "asocials" or "community aliens" (*Gemeinschaftsfremde*). A November 1933 decree ("against dangerous habitual criminals") empowered the police

---

[88] For reactions to the pogrom, see Ian Kershaw, "The Persecution of the Jews and German Popular Opinion in the Third Reich," *Leo Baeck Institute Yearbook*, 26 (1981): 275–81; David Bankier, *The Germans and the Final Solution: Public Opinion under Nazism* (New York: Oxford University Press, 1992), 85–8; Friedländer, *Nazi Germany and the Jews*, vol. 1, 294–8.

[89] On the broader acceptance of economic measures against the Jews, see Stöver, *Volksgemeinschaft im Dritten Reich*, 246–55, 420–1. For the broad spectrum of beneficiaries within German society, see Bajohr, *"Aryanisation" in Hamburg*, 222–72, 277–82. For the most recent study of the systemic relationship between Nazi policies of racial persecution, conquest, and genocide, on the one hand, and materialistic benefit to Germans, on the other, see: Götz Aly, *Hitler's Beneficiaries: Plunder, Racial War, and the Nazi Welfare State* (New York: Metropolitan Books, 2006).

[90] Reiner Pommerin, *"Sterilisierung der Rheinlandbastarde": Das Schicksal einer farbigen deustchen Minderheit 1918–1927* (Düsseldorf: Droste, 1979).

to take into unlimited "preventive detention" anyone with two or more criminal convictions. A December 1937 decree extended the powers of preventive detention to include "asocials," namely, those "who demonstrate through behavior towards the community, which may not in itself be criminal, that they will not adapt themselves to the community." Specifically included were beggars, tramps, whores, and alcoholics; those with contagious, especially sexually transmitted diseases who evaded public health measures; and the "workshy" or chronically unemployed. These people were seen not only as aesthetic blemishes on the Nazi image of the racial community, but also as stubborn nonconformists who constituted a dissident threat to the Nazis' capacity to impose both uniform and productive behavior.[91] The tendency was always to subsume "asocial" behavior, when judged irremediable, within the biologically defective. Also exiled from the *Volksgemeinschaft* but persecuted on different legal grounds were homosexuals. They were perceived as offensive to public morality, symbolic of the sexual license of Weimar, subversive of Nazi notions of manly camaraderie, and treasonously withholding their procreative powers from the community.[92] Thus those deemed habitual criminals or incorrigible homosexuals ("seducers") were subjected not only to indefinite incarceration but also to sterilization, castration, or execution.[93] The strength of this tendency to remove what was deemed unaesthetic, deviant, and irremediable through ever-escalating measures can be seen in the November 1944 recommendation of the Bamberg state prosecutor that particularly ugly asocial prisoners should also be eliminated.[94]

Nowhere can the tendency of the Nazi regime to merge its categories of habitual criminal, feebleminded, asocial, and racial alien be seen more clearly than in its treatment of Sinti and Roma, pejoratively referred to as *Zigeuner*.[95]

---

[91] Michael Burleigh and Wolfgang Wippermann, *The Racial State: Germany 1933–1945* (New York: Cambridge University Press, 1991), 167–97; Wolfgang Ayass, "'Ein Gebot der nationalen Arbeitsdisziplin': Die Aktion 'Arbeitsscheu Reich' 1938," *Feinderklärung und Prävention: Kriminalbiologie, Zigeunerforschung und Asozialpolitik* (Berlin: Rotbuch Verlag, 1988); *Beiträge zur nationalsozialistischen Gesundheits- und Sozialpolitik*, VI, 43–74; Klaus Scherer, "*Asozial*" *im Dritten Reich: Die vergessenen Verfolgten* (Munich: VOTUM Verlag, 1990).

[92] Geoffrey Giles, "The Institutionalization of Homosexual Panic in the Third Reich," in *Social Outsiders in Nazi Germany*, eds. Robert Gellately and Nathan Stoltzfuss (Princeton, NJ: Princeton University Press, 2001), 233–55; and "Männerbund mit Homo–Panik: Die Angst der Nazis vor der Rolle der Erotik," *Nationalsozialistischer Terror gegen Homosexuelle: Verdrängt und ungesühnt*, eds. Burkhard Jellonnek and Rüdiger Lautmann (Paderborn: Ferdinand Schönigh, 2002), 105–18.

[93] Nickolaus Wachsmann, "From Indefinite Confinement to Extermination: 'Habitual Criminals' in the Third Reich," *Social Outsiders in Nazi Germany*, eds. Robert Gellately and Nathan Stoltzfuss (Princeton, NJ: Princeton University Press, 2001), 165–91.

[94] Raul Hilberg, *The Destruction of the European Jews* (Chicago: Quadrangle Press, 1961), 642–3.

[95] The two most detailed and invaluable studies of the Nazi persecution of the "Gypsies" are Guenter Lewy, *The Nazi Persecution of the Gypsies* (New York: Oxford University Press, 2000), and Michael Zimmerman, *Rassenutopie und Genozid: Die nationalsozialistische "Lösung der Zigeunerfrage"* (Hamburg: Christians, 1996). For a short summary, see Sybil Milton, "'Gypsies'

The victims of widespread prejudice and discrimination before 1933, the Sinti and Roma were stereotypically characterized as parasitical, criminal, lazy, and rootless. After 1933 in Germany they were disproportionately subjected to the Nazi regime's measures against "asocial" habitual criminals, vagrants, and beggars. In fact, one category of asocial behavior subject to "preventive detention" was simply exhibiting a "Gypsy-like" lifestyle, even when those involved were not "Gypsies." The Sinti and Roma were likewise disproportionately subjected to compulsory sterilization on the grounds of feeblemindedness. For cases when the victims were obviously too bright for such a pretext, several public health officials developed the concept of "disguised mental retardation," in which indifference and nonconformity to societal norms, on the one hand, and cleverness and cunning, on the other, were declared to be the very symptoms that confirmed an alleged hereditary mental retardation justifying sterilization.[96] The Nuremberg Laws did not mention *Zigeuner*, but subsequent commentaries declared them to be of "alien blood" and subject to the same prohibitions that affected Jews. Himmler in turn set up a Central Office for the Fight against the Gypsy Nuisance and declared the "Gypsy problem" to be a "matter of race." Thereafter the Sinti and Roma were pulled inexorably into the vortex of persecution modeled on the regime's anti-Jewish measures.

As Robert Gellately has shown, Nazi self-representation proclaimed and German popular memory acknowledged that the regime's war on crime was one of its most successful accomplishments.[97] Thus, the identification of criminality with those excluded from the *Volksgemeinschaft* was both pervasive and intentional. Jews were not spared in this regard. For example, Heydrich ordered the arrest of all Jewish males with any past criminal conviction resulting in at least one month's detention as part of a major arrest wave of "asocials," especially the "work-shy," that he initiated in June 1938. (This particular razzia bore striking similarity to two notorious aspects of Stalinist practice, in that each police district was assigned a minimum quota of two hundred arrests, and one explicit goal was to swell the labor force in the concentration camps.)[98] The popular "preventive war" on crime both appropriated pre-Nazi conceptions about the biological determinants of habitual criminals and provided yet another gloss that invoked support for the Nazi construction of the

---

as Social Outsiders in Germany," *Social Outsiders in Nazi Germany*, eds. Robert Gellately and Nathan Stoltzfuss (Princeton, NJ: Princeton University Press, 2001), 212–32. Three studies that place the persecution and murder of the "Gypsies" within the wider context of Nazi racism and genocide are Friedlander, *The Origins of Nazi Genocide*; Burleigh and Wippermann, *The Racial State: Germany 1933–1945*; and Wolfgang Wippermann, "*Wie Die Zigeuner*": *Antisemitismus und Antiziganismus im Vergleich* (Berlin: Elefanten Press, 1997).

[96] Friedlander, *The Origins of Nazi Genocide*, 254–5; Lewy, *The Nazi Persecution of the Gypsies*, 20–3.

[97] Robert Gellately, *Backing Hitler: Consent and Coercion in Nazi Germany* (New York: Oxford University Press, 2001).

[98] Ayass, "'Ein Gebot der nationalen Arbeitsdisziplin,'" 53–5.

Volksgemeinschaft as well as the commensurate exclusion and persecution of marginal, stigmatized groups.[99]

Even with the expansion of Nazi exclusion to encompass the "asocials," the potential number of victims in German society was still minuscule in comparison to the "mass" and "national operations" in the Soviet Union. The vast majority of Germans had little reason to fear the police, who were celebrated as "friends and helpers" and were helped by a "self-policing" ethos in German society, especially in the form of denunciations.[100] This did not, of course, preclude Germans from grumbling or dissenting from the regime on single issues. As Eric Johnson has argued, a tacit agreement seemed to exist whereby Germans were free to complain about and criticize minor matters as long as they gave the regime autonomy to pursue ferociously its racial agenda.[101] There was police terror, but its social impact was utterly asymmetrical. It did not weaken support for the regime; if anything, by targeting clearly delineated outcasts from the *Volksgemeinschaft*, it strengthened it.

WAR AS THE APOTHEOSIS OF IDENTITY

After the Nazi invasion, as Soviet territories fell under occupation, were liberated, and were seized and liberated again, the meaning of Soviet patriotism – and identity – changed irrevocably. Class meant little as all who passed the test of loyalty were inscribed into "the toiling sons and daughters" of the constituent nations of the Union. Stalin could thank the "Russian people" in May 1945 for not having cast their government aside during the war, and the "great Russian people" continued to play the central unifying role within the friendship of the peoples after the war. But the maintenance of that friendship dictated that space be provided for (most but not all) other Soviet nations to share in the retrospective communities of heroism and suffering.[102]

Wartime service in the Red Army could expunge the stain of prewar stigmatization. In the course of the war, former kulaks were subject to the draft, and if they were inducted, their spouses and children received passports that enabled them to leave the special settlements. In 1946, all restrictions on those who had served or had children who served in the Red Army were removed.[103]

[99] Patrick Wagner, *Volksgemeinschaft ohne Verbrecher: Konzeptionen und Praxis der Kriminalpolizei in der Zeit der Weimarer Republik und des Nationalsozialismus* (Hamburg: Christians, 1996).

[100] Robert Gellately, *Backing Hitler* and *The Gestapo and German Society: Enforcing Racial Policy, 1933–1945*.

[101] Eric Johnson, *Nazi Terror: The Gestapo, Jews, and Ordinary Germans* (New York: Basic Books, 1999).

[102] We are following here the formulation and argument of Amir Weiner, *Making Sense of War: The Second World War and the Fate of the Bolshevik Revolution* (Princeton, NJ: Princeton University Press, 2001).

[103] Amir Weiner, "Nature, Nurture, and Memory in a Socialist Utopia: Delineating the Soviet Socio-Ethnic Body in the Age of Socialism," *American Historical Review*, 104, no. 4 (1999): 1132–3.

The return of these "formers" to their native villages must have revived old tensions, but the war and the officially sponsored myths surrounding it permitted them and others with prewar blemishes on their records, in effect, to start over. They could now rewrite their biographies, for they were identified as, and therefore could assume the identities of, fully fledged Soviet citizens. Referring to Red Army veterans, former partisans, and their families in Vinnytsia *oblast'* (Ukraine), Amir Weiner noted that they made up "hundreds of thousands of peasants defining their political and social identity on the basis of their sacrifice for the Soviet motherland and in juxtaposition to those who had not gone through the same ordeal of war or did not identify themselves with the Soviet cause."[104] This undoubtedly was true of many other parts of the Soviet Union.

Redemption was not so clearly at hand for those who had lived passively under Nazi occupation or had withdrawn to the Soviet interior out of harm's way. Still less could repatriated former *Ostarbeiter* and soldiers who had survived the horrors of Nazi POW camps expect to share in the benefits of Soviet victory or avoid incarceration upon their return.[105] Those who had collaborated with the enemy while under occupation generally were denied the possibility of political or social rehabilitation, even if they subsequently had enlisted in the Red Army and performed acts of bravery. Moreover, as in the case of collectivization-era kulaks and purge-era enemies of the people, their punishment was transferable to blood relatives. Deportations to Kazakhstan and Siberia awaited "kulaks" along with members of their families from western Ukraine and the Baltic republics; in the case of an order from April 1949 referring to the inhabitants of the reabsorbed Moldavian republic, the categories of deportees represented a virtual recapitulation of enemies from throughout Soviet history: former landowners, large merchants, members of profascist parties, former White Guardists, members of illegal religious sects, supporters of Nazi occupiers.[106]

Finally, those who actively had fought against the Soviet cause and continued to do so in the name of their "nation" after the Nazis' surrender were faced with extermination at the hands of the Red Army and the NKVD. This was not only a matter of collective retribution for atrocities committed against loyal Soviet citizens, but because such organizations as the Organization of Ukrainian Nationalists, its Ukrainian Insurgent Army, and the various Baltic home guards embodied the kind of anti-Soviet nationalism against which Soviet nationality policies had been constructed and pursued since the early 1920s. Weiner contends that the ideologically induced mania for purification of the political and social bodies drove both postwar verification campaigns within the

---

[104] Weiner, *Making Sense of War*, 325.
[105] Robert W. Thurston, "Cauldrons of Loyalty and Betrayal: Soviet Soldiers' Behavior, 1941 and 1945," in *The People's War: Responses to World War II in the Soviet Union*, eds. Robert W. Thurston and Bernd Bonwetsch (Urbana and Chicago: University of Illinois Press, 2000), 245–50.
[106] Mironenko and Vert, *Massovye repressii*, 515–16, 522–4.

Communist Party and the war against remnants of nationalist-guerrilla groups. This may be so, but at least at the local level – "in the intimate environment of the village" and the towns – personal score settling and an unquenched thirst for vengeance were much in evidence as well.[107] Rather than stemming from a single source, wartime and postwar Soviet schemas of identification arose out of a combination of deeply rooted prejudices and fears, the differential treatment by Nazi occupation forces of Soviet citizens according to their nationality or "race," the Soviet state's anxieties with respect to its place in the postwar international arena, and its propensity to interpret internal security risks in ethnonational terms and, where convenient or possible, to subject all members of such national groups to collective punishment.

All these factors seem to have been involved in the deportations to Kazakhstan, Uzbekistan, and Kirgizia of virtually all Chechens, Ingush, Crimean Tatars, Kalmyks, and other north Caucasus and Transcaucasian national groups in 1944.[108] These deportations evidently were intended to eradicate the territorial if not the ethnocultural identities of the affected nations. That they did nothing of the kind must be acknowledged to have been one of Stalin's more spectacular failures. Yet, whether eventually permitted to return to their homelands or not, the vast majority among these "punished peoples" were hardly less Soviet in their self-identities than those whose place within the communities of heroism and suffering was secure.

This brings us finally to the identification of Jews and their perilous situation in the postwar era. Jews, it seems, represented the obverse case of the punished peoples of the north Caucasus and Transcaucasia. Their "crime" was not collaboration with the enemy (though some postwar depictions of Jews in popular literature implied this), but rather attempts after the war by prominent Jews to commemorate the uniqueness of Jewish suffering combined with Jews' brazenly unauthorized celebration of Israeli independence in 1948. Even as individual Jews were decorated for their wartime bravery and achieved prominence in various walks of postwar life, the Jewish people were "excised" from the friendship of peoples that composed the USSR.[109] In another interpretation, Jews became vulnerable after the war (or at least after 1948) to two distinct if not contradictory claims of disloyalty. First, the creation of Israel and the Cold War made Jews a diaspora nationality analogous to those subjected to the national operations during the Great Purges. The Jewish "national form" thus "had become the symptom of a hostile bourgeois content." Second, the very lack of ethnic transparency on the part of those who dominated science, education, medicine, and other professions meant that "every Russian in high

---

[107] Weiner, *Making Sense of War*, 171–82.

[108] Aleksandr M. Nekrich, *The Punished Peoples: The Deportation and Fate of Soviet Minorities at the End of the Second World War* (New York: W. W. Norton, 1978); Norman M. Naimark, *Fires of Hatred: Ethnic Cleansing in Twentieth-Century Europe* (Cambridge, MA: Harvard University Press, 2001), 89–107.

[109] Weiner, *Making Sense of War*, 191–235, 375–7.

position was a potential Jew, and every Jew without exception was a potential enemy."[110] The analogy with (if not adaptation of) Nazism's extensive practice of "investigative genealogy" is fairly obvious.

In Nazi Germany the war led not to a reshuffling of identity, with new priority given to loyalty, military service, and sacrifice, but rather to an exponential increase in both the number of victims – now millions of Jews, Slavs, and others in the conquered territories – and the severity of persecution – now "ethnic cleansing," enslavement, and extermination.[111] For Hitler the *Volksgemeinschaft* as racial community was both the means and end of politics. Creating a unified racial community in which alien and inferior elements were eliminated and individuals renounced other ties and loyalties and were prepared to sacrifice themselves for the community would produce an irresistible instrument of expansion and conquest. The attainment of *Lebensraum* through expansion and conquest was in turn essential for the maintenance and growth of the racial community. Stalin might conceive of "socialism in one country," but Hitler never conceived of a unified German racial community surviving and prospering within the confines of the state boundaries bequeathed by Versailles or indeed any fixed boundaries.

Alongside policies of exclusion and destruction, policies of inclusion were central to the adaptation of the *Volksgemeinschaft* to its expanding *Lebensraum*. Within Germany and among the German-speaking peoples of Austria, the Sudetenland, Luxembourg, and Alsace-Lorraine, membership in the *Volksgemeinschaft* was open to virtually anyone who was not deemed racially alien or biologically defective. The requirement of certifying one's racial background was built into any number of ordinary bureaucratic procedures to which all Germans were subjected. It threatened so few that repeated compliance became a normal part of life as well as a ritual through which the population accepted and internalized "race" as a defining reality. But policies of inclusion became much more complex and contested with German conquests in the east. A great irony quickly emerged. Conquest of empire had been justified by portraying Germans as a *Volk ohne Raum*, a people without land. Now the Germans confronted the reality of having *Raum ohne Volk*, vast conquered territories without Germans to inhabit them. It was Himmler's dictum that "one only

[110] Yuri Slezkine, *The Jewish Century* (Princeton, NJ: Princeton University Press, 2004), 297–312. See also Genadii Kostyrchenko, *Tainaia politika Stalina: Vlast' i antisemitizm* (Moscow: Mezhdunarodnye otnosheniia, 2001).

[111] For the emergence of the policy of extermination against the Jews, see: Christopher R. Browning (with contributions by Jürgen Matthäus), *The Origins of the Final Solution: The Evolution of Nazi Jewish Policy, September 1939–March 1942* (Lincoln: The University of Nebraska Press, 2004); Peter Longerich, *Politik der Vernichtung:Eine Gesamtdarstellung der nationalsozialistischen Judenverfolgung* (Munich: Piper, 1998). For implementation of the "Final Solution," see Raul Hilberg, *The Destruction of the European Jews* (New Haven, CT: Yale University Press, 2004). For an overview that integrates the victim experience, Saul Friedländer, *The Years of Extermination*, Vol. 2: *Nazi Germany and the Jews, 1933–1945* (New York: HarperCollins, 2007).

possesses a land when even the last inhabitant of this territory belongs to his own people."[112] But neither the inclusion of the *Volksdeutschen* or ethnic Germans on the conquered territories, the repatriation of ethnic Germans from Soviet territory and Southeast Europe, nor even the ruthless kidnapping of children deemed racially suitable to be raised by German parents could begin to fill the void. At its most expansive, Generalplan Ost envisaged both the "Germanization" of selected East Europeans (a hotly disputed issue among Nazi racial experts and demographic engineers) and the recruitment of Dutch, Scandinavian, English, and overseas ethnic German colonists to populate Germany's *Lebensraum*.[113] In the meantime the Germans made use of local auxiliaries whom they referred to as "Askaris," the term for the native troops who had served in the German colonial armies in Africa before 1918.

The fate of the conquered populations of East Europe that were not to be included in the *Volksgemeinschaft* was either systematic destruction (for the Jews everywhere and the mentally and physically handicapped as well as Roma and Sinti within German *Lebensraum*) or first subjugation and then, for many millions, starvation or expulsion to Siberia to make way for German settlement.[114] And by subjugation the Nazis meant both reduction to a "helot status" or enslavement, on the one hand, and denationalization or cultural genocide, on the other. The Nazi assertion of German identity as the "master race" meant the destruction of both the freedom and the identity of those whom they ruled.

If in the 1930s the cohesiveness of the *Volksgemeinschaft* was based in no small part on the illusion of restoring a mythical unity through the repression of all political pluralism and the exclusion of stigmatized minorities, the war years posed a new challenge by unleashing the regime and revealing the vast magnitude and radical nature of its racial revolution. For ordinary Germans participation in the conquest and occupation of Europe, especially "in the east," was a quite different experience from the relative domestic tranquility of the prewar years.[115] The polarizing effect of war itself, binding the Germans and their regime together, was reinforced by the heady and corrupting effect of dominating the conquered territories as the "master race." Victory and empire completed the transition of the *Volksgemeinschaft* from the restoration illusion of a unified community of the German people to the Nazi vision of a racial community waging eternal struggle – a *Kampfgemeinschaft*. The vital cohesive

---

[112] Himmler memorandum, June 24, 1940: National Archives microfilm, T175/122/266598ff.

[113] Helmut Heiber, "Der Generalplan Ost," *Vierteljahrshefte für Zeitgeschichte* 3 (1958): 283–325, esp. 288.

[114] For two model regional studies of the incredibly destructive Nazi occupation policies in Eastern Europe, see Dieter Pohl, *Nationalsozialistische Judenverfolgung in Ostgalizien 1941–1944: Organisation und Durchführung eines staatlichen Massenverbrechens* (Munich: Oldenbourg, 1996); Christian Gerlach, *Kalkulierte Morde: Die deutsche Wirtschafts- und Vernichtungspolitik in Weissrussland 1941 bis 1944* (Hamburg: Hamburger Edition, 1999).

[115] Christopher R. Browning, *Ordinary Men: Reserve Police Battalion 101 and the Final Solution in Poland* (New York: HarperCollins, 1992).

power of "camaraderie" (*Kameradschaft*) – so effectively appropriated by the Nazi regime as a companion notion of *Volksgemeinschaft* – helped preserve the staying power of military units,[116] and even the industrial working class, whose disaffection the regime had feared, proved to be loyal soldiers who fought tenaciously to the bitter end.[117] The bonds of identity between regime and people held, and ordinary Germans who had been supportive of the regime now also became willing accomplices in its crimes. Himmler in various speeches tried to cloak the perpetration of these crimes in the guise of traditional values: idealism, heroic toughness, sobriety, and selfless incorruptibility. The real experience of those implementing German racial imperialism was the total opposite: unfettered sadism and cruelty, cowardly conformity, widespread drunkenness, and pervasive self-enrichment and corruption. If German expansion made German soldiers and occupation officials into a "master race" abroad, on a much smaller scale the importation of millions of foreign workers provided Germans domestically with the concrete experience of racial domination as well.[118] And German women not only provided moral support for their men, but participated directly in racial imperialism as pioneers in the "Germanization" of conquered territories.[119]

After the tide of war turned and the defeat of the Third Reich loomed ever nearer, the notion of the *Volksgemeinschaft* was transformed once again, from a racial community establishing imperial dominion over Europe into a *Schicksalgemeinschaft* or "community of fate." The Germans were once again victims, who suffered the devastation of allied bombing, the uprooting of millions from their ancestral homes in the east, pillage and rape at the hands of a vengeful Red Army, and geographical partition and dismemberment. Collectively, they were also the victims of Hitler and the Nazis, who left them with the consequences of defeat and burdened them with the guilt and shame of the regime's crimes. And as individuals within that community of fate, they were victims of the misfortune or bad luck that had seen them assigned to an antipartisan unit in the Balkans, a police battalion in Poland, an *Einsatzgruppe* in Russia, or guard duty in one of the myriad camps spread all over Europe. With the end of the war, the community of fate had become also a community of self-pity. For all the rupture of 1945, at least, one continuity stood out. As

---

[116] Thomas Kühne, *Kameradschaft: Die Soldaten des nationalsozialistischen Krieges und das 20. Jahrhundert* (Göttigen: Vandenhoeck & Ruprecht, 2006).

[117] Omer Bartov, "The Missing Years: German Workers, German Soldiers," *German History* 8, no. 1 (1990): 46–65. Tim Mason, *Social Policy in the Third Reich: The Working Class and the "National Community"* (Providence, RI: Berg, 1993), 276–8, 331–69.

[118] Ulrich Herbert, "Der 'Ausländer–Einsatz' in der deutschen Kriegswirtschaft," *Arbeit, Volkstum, Weltanschauung* (Frankfurt am Main: Fischer, 1995), 135; and *Hitler's Foreign Workers: Enforced Foreign Labor in Germany under the Third Reich* (Cambridge: Cambridge University Press, 1997), 395–6.

[119] Koonz, *Mothers in the Fatherland*. Elizabeth Harvey, *Women in the Nazi East: Agents and Witnesses of Germanization* (New Haven, CT: Yale University Press, 2003). In numerous publications Gundrun Schwarz has also documented women's involvement in the SS.

Robert Moeller has observed, German victims of the war were still perceived as part of the new postwar community, but victims of the Nazi regime were not.[120]

CONCLUSION: THE PURSUIT OF LETHAL UTOPIAS

The trajectories of ascribed social identity in the Soviet Union under Stalin and Nazi Germany were quite different, and no attempt has been made here to argue for an essential homology or to force them into a unitary interpretive framework. Nevertheless, it seems incontestable that both regimes assumed the right to inscribe identity and impose categorization for the purpose of social engineering through exclusion and purification, and that they did so with unfettered use of force and violence. Aside from lacking all inhibitions about the use of violence, both regimes assumed they not only should but also could accomplish such ambitious projects of social engineering because their ideologies emphasized a key determinative factor – class or race – in making history. Unlike many Europeans who were chastened by the catastrophe of World War I, Stalinists and Nazis thought the "realization of Utopia"[121] was within their grasp. In both cases, as well, the relentless, if not chiliastic, pursuit of the ideal society via the annihilation of class enemies and the isolation of enemy nations, in the case of the Soviet Union, and the elimination of racially and biologically "defective" elements, in Nazi Germany, consumed enormous resources that proved counterproductive to the achievement of other declared objectives. These, then, are the major similarities at the level of state practices.

The differences are no less striking. In the USSR, the state's identification of the population according to the criterion of class was particularly prominent in the late 1920s and early 1930s. This criterion gave way by the mid-1930s to more complex, multifaceted forms of identification in which distinctions among nations constituted an especially important role. With the war, Soviet citizens had the possibility for the first time since the civil war of choosing to fight for the regime or collaborate with its declared enemy – the Nazi invader – and thereby of defining their own identities. In Germany in the 1920s, the people's own sense of identity and their yearning for the sublimation of conflicting identities into the *Volksgemeinschaft* were key. After 1933 the regime's escalating practice of ascribing identity and categorizing enemies became increasingly prominent and fateful, eventually extending to the occupied territories as well.

Secondly, Soviet policies of ascribing and stigmatizing certain identities, which were executed by means of persecution and exclusion, affected large portions of the population. In Germany, those excluded were a small minority, which allowed for enthusiastic support for the regime and a strong sense of

---

[120] Robert Moeller, *War Stories: The Search for a Usable Past in the Federal Republic of Germany* (Berkeley: University of California Press, 2001), 7.

[121] We borrow this phrase from Hans Mommsen, "Die Realisierung des Utopischen: Die 'Endlösung' im Dritten Reich," *Geschichte und Gesellschaft* 9 (1983): 381–420.

security and well-being by the majority, as well as the majority's relative indifference to the fate of the minorities. Only with the conquest of non-German territories did the numbers of Nazi victims increase exponentially. In the Soviet Union, by contrast, the war enabled previously stigmatized groups to expunge the stains on their records through service in the Red Army or participation in partisan groups resisting Nazi occupation. More generally, the blending of Soviet with more traditional patriotic appeals broadened popular support.

Finally, after following different trajectories for so long, Soviet and German societies experienced an ironic convergence: Soviet victory and German defeat created a situation in which sacrifice and suffering in war were the defining experience for both, even if general acknowledgment of that equivalence would have to wait until after the end of the Cold War.

7

Energizing the Everyday

On the Breaking and Making of Social Bonds in Nazism and Stalinism

Sheila Fitzpatrick and Alf Lüdtke

Hannah Arendt's suggestion that social "atomization" was fundamental to totalitarian domination has appealed greatly to many scholars and intellectuals.[1] Despite, or perhaps because of, this, it is a hypothesis whose empirical fit with the societies it purports to describe has never been seriously scrutinized. We took it as starting point for our comparative inquiry into the everyday in Nazi Germany and Stalinist Russia that in each case some kind of breakdown (but perhaps also a reconfiguration?) of social relationships took place.

Arendt's analysis focuses not only on the apparatus of domination and its manipulative and represses tactics. In her view more fundamental is the "movement" of "masses of lonely men" looking for shelter from a world they encountered as "wilderness." Thus, Arendt finds that the appeal of totalitarian movements and regimes is not fabricated from "above." Rather, she contends, the rulers "rely on that compulsion with which we can compel ourselves." Recent research has shown that it is this urge which drives people to participate actively in the "great cause" of the respective regimes. It is here that the "inner face" of the many who accepted, if not supported, them comes into view. In our view it is central for understanding the productive and even more the destructive potential of these regimes to address the emotional charges that drove their respective dynamics "from within": what were the practices of (self-)energizing which people employed or encountered?

The perspective Arendt pursues needs debate in another regard. In her appraisal of the "redeeming grace of companionship"[2] she portrays such bonds as restraining people from practicing that violence which is the most striking

---

[1] Hannah Arendt, *The Origins of Totalitarianism*, 2nd ed. (San Diego, New York: Harvest/Harcourt, 1966) (1st ed. 1951), 14. While Arendt refers to processes that prestructure the terrain for totalitarian movements other researchers have taken her point on "atomization" as the striking characteristic of Nazi and Stalinist policies; see Detlev Peukert, *Inside Nazi Germany: Conformity, Opposition, and Racism in Everyday Life*, trans. Richard Deveson (New Haven, CT, and London: Yale University Press, 1987, 241, cf. 240 and 248.

[2] Arendt, 174.

component of totalitarian regimes. Here, Arendt's moral stance may limit the explorative capacity of her approach. Close inspection of actual forms and meanings of social bonds shows their inherent ambivalence. Family ties or, for that matter, comradeship at the workplace or in a military unit offers not only comfort but also function as last resort in times of hardship or distress. Thus, the very intensity of these bonds makes possible violence against "others."

Our approach in this essay is to focus on an issue centrally relevant to Arendt's perspective: bonds between people, on the one hand, and people's bonds to the Nazi and Stalinist sociopolitical projects, on the other. We look first at practices of *inclusion*: bonding with the state project and its energizing "charges" followers claimed or encountered; then we turn to the severing of bonds associated with *exclusion*; we go on to consider *family bonds and sociability* at and outside the workplace; and finally focus on the process of *creation or renewal* of bonds, which, while consonant with the state project, also constitutes an effort to carve out social and emotional space for a sphere of one's own.

Since generalizations are particularly suspect in a realm like the everyday, we will do our best throughout to show the *range* of possibilities. For this purpose, we have included short individual biographies in boxes at more or less random intervals: their purpose is not directly to illustrate the text but to indicate how complex and sometimes contradictory individual practices and relationships tend to be.

First, however, it is necessary to establish crucial features of social-historical context for our inquiry.

GERMAN AND SOVIET SOCIETIES AFTER THE FIRST WORLD WAR

Two major ruptures affected German society in the period from 1914 to 1933.[3] The first was the war of 1914–18, which gave Germans the new and shocking experience of total warfare. The effort to mobilize all personal and material resources dramatically blurred boundaries between civilians and the military, especially after 1916, and transformed people's everyday life in both urban and village settings. Men and women experienced the war rather differently. While men serving in the military had direct experience of violence and bloodshed, women suffered from the strain of single-person householding and the hardships of making do in times of severe food shortage.

The second rupture was economic, and it hit various groups of Germans in different ways and at different times. Property holders, especially those of modest wealth without landed property, found themselves deprived of a large part of their savings in the course of the (hyper)inflation that reached its

---

[3] Richard Bessel, *Germany after the First World War* (Oxford: Clarendon, 1995); Detlev Peukert, *The Weimar Republic: The Crisis of Classical Modernity*, trans. Richard Deveson (New York: Hill & Wang, 2002); Cornelie Usborne, *The Politics of the Body in Weimar Germany: Women's Reproductive Rights and Duties* (Basingstoke: Macmillan, 1992).

height in the autumn of 1923; middle-class households could no longer keep maids. Working-class people fared comparatively better than the middle class in the first half of the 1920s, but their turn came with devastating force when unemployment rose sharply in the fall of 1929. Every third wage worker was sacked and often stayed jobless for two or three years, his social benefits long since expired.

The dramatic economic crisis sharpened the "generational" divide. During the Great Slump, children of the soldiering fathers of 1914–18 found themselves excluded from the workforce, waiting for the fathers' generation to retire. Some of the "sons," particularly those who had no chance for vocational training, wound up roaming the streets in militant groups affiliated with the Nazis (SA) and the Communist Party.[4]

Gender divisions were embittered as unemployed men saw themselves deprived of meaningful activity and self-respect, and women, including those previously employed, were forced to focus ever more on domestic chores. On another plane, the bobbed hair of young single females earning their living as clerks in shops and offices became a familiar sight not only on the streets of Berlin but also in smaller towns, dismaying those who were nostalgic for the good old days before 1914.[5] "Americanization" was another bugbear, especially in the cultural sphere, with jazz and its predominantly black musicians becoming a special target of attack which resonated in all segments of society.[6]

In Russia (from 1924, the Soviet Union), the disruptions were even greater because of the revolution, which produced radical changes in political and governmental institutions and economic structures.[7] In their early antiauthoritarian phase, the Bolsheviks despised all forms of hierarchy and behaviors of deference. One hierarchy that they set out to overturn (literally, in accordance with the "dictatorship of the proletariat" principle) was the class hierarchy of prerevolutionary Russia. They also fostered the emancipation of women not only rhetorically, through a discourse on the oppression of the patriarchal family, but also practically, via the large-scale recruitment of women into the workforce.

---

[4] Dirk Schumann, *Politische Gewalt in der Weimarer Republik 1918–1933: Kampf um die Strasse und Furcht vor dem Bürgerkrieg* (Essen: Klartext, 2001); Pamela Swett, *Neighbors and Enemies: The Culture of Radicalism in Berlin, 1929–1933* (Cambridge: Cambridge University Press, 2004).

[5] See Atina Grossmann, *Reforming Sex: The German Movement for Birth Control and Abortion Reform, 1920–1950* (New York: Oxford University Press, 1995).

[6] Adelheid von Saldern, *The Challenge of Modernity: German Social and Cultural Studies, 1890–1960*, trans. Bruce Little (Ann Arbor: University of Michigan Press, 2002), 299–347.

[7] On the social history of the interwar period in the Soviet Union, see Vladimir Andrle, *A Social History of Twentieth-Century Russia* (London: Edward Arnold, 1994); Lewis H. Siegelbaum, *Soviet State and Society between Revolutions, 1918–1929* (Cambridge and New York: Cambridge University Press, 1992); Sheila Fitzpatrick, *Everyday Stalinism: Ordinary Life in Extraordinary Times: Soviet Russia in the 1930s* (New York: Oxford University Press, 1999); and Lewis Siegelbaum and Andrei Sokolov, *Stalinism as a Way of Life: A Narrative in Documents* (New Haven, CT: Yale University Press, 2000).

VLADIMIR KABO[8] *was born in Moscow circa 1925 to a Jewish intelligentsia family with revolutionary credentials. Closeness to his parents, especially his mother (the economist Elena Kabo), was a constant in Kabo's story of his life. In recalling the years before the great break at the outbreak of war, he drew a sharp distinction between his happy childhood and youth and the "grim mood" of the Great Purge years of the late 1930s, which coincided with his adolescence. In childhood, there was "a feeling of bliss and the fullness of life . . . a joyful anticipation of a happiness which is very close by, within's arm's reach." Home, school, the countryside around Moscow, and the city itself were all suffused with this sense of well-being and happy anticipation. He remembered eagerly awaiting the big holidays (May Day, Revolution Day, and so on). "When at last the morning came, the sounds of a brass band would be heard over the wall between our courtyard and the Bol'shevichka clothing factory, where the working girls were mustering to take part in the day's parade. In the evening, mother would take me to see the illuminations, another vivid recollection of childhood: the buildings, bridges and squares sparkling with multi-colored electric lamps and a huge full-length portrait of Stalin, almost taller than the Bol'shoi Theatre, lit up by searchlights. Only many years later did I find out the strolls through Moscow on those holiday evenings, which gave me so much pleasure, were a painful burden for my mother."*

"At thirteen or thereabouts, my radiant mood was suddenly replaced by a somber and gloomy state. I began to look attentively at the dark sides of life, of which there were plenty, and wanted to write only about them. I was haunted by thoughts of suicide. This state is often found in adolescents of this age. It comes with their growing up, not only sexual but also spiritual. It coincided with a grim mood which pervaded the house from all that had happened in it and the sad affair of Liuba [his sister had lost a leg in a street-car accident]. At that time my father turned rapidly grey, his hair becoming quite white. His grim silence was occasionally broken by a sharp, guttural sound accompanied by his fist thumping the table, as if he had suddenly remembered something irremediable. Only Mother retained her calm and presence of mind."

The Bolshevik revolution came in two stages, the first being the seizure of power in 1917, and the second the economic "revolution from above" set in train in the late 1920s, which included forced-pace industrialization, the outlawing of the urban private sector, and collectivization of agriculture. The dimensions of the second may be judged from the fact that the urban population of the Soviet Union more than doubled between 1926 and 1939, while the number of wage- and salary earners almost tripled over the same period.[9] The geographical and social displacement, separation, and relocation

---

[8] Vladimir Kabo, *The Road to Australia*, trans. Patrick Rosh Ireland and Kevin McNeill Windle (Canberra: Aboriginal Studies Press, 1998). His memoirs were written after his emigration to Australia in the 1990s.

[9] Figures from Iu. A. Poliakov, ed., *Vsesoiuznaia perepis' naseleniia 1939 goda: Osnovnye itogi* (Moscow: "Nauka," 1992), 20; *Trud v SSSR: Statisticheskii sbornik* (Moscow: "Statistika," 1968), 22.

implied are enormous. In addition, we should note the emigration of at least a million Russians, disproportionately from Russia's thin educated-elite stratum, by the end of the Civil War.

When the Bolsheviks took power, they had strong support in the big industrial cities. Peasants, four-fifths of the population before collectivization, generally neither supported nor actively opposed the new regime in the 1920s. After collectivization, the regime's popularity plummeted in the villages and also suffered in the towns because of the sharp drop in living standards.

The regime relied heavily on terror to carry out the "revolution from above" and continued to use terror against various groups and against the population as a whole throughout the 1930s. This is not to say the regime and more broadly the Soviet project were without their supporters, including much of the "old" working class that had fought in the revolution and Civil War, especially those many from this group who had been upwardly mobile into the new administrative and professional elite.

BONDING WITH THE STATE PROJECT

Inclusion

In both the Soviet Union and Germany, idealistic aspirations[10] toward a "new beginning" for society and, by the same token, transformation of the individual citizen into a "new man" or woman impressed contemporaries inside and outside the two countries. In both cases, mass rallies recurrently assembled tens or hundreds of thousands in meetings on public squares or sports arenas. Equally important were the "larger than life" spectacles staged even in small towns and villages, with forests of flags (red, in both cases), boisterous music, collective clapping, shouting, and singing taking place before, during, and after the speeches of party or state dignitaries. All this was greatly enhanced when the leader, Stalin or Hitler himself, appeared in person. These events, which were staged at the national as well as regional and local levels, marked a new calendar punctuated by anniversaries, for instance, the Day of the Revolution (November 7, in the USSR) or the Day of the Seizure of Power (January 30, in Germany), as well as politically coded festivals such as May Day. Almost every Soviet oral history from the 1990s recalling the Stalin period, regardless of the

---

[10] Here, the focus is on people's behavior and less on their "mood"; studies of public mood often miss crucial dimensions. For one, they tend to homogenize the many and their manifold forms of accepting, supporting, and cooperating – *or their practices of withdrawing and distancing.* Secondly, this view neglects the distinction between people's motives and the results of their respective actions and doings. In particular, forms of accepting in one's job performance and, more generally, in professional practices were often inspired by the goal to find fulfillment in "just doing a good job" – or to sustain normalcy, or to exploit new venues that had not been available (or were beyond imagination) prior to the new regime. Nevertheless, one way or the other all of these attitudes allowed the pursuit of the workings of the regime as a whole – thus supporting its actions including totalizing warfare and deportations in the Soviet and warfare of extermination and genocide in the German case.

political stance of the respondent, includes at least one memory of a moment of pride and identification with the collective and the regime (on receiving an award or some kind of recognition for work, winning a competition, attending a ceremony, watching Soviet planes in an air show, cheering returning Polar explorers, and so on).[11]

In Germany, historians have seen bonding with the regime as characteristic of people who, for diverse reasons (often resulting from ruptures of social relations and ties originating from the First World War or the economic depression after 1929) were "not yet settled in"; such people, having previously seen only a bleak future before them, ferociously embraced the new vistas.[12]

In both societies, enthusiasm was most commonly to be found among young people. In Germany, membership in youth associations had become widespread during the 1920s, though it was mainly an urban phenomenon. The youth associations of confessional groups, drawing in roughly 40 percent of the relevant age group, were the exception: under the tutelage of the local pastor or priest, the Christian ones were at least as present in villages and small towns. The activities of these groups and associations covered a wide range. But even in the confessional and political (socialist and Communist) youth associations, the activities revolved to a large extent around sports, mainly soccer, and attracted mainly boys. When the Nazi regime prohibited sports activities within confessional youth associations early in 1934, their membership drastically declined.

Sports were the primary attraction for youth from all backgrounds in the 1920s and the 1930s as well, almost exclusively for males, however.[13] Before 1933, however, efforts of working-class activists to keep the children from

---

[11] A useful publication of oral histories with much material on the 1930s is Barbara A. Engel and Anastasia Posadskaya-Vanderbeck, eds., *A Revolution of Their Own: Voices of Women in Soviet History*, trans. Sona Hoisington (Boulder, CO: Westview Press, 1997). For diaries, see *Intimacy and Terror: Soviet Diaries of the 1930s*, eds. V. Garros, N. Korenevskaya, and T. Lahusen (New York: The New Press, 1995) and Jochen Hellbeck, *Revolution on My Mind: Writing a Diary under Stalin* (Cambridge, MA: Harvard University Press, 2006).

[12] A telling regional case is under scrutiny in Richard Bessel, *Political Violence and the Rise of Nazism: The Stromtroopers in Eastern Germany, 1925–1934* (New Haven, CT: Yale University Press, 1984; life-course aspects are prominent in both Detlev Peukert et al., eds., *Die Reihen fast geschlossen: Beiträge zur Geschichte des Alltags unter dem Nationalsozialismus* (Wuppertal: Hammer, 1981), and Peter H. Merkl, *Political Violence under the Swastika: 581 Early Nazis* (Princeton, NJ: University Press, 1985); for an autobiographical take written in exile at about 1939/40 see Sebastian Haffner, *Geschichte eines Deutschen: die Erinnerungen 1914–1933* (Stuttgart: Deutsche Verlagsanstalt, 2000).

[13] One popular male sport was soccer; cf. Nils Havemann, *Fussball unterm Hakenkreuz: Der DFB zwischen Politik, Sport und Kommerz* (Frankfurt am Main: Campus, 2005); as a local case in point Markwart Herzog, *Der "Betze" unterm Hakenkreuz: Der 1. FC Kaiserslautern in der Zeit des Nationalsozialismus* (Göttingen: Werkstatt, 2006); Rudolf Oswald, "'Ein Gift, mit echt jüdischer Geschicklichkeit ins Volk gespritzt': Nationalsozialistische Judenverfolgung und das Ende des mitteleuropäischen Profifußballes, 1938–1941," in *Emanzipation durch Muskelkraft: Juden und Sport in Europa*, eds. Michael Brenner and Gideon Reuveni (Göttingen: Vandenhoeck & Ruprecht, 2006), 159–72.

working-class families in the domain of class and its bonds proved largely futile. Their calls to join "labor sports associations" had only limited success: large numbers of children from these neighborhoods, but especially soccer players – at that time all male – successfully strove for entry into "bourgeois" clubs. Other youth associations like Boy or Girl Scouts or the less acquiescent Youth Movement groups drew mostly juveniles from families of shopowners, officials and teachers, academics, doctors, and other professionals, that is, the vast array of the middle classes.

This points in two directions as far as the maintenance of old bonds and the creation of new ones are concerned. In "bourgeois" families with political and ideological affinities with the "Third Reich," young people who joined the official youth organizations did so with their parents' blessing. But in other cases, parents disapproved (see the case of Melita Maschmann, whose parents strictly forbade her to join!), so that joining meant rupture of familial bonds. However, it was just such parental interdiction that stimulated many to join or, at least, to become active. To these young people, the Nazi organizations provided space for exploration and maneuver and facilitated the establishment of distance from previous bonds or encroachments. This emancipatory dimension can hardly be overestimated. Whether and to what extent youth association membership stimulated the development of new bonds is another matter. Accounts of the time suggest that young activists focused more on their relationship with distant leaders and a similarly distant "great cause" than on any relationship with their peers in the movement.[14]

Association in informal tightly connected groups, sometimes operating as a "gang" on streets and other public spaces, had been a familiar feature of male and even female youth cultures. Such informal associations – each strictly observing the boundaries of class, milieu, and religion – were widespread throughout society. In contrast, the Nazi youth organizations set out to regulate, police, and, in the end, to wipe out such claims to a sphere of one's own. It was precisely this policing aim – and the often rude or clumsy tactics used – that tended to discredit the Nazi youth associations, at least in the eyes of some young people. At any rate, youth gangs continued to exist or, more precisely, to be started anew as boys and girls reached the appropriate age: for example, the "Kittelbach-Piraten" and "Edelweiss-Piraten" of the Rhein and the Ruhr, which had a proletarian ring, and "Swing-Youth" in metropolitan centers like Hamburg or Berlin during the war, who conspicuously displayed "bourgeois"

---

[14] For this in general and also as a case study for the administrative district of Düsseldorf, see Alfons Kenkmann, *Wilde Jugend: Lebenswelt großstädtischer Jugendlicher zwischen Weltwirtschafts-krise, Nationalsozialismus und Währungsreform* (Essen: Klartext, 1996), 55–9, 83–98, 164–7, 228–31; for the focus on individual achievement and its possible long-term consequences (past 1945) see Nori Möding, "Ich muss irgendwo engagiert sein – fragen Sie mich bloss nicht, warum," Überlegungen zu Sozialisationserfahrungen von Mädchen im NS-Organisationen *"Wir kriegen jetzt andere Zeiten": Auf der Suche nach der Erfahrung des Volkes in nachfaschistischen Ländern* (Berlin: Verlag J. H. W. Dietz, 1985), 291–5.

clothes, tastes, and habits. Intensified surveillance of informal activities outside the officially demarcated arenas, including patrolling suspicious areas by the HJ and police, widened the gulf and led some young people into concrete counterregime activities.[15]

For the Soviet Union, the time of acute generational conflict was the 1920s.[16] The Komsomol (for adolescents and young adults) and the Young Pioneers (for the ten to fourteen age group) were then new organizations, emancipatory in their message and impact and selective in their recruitment (children of "alien" social origins were not admitted). Komsomol ideology involved a head-on challenge to the authority of parents as well as others of the older generation (teachers suffered particularly from this). Sexual liberation was a major part of the Komsomol message, to the alarm of high Party organs. The Komsomol led the charge against religion, often engaging in what their Communist elders defined as "hooligan" behavior such as taunting priests on the street or marching around the church during service singing revolutionary songs. Komsomol members strove to distinguish themselves from other ("unconscious") youth by their dress: girls with short hair, eschewing makeup and femininity, dressing as much like men as possible; boys preferring an army-surplus look. Marriage and domesticity were scorned as bourgeois. If two young activists produced a child, they would either expect one of their mothers to look after it or hire a nanny from the village, without interrupting their education, work, or Komsomol activism.[17]

Soviet youth organizations were by no means sports clubs writ large, as their German counterparts sometimes were. Youth sports clubs had not been well developed in prerevolutionary Russia and were hence not part of an acknowledged or unacknowledged substructure of the new organization (as the Boy Scouts, which had begun to make a little headway in Russia in the early twentieth century, may sometimes have been, though condemned root and branch as "bourgeois" by the newly founded Komsomol). The Komsomol held sport in high regard, but the extreme shortage of even the most basic equipment and prerequisites (sports fields, soccer and volley balls) restricted their practice of it in the prewar period. For some urban boys and girls, training took place in Osoaviakhim (Union of Societies of Assistance to Defense and Aviation-Chemical Construction), a voluntary society that taught military skills to young people.

---

[15] Kenkmann, *Wilde Jugend*, Part B, 129–205, and Part C, 208–341.

[16] On Soviet youth, see N. K. Novak-Deker, ed., *Soviet Youth: Twelve Komsomol Histories*, trans. Oliver J. Frederiksen (Munich: Institut zur Erforschung der UdSSR, 1959); and Anne E. Gorsuch, *Youth in Revolutionary Russia: Enthusiasts, Bohemians, Delinquents* (Bloomington: Indiana University Press, 2000).

[17] See, for example, the autobiography of Sofia Nikandrovna Pavlova, "Taking Advantage of New Opportunities," in *A Revolution of Their Own*, 47–84; also John Scott's account of his Russian activist wife's response to having a child in his *Behind the Urals: An American Worker in Russia's City of Steel* (Bloomington: Indiana University Press, 1989), 128–33.

The Komsomol in the 1920s was above all a *political* organization, proudly identifying itself as the junior branch of the Communist Party. Joining the Komsomol in the 1920s often led to clashes with parents, sometimes even severing of bonds, especially in the villages (where Komsomol cells were few, but the more radical and restless young people sometimes emulated Komsomol behavior without the benefit of any formal organization – "Komsomols by conviction"). Bonding of young people in the organization seems to have been strong; indeed, in later mythology it extended beyond the Komsomol and Pioneers to the whole cohort of youth – hailed in the media as the chosen generation, builders of the socialist future, free of the habits of prerevolutionary bourgeois philistinism and mental "survivals of the past" that their elders might unwittingly have absorbed. The 1920s and early 1930s cohort would later look back with great nostalgia to their idealist, activist youth. Memories of Komsomol activism and the idealism perceived as its milieu were so strong that that they found reflection even in interviews with wartime defectors conducted by Radio Free Europe in Munich in the 1950s.[18]

Komsomol activism reached its height during the Cultural Revolution of the late 1920s and early 1930s, when the organization spearheaded a boisterous campaign against "bureaucracy" and routinism in government agencies and provided many volunteers for the collectivization drive in the countryside.[19] The radicalism of the organization, its implicit ideology of youth as the "vanguard," and the political ambitions of the leaders of the Komsomol Central Committee led to conflicts with the Party's own leaders. In the mid-1930s, under pressure from Stalin and other Party leaders, the Komsomol underwent an unwilling restructuring which made it a "mass" rather than selective organization (not socially discriminatory in recruitment) and, to the regret of the Komsomol Old Guard and the relief of the Party leaders, a less revolutionary one. Much of the old spirit survived up to the Second World War, however. Komsomol members volunteered to go out and "build socialism" (that is, develop new towns and industrial plants, like the famous Magnitogorsk or Komsomolsk-na-Amure) in remote and dangerous locations, preserving the spirit of adventure that had so powerfully attracted young people since the Revolution. During the war, the fabled exploits of young "partisans" against the enemy[20] continued this tradition.

In both countries, the beginning of the war – as different as it was – marked a crucial shift and an intensification of the sense of inclusion in the national

---

[18] See Nikolai K. Novak-Deker, ed., *Soviet Youth: Twelve Komsomol Histories*.

[19] See Sheila Fitzpatrick, "Cultural Revolution as Class War," in *The Cultural Front* (Ithaca, NY: Cornell University Press, 1992), 132–6; and idem, *Stalin's Peasants: Resistance and Survival in the Russian Village after Collectivization* (New York: Oxford University Press, 1994), 60–1.

[20] See, for example, Aleksandr Fadeev's *Molodaia gvardiia* (Moscow: TsK VLKSM, 1946), a postwar novel about young partisans that he had to rewrite because of his initial underestimation of the guiding role of the Party. Arkady Gaidar's enormously popular *Timur i ego komanda* [Timur and his team] (Moscow: TSK VLKSM, Izd-vo detskoi lit-ry, 1941) about adventurous young activists catches this spirit even better.

project. In the Soviet case, to be sure, the sense of identification among certain groups (the Party, urban youth) was already high, particularly in connection with the industrialization drive, which was conducted rhetorically and to some degree actually as if it were a war; but with the coming of a real war, the identifying population greatly broadened. There was also a sense of relief (in the wake of the Great Purges) that finally there was an identifiable foreign enemy to fight. Now the endangered "fatherland" – exclusively male in German (*Vaterland*), both male (*otechestvo*) and female (*rodina* or *rodina-mat'*) in Russian – dominated in people's minds. This was not only an effect of propaganda, though the media, film, and other arts, and the respective branches of the ruling party and state apparatus actively aimed at cultivating patriotic sentiments. Regime propaganda blended with long-standing resentment against the "West" in the USSR (which is not to deny the existence of an equally powerful strain of popular attraction and envy) or, on the part of Germans, "the East" and its supposedly barbaric people (attitudes easily recast in racial terms).

Popular moods in both countries changed with the fortunes of war: triumphant in Germany in June–July 1940 and (though perhaps more tainted by skepticism) in the spring and summer of 1941; panicky in the Soviet Union after the German attack in 1941 and fatalistically pessimistic following the defeats of 1942; more buoyant in the Soviet Union after the victory at Stalingrad in early February 1943. From the behavior of the population in Soviet territory occupied by the Germans, it is evident that "acceptance" of the "rule of them" was a state of mind that was potentially transferable from one regime to another, at least as far as many Ukrainians were concerned. But there were also many Soviet citizens in occupied territory who were ready to upgrade their level of commitment to the point of active resistance and death. Whatever the mix of coercion, desperation, and loyalty, the Soviet army somehow survived a massive shameful, disorderly retreat in the summer of 1941 and another eighteen months of less dramatic setbacks. In the German case, remarkably, military defeat scarcely changed the focus or intensity of popular support or acceptance. In fact, in the German case the long haul of the army's retreat to the Reich proper only intensified determination to continue fighting, both in the combat zones and in many areas of the home front.

Exclusion

For both Nazi and Soviet regimes, exclusion – non-Aryans for the Nazis, "class enemies" for Soviet Communists – was a basic principle. This had consequences which, for the purpose of our inquiry, point in different directions. On the one hand, those stigmatized and excluded experienced the breaking of old social bonds in particularly bitter form. On the other, the process of exclusion undoubtedly acted as a bonding force for those within *Volksgemeinschaft* and its Soviet equivalent (the national community engaged in building socialism).

Both governments established legislative and administrative regimes of exclusion, but their successful implementation depended on popular support and indeed popular initiative, which were generally speaking forthcoming in both societies. This no doubt reflected existing resentments against the stigmatized groups but also demonstrated the dynamics of group formation by closing ranks and excluding others, especially in times of turmoil and rapid transformation. Denunciation, a matter of individual initiative, was widely practiced in both countries.[21] In Germany, Jews were the main targets, though others might be denounced for infractions like listening to foreign radio.[22] In the Soviet context, political as well as class enemies were targeted – though this often meant that the denouncer's private enemy was given the damaging label of "Trotskyite" or "kulak." Concealment of true identity was a leitmotif of Soviet denunciation, just as it was of the public rituals of purging "aliens" from the Communist Party and state institutions that were regularly held in the 1920s and early 1930s.

While in Germany the Nazi seizure of power did not directly affect most people's ways of making their living or socializing, the situation was different for those who were excluded from the project of "National Revolution": "political enemies," especially Communists and Social Democrats (not to forget union activists) but also Catholic and, to a lesser extent, Protestant church members. Primarily, however, the new regime ruthlessly persecuted and terrorized all who were stamped "non-Aryans." Humiliating as it was for those excluded to be subject to physical assaults by fist blows or spitting, for many it was even more poignant that close neighbors, good colleagues, and even dear friends almost instantaneously abandoned their relationships. From one day to the next most of them did not "know" or "recognize" former acquaintances or colleagues, at least in public.

From the very beginning of the regime, the vast majority of Germans displayed conformity to, if not support of, practices of exclusion of those designated as Jews. Efforts to boycott Jewish shops began even prior to its "official" call in April 1, 1933. A law of April 7 allowed the expulsion of those defined according to Nazi racist criteria as Jews from national, state, or local government, and many private organizations and companies followed suit. Critical comments on the "rather harsh measures" against Jews or the related "waste of resources" remained subdued and circulated only in private conversation or pub chats,[23] thus leaving no visible trace, though later recollections of the

---

[21] On denunciation, see Sheila Fitzpatrick and Robert Gellately, eds., *Accusatory Practices: Denunciation in Modern European History 1789–1989* (Chicago: University of Chicago Press, 1997).

[22] See Robert Gellately, *The Gestapo and German Society: Enforcing Racial Policy, 1933–1945* (Oxford: Clarendon, 1990); while Gellately shows a widespread readiness of non-Jews in Germany to denounce people for being "Jews" Eric Johnson has emphasized that the intensity of such denunciations does not confirm that the vast majority of the population generally engaged in denunciation: Eric Johnson, *Nazi Terror: The Gestapo, Jews, and Ordinary Germans* (London: John Murray, 2000); on the issue of female activity and participation, cf. Vandana Joshi, *Gender and Power in the Third Reich: Female Denouncers and the Gestapo (1933–45)* (Basingstoke: Palgrave Macmillan, 2003).

[23] Cf. David Bankier, *The Germans and the Final Solution: Public Opinion under Nazism* (Oxford: Blackwell, 1993).

VICTOR KLEMPERER,[24] *a Jewish professor of Romance languages married to a Gentile, describes "one single working day" in his book* Lingua Tertii Imperii. *Those designated as "Jews" by Nazi law had been forced into labor since spring 1939, and Klemperer had been assigned a job in a Dresden factory that produced paper envelopes. He recalls that the atmosphere was not "particularly Nazi" in this company. The entrepreneur was a member of the SS but, so Klemperer again, "he supported the Jews in the factory wherever it was possible, he politely talked to them and occasionally he gave them something from the canteen [which the letter of the law prohibited.]" Klemperer also recalls that he is not sure what was more of a consolation, a piece of horse sausage or if once in a while he was called not only by his (last) name but "Herr Klemperer" or even "Herr Professor."*

According to his recollection also the workers were by no means "Nazi" at least not any more in winter 1943/4, one year after Stalingrad. One of the workers was a man by the name of Albert, who was skeptical of the German (Nazi) government and not fond of the war. He had lost a brother, and he himself had been released from the military because of stomach problems and was anxious to avoid being redrafted to the military before "this bloody war has come to an end." Klemperer overheard a talk with one of the mates where the other responded to such remark: "But how shall this war come to an end? Nobody gives in!" Albert responded: "Well isn't that clear? The others have to accept that we are invincible, they cannot conquer us, we are so extremely well organized!"

Klemperer describes another mate, too. This woman, Frieda, occasionally asked about his wife and also once in a while gave him an apple. Many times she ignored strict decrees not to talk to "the Jews." Once, she came over and said: "Albert says your wife is a German. Is she really a German?" "Immediately I lost any joy in the apple," Klemperer recalled. "This friendly person who was not a Nazi at all and had human feelings, even here the Nazi poison had made its way; she had identified Germans with the magical notion of Aryan. She could not grasp that my wife would be a German."

period include many examples of breaking the boycott or exchanging greetings with neighbors and former colleagues. Although such symbolic gestures of recognition could mean a lot to the addressees, they never constituted a body of practices that visibly demonstrated nonacceptance.

Many people were uneasy about the destruction of Jewish property that occurred repeatedly by street violence, even before *Reichskristallnacht* of November 9–10, 1938,[25] but their concern was apparently not for the loss to the proprietors but rather the loss to the "German *Volk*'s common weal."[26] The same people "stood by" when SA and Nazi activists denounced people

[24] Victor Klemperer, *LTI: Notizbuch eines Philologen*, 3rd ed. (Halle: M. Niemeyer, 1957), 101–6.
[25] Michael Wildt, "Gewalt gegen Juden in Deutschland 1933 bis 1939," *WerkstattGeschichte* 8, no. 18 (1997): 59–80.
[26] Saul Friedlander, *The Years of Persecution, 1933–1939*, Vol. 1: *Nazi Germany and the Jews* (New York: HarperCollins, 1997); idem, *The Years of Extermination, 1939–1945*, Vol. 2: *Nazi Germany and the Jews* (New York: HarperCollins, 2007).

for committing *Rassenschande*, that is, having intimate relations with a Jew.[27] The vast majority of *Reichsdeutsche* looked the other way, while others did not hesitate to denounce possible "non-Aryans." Moreover, when Jews were deported, former neighbors often looted or snapped up bargains at the regular auctions of "confiscated" (that is, stolen) property held all over the country; and in 1942 and early 1943, Nazi agencies were swamped with claims for the houses and apartments of deportees (in the spring of 1943, following orders from the top, these claims were suspended until the "final victory").

In many places, local officials and clerks administering welfare programs interpreted laws regulating marital and sexual relationships between "Aryans" and "Jews" as a pretext to exclude Jewish recipients or reduce their benefits. The same range of (non)arbitrary action characterized the administrations of public health and hygiene and of public order as well. It was local or regional agents who decided, for instance, to ban Jews from park benches, public baths, or tramways. Racism also triggered exclusion of those parents and/or children evaluated by local public health authorities as *erbkrank* (hereditarily diseased) or *erbunwert* (hereditarily unfit). Between 1935 and 1937 around 15 percent of the applicants for financial support under the law providing for families of four and more children were deemed "unworthy" on these grounds, depriving about one hundred thousand families and more than four hundred thousand children of benefits.[28]

In addition to the measures already discussed expelling Jews from employment in the public and private sectors, the Internal Revenue Service and Customs extracted confiscatory portions from assets and other fortunes being transferred to foreign countries, and officials and border guards set out to collect as much as possible from those emigrating legally. From early 1934, administrative orders increasingly reduced the amount of assets that could legally be transferred out of the country (bringing it down to 10 RM to be carried by one person later that year). Through assessments of the amount to be paid as *Reichsfluchtsteuer* that were often arbitrarily high, the amount of cash left to the exiles was often reduced to zero. Local IRS officials acted with even less restraint against those who left illegally in response to warnings or rumors. Whether or not they were caught, the authorities immediately confiscated all their remaining property as a whole, and if such cases came to court, judges confirmed these actions.[29]

Practices of exclusion resonated with special intensity in and with Germans every day when partnerships were affected: whether heterosexual or unisexual,

[27] Alexandra Przyrembel, *Rassenschande: Reinheitsmythos und Vernichtungslegitimation im Nationalsozialismus* (Göttingen: Vandenhoeck & Ruprecht, 2003), 185–227.

[28] Asmus Nitschke, *Die "Erbpolizei" im Nationalsozialismus: zur Alltagsgeschichte der Gesundheitsämter im Dritten Reich: Das Beispiel Bremen* (Opladen: Westdeutscher Verlag, 1999), 130–7.

[29] Alfons Kenkmann and Bernd-A Rusinek eds., *Verfolgung und Verwaltung: die wirtschaftliche Ausplünderung der Juden und die westfälischen Finanzbehörden*, Exhibiton catalogue Villa ten Hompel (Münster: Oberfinanzdirektion Münster, 1999).

short- or long-term, or formalized by marriage or practiced informally. Local Nazi Party functionaries or Hitler Youth leaders literally staged public chases of individuals who had been denounced by neighbors or colleagues for sustaining such a partnership (*Rassenschande*). When the Nuremberg Laws of September 1935 incorporated *Rassenschande* into criminal law, state prosecutors and judges cracked down sharply on all suspects, as did criminal police and Gestapo. Thousands of individuals were tried for *Rassenschande*, while others went into exile or committed suicide. "Jewish" men, the main victims, were sentenced to several years of prison often followed by unlimited detention in a concentration camp.[30]

In general, those being targeted by ever intensified measures of racist exclusion reacted with efforts to establish or expand networks of support. Still, even well after the Nuremberg Laws of 1935 many of those marked as "Jews" considered the persecution as temporary – especially those born around and before 1900 who were not members of a synagogue congregation. Those who had been vigorous advocates of German nationalism or fought in World War I often ignored or belittled the threat despite widespread and repeated violence. (Klemperer, who had no doubt about the deadliness of the threat, was an exception.) Only younger people tended to understand the exclusion as permanent and a matter of life and death, and they were the ones who mainly resorted to exile. Those who found themselves trapped and excluded made all sorts of efforts to strengthen relationships with family and Jewish neighbors. Maintaining or (re)inventing bonds did not, however, overcome ingrained fissures of class or politics. Accordingly, these communities of exclusion remained necessarily fragile. Bitter and often brutal struggles for survival penetrated their everyday, limiting even more the liminal space Nazi persecution left for retreat.

In the Soviet case, exclusion was on grounds of class, not race. From 1918 to 1936 a legal category of stigmatization – *lishentsy*, or those deprived of the vote, often on grounds of class – existed.[31] If you were a *lishenets* – and even sometimes if you were not, but were nevertheless suspected of bad class origins or attitudes – you were generally deprived not just of the right to vote but also of access to higher education, membership of the Communist Party and the Komsomol, and state housing; liable to special punitive taxation, disadvantaged in court (which operated according to the principles of "class justice"), and always vulnerable to being fired from your job (especially a white-collar one) in one of the periodic institutional purges held in the 1920s and early 1930s. Members of certain widely recognized categories like the clergy (including family of priests and other church officers), *byvshie* ("former people" = *ci-devants*), and persons who had been dekulakized often tried to hide their origins, which in turn made the "unmasking" of those who "concealed their class face" a favorite pastime of Communists and Komsomols.

---

[30] Przyrembel, "*Rassenschande*," 389–443.

[31] On *lishentsy*, see Golfo Alexopoulos, *Stalin's Outcasts: Aliens, Citizens, and the Soviet State, 1926–1936* (Ithaca, NY: Cornell University Press, 2003).

Whereas in the case of Nazi Germany, it was relatively clear whether you fell into an outcast category (Jews, homosexuals, the mentally and physically impaired, and "asocials"), in the Soviet Union the situation was more complicated: stigmatization was even more widespread than in Germany, but less stable in its targets. Being a "class enemy," that is, belonging to one of the social classes (bourgeoisie, nobility, clergy, kulaks) that were officially regarded as hostile to the Soviet state, was the main reason for stigmatization (along with past political affiliations, adherence to religion, relationship to "enemies of the people," and so forth). But in a rapidly modernizing, highly mobile, unsettled society like that of Russia in the first half of the twentieth century, an individual's class was not so easy to determine. What was the social class of someone born in a peasant family, apprenticed in youth to a blacksmith, who had a job in the private retail sector during NEP and then worked as a cook in a state-run cafeteria? Or of a woman married to a worker, herself a librarian, whose father had been a member of the nobility before 1917 and later worked as an accountant in a state firm? Or even of the *kolkhoznik* whose parents had been classified as "poor peasants" but whose uncle had been dekulakized? Almost everybody's biography had elements of ambiguity as far as class was concerned; hence, many people were at risk of stigmatization if (as often happened) they were denounced as "kulaks" or "nobles." For this reason, it was standard practice to edit one's biography to leave out the black marks like dekulakized uncles, and equally standard practice for ill-wishers to denounce one for such concealments.[32]

At moments of political tension, or simply as the result of bad luck, the priest father, kulak uncle, or aunt in emigration might come back to haunt any Soviet citizen, resulting in punishments ranging from rebukes for concealment, through expulsion from university or the Communist Party, to deportation (for example, in the case of former nobles in Leningrad after Kirov's murder) or arrest as an "enemy of the people." But at other times, these black marks would be forgotten (sometimes even as a matter of state policy, as when Stalin in 1935 dropped the remark that "a son does not answer for his father," thus temporarily sanctioning the lifting of stigma from kulaks' children). Of course, black marks were never forgotten by those at risk of having them revealed. More than half the women respondents in a small oral history project of the 1990s remembered such a "sword of Damocles" hanging over their heads in the 1920s and 1930s.[33]

It could also happen that those who were hiding some black mark in their family history were the most vociferous and apparently convinced enthusiasts. Stepan Podlubnyi, the son of a dekulakized kulak, was only one of many who reacted to his own threatened exclusion by passionately embracing Soviet

---

[32] See Sheila Fitzpatrick, *Tear Off the Masks! Identity and Imposture in Twentieth-Century Russia* (Princeton, NJ: Princeton University Press, 2005).

[33] Engel and Posadskaya-Vanderbeck, eds., *A Revolution*: four out of eight respondents fell into this category (Dubova, Fleisher, Berezhnaia, Dolgikh).

values and attempting to rid himself of the "kulak" within.[34] Raisa Orlova, who belonged to the suspect class of "bourgeois intelligentsia" and for that reason was initially rejected for membership of the Komsomol, reports a similar feeling of having to work doubly hard on herself to overcome a taint, as well as a similar (and in her case even longer-lasting) sense of identification with the Soviet project.[35] Even émigré oral histories of former Komsomol activists taken in Munich after the war catch that same emotional drive to belong, to overcome the resistance of the collective to admitting them. This reflected the pervasiveness of the Soviet "remaking" myth, even though in practice the black marks that resulted from "bad" social origin were hard to expunge. Here we find a clear contrast to the German situation, where those excluded had no realistic hope of ever belonging and rarely if ever developed an emotional attachment to the regime that excluded them.

FAMILY BONDS

There are different approaches to the bonds of families. One is to find out what people say about the importance of family bonds, for example, in letters from the front or answers to surveys. However, this approach does not account for possible discrepancies between articulations of the desirability of close family bonds and their actual (non)existence or form. Furthermore, people are not always asked to give an opinion on this sort of topic, and, if asked, they may not respond if they regard it as either as self-evident or, on the contrary, particularly touchy. A second approach is to try to test the strength of family bonds through observations of behavior and social environment. If, for example, it were demonstrable that in Nazi and/or Soviet society people habitually denounced close family members to the authorities (as Arendt and others assume), that would surely indicate a weakening of bonds. The social environment is relevant to the question of family bonds in that certain circumstances are likely to put practical obstacles in the way of maintaining them: for example, societies in upheaval, with high rates of geographical and social mobility.

A third approach would look at life courses and life cycles, since even within the one family, "family bonds" mean something different to the different members and even different to the same person at various stages of life. This is all the more true of nonfamily bonds like friendship and workplace comradeship: it is impossible to imagine general statements on this topic that satisfactorily covered, for example, a schoolgirl daughter, a nonworking mother, a working father, and a grandmother who are all members of the same family. If we combine these approaches in inquiring about the Nazi and Stalinist cases, we get a mixed picture.

---

[34] Podlubnyi's story is told by Jochen Hellbeck in his *Revolution on My Mind*, 165–221.
[35] Raisa Orlova, *Memoirs*, trans. Samuel Cioran (New York: Random House, 1983), 12–13.

In Germany, during the Nazi period as well as before and after, the importance of close family bonds was generally self-evident.[36] Most of the time, therefore, people were not moved to affirm their significance. The exception occurred in wartime, when soldiers' letters from the front – not just in the German case, but also in the Soviet and probably that of every other belligerent – strongly affirmed the importance to them of the family tie. Most of the rank and file had, in fact, encountered the Nazi regime as profamily, at least profamily as a reproductive unit. Interviewees from working-class families emphasize that marriage and starting a family became viable again from the mid-1930s. At that time more and more males (but also females) found wage work. They were reemployed or employed for the first time since the bleak years of unemployment and depression, not the least in new or expanded centers of industry such as building of aircrafts, trucks, tanks, and ships, which heavily relied on the armament program of the Nazi government. Statistical data corroborate such individual recollections: in the mid-1930s the proportion of the population that was married returned to the levels of the prewar period and late 1920s.[37]

Both Nazi propaganda and social policies heavily stressed the importance of family for the German *Volk* and, thus, German empire for its presumed grandiose future. Still, at least in the short run the result of such pressuring (accompanied by such social policies as granting financial support for young families) was no more than the return to "normality" as far as marriage and birthrates are concerned.[38] In fact, at the same time divorce became somewhat more common, though the change began prior to 1933. Between 1928 and 1938 there was a steady, moderate increase in the divorce rate, from 58 to 72 per 1,000, but in 1939 it shot up to 89 per 1,000. In agrarian regions of the country the increase was higher, regardless of confession: Protestant Mecklenburg and Catholic Bavaria, for instance, did not differ much. Still this change cannot be taken as an indicator of diminishing wishes, efforts, or, in particular, concrete practices of bonding as nonlegalized cohabitation.

In the Soviet Union, the importance of family bonds was a more problematic issue, given the early Soviet rhetoric against the "bourgeois patriarchal family" (which meant, by extension, the family per se) and its oppression of women and

---

[36] Gabriele Czarnowski, *Das kontrollierte Paar: Ehe- und Sexualpolitik im Nationalsozialismus* (Weinheim: Deutscher Studien Verlag, 1991); Dagmar Herzog, ed., *Sexuality and German Fascism* (New York: Berghahn Books, 2004.

[37] See interviews from the Ruhr area, a center of heavy industry, in *"Die Jahre weiss man nicht, wo man die heute hinsetzen soll": Faschismuserfahrungen im Ruhrgebiet: Lebensgeschichte und Sozialkultur im Ruhrgebiet 1930 bis 1960*, ed. Lutz Niethammer (Berlin and Bonn: Dietz Verlag, 1983); Länderrat des Amerikanischen Besatzungsgebietes, ed., *Statistisches Handbuch von Deutschland, 1928–1944* (Munich: F. Ehrenwirth, 1949), 47–55.

[38] Cf. Länderrat des Amerikanischen Besatzungsgebiets, ed. *Statistisches Handbuch von Deutschland, 1928–1944* (Munich: F. Ehrenwirth, 1949), 47, 63; Statistisches Bundesamt, ed., *Bevölkerung und Wirtschaft 1872–1972* (Stuttgart: Kohlhammer, 1972) 96; cf. 102–3.

VERA FLEISHER[39] *grew up in a small town in the Urals, daughter of a priest. "I was a rather good student, but there was no opportunity to further my education [in Akhansk]. Our social origins weighed on me and my brothers and sisters like a stigma. And all of them, one by one, left Akhansk. We had relatives in Perm; whoever could, settled there. My older brother was studying in the pedagogical institute. He was in charge of a detskii dom [children's home] and he wrote to me: 'Come. You can finish high school here and then you will be able to continue your studies.' So in December 1924, I left Akhansk for Perm."*

Vera completed school and teacher's college, became a teacher, and married a doctor. Keeping up contact with her parents was difficult – "It was like having a tie with an 'alien element'" – but nevertheless she continued to correspond with them. A few years after her marriage, "I made up my mind to risk going to my parents, to visit them. A very sorry sight greeted me: Mama was seriously ill. She was paralyzed.... At the time, my little sister... wasn't yet ten. Mama was fifty when she was born. And so my sister, of course, was neglected. You can well imagine what sort of girl she was – wild, you could say – she ran around with peasant kids."

At her father's request, Vera took her sister, Lenochka, home with her. "I remember when we were on the train, the other passengers asked: 'Is this girl from a detskii dom [orphanage]...?' she was so badly dressed, you know.... When we arrived, the very first thing I did was to take the girl to a beauty parlor; they fixed her up. Then I went to the store and bought her a dress, a coat, shoes. The girl was transformed. I could show her to my relatives."

Vera's father was arrested in 1937 and died shortly thereafter, out of contact with his family. "Mama's life turned out to be even more tragic. We couldn't be with her. You see, I was expecting my second child.... In December 1937, I received a telegram: 'Mama has died.' Here's what happened: she died in the arms of that woman who took care of her. She gave birth to and brought up, as best she could, seven children. Yet she died in the arms of someone else."

children.[40] Although such rhetoric was firmly dropped by the mid-1930s and had in any case always been contradicted by Soviet legal and administrative practice (which made families financially responsible for the welfare of their members, until such distant time as the cash-strapped state could assume these responsibilities), some popular sense persisted that too conspicuous or assertive insistence on the importance of family could be construed as anti-Soviet. The regime strongly endorsed the family as a reproductive unit in connection with

---

[39] Vera Konstantinovna Fleisher, "Daughter of a Village Priest," in *A Revolution of Their Own*, 85–100, passim.

[40] On the Soviet family, see Kurt Geiger, *The Family in Soviet Russia* (Cambridge, MA: Harvard University Press, 1968) and Wendy Z. Goldman, *Women, the State, and Revolution: Soviet Family Policy and Social Life, 1917–1936* (Cambridge: Cambridge University Press, 1993).

the ban on abortion, restrictions on divorce, and encouragement of childbearing of the 1936 law. At the same time, the regime also gave considerable propaganda weight to the Pavlik Morozov story, which in its propaganda (mythical) version was a morality tale of a son who understood that his duty to the state was greater than his duty to an erring father and therefore denounced him; and during the Great Purges of 1937–8,[41] there was official encouragement for wives and children of arrested "enemies of the people" to repudiate them publicly.

We might conclude from all this that while there is little if any reason to conclude that family bonds were generally weakened in Nazi Germany, such a conclusion might legitimately be drawn about Stalinist Russia. As it happens, however, we do have some additional evidence to adduce on attitudes to the family, namely, the postwar Harvard Interview Project on the Soviet Social System (Harvard Project), which asked respondents exactly this question, that is, whether family bonds had grown stronger or weaker after the Revolution. The majority of respondents in all social classes but the peasantry said they had grown stronger (citing the importance of mutual support in difficult conditions). A slight majority of peasant respondents said they had grown weaker but attributed this to the practical circumstance of geographical separation of family members after collectivization.[42]

The Soviet case is not so clear-cut because in the 1920s and early 1930s the state's acceptance of de facto marriage and the easy availability of divorce undoubtedly weakened the institution of marriage, although state policy on this matter was reversed in the mid-1930s. Many couples with long-standing de facto marriages and children married formally only on the outbreak of war, to regularize the legal and benefits situation when the man went away to fight. The Soviet press of the 1930s is full of stories of fathers who had abandoned their families and were hiding from their wives' demands for child support payments (though the point of publishing such stories was to vilify the delinquent men). At the same time, we have some countervailing evidence from the 1937 Soviet census, which shows that a very high proportion of all men identified themselves as married (this presumably includes de facto marriages). The proportion was slightly lower for women as a result of war- and upheaval-related gender imbalance in key age groups: even so, the absolute number of women declaring themselves married was greater than the absolute number of men, suggesting that women were more inclined than men to interpret cohabitation as marriage.[43]

---

[41] On the Pavlik Morozov myth, see Catriona Kelly, *Comrade Pavlik: The Rise and Fall of a Soviet Boy Hero* (London: Granta Books, 2005).

[42] Alex Inkeles and Raymond Bauer, *The Soviet Citizen: Daily Life in a Totalitarian Society* (New York: Athenaeum, 1968), 211–16.

[43] Iu.A. Poliakov et al., eds., *Vsesoiuznaia perepis' naseleniia 1937 g. Kratkie itogi* (Moscow: Akademia nauk SSSR, In-t istorii SSSR, 1991), 82.

Of course, figures like the Soviet ones reflect only the external side of family life. For the internal side, one possible indication of a weakening of bonds would be a demonstrated propensity of family members to denounce each other to the authorities. Such "reporting" did happen in Germany – however, not only under the Nazi dictatorship. Parental demands that the state assume custody of an unruly son or daughter regularly occupied Berlin police and welfare authorities in the 1920s.[44] In the early 1920s in the areas of allied occupation "good Germans" were expected to denounce and, often, harass those who apparently "collaborated" with the enemy; Communists were encouraged to report to the Party on "comrades" who might be "traitors," whether kin or not.[45] Still, people in their semipublic chats in pubs or at coffee tables were scandalized by such cases when they became known, reflecting a sense of transgression: the informers had violated the neighborhood's (or the community's) line of respectability and social honor.[46] Memoirs and oral recollections confirm both the durability of bonds revolving around household and family and their limited impact on individual behavior and attitudes, since they sometimes feature spouses or siblings engaged on opposite ends of the political spectrum (for instance, one son being active in the Rote Front Kämpferbund before 1933, while the other was a member of a local SA unit).[47]

In the Soviet Union, despite the Pavlik Morozov myth, denunciation of close family members seems to have been rare in the 1930s, even though the practice of denunciation in general was flourishing.[48] We can only speculate on the reasons for this, but one likely reason is that when the regime punished an individual – as a kulak, enemy of the people, or whatever – it generally directly punished the whole family or household, and indirectly punished or put at risk a broader family group (including ex-spouses and children living apart from the punished person), who could be considered guilty by association. (In the real-life Pavlik Morozov case, the family was no longer one household because of a nasty divorce that pitted Pavlik and his mother against his father.) But even divorce or acrimonious separation did not produce many denunciations in the 1930s, though this was to change after the war, when the 1944 law restricting

---

[44] Kerstin Kohtz, "Väter und Mütter im Dialog mit der Berliner Jugendfürsorge in den 1920er Jahren," *SOWI Sozialwissenschaftliche Informationen* 27 (1998): 113–18.

[45] Michael Ruck, *Die freien Gewerkschaften im Ruhrkampf 1923* (Cologne: Bund Verlag, 1986); Gerd Krüger, "Straffreie Selbstjustiz: Öffentliche Denunzierungen im Ruhrgebiet 1923–1926," *SOWI Sozialwissenschaftliche Informationen* 27 (1998): 119–25.

[46] Swett, *Neighbors and Enemies*, 214–31.

[47] See the recollection of Theo Pirker, born 1922 in Munich, about his brothers in Martin Jander, ed., *Theo Pirker über Theo Pirker* (Marburg: SP-Verlag N. Schüren, 1988), 25–7; cf. recollections from the Ruhr area, especially Alexander von Plato, "Ich bin mit allen gut ausgekommen" in *"Die Jahre weiss man nicht, wo man die heute hinsetzen soll": Faschismuserfahrungen im Ruhrgebiet*, ed. Lutz Niethammer (Berlin and Bonn: Dietz, 1983), 31–65.

[48] Fitzpatrick, "Signals from Below: Soviet Letters of Denunciation in the 1930s," in *Accusatory Practices: Denunciation in Modern European History 1789–1989*, eds. Sheila Fitzpatrick and Robert Gellately (Chicago: University of Chicago Press, 1997), 103–5.

access to divorce increased the incentive for spouses desiring divorce to blacken each other's names.[49]

During the Great Purges, wives of arrested "enemies of the people" were sometimes forced to make a public statement repudiating their spouses, and the same kind of thing happened in some schools with the children. At the same time, completely opposite practices were much more widespread: for example spouses and children (and also parents and other relatives) standing in line to get news of the arrested person and send him (her) parcels and money; wives petitioning the authorities for their husbands' release, testifying to their blameless character. The latter practice was standard procedure for wives, and so understood by the authorities, who did not take punitive action in response but treated the requests quite respectfully, even though they were rarely (in the late 1930s) successful.[50] The point here is that the authorities' response to wives' (or mothers' or children's or occasionally husbands') petitions clearly conveyed an assumption that the existence of such family bonds was natural and to be expected.

It should be noted that implicit in this whole inquiry is the assumption that family bonds are sources of support and that any weakening of them makes individuals mentally vulnerable and prone to loneliness. Yet, families are not necessarily harmonious but often the source of pain, distress, and hardship; they may be rent with anger to the point that the family is incapable of offering support to its members and escape may seem highly desirable. Such stifling family situations have often been discussed in societies facing both commodification and individualization of social and cultural relationships (see, for example, novels and memoirs of bourgeois life, but also the scientific focus on "nerves" and individual psychology in Britain, France, and Germany in the nineteenth and early twentieth centuries). In ages of upheaval, we hear less of them. The "stifling family" motif is very rare in Soviet memoirs and literature and, on the German side, less frequent for the Nazi period than earlier.

Where intergeneration family conflict existed in Nazi Germany or the Soviet Union, it was relatively easily resolved: given the external forces supporting the children's choice, the children did not have to remain subordinate to a tyrannical father (or overprotective mother) or trapped within an oppressive family. Another variant of family conflict common in the Soviet Union occurred when the parents' stigmatized status, usually on the basis of class origin, blighted the chances of their children, who therefore felt obliged to renounce them publicly or in some way dissociate themselves. As far as we can tell from scattered reports, however, this was usually not so much a rancorous conflict as a more

---

[49] Fitzpatrick, *Tear Off the Masks!* 254–61.

[50] There are many such letters in the Sovnarkom archive of A. Ia. Vyshinskii, sometime State Prosecutor: See Gosudarstvennyi arkhiv Rossiiskoi Federatsii (GARF), f. 5446, op. 81a, correspondence for 1939.

or less regretful parting, which the parents (for the good of the child) often initiated.

WORKPLACE BONDS

Bonds between workers and employees at the workplaces obviously existed and developed in both societies. The question is, How and in what directions? In German industry from the 1920s various wage schemes stimulated "cooperation of necessity," mostly among fellow workers of similar skill and experience engaged in a common task. Workers tended to consider this cooperation as part and parcel of "doing a good job" and delivering "German quality work." Mutual support remained compartmentalized, however, and focused on the specific shop or work group; thus, "solidarity" meant little more than providing help in personal emergencies.[51] Cooperation remained limited and was dictated by necessity: to avoid injuries and to keep the flow of production going, thus ensuring both one's wage and one's satisfaction. Informal rules bound rank and file to collective standards of pace and intensity of work, thereby channeling both demands of superiors and expectations of colleagues. Still, the social spheres of skilled workers rarely overlapped with those of semi- or unskilled workers, and the same was true of the sociability of male and female workers, blue- and white-collar, not to mention recent recruits to the workforce and second- or third-generation proletarians. Attachment to and participation in formal associations like Social-Democratic, Communist, or Christian (primarily Catholic) unions and political parties varied greatly among different regions and branches of industry. There was intense competition that regularly expressed itself in bitter fights and even physical violence.

Bonds were sectoral, also, among the wide array of clerical workers in state and communal offices and industrial administration as well as of commercial enterprises and department stores. This is one reason why in April and May 1933 the immediate onslaught of SA and other Nazi gangs on the Socialist, Communist, and Christian labor movements met with an apathetic and occasionally approving response outside the inner circles of these organizations. After the early 1920s the notion of a united working class had become a hollow phrase with very limited appeal to the majority of working people. Thus, after 1933 Nazi efforts to organize working people from industry, clerical jobs, and the peasant or estate economy particularly resonated in nonurban areas and outside the centers of big industry, more so in Protestant than in Catholic areas. Here, the programs of *Schönheit der Arbeit* meant tangible improvements that addressed items from the usual wish list of male and female workers: toilets,

---

[51] Alf Lüdtke, "'Deutsche Qualitätsarbeit,' 'Spielereien' am Arbeitsplatz und 'Fliehen' aus der Fabrik: Industrielle Arbeitsprozesse und Arbeiterverhalten in den 1920er Jahren," in *Arbeiterkulturen zwischen Alltag und Politik*, ed. Friedhelm Boll (Vienna: Europa Verlag 1986), 155–97; Alf Lüdtke, "Hunger in der Großen Depression: Hungererfahrungen und Hungerpolitik am Ende der Weimarer Republik," *Archiv für Sozialgeschichte* 27 (1987): 145–76.

running water, clean tables for coffee breaks, better light, and larger windows in the shops. Recollections repeatedly and most vividly mention such innovations as true evidence of a "new era," especially those of workers who never had been connected to any of the labor unions.

Bonds between workers developed for and in the context of limited projects, such as piecework given to several people with similar or matching qualifications (though it also happened that mates would ask for certain tasks they could do as a two-, three-, four-, or eight-man gang). Contrary to the Soviet model, these work teams never were organized formally. In fact, wage schemes aimed at stimulating individual performance and, thus, had to be circumvented when the needs of workflow demanded to operate in a work team. In the 1930s, however, a new wage scheme became popular in industry: group piecework (*Gruppenakkord*). This form of wage rested on the actual cooperation of the respective work team, thus ensuring everyone's share of the total amount granted to the group upon completion of their task.[52]

Individual pride and satisfaction in one's work abilities and the products of one's work were important in Germany both before and after the Nazi period. Indeed, attachment to one's work practice or task tended to be stronger among German workers than attachment to mates or work teams. After the First World War, union functionaries, management representatives, engineers, and politicians had joined in a plea for "German quality work" as the prerequisite for recovery of the German state and nation. Such pleas resonated with workers' aspirations for recognition beyond the cash nexus – longings that were ignored by the political and union organizations aiming at organizing industrial (and agrarian) workers before 1933. While Nazi policies and practices had the goal of controlling and manipulating workers, they nevertheless responded in some degree to these aspirations and tended to stimulate the intensity of individual workers' effort and devotion to their task, whether this was producing standardized screws or an airplane. Thus, the Nazi propaganda about the "honor of labor" connected easily with the concept of "worker's dignity" many workers harbored.

In the Soviet case, the Revolution intensified feelings of working-class identity and its significance (the much-discussed "proletarian consciousness") but also to some degree moved its locus out of the workplace, so how this affected

---

[52] Carola Sachse, *Angst, Belohnung, Zucht und Ordnung: Herrschaftsmechanismen im Nationalsozialismus* (Opladen: Westdeutscher Verlag, 1982); Rüdiger Hachtmann, *Industriearbeit im "Dritten Reich": Untersuchungen zu den Lohn- und Arbeitsbedingungen in Deutschland 1933–1945* (Göttingen: Vandenhoeck & Ruprecht, 1989); Carola Sachse, *Siemens, der Nationalsozialismus und die moderne Familie: Eine Untersuchung zur sozialen Rationalisierung in Deutschland im 20. Jahrhundert* (Hamburg: Rasch und Röhring, 1990); Wolfgang Schäfer, *Die Fabrik auf dem Dorf: Studien zum betrieblichen Sozialverhalten ländlicher Industriearbeiter* (Göttingen: Werkstatt Verlag, 1991); Wolfgang Franz Werner, *Bleib übrig! Deutsche Arbeiter in der nationalsozialistischen Kriegswirtschaft* (Düsseldorf: Schwann Verlag, 1983); as to multiple everyday settings and practices among working people see Alf Lüdtke, "People Working: Everyday Life and German Fascism," *History Workshop Journal*, no. 50 (2000): 74–92.

An anonymous **ENGINEER FROM SMOLENSK**, *Russian by nationality and born around 1913, was interviewed as part of the postwar Harvard Interview Project on the Soviet Social System.*[53] *A beneficiary of Soviet affirmative action for workers' and peasants' children, he was characterized by his interviewer as "exceptionally pro-Soviet." His picture of his work life in the Soviet Union was glowing. "I recall no friction at the plant.... The engineers called the old lathe operators by their names and patronymics; they really consulted them and discussed things seriously together. "There were no obstacles in my way" as far as advancement was concerned. "For us, the idealists, who were itching for action, who still had their romanticism of doing something useful, there were greater opportunities, wider horizons far away, you might say.... Many geologists volunteered to go to Siberia, into the Pamir, the Altai. They were mostly young people." Neither he nor any family members were ever arrested, though some of his friends were.*

He served in the army during the war and after the war worked in Germany dismantling equipment, where he describes bursts of unexpected sympathy for the defeated Germans and disgust at the Soviet army's brutal conduct in East Prussia. An emotional turning point occurred in 1947, when he returned to Moscow on leave. "Somehow the sight of Moscow especially touched my patriotic feelings. Seeing it the way it was, made all my ideals evaporate. On some central square a number of interned women probably from the Balkans were working, repairing something; they were clothed in rags, working under heavy guard. I felt awkward, back home as a hero, on furlough!... In the courtyard I saw women working with obvious physical evidence of famine. When I asked my friend, he said there are many such – they are the widows of soldiers who were killed in the war. At home on furlough, I spent nights without sleeping, thinking about it. All this impressed me so much. What was it we had won this war for?" With regard to his ultimate decision to defect, he said: "For a normal human being it must be difficult to understand why I have come over. I sometimes wondered myself what it is that makes a man change allegiance this way. Europeans are cooler, more rational people. But we Russians, perhaps all the Slavs, are more impressionable, more temperamental." [Nothing earlier in the interview suggests that he possessed these traits.]

bonds between workers in particular shops, workplaces, and union branches remains somewhat unclear.[54] Work was scarce in the 1920s, with the result

[53] Davis Center, Harvard University, "Project on the Soviet Social System. Interview Records. 'A' Schedule Protocols," no. 517 (v. 26, pp. 2ff). Henceforth cited as Harvard Project. The Harvard Project is now accessible online at http://hcl.harvard.edu/collections/hpsss/index.html.

[54] On labor in the 1930s, see Donald Filtzer, *Soviet Workers and Stalinist Industrialization: The Formation of Modern Soviet Production Relations, 1928–1941* (Armonk, NY: M. E. Sharpe, 1986); Hiroaki Kuromiya, *Stalin's Industrial Revolution: Politics and Workers, 1928–1932* (Cambridge: Cambridge University Press, 1988); David L. Hoffman, *Peasant Metropolis: Social Identities in Moscow, 1929–1941* (Ithaca, NY: Cornell University Press, 1994); Lewis R. Siegelbaum, *Stakhanovism and the Politics of Productivity in the USSR, 1935–1941* (Cambridge:

that the trade unions, mainly dominated by male workers with prewar work experience, often tried to enforce "closed shop" rules against women, peasants, and inexperienced young urbanities trying to find employment. The situation was further complicated by the fact that the status of "worker" was a socially valuable one, opening the doors to many opportunities including higher education. With the First Five-Year Plan at the end of the 1920s (accompanied by the unpopular collectivization of agriculture), the urban unemployment problem disappeared and, at the same time, millions of peasants flooded into the urban industrial workforce. Conflicts between "old" and "new" workers, as well as between workers of different nationality in some parts of the country, were frequent at this period. Strikes were not permitted (though they sometimes happened anyway), the scope for collective bargaining on wages was greatly reduced, and the trade unions' role was redefined to focus on welfare administration. In the mid-1930s, official campaigns for "socialist competition" between brigades and the Stakhanovite movement, rewarding individual output, were seen by some as undermining workers' solidarity and encouraging "norm-busting." At the same time, for blue- and white-collar workers alike, the Soviet workplace was becoming increasingly important as a site of sociability.[55] This was probably partly related to the decline of other venues, to be discussed later. But as the Soviet workplace became the primary unit for the distribution of all sorts of benefits, starting with rations and hot meals in the hungry early 1930s, there were intrinsic, functional reasons as well.

Worker solidarity and the existence of close bonds within the workplace community are so much the stuff of Soviet propaganda that it is difficult to get a clear picture on the Soviet side. A wealth of Stalin-period memoirs and oral histories (admittedly composed to a stereotyped pattern) testifies to the importance of blue-collar bonding at enterprises, and there is post-Soviet testimony (mainly from women) on bonding at the office as well as the factory.[56] In 1990s interviews, a woman engineer had fond memories of the bonds she formed with "her girls" in the factory shop,[57] while a male engineer interviewed as an émigré by the Harvard Project spoke eloquently about the bonds between young engineers, as well as with older workers, at his plant.[58] To be sure, there is other testimony about *lack* of harmony in the collective, for example, conflicts between "old" and "new" workers, or between Stakhanovites and

Cambridge University Press, 1988); Lewis H. Siegelbaum and Ronald G. Suny, eds., *Making Workers Soviet: Power, Class and Identity* (Ithaca, NY: Cornell University Press, 1994); Wendy Z. Goldman, *Women at the Gates: Gender and Industry in Stalin's Russia* (Cambridge: Cambridge University Press, 2002); and Jeffrey J. Rossman, *Worker Resistance under Stalin: Class and Revolution on the Shop Floor* (Cambridge, MA: Harvard University Press, 2005).

[55] For a vivid fictional picture of an office community in the late 1930s, see Lydia Chukovskaia's novella, *Sofia Petrovna*, trans. Aline Worth (Evanston, IL: Northwestern University Press, 1988).

[56] There are many such examples in the interviews with Leningraders on the 1930s in *Na korme vremeni: Interv'iu s leningradtsami 1930-kh godov*, ed. M. Vitukhnovskaia (St. Petersburg: "Neva," 2000).

[57] Engel and Posadskaya, eds., *Revolution*, 108 (Berezhnaia).

[58] Harvard Project, no. 517 (v. 26), 11.

MELITA MASCHMANN[59] *was born in Berlin in 1918 to well-established middle-class parents. As a schoolgirl on January 30, 1933, she witnessed the torch-light parade of the NSDAP and its SA troops in Berlin celebrating Hitler's appointment as Chancellor. This march in its mixture of boisterousness and solemnity made a lasting impression on her: "I was overcome by a burning desire to belong to these people for whom it was a matter of life and death," which they expressed in ways "aggressive and sentimental" at the same time. In the ranks of the Nazi organization she saw fulfillment for her longing to be attached "to something that was great and fundamental" and to leave behind matters of "clothing or food or school essays" and other "derisory trivialities." In particular, Nazism and, concretely, Nazi Youth (or BDM) meant to her in the first place to confront the "bourgeois values" represented by her parents and their reliance on the unquestioned obedience of maids and her father's chauffeur. Without her parents' knowledge, she joined the BDM, only to realize quickly that she remained an outcast among these girls of "humble background" and rough manners. However, she "took refuge in a fanaticism for work which kept his hold on me . . . until the end of the Third Reich." Upon graduation in 1937, she did her obligatory BDM stint of a half-year of service, after which she was recruited for a permanent position as a professional leader in that organization. Hard manual work shaped the days (and nights) during her "service year" when she and her mates were commissioned to support small farmers and their families in one of the Eastern provinces. Here, she recalls how "physical exhaustion . . . changed suddenly into a feeling of unquenchable joy." "Profound respect for all those who perform physically hard work" became, so she recalls, crucial to her. Also important was the experience of a working community of mixed social background, as the BDM camp was at that time. Inspired by this, she volunteered for a job in occupied Poland, where in 1942 she was assigned the position of leader of a work camp. A strong "fanaticism of work," as she puts it, informed her activity organizing young German women there. However, in her recollection this fanaticism turned into "cold contempt" for the occupied Poles, especially when she met them suffering as in the case of a devastating fire in a neighboring Polish village.*

others. Memoirs like those of the Stakhanovite Ivan Gudov show what it could feel like to be an outsider in the factory collective, and how outsider resentments might fuel Stakhanovite norm busting.[60] But the hostile reaction to overachievers like Gudov is in its own way also testimony to workplace solidarity. The individual "quality work" motif of the Germans is largely absent on the Soviet side, where the emphasis is either on collective overcoming of difficulties to meet the Plan or on individual record breaking (as in the Stakhanov movement).

[59] The information is drawn from Melitta Maschmann, *Fazit: Mein Weg in der Hitler-Jugend* (Munich: DTV, 1963).
[60] Ivan Gudov, *Sud'ba rabochego* (Moscow: Politizdat, 1970).

There can be little doubt of the depth and significance of the bonds of comradeship forged between soldiers (German and Soviet alike), in particular at the front and in combat zones during World War II. These bonds, however, must surely be of a fundamentally different kind because of the different level of trust involved. Members of a work brigade are not generally entrusting their lives to each other; they probably also do not share with each other certain emotions and opinions for reasons of prudence or simply a sense of appropriateness. Front line brotherhood[61] or comradeship, on the other hand, is often described as a relationship of total trust, involving not only trusting one's life but also entrusting to one's front line brother thoughts and emotions that are not usually shared with anyone. This still leaves the question of whether such front line comradeship in the German and Soviet armies during World War II differed in kind from that prevailing in, for instance, the British armed forces or the U.S. Army at the same time, or from the German and Russian armies in World War I. Even more, the general emphasis on comradeship in the war propaganda on both sides makes it difficult to assess the actual range and profile – even the very existence of relationships of mutual trust among rank and file as between them and their superiors.[62] Especially in the war theaters in the Soviet Union various forms of comradeship were increasingly fueled by encounters with and practices of killing. Closeness to one's buddies increasingly relied on and, in turn, opened one up for brutal action against the "enemy."[63]

SOCIABILITY OUTSIDE THE WORKPLACE

This is an area in which the German and Soviet cases are very different from each other, largely as a result of the striking restriction of associational life (outside the workplace and youth organizations, the Komsomol and Young Pioneers) in Russia in the Stalin period. In Germany, in contrast, existing forms of association survived, though often at least superficially recast into the

---

[61] This term was specific to the Red Army; it did not play any role in and is not even mentioned for the German military.

[62] On Soviet soldiers, see Catherine Merridale, *Ivan's War: Life and Death in the Red Army, 1939–1945* (New York: Henry Holt, 2006). For the German side Theo Schulte, *The German Army and Nazi Policies in Occupied Russia* (Oxford: Berg, 1989); Thomas Kühne, "Kameradschaft – 'das Beste im Leben des Mannes': Die deutschen Soldaten des Zweiten Weltkriegs in erfahrungs- und geschlechtergeschichtlicher Perspektive," *Geschichte und Gesellschaft* 22 (1996): 504–29; Thomas Kühne, *Kameradschaft: Die Soldaten des nationalsozialistischen Krieges und das 20. Jahrhundert* (Göttingen: Vandenhoeck & Ruprecht, 2006), 140–71.

[63] Christopher Browning, "German Killers: Behavior and Motivation in the Light of New Evidence," *Nazi Policies, Jewish Workers, German Killers*, ed. Christopher Browning (Cambridge and New York: Cambridge University Press, 2000), 143–69; Hamburger Institut für Sozialforschung, ed., *Verbrechen der Wehrmacht: Dimensionen des Vernichtungskrieges 1941-1944* (Hamburg: Hamburger Edition, 2002); Ben Shepherd, *War in the Wild East: The German Army and Soviet Partisans* (Cambridge, MA: Harvard University Press, 2004). On the Soviet case, see Catherine Merridale, *Ivan's War: Life and Death in the Red Army, 1939–1945* (New York: Metropolitan Books, 2006), 78, 230–1, 308, 357, and passim.

NS mold, while new forms of association were created, especially via regional tourism under the banner of the KDF.

In Germany, the effort to reorganize shooting associations, sports and athletic clubs, dancing circles, or singing clubs in the context of *Gleichschaltung* in 1933/4 often meant little more than changing the name and incorporating the swastika into the arms and proper *völkisch* terms into the charter. Still, the expulsion of Jewish members or sometimes their (mostly silent) withdrawal was part of the process. In other words, the efforts of reorganization did not affect the inner workings of these associations very much. The parallel to the (*Selbst*)-*Gleichschaltung* of the wide array of professional organizations is striking: most people made a smooth transition, often without even realizing that an important change had occurred. The government-ordered immediate shutdown of all associations attached to the political left, including the SPD and KPD, was a different story, as were efforts to monitor and inhibit much of church-related associational life, especially when they affected children and young adults (an area where the NS organizations were supposed to exercise an unrestricted monopoly). Still, in many areas members of "left" associations and church groups on the parish level adjusted to the imposed changes without much ado: in most cases they were familiar with their new buddies or associates from neighborhood and kin networks even across rigid political divides as those between the "camps" of political Catholicism and Communism.

Other arenas of the pre-Nazi German world of sociability – the male Stammtisch in corner pubs, the female Kaffeeklatsch in a cafe or a neighborhood restaurant – were in no way directly affected by the Nazis' coming to power. In fact, the spread of radios and the emphasis of the new regime on broadcasting the rapid emergence of an "Aryan *Volksgemeinschaft*" expanded such semipublic arenas of conviviality into the neighborhood: people became rapidly accustomed to neighbors' "listening along with them" and, thus, anticipated they would also be "listening in on them."[64]

In Russia, by contrast, associational life was sparser and often of more recent development than in Germany. With the end of the New Economic Policy in the late 1920s, neighborhood bars, cafes, and restaurants that had formerly been in private hands were closed down, and it was decades before the state created substitutes (the state did create cafeterias, mainly workplace-based, where most urban working people ate once a day, but conditions in them were so substandard that they can hardly have furthered enjoyable social interactions). Social life centered on the Orthodox Church was sharply restricted after 1929 (with the mass closing of churches and arrest of priests). People sometimes responded to this by holding religious observances in their homes, with or without a priest in attendance; often these groups drifted away from Orthodoxy into sects, and always such activity was regarded as anti-Soviet and those who participated risked arrest. Thus for a not insignificant minority of the population, especially rural, sociability and illegal meeting acquired a close connection.

---

[64] Andrew Stuart Bergerson, "Listening to the Radio in Hildesheim, 1923–53," *German Studies Review* 24 (2001): 83–113, 102.

FRITZ KIEHN[65] *was informally acclaimed as the new "king" of Trossingen, a center of specialized industries in the Protestant part of Upper Swabia. Kiehn, owner-entrepreneur of a company producing cigarette paper by the brand of "Efka" (i.e., his initials F.K.), who also held multiple posts in the NSDAP, replaced the former "king" Hohner, whose family had for decades run the dominant company in town. Kiehn had literally been a nobody when he entered town in 1908 as a traveling salesman, at the age of 23. But in the early 1920s Kiehn had successfully capitalized on the hyperinflation by producing cigarette paper to meet a skyrocketing demand. However, the local elites led by the Hohner family kept him at bay socially throughout the 1920s, despite his marriage to the daughter of a well-established local family.*

The Nazi movement seemed to offer an arena to this social outcast. Kiehn took the opportunity and became an active organizer in both his town and the county, even winning election to the German Reichstag of July 1932; thus, in 1933 this company owner figured among the "old fighters" of the Nazi movement and swiftly accumulated posts and relations. He used both to expand influence and power, especially in industry in Southwest Germany; at the same time he ruthlessly took advantage of his networks and made a fortune by speculatively trading stocks and, not the least, exploiting of the "Aryanization" in the late 1930s.

Being awarded an officer's rank of the SS and, in 1938, co-opted to the personal staff of Heinrich Himmler, Minister of Interior and head of the SS, Kiehn appeared regularly in public in SS uniform and his car flew the SS emblem. He organized local rallies and parades, which the town's old elites, including the Hohner famliy, were forced to attend. Still, Kiehn's boisterous self-aggrandizing and reckless moneymaking did not go unchallenged, although a party court finally acquitted him in 1939 of accusations of violating "Nazi ethics" for having business contacts with Jews and putting individual interest above that of the party.

As a company owner, Kiehn showed concern for the well-being of his employees, including former Social Democrats and, so the rumor went, individual Jews. After 1945, Hohner did not try to take revenge; thus, Kiehn continued to operate his company. Throughout the 1950s, local politicians treated Kiehn as a most honorable member of the community and even designated public space and buildings in his honor.

Many interest-centered associations like that of the Esperantists were closed down in the early 1930s because of the regime's fear of their use for political conspiratorial purposes. The state assumed control of some of the old associations (for example, chess clubs), though they remained in theory "voluntary" or, in the case of sports clubs, under trade union auspices. With regard to some professional organizations – of writers, composers, artists, and architects – it could even be argued that the 1930s saw an expansion of the scope of their

[65] The biographical information is drawn from Hartmut Berghoff and Cornelia Rauh-Kühne, *Fritz K.: Ein deutsches Leben in zwanzigsten Jahrhundert* (Stuttgart: Deutsche Verlags-Anstalt, 2000).

activities, resources, and importance in the life of their members, even though the organizational diversity of the 1920s had been replaced with one umbrella union for each profession. As far as the organization of leisure was concerned, the Soviet state had rhetoric not dissimilar to the Nazis' with KDF, but its achievements were smaller.

It cannot be assumed that the elimination of some sites of sociability eliminated extra-workplace sociability; the more likely possibility is that it changed its forms. Moving beyond the organized, institutionalized venues of sociability, Soviet people mingled with each other in the open-air bazaars ("kolkhoz markets") in towns, which were sites of second-economy transactions as well as legal trade by collective farmers;[66] in queues; at bus and tram stops; and in railway stations waiting for trains and/or drinking. (These venues, together with workplace cafeterias and the workplace generally, were those that the NKVD monitored for its "mood of the population" reports.) Men drank together, often in stairwells or on the street because of the shortage of bars, splitting a bottle of vodka bought in the state *Gastronom*. (There was an anti-alcohol strain in the Bolshevik leadership early on, but by the mid-1920s the leadership had ended the imperial government's wartime suspension of vodka production – a state monopoly – and by the end of the decade Stalin was firmly committed to increasing vodka production and sales as a way of raising revenue for industrialization.)[67]

Another thing that brought people together was the search for scarce goods, unavailable in state stores. To get basic goods like shoes, clothing, and saucepans, and also services like school places, telephone connections at home, and tickets to the ballet, urban residents needed networks of contacts – people who had access or "pull" with regard to different categories of goods. The term *blat* – emerging from the criminal world into the regular urban world in the 1930s – was used for these contacts. These networks operated on the basis of reciprocal favors, not the exchange of money, and were conceptualized by participants in terms of friendship and mutual respect. Patronage networks, serving similar functions and also the function of protection, were another important locus of social interaction – certainly no less prevalent, and probably more, than in the pre-revolutionary period.[68]

BONDS OUTSIDE *VOLKSGEMEINSCHAFT*

In changed circumstances, new demands and incentives generate, or at least make possible, new social bonds. This seems to have been the case in both the Soviet Union and Nazi Germany. At the same time, however, changes in social

[66] On the bazaars, see Julie Hessler, *A Social History of Soviet Trade* (Princeton, NJ: Princeton University Press, 2004), 252–73.

[67] On early Bolshevik policy, see Laura L. Phillips, *Bolsheviks and the Bottle: Drink and Worker Culture in St. Petersburg, 1900–1929* (De Kalb: Northern Illinois Press, 2000), 17–26.

[68] On *blat* and patronage, see Sheila Fitzpatrick, *Everyday Stalinism* (New York: Oxford University Press, 1999), 62–6, 109–14.

and governmental practice (for example, with regard to association, marriage, and policing) weakened or even destroyed bonds that people had long relied on (and sometimes resented as well). Thus, the impact of "totalitarian" rule on the two societies was more complex and ambivalent than is often recognized.

On the Soviet side, the Gulag experience is, perversely, an interesting example of the generation of new social bonds. Not only do virtually all intelligentsia memoirs of the camps report sustenance from newly and involuntarily formed collectives of "politicals" among the convict population, there is even more striking evidence of the strong community sense of "criminals" in Gulag. In the post-Stalin period, various versions of Gulag fraternity (Solzhenitsyn's zeks, the career criminals known as *vory v zakone*) became visible parts of a complex social fabric. In Germany, by contrast, memoirs of survivors from the concentration or labor camps stress the sense that "each stood for himself." Except for activists of the Communist Party and of some religious sects or groups, such as Catholic priests or Jehovah's Witnesses, survivors do not recall bonds that incorporated fellow inmates in a way similar to recollections of Soviet survivors. And even in these cases the bonds connected and worked solely for the members of the specific group. In no case do they seem to have included the majority of inmates.[69]

But Gulag is not the only Soviet example of new bonding. The majority of the urban population lived in communal apartments (one family to a room, neighbors not of one's own choosing) or in dormitories and barracks. Communal apartments were only rarely collectives of mutual support; more often, they were rent by quarrels over shared facilities and meanness. But bonds and mutual dependency did form within them; children often perceived neighbors as family even if parents hated them. Perhaps the Soviet communal apartment of the 1930s could be compared in its prickly closeness and dysfunctionality to the repressive German bourgeois family often represented in literature and memoirs. The workplace also seems to have functioned as a new or intensified site of bonding in the Soviet case: not necessarily bonding associated with the actual work performed, but with the multitude of other functions (distribution of food and other goods, political meetings, cultural events, and so on) that the workplace developed in the Stalin period.

Practices of exclusion strengthened communities of the stigmatized and stimulated the formation of new ones. In the German case, persecution promoted (among Jews but also, though very differently, among homosexuals, Roma and Sinti, and Jehovah's Witnesses) a sense of common fate but also a wariness about the risks of public association with other outcasts. Those who had thought of themselves primarily as Germans now had to think of themselves primarily as Jews. In the Soviet case, those deprived of the right to vote (*lishentsy*) were probably too big and disparate a category to become a single community,

---

[69] Lutz Niethammer et al., eds., *Der "gesäuberte" Antifaschismus: Die SED und die roten Kapos von Buchenwald: Dokumente* (Berlin: Akademie Verlag, 1994).

but the subgroup of *byvshie* (those from the former privileged classes) surely recognized each other, as did those discriminated against for their connections with the clergy. Those "networks of enemies" that the Stalinist regime so feared were not always purely imaginary: the regime's own discriminatory policies tended to create them.

In both countries, religion had a major impact in generating or reshaping communities outside *Volksgemeinschaft*.[70] In the Soviet Union, the state had a determined atheistic commitment; all religious confessions were subject to persecution (though the level went up and down), until the regime's partial reconciliation with the Orthodox Church during the war. The assault on the Orthodox Church was particularly vicious in Russia during the Cultural Revolution of the late 1920s and early 1930s, when priests were arrested en masse ("dekulakized"), church bells were taken down, many churches were forcibly closed, and rumors of apocalypse and the coming of Antichrist swept the countryside. The campaign against the Orthodox Church pushed many Orthodox Christians into sects, which met secretly in people's houses, usually without priests, but during the Great Purges it was the turn of the sectarians to suffer heavily. The Soviet authorities regarded sects – not without reason – as ipso facto anti-Soviet communities.

In Germany, Nazi leaders and ideologists such as Heinrich Himmler and Alfred Rosenberg called for a religiosity (labeled *Gottgläubigkeit*) strictly disconnected from the Christian churches and operating against them. Parallel to their efforts to exclude church from the public sphere, Nazi Party activists strove to expand state (and party) regulation of elementary schools. Here, however, actions for nonreligious schools met stubborn nonacceptance on the part of many parents (until the state cracked down on them in 1937 and 1938). In other arenas the forms and intensity of confrontation differed, as a result of the different profiles of confessional activities. In the Protestant sphere a considerable segment of pastors and parish members supported the formation of the Nazi-leaning *Deutsche Christen* (DC), praising its claim for a rebirth of the nation that would overcome the onslaught of "Jewish materialism." In

---

[70] On religion in the Soviet Union in the 1930s, see Edward E. Roslof, *Red Priests: Renovationism, Russian Orthodoxy, and Revolution, 1905–1946* (Bloomington: Indiana University Press, 2002), and Daniel Peris, *Storming the Heavens: The Soviet League of the Militant Godless* (Ithaca, NY: Cornell University Press, 1998). On religion and the everyday, see Sheila Fitzpatrick, *Stalin's Peasants: Resistance and Survival in the Russian Village after Collectivization* (New York: Oxford University Press, 1994), pp. 204–14. The everydayness of the metropolitan case of Berlin is at the center of: Manfred Gailus, *Protestantismus und Nationalsozialismus: Studien zur nationalsozialistischen Durchdringung des protestanischen Sozialmilieus in Berlin* (Cologne: Böhlau, 2001); on the "other side" of the confessional divide that had enormous bearing in Germany until the late 1950s; cf. the case study Kevin P. Spicer, *Resisting the Third Reich: The Catholic Clergy in Hitler's Berlin* (DeKalb: Northern Illinois University Press, 2004); on the "German Christian Movement," also in its everydayish aspects, see Doris L. Bergen, *Twisted Cross: The German Christian Movement in the Third Reich* (Chapel Hill: University of North Carolina Press, 1966).

Berlin, a quarter of all parishes quickly came under DC domination, while half were split between DC adherents and dissenters.[71]

The Catholic Church showed a similar restraint with regard to persecution of Jews. However, local priests were often outspoken in their criticism of the "renewed heathendom" of the Nazis, notwithstanding threats by the Gestapo and actual incarceration. In general, persecution of Catholic priests was harsher – since the church authorities tried to defend their sphere (especially in schooling)[72] much more persistently against Nazi interventions than their Protestant counterparts. Concretely, this could mean a struggle for the cross in the classroom. Nazi efforts to ban Catholic youth associations did not have much effect until the late 1930s, when the government shut down the remaining ones. Still, the priests who had presided over these associations could outflank the prohibition by reorganizing these activities as parish based, enabling many groups of young men and women to continue to meet and pursue their church-related commitment. At least in the countryside they sometimes outmaneuvered HJ and BDM. These efforts, however, remained limited to the issue of local control, without impinging upon the "national" and "patriotic" sentiments that were common to fervent Christians (both Catholic and Protestant) and Nazi activists.

In the Soviet case, arguably, villages often became something like passive-resistance communities, particularly in the first half of the 1930s, as a result of the peasants' passionate objections to collectivization – something to which there is no German analogue. Judging by the persistent rumors in the Russian and Ukrainian countryside of imminent rescue by invading foreigners in the prewar years, peasants seem to have been resentfully conscious of being outside the real "Soviet" community of the urban and educated. While Soviet values were not totally absent from the villages (being propagated mainly by the teacher, or sometimes the kolkhoz chairman), acceptance of them by the young was often tantamount to a decision to leave and find one's fortune in the town.[73] No real "peasants into Soviets" process is observable until the war – and then it was most noticeable among peasant men conscripted into military service.

CONCLUSION: BONDING – AND ENERGIZING

This comparative inspection of practices and relationships of the everyday shows that people in both societies bonded and found themselves bound to others in manifold ways. "Mass society" in general, and "totalitarian rule" in particular, may have twisted, devalued, or even destroyed some social

---

[71] Manfred Gailus, *Protestantismus und Nationalsozialismus*, 637–66.

[72] In 1937–8, however, the church was forced to succumb to Nazi pressure and accept the abolition of confessional schooling, Franz Sonnenberger, "'Der neue Kulturkampf': Die Gemeinschafts-schule und ihre historischen Voraussetzungen," in *Bayern in der NS-Zeit*, vol. 3, eds. Martin Broszat et al. (Munich: Oldenbourg, 1981), 235–327, 306–24.

[73] For elaboration of these points, see Fitzpatrick, *Stalin's Peasants*.

relationships – for example, those of kin, class, or milieu – as Hannah Arendt has argued. Concomitantly, though, in both societies people generated new relationships and transformed old ones. The weight of tradition faded and the younger generation was privileged over their elders. In both the Nazi and the Stalinist case, the regimes were inspired by grand schemes of mobilization of the "masses." These required, or at least licensed, the remodeling of bonds. At the same time, the drive for (self-)mobilization gave a stark emotional charge to practices of inclusion and exclusion.

The exclusionary dynamics that adherents of the Nazi and the Soviet regimes simultaneously stimulated and relied upon meant that stigmatized minorities were forced to sever their bonds with *Volksgemeinschaft,* a very painful if not deadly process that generated despair that oftentimes led to existential loneliness among those excluded. As to Jewish Germans, however, bitterness and anger of the excluded fostered activities to withstand the onslaught, in particular among wives and mothers.[74] For those within the realm of *Volksgemeinschaft* and its Soviet equivalent, however, the process of exclusion relied on but also enhanced an emotional charge that cemented bonds among the excluders. Ousting "others," as both German and Soviet experience repeatedly showed, was an effective means of generating community.

Family bonds were not demonstrably weakened in either Nazi Germany or the Soviet Union, though there is more room for argument on the Soviet side because of antifamily rhetoric and the Pavlik Morozov exemplar. But Soviet words and Soviet deeds on family were often contradictory; moreover, in the face of repression and coping with a difficult external environment, families tended to draw together. Bonds outside the family showed little if any change on the German side in peacetime. On the Soviet side, by contrast, the closing down of independent associations had an obvious negative impact on some kinds of sociability. The coming of war, however, definitely strengthened and energized extrafamilial social bonds, especially those of comradeship at the front and also to a lesser extent in the rear. And since war was fundamental to both regimes – a raison d'être on the Nazi side; a long-awaited and feared test of regime legitimacy and national strength on the Soviet – this particular effect should probably be regarded as systemic rather than purely contingent.

The Arendtian notion of atomization turns out to be least satisfactory to the historian in its assumption that new bonds and new types of bonds cannot be generated in "totalitarian" societies. Clearly such new types of bonds *were* generated: those associated with the new Soviet workplace and *blat* are good examples. Of long-term as well as immediate significance was the shared consciousness that developed among young activists in both Germany and the Soviet Union of belonging to a special cohort destined, along with the nation, for greatness. New bonds of particular poignancy were forged in the course of military service during the war. In addition, the practices of both regimes

---

[74] Marion Kaplan, *Between Dignity and Despair: Jewish Women in the Aftermath of November 1938* (New York: Leo Baeck Institute, 1996).

unintentionally generated resistance communities or networks (a new kind of bond), especially among religious believers.

This brings us back to the major deficiency of totalitarianism as a model for historical analysis: the assumption that totalitarianism is a state to which there is an entry but no exit, that (as Friedrich and Brzezinski argued in the social-science version of totalitarianism) the model is self-perpetuating and self-reinforcing, that (uniquely among human societies) there was no possibility of internally generated change or development other than an ever-closer approach to the ideal type. Perhaps this notion was easier to accept with regard to Nazi Germany, often seen as possessing a dynamic of radicalization that inevitably ends in self-destruction (though, assuming German victory in World War II was not an impossibility, can we really regard that self-destruction – and the accompanying loss of a developmental future – as inevitable?). In the Soviet case, it turned out that there was an exit from totalitarianism (post 1953), in other words, that the historian's assumption that things will always change and decay (the historian's equivalent of the physicist's principle of entropy) need not be suspended in this case. Indeed, we can go beyond the entropy principle to reaffirm the historian's truism that things are always "growing new" as well as growing old, for it turns out that the most interesting question concerning social bonds in these two societies is not about their erosion but rather about the forms of their regeneration.

In this context, it may be helpful to return to the issue of energizing the everyday that we have alluded to at various points in this essay. Both contemporary rhetoric and later recollections of both societies stress the importance of the stimulation of intense emotions and energetic action that occurred under these regimes. Activists (many of them young) embraced the regimes' projects and put in all their energies behind them. To cooperate actively and, thus, to propel the great cause: these dynamics of energizing oneself and others provided strong emotional charges reverberating in people's everyday.

The drive to participate had many faces and operated on more than one level. In both societies, people in all segments and groups were caught up in the excitement of active involvement in a process of fundamental transformation of things both large and small.[75] Thus, efforts to improve or boost production in agriculture or industry cannot be detached from the desires of individuals or groups for social promotion or economic bonuses, for example. The same can be shown for professional groups and for women, whether at home or (increasingly in both societies) on the job. In the Soviet Union, this energizing process was clearly manifest during the industrialization drive and Cultural Revolution at the beginning of the 1930s, while in the German case such dynamics shaped

---

[75] In Germany electrical power was rather successfully advertised as energizer for women to speed up housework and connect it with wage work, esp. in 1934–5 (*Elektroangriff*), see Hartmut Berghoff, "Methoden der Verbrauchslenkung im Nationalsozialismus," in *Wirtschaftskontrolle und Recht in der nationalsozialistischen Diktatur*, ed. Dieter Gosewinkel (Frankfurt am Main: Klostermann, 2005), 281–316, 306–9.

activities ranging from economy and rearmament to sports, film, and fashion throughout the prewar Nazi period. In both the Soviet Union and Nazi Germany, it became paramount during the war. Even mounting shocks of violence – on the Soviet side during the recuperation of the torched land by the Red Army in 1944; on the German side by the Red Army's final offensive in late January 1945 as well as by ubiquitous allied bombings in the following weeks – invigorated the potential of self-energizing rather than exhausting it. To be sure, it is the everyday of those actively included in *Volksgemeinschaft* – the "participants in socialist construction," to use the Soviet term – that is illuminated by the energizing paradigm. Those who were excluded and suffered social death found themselves literally "switched off."

8

The New Man in Stalinist Russia and Nazi Germany

Peter Fritzsche and Jochen Hellbeck

This essay explores anthropological ideals and practices in Stalinist Russia and Nazi Germany. Both regimes shared a fundamental commitment to producing a higher human type, and they both sponsored ambitious initiatives to transform, remake, and perfect their populations. But the ideologies that underwrote the "New Man" differed substantially. Whereas the Soviet system conceived of nothing less than the liberation of all humanity, the Nazis sought to create a master race in order to organize a new racial hierarchy in Europe. Yet both regimes cast their policies as answers and solutions to a perceived crisis of the contemporary world. Both identified the "bourgeois" world as an "old," obsolescent order against which they deployed their visions of a New Man. As a result, both regimes stood in dialogue – sometimes implicitly, sometimes explicitly – with each other. Taken together, the visions and policies of these regimes represented a radical and total rejection of liberalism and its pursuit of the freedoms and rights of the individual. The New Man emerged as a constituent of an insistently collective subject, in the case of the Soviet Union, a classless, Communist society; in the case of the Third Reich, the racial union of Aryans. Although they were illiberal, both regimes were profoundly modern precisely because of their dedication to remaking and redefining the human species. Their project encompassed an alternative, illiberal modernity.

The New Man was an alternative, but not completely unfamiliar figure because he was designed with the tools of science and rationality and in accord with basic premises of Western "progress." In exploring this design, we ultimately pose the question about the still dominant assumption that liberalism is the basic default position of the West. We show that liberalism is a highly contingent position, under furious attack for much of the twentieth century.[1] And we follow the deployment of alternative ideals of being and methods of

---

[1] Mark Mazower, *Dark Continent: Europe's Twentieth Century* (New York: Vintage Books, 1999).

striving that will strike readers as unfamiliar, but are contemporaneous to and as modern as the liberal self.

Our essay pursues two goals. While its main focus is on Stalinist and National Socialist practices of remaking man, it also investigates the phenomenon of the modern New Man as such. The New Man was pursued by both regimes but was never exclusively their property. In examining this broader issue of the New Man, we seek to leave behind the totalitarian paradigm that links the New Man and the radical utopian impulses he represents exclusively to the ambitions of Nazism and Stalinism. Instead we present the New Man as a variant of modernity, at home in the Third Reich and the Soviet Union, but rooted in paradigms of bourgeois, liberal society in the nineteenth and twentieth centuries. To show this, our contribution explores the prehistory of Stalinism and Nazism. In Russia, the figure of the New Man was intensely discussed and tried on prior to the revolution of 1917; the same holds true for Germany before 1933. This prehistory exposes the ideological trajectories on which Stalinism and Nazism rested but also the deeper interrelations between the New Man and modern times.

Throughout this essay, our emphasis is on transformation of humanity as project and process. In writing or talking about the New Man, his ideologists had in mind first and foremost the transformation over time of physical human beings. Yet this physical, day-to-day commitment gets lost in most studies of the New Man, which investigate the figure as a merely rhetorical or aesthetic construct and follow the debates about the New Man without delving into the actual work of creating such a figure. Similarly, most scholars conceive this agenda as a top-down narrative in which artists envision or political regimes decree but otherwise sideline the actual life and exertions of the New Man. By contrast, we will pay attention to the labor of doing, and to the incentives, appeals, and the strivings of individuals engaged in their own self-transformation. In other words, we stress the predicates as well as the objects of design. We propose to investigate closely the intersection between verbal or artistic representation and life itself, between political and cultural prescriptions and individual appropriations and accounts of working through.

Illiberal modernity not only demands close attention to the particular historiography and placement of Russia and Germany, it also reveals drastic configurations of time and space. In the case of Russia, early conceptions of the New Man originated from an acute sense of civilizational backwardness, and in the subsequent implementation of the New Man, Soviet Russia claimed for itself the role of humanity's vanguard. In large measure it was the figure of the New Man which justified this temporal leap from deficient modernity to modernity consummated. Germany, by contrast, organized itself spatially against the rest of a racially degenerate Europe. Already after World War I, it conceived of European space as a vast zone of danger which at once needed to be managed and exploited carefully in order to create a greater German empire. The German New Man was not available for the rest of humanity or for the future, but stood as the most able type in the eternal present of the "thousand-year" Reich.

The arrival of the "New Man" depended on an epistemological break with familiar ideas about nature and possibility. It presumed an apprehension of the lightness of being, the startling realization that men and women were not necessarily formed in nature or molded by reason and thus basically alike. The "New Man" appeared as a defiantly secular figure, one who was no longer concerned with religious or moral purification but available nonetheless for the wholesale transformation of both the soul and the body in projects of this worldly transcendence. The "New Man" was also only conceivable after confidence in the Enlightenment project in discovering "Man" had given way to doubt as to the unity nature of social existence. His appearance was thus deeply entangled in the French Revolution, which had left observers uncertain about the compass of human behavior or the direction of history. Burke, for example, found the revolution to be "the most astonishing that has hitherto happened in the world," precisely because it defied "common maxims" and "common means." Robespierre himself declared that "the theory of revolutionary government is as new as the revolution which brought it into being. It is not necessary to search for it in the books of political writers, who did not foresee this revolution."[2] Both the enthusiasts for and detractors of the revolution repeatedly referred to the "new epoch" in human history whose signature was the audacious repudiation of the "common maxims" of the past in the name of the undefined potential of the future.

The New Man outlived the French Revolution because he gained new definition and new prowess amid the energetic motions of nineteenth-century industrial development. What the Industrial Revolution revealed was both the makability and the fragility of the world. If nineteenth-century Europeans served the general cause of improvement, surveying wilderness, clearing forests, draining swamps, digging mines, they also worried obsessively about the imminence of revolution, the breakability of the social order, the disease and poverty of the new industrial cities, and the biological degeneration of the modern individual. At the turn of the twentieth century, it was technological and scientific advance, rather than revolutionary virtue, that invigorated the construction projects of collective subjectivity. Engineers, scientists, as well as intellectuals assembled an array of efficient and eugenic bodies designed to overcome degenerative cycles of history. Social pathology and social experimentation went hand in hand, but, as recent histories of psychiatry, social welfare, public health, and universal education have shown, these efforts were more preoccupied with renovation than transformation and they functioned to discipline, not transcend. A new generation of vitalist and youth groups did seek at this time to transcend the material limits of bourgeois society and to found new postliberal communities based on faith and sentiment rather than interest or civic responsibility.

---

[2] Quoted in Lynn Avery Hunt, *Politics, Culture and Class in the French Revolution* (Berkeley: University of California Press, 1984), 54.

Although these remained confined to small and scattered groups, they retained the transformative idea of the New Man, which socialists had for the most part discarded; by 1914, the most immediate heir to the French revolutionary tradition, the Second International, no longer conceived of a postapocalyptic "new time" or cherished the "New Men" and "New Women" who might inhabit it. The nineteenth century thus ended on a very different note than it began, with more emphasis on up-to-date but nonetheless reliable "common maxims" and "common means" and much less value placed on the potential of revolution to fundamentally remake the world.

Where the idea of the New Man continued to flourish was on the perceived margins of Europe, in Russia, where the notion of fashioning new beings out of nature acquired more and more urgency. Russian thought in the nineteenth century gave the most sustained attention to the New Man as a prototype for a new humanity first glimpsed during the French Revolution and later reanimated by the Communist revolution. Elsewhere, the New Man only inhabited the literary imagination or was confined to small utopian communities. It is only in World War I that a new, authoritative version of the New Man reappeared, this time in Germany, and one designed to secure the survival of a particular racial collective that is eventually realized in National Socialism and therefore quite unlike the universal ambitions of Communism's New Man. Collective responsibilities shaped both the Soviet and the Nazi New Man, but the types were fundamentally different. Whereas the Soviet New Man created himself inside a humanist tradition and offered himself as a prototype to the West, the Nazi New Man fashioned himself against the threats that allegedly besieged the German nation and considered his appearance the guarantee of German survival. He had nothing to offer the West. The very physical conception of danger and possibility meant that the New Man in Germany more resembled a warrior and worked on his body, whereas the New Man in the Soviet Union was to approximate the ideal of a total man, which involved the soul as well as the body.

There was also more stress on the individual process of becoming a New Man in Soviet Russia, whereas the responsibility to accept the larger demands of the racial collective always predominated in Germany. But both visions held out the possibility of transcending liberalism, of working on the self, and of serving larger social entities. In Russia, the New Man expressed the fulfillment of universal potential; he stood out as an exemplar to the rest of the world. The German New Man, by contrast, stood duty-bound to the imperatives of the Aryan race; he was its representative alone. Neither in Russia nor in Germany was the New Man conceived of as a gendered being, as the English translation may lead one to think. *Chelovek* and *Mensch*, the Russian and German renderings of "man" in this context, refer to the generic features of humanity. In spite of the gendered misreadings that the English rendering of *novyi chelovek* or *Neuer Mensch* as New Man may invite, this translation is historically more precise than other variants, such as "new men and women," which projects a gender sensitivity onto historical actors that they lacked, or "new person," which individualizes the transformative vision and elides the principal subject and object of transformation: the collective.[3]

The figure of the New Man has a tradition in Russia dating back to the mid-nineteenth century. It is primarily associated with a lineage of radical thought born of a sense of the country's particularly oppressive social and political structures, which were held responsible for the underdevelopment of personality and society. This diagnosis was tied to visions of individual and social liberation that would restore to Russian citizens their humanity and advance the Russian state along the road of historical progress. The New Man invited more radical expressions as well: the longing for revolution and for the creation of a new world that would catapult Russia into a radiant future. Such visions, and the ethical investment that was required for their realization, were central to the aspirations and the self-legitimation of the radical intelligentsia, a professionally and socially disparate group of people united by their profound disenchantment with the existing sociopolitical order and their overriding moral commitment to changing it. Intellectually the radical intelligentsia stood in the tradition of German idealism, notably the left Hegelian tradition, from which they derived a firm belief in the lawful progression of history according to a scheme of progressive rationality, self-consciousness, and human liberation. The principal task of the intelligentsia was to educate and enlighten, to raise individuals to the stature of true "human beings" (*chelovek*) and critically thinking "personalities" (*lichnost'*), who would then rise up against their oppressors and thus move history along on its preordained emancipatory path.

The enormous "backwardness" inherent in this diagnosis posed no hindrance to the New Man; on the contrary: in dialectical fashion, to conceive Russia as a negation helped clear the way for envisioning a totally different future, a negation of the negation. Similarly the marginal position occupied by the radical intelligentsia in Russian society – their stigma as "superfluous people" in the existing order – could easily be reverted in gestures of self-signification, as these individuals refashioned themselves into exemplars of the New Man, the vanguard of the future. Literature in particular was conceived of as a "socially transformative practice," less to provide aesthetic edification than to show the road to progress and liberation. The ultimate standard for the aesthetic evaluation of a given work of art was History itself. As the influential critic Vissarion Belinskii maintained, "Only the results of the historical development of society" revealed whether a piece of writing was true or false, useful or worthless, good or bad. This was the standard with which the writer Nikolai Chernyshevsky, Belinskii's contemporary, wanted his works to be read and which also shaped the reception of his book *What Is to Be Done?*

---

[3] See Lynne Attwood and Catriona Kelly, "Programmes for Identity: the 'New Man' and the 'New Woman,'" in *Constructing Russian Culture in the Age of Revolution, 1881–1940*, eds. Catriona Kelly and David Shepherd (Oxford and New York: Oxford University Press, 1998), 256–90.

(1863), one of the very first Russian publications to address the "New Man" by name.[4]

Chernyshevsky regarded himself as acting as an "enlightener and a benefactor of humanity." His novel indulged in a vision of a rational and technicized world closely patterned on prescripts formulated by the French utopian socialists St. Simon and Charles Fourier. The focus of the novel was on the "new people" – a group of morally pure and rationally harmonious individuals who were rendered almost indistinguishable from one another, precisely because they were meant as allegorical representations of liberated humanity. The New Man as advocated by Chernyshevsky and other members of his generation was an abstraction standing for the liberated human being of the future. Chernyshevsky greatly shaped the first generations of Russian Marxists and their notions of subjectivity and ideal humanity. *What Is to be Done?* was a virtual bible for Lenin's older brother, Aleksandr Ul'ianov, until his execution for his unsuccessful attempt to kill the tsar. Lenin then became interested in the novel and later declared that it had "overturned" his life. Chernyshevsky's greatest service, according to Lenin, was that his novel showed the particular type of man that a revolutionary should be and specified ways to attain this ideal.[5] The restless activity, the worship of rational consciousness and mastery over the "spontaneous" forces of the body, and the proclivity to interpret human psychology in physiological terms that the Soviets cherished were prefigured by Chernyshevsky. Lenin's indebtedness to Chernyshevsky showed most clearly in a book which he conceived of as a program of political action in the spirit of Chernyshevsky's novel. Lenin's "What Is to Be Done?" (1902) outlined the vanguard of party cadres who by the strength of their consciousness and will were to guide the proletariat to self-knowledge and revolution.

Nevertheless, Lenin and other Russian Marxists at all times stressed their adherence to Marx over any other intellectual influence. Marxism, Lenin declared, was infinitely superior to early, "utopian" socialist theories, including the ideas of Chernyshevsky, because it contained a "scientifically" valid interpretation of man's historical destiny and provided the historical dialectics necessary for reaching the ideal future.[6] The historical nature of the New Man was now buttressed with a "scientific" foundation. Furthermore, no Russian Marxist imagined the road to the New Man separate from the proletariat. Representations of the factory, factory workers, and scenes of collective labor

---

[4] V. G. Belinskii, *Polnoe sobranie sochinenii*, vol. 7 (Moscow: Akademiia Nauk, 1955), 101. *What Is to Be Done?* bore the subtitle: "Tales about New People." We capitalize the term "History" when seeking to convey the actorial sense that Chernyshevsky and other Russian progenitors of the New Man (many of them standing in a Hegelian tradition) connoted with its usage.

[5] Irina Paperno, *Chernyshevsky and the Age of Realism: A Study in the Semiotics of Behavior* (Stanford, CA: Stanford University Press 1988), 30–3; see also Bianka Pietrow-Ennker, *Russlands "neue Menschen": Die Entwicklung der Frauenbewegung von den Anfängen bis zur Oktoberrevolution* (Frankfurt: Campus, 1999).

[6] Ark. Lomakin, "Lenin o Chernyshevskom," *Revoliutsiia i kul'tura*, no. 22 (1928): 5–12, esp. 12.

eventually displaced earlier views of the intelligentsia circle and the solitary university student as molds for the New Man.[7] Finally, Marxism complemented an emotionally detached narrative of rationally minded individuals calmly progressing toward the ideal future with a story rich in historical drama, saturated with notions of struggle and a mythical yearning for self-completion.[8] While the proletariat, according to Marx, led humanity's struggle for freedom and self-realization, it was not destined to incarnate the New Man of communist society. The proletariat represented History's negation, as it struggled toward synthesis. The synthetic New Man was a transformed worker with rich intellectual and artistic powers. Marx's aesthetic utopia was markedly romantic and idealist in spirit, betraying his early nineteenth-century influences. Economic activity would turn into an act of artistic creation, on a planetary scope. Capitalist alienation and suffering would give way to "free conscious activity," with mankind proceeding to remake the human species and the world "in accordance with the laws of beauty"[9] This romantic image would resurface in strikingly literal fashion nearly a century later, in Stalin era representations of the ideal New Soviet Man.

The Stalinist regime cited Chernyshevsky, Marx, and Lenin as intellectual and political forefathers of the New Man. But it was the writer Maxim Gorky who more than any other individual thinker contributed to the contours and the meaning of the Stalinist New Man. If Chernyshevsky and Lenin emphasized rationality and historicity, Gorky endowed the New Man with two further traits: heroism and collectivism. Every individual was a potential hero, had an inborn fullness of life, strength, and beauty, which were realized by mobilizing the will and serving a larger, transindividual whole: society, humanity, or the course of history. Life, conceived by Gorky in Nietzschean vitalist terms, was realized in an expressive dynamic that propelled the individual "forward and higher" and raised him to the level of a "MAN with capital letters." Those who did not strive toward this ideal did not truly live. Gorky expressed nothing but disdain for "bourgeois" individualism, narrow-minded, property-seeking "philistines," who lived to the detriment of fellow humanity.[10]

Of the many competing visions of the New Man proposed before the Soviet revolution, only those would later be amalgamated into Stalinist representations of ideal humanity which could present themselves as being historical in

---

[7] The new focus on the proletariat imparted considerably more maleness to notions of the New Man, who up to then had often been represented as a female individual. Still, the proletariat was conceived of as a universal human type, expressing a universal human quest for liberation, and thus comprising men as well as women.

[8] Robert Tucker, *Philosophy and Myth in Karl Marx*, rev. ed. (Cambridge: Cambridge University Press, 1972), Igal Halfin, *From Darkness to Light: Class, Consciousness, and Salvation in Revolutionary Russia* (Pittsburgh, University of Pittsburgh Press, 2000).

[9] Karl Marx and Friedrich Engels, *Historisch-Kritische Gesamtausgabe, erste Abteilung*, vol. 3 (Frankfurt am Main: Marx-Engels-Archiv, Verl.-Ges, 1932), 88; Tucker, 158, 234, 236.

[10] See especially Hans Günther, *Der sozialistische Übermensch: M. Gor'kij und der sowjetische Heldenmythos* (Stuttgart: J. B. Metzler, 1993).

nature and in accordance with History's continued progression toward the Communist future.[11] Reason – defined as an understanding of the course of history – and will – indispensable to implement revolutionary politics – were two inalienable qualities of the new Soviet Man. For reasons specific to Russian history in the nineteenth century, the demonstration of the laws of history was a privileged domain of writers and critics, and it was these writers and critics who became chief "engineers" of the New Man. The privileging of both historical consciousness and the writer as its chief disseminator also explains why the textual mode – literature – was so important, both as prescriptive mirror and as working tool in the creation of the New Man. History, literature, and textuality form an inextricable whole, central for the definition of the New Man in the Russian and Soviet contexts.

In Germany, the combination of the mass experience of total war and the disaster of military defeat prompted an intensive scrutiny of new forms of warfare, new types of warriors, and, ultimately, new modes of civic responsibility. More than anything, the war created entirely new zones of danger and made urgent the design of new social, political, and psychological fortifications. It was in the conditions of Carl Schmitt's division of the world into friends and foes and his demand that politics develop the capacities of the nation that the New Man flourished. Older genealogies of youth and Nietzschean vitality were rearticulated, but it was the experience of the war that armed the imagination, made urgent the search innovation, and made available a scarred, but politicized generation to carry out the task of national redesign. This was an insistently German project. In this case, the New Man was not available as an international model but rather regarded as a necessity for national survival. Even before the war ended, observers identified a distinctive twentieth-century soldier whose movements became more closely calibrated to the intensity of technological battle. Increasingly, the harsh struggle on the front, rather than the national cause, defined the physical features of Germany's fighting men. Hard, resolute, depersonalized faces correspond to the steel helmets that nearly covered them: the man of steel.[12] The unrelenting demands and unprecedented horrors of the war fascinated observers who reported from the front on the new elites of the twentieth century. Aviators, in particular, appeared as bold explorers of a New World of danger and destruction, and they returned to Earth fundamentally transformed with "iron nerves, steady eyes, [and] quick decisiveness." They were imagined as steeling and training their nerves, thereby cultivating the virtues required in this brutal war of existence. As a new species

---

[11] For early-twentieth-century Russian debates about the new man, see Bernice Glatzer Rosenthal, *New Myth, New World: From Nietzsche to Stalinism* (University Park: Pennsylvania State University Press, 2002); and Irina Gutkin, *The Cultural Origins of the Socialist Realist Aesthetic, 1890–1934* (Evanston, IL: Northwestern University Press, 1999); Derek Müller, *Der Topos des Neuen Menschen in der russischen und sowjetrussischen Geistesgeschichte* (Bern: P. Lang, 1998).

[12] Bernd Hüppauf, "Langemarck, Verdun and the Myth of a New Man in Germany after the First World War," *War and Society* 6 (1988): 70–103.

of machine men, aces fascinated because they adhered to the harsh injunctions of modern war.[13] These wartime sightings were elaborated by postwar writers such as Ernst Jünger, who announced the creation of a new breed of machine men: "fearless and fabulous, unsparing of blood and sparing of pity – a race that builds machines and trusts to machines, to whom machines are not soulless iron, but engines of might which it controls with cold reason and hot blood. This puts a new face on the world."[14]

In Jünger's accounts, the battlefield itself overshadows the national arenas of Germany, France, and Britain, which are hardly named in *Storm of Steel* or *Copse 125* or later in *Der Arbeiter*. Rather, it was the mobilization of material, physical, and psychological resources that fascinated Jünger and convinced him that Europeans had entered a new, more dangerous, and vastly more powerful epoch. The war, he wrote, has "dug itself permanently into us": "This hard and pitiless landscape of the war...will brand those who are strong enough not to be crushed beneath its impress with an imprint that will never be erased."[15] And it is a measure of the authority and credibility of the image of this "New Man" that Jünger's books were best-sellers and translated into English already in the 1920s, and that Jünger himself, without any literary pedigree, emerged as the most visible representative of the front generation. The technological imperatives and the mass aspect to twentieth-century Europe remained clearly in view for all the "new age" diagnosticians from Spengler to Ortega y Gasset. The most popular contemporary history of the postwar period, H. G. Wells's *The Outline of History* (1920), left no doubt that Europe had entered a dramatically new time zone. He forecast a future conflict that would leave the continent ravaged by air attacks, making the "bombing of those "'prentice days," 1914–18, look like mere "child's play."[16] It is often forgotten that the fear of massive air attack rooted itself as deeply among Europeans in the 1920s and 1930s as did the terror of all-out nuclear war during the Cold War. The horrible specter of air war led to a growing interest in the psychological mobilization of the civilian population, which throughout this period was imagined, in the pages of the *Berliner Illustrierte Zeitung*, for example, either as an unstable, vulnerable mass or as a disciplined, gas-masked collective that had learned to adapt to the remorseless demands of international warfare. Modern technology in the 1920s arguably served as a vast metonym for war itself. The constant iterations of the "New Man" or the "new type," the athlete, the race-car driver, and the aviator to which popular magazines introduced readers, can be seen as civilian projections of the new warrior. The circulation of big-city traffic, the discipline of rationalization, and the fine calibration of

---

[13] See Peter Fritzsche, *A Nation of Fliers: German Aviation and the Popular Imagination* (Cambridge, MA: Harvard University Press, 1992), 96–7.

[14] Ernst Jünger, *Copse 125: A Chronicle from the Trench Warfare of 1918* (New York: Howard Fertig, 1988), 21.

[15] Ibid., viii, 58.

[16] H. G. Wells, *The Outline of History: Being a Plain History of Life and Mankind* (New York: Macmillan, 1920), 1084–5, quoting the Royal United Service Institution's Sir Louis Jackson.

larger and more powerful machines retold the storyline of wartime innovation and wartime necessity again and again. That women or androgynous figures frequently represented the new type dramatizes how the imagined imperatives of the technological present revised even familiar categories of gender and smudged the boundaries between the public and the private and the domestic and the political.[17] Although much of the armor of the New Man and the New Woman was no different from that of their counterparts in the Russian imagination – steely nerves, sophisticated circuitry, sheer durability – the German project was primarily biological or biotechnological and was pursued in order to build a new warrior type. The site of the production of the New Man was the body, and the collective it was to serve was the imperiled nation.

By the early 1930s, the characteristics of the individualized "Man of Steel" were projected onto the *Volk* itself. In the new collective practices of sports, mass entertainment, and political mobilization, the *Volk* appeared as a subject available for national transformation. It was this collective ideal that Ernst Jünger celebrated in *Der Arbeiter* and that the Nazis eventually racialized. "The survival strategies of those who escaped the war existed as a flight into fantasies of coldness and body armor," as Jünger described, and then "into the daydream of the nation," which was animated in the political labor and collective dreams of thousands of Germans in the years before Hitler's seizure of power.[18] The New Man became the means to realize the New *Volk*.

If Russian ideologues of the New Man worked on their souls, their German counterparts worked on their bodies to serve the nation. Yet both types strained to leave behind familiar practices and familiar precincts. The New Men in the Soviet Union and in Germany conceived their work in epochal historical terms. The movement from the secure and knowable confines of the family onto the still indefinite terrain of the nation was accelerated by the sense of having been cut off from the past: Jünger's "peasant boys" tumble into "world history." In this respect, the autobiographical statements of old Nazi fighters assembled by the American sociologist Theodor Abel in 1936 are quite revealing. Activists remembered straining to discern historical itineraries in the years after 1918 and described the profound unsettlement of their individual lives in the light of new social relations and new collective commitments. They indicate considerable self-reflection about the disjunction between past and present and the transitory nature of the present day. To account for his journey to National Socialism, an East Prussian farmer began his memoirs with the day "exactly twenty years ago, when I was only five years old. I first saw field-grey-clad soldiers with sabres and guns, and my own father dressed the same way. My mother watched, serious and worried. War! I heard this

---

[17] Lynne-Marie Hoskins Frame, "Forming and Reforming the New Woman in Weimar Germany" (Ph.D. diss., University of California, Berkeley, 1997).

[18] Hannes Heer and Klaus Naumann, "Introduction," in *War of Extermination: The German Military in World War II, 1941–44*, eds. H. Heer and K. Naumann (New York: Berghahn Books, 2000), 4.

word then for the first time, but I soon understood it."[19] A sense that an older world had been left behind shaped these narratives: "My old world broke asunder in my experiences" in the war, recalled one Catholic National Socialist.[20] Future party members remembered themselves as ravenous readers, fascinated with history already in school, and later browsing among newspapers until they reported finally picking up a Nazi edition or visiting all sorts of political meetings until they found themselves in agreement with one or another Nazi orator. "Learning, reading, comparing" was the way one future Nazi, a teacher from Vorsfelde, explained his task; in the 1920s two books stood on his desk: "Adolf Hitler's *Mein Kampf* and Karl Marx. Jawohl Karl Marx!" Eventually, he admitted, "Karl Marx disappeared"; Hitler did not.[21] This stock taking, which echoes throughout autobiographies in this period – from *Mein Kampf* to Ernst von Salomon's fictionalized memoir, *Die Geächteten* – is remarkable evidence for the visualization of the indeterminate, but sensible forces of a historical new time.

Nazi activists, who are the only ones for whom we have a large set of autobiographies, recalled as well the sheer strain of discovering the nation. "Almost daily I cycled five miles of bad road into town to listen to a Nazi speech, and then home again alone," recalled one old fighter.[22] "Night after night, Sunday after Sunday, in wind and rain," activists spread the Nazi word on bicycles and trucks in the late 1920s and early 1930s.[23] Hiking, bicycling, and motoring to the next village, and eventually on to the regional center for larger rallies and to big cities for national events are references that recur repeatedly in Nazi autobiographies and indicate just how nonlocal the identifications of the new political self had become. The Abel respondents also testified to their explorations of unfamiliar social precincts: "I walked through the city. I wandered through the Communist district. I talked to the people there a number of times," recalled a young middle-class youth.[24] What Nazi campaigners endeavored to realize was the myth of the trenches, in which soldiers from a variety of social backgrounds allegedly discovered their common German being, or the experience of the Weimar era *Werkstudent*, the impoverished middle-class students who spent summers working in factories and living among workers.[25] This folksy

---

[19] "The Story of a Farmer," in Theodore Abel, *The Nazi Movement: Why Hitler Came to Power* (New York: Atherton Press, 1966), 289.

[20] Peter H. Merkl, *Political Violence under the Swastika: 581 Early Nazis* (Princeton, NJ: Princeton University Press, 1975), 53.

[21] Rudolf Kahn, folder 31, box 1, Theodore Abel Papers, Hoover Institution Archives, Stanford, CA. See also Fritz Junghanss, folder 526, box 7, Theodore Abel Papers, Hoover Institution Archives, Stanford, CA.

[22] Merkl, *Political Violence*, 132.

[23] Friedrich Kurz, "Meine Erlebnisse in der Kampfzeit," 25 Dec. 1936, Bundesarchiv, NS26/529.

[24] "The Story of a Middle-Class Youth," in Abel, *Nazi Movement*, 269.

[25] In his *Michael: A Novel*, trans. J. Neugroschel (New York: Amok Press, 1987), Goebbels thematizes the work student. See also Michael Kater, "The Work Student: A Socio-Economic Phenomenon of Early Weimar Germany," *Journal of Contemporary History* 10 (1975): 71–94.

evidence is undoubtedly sentimentalized, but it indicates the value placed on cross-class experiences in narratives of political awakening.

The journey of political discovery in the service of a larger, national collective was usually not explained in racial terms, or only vaguely so. Indeed, one of the challenges that Nazi revolutionaries and their sympathizers faced when Hitler came to power in 1933 was to learn how to think racially, to act in racially desirable ways, and thus to become a complete Nazi and an identifiable Aryan. Nonetheless, the political journey in the 1920s was accompanied by an openness to the fact that there were harsh new lessons that had to be followed if the collective good of the nation was to be secured; this epistemological openness before 1933 prepared the ground for the acceptance of a racialized worldview after 1933. The prevalent physiognomical practices of the Weimar era derived from the endeavor to get at the true workings of things. "It was as if one can see the epoch standing in front of the mirror searching for its face," write Claudia Schmölders and Sander L. Gilman: "Left and Right, the political elite sought, if even in vain, for the singular character or the true portrait," whether it was of Bolshevism, the century, or Germans themselves.[26] Scholars have emphasized the ways in which physiognomic typologies added up to a defensive maneuver to give knowable contours to a "society in disarray."[27] But the proliferation of physiognomic readings should also be regarded as an effort to reclassify, to retrieve, and to reach beneath the surface or behind appearances in order to find a new order and a new subjectivity. The "new visuality" (*die neue Schau*), in the words of the racial scholar E. Guenther Gründel, pierced through the insubstantial illusions of the present order to reveal thresholds to another place, new, "the new historical acting subject [*Aktionseinheit*] at the very threshold of a new era." Although Gründel took note of an emerging racial selfhood, conceptions of "social biology" and "racial hygiene" remained indefinite. What was consequential, however, was the general acknowledgment that the fate of the nation depended on the recognition of the true or deep dynamics of history. An emphasis on depth and "vertical thinking" underscored just how incomplete Germany's journey to political self-determination remained; how indebted it was to visual, physiognomical expertise; and how heavy the labor involved in transforming the self to serve the new collective needed to be.[28]

In Germany as well as in Russia, the New Man was deployed amid intense engagement with history. Yet the respective understandings of what actually constituted history differed. Russian, later Soviet, ideologues exuded a striking confidence in the laws of history, which, they knew, animated their revolutionary project. They did not waste time probing the surface for possible alternative meanings, but impatiently proceeded to bring the new world into being. Their

---

[26] Claudia Schmölders and Sander L. Gilman, eds., *Gesichter der Weimarer Republik: Eine physiognomische Kulturgeschichte* (Cologne: DuMont, 2000), 8

[27] Frame, 3.

[28] Gründel, *Die Sendung der jungen Generation: Versuch einer umfassenden revolutionären Sinndeutung der Krise* (Munich: Beck, 1932), 305, 327.

task was to eliminate the developmental gap that separated backward Russia from more advanced industrialized countries, to "catch up and overtake" the bourgeois West. In Germany, by contrast, these very certainties had been under modernist attack since the turn of the century, and their remnants were shattered in the trenches of the Great War. Temporally, Germany was under way to new shores in the wake of the war, while contemporary Russia continued to move on a linear axis of developmental time rooted in the Enlightenment tradition. These different trajectories account for the different shapes of the new man in both systems. Russian ideologues, who placed all their belief in the salvational potential of history, were keen on molding citizens into historical agents who likewise understood the laws of history and acted on their behalf. Hence the orientation toward individuals' "consciousness," their "souls," as the decisive realm in which the new man became manifest. In Germany, on the other hand, the realization that historical certainties had been broken made it necessary to arm the nation and individuals against the vagaries of modern time, a time in which history itself had become delinquent. It was in this danger zone of unprecedented anxiety and possibility that German thinking and acting about the new man developed. It invoked ideals of physical strength, alertness, and a ruthless disposition which were to shield the German nation against frightful processes of erosion and degeneration.

The Soviet regime that came to power in 1917 declared the revolution to be the watershed of world history. The revolution was to mark, in Marxist parlance, the end of mankind's prehistory and the beginning of real humanity. This was of course a self-created myth, which glossed over the fact that the New Man as a concept preexisted 1917, and that most Soviet projects to implement this program were based on preexisting designs. Nevertheless the revolution was a turning point in a political sense: it brought to power a movement which was defined by its commitment to produce an "improved edition of mankind" (Trotsky). In this process, Marxist ideology, the script of humanity's rebellion and self-becoming, turned into a statewide prescription for political action. Thus 1917 was a watershed, not in an empirical sense of producing actual new people, but conceptually, as a marker in historical time. As such the revolution was a real point of origin for a regime committed to transforming the world, and to transforming it according to scientifically measurable laws of historical progress. The Bolshevik state preached a utilitarian morality that legitimated, and in fact demanded, the forcible removal of obstinate remnants of old life, in order to clear the path for the emergence of the new. In the atmosphere of the Civil War, the calls by leading Bolsheviks to "knock out the teeth from old traditions" or to "punch" every "*burzhui* in the mug" (Bukharin) who insulted Soviet power were bound to be read in more than just metaphorical ways.[29] As Bukharin's words suggested, much of the Bolshevik regime's organized violence was directed against the "bourgeoisie," a label that could target anyone who

---

[29] Both quotations from Bukharin, cited by Gerd Koenen, *Utopie der Säuberung: Was war der Kommunismus?* (Berlin: A. Fast, 1998), 129–30.

hailed not from workers or poor peasants or was occupationally tied to tsarist era political, economic, or social structures. In Germany, by contrast, the effort was directed at racial reclamation in the name of the *Volk*, rather than a clearing of debris in order to move forward.

The first decade of Soviet rule was rich in thinking and experimenting with the New Man. This experimental phase was defined by the search for an idealized proletarian subject. Most contemporary visions of the New Man in one form or another incorporated proletarian attributes. Especially prevalent were notions of the machine man. Proletarian poets Vladimir Kirillov, Mikhail Gerasimov, and Aleksei Gastev poeticized the factory and heralded a new type of proletarian superman, an "iron messiah," who had blended with his machines, "an iron demon of the age with a human soul / with nerves like steel / with muscles like rails."[30] These visions of a machine man only superficially resembled Ernst Jünger's armored worker-soldier who appeared at roughly the same time. The proletarian's metal skin was not meant to shield him against his unpredictable environment. Rather it expressed an exuberant vision of a fully industrialized world that produced human beings in its own mechanized image. Underlying these visions was a materialist assumption, deriving from Marxism and later behavioralism, that man's nature was entirely conditioned by an environment toward which he merely reacted. This premise meant that technological fixes could solve social problems. The metal purity and rhythmic discipline of the technological age would mold disorganized human individuals into a gigantic collective machine; in turn, the collective machine-man would educate the chaotic physiological apparati of every individual worker. The machine man was especially the domain of Proletkul't, an organization inspired by Bogdanov and dedicated to the creation of a distinctly proletarian culture to buttress the dictatorship of the proletariat. Once in place, proletarian culture would bring about a spiritual revolution, renewing the consciousness of the working class. Before being outmaneuvered by the Communist Party, which feared for its hegemony, Proletkul't numbered over half a million workers.[31]

One of the most radical and influential proponents of Proletkul't, Aleksei Gastev, created a "Central Institute of Labor" in which he conducted research on the ability of rhythmic and mechanically precise labor processes in the factory to "educate" the muscles and nerves of the proletariat.[32] Gastev's teachings

---

[30] Cited by Rosenthal, 159; see also Rolf Hellebust, *Flesh to Metal: Soviet Literature and the Alchemy of Revolution* (Ithaca, NY: Cornell University Press, 2003); Mark Steinberg, *Proletarian Imagination: Self, Modernity, and the Sacred in Russia, 1910–1925* (Ithaca, NY: Cornell University Press, 2002).

[31] Rosenthal, 156; Lynn Mally, *Culture of the Future: The Proletkult Movement in Revolutionary Russia* (Berkeley: University of California Press, 1990).

[32] Toby Clark, "The 'New Man's' Body: A Motif in Early Soviet Culture," in *Art of the Soviets: Painting, Sculpture and Architecture in a One-Party State, 1917–1992*, eds. M. Cullerne Bown and B. Taylor (Manchester: Manchester University Press, 1993), 37; Vladislav Todorov, *Red Square, Black Square: Organon for Revolutionary Imagination* (Albany: State University of New York Press, 1995), 69–70; Stefan Plaggenborg, *Revolutionskultur: Menschenbilder und*

were far reaching: by 1938 more than 1 million workers had received training
in his institute and its branches. The founder of Proletkul't, Bogdanov, exper-
imented with, and eventually died from, transfusions of filtered blood among
workers to create a communal proletarian body – a literal attempt to substanti-
ate the notion of an enlarged laboring self that he and other "Godbuilders" had
advocated before the revolution. Beyond Proletkul't, other Soviet activists conceived of ideal humanity in mechanical and technological terms. They included
the theater director Vsevolod Meyerhold and the "biomechanical" training he
devised for his actors, and the filmmaker Dziga Vertov, who dreamed of a "perfect electric man"[33] – an individual whose soul was no longer subject to chaotic
and ineffectual psychological impulses but functioned with the directed energy
and precision of machines: "We bring people into closer kinship with machines,
we foster new people. The New Man, free of unwieldiness and clumsiness, will
have the light, precise movements of machines."[34]

The sense that, if left to itself, human psychology was chaotic or passive and
therefore required rational intervention in order to be activated and directed
was shared by all revolutionary actors at the time and applies equally to Nazi
Germany and the Soviet Union. A similar consensus also applied to the disdain
Vertov expressed for "contemporary man," his "inability to control himself,"
and "the bungling citizen's" alternating states of "disorderly haste" and pas-
siveness.[35] Existing man comprised "old human material" that was in need of
rebuilding, which was the socialist construction project.[36] In this regard, Vertov's contemporary man was not so different from the racial types that ideologists of the Third Reich such as Walter Gross and Heinrich Himmler inherited
in 1933. They too had mismanaged their selves, although in the German case it
was a question of bodies and marriages and racial lineages. Without the racial
discipline of the National Socialist state and the self-discipline it sought to
inculcate, Germany was doomed. The way ahead was to transform old bodies
into new through state regulation and, more importantly, race consciousness

kulturelle Praxis in Sowjetrussland zwischen Oktoberrevolution und Stalinismus (Cologne:
Böhlau, 1998), 35–45.

[33] This expression was coined by the filmmaker Dziga Vertov. Members of the Soviet avant garde
literally related individuals' social consciousness to electricity, regarding weak consciousness
as an effect of low-voltage activity in the body. They advocated communal housing, so-called
"social condensers," as catalysts of attaining a high-voltage current in individuals' bodies and
the social body as a whole. See Katerina Clark, *Petersburg: Crucible of Cultural Revolution*
(Cambridge, MA: Harvard University Press, 1995), 251.

[34] From the manifesto, "The New Man" (1922), in *Kino-Eye: The Writings of Dziga Vertov*, ed.
Annette Michelson and trans. Kevin O'Brien (Berkeley: University of California Press, 1984),
7–8.

[35] Ibid.

[36] "Lenin i vospitanie novogo cheloveka," *Revoliutsiia i kul'tura*, no. 1 (1928): 5–10, here 5.
Even the pedagogue Anton Makarenko, who saw himself working in the tradition of Gorky
and his concept of the human personality, deplored the absence of a "science of human raw
material" which would enable him to distinguish "precious raw material" from "junk." See
Anton Makarenko, *Pedagogicheskaia poema* (Moscow: Khudozh. literatura, 1964).

on the part of individuals. But a rejection of liberalism, and of the chaos of a purely individual point of view that accompanied it, was common to both construction projects.

Yet inside the Soviet Union these mechanicist conceptions of man were increasingly criticized for their inability to account for the human soul as a hearth of individual consciousness. Indeed Gastev militated for a "radically objective demonstration of things, of mechanized human masses, which acquires gigantic dimensions and has no personal, intimate, or lyrical residues."[37] Some of his critics understood Gastev's attack against the bourgeois individual as an attack against individuality, the individual soul as such. As one of them noted, he sought to "transform the living person into an unreasoning and stupid instrument without any general qualifications or sufficient all-round development."[38] The idea of a well-rounded development was a nod to Marx's humanism, which many of those critical of the machine cult and an exclusively proletarian culture upheld as the normative frame for the future New Man. It was difficult for constructivists and other proponents of the machine man to legitimate their project in Marxist terms, because for Marx the soul was an indispensable part in the human process of self-becoming. For Marxists, the New Man required subjectivity, which was central for his historical evolution from nonman to man.

The emphasis on the individual, the soul, and the will was consistent with Stalinism. The onset of the Stalinist era in Soviet history is usually associated with the late 1920s, when the Party majority led by Stalin broke with the compromises of the NEP order and decided to industrialize the country at breakneck speed, to collectivize the peasantry, and to intensify the war against all class enemies, all in the service of constructing a socialist society. This "Great Break" also entailed the emergence of new, more humanist conceptions of the New Man. The anthropological ideal of the Stalinist state was voluntarist, it focused on the individual rather than the collective as the defining basic entity of human behavior, and it also rehabilitated the individual soul as the vessel of the conscious will. The Stalinist ideological apparatus cultivated individual biographies, emphasizing the making of exceptional personalities rather than the exceptional deeds of inanimate machines. Soviet activists now proclaimed that the New Man was coming into being as an empirical reality, and they linked his appearance to a crucial stage in historical development that the Soviet state had just passed. In so doing they created their own teleology of the New Man, which reached back via the machine man of the 1920s to radical thinkers like Chernyshevsky as the first distant heralds of the perfect, socialist present.

The beginning of the Stalin era was coterminous with the fantastic decision to build utopia, in a very material sense. As early as 1930, participating actors discerned the epochal quality of the Stalin era as the particular stage in Soviet

---

[37] Plaggenborg, 35–45.
[38] Toby Clark, 38.

history when Bolshevism's long-held, but long dormant, dreams of social engineering were being fully enacted. There was a shift in acceleration in Germany as well, but it was prompted not by a new leader such as Stalin or a new incentive such as the rejuvenation of Italian fascism after 1935. Rather, it was the outbreak of the war that replenished the New Man. The principal change from Lenin to Stalin was a change in historical diagnosis. Stalin and his followers deliberately sought to accelerate the course of historical development. Speaking in 1931, Stalin surveyed the historical development of the Soviet Union and found it lagged fifty or a hundred years behind that of advanced capitalist countries: "We must make good this lag in ten years. Either we achieve this or we will be crushed."[39] Stalinist culture was filled with a renewed urge to activate citizens to speed up the construction of socialism. Stalin's appeal resonated intensely with Communists who yearned for revolutionary action and a break with the frustrating compromises of NEP. There was also a widespread sense that the international revolution was not to occur in the near future and that the Soviet regime had no choice but to mobilize its own resources. The stress on individual consciousness and willpower was the innovation of Stalinism and broke decisively with 1920s mechanicist ideals.

Maxim Gorky played an instrumental role in recognizing the need for the self-deployment of revolutionaries, and in so doing he provided one of the first formulations of the Stalinist New Man. Gorky had left the Soviet Union in the early 1920s, but even while residing abroad he maintained active correspondence with Soviet writers and other activists, among them the pedagogue Makarenko and his colony of young delinquents. He returned to the Soviet Union for two widely publicized visits, in 1928 and 1929, before settling for good in 1931. In a widely featured report on his travels "across the Union of Soviets," he showed himself amazed by the psychic changes that he observed in the Soviet population since the revolution. The people were saturating themselves with political ideas, and "political consciousness" was becoming "an everyday phenomenon." "Everybody had become younger in essence." It was an image that Gorky placed in deliberate contrast to the sentiment he recalled from journeys to the very same places prior to the revolution: "Russian feebleness and spiritual mourning" and the "specifically Russian bent for sadness."[40] Gorky elaborated his ideas in an editorial published in both *Pravda* and *Izvestiia*, in 1932: "On the Old and the New Man." While the old man was described as petty bourgeois, atomistic, and hostile toward progress, residing predominantly in capitalist societies, the Soviet Union was the habitat of the energetic and creative New Man, who derived his self-confidence from knowing his role and future in history: "In the Union of Soviets a New Man is coming of age, . . . He is young, not only biologically, but also historically. He is a force that has only begun to become aware of its path and significance in history."[41]

[39] I. V. Stalin, *Sochineniia*, vol. 13 (Moscow: Gos. izd-vo polit. Lit-ry, 1951), 39.
[40] *Pravda*, 13 June 1928, 5.
[41] Maksim Gor'kii, "O starom i o novom cheloveke" (1932), in idem, *Sobranie sochinenii v tridtsati tomakh*, vol. 26 (Moscow: Gos. izd.-vo Khudozh lit-ry, 1953), 289.

To make this New Man fully aware of himself he needed a guiding, helping hand. Again it was Gorky who in great measure defined the medium which was to instill the man with full self-consciousness: literature. This was the medium by which intellectuals had introduced the New Man in the first place a century earlier. It was at Gorky's Moscow residence, in October 1932, that Stalin called on leading Soviet writers to work as "engineers of human souls."[42] The Stalinist regime invested in literature more than in any other artistic sphere to promote the features of the New Man; simultaneously literature advanced to the regime's artistic medium of choice. Literary works were both to "reflect" the achievements of new Soviet men and women and to provide the biographical mold according to which readers were to pattern their personal life experience. This emphasis on the heroic biography was what for the writer Aleksei Tolstoi distinguished Soviet literature from its counterpart in the declining bourgeois West. "From this point on, the paths of Russian and European literature part.... Hero! We need a hero of our time."[43]

These literary patterns acquired material power as they were assimilated into coercive practices of the Stalinist regime. The construction of the Belomor Canal, linking the Baltic to the White Sea, as well as other construction projects built with the expanding Gulag workforce, were propagated as initiatives to "reforge" criminals into useful socialist citizens. A propaganda volume composed by thirty writers, who included some of the most venerated literary figures of the time, presented stories of individuals bent down by capitalist exploitation whose personalities were straightened out after exposure to forms of collective, purposeful labor. The image that the book presents of Belomor as a harsh yet nurturing place clashes with the evidence of exhaustion, death, and cruel regimentation that characterized the social reality of Belomor in the first place and found no entry into the pages of the propaganda volume. While the extent to which the ideology of reforging shaped the subjective horizons of the forced laborers themselves is uncertain, several of the artists who helped produce the volume tied their involvement in the elaboration of the Stalinist myth of rebirth to agendas of personal transformation that their participation in this project appeared to assure.[44]

Increasingly in the course of the 1930s, the New Man was declared to be a contemporary social reality. The extraordinary exploits of Stakhanovite

---

[42] Although the term "engineering of souls" had been coined by experimental writers already in the 1920s, it did bring out the understanding Stalin applied to it, of the fully developed individual (the writer producing under the direction of the Party) who used technology as a tool of social transformation; see O. Ronen, "'Inzhenery chelovecheskikh dush': K istorii izrecheniia," *Lotmanovskii sbornik* 2 (1997): 393–400.

[43] Quoted by Gutkin, 77.

[44] This applied, notably, to the writer Mikhail Zoshchenko and the photographer Rodchenko. See Elizabeth A. Papazian, "Reconstructing the (Authentic Proletarian) Reader: Mikhail Zoshchenko's Changing Model of Authorship, 1929–1934," *Kritika* 4, no. 4 (2003): 816–48; Leah Dickerman, "The Propagandizing of Things," in *Aleksandr Rodchenko*, eds. Magdalena Dabrowski et al. (New York: Museum of Modern Art, 1998), 96; see also Thomas Lahusen, *How Life Writes the Book: Real Socialism and Socialist Realism in Stalin's Russia* (Ithaca, NY: Cornell University Press, 1997).

coal miners, milkmaids, and polar aviators proved to Stalin that the socialist personality had come into being. While in the earlier phase of the Soviet system, "technology [had] decided everything" (a reference to the mechanicist ethos of the 1920s), now "cadres decide[d] everything." The quantitative rise in productivity, which the Stakhanovites demonstrated so poignantly, signified a qualitative leap in historical development, meaning that qualitatively new people were now appearing on Soviet soil. As Stalin indicated, the New Man of the 1930s superseded the former ideal of the machine man. The machine threatened to enslave man, Aleksei Stakhanov noted in his autobiography, and therefore had to be mastered.[45] Against the synthetic present of socialist society, the ideals of the recent past appeared as incomplete ideals, generated in a historical state of dialectical negation. The ideal Communist propagated by Lenin during his entire life, the ascetic puritanical saint, was now reconsidered as a self-abnegating, incomplete figure, who was historically deprived of a rich personal life. The androgynous ideal of the early Bolshevik regime gave way to distinctly gendered notions of the socialist man and woman. These aesthetic changes were to connote a transition from a period of all-out struggle and self-sacrifice, encapsulated in the image of a faceless collective of proletarian workers, to a socialist civilization which cultivated unfettered male and female individuals.[46]

Ultimately, it was not an individual's gender but his or her dedication to socialist values that determined whether one was old or new, a reactionary, philistine, or progressive citizen. Socialist citizens were supposed to be physically fit, but they were to combine proletarian muscle with the pursuit of cultural interests. Their trimmed bodies, encapsulated in the formations of gymnasts clad in white who paraded across Red Square, were an important though ultimately secondary component part of an ideal of selfhood defined exclusively in terms of self-possession and voluntarist striving, which could

---

[45] A. Stakhanov, *Rasskaz o moei zhizni* (Moscow: Gos. sots-ekon. izd-vo, 1937). On mythic images of Stakhanovites as first living exemplars of the New Man, see Lewis Siegelbaum, *Stakhanovism and the Politics of Productivity in the USSR, 1935–1941* (Cambridge: Cambridge University Press, 1988); Robert Maier, *Die Stachanov-Bewegung 1935–1938: Der Stachanovismus als tragendes und verschärfendes Moment der Stalinisierung der sowjetischen Gesellschaft* (Stuttgart: F. Steiner, 1990), 182–3.

[46] David L. Hoffmann, *Stalinist Values: the Cultural Norms of Soviet Modernity, 1917–1941* (Ithaca, NY: Cornell University Press, 2003). Significantly, the agenda of the "new woman" disappeared in the course of the Stalin era. The term had originated in the European women's movement at the turn of the twentieth century and was actively propagated by the Soviet regime during the 1920s, particularly in Central Asia, where it appealed to women as a surrogate proletariat, calling upon them to become literate, throw off their veils, and fight their male oppressors. The term *new woman* indicated a progressive stance, but it never evoked the utopian ideal inherent in the "new man" (*novyi chelovek*). During the 1930s, as the struggle against backwardness was supposed to be completed and Soviet society entered the socialist age, men and women alike were called upon to mold themselves in the image of a socialist personality. Elizabeth Wood, *The Baba and the Comrade: Gender and Politics in Revolutionary Russia* (Bloomington: Indiana University Press, 1997); Douglas Northrop, *Veiled Empire: Gender and Power in Stalinist Central Asia* (Ithaca, NY: Cornell University Press, 2004).

equally animate a physically crippled individual (witness Pavel Korchagin in Nikolai Ostrovskii's *How the Steel Was Tempered*).[47] Finally, the emblematic new men and women of the Stalinist age – whether as coal miners, tractor drivers, or aviators – were all individuals in dialogue with technology. Their miraculous records were explained by the fact that they infused and directed technology with the power of an unfettered socialist consciousness. This constituted the qualitative difference from the Western pilots and workers who were represented as a "class without consciousness" that could not "think for itself" and was thus inherently incapable of such voluntarist feats.[48] Comparisons such as this one suggest that the Soviet New Man could conceivably be formulated only with the contemporary Western world in mind, whereas the Nazis would completely reject the West in favor of German particularism. Much of the thrust of Stalinist human engineering was derived from the specter of a capitalist world in decline, epitomized in the stock market crash of 1929, and the rise of an alternative model of fascist subjectivity. In a letter to Gorky, Aleksei Tolstoi described the Soviet government's decision to build a Volga dam as the "opening of a new page in world history. And this is how, at some point in the future, it will be described: during a time when in the West civilizations were decaying, throwing millions of people out onto the streets, and when the East was being filled with blood and the countries were seeking salvation in war and annihilation, the [Soviet] Union elevated itself above time and published the decree on the Volga Dam."[49] The transnational dimensions of the creation of the "new Soviet man" was also illustrated in the many pilgrimages by Western observers to the Soviet Union during the late 1920s and 1930s, whose admiring reports circulated widely in the Soviet press.[50]

---

[47] Karen Petrone, *Life Has Become More Joyous, Comrades: Celebrations in the Time of Stalin* (Bloomington: Indiana University Press, 2000); Lilya Kaganovsky, "How the Soviet Man Was (Un)Made," *Slavic Review* 63, no. 3 (2004): 557–96.

[48] Soviet ideologues were greatly interested in fascist subjectivity. Fascism, they acknowledged, resembled the Soviet system in its emphasis on mass mobilization, but it sought to mobilize the masses into a collective machine (A. Vedenov, quoted in Raymond Augustin Bauer, *The New Man in Soviet Psychology* [Cambridge, MA: Harvard University Press, 1952]), 98; see also diary of Vsevolod Vishnevskii, entries of 31.12.1940, 3.3.1942, in idem, *Sobranie sochinenii v 5-ti tomakh* (dopolnitel'nyi): *Vystupleniia i radiorechi: Zapisnye knizhki: Pis'ma*, vol. 6 (Moscow: Gos. izd-vo khudozh. Lit-ry, 1961). This view is borne out by the self-representation of the Soviet and Fascist states at the time. A Soviet photomontage from the 1930s (by Gustav Klutsis) uses the synecdoche of the human body to suggest the individual's active participation in the political system, whereas a photomontage of the same period from Fascist Italy portrays a machine which subjugates the mass of individuals. An inscription on this poster reads, "See how the inflammatory words of Mussolini attract the people of Italy with the violent power of turbines and convert them to Fascism." Benjamin Buchloh, "From *Faktura* to Factography," *October* 30 (Fall 1984): 113–14; see also Simonetta Falasca-Zamponi, *Fascist Spectacle: The Aesthetics of Power in Mussolini's Italy* (Berkeley: University of California Press, 1997).

[49] Maksim Gor'kii, *Gor'kii i sovetskie pisateli: Neizdannaia perepiska* (Moscow: Izd-vo Akademii nauk SSSR, 1963), 410 (letter of May 23, 1932).

[50] See especially Klaus Mehnert, *Youth in Soviet Russia*, trans. Michael Davidson (New York: Harcourt, Brace, 1933), as well as Maurice Hindus, who traveled to newly collectivized Russian

As an ideological construct, the New Man was an essential component of the Soviet revolutionary project and a device wielded by a revolutionary regime in need of self-legitimation. Yet the allure of this figure extended beyond the leadership of the Communist Party and beyond those whom the Soviet regime identified as model inhabitants of the new world. The incentive and urge to transform oneself, expressed in the shorthand term of the "New Man," were shared by Soviet citizens of different backgrounds and ages. They manifested themselves above all in a historical consciousness, a commitment to work on oneself so as not to be left aside by, or drown in the current of History. But this labor also promised moral and existential rewards, the certainty of contributing to the creation of a perfect future. Ultimately, by taking up the injunction to rework oneself individuals acquired a sense of biographical continuity and purpose that acquired particular meaning in the cataclysmic environment of war and revolution.

The Stalinist turn toward willing the new world into being began with an all-out attack on all remnants of the old world. Correspondingly the New Man, who appeared as a positive ideal in the early 1930s, was preceded by a struggle against remnants of the Old Man within. The institutionalized campaign waged by the Party and state against all social groups identified with the old world – "kulaks," private artisans, traders, "speculators," and the "bourgeois" intelligentsia – was sweeping and powerful. It did not limit itself to destroying the social and economic structures – villages, trading networks, professional associations – on which the functioning of these groups had rested but demanded that all members of these groups renounce their past and prove their allegiance to the Soviet cause in deeds and words.[51] It was in the context of this campaign that individuals associated with the old order proceeded to confront the enemy within themselves. As the explosion of personal confessional texts during this period demonstrates, the onset of the Stalin period marked a utopian threshold, when all citizens were expected to align themselves to the emerging new world, when every individual was to mark the transition from the old to the New Man in his or her personal life.[52]

Members of the intelligentsia most clearly articulated the steady destruction of the Old Man within. To some extent, this had to do with their superior grasp

---

villages and believed he was glimpsing the world's future: "Man, under the impetus of the new changes, is destined to acquire a body of motives, aims, relationships, which in time will make Russia an anomaly among the nations, a real Mars on earth. Limitless and fantastic are the social transmutations inherent in collectivization." See Maurice Hindus, *Red Bread* (New York: J. Cape & H. Smith, 1931), 8–9; see also Sophie Coeure, *La grande lueur à l'Est: Les Français et l'Union soviétique, 1917–1939* (Paris: Seuil, 1999).

[51] During this period scores of disenfranchised individuals, who had been stripped of Soviet citizenship on account of their "bourgeois" class background, petitioned for rehabilitation by invoking their alignment with the course of the revolution and, ultimately, with history. See Golfo Alexopoulos, *Stalin's Outcasts: Aliens, Citizens, and the Soviet State, 1926–1936* (Ithaca, NY: Cornell University Press, 2003).

[52] Igal Halfin, *Terror in My Soul: Communist Autobiographies on Trial* (Cambridge, MA: Harvard University Press, 2003).

of the syntax of self-expression, but at least equally important was the fact that they, unlike less educated groups in Soviet society, continued to inhabit formed, yet problematic "personalities" which were shaped by prerevolutionary culture. To be sure, workers and peasants also grappled with the struggle between old and new codes of thinking and behavior, but they rarely reified their lapses into "old" habits – such as heavy drinking, cursing, or mistreating their spouses – into a full-fledged figure of an "Old Man" who had to die in order for the New Man to emerge. For intellectuals these habits represented the very essence of backwardness, and they referred to the feudal-capitalist enslavement of the laboring people's souls, an enslavement that had kept them on the verge of a subhuman existence. Moreover, before the intellectual could join the "proletarian fighting army," he had, in the words of Johannes Becher, to "burn most of what he owes to his bourgeois genealogy," particularly "all the capricious and moody posturing."[53] It was precisely the intelligentsia who admitted to feeling weighed down by the Old Man within and who, at the same time, actively involved themselves in the creation of the New Man. It may even be fair to say that the New Man as a figure of utmost perfection was most pronouncedly advocated by individuals who suffered from impure backgrounds, such as class alien origins, a previous oppositionist record, or prolonged stays in the capitalist West.[54]

In extreme situations where individuals were targeted as old and outlived, the urge to tie one's life to the mythology of the New Man acquired existential relevance. Consider the case of Nikolai Ustrialov, an erstwhile White officer who had emigrated to Harbin in the wake of the Civil War. Already during the Civil War Ustrialov confessed to a fellow White officer that he envied the Soviet revolutionary project for its "historical pathos." The future, he believed, was on the Reds' side; the White camp, by contrast, was composed only of "former people."[55] Ustrialov's ascription of this derogatory Soviet term to himself and other members of the White camp shows how impressed he was by the Soviet narrative of revolution and historical progress. The pathos of History that in his eyes animated the Soviet state kept tormenting Ustrialov for years to come and prompted him to return to Soviet Russia in 1935 – precisely at the junction when the "socialist personality" had been declared to have emerged. The diary in which Ustrialov documented his return to the USSR reveals his urge to participate in the construction of the New World. In the diary he constantly tested his inner disposition toward the Soviet system: was he truly inspired by the enthusiasm and belief that characterized the ideal Soviet citizen, and was he

[53] J. R. Becher, *Der gespaltene Dichter: Johannes R. Becher: Gedichte, Briefe, Dokumente* (Berlin: Aufbau Taschenbuch Verlag, 1991); see also Francois Furet, *The Passing of an Illusion: The Idea of Communism in the Twentieth Century*, trans. Deborah Furet (Chicago: University of Chicago Press, 1999).

[54] See, for example, the odes to the socialist personality composed by Nikolai Bukharin in prison, while he awaited his trial (N. I. Bukharin, *Tiuremnye rukopisi N. I. Bukharina*, 2 vols. [Moscow: AIRO-XX, 1996].

[55] N. Ustrialov, *Pod znakom revoliutsii*, 2nd rev. ed. (Kharbin [Poligraf], 1927), 87.

thus in a position "to earn a Soviet biography"? All his doubts and moments of despair, of which there were many, because his attempts to earn employment and trust went to nil, were evidence to him of the "old," "heretical" subject in him which had to be ruthlessly suppressed.

Particularly striking about Ustrialov's narrative is its historical conscious-ness. Ustrialov was aware of the historical threshold that was being crossed in the Soviet Union in the year of his return. Walking through the streets of Moscow while an international youth festival was being held, he observed the "cohorts and legions of youth, the wonderful early autumn sun, the sounds of orchestras screaming from the loudspeakers, sounds filled with bravura and fighting spirit, resounding in a major key.... An existential pathos. Yes, it is so clear that our revolution is an upsurge, a beginning, a thesis in a new dialectical cycle." Consistently with his belief in historical progression Ustri-alov apprehended the young athletes at the youth festival as epitomes of the New Man. There was a strong self-reflexive component in this observation, for Ustrialov's ability to see and believe in the existing New Man was proof to him of the purity of his own consciousness as a Soviet citizen. But Ustrialov perfectly knew that he himself could not incarnate the ideal which he jealously observed from a distance. Worse even, observing the perfect young people only reinforced his own sense of being old and historically doomed ("We are a dying generation. The Soviet epoch is the sunset for us and our lives"). Nonetheless he felt the duty to "work on myself, to educate and drill myself" because it was in this act of repressing the Old Man in himself that he, too, could feel the "pathos of the great state and of potential humanity." Not to be able to align oneself with the collective and assume the shape of the vaunted new man was tantamount to being discarded into the garbage pail of history. Seen in this context, individual projects of self-organization and transformation in tune with the revolutionary state resonated with an intensity that the lines of an autobiographical narrative alone may not fully disclose. In the case of Nikolai Ustrialov, his attempts to inhabit the Soviet mold ultimately failed to convince the Soviet regime. Ustrialov was arrested on conspiracy charges in fall 1937 and shot.[56]

The New Man of the 1930s was a present-day ideal, but it was fully embod-ied only by preciously few outstanding individuals and not – not yet, as many commentators would emphasize – a mass phenomenon.[57] This was also true in Nazi Germany, where even the SS was regarded as a vanguard formation. Young people who appeared as exemplars of a new, supposedly pure generation themselves often described a sense of falling short of the ideal of concentrated

---

[56] "'Sluzhit' rodine prikhoditsia kostiami...' Dnevnik N. V. Ustrialova 1935–1937 gg.," *Istochnik*, no. 5–6 (1998): 3–100, entries for June 20, 1935; September 3, 1935'; July 5, 1936.

[57] Andrei Platonov's novel, *Schastlivaia Moskva*, expresses existing humanity's inability to live up to utopian ideals through the metaphor of cut limbs. On the meanings of amputation in the Soviet 1930s, see Kaganovsky, "How the Soviet Man Was (Un)Made."

willpower and consciousness that defined the rich socialist personality. This hierarchical distinction between a mass of ordinary and a small but growing number of extraordinary Soviet citizens is reflected in literature from the 1930s and 1940s. Novels such as Veniamin Kaverin's *Two Captains* (1936–44) or Aleksandr Fadeev's *Young Guard* (1946), suggested that all Soviet citizens, by virtue of residing in the fertile socialist habitat, possessed the germ of the New Man in them. Yet far from all mobilized their inherent powers to the fullest possible extent to become living prototypes of the New Man. Most good Soviet citizens remained mortal beings, with human limitations and weaknesses. Only a few extraordinary individuals had the energy and devotion to renounce the new material pleasures of Soviet life (high income, one's own apartment, and a family) and to strive further, often in the form of lonely travel, toward the ideal future.[58]

A striking real life adaptation of this social ideal can be found in the biography of Leonid Potemkin, born in 1914, one of countless social upstarts of the Stalin period. After graduating from the Sverdlovsk Mining Institute, with distinction, in 1939, Potemkin embarked on a steep career that raised him to the post of Party Secretary of Moscow's Lenin district in the 1950s and of Deputy Minister of Geology of the RSFSR a decade later. In his diary as well as in his personal letters of the Stalin period he referred to himself as a paradigmatic New Man. His descriptions of how he transformed himself from a destitute villager into a culturally and aesthetically rich socialist citizen were patterned on the mythical story of the Marxist proletariat that evolved historically from nothing to becoming everything.[59] To be "worthy" of his "time and role in history," Potemkin noted in his diary, he had to be "greater than the great people of the past." These past luminaries included Pushkin and Goethe, who "learned foreign languages in a matter of months, they knew 30 languages, whereas we spend years in language classes and can't even master one." A fellow student to whom he related his urgent ambitions was impressed; others laughed at him or called him a dreamer.

A devoted Communist, Potemkin sought to transform not only himself but also other young people into prototypes of the New Man. He pursued this mission in his activities as Communist agitator, but also privately, in his love relationships. Away from Sverdlovsk on a summer internship in 1936, he had a romance with a certain Liudmila, a woman he described as cold and cynical whom he tried to educate like a "comrade." During their encounters, Leonid lectured Liudmila "on the traits of the New Man with strong and renewed feelings, the creator of a new life." Every socialist citizen, he implied, had a potential to become a New Man, but the realization of this potential entailed

---

[58] Gutkin, 146.

[59] Potemkin's diary and letters are in his personal archive in Moscow. Excerpts from the diary have been published in Véronique Garros, Natalia Korenevskaya, and Thomas Lahusen, eds. *Intimacy and Terror: Soviet Diaries of the 1930s*, trans. Carol A Flath (New York: New Press, 1995).

sustained education of one's conscious faculties and the will. Trying to "force her to reflect on her life," Potemkin referred to biography as the proper vessel of self-understanding. In reading this account one is reminded of nineteenth-century literary precursors of the New Man, particularly the male heroes in Chernyshevsky's novel, for whom love for a woman was inextricably inter-twined with the duty to educate and humanize her.

It is not clear whether Potemkin was aware of this lineage, but he did consider at one point publishing his encounter with Liudmila. In any case, his self-fashioning amounted to more than the echoing of literary stereotypes. Potemkin's written record – his diary, private letters, and autobiographies from the Stalin period, as well as his memoirs, written in old age – forms a corpus striking in coherence and univocality. The trajectory of his career which sent him on assignments throughout the Soviet Union, made him explorer of the greatest nickel deposits in Europe, and awarded him with ministerial honors further testifies to the degree to which he self-consciously saw himself as an extraordinary man of the Soviet age. Few Soviet citizens went as far as Leonid Potemkin to cast the totality of their lives in the mold of the new man. Even Potemkin, in his diary and in personal letters to friends, admitted to lapses and bouts of depressions in his pursuit of the ideal, and his admissions only under-scored the utopian quality of Stalinist anthropological standards, for nobody was able to live up to the mandated state of permanent enthusiasm, labor activism, and hyperconsciousness which transformed self-contained individuals into truly collectivist historical subjects. Nonetheless, these standards mapped the default position of self-definition in the Soviet realm. If we understand the New Man not as a set of given, empirical qualities but as an embodiment to strive for, he was an unquestioned social reality of the Stalin period. His fea-tures revealed himself in ubiquitous gestures to disavow the past, to denounce the individualized and selfish forms of "bourgeois" life as morally reprehensi-ble and economically ineffectual, and to align oneself in new, collective forms of work and life.

As in the Soviet case, the German New Man required strenuous work and discipline. Nazi ideologues believed that the transformation of the *Volk* into racially superlative Aryans would not be completed for several generations. In part to accelerate this process, the Nazis nourished and trained a political elite, the SS, as a racial vanguard, and it was here, among these 800,000 Germans, that the most fully realized New Man resided. But the Nazi regime also facilitated the efforts of more ordinary Germans to realize their Nazi selves, and ultimately the success of the Nazi racial project depended on the racial discipline and racial consciousness of Germans at large.

When Hitler came to power in 1933, the Nazi revolution had just begun. National Socialists believed they stood at the very edge of history, poised to redirect the nation to fit the grooves of an envisioned Aryan future. The whole previous itinerary of Germany, in which a liberal sphere had been elaborated, in which public claims had been put forward by political parties and interest groups, and in which various ethnic groups, provincial identities, and religious communities had survived and commingled, was to come to an abrupt end. From the perspective of the Nazis, the year 1933 marked a sharp break. In place of the quarrels of party, the contests of interest, and the divisions of class that had supposedly compromised the ability of the nation to act, the Nazis proposed to build a unified racial community guided by modern science. The biological politics to which the Nazis adhered corresponded to the achievement of the *Aktionseinheit* they believed necessary to survive and prosper in the dangerous conditions of the twentieth century.

However, the Nazis did not vigilantly identify Old Men who had to be suppressed or eliminated as was the case in the Soviet Union. They stressed the basic good working material of Aryan Germans. Although Nazi officials sometimes noted that as many as 20 or 30 percent of the German population were biologically deficient in some way, reclamation rather than elimination was the primary goal of Nazi eugenic policy for the population as a whole. Mass murder was reserved for those Germans unable to be productive – the mentally or physically impaired – and for the Jews.

The task ahead was to make Germans into Aryans. Although this was a difficult task, and one that was never fully realized, the racial project should not be seen exclusively in terms of prescription and compulsion. It rested on the growing credibility of the Nazi worldview and on the efforts of millions of Germans to recognize themselves as Aryans and to nurture their newly recognized racial selves. That this labor of self-transformation was widespread does not mean that ordinary Germans fully accepted or even completely understood the racial tenets of the regime. But they proved willing to try and over time increasingly shifted the conduct of their lives to accord with the racial future. The degree of self-mobilization into the Nazi sphere is impressive. In each of the last years before the war, over 1 million volunteers participated in the annual Winterhilfe charity drive, several million more young people were happily recruited into the Hitler Youth, more than 2 million workers enrolled in German Labor Front apprenticeship programs, as many as 8 million Germans joined local civil-defense leagues, and an astonishing 54 million had, in the single year 1938, participated in some sort of Kraft durch Freude activity.[60] Wartime service only strengthened the role of National Socialist institutions and the validity of its pitiless racialized worldview in daily life.[61] Without relinquishing familiar ties to family, work mates, and neighbors, Germans moved relatively easily from one to the other world, adopting as they did the vocabulary of national integration, racial exclusiveness, and the terms of constant racial struggle.[62] That the National Socialist world crumbled so quickly in 1945, even to the

---

[60] Ronald Smelser, *Robert Ley: Hitler's Labor Front Leader* (New York: St Martin's Press, 1988), 191–216; Herwart Vorländer, *Die NSV: Darstellung und Dokumentation einer nationalsozialistischen Organisation* (Boppard am Main: H. Boldt, 1988).

[61] Omer Bartov, *Hitler's Army: Soldiers, Nazis, and War in the Third Reich* (New York: Oxford University Press, 1991).

[62] Smelser, 302–3; Ian Kershaw, *The "Hitler Myth": Image and Reality in the Third Reich* (Oxford: Oxford University Press, 1987); Detlev Peukert, *Inside Nazi Germany: Conformity, Opposition*

point where the 1949 elections appeared to revive the electoral parochialisms of the Weimar era, surely revealed the limits to the fascist dream world.[63] But it would be a mistake to assume that the Nazi world was superficial because it was incomplete: the alacrity with which Germans assumed identities as Aryans and then shed them indicates that neither liberal nor illiberal subjectivity was stronger than the other and suggests as well that the experiences of both persisted as an unofficial half-life even when one or the other was no longer officially sanctioned.

"It is not a party badge or a brown shirt that makes you a National Socialist, but rather your character and the conduct of your life," announced the eugenic journal *Neues Volk* in July 1933.[64] A "spiritual revolution" had to follow the accomplishments of the political revolution, insisted Walter Gross, director of the Rassenpolitisches Amt of the Nazi Party, in 1934: it will "fundamentally remodel and reform" – "even all those things that seem today completely solid," he added.[65] What was necessary was to "recognize yourself" (*Erkenne dich selbst*), which meant following the tenets of hereditary biology to find a suitable partner for marriage and marry only for love, to provide the *Volk* with healthy children, and to accept "the limits of empathy" as a revitalized Germany weeded out racial undesirables.[66] Both the projects of racial reclamation and of racial extermination are hinted at here. Not only would the Aryan body have to be protected through vigorous eugenic measures, but the Aryan self had to be strengthened by public recognition of the individual's responsibility to the collective racial whole. Since the German people were a mixture of various races, Nazi biopoliticians pointed out, the lessons of racial hygiene had to be learned quickly and thoroughly, lest the contamination of the whole run out of control. This put the emphasis on the efforts of ordinary, racially desirable Germans to practice what may be called racial grooming.

The Nazi regime undertook a massive campaign to propose the new language of race. Beginning in August 1933, the *Illustrierter Beobachter*, the party publication with the highest circulation (840,000 in December 1933, up from 302,000 in January), began the regular series "*Was ist Rasse?*" that ran for the rest of the year. Images of racial health and degeneration became part of the aural and visual space of the new Germany, circulating in calendars, school books, newspapers, and the hundreds of thousands of pamphlets distributed by the Rassenpolitisches Amt of the NSDAP. By 1938, *Neues Volk*, the journal directed at biopolitical professionals, attained an astonishing circulation of

---

and Racism in Everyday Life, trans. Richard Deveson (New Haven, CT, and London: Yale University Press, 1987), 125–55; and Bartov, *Hitler's Army*, esp. 144–78.

[63] Jürgen Falter, "Kontinuität und Neubeginn: Die Bundestagswahl 1949 zwischen Weimar und Bonn," *Politische Vierteljahresschrift* 22, no. 3 (1981): 236–63.

[64] Introductory editorial in the first issue of the journal *Neues Volk* 1 (July 1933).

[65] Walter Gross, "Von der äusseren zur inneren Revolution," *Neues Volk* 2 (August 1934).

[66] Hans F. K. Günther, "Was ist Rasse?" *Illustrierter Beobachter* 8 (12 Aug. 1933): 32; "Grenzen des Mitleids," *Neues Volk* 1 (July 1933).

three hundred thousand.[67] The campaign to tell "who is who" – "Who Is A Jew? – Who Is Mixed Race? – Who Can Be a German Citizen and Who Cannot?" – intensified in November 1935, with the publication of the Nürnberg Laws.[68] They regulated not only who could marry whom but how Germans were to marry, thereby adding the expectation of proper conduct to the definition of race. The signals for correct "Aryan" behavior became even more explicit when, in fall 1941, the public suddenly unmistakably "saw" Jews who had been required to wear a yellow star. "Who among us even had a clue that the enemy stood so directly next to us... in the street, in the subways, in line in front of the tobacco shop," averred Goebbels in a front-page article in *Das Reich*.[69] The implication was obvious: racial vigilance had to be exercised even in the most ordinary places and the most ordinary ways. Life more and more resembled the "continual special news bulletin" that Christa Wolf's Nelly remembered.[70] For Germany's remaining Jews the result was "social death."

To be a proper German meant representing the self as an ongoing biological project, which means that there must have been a rather elaborate performative aspect to National Socialism, although this has scarcely been addressed by scholars. It is worth contemplating the extent to which Nazi activists and sympathizers groomed themselves in the years after 1933. The Nazi era "body project" included guidelines on makeup, fashion, and hair styling; on calisthenics and exercise; and on a proper diet. It revealed a keen sense of style in order to carry the presumption of racial superiority. And it embraced what has become to us the familiar politics of lifestyle, as the Nazi war on cancer so well reveals.[71] There are a few tantalizing clues as to how this worked itself out. We know that Germans learned to coordinate their vocabulary to the biological worldview. There is evidence that fashion expressed a more deliberately work- or sports-oriented comportment as might be expected in a more self-conscious *Volksgemeinschaft*. Did more girls wear "thick long braids," as Christa Wolf recalls? Fashion advertisements certainly celebrated blondes, *"überall die schönsten."*[72] Advertising pages also reveal that paramilitary apparel became part of the everyday look for both men and boys.[73] The growing popularity of fedoras also suggested the appeal of more uniform, less socially characteristic apparel; more and more men took the effort to include themselves in a national public that was modern and socially undifferentiated. In the home itself, there was often a "brown corner" (Braunecke), in which

---

[67] *Illustrierter Beobachter*, no. 1 (6 Jan. 1934): 19; Walter Gross, "Drei Jahre rassenpolitische Aufklärungsarbeit," *Volk und Rasse* (1936), 331–7; *Neues Volk* 6 (Oct. 1938).

[68] *Berliner Morgenpost*, 16 November 1935.

[69] Goebbels, "Die Juden sind schuld!" *Das Reich*, 16 November 1941.

[70] Wolf, 172.

[71] Robert N. Proctor, *The Nazi War on Cancer* (Princeton, NJ: Princeton University, 1999).

[72] Wolf, 98, and "Schwarzkopf Extra-Blond," *Illustrierter Beobachter*, 8 July 1933; "Roberts Nur-Blond," *Illustrierter Beobachter*, 29 July 1933.

[73] See, for example, *Illustrierter Beobachter*, 6 May 1933 (ad for Quaker oats); 20 May 1933 (Quaker oats), 16 Dec. 1933 (Saba radio).

the photograph of the Führer and other Nazi memorabilia were displayed, but we do not know how common this was. Over 10 million copies of Hitler's *Mein Kampf* circulated by 1945, although again it is not clear how this difficult – for Gründel "unfortunately still unabridged" – text was read and studied.[74] Much of the evidence that Germans endeavored to become Aryans was in fact deliberately destroyed, a fact that in itself is revealing. After twelve years, scores of family photographs documented men in work camps, dressed in uniforms, and outfitted with telltale swastikas and other clues of racial identity. "When you have two military brothers and a like-minded brother-in-law, you can imagine what sort of stuff has collected around the house," wrote one woman in besieged Gleiwitz in late January 1945 as she tore up incriminating photographs before the arrival of the Russians.[75] This record of destruction provides a further glimpse of the knowing entanglement of individuals in the racial categories of Nazism.

The perspective of the victim is perhaps the most useful to assess the degree to which racial categories were adopted in everyday social exchanges. Victor Klemperer's diaries detail the ease with which Germans extracted themselves from relations with Jews and comfortably inhabited their Aryan identity. Sebastian Haffner, not a Jew, but a liberal, was astonished, after just a few weeks, at how many people "now felt uninhibited and justified" to discuss the "Jewish question," "whereby the allegedly disproportionate percentage of Jewish doctors, lawyers, journalists etc. was accepted by even formerly 'educated' people as a valid argument."[76]

With the Nuremberg Laws racial categories governed the most important aspects of everyday life, particularly the permission to marry and the registration of births and deaths. Just how willingly the identity of German or Aryan or Jew was accepted is not clear, but these certainly became part of ordinary existence. Since vigorous public interest in genealogy went hand in hand with legal requirements to prepare an *Ahnenpass*, or genealogical passport, there seems to have been broad legitimacy of the idea of German kin and the notion of racial insiders and outsiders. The popular *Illustrierter Beobachter* imagined Germans searching through "attics" and "dusty chests": "That is where you will find old, faded letters... passports, residence certificates, marriage licenses... a large leather-bound album: its great-grandmother's *Poesiealbum*!" And "soon enough contact is made with your ancestors." In his *Genealogische Plauderei*, Oscar Robert Achenbach went on to recommend a trip to local *Pfarrämter*, where before 1874 all births, marriages, and deaths had been registered. Although most contemporaries were familiar with a "family tree," in which relatives are organized from the oldest ancestors, usually an

---

[74] Gründel, 271.

[75] Quoted in Walter Kempowski, *Das Echolot: Fuga furiosa: Ein Kollektives Tagebuch, Winter 1945*, vol. 2 (Munich: A. Knaus, 1999), 650.

[76] Michael Wildt, *Generation des Unbedingten: Das Führungskorps des Reichssicherheitshauptamtes* (Hamburg: Hamburger Edition, 2002), 156.

ancient husband and wife, down to the family clusters of the living generation, Achenbach urged National Socialists to prepare something rather different, an *Ahnentafel* that worked from the contemporary individual backward to include all lineal relatives. "If the family tree is colorful and many-sided, depending on the number of children and the structure of the family, the *Ahnentafel*," Achenbach wrote, "has an architectonic layout characterized by strict discrimination and mathematical uniformity." Beginning with the individual in question, the *Ahnentafel* "reveals the direction of maternal and paternal bloodlines" in order to serve as a certification of blood purity and thus the inclusion of the individual in the *Volksgemeinschaft*.[77] This was no easy task. Germans needed the "nose of an accomplished detective" in order to gather up all the data to track bloodlines into the past. "State archives and libraries have to be trawled . . . and also ranking lists, muster roles, telephone books, bills of lading, guild records. We also have to make our way to old cemeteries where tumbledown graves might reveal yet another clue."[78] "Tumble-down graves" – there is an uneasy resemblance between the effort to document Aryan identity before 1945 and the recovery of traces of Jewish life in Germany and Poland after 1945.

All this busywork was a matter of life and death once the Nuremberg Laws required all Germans to prove the "Aryan" identity of all four grandparents. This demonstration entailed a huge effort, which individual Germans had to undertake by themselves. Now it was not thousands of amateurs poking around local archives, but millions of presumed "Aryans" who needed an official validation of Aryan births and marriages, which *Pfarrerämter and Standesämter* provided against a nominal fee of ten to sixty pfennigs, usually paid in postage stamps. For those individuals who encountered difficulty locating all four grandparents, the documentation could take longer and become rather expensive. In one case, the local pastor did not recognize the last name, sending one Herbert Fuhst on a chase that lasted one and one-half years and cost 150–200 marks.[79] Not surprisingly, among the new professions in the Third Reich was that of genealogical researcher. What is noteworthy about this genealogical effort is that almost every German had to undertake it individually. To procure documentation for oneself, two parents, and four grandparents added up and demanded that the individual create a permanent binder. After 1936, being a German implied the effort of archiving the racial self. The process of documentation had become so familiar that it served as the raw material for everyday humor. Legion were the whispered stories of faithful party members offended by pastors who had provided them with literal transcriptions of the old-fashioned and often moralistic entries in the church books that described

---

[77] Oscar Robert Achenbach, "Eine Viertelstunde Familienforschung," *Illustrierter Beobachter* 9 (19 May 1934): 812, 814.
[78] Udo R. Fischer, "Familienforschung; ein Gebot der Stunde," *Neues Volk* 1 (July 1933): 20–1.
[79] Herbert Fuhst to Reichsstelle für Sippenforschung, 8 Jan. 1937, in BA-B, Reichssippenamt, R 1509/565a.

the illegitimate birth of a beloved grandmother.[80] Of course, jokes mocked the high seriousness of the genealogical enterprise, but they also made "Aryan" identities more homespun. "I am of agrarian background," began the inquiry of one petitioner. Another insisted: "I looked up Aryan in the encyclopedia. They live in Asia. We don't have family there, we're from Prenzlau." "Thank God Grandma is illegitimate," commented a relieved genealogist, "now I don't have to look for a marriage certificate."[81]

Beginning in 1936, anyone getting married also assumed an "Aryan" identity. Prospective husbands and wives needed to document their own Aryan racial status with notarized citations of the registrations of the birth, marriage, and death of each of their parents and grandparents. Moreover, prospective newlyweds had to certify their genetic health, which often meant a visit to the local public health office and the acquisition of additional documents. In addition to handing out *Mein Kampf*, the registrar's office provided couples with pamphlets on maintaining and reproducing good racial stock, "Germans, Think of Your and Your Children's Health, Handbook for the German Family, and Advice for Mothers," and instructions on how to maintain proper genealogical records. Finally, German newlyweds received a coupon for a one-month trial subscription to a newspaper, preferably the Nazi Party daily, *Völkischer Beobachter*.[82] All this added up to a broad effort to push Germans to document and comport themselves as Aryans. Piece by piece, even ordinary Germans assembled their own private archives, and as they did they invariably became more recognizable as Aryans in Hitler's eyes and in their own. Considerable attention was paid to the racial responsibilities of women, who oversaw child rearing, family health, and domestic expenses. Between 1934 and 1937, 1,139,945 women took part in the *Mutterschulungskurse* offered by the NS-Frauenschaft.[83]

The creation of a new Aryan elite by the SS was a gigantic enterprise. The SS self-consciously thought of itself as a new breed of leaders who were politically and morally more advanced and more racially pure than the German population as a whole, although it should not be isolated from the general effort, on the part of the regime and the public, to achieve an Aryan subjectivity. The SS put great emphasis on the training of ruthless political soldiers whose primary responsibility was to the realization of the racial community. In particular, the SS hoped to break more traditional affinities to religious communities and the conventional principles of Christian love and mercy which

[80] See the articles in *Schwarzes Korps*, 3 Mar. 1939 and 16 Feb. 1939, in BA-B, Reichssippenamt, R 1509/565.

[81] "Anfragen beim Kusteramt," *Neues Volk* 4 (July 1936): 47.

[82] Reichsministerium des Innern, "Dienstleistungen für die Standesbeamten und ihre Aufsichtsbehörden (1938)," BA-B, R1501/127452.

[83] Stefan Schnurr, "Die nationalsozialistische Funktionalisierung sozialer Arbeit: Zur Kontinuität und Diskontinuität der Praxis sozialer Berufe," in *Politische Formierung und soziale Erziehung im Nationalsozialismus*, eds. Hans-Uwe Otto and Heinz Sünker (Frankfurt: Suhrkamp, 1991), 121–2.

continued to sway most Germans. Moreover, the SS quite resolutely demanded of its members new, more racially self-conscious codes of private behavior. Not only were unmarried SS men pressured to find appropriate love matches and to bear children, and to remain faithful to their wives once married, but all prospective wives had to go to considerable lengths to prove their Aryan origins and German comportment. According to Himmler, "In the old days it was often said: 'you must marry so-and-so;' we say: 'you are permitted to marry her and not her.'" In other words, "to fall in love, get engaged, and then marry is no longer a personal matter."[84] Even after the start of the war loosened racial prescriptions, hundreds, if not thousands of prospective brides were deemed unsuitable. This rigorous process of selection conformed to a highly gendered division of responsibilities in which the husband served the racial community as political soldier and the wife as mother and helpmate, but it also underscored the crucial role assigned to women in fashioning the new race. As Gudrun Schwarz demonstrates, SS wives willingly accepted their role as racial superiors, both before the war as privileged members of an elect "community of lineage" and during the war as active enforcers of the racial hierarchy, especially in the occupied territories.

Yet the boundaries between the SS *Sippengemeinschaft* and the German population in general should not be drawn too sharply. Nearly 800,000 German men, more than 1 percent of the total population of "Greater Germany," joined the SS between 1931 and 1945; over the same time, over 240,000 women married SS men. SS members interacted with local German populations when they resettled to run the concentration and work camps that were scattered across German as well as German-occupied territory. More importantly, the SS ethic of mercilessness corresponded to the much broader, if always less resolute recognition of "the limits of empathy" that accompanied the regime's media campaigns in favor of sterilization and euthanasia. Images of supposedly unproductive or worthless lives saturated popular culture, particularly movies, schoolbooks, and prescriptive homemaking texts. Moreover, by 1936, all persons classified as Germans needed to adjust their lives in order to adhere to racial guidelines; SS expectations were more severe, but not fundamentally different. Finally, the majority of Germans participated in the rituals of the racial community. It is estimated that nearly every German spent at least some time in a work or education camp (*Lager*) between 1933 and 1945. Young people had the most sustained and frequent camp experiences. With the introduction of one half-year obligatory community service for all young between the ages of eighteen and twenty-five in June 1935 (*Reichsarbeitsdienst*) and the requirement that all adolescent boys join the Hitler Youth, the Nazis created a political itinerary that structured the experiences of an entire generation. School year upon school year was handed to the Hitler Youth, community service, and then the Wehrmacht itself. Community service was extended in September 1939 to

---

[84] Gudrun Schwarz, *Eine Frauan seiner Seite: Ehefrauen in der "SS-Sippengemeinschaft"* (Hamburg: Hamburg Edition, 1997), 26.

include young women, who as adolescents were also encouraged to join the Bund deutscher Mädel. "What this produced was the structural coordination of the biographies of young people in Nazi Germany," comments Klaus Latzel.[85]

The Lager experience was not limited to the young, although it is certainly true that it was the generation born between 1925 and 1935 that most thoroughly identified with National Socialism. According to Adolf Mertens, who pioneered the pedagogy of the camp, "a network of camps covers our country from the sea to the mountains, for the heaths and forests of the East to the industrial regions of the West. Camps for party officials, for SA, SS, and HJ, for lawyers, artists, doctors, civil servants, corporate directors, for men and for women, for young people and for those much older."[86] "There are camps in tents and in houses, camps for thirty and for several hundred and even one-thousand participants." "When the sun sets," concluded one astonished observer, "camp crews all over Germany are standing at attention in flag parades."[87] Not surprisingly, "camp leader" and "Rural Service Educator" became recognized careers in the Third Reich. The central experience of the camp was the continuous rehearsal of the racial community. With the stress on comradeship, soldierly discipline, and paramilitary uniformity, camps were the sites where National Socialism could best be experienced. They promoted Volkswerdung, or "becoming a people," by substituting comradely for bourgeois social relations. "Title and rank are put aside," wrote a smitten camp participant in retrospect: "Here we recognize only one form of address: Comrade and You!"[88] The camps are quite rightly described as "total institutions," even if they did not all at once transform social relations or recreate German citizens into racial comrades. They made credible the "second world" of National Socialism and demanded and encouraged Germans to think and talk about and to comport themselves as members of a vigilant racial community.

It was on the battlefield, rather than in the camps, that the "New Man" of the Third Reich was most closely realized. The increasingly brutal fighting on the Eastern Front, in particular, made the world in view correspond more and more closely to the Nazi worldview. The titanic race war between Germany and Russia stylized in the propaganda the Nazis directed both to the home front and to the fighting lines was in fact what millions of soldiers thought they were fighting. In the isolated and frightening circumstances of military engagement, it is not always easy to disentangle what ordinary soldiers believed from what they were ordered to do, but a recent generation of military historians emphasizes the degree to which the racialization of combat morale came to regulate extremely

[85] Klaus Latzel, *Deutsche Soldaten–nationalsozialistischer Krieg? Kriegserlebnis–Kriegserfahrung 1939–1945* (Paderborn: Schöningh, 1998), 86.

[86] Mertens quoted by Jürgen Schiedeck and Martin Stahlmann, "Die Inzenierung 'totalen Erlebens': Lagererziehung im Nationalsozialismus," in *Politische Formierung und soziale Erziehung im Nationalsozialismus*, eds. Hans-Uwe Otto and Heinz Sünker (Frankfurt: Suhrkamp, 1991), 173.

[87] Günther quoted by Schiedeck and Stahlmann, 173.

[88] Schiedeck and Stahlmann, 194, 172.

brutal conduct toward the uniformed enemy; toward Polish, Russian, and Ukrainian civilians; and, of course, toward Europe's Jews. The gestures of racial superiority were more obvious among SS men and their wives, but also present in the behavior of Wehrmacht soldiers and officers. What is noteworthy is not only the overall effect of race war, which from the perspective of victims appeared quite seamless, yet from the perspective of the soldiers was perhaps more threadbare, but also the general effort to assume the racial identity of an Aryan combatant.

In the Soviet Union, too, the war marked a threshold in the making of the New Man. The relentless calls for human transformation and self-sacrifice in struggle, which pervaded the political culture of the 1930s and shaped the personal lives of thousands of Communists, assumed an even greater momentum in the context of wartime mobilization. The injunction to prove one's moral worth in combat now extended to large segments of the population who served in the Red Army or worked at the "home front." Before the war, the feverish campaign to build the new world had relied on elusive images of "enemies" – the "old bourgeoisie," "counterrevolutionary wreckers," and "foreign spies" – who allegedly obstructed the building of the Communist paradise. These images did not always convince individuals to join in the battle.[89] With the German invasion of the Soviet Union, the mythical struggle between the "dying old world order" and the emerging new world came to life for countless Soviet citizens in urgent and existentially relevant ways.[90] Unlike in Nazi Germany, however, the physical act of warfare itself was not the principal site of the New Man's creation. What happened instead was that practices of Soviet political and moral education, established before the war, were carried to the battleground and put to work in a wartime environment.

Many of those who oversaw the Soviet war effort – political officers attached to Red Army units, NKVD surveillance stationed behind the front, military correspondents, and individual officers and soldiers themselves – evaluated the performance of Soviet fighters during the war in terms of their personal moral growth under fire. NKVD officials read soldiers' mail, grouping it according to a given author's moral strength or weakness. Political officers lectured their soldiers on desired personality traits, and they applied disciplinary sanctions with soldiers' moral transformation in view.[91] Military historians have remarked on the ruthless culture of violence that reigned inside the Red Army during the war, but they have paid less attention to the moral framework in which the disciplinary measures were rooted. The standard against which Red Army soldiers

[89] Veronique Garros, Natalia Korenevskaya, and Thomas Lahusen, eds., *Intimacy and Terror: Soviet Diaries of the 1930s.*

[90] Amir Weiner, *Making Sense of War: The Second World War and the Fate of the Bolshevik Revolution* (Princeton, NJ: Princeton University Press, 2001).

[91] Ia. F. Pogonii et al., eds., *Stalingradskaia epopeia: Vpervye publikuemye dokumenty, rassekrechennye FSB RF* (Moscow: "Zvonnitsa-MG," 2000); Vasilii Chekalov, *Voennyi dnevnik: 1941, 1942, 1943* (Moscow: Rossiiskoe gumanisticheskoe ob-vo, 2003).

were measured and punished was that of a Stakhanovite worker at war, an individual fueled by inexhaustible willpower, who burned with a desire to sacrifice himself for the larger cause. Professional writers and critics, who for decades had played an enormous role in the propagation of the new socialist world and the New Man, took this mission into the war years. Many of them volunteered to serve as military correspondents. Their portrayals of heroic Soviet soldiers were intensely received by Red Army soldiers and assimilated into their personal experience of the war. The writer and critic Ilya Ehrenburg wrote daily columns in the Red Army newspaper, lecturing Soviet soldiers about who they were, what kind of battle they were engaged in, and what sort of beastly enemy they were fighting. At the front Ehrenburg's articles proved so popular that there were decrees forbidding the paper on which they were printed to be used for rolling tobacco; his articles had to be cut out and preserved for others to read.[92] As he covered the war, Ehrenburg was interested above all in gauging the transformative effect it had on Soviet men and women. "While we have gone through great losses during the war," he noted in 1943, "we have gained from it the new man, a superior human type. The war has been imposed on us by a cruel and immoral enemy. This is a heavy burden. We have never idealized the war and we are not idealizing it. We are not fascists for whom war is the apex of civilization."[93] War, especially a war waged against an enemy who denounced the universal values of Western humanity, could act as a powerful moral agent. At the same time, Ehrenburg distanced himself from the pursuit of warfare in and of itself. The focus on moral growth and transformation that he shared with Soviet political officers revealed a striking continuity in wartime Russia of the Soviet Communist belief in the malleability and perfectibility of human nature. In Nazi Germany, the war had a fundamentally different standing. It was on the battlefield that the racialized properties and imperial ambitions of the new man were to materialize.

The quick victories of the Germans first against Norway, Holland, Belgium, and France in spring 1940, and then Yugoslavia a year later, and, in the first five months after the June 1941 invasion, the Soviet Union created an extraordinary familiarity with empire which worked itself into everyday exchanges. The features of this new imperial identity can be seen most plainly in the self-assured geopolitical analyses of Goebbels's weekly, *Das Reich*, which began publication in the victorious summer of 1940. It introduced an insistently global perspective to German readers to take the measure of British isolation and to identify the resources of Germany's power and that of its allies. Spokesmen for the Third Reich such as Carl Schmitt outlined the reasoning behind "the Reich as the force for European order," while others surveyed the colonial administration in Poland, describing the *Generalgouvernement* as "a field

[92] Joshua Rubenstein, *Tangled Loyalties: the Life and Times of Ilya Ehrenburg* (New York: Basic Books, 1996), 193.

[93] Ilya Ehrenburg, *Cent Lettres*, trans. A. Roudnikov (Moscow: Editions en langues étrangères, 1944), 12.

for experiments in imperial structuring" and the new settlements of German colonialism that spread out from Litzmannstadt.[94] In their mind's eye, soldiers moved across Germany's imperial space with astonishing ease, even looking upon their assignments abroad as an opportunity for tourism. As new mobilization orders came through in spring 1941, soldiers took turns guessing: "We're guessing and wondering: the South of France? Holland or Poland? Over Italy to Africa? Home–Home? No one believes that," recalled Hans Hoeschen in one of his early reportages: "What would we be doing Home?"[95] Even civilians wandered vicariously along the outposts of empire. For the first time, wrote *Die Mode*, fashion was fitted to new political borders: new Berlin collections in 1942 featured "colorful stitches in the style of South Eastern costumes – short, loose fleece coats like those worn by Hungarian shepherds – caps first inspired by Sicilian fishermen – the white hood of the Dutch – narrow black shawls worn around the head and the stepped, layered skirts of the Spaniards."[96] And what were Berlin housewives preparing for dinner? "This year, for the first time, green peppers, and also eggplants and chicory have been conquered by Germany's kitchens," noted *Das Reich* about "Berlin in autumn 1941": "Sauces or stuffing for paprika halves is the more likely topic of conversations between neighbors than the last film."[97]

The dramatic reordering of European space also established striking confidence in a racialized anthropology of subject peoples. Tarnopol, for example, was known to Hans Hoeschen to be a "city with two faces. Some things were formed by the German spirit, which is expressed in Bohemian and Frankish forms. This was once a outpost of a courageous German *Bürgertum*, whose colonial endeavors gave the cities of the East their character for centuries." The rest of the city, however, is "eastern [*ostisch*], strange, and gloomy."[98] German soldiers in both world wars deployed hierarchical categories classifying friend and foe in terms of cleanliness and dirtiness, but in World War II, the letters posted from the Eastern Front were much more apt to make physiognomical judgments on the population rather than the landscape. An increasingly racialized point of view was expressed in the proportion of negative references to hygiene and in the drastic pejoratives that dismiss people as everything from "'dull,' 'dumb,' 'stupid' all the way to 'depraved' und 'barely humanlike,'" against which Klaus Latzel adds, "the vocabulary of the First World War seems almost harmless." Latzel concludes:

> That the French were arrogant, the Jews money-hungry, the Poles lazy and dirty, the Russians dull, and the Serbs highway robbers, all that previous generations had 'known,' and there was little need for remedial lessons. But that these traditional

[94] Carl Schmitt, "Das Meer gegen das Land," *Das Reich*, 9 Mar. 1941; also *Das Reich*, 5 Jan. 1941.
[95] Hans Hoeschen, *Zwischen Weichsel und Wolga* (Gütersloh: C. Bertelsmann, 1943), 8.
[96] "Aus den Kollektionen," *Die Mode* 2 (Jan./Feb. 1942).
[97] Jürgen Schüddekopf, "Berlin im Herbst 1941," *Das Reich*, 26 Oct. 1941.
[98] Hans Hoeschen, 46–7.

stereotypes not only classified the people for whom they were minted, but ranked them in hierarchies, biologically justified their dehumanization, and in extreme cases opened the way for their destruction, this was a lesson that only the Nazis felt capable of successfully teaching.[99]

The new knowledge that ordinary soldiers on the front had acquired earned the unabashed praise of Goebbels. "Their judgement of the enemy," he stressed, "was sober, objective, without a trace of arrogance, but always superior. They offered opinions about the mentality of the Bolsheviks or the English that would put a practiced social psychologist to shame."[100]

The new knowledge of race war did not always come easily. The military historian Hannes Heer stresses the moment of "shock" and the subsequent process of "renormalization." "The tale told by the letters written by the majority of soldiers who invaded the Soviet Union in summer 1941," he explains is of the "experience having turned them 'into a different person,' of a process of 'inner change' having occurred, of being forced to 'completely readjust,' and also of having to 'throw overboard several principles held in the past.'" While Heer concedes that "a minority of men experienced this 'adjustment' as a harrowing process of 'split consciousness' which ended either in their resigned withdrawal into a world of subjective privacy . . . most soldiers managed to adapt effortlessly to the shock: they became 'hard,' 'indifferent,' and 'heartless.'"[101]

A "New Man" became more and more recognizable. According to Kleo Pleyer, a reporter on the Eastern Front:

> The battle-grey German was spared nothing in the Soviet Union. He did not just go through a triumphant offensive attack, as in France, he also had to keep his head amidst enemy artillery that lasted hours, days, weeks. He has seen one comrade after another fall bloody to the ground, he has seen the shredded corpse of a friend. For months he lived in hell. Countless nights he stood guard with his machine gun without relief, from dusk to dawn, shaking with cold and drenched by rain. . . . But for all that he only became stronger, harder.[102]

What emerged was a new kind of heroism that had been incubated ideologically in the 1920s but only put into practice a half-generation later; the combat soldier increasingly assumed the virtues of unsparing and ruthless hardness, and whose brutality was justified not any longer in general terms of Christian

---

[99] Klaus Latzel, 177, 181. See also Klara Löffler, *Aufgehoben: Soldatenbriefe aus dem Zweiten Weltkrieg: Eine Studie zur subjektiven Wirklichkeit des Krieges* (Bamberg: WVB, 1992), 122.

[100] Goebbels, "Gespräche mit Frontsoldaten," *Das Reich*, 26 July 1942.

[101] Hannes Heer, "How Amorality Became Normality: Reflections on the Mentality of German Soldiers on the Eastern Front," in *War of Extermination: The German Military in World War II, 1941–44*, eds. Hannes Heer and Klaus Naumann (New York: Berghahn Books, 2000), 331–32. See also Omer Bartov, *Hitler's Army: Soldiers, Nazis, and the War in Third Reich* (New York: Berghahn Books, 1991), 26; and Hanns Wiedmann, *Landser, Tod, und Teufel: Aufzeichnungen aus dem Feldzug im Osten* (Munich: Piper, 1943), 11.

[102] Kleo Pleyer, *Volk im Feld* (Hamburg: Hanseatische verlaganstalt, 1943), 227.

duty or national service, but in much more precise ideological allegiances to the Führer or to "*Volk*, Fatherland, and Destiny."[103] "Here war is pursued in its pure form," reflected one soldier in July 1941; "any sign of humanity seems to have disappeared from deeds, hearts, and minds." "With the senses of a predator we recognize how the rest of the world will be ground between the millstones of this war."[104] The absolute terms of the engagement on the Eastern Front became more drastic after Stalingrad, when explicit references to the very survival of Germany betrayed the new defensive situation of the racial empire in early 1943. The huge casualty rate that accompanied Germany's long defeat actually produced more and more New Men: officers newly promoted from the ranks wore distinct uniforms of an increasingly lawless, terrifying elite whose seeming invincibility except at the very end remains a familiar media fantasy to this day. New professionals also proliferated in the Reich's "ethnic cleansing" operations in which hundreds of thousands of allegedly ethnic Germans were reclaimed and resettled, racially undesirable Poles pushed aside and forcibly put to work, and racially unacceptable Jews isolated and then murdered. Germany's New Man is most completely visible, most concretely realized, across the vast killing field which he laid out in the war years.

Nazi Germany's war against the Soviet Union brought the Third Reich's New Man fully to life. Engaged in what they believed was a brutal race war against inferior people, Germany's soldiers increasingly identified with the tough, remorseless figure that had been the Nazi ideal. But this New Man was fundamentally different from his Soviet counterpart. In the Soviet Union, the New Man fashioned himself in accordance with the stringent but lawful movements of progressive history and was available as an exemplar to be emulated around the world. If the demands of history left behind Old Men, and literally condemned them to death, the promise of history also recreated a new socialist being. In contrast, the New Man in Germany mistrusted history. It was precisely the danger zones of World War I, the awful, hidden potentials of technological mobilization, and the international jeopardy in which postwar Germany found itself that made the New Man both possible and necessary. The adherents of Nazi racial suprematism mobilized in lieu of history, while the Stalinist citizen believed himself to be the embodiment of historical progression. It is not surprising, then, that for all the violent dissociation of the New Man from the Old Man under Stalinism, the process of creation was regarded as consistent with universal Enlightenment principles. In Germany, the New Men were Aryans first and foremost, serving the particular interests of Germany, not the general ideas of revolution and liberation. Socialist New Men could find each other around the globe; Aryan New Men knew only each other. In this sense, the New Man in the Soviet Union was more optimistic, while the New Man in Nazi Germany could only rely on the bloodlines of his own people, reclaiming Aryans out of Germans and ethnically "lost" Germans,

[103] Latzel, 367–8.
[104] Quoted in Bartov, 26.

but uninterested in and uninteresting to the rest of the world. If the enemy of the Soviet Union lay in the dead hand of the past, which did not release all contemporaries and condemned them as useless, the enemy of the Third Reich was spatial: what was around Germans, what threatened to contaminate Germans. This self-absorption with the racial body meant that there was no developed category of Old Men in Nazi Germany: Germans as such were Aryans who needed to be taught to recognize their racial selves; those political groups that had misled the country in the decades before the Nazi revolution were not regarded as incorrigible as was often the case in the Soviet Union. But this self-absorption with the Aryan self also meant a fanatical concern with eliminating racial impurities, Jews, first and foremost, but also people who were deemed to be impaired with heritable physical and mental defects.

The Soviet New Man cultivated the self both physically and intellectually and sought a rational and critical praxis of the individual. There was great stress on the soul and on the process of recognizing and unlearning bourgeois habits and on recognizing and assuming socialist virtues. It was the individual's intellectual responsibility to remake himself, a labor that was exposed in and advanced by textual analysis, diaries, autobiographies, and other instruments of self-reflection. The emphasis on the text stands in contrast to Nazi Germany's suspicion of books and letters. In Hitler's words, blood could blot out paper.[105] Germany's New Men worked on their bodies and on their relations with other bodies, whether these were Aryan spouses and the German *Volk* or Russian "subhumans" and Jewish "parasites." Although early Nazis produced autobiographical texts, *Mein Kampf* first and foremost among them, Nazi Germany did not cultivate intellectual self-examination. The huge paper trail that the Nazis left behind aimed to index the physical body and technical and physical capacities and to ensure the separation of healthy Aryans from dangerous others. As a result, the New Men of the Soviet Union and the New Men of Nazi Germany did not recognize each other as elites, although each cited the peril of the other in order to accelerate the process of self-fashioning at home.

Stalinist and Nazi New Men did share a common commitment to discipline, whether intellectual or physical, and thus a belief in the ability to leave behind the liberal world. They both put a premium on organized collectivities – their marching order expressing, alternatively, the powerful march of history or the strength and beauty of the master race. Only through synchronic collective exertions could history be propelled forward, as the Soviets believed, or the degenerate tumble of history be reversed, as in the German case. Both scorned liberalism for its weakness and inability to cope with the demands of the modern world. Their pretense to transform the world in systematic fashion and grandiose ways legitimated their claim to being vanguards of two distinct variants of an illiberal modernity. In the Soviet case, the liberal world had

---

[105] See Katerina Clark and Karl Schlögel's contribution on the Soviet image of Nazi Germany in this volume.

become obsolescent and a grander future could be achieved; in the Nazi case, the liberal world obscured more fundamental racial identities. There was a dizzying audaciousness in the assumption that new collective identities could be claimed in the twentieth century. However, this audaciousness also revealed itself in the vast destructive energies that the creation of the New Man entailed. In the Soviet Union, New Men presupposed Old Men abandoned by history who needed to be cleared away; in Nazi Germany, New Men revealed themselves in their willingness to eliminate any and all racial perils. The assumption of new identities was ultimately a ferocious attack on and a frightening alternative to liberal modernity, a state of being that is possible and demands scrutiny.

PART IV

ENTANGLEMENTS

9

States of Exception

The Nazi-Soviet War as a System of Violence, 1939–1945

Mark Edele and Michael Geyer

> Step forward: We hear that you are a good man. . . . Listen, we know you are our
> enemy. Therefore we now shall put you against a wall. But in consideration of
> your merits and virtues, it will be a good wall, and we shall shoot you with good
> bullets from good guns, and we shall bury you with a good shovel in good soil.
>
> (Bertolt Brecht, "Verhör des Guten")
>
> And as to you, when the time has come that man will be his brother's keeper,
> look back on us with forbearance.
>
> (Bertolt Brecht, "An die Nachgeborenen")[1]

The trouble is that neither the Wehrmacht nor the Red Army considered merit
and virtue and, inasmuch as they buried the dead, they did not bury them in
good soil. Neither did those born afterward show forbearance, for they were
either too caught up in the dark times they tried to escape after defeat or
never saw the darkness in the bright light of victory. The Soviet Union and the
German Reich fought a war that denied virtue and honor to enemy soldiers and
set entire people against each other in a life-and-death struggle. Memorializing

---

[1] Tritt vor: Wir hören / Daß Du ein guter Mann bist. . . . So höre: Wir wissen / Du bist unser Feind.
Deshalb wollen wir Dich / Jetzt an eine Wand stellen. Aber in Anbetracht deiner Verdienste /
Und guten Eigenschaften / An eine gute Wand und dich erschießen mit / Guten Kugeln guter
Gewehre und dich begraben mit / Einer guten Schaufel in guter Erde. Bertolt Brecht, "Verhör Des
Guten [Me-Ti/ Buch Der Wendungen]," in *Gesammelte Werke*, ed. Bertolt Brecht (Frankfurt am
Main: Suhrkamp Verlag, 1967), 462–3. Ihr aber, wenn es so weit sein wird / Daß der Mensch
dem Menschen ein Helfer ist / Gedenkt unserer / Mit Nachsicht. Idem, "An die Nachgeborenen
[Svedenborger Gedichte]," in *Gesammelte Werke*, vol. 9, 722–5, here 725.

Research for this essay was made possible in part (for Mark Edele) by a University of Western
Australia Research Grant (UWARG) (2006) and (for Michael Geyer) by a fellowship of the American Academy in Berlin (2004) and a Humboldt Forschungspreis (2007). Thanks to Josh Sanborn
and Elena Shulman for kind permission to quote from unpublished work. Special thanks to Peter
Holquist for his contributions to this essay in an early stage of the discussion.

the war did not bring, or has not brought yet, together what the war had torn asunder.[2] In the new century, there are some indications that the time for forbearance or, in any case, for commemoration in the spirit of mutuality may yet come.[3] However, the moment is most certainly right for a reconsideration of the single most destructive war of the twentieth century, the war between Nazi Germany and Soviet Russia, and to approach this war not as a German or a Soviet affair, respectively, but as a ferocious and brutal antagonism in a wider field of European and global war.[4]

The lethal encounter between the militarized polities of Germany and the Soviet Union on what the Germans called the "Eastern Front" (*Ostfront*) and the Soviets the "Great Patriotic War" (*Velikaia Otechestvennaia voina*) can only be essayed in the literal sense; that is, as an experiment or, in one of the OEDs definitions, a "first tentative effort in learning."[5] The reasons differ. Simply put, our knowledge about the Soviet side, judges one of the premier military historians of this conflict, "remains appallingly incomplete."[6] Notwithstanding manifestos calling for historians of Russia finally to focus on the war,[7] so far only few studies have emerged that go beyond the excellent operational studies of John Erickson, David Glantz, and Jonathan House.[8] As Catherine Merridale – whose work is among the few exceptions to that rule – has

---

[2] "Kluften der Erinnerung: Rußland und Deutschland sechzig Jahre nach dem Krieg." *Osteuropa* 55, no. 4–6 (2005).

[3] Margot Blank, ed., *Beutestücke: Kriegsgefangene in der deutschen und sowjetischen Fotografie, 1941–1945, Katalog zur Ausstellung im deutsch-russischen Museum Berlin Karlshorst* (Berlin: Ch. Links, 2003); Olga V. Kurilo, ed., *Der Zweite Weltkrieg im deutschen und russischen Gedächtnis* (Berlin: Avinus, 2006).

[4] Gerhard L.Weinberg, *A World at Arms: A Global History of World War II* (Cambridge and New York: Cambridge University Press, 1994); Evan Mawdsley, *Thunder in the East: The Nazi-Soviet War 1941–1945* (London: Hodder, 2005); Norman Davies, *No Simple Victory: World War II in Europe, 1939–1945* (New York: Viking, 2007).

[5] For starting points see Jörg Baberowski and Anselm Doering-Manteufel, *Ordnung durch Terror: Gewaltexzesse und Vernichtung im nationalsozialistischen und stalinistischen Imperium* (Bonn: Dietz, 2006), 71–90; Richard Overy, *The Dictators: Hitler's Germany, Stalin's Russia* (New York: Norton, 2006), 512–25; and Ian Kershaw, *Fateful Choices: Ten Decisions that Changed the World, 1940–1941* (New York: Penguin Press, 2007).

[6] David M. Glantz, *Colossus Reborn: The Red Army at War, 1941–1943* (Lawrence: University Press of Kansas, 2005), 611.

[7] Amir Weiner, "Saving Private Ivan: From What, Why, and How?" *Kritika: Explorations in Russian and Eurasian History* 1, no. 2 (2000): 305–36. He repeated the charge in "In the Long Shadow of War: The Second World War and the Soviet and Post-Soviet World," *Diplomatic History* s25, no. 3 (2001): 443–56.

[8] David M. Glantz and Jonathan House, *When Titans Clashed: How the Red Army Stopped Hitler* (Lawrence: University Press of Kansas, 1995); David M. Glantz, *Barbarossa: Hitler's Invasion of Russia, 1941* (Stroud: Tempus, 2001); id., *The Battle for Leningrad: 1941–1944* (Lawrence: University Press of Kansas, 2002); John Erickson, *The Road to Stalingrad: Stalin's War with Germany*, vol. 1 (New Haven, CT, and London: Yale University Press, 1975); id., *The Road to Berlin: Stalin's War with Germany*, vol. 2 (New Haven, CT, and London: Yale University Press, 1983). Recent additions to the genre include Mawdsley, *Thunder*; and Chris Bellamy, *Absolute War: Soviet Russia in the Second World War* (New York: Alfred A. Knopf, 2007).

recently pointed out, we still know very little "about the lives, background and motivation of the [Soviet] troops themselves."[9] The main struggle is to find sufficient evidence to back up the vast claims popular historians have made about Stalin and the Soviet Union at war.[10] In contrast, we know much, much more about the German side. In fact, the density of historical research on the "Eastern Front," on occupation and collaboration, as well as on annihilation and extermination is staggering.[11] Moreover, the Nazi-Soviet war has been subject to a host of documentaries, films, exhibitions, often with extensive Russian footage and documentation that have engendered intense public debates.[12] Germans now know, or can know, what kind of war their war on the Eastern Front was. But knowledge of the German war, deep and vast as it is, can only become insight if and when it is matched and, indeed, entangled with the knowledge of the other side. For war, and surely war of this

---

[9] Catherine Merridale, "Culture, Ideology and Combat in the Red Army, 1939–45." *Journal of Contemporary History* 41, no. 2 (2006): 305–24; here: 305. See also her seminal *Ivan's War: Life and Death in the Red Army, 1939–1945* (New York: Metropolitan Books, 2006); Kenneth Slepyan, *Stalin's Guerrillas: Soviet Partisans in World War II* (Lawrence: University Press of Kansas, 2006); and Amir Weiner, "Something to Die For, a Lot to Kill For: The Soviet System and the Barbarisation of Warfare, 1939–1945," in: *The Barbarization of Warfare* ed. George Kassimeris (New York: New York University Press, 2006), 101–25. Important Russian-language contributions include *Velikaia Otechestvennaia voina 1941–1945*, Kniga 4: *Narod i voina* (Moscow: Nauka, 1999) (quoted hereafter as: *Narod i voina*); and Elena S. Seniavskaia, *Frontovoe pokolenie 1941–1945. Istoriko-psikhologicheskoe issledovanie* (Moscow: RAN institut Rossiiskoi istorii, 1995).

[10] Television has superseded historiography in this respect. John Erickson handles the relative lack of sources quite well in *The Russian Front, 1941–1945*, four videocassettes (182 min.), directed by John Erickson, Michael Leighton, Lamancha Productions, and Cromwell Productions, 1998, while later Western TV productions are rather weaker. However, see the remarkable hit on Russian TV, *Štrafbat* [Penal Battalion], dir. Nikolaj Dostal', perfs. Aleksei Serebriakov, Iurii Stepanov, and Aleksandr Bashirov, 525 min., Kachestvo DVD, Russia 2004; or the film *Svoi*, dir. Dimitrii Meskhiev, perfs. Bogdan Stupka, Konstantin Khabensky, and Sergei Garmash, color, 105 min., DVD (Moscow: ORT Video 2004).

[11] Rolf-Dieter Müller and Gerd R. Ueberschär, eds., *Hitlers Krieg im Osten 1941–1945: Ein Forschungsbericht* (Darmstadt: Wissenschaftliche Buchgesellschaft, 2000). The list has grown considerably since. See Rolf-Dieter Müller and Hans Erich Volkmann, eds., *Die Wehrmacht: Mythos und Realität* (Munich: Oldenbourg, 1999); Bruno Thoß and Hans-Erich Volkmann, eds., *Erster Weltkrieg – Zweiter Weltkrieg, ein Vergleich: Krieg, Kriegserlebnis, Kriegserfahrung in Deutschland.* (Paderborn: Ferdinand Schöningh, 2002). See the comprehensive series Militärgeschichtliches Forschungsamt, ed., *Das Deutsche Reich und der Zweite Weltkrieg*, 10 vols. (Stuttgart: Deutsche Verlags-Anstalt, 1979–2008). See also the essays by Gerlach and Werth, Baberowski and Doering-Manteuffel, Browning and Siegelbaum, as well as Fitzpatrick and Lüdtke in this volume.

[12] Wulf Kansteiner, *In Pursuit of German Memory: History, Television, and Politics after Auschwitz* (Athens: Ohio University Press, 2006); Eike Wenzel, *Gedächtnisraum Film: Die Arbeit an der deutschen Geschichte in Filmen seit den sechziger Jahren* (Stuttgart: Metzler, 2000); Hannes Heer, *Vom Verschwinden der Täter: Der Vernichtungskrieg fand statt, aber keiner war dabei*, 2nd ed. (Berlin: Aufbau Verlag, 2004); Christian Hartmann, Johannes Hürter, and Ulrike Jureit, eds., *Verbrechen der Wehrmacht: Bilanz einer Debatte* (Munich: C. H. Beck, 2005).

magnitude, is only accounted for inasmuch as both sides see each other and see themselves reflected in the other in their deadly encounter. We may doubt on practical and philosophical grounds that they will ever see the same, but as long as the two sides perceive and, thus, recognize each other, they can at least begin recalling and writing a history in which Brecht's wisdom may apply – in hindsight if not necessarily with forbearance. Whether this history will then be a suitable instrument for mending the tear that ruptured the bond between the two nations is another question.[13]

Given the unequal development of historiography, the ambition of this essay may be foolish – not only to provide a sketch of a history of the adversaries' conduct of war, but also to reflect on the peculiar, expansive, and intensive system of violence that made both German and Soviet societies subjects and objects of destruction. That is, we have to account for a war that reached inside to remake the respective war-fighting society in a war of excisions much as it reached outside in order to subjugate and, indeed, destroy, annihilate, and exterminate the enemy – all the while it was fought in bloody battles by huge armies with utmost intensity along a hyperextended front. We think of the former as a "civil war," that is, a war that aimed at remaking (and obliterating) entire populations, and the latter as a "war of destruction" with its own dynamic toward all-out annihilation. And this does not even account yet for the fusion of interior and exterior war in the territories and with the people in between that became pawns in the hands of both sides.[14]

Our argument unfolds in a number of steps.

First, the unparalleled lethality of this theater of war had its roots not simply in the destructive ideology of the one or the other side, or in a universal dynamic of total war. Rather, the devastating nature of this war, we suggest, is the consequence of the inimical interrelationship of Nazi Germany and the Soviet Union. This was a war fought with utter unrestraint from the start, the result of the assessment of the enemy as peculiarly heinous. From the start, this was not a "conventional" war, but a war in which the imperative was to win by whatever means necessary or to perish entirely.

Military institutions and militarized societies are highly self-contained and self-involved, and this is quite apart from the self-encapsulation of the two

---

[13] Heinrich Böll, Lev Kopelev, and Klaus Bednarz, *Warum haben wir aufeinander geschossen?* (Bornheim-Merten: Lamuv-Verlag, 1981), is the conciliatory version of the story.

[14] One of the sites for this debate is the German and Soviet occupation of Poland. See Marek Jan Chodakiewicz, *Between Nazis and Soviets: Occupation Politics in Poland, 1939–1947* (Lanham, MD: Lexington Books, 2004); Maria Szonert-Binienda, *World War II through Polish Eyes: In the Nazi-Soviet Grip* (Boulder, CO, and New York: Columbia University Press, 2002). Another site is the ornery question whether the Red Army could have intervened to prevent the destruction of Warsaw in 1944. See the newest assessment by David M. Glantz, "The Red Army's Lublin-Brest Offensive and Advance on Warsaw (18 July–30 September 1944)," *Journal of Slavic Military Studies* 19, no. 2 (2006): 401–44. On the question of absolute war, see Alan Kramer, *Dynamic of Destruction: Culture and Mass Killing in the First World War* (Oxford, New York: Oxford University Press, 2007).

regimes.[15] Their mutual hatred sufficed to unleash extreme violence. However, they always also engage the other – if only to learn how better to destroy the enemy. In this case, both sides needed the other (the image and, as it turns out, combat and occupation practice) in order to perpetuate and deepen their respective practices of "destructive war" or what some scholars call "degenerate war," that is, first and foremost extreme and unrestrained violence.[16] This unrestraint had its own dynamic – an escalation that emerged locally and from the bottom up as it were. By deliberately removing checks on violence, the two combatants set in motion – each in its own time – a relentless process of escalation that was near impossible to stop, even when and where restraint appeared strategically or politically prudent. It is commonly overlooked, given the atrocities of 1941, that the conduct of war got more ferocious, and more deliberately ferocious, as the war progressed.

Second, the Nazi-Soviet war was an all-out civil war between two militarized polities. That is, this war was fought as a war on an interior and on an exterior front, a deliberate overthrow of military tradition (and in this sense quite literally a revolution in military affairs).[17] It was a war between two armed camps from the outset but was fought with and against society from the start. Again, this war had its own logic of escalation. At its most intense, it became radicalized into a war of all-out extermination – either threatened as in the Soviet case or practiced as in the German one. The Holocaust, we argue, is the literally pivotal aspect of this civil war of all-out extermination. Inasmuch as this radicalization turned war into a life-and-death struggle, not of armies, but of entire people and nations, we might also characterize this

---

[15] On German autism: Michael Geyer, "Restaurative Elites, German Society and the Nazi Pursuit of War," in *Fascist Italy and Nazi Germany: Comparison and Contrast*, ed. Richard Bessel (Cambridge: Cambridge University Press, 1996), 134–64; Gerd Koenen, "Zwischen Antibolschewismus und 'Ostorientierung': Kontinuitäten und Diskontinuitäten," in *Strukturmerkmale der deutschen Geschichte des 20. Jahrhunderts*, ed. Anselm Doering-Manteuffel (Munich: R. Oldenbourg Verlag, 2006), 241–52. On parallel, but separate military development, see Mary R. Habeck, *Storm of Steel: The Development of Armor Doctrine in Germany and the Soviet Union, 1919–1939* (Ithaca, NY: Cornell University Press, 2003). On Soviet isolationism, see Raymond A. Bauer, Alex Inkeles, and Clyde Kluckhohn, *How the Soviet System Works: Cultural, Psychological, and Social Themes* (Cambridge: Harvard University Press, 1956), 26; Stephen Kotkin, *Magnetic Mountain: Stalinism as a Civilization* (Berkeley, Los Angeles, and London: University of California Press, 1995), 225; Sheila Fitzpatrick, *Everyday Stalinism: Ordinary Life in Extraordinary Times: Soviet Russia in the 1930s* (New York and Oxford: Oxford University Press, 1999), 5.

[16] The former, very useful term and concept was coined, in the context of the American Civil and Indian wars, by Charles Royster; see Charles Royster, *The Destructive War: William Tecumseh Sherman, Stonewall Jackson, and the Americans* (New York: Random House, 1991). The latter, more problematic term can be found in Martin Shaw, *War and Genocide: Organized Killing in Modern Society* (Cambridge: Polity Press in association with Blackwell, 2003).

[17] A similar case is argued, albeit for October 1942, by MacGregor Knox, "1 October 1942: Adolf Hitler, Wehrmacht Officer Policy, and Social Revolution," *The Historical Journal* 43, no. 3 (2000): 801–25.

process as "barbarization."[18] Rather than denoting sheer lethality (escalation) or extermination (radicalization), "barbarization" captures the mythical or, as it were, "barbarian" understanding of a war locked in a state of exception, in which each side fights (or insists they must fight) until one side is utterly and completely subjugated, incapable of renewing itself on its own devices. The victor survives as "the last man standing"; the vanquished is not only dead, but also ravished. We should note in passing that this barbaric "ideology" is a persistent potential of modern, Western war.[19]

Third, useful as these distinctions may be, they do not capture the fundamentally asymmetric nature of the conduct of war between the two combatants. Seen as a totality, the war in the "East" started with a rapid-fire escalation of unrestraint on the German side (in which practice surpassed ideology) and was countered by a distinct radicalization and barbarization in the context of defense measures by the Soviets, which in turn triggered a radicalization and barbarization process on the side of the aggressor. The all-out defensive war of the Soviets in response to the German onslaught mobilized the entire nation and was fought on an interior and an exterior front. It was fought as a civil or, in view of the French precedent in 1792/3, as a national-revolutionary war, as an upheaval of the nation to wipe out its interior and exterior enemies. The German equivalent became fully apparent in 1941–2, when German warfare was recalibrated into a war of extermination – also a war against interior and exterior enemies but single-mindedly focused on eradicating them with the Holocaust serving as its aggressive prong and the utter despoliation of the people and the territory of the Soviet Union as its regressive or retreating one. In the German, as in the Russian, case we need to remember that 1941 was just a beginning. The war reached its zenith in 1943–4.

Fourth, the corollary of both escalation and radicalization on a subjective and psychological level was a process of "brutalization," a term that is most appropriate for describing and analyzing the "passions of war" to use Clausewitzian terminology. Soldiers on both sides committed extraordinary atrocities and the likelihood of their doing so increased with their sense of impunity and just cause, such as revenge. Beyond a sizable core of what we call cadres of totalitarian violence, who were prepared for and ideologically committed to this kind of brutalized conduct, the majority of soldiers and officers were drawn into and out of acts of brutalization, largely dependent on time and place. Hate propaganda, word of mouth, and experience interacted to incite slaughter and atrocity, a compulsion to destroy, ravage, and kill.

Again asymmetry prevails. On the German side even the passions of war were driven, more often than not, by cold calculation and the deliberate, and

---

[18] George Kassimeris, ed., *The Barbarization of Warfare* (New York: New York University Press, 2006).

[19] David A. Bell, *The First Total War: Napoleon's Europe and the Birth of Warfare as We Know It* (Boston: Houghton Mifflin, 2007) calls this same phenomenon "total war."

efficacious, use of extreme unrestraint. Anger, fear, and rage of individual soldiers were a subsidiary to this calculus.[20] An extreme level of discipline prevailed, and was demanded, in the midst of utter destruction – certainly in terms of self-image, but also in practice. On the Soviet side, by contrast, the passions of war were systematically unleashed, coupled with brutal coercion against one's own, as this turned out to be the most successful means to make peasant soldiers fight and die for a regime which only a decade earlier had declared all-out war on this same majority of the population. Alas, these passions, once unleashed, could not be stopped, when it mattered politically, in 1944–5. Soviet soldiers went on a rampage when prudence dictated restraint by a victor who had long abandoned its initial, irrational, and utterly panicked call for an all-out war of extermination.

WHEN PRACTICE EXCEEDS EXPECTATION: OPERATION BARBAROSSA

Preparations for the war against the Soviet Union commenced on 31 July 1940 with Hitler's order "to finish off Russia" amidst wider strategic deliberations concerning the continuation of war.[21] Directive 21, of 18 December 1940, established the goal of the military operation: to envelop and destroy the vast majority of Soviet forces "in a quick campaign" while preventing their retreat by way of deep penetration. With the Red Army annihilated, a new defense perimeter against "Asian Russia" would be established along a general line reaching from Arkhangel'sk to the river Volga.[22] Although there were cautionary voices, the goal seemed attainable, because the Red Army appeared ill equipped and badly trained, and the Soviet Union was expected to fall apart once the Communist regime was destroyed.[23]

---

[20] An interesting case of German self-perception that sets calculated institutional terror against savage, social terror is Jonathan E. Gumz, "Wehrmacht Perceptions of Mass Violence in Croatia, 1941–1942," *Historical Journal* 44, no. 4 (2001): 1015–38.

[21] The following is greatly indebted to Jürgen Förster, whose work on Barbarossa may well be considered the *Urtext* of all subsequent studies on Barbarossa. While the English translation of the 10-volume series is solid, we prefer the German edition. Jürgen Förster, "Unternehmen 'Barbarossa' als Eroberungs- und Vernichtungskrieg," in *Das Deutsche Reich und der Zweite Weltkrieg*, Vol. 4: *Der Angriff auf die Sowjetunion*, eds. Horst Boog et al. (Stuttgart: Deutsche Verlags-Anstalt, 1983), 498–538; id., "Die Sicherung des 'Lebensraumes,'" in *Der Angriff auf die Sowjetunion*; id., "'Verbrecherische Befehle,'" in *Kriegsverbrechen im 20. Jahrhundert*, eds. Wolfram Wette and Gerd R. Ueberschär (Darmstadt: Wissenschaftliche Buchgesellschaft, 2001), 137–51.

[22] Gerd R. Ueberschär and Wolfram Wette, *"Unternehmen Barbarossa": Der deutsche Überfall auf die Sowjetunion, 1941: Berichte, Analysen, Dokumente* (Paderborn: F. Schöningh, 1984),18–22; Hamburger Institut für Sozialforschung, ed., *Verbrechen der Wehrmacht: Dimensionen des Vernichtungskrieges 1941–1944, Ausstellungskatalog* (Hamburg: Hamburger Edition, 2002), 39–41, with the first three pages.

[23] Jürgen Förster, "Hitlers Wendung nach Osten: Die deutsche Kriegspolitik 1940–1941," in *Zwei Wege nach Moskau: Vom Hitler-Stalin-Pakt zum "Unternehmen Barbarossa,"* ed. Bernd Wegner (Munich; Zurich: Piper, 1991), 113–32.

The rationale for aggression was strategic: Control of the Russian space and its resources made Germany "invulnerable" in an age of global power.[24] The goal was not occupation, certainly not liberation, but imperial and colonial conquest – the "securing and ruthless exploitation of the land" and settlement in choice areas.[25] Expectation dictated a war without regard for the enemy. Instead of peace there would be subjugation. By the same token, the Nazi and military leadership agreed that Operation Barbarossa would be war in a new key.[26] This was to be war against a fanatical regime whose agents counted on subversion and treachery and held society in an iron grip. Such wars had for a long time been the staple of nationalist myth, which made war into a heroic life-and-death struggle between races.[27] But it was World War I that set the mold, forming the experience that haunted the Nazis' and the Wehrmacht's leadership in their preparations for an attack on the Soviet Union. In their view Operation Barbarossa was, at one and the same time, an eminently "just war" that ascertained the sovereignty and well-being of the German people in a hostile world and a highly unconventional war.[28] Much could be learned from the past, and especially the German military leadership did not step out of tradition lightly. But there was also a sense that this war would break the mold.

Three initiatives in particular established the ground rules for the conduct of war. First, war would be fought as a combined strategic operation with a military, a security, and an economic component. To this end, a division of labor – typically haphazard, but overall effective – was worked out between the Wehrmacht, Himmler's security forces, and an economic apparatus (to which we should add the civilian occupation apparatus). What matters is less the division between the military, security, and political and economic institutions than the shared preparation for the destruction on the Soviet regime and its roots in society and the instant wholesale pillage of people and territory. There was agreement not only on the principle (that enemy groups within the civilian populations must be destroyed), but also on the substance (that Jews and Bolsheviks were the agents of the regime to be annihilated).[29] Further, it was understood that German requests for provisions were to be satisfied before

---

[24] Andreas Hillgruber, *Hitlers Strategie; Politik und Kriegführung, 1940–1941* (Frankfurt am Main: Bernard & Graefe Verlag für Wehrwesen, 1965).

[25] Andreas Hillgruber, "Die 'Endlösung' und das deutsche Ostimperium als Kernstück des rassenideologischen Programms des Nationalsozialismus," *Vierteljahrshefte für Zeitgeschichte* 20 (1972): 133–53.

[26] As mentioned, Poland served as precedent. Alexander B. Rossino, *Hitler Strikes Poland: Blitzkrieg, Ideology, and Atrocity* (Lawrence: University Press of Kansas, 2003).

[27] Richard Bessel, *Nazism and War* (New York: Modern Library, 2004); Felix-Lothar Kroll, *Utopie als Ideologie: Geschichtsdenken und politisches Handeln im Dritten Reich* (Paderborn: Schöningh Verlag, 1998).

[28] Birgit Kletzin, *Europa aus Rasse und Raum: Die nationalsozialistische Idee der neuen Ordnung* (Münster: Lit, 2000); Jürgen Förster, "Hitlers Entscheidung für den Krieg gegen die Sowjetunion," in *Der Angriff auf Die Sowjetunion*, 27–68.

[29] Jürgen Förster, "Wehrmacht, Krieg und Holocaust," in *Die Wehrmacht: Mythos und Realität*, eds. Rolf-Dieter Müller and Erich Volkmann (Munich: Beck, 1999), 948–63.

those of the occupied.[30] The debate on these preparations remains unsettled, but the basic fact is that the German leadership prepared a war against an entire society, attacking with the purpose of destroying the regime and killing its agents in order to exploit what was expected to be inchoate masses – the human and natural resources of the Soviet territory. The utter disregard for Soviet human life was built into the combined operation to subdue the Soviet Union.

The second thrust of preparations focused on generating the "ruthlessness" necessary for fighting a treacherous enemy. Soldiers were to be made ready to fight – not only an enemy army and society, but so-called fanatics and criminals amidst the enemy. Propaganda about the Soviet regime grotesquely played up Jewish-Bolshevik cadres and thus contributed to the everyday brutality of the war.[31] But the German military had never really banked on images and motivations and did not do so in this case either.[32] Instead, they granted preventative immunity for criminal conduct in the pursuit of war and, because war making targeted the civilian population, impunity also pertained to the "treatment of the local population."[33] The Decree on the Exercise of Military Jurisdiction put "military necessity over a consideration what is lawful."[34] The power of definition rested entirely with the commanding officer, who was also called upon to ascertain military discipline. The purpose was to create an armed force that was at one and the same time unrestrained in pursuit of its goals and a uniquely disciplined instrument in their conduct. The combination of sheer destructiveness and extreme discipline remained tenuous, but much as we might emphasize bloodlust or the compulsion to kill ("Shoot every Russian that looks askance"),[35] the cold rage of disciplined annihilation was the order of the day and defined German warfare.[36] No doubt, the latter also served as cover for individual and group brutalization.

The third strand of war preparations authorized targeted murder. The Decree for the Treatment of Political Commissars, the famous Commissar

---

[30] Christian Gerlach, *Kalkulierte Morde: Die deutsche Wirtschafts- und Vernichtungspolitik in Weissrussland 1941 bis 1944*, 2nd ed. (Hamburg: Hamburger Edition, 2000); Klaus Jochen Arnold, *Die Wehrmacht und die Besatzungspolitik in den besetzten Gebieten der Sowjetunion: Kriegführung und Radikalisierung im "Unternehmen Barbarossa"* (Berlin: Duncker & Humblot, 2004).

[31] Förster, "Unternehmen "Barbarossa" als Eroberungs- und Vernichtungskrieg." 440–7.

[32] Michael Geyer, "Vom massenhaften Tötungshandeln, oder: Wie die Deutschen das Krieg-Machen lernten," in *Massenhaftes Töten: Kriege und Genozide im 20. Jahrhundert*, eds. Peter Gleichmann and Thomas Kühne (Essen: Klartext Verlag, 2004), 105–42.

[33] Hamburger Institut für Sozialforschung, *Verbrechen der Wehrmacht: Dimensionen des Vernichtungskrieges 1941–1944, Ausstellungskatalog*, 49.

[34] Ibid., 46–8. Förster, "Unternehmen 'Barbarossa' als Eroberungs- und Vernichtungskrieg," 435: "Return to old customs of war. One of the two enemies must fall; do not conserve the incubators of hostile attitudes, but liquidate" (Gen. Müller).

[35] Hitler, according to *Aktenvermerk*, 16 July 1941, International Military Tribunal, *Trial of the Major War Criminals before the International Military Tribunal, Nuremberg: 14 November 1945–1 October 1946* (Nuremberg: Secretariat of the Tribunal, 1947), 86–94, here 92.

[36] Discipline as a key element in unleashing extraordinary violence is rather understudied. But see the impressive study by Birgit Beck, *Wehrmacht und sexuelle Gewalt: Sexualverbrechen vor deutschen Militärgerichten 1939–1945* (Paderborn: Schöningh, 2007).

Order, ordered that Soviet commissars and other undesirables such as Jews were to be separated in order to be killed.[37] The targeted groups in the Commissar Order were specific, but the Guidelines for the Behavior of Troops in Russia widened the list, demanding "ruthless and energetic measures against Bolshevik agitators, partisans, saboteurs, Jews, and [the] complete eradication of any active or passive form of resistance."[38] In the end, the list of people and groups to be executed remained fuzzy. But the main enemy was racial: because the cruel and perfidious war was instigated by the Jewish-Bolshevik regime and its agents, so the main rationale, extermination of Jews and Commissars, was the chief priority. Others – such as female soldiers, Asian minorities, "asocials" – were associated with the main target group, the common military denominator being that they lacked honor and were by their very nature suspect of perfidy. Targeted killing thus appears both as the prerequisite for bringing down the regime and the means for (re)establishing a more natural order of things. Specific task groups (*Einsatzgruppen*) were set up in order to expedite the process. Typically, they facilitated killing away from the troops and were supposed to minimize the opportunity for "atrocities" (*Metzeleien*).[39] As far as the military leadership was concerned, maintaining discipline and, whenever possible, distance was the only qualification for deliberate murder, which otherwise found ready support.

The fervor to get the Army of the East set up for a quick and decisive campaign and the cold passion of avenging defeat and revolution remade the Wehrmacht into a school of extreme violence. Much of what was planned, built on older precedent; a great deal emerged from interwar learning processes about World War I and about the postwar civil wars;[40] but the entire setup amounted to a distinct revolution in military affairs. First, the plan for a quick and decisive victory that relied on overwhelming force fit the German military tradition.[41] But now any restraints on the use of force were lifted in the pursuit of the war's goals. Extreme violence was built in as it were. Second, the pursuit of quick and overwhelming victory had produced a great deal of collateral (civilian) death and damages in the past (as in Belgium),[42] but now the murder

[37] Hans-Adolf Jacobsen, "Kommissarbefehl und Massenexekutionen sowjetischer Kriegsgefangener," in *Anatomie des SS-Staates: Gutachten des Instituts für Zeitgeschichte*, ed. Hans Buchheim (Olten: Walter-Verlag, 1965),161–278. See also Hamburger Institut für Sozialforschung, ed., *Verbrechen der Wehrmacht: Dimensionen des Vernichtungskrieges 1941–1944, Ausstellungskatalog*, 52–3.

[38] Hamburger Institut für Sozialforschung, ed., *Verbrechen der Wehrmacht: Dimensionen des Vernichtungskrieges 1941–1944, Ausstellungskatalog*, 54–5.

[39] Förster, "Unternehmen 'Barbarossa' als Eroberungs- und Vernichtungskrieg," 438.

[40] On right-wing German violence, Richard Bessel, *Political Violence and the Rise of Nazism: The Storm Troopers in Eastern Germany, 1925–1934* (New Haven, CT: Yale University Press, 1984); Dirk Schumann, *Politische Gewalt in der Weimarer Republik 1918–1933: Kampf um die Straße und Furcht vor dem Bürgerkrieg* (Essen: Klartext, 2001).

[41] Isabel V. Hull, *Absolute Destruction: Military Culture and the Practice of War in Imperial Germany* (Ithaca, NY, and London: Cornell University Press, 2005).

[42] Wolfgang Schivelbusch, *Die Bibliothek von Löwen: Eine Episode aus der Zeit der Weltkriege* (Munich: C. Hanser, 1988).

of entire enemy groups, foremost Bolsheviks and Jews, was premeditated and deemed an essential and necessary condition for victory. The German conduct of war fused military and civilian elements into an unprecedented, murderous totality. Third, the desire to establish the security of the territory, especially the fear of partisans, had led to hostage taking and shooting already in Belgium in 1914.[43] But the plans for pacification of the occupied territory once again broke the mold in that they made terror the operative principle in the short run and counted on the permanence of violent subordination in the long run (for which task forty to fifty divisions were to be readied after victory). The colonial precedent looms large,[44] but terror as a tool of pacification was novel. Military planners broke the mold of experience in preparing for Barbarossa. Hitler's intervention and his overarching rationale were responsible for this development inasmuch as he opened up the opportunity for the all-out pursuit of quick victory. Thus, while military preparations were utilitarian (how best to achieve quick victory), the recourse to absolute, unrestrained violence was entirely ideological. *Not kennt kein Gebot* is, of course, an old maxim, but the Wehrmacht leadership prepared for extreme violence because they held that they had to exterminate in order to subject, and not just defeat and occupy, the enemy and its territory.

If the general rule holds that nothing is ever quite as extreme in practice as it is in theory, this rule was the first thing to go, when Operation Barbarossa commenced on 22 June 1941. Historians have rightly cautioned us that the war in the East had many faces, that accommodation was as much an aspect of the war as brutalization.[45] But during Barbarossa the inherent frictions of war did not moderate, but rather unleashed and escalated extreme violence. Accommodation, wherever and whenever it occurred, was pierced by mass murder and sooner or later gave way to destructive war. Newest research shows how unsettled midlevel German officers in the field were about the unrelenting violence especially against the civilian population and how counterproductive many of them considered it to be.[46] But in 1941 none of this altered the ratcheting up of violence both at the front and behind the front.[47]

[43] John N. Horne and Alan Kramer, *German Atrocities, 1914: A History of Denial* (New Haven, CT: Yale University Press, 2001).

[44] Jürgen Zimmerer, "Die Geburt des "Ostlandes" aus dem Geiste des Kolonialismus: Die nationalsozialistische Eroberungs- und Beherrschungspolitik in (post)kolonialer Perspektive," *SozialGeschichte: Zeitschrift für die historische Analyse des 20. und 21. Jahrhunderts* 19, no. 1 (2004): 19–43.

[45] One of the first and still the most important contribution is Theo J. Schulte, *The German Army and Nazi Policies in Occupied Russia* (Oxford and New York: Berg, 1989).

[46] Christian Hartmann, "Verbrecherischer Krieg – Verbrecherische Wehrmacht? Überlegungen zur Struktur des deutschen Ostheeres 1941–1944," *Vierteljahrshefte für Zeitgeschichte* 52, no. 1 (2004): 1–75; Johannes Hürter, "Die Wehrmacht vor Leningrad: Krieg und Besatzungspolitik der 18. Armee im Herbst und Winter 1941/42," *Vierteljahrshefte für Zeitgeschichte* 49, no. 3 (2001): 377–440.

[47] Bernhard Chiari, *Alltag hinter der Front: Besatzung, Kollaboration und Widerstand in Weißrußland 1941–1944* (Düsseldorf: Droste Verlag, 1998); Manfred Oldenburg, *Ideologie und*

Two points are worth making. First, the actual practice of Operation Barbarossa exceeded what had been prepared. Within months, Operation Barbarossa turned from its preplanned security measures to a free fall into utter
destruction, callous and inhuman negligence, and all-out extermination.[48] The
murder of targeted enemy groups escalated from the first days of the campaign
on. The rapid German advance and the occupation of major cities created
conditions of endemic famine – not unlike the "hunger plan" for Soviet cities
that had come up in the context of economic preparations for Barbarossa.[49]
There is a heated debate whether such a "plan" existed in the first place, but
the practice of war made real what preparations had left in the realm of potentialities. Second, the killing and dying of soldiers and civilians – and there were
more civilian casualties than military ones – during the first six months of the
war were so horrendous that many historians treat the rest of the war as a
continuum of violence. But the difficult truth is that the escalation of violence
during Operation Barbarossa was followed by much worse between 1942 and
1944 – and again in 1944/5.[50] While war rarely follows a linear path, in this
war – German and Soviet soldiers agreed[51] – the crooked line led straight to
hell.

The reasons for this escalation – alternatively called "barbarization" or
"radicalization" by historians – in the conduct of war in summer and fall 1941
are still debated. Was it the preemptive, ideologically motivated overkill of the
directives, the criminal decrees, and the guidelines for the troops that were
responsible?[52] Or was it the situation on the ground, the exigencies of a harsh
war against an implacable enemy that led from planned overkill to a free fall

militärisches Kalkül: Die Besatzungspolitik der Wehrmacht in der Sowjetunion 1942 (Cologne: Böhlau, 2004).

[48] Andrej Angrick, "Das Beispiel Charkow: Massenmord unter deutscher Besatzung," eds. Christian Hartmann, Johannes Hürter, and Ulrike Jureit (Munich: Verlag C. H. Beck, 2005), 117–24.
Hamburger Institut für Sozialforschung, ed., *Verbrechen der Wehrmacht: Dimensionen des Vernichtungskrieges 1941–1944, Ausstellungskatalog*, 179–85.

[49] Norbert Kunz, "Das Beispiel Charkow: Eine Stadtbevölkerung als Opfer der deutschen Hunger-
strategie 1941/42," eds. Christian Hartmann, Johannes Hürter, and Ulrike Jureit (Munich: Verlag C. H. Beck, 2005), 136–44. Hamburger Institut für Sozialforschung, ed., *Verbrechen der
Wehrmacht: Dimensionen des Vernichtungskrieges 1941–1944, Ausstellungskatalog*, 328–46.

[50] For an overview and discussion of Soviet civilian and military casualty figures see Michael
Ellman and S. Maksudov, "Soviet Deaths in the Great Patriotic War: A Note," *Europe-Asia
Studies* 46, no. 4 (1994): 671–80; for detailed figures of military casualties see G. F. Krivosheev,
ed., *Grif sekretnosti sniat: Poteri vooruzhennykh sil SSSR v voinakh, boevykh deistviiakh i
voennykh konfliktakh: Statisticheskoe issledovanie* (Moscow: Voennoe izdatel'stvo, 1993); and
the discussion in G. F. Krivosheev and M. F. Filimoshin, "Poteri vooruzhennykh sil SSSR v
Velikoi Otechestvennoi voine," in *Naselenie Rossii v xx veke: Istoricheskie ocherki, 1940–
1959*, Vol 2, eds. Iu. A. Poliakov and V. B. Zhiromskaia (Moscow: Rosspen, 2001), 19–39.

[51] Stephen G. Fritz, *Frontsoldaten: The German Soldier in World War II* (Lexington: University
Press of Kentucky, 1995); Merridale, *Ivan's War*.

[52] Hannes Heer, "The Logic of the War of Extermination: The Wehrmacht and the Anti-Partisan
War," in *War of Extermination: The German Military in World War II 1941–1944*, eds.
Hannes Heer and Klaus Naumann (New York and Oxford: Berghahn Books, 2000), 92–126.

into extreme violence?[53] There is general agreement that Omer Bartov's once dominant interpretation does not hold, because the "barbarization" of the conduct of war he describes takes hold before the preconditions he sets for this turn (destruction of small groups, depletion of materiel) become apparent.[54] We rather see a willful destructiveness at work that escalates relentlessly. This spiral of violence is made more explicit by the internal doubts about the usefulness and, less so, moral appropriateness of ratcheting up violence especially behind the front, without ever being able to stop it.[55] In our view, this escalation across the board during the first months of Barbarossa was conditioned first and foremost by the imperative of decisive victory and the unrestraint that was meant to achieve this end. This imperative generated a groundswell of violence from the bottom up that was further advanced by the pervasive insecurity due to the quick advance. This situation reminds us of 1914. But again, the difference is telling. The German military had learned from the failure of the Schlieffen Plan that only utmost unrestraint, deliberate overkill, would lead to victory and, therefore, escalation preceded frictions rather than followed them. However, we must keep in mind that what followed escalation was much worse: a radicalization and recalibration of violence, still in the expectation of victory, but in the knowledge that the war would continue beyond Barbarossa.

In 1941, even the victorious advance of the Army of the East was a double-edged affair. The Wehrmacht appeared to be absolutely invincible and the Soviet enemy infinitely inferior. Even when the military advance was slowed down at Smolensk, there seemed to be nothing that could stop it. A sense of elation captured not just Hitler and the military leadership, but also the rank and file and the people at home. This euphoria gave rise, in summer 1941, to some of the more elaborate fantasies of turning Russia into a veritable Garden of Eden – a paradise, from which evil was to be expelled once and for all. In Hitler's flights of rhetoric German happiness unmistakably was linked

---

[53] K. Arnold, *Die Wehrmacht und die Besatzungspolitik in den besetzten Gebieten der Sowjetunion: Kriegführung und Radikalisierung im "Unternehmen Barbarossa."*

[54] Omer Bartov, *The Eastern Front, 1941–45: German Troops and the Barbarisation of Warfare*, 2nd ed. (New York: Palgrave, 2001). Christoph Rass, *Menschenmaterial: Deutsche Soldaten an der Ostfront – Innenansichten einer Infanteriedivision 1939–1945* (Paderborn: Schöningh, 2003); Christian Gerlach, "Verbrechen deutscher Fronttruppen in Weißrußland 1941–1944: Eine Annäherung," in *Wehrmacht und Vernichtungspolitik; Militär im nationalsozialistischen System*, ed. Karl Heinrich Pohl (Göttingen: Vandenhoeck & Ruprecht, 1999), 89–114.

[55] Hamburger Institut für Sozialforschung, ed., "Handlungsspielräume" in *Verbrechen der Wehrmacht: Dimensionen des Vernichtungskrieges 1941–1944, Ausstellungskatalog*, 579–627. Compare with Bernd Boll and Hans Safrian, "On the Way to Stalingrad: The 6th Army in 1941–42," in *War of Extermination: The German Military in World War Ii 1941–1944*, eds. Hannes Heer and Klaus Naumann (New York and Oxford: Berghahn Books, 2000), 237–71; Johannes Hürter, "Auf dem Weg zur Militäropposition: Treskow, Gersdorff, der Vernichtungskrieg und der Judenmord: Neue Dokumente über das Verhältnis der Heeresgruppe Mitte zur Einsatzgruppe B im Jahre 1041," *Vierteljahrshefte für Zeitgeschichte* 52, no. 3 (2004): 527–62; Timm C. Richter, "Handlungsspielräume am Beispiel der 6. Armee," in *Verbrechen der Wehrmacht: Bilanz einer Debatte*, eds. Christian Hartmann, Johannes Hürter, and Ulrike Jureit (Munich: Verlag C. H. Beck, 2005), 60–8.

to purging evil and that was to exterminating the Jewish and the Bolshevik enemy.[56] We see a rapid escalation of the murderous aspects of the German conduct both from the bottom up and from the top down. Within months the murder of Jews escalated from pogroms and the killing of adult males to the extermination, in September/October 1941, of entire communities of men, women, and children – the beginnings of a systematic and comprehensive practice of extermination.[57]

These murderous effusions of invincibility were also always tinged by the recognition of utter vulnerability. The Army of the East did not slice through the Soviet forces and the Soviet regime did not crumble as was expected. While the Red Army lost nearly 4 million of its soldiers in the German onslaught, it fought tenaciously in an armed retreat. It never folded and radicalized self-defense into all-out destruction. The frontline troops fought with utter brutality. While more than 3 million soldiers ended in captivity, there were many – especially in the later battles in October and November – who were not captured and formed the nucleus of partisan units – or rather of groups of armed young men roaming the countryside – increasing the insecurity of the territory.[58] German forces did not suffice to control the hinterland. They were inadequate to guard the prisoners of war. They were unable to supply themselves and the population. And not least, they were outmanned and even outgunned at the front increasingly in November/December 1941. The response was unequivocal across the board. Deficiencies were mastered with recourse to more brutal fighting at the front, a worsening regime of death marches and mass starvation for prisoners of war, more starvation for the urban population in occupied areas, and more terror in the occupied territories. Extreme unrestraint was the answer to all frictions. In the last quarter of 1941, practice evolved faster than ideology, but escalatory practice was inconceivable without its underlying ideological justification in the first place.

When victory faded out of sight, the deficiencies of Barbarossa became glaringly obvious.[59] In racing from battle victory to battle victory, the Army of the

---

[56] Hugh Trevor-Roper, ed., *Hitler's Secret Conversations, 1941–1944* (New York: Farrar Straus and Young, 1953), 4; Christopher R. Browning and Jürgen Matthäus, *The Origins of the Final Solution: The Evolution of Nazi Jewish Policy, September 1939–March 1942* (Lincoln and Jerusalem: University of Nebraska Press and Yad Vashem, 2004); Peter Longerich, *Politik der Vernichtung: Eine Gesamtdarstellung der nationalsozialistischen Judenverfolgung* (Munich: Piper, 1998), 352–410.

[57] Browning and Matthäus, *The Origins of the Final Solution: The Evolution of Nazi Jewish Policy, September 1939–March 1942*.

[58] Slepyan, *Stalin's Guerrillas*.

[59] Bernard R. Kroener, "Der 'Erfrorene Blitzkrieg': Strategische Planungen der deutschen Führung gegen die Sowjetunion und die Ursachen ihres Scheiterns," in *Zwei Wege nach Moskau: Vom Hitler-Stalin-Pakt zum "Unternehmen Barbarossa,"* ed. Bernd Wegner (Munich; Zurich: Piper, 1991), 133–48; Karl-Heinz Frieser, "Die deutschen Blitzkriege: Operativer Triumph – Strategische Tragödie," in *Erster Weltkrieg – Zweiter Weltkrieg: Krieg, Kriegserlebnis, Kriegserfahrung in Deutschland*, eds. Bruno Thoß and Hans-Erich Volkmann (Paderborn: Ferdinand Schöningh, 2002), 182–96.

East dug an ever deeper hole for itself. The troops up front were called upon to fight more relentlessly, the economic agencies plundered more egregiously, and the security forces expanded their mass killings in leaps and bounds. This escalation of violence was not some kind of anonymous "dynamic," but it was driven by the precepts that Wehrmacht and Nazi leadership had set for themselves: to fight without mercy, to treat the conquered population as dispensable, and to kill Jews and Bolsheviks as the instigators of resistance. Especially between September and November 1941, the entire spectrum of violence was relentlessly ratcheted up.[60]

The deleterious reality of the war overtook even the vilest imagination.[61] Long before the situation became truly critical, in the winter counteroffensive of 1941–2, German soldiers, security forces, and occupiers were ready to think of the war they fought as a life-or-death struggle. It was either win and live or lose and die.[62] And they acted accordingly. The German term for this sentiment was *Verbitterung* (embitterment). Against all dictates of prudence and against any pangs of mercy, German forces fought with "increasing bitterness."[63] A series of midlevel orders, most famously the one by General Reichenau, expressed this general sentiment in their own, more or less Nazified language, but they all expressed the conviction that only utter ruthlessness would defeat the enemy.[64] Quite on their own, the soldiers did the Nazis' bidding and sought their own final solutions for bringing this war to an end.

It is harebrained to deduce that the Soviet Union's striking back was responsible for the German escalation of violence.[65] The Red Army was responsible for withstanding the German onslaught. It was responsible for undoing the German battle plan and the expectations for a quick victory. It certainly contributed to the feeling of insecurity and the growing bitterness, but if anything German duress reinforced ideology. German soldiers had come to find an exceptional enemy – and they found more of it than they had ever dreamed. Therefore, we must now turn to the Soviet side with the simple caveat to readers that, at this point, they desist from making premature conjectures about the German

---

[60] Geoffrey P. Megargee, *War of Annihilation: Combat and Genocide on the Eastern Front, 1941* (Lanham, MD: Rowman & Littlefield, 2006), 73–128.

[61] See the material in Klaus Latzel, *Deutsche Soldaten–Nationalsozialistischer Krieg?: Kriegserlebnis, Kriegserfahrung 1939–1945* (Paderborn: Schöningh, 1998); Walter Kempowski, *Das Echolot: Barbarossa '41: Ein kollektives Tagebuch* (Munich: Knaus, 2002); K. Arnold, *Die Wehrmacht und die Besatzungspolitik in den besetzten Gebieten der Sowjetunion: Kriegführung und Radikalisierung im "Unternehmen Barbarossa."*

[62] Omer Bartov, "Von unten betrachtet: Überleben, Zusammenhalt und Brutalität an der Ostfront," in *Zwei Wege nach Moskau: Vom Hoitler-Stalin-Pakt zum "Unternehmen Barbarossa,"* ed. Bernd Wegner (Munich and Zurich: Piper, 1991), 326–44.

[63] K. Arnold, *Die Wehrmacht und die Besatzungspolitik in den besetzten Gebieten der Sowjetunion: Kriegführung und Radikalisierung im "Unternehmen Barbarossa,"* 180.

[64] Hamburger Institut für Sozialforschung, ed., *Verbrechen der Wehrmacht: Dimensionen des Vernichtungskrieges 1941–1944, Ausstellungskatalog*, 331.

[65] Joachim Hoffmann, *Stalins Vernichtungskrieg 1941–1945*, 3rd rev. ed. (Munich: Verlag für Wehrwissenschaften, 1996).

radicalization of violence that ensued when the spell of German invincibility was broken.

WAR BY ANY MEANS

When, on 22 June 1941, the Third Reich invaded the Soviet Union with overwhelming force, it crushed through the mass of Soviet forces deployed along the western border in the newly occupied territories and in three prongs pushed deep into Soviet territory. Soviet casualties were enormous. Time and again, the Red Army appeared to be teetering on the abyss. The Red Air Force was nearly wiped out. But although German forces pushed ever deeper, the Soviet defenders fought tenaciously and slowed the German thrust sufficiently to overthrow German expectations. Many historians consider the Battle of Smolensk a key turning point in this respect. By the same token, as horrific as Soviet casualties were, the Red Army and the Soviet regime managed to stage a fighting retreat. Neither the army nor the regime shattered as Hitler had expected. That they proved to be far sturdier than foreseen exacerbated the debate within the German military and political leadership of how, if at all, this enemy could be defeated. The Soviet army and the regime fought back and they fought aggressively to a fault. They took on the enemy by whatever means available ("pikes, swords, home-made weapons, anything you can make in your own factories")[66] and they drove home the point as quickly as possible that anyone who did not do likewise would be treated as an enemy as well.[67]

The immediate reflex of the Soviet military was not to organize defensive battles or retreat to defense positions, but to attack. The goal of battle, not unlike the German doctrine, was the complete destruction of the enemy. On 22 June 1941, at 0715 hours, the People's Commissar of Defense ordered "the Soviet forces to engage the enemy with all means at their disposal and annihilate them."[68] This strategy of relentless counterattack was improved over time, but never abandoned, as the fighting at Moscow in 1941–2, Operation Mars in 1942, and the battles of Stalingrad and Kursk in 1942 and 1943 show. While many rank and file soldiers made a run for it or surrendered, enough refused to give up and kept on fighting doggedly.[69] A small minority of civilians (largely communists), NKVD personnel, and some surrounded Red Army units went

---

[66] Moscow's answer to request for weapons, related by Khrushchev in his memoirs. Quoted in Geoffrey Hosking, *A History of the Soviet Union 1917–1991*, final ed. (London: Fontana Press, 1992), 271.

[67] The most in-depth study of the first phase of the war is Glantz, *Colossus Reborn: The Red Army at War, 1941–1943*.

[68] Anatoli Chor'kov, "The Red Army during the Initial Phase of the Great Patriotic War," in *From Peace to War: Germany, Soviet Russia and the World, 1939–1941*, ed. Bernd Wegner (Oxford: Berghan Books, 1997), 417.

[69] On the German reaction see K. Arnold, *Die Wehrmacht und die Besatzungspolitik in den besetzten Gebieten der Sowjetunion: Kriegführung und Radikalisierung im "Unternehmen Barbarossa."*

into hiding and started partisan warfare behind the enemy's lines. These were, to be sure, futile attempts at this stage of the war, but they did have the desired effect of provoking disproportionate German reprisals.[70]

The standard accounts of the beginning of the war stress the lack of Soviet preparations, the chaos, and incompetence.[71] As far as military and strategic readiness is concerned, this is very much to the point. The Soviet armed forces were in the middle of an enormous expansion and a partial redeployment to new positions. Equipment had not arrived and the available technology was substandard. Trained personnel was lacking as were the necessary technology and infrastructure to keep the tanks rolling and the planes flying; because radios were a rarity, communication in battle both within a branch of arms and across different arms was hard or impossible. The officer corps had been subjugated (and partially decimated) in the Great Purges; there was a lack of qualified leadership on all levels, at times including such basic "qualifications" as mere literacy or the ability to read a map; and the power of political officers (reintroduced shortly after the invasion) predominated over that of military specialists. The army was, in other words, in shambles.[72]

However, seen from a different vantage point, the Soviet Union was very much ready for war. This was a society which in many ways resembled a wartime economy in peacetime. The Soviet system was conceived during what Peter Holquist has called a "continuum of crisis" stretching between World War I and the end of the Russian civil war in 1921. The mono-organizational society which emerged in this cauldron of violence was, in terms of institutional structure and a whole range of practices, a child of total war. The language and thought of Bolshevism were highly militaristic, too. Communists loved to talk of "fronts" and "assaults" even when talking about plainly civilian matters. The party itself was understood in military terms as the "vanguard" of the

---

[70] The literature on partisan warfare is huge but largely focuses on the German side. For a recent and archivally based view of the Soviet side see Slepyan, *Stalin's Guerrillas*. See also Karel C. Berkhoff, *Harvest of Despair: Life and Death in Ukraine under Nazi Rule* (Cambridge, MA: Harvard University Press, 2004), 275–85. Ben Shepherd, *War in the Wild East: The German Army and Soviet Partisans* (Cambridge, MA: Harvard University Press, 2004). On NKVD behind German lines see V. N. Khaustov et al., eds., *Lubianka. Stalin i NKVD-NKGB-GUKP "Smersh." 1939–mart 1946* (Moscow: Demokratiia, 2006), 330–4; 345–7.

[71] Aleksandr M. Nekrich, *1941, 22 iiun'ia*, 2nd rev. ed. (Moscow: Pamiatniki istoricheskoi mysli, 1995). The theme has reemerged in the discussion about whether or not there was a Soviet plan to attack Germany. The latest English-language overview is in Bellamy, *Absolute War*, 99–135. For a good sample of the controversy see Iu. N. Afanas'ev, ed., *Drugaia voina 1939–1945* (Moscow: RGGU, 1996), 32–224. See also Gabriel Gorodetsky, *Grand Delusion: Stalin and the German Invasion of Russia* (New Haven, CT, and London: Yale University Press, 1999).

[72] A. A. Pechenkin, "Byla li vozmozhnost nastupat'?" *Otechestvennaia istoriia*, no. 3 (1995): 44–59; Richard Overy, *Russia's War: A History of the Soviet War Effort: 1941–1945* (New York: Penguin, 1997), 30–3, 89–90; Roger Reese, *Stalin's Reluctant Soldiers: A Social History of the Red Army 1925–1941* (Lawrence: University Press of Kansas, 1996); id., *Red Commanders: A Social History of the Soviet Army Officer Corps, 1918–1991* (Lawrence: University Press of Kansas, 2005), 134–57; Glantz, *Colossus Reborn*, 466–71; Glantz and House, *When Titans Clashed*, 5–45.

proletariat. Stalin's Revolution from Above was a reaction to perceived military threats, and the explicit goal was the creation of an industrialized society which could withstand modern warfare. The result was a highly centralized polity already mobilized in peacetime and thus well prepared for war.[73]

In terms of mentality, also, much of Soviet society was already mobilized. War had been a recurrent phenomenon in the forty years since the turn of the century. And these wars became more and more total: the Russo-Japanese War of 1904–5 was still a relatively conventional conflict, although it already drew in enough of civilian society to trigger a first revolution in 1905. World War I necessitated the mobilization of all resources for the war effort and overtaxed the imperial political system; Russia imploded into two revolutions in 1917 which triggered the civil war of 1918–21 – a truly total, if not "totalitarian" war that not only called for the complete mobilization of resources by the warring parties, but also undid the distinction between combatant and noncombatant. In this war, the goal was not to force concessions out of the adversary ("politics by other means"), but to produce complete physical destruction of the enemy and all his allies. In the mentality born of this conflict – which would form part of the ground on which Stalinism was built – politics became an extension of war, not the other way around.[74]

The experience of unfettered violence formed the mental background to the peculiarly Soviet reaction to the German invasion. This was not a society where

---

[73] Roger Pethybridge, *The Social Prelude to Stalinism* (London and Basingstoke: Macmillan, 1974), 73–131; Sheila Fitzpatrick, "War and Society in Soviet Context: Soviet Labor before, during, and after World War II," *International Labor and Working-Class History* 35 (Spring 1989): 37–52; John Barber and Mark Harrison, *The Soviet Home Front, 1941–1945: A Social and Economic History of the USSR in World War II* (London and New York: Longman, 1991), 13–18; Mark von Hagen, *Soldiers in the Proletarian Dictatorship: The Red Army and the Soviet Socialist State, 1917–1930* (Ithaca, NY: Cornell University Press, 1990); Peter Holquist, *Making War, Forging Revolution: Russia's Continuum of Crisis, 1914–1921* (Cambridge, MA: Harvard University Press, 2002); Joshua Sanborn, *Drafting the Russian Nation: Military Conscription, Total War, and Mass Politics 1905–1925* (DeKalb: Northern Illinois University Press, 2003).

[74] On the role of the Civil War in the mentality of Bolshevism and Stalinism see, for example, Robert C. Tucker, "Stalinism as Revolution from Above," in *Stalinism: Essays in Historical Interpretation*, ed. R. C. Tucker (New York: Norton, 1977), 77–108; esp. 103. Sheila Fitzpatrick, "The Legacy of the Civil War," in *Party, State, and Society in the Russian Civil War: Explorations in Social History*, eds. William Rosenberg, Diane P. Koenker, and Ronald G. Suny (Bloomington and Indianapolis: Indiana University Press, 1989), 385–98; and id., "The Civil War as a Formative Experience" in *Bolshevik Culture*, eds. Abbott Gleason, Peter Kenez, and Richard Stites (Bloomington: Indiana University Press, 1985), 57–76. On the replay of Civil War traditions – often by those who had "missed" it – see id., "Cultural Revolution as Class War," *Cultural Revolution in Russia, 1928–1931*, ed. S. Fitzpatrick (Bloomington: Indiana University Press, 1978), 8–40, esp. 18, 25. For broader perspectives on the history of violence and violent *mentalités* see Stefan Plaggenborg, "Weltkrieg, Bürgerkrieg, Klassenkrieg: Mentalitätsgeschichtliche Versuch über die Gewalt in Sowjetrußland," *Historische Anthropologie* 3 (1995): 493–505; id., "Gewalt und Militanz in Sowjetrussland 1917–1930," *Jahrbücher für Geschichte Osteuropas* 44, no. 3 (1996): 409–30; and E. S. Seniavskaia, *Psikhologiia voiny v xx veke: Istoricheskii opyt Rossii* (Moscow: ROSSPEN, 1999). For the importance of these for the war see Weiner, "Something to Die For."

peace was normal and war best avoided. This was a political system "whose innate harshness replicated life in the military in many ways."[75] In principle, war was seen as inevitable and had been expected for decades. A children's novel of the 1920s not only predicted world Communism to arrive by the late 1950s, but also made it clear to its young readership what to expect between the miserable present and the bright future – revolutionary war as world war.[76] The Civil War in Spain was a major staple of popular culture in the 1930s, and movies with titles like *If Tomorrow Brings War* (1938) celebrated the coming conflict.[77] Soviet citizens fantasized about "Spain" in their daydreams, which they recorded in their diaries; at night they sometimes dreamed their way into the slaughter, participating in a more heroic reality than their mundane and often numbing everyday existence afforded. Soon, they could act out such wishes in real life.[78] A particularly impressive example of this psychological-cum-cultural preparation for the coming conflict and one's own likely violent death was the writer Alexander Afinogenov. In 1940 he started writing a play called *On the Eve*. It documented "the eve and the first days of the great war that, he was sure, was imminent." Within days of the beginning of Barbarossa, the play was commissioned and the author "had only to endow the abstract enemy forces of his first draft with the faces of the invading Nazi forces."[79]

The symbolic means to engage the coming violence were thus readily available.[80] Russian nationalism had developed as a strong theme throughout the 1930s, which explains why the conflict could be termed the (*Great*) *Patriotic War* right from the outset.[81] The corollary – the repression, deportation, or

[75] Glantz, *Colossus Reborn*, 589.

[76] Innokenty Zhukov, "Voyage of the Red Star Pioneer Troop to Wonderland" (1924), in *Mass Culture in Soviet Russia: Tales, Poems, Songs, Movies, Plays, and Folklore, 1917–1953*, eds. James von Geldern and Richard Stites (Bloomington and Indianapolis: Indiana University Press, 1995), 90–112.

[77] Seniavskaia, *Frontovoe pokolenie*, 75–6; A. B. Zubov, "Pobeda, kotoruiu my poteriali," *Drugaia voina*, 384–5; von Geldern and Stites, eds., *Mass Culture in Soviet Russia*, 316–18; Sheila Fitzpatrick, *Everyday Stalinism*, 10, 69, 171; Marius Broekmeyer, *Stalin, the Russians, and Their War*, trans. Rosalind Buck (Madison: The University of Wisconsin Press, 1999), 3–5.

[78] Jochen Hellbeck, *Revolution on My Mind: Writing a Diary under Stalin* (Cambridge, MA, and London: Harvard University Press, 2006), 92–3.

[79] Hellbeck, *Revolution on My Mind*, 340.

[80] On the war preparations of the propaganda apparatus see Vladimir Aleksandrovich Nevezhin, "Rech' Stalina 5 maia 1941 goda i apologiia nastupatel'noi voiny," *Otechestvennaia istoriia*, no. 2 (1995): 54–69.

[81] Iu. A. Poliakov, "Istoki narodnogo podviga," in *Narod i voina*, 13; David Brandenberger, *National Bolshevism: Stalinist Mass Culture and the Formation of Modern Russian National Identity, 1931–1956* (Cambridge, MA, and London: Harvard University Press, 2002). The comparison with the "patriotic war" (*otechestvennaia voina*) against Napoleon was already made in Molotov's radio address of 22 June 1941. *Izvestiia*, 24 June 1941, reprinted in V. P. Naumov, ed., *1941 god. V 2-kh knigakh*, vol. 2 (Moscow: Mezhdunarodnyi fond "Demokratiia," 1998), 434–5, here: 435. Although historians sometimes claim otherwise, this war soon became "Great" in Soviet propaganda, which used the terms *Velikaia Otechestvennaia voina* and *Otechestvennaia voina* interchangably for war. Compare the uses of the term in the documents from 1941 and 1943 in V. A. Zolotarev, ed., *Glavnye politicheskie organy vooruzhennykh*

execution of members of "enemy nations" – was also not a result of the war but an escalation of practices of the past decade.[82] The criminalization of captivity was, likewise, in place. Already the Criminal Code of 1926 had defined "giving oneself over to the enemy" (*sdat'sia v plen*) as treason, if it was not caused by the "battle situation"; in the 1930s, the security organs were keenly interested in people who had been POWs during World War I or in the Soviet-Polish war; and during the winter war with Finland in 1939-40 recovered captives had been treated as traitors.[83] The Red Army's propaganda apparatus threatened soldiers already on 24 June 1941 with "the highest form of punishment" for the "treason and betrayal" of "giving oneself into captivity."[84] The repressive policies against POWs connected to Stalin's order No. 270 of 16 August 1941 were thus just reinforcements and radicalizations of what was already in place.[85] Something similar can be said about the brutality against their own troops, which would characterize the wartime Red Army and which was symbolized in the famous "blocking detachments" (*zagraditel'nye otriady*). New disciplinary regulations introduced on 12 October 1940 had given commanders far-reaching authority to punish subordinates – including "employing force or weapons."[86]

---

sil SSSR v Velikoi Otechestvennoi voine 1941–1945 gg. Dokumenty i materialy. Vol. 17–6, Russkii Arkhiv. Velikaia Otechestvennaia (Moscow: Terra, 1996), 20, 39, 45, 69, 235, with Mawdsley, *Thunder*, 460 fn. 3, and Bellamy, *Absolute War*, 3.

[82] Terry Martin, "The Origins of Soviet Ethnic Cleansing," *The Journal of Modern History* 70, no. 4 (1998): 813–61; Pavel Polian, *Ne po svoei vole... istoriia i geografiia prinuditel'nykh migratsii v SSSR* (Moscow: OGI, 2001); Kate Brown, *A Biography of No Place: From Ethnic Borderland to Soviet Heartland* (Cambridge, MA: Harvard University Press, 2003); N. L. Pobol' and P. M. Polian, eds., *Stalinskie deportatsii 1928–1953*, Rossiia XX vek. Dokumenty (Moscow: Demokratiia, 2005); Jeffrey Burds, "The Soviet War against 'Fifth Columnists': The Case of Chechnya, 1942–4," *Journal of Contemporary History* 42, no. 2 (2007): 267–314.

[83] L. G. Ivashov and A. S. Emelin, "Nravstvennye i pravovye problemy plena v Otechestvennoi istorii," *Voenno-istoricheskii zhurnal*, no. 1 (1992): 47–8; V. Danilov, R. Manning, and L. Viola, eds., *Tragediia sovetskoi derevni: Kollektivizatsiia i raskulachivanie: Dokumenty i materialy v 5 tomakh 1927–1939. Tom 5, kn. 2: 1938–1939* (Moscow: Rosspen, 2006), 53–5; V. K. Luzherenko, "Plen: tragediia millionov," in: *Narod i voina*, 188.

[84] Zolotarev, ed., *Glavnye politicheskie organy vooruzhennykh sil SSSR*, 24.

[85] There is a large literature on Soviet POWs during and after the war. For a guide up to the mid-1990s see Jörg Osterloh, *Sowjetische Kriegsgefangene 1941–1945 im Spiegel nationaler und internationaler Untersuchungen: Forschungsüberblick und Bibliographie*, 2nd rev. ed. (Dresden: Hannah-Arendt-Institut für Totalitarismusforschung e.V. and der TU Dresden, 1996). Basic Russian-language reading includes Pavel Polian, *Zhertvy dvukh diktatur: Ostarbaitery i voennoplennye v tret'em reikhe i ikh repatriatsiia* (Moscow: Vash Vybor TsIPZ, 1996); V. P. Naumov, "Sud'ba voennoplennykh i deportirovannykh grazhdan SSSR. Materialy komissii po reabilitatsii zhertv politicheskikh repressii," *Novaia i noveishaia istoriia* no. 2 (1996): 91–112; Luzherenko, "Plen: tragediia millionov," and Aron Shneer, *Plen: Sovetskie voennoplennye v Germanii, 1941–1945* (Moscow: Mosty kultury, 2005). The German classic is Christian Streit, *Keine Kameraden: Die Wehrmacht und die sowjetischen Kriegsgefangenen 1941–1945* (Bonn: Dietz, 1997).

[86] Pechenkin, "Byla li vozmozhnost nastupat'?" 48–49; Zolotarev, ed., *Glavnye politicheskie organy vooruzhennykh sil SSSR*, 325 n.11.

Finally, the hate propaganda which became so central to the war effort of the Soviets had a history which went back at least as far as World War I and the Civil War.[87] The representation of the animallike German soldier in wartime posters was not simply a symbolic expression of the enemy's real-life monstrosity. It was that, too, but it also drew on an established pictorial repertoire – the fascist monster of the 1930s.[88] Soviet propagandists were thus ready for this war, and the atrocity agitation was at full pitch long before German behavior could confirm these expectations.[89] Moreover, important groups of Soviet citizens – what we might call the cadres of totalitarian violence – were not only mentally, but also practically prepared for this war. A (due to the purges) thinning, but nevertheless important section of the officer corps had gained prior wartime experience in the fierce Russian and Spanish Civil Wars.[90] In fact, the top circles of power during the war years included many men whose worldview was deeply influenced by the savage fighting of 1918–21 – Timoshenko, Voroshilov, Kulik, Budennyi, Zhukov, and of course Stalin himself.[91] The latter's conduct during the Civil War pointed to things to come – preference for severe discipline and force over persuasion, callous sacrifice of soldiers, and disregard for obscene casualty numbers.[92]

Likewise, the civilian population included people like Iosif Prut, an utterly peaceful scriptwriter, who two decades earlier had liquidated anti-Soviet rebels

[87] Frank Kämpfer, *Der rote Keil: Das politische Plakat: Theorie und Geschichte* (Berlin: Gebr. Mann Verlag, 1985); Hubertus Jahn, *Patriotic Culture in Russia during World War I* (Ithaca, NY, and London: Cornell University Press, 1995); Richard Stites, ed., *Culture and Entertainment in Wartime Russia* (Bloomington and Indianapolis: Indiana University Press, 1995); Victoria Bonnell, *Iconography of Power: Soviet Political Posters under Lenin and Stalin* (Berkeley, Los Angeles, and London: University of California Press, 1997); Mark Edele, "Paper Soldiers: The World of the Soldier Hero According to Soviet Wartime Posters," *Jahrbücher für Geschichte Osteuropas* 47, no. 1 (1999): 89–108; Jeffrey Brooks, *Thank You, Comrade Stalin! Soviet Public Culture from Revolution to Cold War* (Princeton, NJ: Princeton University Press, 2000); Stephen M. Norris, *A War of Images: Russian Popular Prints, Wartime Culture, and National Identity 1812–1945* (DeKalb: Northern Illinois University Press, 2006); E. S. Seniavskaia, *Protivniki Rossii v voinakh xx veka: Evoliutsiia 'obraza vraga' v soznanii armii i obshchestva* (Moscow: ROSSPEN, 2006); Denise J. Youngblood, *Russian War Films: On the Cinema Front, 1914–2005* (Lawrence: University Press of Kansas, 2007).
[88] For example, see the folowing posters: V. Deni and N. Dolgorukov, "Fashizm – eto voina" (1936); reprinted in *Simvoly epokhi v sovetskom plakate*, ed. T. G. Koloskova (Moscow: Gosudarstvennyi istoricheskii muzei, 2001), #81; or I. Dolgopolov and Iu. Uzbekov, "Doloi fashistskikh podzhigatelei voiny!" (1938); reprinted in *Plakaty pervykh let sovetskoi vlasti i sotsialisticheskogo sotrudnichestva (1918–1941): Katalog*, eds. I. P. Avdeichik and G. K. Iukhnovich (Minsk: "Polymia," 1985), 112.
[89] See, for example, *Krasnaia zvezda*, 26 June 1941, 1 and 3.
[90] Reese, *Red Commanders*, 150.
[91] V. A. Torchinov and A. M. Leontiuk, *Vokrug Stalina: Istoriko-biograficheskii spravochnik* (St. Petersburg: Filologicheskii fakul'tet Sankt-Peterburgskogo gosudarstvennogo universiteta, 2000), 479; Kevin McDermott, *Stalin: Revolutionary in an Era of War* (Basingtoke and New York: Palgrave Macmillan, 2006), 34–40; Robert Service, *Stalin: A Biography* (Cambridge, MA: Belknap Press of Harvard University Press, 2005), 163–75, 337.
[92] Service, *Stalin*, 170. On the Civil War legacy and Stalin's learning process during the war see also Mawdsley, *Thunder*, 207.

in Central Asia, delivering the head of one of these "bandits" as proof of an accomplished mission to his commander.[93] Such men brought their knowledge of all-out civil warfare with them into the army. They joined thousands of younger communists who had participated in the civil war against the peasantry in the early 1930s and had been well-enough schooled in dialectics to see the violence of collectivization and the ensuing mass famine as historically necessary and thus progressive.[94] Finally, large numbers of NKVD personnel had learned during the Great Purges that the physical destruction of enemies – even potential foes – was part of the course of revolutionary action. And, of course, Stalin himself thought of violence as a normal ingredient of political struggle.[95] Once his empire expanded beyond its initial borders (Poland 1939, the Baltic states and Bessarabia in 1940), the subjected peoples were treated to a terror regime at times bordering on genocide. The forest of Katyn, where in 1940 several thousand Polish officers were buried after their execution on direct orders by the Politburo, became the symbol for the brutality of Stalin's "revolution from abroad."[96] While the Nazi fantasy world of Aryan people of light locked in mortal combat with bloodthirsty Jewish-Bolshevik subhumans of the night has little to recommend itself as a description of reality, the Germans did not need to invent much when it came to the brutality of Stalin's regime. The Katyn mass graves, as well as the 1941 slaughter of at least 8,789 and maybe as many as 100,000 prisoners, whose corpses were left behind by retreating NKVD troops, are the most infamous examples.[97] These horrific episodes, which German propagandists quickly seized upon and the Soviets immediately denied, were consistent with the "mass operations of repression of anti-Soviet elements" in 1937 and 1938, when all kinds of undesirables had been liquidated. The main difference was that in the late 1930s carefully planned quotas for shootings were distributed, while in 1941 the massacres

---

[93] Iosif Prut, *Nepoddaiushchiisia o mnogikh drugikh i koe-chto o sebe* (Moscow: "Vagrius," 2000). On the incident with the "bandit's" head see ibid., 117–18.

[94] A famous example is the later dissident Lev Kopelev. See his memoirs *The Education of a True Believer*, trans. Gary Kern (London: Wildwood House, 1981); and *No Jail for Thought*, trans. Anthony Austin (London: Secker & Warburg, 1977). On the collectivizers see also Lynne Viola, *The Best Sons of the Fatherland: Workers in the Vanguard of Soviet Collectivization* (New York and Oxford: Oxford University Press, 1987).

[95] Service, *Stalin*, 336–56.

[96] Ch. Magaichik, "Katyn';" N. S. Lebedeva, "Chetvertyi razdel Pol'shi i katyn'skaia tragediia," both in *Drugaia voina*, 225–95; Jan T. Gross, *Revolution from Abroad: The Soviet Conquest of Poland's Western Ukraine and Western Belorussia*, expanded ed. (Princeton, NJ, and Oxford: Princeton University Press, 2002), 228–9; R.W. Davies, *Soviet History in the Yeltsin Era* (New York: St. Martin's Press in association with Centre for Russian and East European Studies, University of Birmingham, 1997), 18–19, 45.

[97] Robert Conquest, *The Great Terror: A Reassessment* (Oxford and New York: Oxford University Press, 1990), 456–7; Gross, *Revolution from Abroad*, 228; Berkhoff, *Harvest of Despair*, 14–17 (with the more conservative number of executions, those accounted for in Soviet archives, p. 14). The most in-depth study of these episodes is Bogdan Musial, *"Konterrevolutionäre Elemente sind zu erschießen": Die Brutalisierung des deutsch-sowjetischen Krieges im Sommer 1941*, 2nd ed. (Berlin and Munich: Propyläen, 2001).

happened in the chaos of retreat.[98] Also reminiscent of the Great Terror was the initial hunt for scapegoats for the military catastrophe of the first weeks of war – frontline generals were accused of treason, arrested, and shot.[99]

In this immediate escalation of self-defense into a civil war against enemies within as well as without, the Soviet leadership could rely on the loyalty of a core group of cadres ready to defend "the revolution," cost it what it may. Such support, however, was not enough to win this war. It was clear that the majority of Soviet citizens – the peasants and ex-peasants against whom the regime had waged war since collectivization – were unlikely to fight for Bolshevism.[100] Already in 1928 Stalin had predicted that in case of an attack, the regime needed to be prepared to hold out for six months, as this was the time "the peasant" needed "to come to his senses, become familiar with the dangers of war, to understand what's going on and pull himself together for the common task of defending the country."[101] In order to help the *muzhiki* familiarize themselves with these dangers the regime immediately radicalized the conduct of war, once it became clear that the Red Army was unable to stop the German juggernaut at the border. All-out war would, it was hoped, slow the German advance long enough for "the peasant" to come "to his senses." On 29 June the government ordered the complete evacuation or destruction of "all valuable property" and the immediate organization of guerrilla warfare if a region had to be abandoned to the enemy.[102] Shortly thereafter, in his first public appearance after the invasion, the Supreme Commander called the German challenge a "matter of life and death of the Soviet state, of life and death of the peoples of the USSR." This was "no ordinary war" and it would be fought with all means necessary. All of society immediately was to be mobilized for war; soldiers and civilians were told to "defend every inch of Soviet soil, fight to the last drop of blood for our towns and villages," while those who refused to do so – "whiners and cowards, panic-mongers and deserters" – had

[98] See Paul Hagenloh, "'Socially Harmful Elements' and the Great Terror," in *Stalinism: New Directions*, ed. Sheila Fitzpatrick (London and New York: Routledge, 2000), 286–308; J. Arch Getty and Oleg V. Naumov, eds., *The Road to Terror: Stalin and the Self-Destruction of the Bolsheviks, 1932–39* (New Haven, CT, and London: Yale University Press, 1999), 470–80. For an example that engages German atrocity propaganda, see M. Lesnov, "Dokumenty odnogo srazheniia," *Krasnaia zvezda*, 22 October 1941, 3.

[99] See the interrogation protocol of General D. G. Pavlov and the State Defense Committee resolution of 16 July 1941. Both reprinted in: *1941 god. Dokumenty v 2-kh knigakh*, ed. L. E. Reshin et al., Vol. 2 (Moscow: Demokratiia, 1998), 455–68; 472–3. For a summary Merridale, *Ivan's War*, 85–8.

[100] This was in fact the case, as recent research shows: Berkhoff, *Harvest of Despair*, 12–13. On the war with the peasantry see Lynne Viola et al., eds., *The War against the Peasantry, 1927–1930: The Tragedy of the Soviet Countryside* (New Haven, CT: Yale University Press, 2005); V. Danilov, R. Manning, and L. Viola, eds., *Tragediia sovetskoi derevni*.

[101] Stalin's speech at the July Plenum of the Central Committee, evening of 9 July 1928, reprinted in *Tragediia sovetskoi derevni*, vol. 1: 319–31, here: 326–7.

[102] SNK and CC directive, signed by Molotov and Stalin, 29 June 1941, reprinted in *1941 god. Dokumenty*, vol. 2, 446–8, here: 447.

no place "in our ranks." When retreat was unavoidable, anything the enemy could use – from means of transport to fuel, from cows to grain – was to be either evacuated or destroyed; in the occupied territories a partisan war was to be unleashed, destroying infrastructure, attacking the German troops and their collaborators, killing them wherever they were to be found and thus to "create unbearable conditions for the enemy."[103]

This was a program for total war and a radicalization of the initial response, formulated by Molotov immediately after the German invasion. Still expecting that the Red Army could stop the aggressor quickly, the Commissar for Foreign Affairs focused on "bloodthirsty fascists" as the enemy, who had forced "the German people" into this war. He asked for discipline and patriotism, but not for an all-out war.[104] This was on 24 June. By early July, the Soviets had clearly taken off whatever gloves they might have worn. However, it was not yet a program for a war of extermination against the invaders. That was the next step, a further radicalization caused by the experience with the German conduct of war. Four months after his initial address to the Soviet people, in a speech on 6 November 1941, Stalin quoted from captured Wehrmacht documents and accepted warfare on German terms:

> The German invaders want a war of extermination (*istrebitel'naia voina*) with the peoples of the USSR. Well, then, if the Germans want a war of extermination, they will get it. (Thunderous, lengthy applause.)
>   Henceforth our task, the task of the peoples of the USSR, the task of the soldiers, commanders and political workers of our army and navy will be to exterminate (*istrebit'*) each and every German who has forced his way as an occupier onto our homeland. (Thunderous applause; exclamations: "'That's right!" Shouts of "Hurray!")
>   No mercy to the German occupiers!
>   Death to the German occupiers! (Thunderous applause).[105]

This speech was widely propagated at the front, flanked by talks with titles such as "Atrocities of the Fascist cannibals towards captured and wounded Red Army soldiers, commanders, and political workers."[106] In the process, the few subtleties of the message quickly got lost – in Stalin's careful wording this was a program to exterminate, not "each and every German" but "each and every German who has forced his way as an occupier onto our homeland." "Excesses" could thus be blamed on subordinates, but the main goal was reached. Confronted with an enemy who promised not just to defeat the Bolsheviks but to annihilate them and enslave whatever was left of the Soviet people the response was a complete, total war of annihilation of the enemy

---

[103] Stalin's radio address from 3 July 1941, reprinted in Stalin, *O Velikoi Otechestvennoi voine Sovetskogo Soiuza* (Moscow: Izd-vo "Kraft," 2002), 11–16.

[104] Molotov's radio address, 22 June 1941, *Izvestiia*, 24 June 1941.

[105] *Pravda*, 7 November 1941, 1–2, here: 2.

[106] "Direktiva GlavPU RKKA, no. 0178," (14 November 1941), reprinted in *Glavnye politicheskie organy vooruzhennykh sil SSSR*, 83–4; see also "Direktiva GlavPU RKKA, no. 268," (7 December 1941), in ibid., 87–90.

by whatever means necessary and at whatever cost to their own side. As the Supreme Commander advised his military leaders on 13 November 1941, the best way to deal with Germans entrenched in a village was to "completely destroy the settlement and burn it to the ground," burying the enemy under the rubble.[107]

This radicalization of war making was one aspect of the attempt to concentrate the mind of "the peasant." Brutal discipline, the threat and actual administration of violence against those unwilling or unable to fight, and the systematic unleashing of the passions of war through a savage atrocity propaganda were the other aspects of the program. The results were at times so counterproductive that by early 1942, Stalin tried to pull back a little. In an order to the troops on the anniversary of the founding of the Red Army, the Supreme Commander stressed that the Soviet Union was waging a defensive war of liberation, not an offensive, imperialist war of conquest:

> Sometimes the foreign media jabber, that the Red Army has the goal to exterminate (*istrebit'*) the German people and to destroy the German state. That, of course, is stupid nonsense and silly slander of the Red Army. The Red Army could not have such idiotic goals... It would be funny to identify Hitler's clique with the German people, the German state. History teaches that the Hitlers come and go, but the German people, the German state, live on.
>
> ... The Red Army captures German soldiers and officers and saves their lives, if they surrender. The Red Army destroys German soldiers and officers, if they refuse to put down their weapons and [continue] to attempt, gun in hand, to enslave our Homeland.... "If the enemy does not surrender, he will be destroyed."[108]

It seems that this was meant as a real deescalation of the war of extermination, not just as an address to the Allies or enemy soldiers. German military intelligence learned in December 1941 that officers had prohibited the wild shooting of prisoners.[109] Ambiguities remained, however. The new pronouncement was promoted to the troops together with the November call for a war of extermination. Speeches and lectures, talks and articles informed the front line that the Red Army "destroys German soldiers if they refuse to put down their weapons and [continue] to attempt to enslave our Homeland." The stress was still on destruction, and the alternative was hidden in incomplete excerpts: "If the enemy does not surrender, he will be destroyed." (Toward the enemy lines, the message was more straightforward: "The Red Army captures German soldiers and officers and saves their lives, if they surrender.")[110] Still, this was a partial deescalation, flanked also by attempts to change the approach to senseless

---

[107] Quoted in *Drugaia voina*, 154.

[108] "Prikaz Narodnogo komissara oborony, no. 55" (23 February 1942), reprinted in Stalin, *O Velikoi Otechestvennoi voine Sovetskogo Soiuza*, 40–4, here: 43, 44.

[109] Jörg Friedrich, *Das Gesetz des Krieges: Das deutsche Heer in Russland, 1941 bis 1945: Der Prozess gegen das Oberkommando der Wehrmacht* (Munich: Piper, 1993), 586.

[110] "Direktiva GlavPU RKKA, no. 30;" and "Direktiva GlavPU RKKA, no. 31" (both 26 February 1942), reprinted in *Glavnye politicheskie organy vooruzhennykh sil SSSR*, 115–17. See also the "passes" (*propuski*) for German soldiers, promising fair treatment in captivity, "Direktiva GlavPU RKKA, no. 58," (18 April 1942), ibid., 129.

sacrifice of men. A month after Stalin's speech, a directive of the Military Council of the Western Front ordered commanders to stop the "thoughtless" and "abnormal" approach to infantry losses and punish those guilty.[111] In May 1942, Stalin advised the leaders of the South-Western front to learn to fight less bloodily, "as the Germans do it."[112]

Meanwhile the Soviet regime in general and Stalin in particular had reasserted control and discipline after months of ferocious fighting. All energies were now concentrated on winning the war, and the control of many nonessential sectors was all but given up. The management of housing and the consumption of the civilian population devolved onto the local and sometimes enterprise level, cultural policies were relaxed, the Orthodox Church was drafted into the war effort, and after an initial reinstatement of the authority of the irritating commissars (*voennye komissary; politruki*) on 16 July 1941, unity of command was firmly given to the officer corps from 9 October 1942 onward.[113] At the top, the party-state had been centralized in the new State Defense Committee (GKO) with Stalin at its head, but its members, bestowed with plenipotentiary powers, were much freer to act than they had been in the 1930s. They became "semiautonomous leaders." Access to the top decision makers was relatively unrestricted for high-level military as well as civilian leaders, who could now show up uninvited if matters demanded. Republic and regional authorities were strengthened, too, to help them solve problems and reach production targets. Stalin did meddle with military affairs, but by and large he functioned as a central coordinator and let the professionals do their work.[114]

---

[111] 30 May 1942. Reprinted in *Skrytaia pravda voiny: 1941 god. Neizvestnye dokumenty* (Moscow: Russkaia kniga, 1992), 228–9.

[112] 27 May 1942, quoted in *Drugaia voina*, 154.

[113] On devolution of control during the war see P. Charles Hachten, "Property Relations and the Economic Organization of Soviet Russia, 1941–1948" (Ph.D. diss., The University of Chicago, 2005). On the organization of the home front see John Barber and Mark Harrison, *The Soviet Home Front, 1941–1945: A Social and Economic History of the USSR in World War II* (London and New York: Longman, 1991). On food supply see William Moskoff, *The Bread of Affliction: The Food Supply in the USSR during World War II* (Cambridge: Cambridge University Press, 1990). On the cultural relaxation see Stites, *Culture and Entertainment in Wartime Russia*; on religion see Daniel Peris, "'God Is Now on Our Side': The Religious Revival on Unoccupied Soviet Territory during World War II," *Kritika: Explorations in Russian and Eurasian History* 1, no. 1 (2000): 97–118; and Tatiana A. Chumachenko, *Church and State in Soviet Russia: Russian Orthodoxy from World War II to the Khrushchev Years*, trans. Edward E. Roslof (Armonk, NY, and London: M. E. Sharpe, 2002). On commissars and single command in the army see Zolotarev, ed., *Glavnye politicheskie organy vooruzhennykh sil SSSR*, 326 n. 17, 331 n. 48; Merridale, *Ivan's War*, 107–8; Glantz, *Colossus Reborn*, 475.

[114] On the GKO see Yoram Gorlizki and Oleg Khlevniuk, *Cold Peace: Stalin and the Soviet Ruling Circle, 1945–1953* (Oxford and New York: Oxford University Press, 2004), 17, 46–7; Mawdsley, *Thunder*, 206–9; Bellamy, *Absolute War*, 228–30. On Stalin during the war see Service, *Stalin*, 410–87. On the management of the wartime economy see G. Kumanev, *Govoriat stalinskie narkomy* (Smolensk: Rusich, 2005).

Everything was now geared toward making the Red Army, not least with Lend & Lease support, into a more efficient, more motorized, more industrial, and more lethal force – nothing else mattered.[115] In the end, in 1943–4 Stalin did get what he had spoken of in 1941 – a mass army with an industrialized core. It is easy to overstress the level of mechanization – the "army of quality" made up maybe 20 percent of the overall forces; cavalry played an important role in the war of movement until the end; and requisitiond peasant carts rather than Studebaker trucks made infantry units able to keep up with the tank forces. This war was won by the horse as much as the tank.[116] Nevertheless, this (given the casualties) new army was now able to use tank forces "effectively" and implement prewar theories of "deep battle" – the Soviet equivalent of the Blitzkrieg.[117] It was, if not better trained, better equipped, more mobile, and altogether more efficient and effective in fighting war. It was the army that overwhelmed the defenses of Army Group Center in 1944 in the most stunning battle victory of World War II and in January 1945 began its fighting advance toward Berlin that crushed the remnants of the German Army of the East.[118] This military recovery allowed a deescalation of the all-out war against enemies within and without. A more forward-thinking military now began to view civilians and soldiers left behind the front in German-occupied territory not only as likely traitors but also as potential partisans.[119] And not least, the Soviet regime began to pursue a more active, revolutionary politics that aimed to draw Germans in POW camps, at the front, and even back in Germany (by way of letters written by prominent POWs)[120] onto their side,

---

[115] A. S. Iakushevskii, "Arsenal pobedy," in *Narod i voina*, 73–114; A. S. Orlov, "My i soiuzniki," in ibid., 205–17; Mawdsley, *Thunder*, 185–223; Mark Harrison, "The USSR and Total War: Why Didn't the Soviet Economy Collapse in 1942?" in *A World at Total War: Global Conflict and the Politics of Destruction, 1937–1945*, eds. Roger Chickering, Stig Förster, and Bernd Greiner (Cambridge: Cambridge University Press, 2005), 137–56.

[116] For an illuminating memoir about the life in the infantry see Gabriel Temkin, *My Just War: The Memoirs of a Jewish Red Army Soldier in World War II* (Novato, CA: Presidio Press, 1998). On the two armies – the 80 percent "imposing bludgeon" and the 20 percent mobile forces constituting "the swift sword" – see Glantz, *Colossus Reborn*, 618–19. "Army of quality" and "army of quantity" are John Erickson's terms. See *Stalin's War with Germany*, vol. 2: *The Road to Berlin*, 84. For the continued importance of cavalry and the horse see Bellamy, *Absolute War*, 169, 249, 283, 333–4, 602, 603, 678–9, 680; and Mawdsley, *Thunder*, XVII, 26, 64, 122, 127, 217–18, 303. For life in the cavalry see Aleksandr Rodin, *Tri tysiachi kilometrov v sedle* (Moscow: IPO Profizdat, 2000).

[117] David M. Glantz, "Developing Offensive Success: The Soviet Conduct of Operational Maneuver," in *Soviet Military Doctrine from Lenin to Gorbachev, 1915–1991*, ed. Willard Frank and Philip Gillette (Westport, CT, and London: Greenwood Press, 1992), 133–73; Mawdsley, *Thunder*, 22, 175, 221–3; Bellamy, *Absolute War*, 490–1, 602–3.

[118] Antony Beevor, *The Fall of Berlin, 1945* (New York: Viking, 2002).

[119] Slepyan, *Stalin's Guerrillas*. Alexander Hill, *The War behind the Eastern Front: The Soviet Partisan Movement in North-West Russia, 1941–1944* (London and New York: Frank Cass, 2005).

[120] Frank Biess, *Homecomings: Returning POWs and the Legacies of Defeat in Postwar Germany* (Princeton, NJ: Princeton University Press, 2006).

having abandoned its initial internationalism following the first flush of the
German attack.[121] By the same token, the Soviet regime was the first major
combatant to turn to war crimes trials in the effort to separate (military and
civilian) criminals from the mass of Germans that fought the war.[122]

We telescope this entire development because the problem that we face
is how and why this militarily superior and, effectively, newly recruited and
trained army turned out to be the one that engaged in massive atrocities, rape,
pillage, and sadistic murder in its sweep into central Europe and into the
German lands long after the initial call for a war of extermination against the
aggressor had been given up – and this is quite apart from the systematic pursuit
of a political strategy that aimed at securing Soviet control of the liberated and
occupied territories. Again, we ask our readers to hold their judgment for the
moment, because part and parcel of this story is the way in which the German
conduct of war reacted first to the tenacity of the Soviet retreat, which turned
the notion of a short war into an illusion, and, after 1942–3, to the inexorable
advance of Soviet forces against a retreating Wehrmacht.

EXTREME VIOLENCE

The sense of vulnerability even in victory was greatly exacerbated by the nature
of the Russian retreat.[123] It confirmed the prejudices many of the Wehrmacht
officers and soldiers harbored and played into the hands of Nazi propaganda.
As before with the German escalation of violence, reality (of Soviet ruthlessness)
trumped imagination. There was an element of protective rhetoric involved,
but German soldiers and officers also recognized, as they did with increasing
frequency in late fall and winter 1941–2, that they confronted their own escalation of violence when encountering starving and freezing women, children, and
emaciated Soviet POWs.[124] At this point, not unlike in World War I, soldiers
entered a space of combat, in which they only had themselves and their value
judgments to depend on.[125] In this situation, it mattered immensely that the

---

[121] Sabine R. Arnold and Gerd R. Ueberschär, *Das Nationalkommittee "Freies Deutschland" und
   der Bund deutscher Offiziere* (Frankfurt am Main: Fischer Taschenbuch Verlag, 1995).
[122] Earl Frederick Ziemke, *Stalingrad to Berlin: The German Defeat in the East* (Washington, DC:
   Office of the Chief of Military History, 1968).
[123] K. Arnold, *Die Wehrmacht und die Besatzungspolitik in den besetzten Gebieten der Sowjetunion: Kriegführung und Radikalisierung im "Unternehmen Barbarossa,"* overstates his case
   about effects, but he is right in his insistence that the Soviet reaction left a deep imprint on
   German soldiers. See the supporting evidence in Latzel, *Deutsche Soldaten – Nationalsozialistischer Krieg?: Kriegserlebnis, Kriegserfahrung 1939–1945*; Martin Humburg, *Das Gesicht des
   Krieges: Feldpostbriefe von Wehrmachtssoldaten aus der Sowjetunion 1941–1944* (Opladen:
   Westdeutscher Verlag, 1998).
[124] Hürter, "Die Wehrmacht vor Leningrad: Krieg und Besatzungspolitik der 18. Armee im Herbst
   und Winter 1941/42."
[125] Thomas Kühne, *Kameradschaft: Die Soldaten des nationalsozialistischen Krieges und das 20.
   Jahrhundert* (Göttingen: Vandenhoeck & Ruprecht, 2006).

only "virtue" drilled into them and repeated by propaganda was unrestrained ruthlessness in pursuit of victory – or utter defeat.

The immediate response to Soviet atrocities was a brutalization of war making. We tend to think of brutalization in terms of mass murder and of the mindset of perpetrators.[126] But mass murder, in which Wehrmacht units although frequent participants were not the main actors, occurred in the context of a groundswell of military acts of cruelty. A typical case in point was the use of human shields, as, for example, in the effort to seize Brest against desperate resistance;[127] typical also was the murder of prisoners of war who seemed dangerous or were ballast for the advancing troops (or for the detachments that guarded them);[128] reckless destruction and unstoppable pilfering in the guise of living off the land were frequently mentioned.[129] Hostage taking and shooting were routine, as were the seizure, internment, and murder of suspect civilians and the bombardment of civilian evacuees in flight.[130] We know of many of these incidents only because commanding officers perceived of them as threats to their unit's discipline. In the first instance, these acts of cruelty indicate the everyday reality of the "criminal orders" among frontline units. They made cruelty a routine matter.

Cruelty was justified with reference to Soviet atrocities. German soldiers responded fiercely to the shooting of wounded soldiers and especially to (the actual experience and rumors of) mutilations of their bodies.[131] They retaliated in kind and closed ranks for fear of falling into the hands of the enemy. The presumption of treachery in the civilian population, again backed up mostly by rumor, increased the readiness to destroy and kill. German soldiers reacted violently to the fighting retreat of the Soviet forces with their scorched earth tactics. Soldiers came to anticipate booby-trapped buildings or delayed mines in towns; they faced the decomposing victims of Soviet political murders with mind-numbing regularity; they were confronted with a remarkably efficient system for the evacuation of people and things and the systematic destruction of what was left behind; they abhorred the sheer destructiveness of the Soviet

---

[126] Christopher R. Browning, *Ordinary Men: Reserve Police Batallion 101 and the Final Solution in Poland* (New York: HarperCollins, 1993); Christopher Browning, "German Killers: Behavior and Motivation in the Light of New Evidence," in *Nazi Policy: Jewish Workers, German Killers,* ed. Christopher Browning (Cambridge and New York: Cambridge University Press, 2000), 143–69.

[127] Gerlach, "Verbrechen deutscher Fronttruppen in Weißrußland 1941–1944: Eine Annäherung."

[128] Hamburger Institut für Sozialforschung, ed., *Verbrechen der Wehrmacht: Dimensionen des Vernichtungskrieges 1941–1944, Ausstellungskatalog,* 218–26.

[129] Ibid., 298–9.

[130] See Niemiecki Instytut Historyczny w Warszawie, ed., *"Grösste Härte–": Verbrechen der Wehrmacht in Polen September–Oktober 1939: Ausstellungskatalog* (Osnabrück: Fibre, 2005).

[131] Examples for this process can be found in Latzel, *Deutsche Soldaten–Nationalsozialistischer Krieg?: Kriegserlebnis, Kriegserfahrung 1939–1945;* Heer, *Vom Verschwinden der Täter,* 118.

retreat.[132] The shocking reality of Soviet retreat clearly excited their imagination.[133] It led to a brutalization of their conduct, a readiness to use excessive force, and rallied them behind calls for an escalation of violence. In response to Soviet self-defense, German soldiers, whether Nazis or not, developed a dogged determination to crush a fiendish enemy – exactly the kind of image that the propaganda for Barbarossa had insinuated. This shared resolve made it easier, much easier, for the many and diverse human beings that made up the Army of the East to think of the war against the Soviet Union as "another place" in which only the ruthless would survive and norms of civility could and would be set aside. It generated a kind of solidarity that over time would make the Wehrmacht into a people's army – a fighting body unified by their experience of a war of survival.[134]

However, it was fear, the sheer terror of survival, that made the Army of the East into a "community of fate" that was ready to use extraordinary violence as a matter of course. If you are in hell, you do as the devil does:

> We are a sworn community of fate, together we know how to find a way to die.... I give orders to shoot so and so many commissars and partisans without even blinking (*besinnungslos*); it is him or me – it is damned simple.... [W]e are fighting here for our own naked lives, daily and hourly, against an enemy who in all respects is far superior.[135]

This was the *cri de coeur* not of a simple soldier, but of Lieutenant General Stieff writing home on 7 December 1941. The Soviet counteroffensive had broken his sense of invincibility; he hung on for dear life and fought a merciless war. Panic and a good deal of hysteria replaced the sense of invincibility that had predominated only months earlier.[136] "Who ever talks about

---

[132] Berkhoff, *Harvest of Despair*, 17–34; Rebecca Manley, "The Evacuation and Survival of Soviet Civilians, 1941–1946" (Ph.D. diss., University of California, Berkeley, 2004); Hamburger Institut für Sozialforschung, ed., *Verbrechen der Wehrmacht: Dimensionen des Vernichtungskrieges 1941–1944, Ausstellungskatalog*, 91–185. Klaus Jochen Arnold, "Die Eroberung und Behandlung der Stadt Kiew durch die Wehrmacht im September 1941: Zur Radikalisierung der Besatzungspolitik," *Militärgeschichtliche Mitteilungen* 58, no. 1 (1999): 23–63.

[133] Evidence collected in Latzel, *Deutsche Soldaten – Nationalsozialistischer Krieg?: Kriegserlebnis, Kriegserfahrung 1939–1945*; Humburg, *Das Gesicht des Krieges: Feldpostbriefe von Wehrmachtssoldaten aus der Sowjetunion 1941–1944*; Hans Joachim Schröder, *Die gestohlenen Jahre: Erzählgeschichten und Geschichtserzählung im Interview: Der Zweite Weltkrieg aus der Sicht ehemaliger Mannschaftssoldaten* (Tübingen: Niemeyer, 1992); Thilo Stenzel, *Das Rußlandbild des 'kleinen Mannes': Gesellschaftliche Prägung und Fremdwahrnehmung in Feldpostbriefen aus dem Ostfeldzug (1941–1944/45)* (Munich: Osteuropa-Institut, 1998).

[134] Bernard R. Kroener, "Auf dem Weg zu einer 'nationalsozialistischen Volksarmee': Die soziale Ordnung des Heeresoffizierkorps im Zweiten Weltkrieg," in *Von Stalingrad zur Währungsreform: Zur Sozialgeschichte des Umbruchs in Deutschland*, ed. Martin Broszat (Munich: Oldenbourg, 1988), 651–82; Kühne, *Kameradschaft: Die Soldaten des nationalsozialistischen Krieges und das 20. Jahrhundert*.

[135] Hellmuth Stieff, *Briefe*, ed. Horst Mühleisen (Berlin: Siedler, 1991), 140.

[136] Johannes Hürter, *Hitlers Heerführer: Die deutschen Oberbefehlshaber im Krieg gegen die Sowjetunion 1941/42* (Munich: Oldenbourg, 2006), 318–50.

winning? Surviving is everything!"[137] Stieff's response marks in an exemplary fashion the end point of a process, in which experience and expectation had been adjusted, within the bounds of common prejudice, in the rapidly escalating violence of Operation Barbarossa. His comment was an early sign of things to come. German soldiers increasingly fought without hope for a future – and with few escapes. Survival was the rule of the game – and now the old rule did apply: *Not kennt kein Gebot*. Alas, it still mattered who defined the exception.

The winter panic, while important for reshuffling the military leadership and putting Hitler in command of the army, was momentary. The more important aspect was the replacement of the programmatic overkill of Operation Barbarossa, by what many historians quite correctly perceive as a more pragmatic conduct of war.[138] The only problem is that – contrary to the meaning of pragmatism – this more pragmatic approach also turned out to be the far more radical one.[139] In 1941–2 Nazi Germany and, in this context, the Army of the East, entered a phase of extermination warfare. Three dimensions of this warfare require our attention: the war against the Jews, which reached its apogee in 1942–3; the war with and against the Soviet population, which climaxed in the same two years; and the systematic pursuit of scorched earth tactics in 1943–4. In these years, war radicalized – in actual fact was radicalized – by a series of German decisions that defined the exception as a murderous life-or-death-struggle across the entire territory of the Soviet Union.[140] This three-pronged radicalization was the distinctly German imprint on the war. When the Red Army finally gained the upper hand in summer 1944, war continued to be exceedingly cruel in the subjection of German civilians. It was certainly deadlier than ever for the German forces, but it ceased to be a life-and-death struggle. Germany and the Germans, contrary to what Nazi ideologues believed, would suffer grievously under Soviet control, but they would survive.[141]

---

[137] Comment of an ordinary soldier, quoted in Christian Hartmann, *Halder: Generalstabschef Hitlers 1938–1942* (Paderborn: Ferdinand Schöningh, 1991), 294.

[138] Oldenburg, *Ideologie und militärisches Kalkül: Die Besatzungspolitik der Wehrmacht in der Sowjetunion 1942*.

[139] On German casualties, Rüdiger Overmans, *Deutsche militärische Verluste im Zweiten Weltkrieg* (Munich: R. Oldenbourg, 1999). On Soviet casualties, see above.

[140] For a similar argument, see Hew Strachan, "Time, Space and Barbarisation: The German Army and the Eastern Front in Two World Wars," in *The Barbarization of Warfare*, ed. George Kassimeris (New York: New York University Press, 2006), 58–82. See also Omer Bartov, "From Blitzkrieg to Total War: Controversial Links between Image and Reality," in *Stalinism and Nazism: Dictatorship in Comparison*, eds. Ian Kershaw and Moshe Levin (Cambridge and New York: Cambridge University Press, 1997), 158–84; Christian Gerlach, "La Wehrmacht et la radicalisation de la lutte contre les partisans en Union Soviétique," in *Occupation et répression militaire allemandes: La politique de "maintien de l'ordre" en Europe occupée, 1939–1945*, eds. Gaël Eismann and Stefan Martens (Paris: Institut historique allemand, 2007), 71–88.

[141] Norman M. Naimark, *The Russians in Germany: A History of the Soviet Zone of Occupation, 1945–1949* (Cambridge, MA: Belknap Press of Harvard University Press, 1995).

The strategic background for this transition was the recognition that the Soviet Union would not fall and that the Nazi-Soviet war would continue. It was equally shaped by the fact that, beginning in December 1941, the Third Reich fought a global war. The main consequence at home was a reluctant mobilization of the civilian population.[142] This mobilization was accompanied by an initially hesitant reconsideration of the industrial labor and, more unwillingly, the military value of populations in the East, including prisoners of war.[143] Ideological reluctance, foremost expressed by Hitler, was bested by crude efficiencies. Women were mobilized; "Slavic" auxiliaries were used in the Wehrmacht and recruited by force for work behind the front (*Organisation Todt*), as well as for industry and agriculture in the Reich.[144]

We find a parallel recalibration of the conduct of war – from a Barbarossa-type overkill to the systematic pursuit of extermination of all those whom the Nazi (and military) leadership defined as their deadly enemies. What emerged from this recalibration of war was a thoroughly racialized and mobilized Nazi "community of fate." This war of extermination was fractured into many microtheaters. Systematic destruction bent to local circumstances. But effectively a military and eventually a German "community of fate" fought war as an all-out life-and-death struggle, a war of bare life as it were, on both an external and an internal front.[145] This was not a war imposed on Germany. Typically, it was a war the military and political leadership chose to fight – and chose preemptively to fight in a situation in which they were no longer in full control of their future, although the possibility of defeat was still far off.

The key to the recalibration of war was the extermination of any and all Jews in the German sphere of control.[146] Indications for this radicalization of the war against the Jews were omnipresent in October/November 1941 – with the mass killings of Jews as hostages in Serbia, mass executions of entire communities (men, women, and children) in Galicia, the beginning deportation

---

[142] Adam Tooze, *The Wages of Destruction: The Making and Breaking of the Nazi Economy* (New York: Viking, 2006).

[143] Ulrich Herbert, *Hitler's Foreign Workers: Enforced Foreign Labor in Germany under the Third Reich* (Cambridge and New York: Cambridge University Press, 1997).

[144] Bernhard R. Kroener, "'Menschenbewirtschaftung,' Bevölkerungsverteilung und personelle Rüstung in der zweiten Kriegshälfte (1942–1944)," in *Das Deutsche Reich und der Zweite Weltkrieg*, Vol. 5/2, *Kriegsverwaltung, Wirtschaft und personelle Ressourcen 1942–1944/45*, ed. Militärgeschichtliches Forschungsamt (Munich: Deutsche Verlagsanstalt, 1999), 777–995. A critical study on the Organisation Todt is still missing. Franz Wilhelm Seidler, *Die Organisation Todt: Bauen für Staat und Wehrmacht, 1938–1945* (Koblenz: Bernard & Graefe, 1987).

[145] Martin Dean, "The German Gendarmerie, the Ukrainian Schutzmannschaft and the 'Second Wave' of Jewish Killings in Occupied Ukraine: German Policing at the Local Level in the Zhitomir Region, 1941–1944," *German History* 14, no. 2 (1996): 168–92.

[146] Christopher R. Browning, "The Euphoria of Victory and the Final Solution: Summer–Fall 1941," *German Studies Review* 17, no. 3 (1994): 473–81; Tobias Jersak, "Die Interaktion von Kriegsverlauf und Judenvernichtung: Ein Blick auf Hitlers Strategie im Spätsommer 1941," *Historische Zeitschrift* 268, no. 2 (1999): 311–74; Klaus Jochen Arnold, "Hitlers Wandel im August 1941: Ein Kommentar zu den Thesen Tobias Jersaks," *Zeitschrift für Geschichtswissenschaft* 48, no. 3 (2000): 239–50.

of German Jews into eastern ghettos, and not least the establishment of camps designed for the purpose of murdering people en masse.[147] This turn was firmed up in December 1941 with explicit reference to the strategic situation and, subsequently, worked into a bureaucratic modus operandi under the leadership of Himmler and his security apparatus at the Wannsee Conference in January 1942.[148] What matters about these deliberations is the recognition by the Nazi leadership that the "final solution" of the "Jewish problem" could not wait until after victory. "In the final analysis," Hermann Göring made clear, the war "is about whether the German and Aryan prevails here, or whether the Jew rules."[149] Therefore, the comprehensive and systematic campaign against the Jewish populations in Europe was fought, as a war on the interior front, in its own theater of war, and it was fought as a war of extermination, the killing of any and all. It reached its high point in 1942, when nearly one-half of all Jews killed in the entire war were murdered. But the campaign did not let up until the Third Reich was defeated and conquered.[150] This was neither extermination under the guise of war nor extreme violence accompanying "ethnic cleansing." Rather Jews were identified as "the most perilous enemy" in a war that the Nazis fought to the death.[151] The campaign for the extermination of the Jewish population also proved to be the most lethal campaign of the entire war.

It is no coincidence that the first people killed in the new extermination facility in Auschwitz were politically suspect Soviet prisoners of war. The destruction of the social institutions and agents of the Soviet regime had been the war plan for the campaign against the Soviet Union all along. But in late 1941 this war began to stretch and was fought without fronts. While the war planners had a highly developed sense of racial (and political, ethnic, religious) differences and while the theaters of war were institutionally subdivided between security forces and military forces, all enemies of the Third Reich and any conceivable form of overt or covert opposition came under attack in a war that covered with increasing ferocity and lethality all fronts and stretched from the zone of "combined" (military and security) operations all the way back to Germany with its millions of slave laborers. In this war "pragmatism," the concentration on military functionality, proved to be the crooked path to hell, because

---

[147] Longerich, *Politik der Vernichtung: Eine Gesamtdarstellung der nationalsozialistischen Judenverfolgung*, 352–400, 441–60.

[148] Christian Gerlach, "The Wannsee Conference, the Fate of German Jews, and Hitler's Decision in Principle to Exterminate All European Jews," *Journal of Modern History* 70, no. 4 (1998): 759–812. Somewhat different readings by Browning and Matthäus, *The Origins of the Final Solution: The Evolution of Nazi Jewish Policy, September 1939–March 1942*, and by Peter Longerich, *The Unwritten Order: Hitler's Role in the Final Solution* (Stroud and Charleston, SC: Tempus, 2001).

[149] Quoted in Peter Fritzsche, *Life and Death in the Third Reich* (Cambridge, MA: Harvard University Press, 2008), 187.

[150] With the proper emphasis on 1942–4: Longerich, *Politik der Vernichtung: Eine Gesamtdarstellung der nationalsozialistischen Judenverfolgung*.

[151] Ibid., 221.

pragmatism was always already front loaded.[152] Hell was a place, in which small "communities of fate," outmatched frontline troops, undermanned security forces in the rear areas, and an increasingly brutal security force in the occupied territories as well as overage police forces at home, did whatever it took to terrorize an unruly enemy population into submission and to keep the Red Army at bay by all means available.

There was always concern that more violence, an even harsher regime of fighting, could only worsen the situation by strengthening resistance.[153] Starvation plans were modified; collaboration was encouraged. The German appeals, much to the chagrin of the more ideologically committed leadership (above all Hitler), met with considerable success even in 1943–4. Stalin's fears about the unreliability of Soviet peoples were quite warranted because collaboration proved essential for the German war effort (and is still understudied). The Army of the East alone came to use more than a half-million Soviet workers, and likely many more, and that does not account for all those who were dragooned into labor services for the armed forces behind the front and in the rear.[154] But none of this altered the fact that the war at the front and in the rear became not less, but more destructive. Indeed, it turned into a war of extermination in its own right. The ideologically preplanned subjection of the local populations, the use of selective terror to deter resistance was "radicalized" into a pervasive regime of massacre, starvation, and spoliation.

The Wehrmacht and the rear administration had every reason to be more prudent in their treatment of the local population – and this is what many frontline and rear formations set out to do, only to push themselves ever deeper into a quagmire of their own making.[155] There was never enough food for everyone. Because locals resisted labor recruitment and demand increased exponentially, German authorities turned ever more violent in their

---

[152] This is the dilemma that generated military opposition. Hürter, "Auf dem Weg zur Militäropposition: Treskow, Gersdorff, der Vernichtungskrieg und der Judenmord: Neue Dokumente über das Verhältnis der Heeresgruppe Mitte zur Einsatzgruppe B im Jahre 1041," 527–62.

[153] Ben Shepherd, "Hawks, Doves and Tote Zonen: A Wehrmacht Security Division in Central Russia, 1943," *Journal of Contemporary History* 37, no. 3 (2002): 349–69; Peter Lieb, "Täter aus Überzeugung? Oberst Carl von Andrian und die Judenmorde der 707: Infanteriedivision 1941/42," *Vierteljahrshefte für Zeitgeschichte* 50, no. 3 (2002): 523–57.

[154] Franz Wilhelm Seidler, *Die Kollaboration, 1939–1945* (Munich: Herbig, 1995); Hamburger Institut für Sozialforschung, ed., *Verbrechen der Wehrmacht: Dimensionen des Vernichtungskrieges 1941–1944, Ausstellungskatalog*, 398–409. S. I. Drobiazko, *Pod znamenami vrage: Antisovetskie formirovaniia v sostave germanskikh vooruzhennykh sil, 1941–1945* (Moscow: Exmo, 2005). It is usually argued that the Wehrmacht units did not have a "tail." The reality is that they had an invisible one, which was not counted because it consisted of "Slavic" auxiliaries.

[155] Bernhard Chiari, "Grenzen deutscher Herrschaft: Voraussetzungen und Folgen der Besatzung der Sowjetunion," in *Das Deutsche Reich und der Zweite Weltkrieg*, Vol. 9/2, *Ausbeutung, Deutungen, Ausgrenzungen*, ed. Militärgeschichtliches Forschungsamt (Munich: Deutsche Verlagsanstalt, 2005), 877–976.

efforts.[156] On top of all this were extra requisitions, surtaxes, and a host of restrictions that defined the situation on the ground: the wasteful neglect of the colonial fantasies of 1941 gave way to ever more unconstrained and out-right vicious forms of exploitation and spoliation that covered everything and everybody and made a mockery out of professions of prudence. By 1942–3, the comprehensiveness and severity of exploitation ran well ahead of all but the most hard-core ideological imagination – again not everywhere and all the time, but enough to taint German rule forever.[157]

Systematic and violent coercion became the pervasive feature of exploitation. If pillage, living off the land, was the political and economic end of violence, it merged increasingly with the sheer physical destruction of people and habitat in the war against partisans. Antipartisan warfare has received a great deal of attention, which tends to focus on the gradations of brutality.[158] As it turns out even the most unrelenting commanders in the antipartisan effort had second thoughts and units acted according to their own judgment of the situation more or less brutally.[159] But differential brutality only matters inasmuch as it occurs in a spectrum of violence, which overall shifted dramatically. We discover in the context of antipartisan warfare that there is a distinct "grammar" of extreme violence.

Again, we need to recapitulate the situation in 1941. Even then the danger of partisans was not entirely made up by the German conquerors.[160] Mostly undermanned German security forces, which were primed to ferret out racial enemies, faced huge numbers of armed men in an situation in which they were incapable of controlling the conquered territory. Himmler's famous notation of 18 December 1941, "Jewish question/exterminate as partisans," shows the racialized intent of partisan warfare.[161] Himmler and others like Heydrich, quite typical for the Berlin leadership, indeed thought that they could use the war as subterfuge for their final solution of the Jewish problem. But these ideas also exuded a sense of superiority and control that was even fantastic in 1941 and was slipping away in 1941–2 and was completely gone in 1943. As we

---

[156] Hamburger Institut für Sozialforschung, ed., *Verbrechen der Wehrmacht: Dimensionen des Vernichtungskrieges 1941–1944, Ausstellungskatalog,* 361–428.

[157] Chiari, *Alltag hinter der Front: Besatzung, Kollaboration und Widerstand in Weißrußland 1941–1944;* Berkhoff, *Harvest of Despair: Life and Death in Ukraine under Nazi Rule.*

[158] Shepherd, *War in the Wild East;* Timm C. Richter, "Die Wehrmacht und der Partisanenkrieg in den besetzten Gebieten der Sowjetunion," in *Erster Weltkrieg–Zweiter Weltkrieg: Krieg, Kriegserlebnis, Kriegserfahrung in Deutschland,* eds. Bruno Thoß and Hans-Erich Volkmann (Paderborn: Ferdinand Schöningh, 2002), 837–57.

[159] Lieb, "Täter aus Überzeugung? Oberst Carl von Andrian und die Judenmorde der 707. Infanteriedivision 1941/42"; Sheperd, "Hawks, Doves and Tote Zonen: A Wehrmacht Security Division in Central Russia, 1943."

[160] Hill, *The War behind the Eastern Front: The Soviet Partisan Movement in North–West Russia, 1941–1944;* Slepyan, *Stalin's Guerillas,* 5–59.

[161] Richter, "Die Wehrmacht und der Partisanenkrieg in den besetzten Gebieten der Sowjetunion," 845.

discovered, the "Jewish question," notwithstanding Himmler's comment to that end, was not resolved as a partisan issue.

In turn, the partisan question gained urgency in its own right – and it was resolved with an all-out war of terror against partisans and increasingly against the entire civilian population in partisan-controlled or endangered territories. By and large the commanders of the rear security forces were keenly aware of the dilemma they faced. They depended on the goodwill of the population, but goodwill, which was already tested by requisitioning, labor recruitment, and corvées, was undermined by brutal antipartisan tactics.[162] The more prudent commanders resolved the problem by prohibiting excess, disciplining arbitrariness and brutality. But they were moving – and driven by Führer directives in 1942 – to ever harsher measures all the same. Directive 46 of 28 October 1942 stated unequivocally: "In the entire eastern territory the war against the partisan is a fight for the complete extermination." Therefore it had to be fought with "utter brutality," which was made possible by granting complete immunity in the fight against partisans.[163]

In 1942–3 antipartisan warfare became the quintessence of what we call the "radicalization of war." Harshness defined as "complete extermination" is certainly one feature. But there is more. First, all Germans on site (and collaborators, although the use of local forces remained a divisive issue) irrespective of function and status were called upon to partake in partisan warfare. Second, partisan territory and its entire population were made into targets of German all-out attacks. That is, partisans were killed, the population deported, animals and foodstuffs were requisitioned, and villages, towns, as well as infrastructure were destroyed. The end result, particularly in the partisan-controlled areas of Belorussia, was so-called *Tote Zonen*, dead zones, which were stripped bare and made uninhabitable. The term for this, *Verwüstung* (desertification), is telling and entirely appropriate.[164] Under these circumstances pacification was impossible and was no longer even intended. This was extreme violence, in which the winner took all – all male and female labor, all foodstuffs, all animals, all shelter – and fought the enemy "without restraint (*ohne Einschränkung*) also against women and children with every means."[165]

In February 1943, Himmler suggested that all males suspected of partisan activities should be deported as forced labor; in summer 1943 Hitler ordered

[162] Hamburger Institut für Sozialforschung, ed., *Verbrechen der Wehrmacht: Dimensionen des Vernichtungskrieges 1941–1944, Ausstellungskatalog*, 461–505; Ruth Bettina Birn, "'Zaunkönig' an 'Uhrmacher': Große Partisanenaktionen 1942/43 am Beispiel des 'Unternehmens Winterzauber,'" *Militärgeschichtliche Zeitschrift* 60, no. 1 (2001): 99–118.

[163] Walther Hubatsch, *Hitlers Weisungen für die Kriegführung 1939–1945: Dokumente des Oberkommandos der Wehrmacht*, unabridged ed. (Munich: Deutscher Taschenbuch Verlag, 1965), 207–9.

[164] Hamburger Institut für Sozialforschung, ed., *Verbrechen der Wehrmacht: Dimensionen des Vernichtungskrieges 1941–1944, Ausstellungskatalog*, 386–95, 421–8.

[165] Quoted in Richter, "Die Wehrmacht und der Partisanenkrieg in den besetzten Gebieten der Sowjetunion," 854.

the full-scale evacuation of the "partisan-infected" territory of the northern Ukraine.[166] Such "evacuations" of entire territories had been practiced by the retreating Red Army in 1941 and they had become a German tactic in the first Soviet counterattack in winter 1941–2. Again, we have the typical warnings over a lack of discipline, arbitrary plunder and pilfering, and the "by now customary burn-offs."[167] But practice pointed in the opposite direction, the ever more comprehensive and encompassing use of scorched earth tactics that aimed at utter spoliation and desertification of the country left behind. The forced evacuation – in September 1943 of 900,000 in the area of Army Group Center – and destruction left behind a territory that was made uninhabitable, populated by the weak and unproductive, who were pushed toward the enemy and were lucky if they were not used as human shields. In 1943, radical partisan warfare and scorched earth retreat combined in a conduct of war that only knew survivors and vanquished.

The year 1943 is the culmination point of a war that was started as the ideological fantasy of colonial conquest and ended in the extreme violence of a deliberately chosen life-and-death struggle, a war by all means against an entire territory and its people. It is in this situation that the distinction between brutalization and radicalization of war collapses (much as it collapsed in the Holocaust). Brutality had become an aspect of the grammar of war. There was no escape and little room for decency. It was the German conquerors and their collaborators against the rest of the population and against the Soviet regime – and it was the German side that set out to eradicate sustainable life on their retreat. This war was won by the Soviet regime – and not simply in a metaphorical sense. When finally on 22 June 1944 (Operation Bagration), three years after the war began with the German conquest, Soviet forces smashed through Army Group Center in the greatest victory of Soviet forces, the ground was prepared by Soviet partisans who effectively destroyed the communications and transportation infrastructure, blinding the enemy, and thus liberated Soviet territory from the German yoke. There was still a long way to Berlin, but now the definition of the exception lay in Soviet hands. The question, therefore, was whether there would be survival for the defeated Germans – life which the Germans had denied to their enemy first in a bout of ideological overkill and subsequently in a pragmatic radicalization of war into a life-and-death-struggle, which the Nazi leadership firmly believed could only end in the complete destruction of one or the other and, hence, prepared for self-destruction.[168]

---

[166] Ibid., 856.

[167] Bernd Wegner, "Die Aporie des Krieges," in *Das Deutsche Reich und der Zweite Weltkrieg.* Vol. 8, *Die Ostfront 1943/44*, ed. Militärgeschichtliches Forschungsamt (Munich: Deutsche Verlagsanstalt, 2007), 211–76, here 259.

[168] Bessel, *Nazism and War*, 170–981; Michael Geyer, "Endkampf 1918 and 1945: German Nationalism, Annihilation, and Self-Destruction," in *No Man's Land of Violence: Extreme Wars in the 20th Century*, eds. Alf Lüdtke and Bernd Weisbrod (Göttingen: Wallstein, 2006), 35–68.

PASSIONS OF WAR

We noted above that the Soviet leadership immediately radicalized the war
into an all-out war of defense, that the propaganda apparatus as well as hard-
core cadres were ready for this kind of a war and enacted it. However, this
does not explain yet how the majority of the population was made to fight –
the regime's approach was one thing; compliance and cooperation of the majority of Soviet citizens in this project another one altogether. The cadres of totalitarian violence, after all, formed only the inner core of a destructive movement
that still had to draw in less radical layers of society – including many victims of
Stalinism. Propaganda, even good propaganda, does not simply work because
it is there. It needs to be appealing and those addressed by it need to react to its
message. Most did, in the end, respond to the call; most did fight, and fought
hard and brutally, breaking the Wehrmacht's back. Why? One explanation
focuses on political religion.[169] "Today it is fashionable," wrote the former
paratrooper Grigorii Naumovich Chukhrai in 2001, "to remember that when
we went to fight we yelled 'For the Motherland, for Stalin!' . . . I went through
the whole war and just cannot remember that cry. I remember curses [*mat*].
But the main point is not what we yelled when we attacked – many of us
really were Stalinists."[170] This son of a communist, a party member himself,
who fought in an elite unit took his own experience *pars pro toto* for Soviet
soldiers in general. At the same time, however, his recollections – full of deserters,[171] people who wound themselves to escape fighting,[172] and people who
try to get away from heroic frontline service by getting into a "Red Army song
and paratrooper dance ensemble"[173] – undermine these claims at universality.
He meets a heavily wounded soldier, son of a *kulak*, who spent much of his
life under false identity, hated the collective farms, and thought that Stalin
was a demon or, quite possibly, the antichrist himself ("instead of toes he has
grown hoofs").[174] In this episode clashed two cultures – the urban Bolsheviks
and the rural civilization they abhorred. It illustrates the huge diversity of the
Soviet fighting forces, who were "divided by everything from generation to
class, ethnicity, and even politics."[175] Young fought next to old, victims of

---

[169] Robert W. Thurston, "Cauldrons of Loyalty and Betrayal: Soviet Soldiers' Behavior, 1941 and
1945," in *The People's War: Responses to World War II in the Soviet Union*, eds. Robert
W. Thurston and Bernd Bonwetsch (Urbana and Chicago: University of Illinois Press, 2000),
235–57; and Weiner, "Saving Private Ivan;" more nuanced: id., "Something to Die For."

[170] Grigorii Chukhrai, *Moia voina* (Moscow: Algoritm, 2001), 281. For similar recollections by
other veterans see also Merridale, "Culture, Ideology and Combat," 317.

[171] Chukhrai, *Moia voina*, 170–2.

[172] For the "small minority" of *samostrel'tsy* see Chukhrai, *Moia voina*, 284.

[173] For the intriguing *ansambl' krasnoarmeiskoi pesni i pliaski vozdushno-desantskikh voisk*, see
Chukhrai, *Moia voina*, 228–9.

[174] Chukhrai, *Moia voina*, 194–6.

[175] Merridale, *Ivan's War*, 211; also: id., "Culture, Ideology and Combat," 307; Glantz, *Colossus
Reborn*, 620; and Mark von Hagen, "Soviet Soldiers and Officers on the Eve of the German
Invasion: Toward a Description of Social Psychology and Political Attitudes," in *The People's
War*, 186–210.

Stalinism next to its beneficiaries, women next to men, barely literate peasants next to literati, anti-Semites next to Jews, Kazakhs next to Russians. The list of differences could go on and include differentiation according to rank, front, and arms that typically stratify combat experience and type of motivation in any modern army. How might Soviet soldiers of such immense diversity have shared a single motivation? How could we ever think of them in the collective singular?[176]

First we need to take a step back from the assumption that "the Soviet soldier" fought in the first place. In a combat situation fighting is only one of many options, and not the most likely one, given the trauma of killing and the danger to life and limb this choice entails. Indeed, the other main choices – flight, submission – were real problems of the Soviet fighting forces.[177] At the beginning of the war, millions opted for submission. The tally of Soviet soldiers taken prisoner by the Germans was, indeed, staggering. "Never in modern European military history had an army in the field lost such a high proportion of its men with so little resistance."[178] Whether one interprets this phenomenon as motivated by the hopeless military situation or as a result of anti-Stalinism, or as a combination of the two – the fact itself is plain enough.[179] As the war went on, the likelihood of submission decreased. The majority of Soviets who became POWs did so during the catastrophic year of 1941. After the victories at Stalingrad and Kursk in 1943, only a small minority (4 percent of the total) surrendered. Nevertheless, we still speak of a mass phenomenon – 181,000 soldiers during the years 1944 and 1945.[180]

Those who argue for a thoroughly "Bolshevik Ivan" should find at least this number – over 400 per day in 1944 – hard to explain. That disgruntlement

---

[176] On the many lines of division among those who fought on the Soviet side see Seniavskaia, *Frontovoe pokolenie*, 76–77; 93–125; Glantz, *Colossus Reborn*, chapter 13, esp. 588; Mark Edele, "Soviet Veterans as an Entitlement Group, 1945–1955," *Slavic Review* 65, no. 1 (2006): 111–37, esp. 113–21; ibid., also larger bibliographical footnotes on literature on women soldiers (fn. 27, 29). The standard work on the latter is still Svetlana Aleksievich, *U voiny – ne zhenskoe litso* (Moscow: Sov. Pisatel', 1987; reprint 1988, 1998), translated as Svetlana Alexiyevich, *War's Unwomanly Face* (Moscow: Progress Publishers, 1988). On the recruiting base of Guards and mechanized formations, see John Erickson, "Red Army Battlefield Performance, 1941–1945: The System and the Soldier," in *Time to Kill: The Soldier's Experience of War in the West, 1939–1945*, eds. Paul Addison and Angus Calder (London: Pimlico, 1997), 234.

[177] Dave Grossman, *On Killing: The Psychological Cost of Learning to Kill in War and Society* (Boston: Little, Brown, 1995), 5–16.

[178] Martin Malia, *The Soviet Tragedy: A History of Socialism in Russia, 1917–1991* (New York: The Free Press, 1994), 284.

[179] See Thurston, "Cauldrons of Loyalty and Betrayal," 239 ("the argument that surrendering troops acted out of disloyalty is unacceptable"). For a more nuanced discussion see Shneer, *Plen*, 93–172.

[180] Calculated from Alexander Dallin, *German Rule in Russia: 1941–1945: A Study of Occupation Policies* (New York: St. Martin's Press, 1957), 427, fn. 2. There is a range of data circulating in the literature, but the differences are minor and do not change the assessment presented here. See, e.g., Streit, *Keine Kameraden*, 83, 244. The most recent account uses Dallin's data: Shneer, *Plen*, 96.

with the regime might have played a role is suggested by individual examples of soldiers who repeatedly refused to fight and who were also on record as disconcerted about the Soviet order. Consider the POW who explained that the "motherland was no longer mine from the first days of the October Revolution."[181] Or take the peasant from Vynnitsia region in the Ukraine who disliked the collective farm, grumbled about the hard service in the Red Army, the poor food, and the bad uniforms (he liked the German equivalents better). He also thought it would be best to let the political leaders fight it out among themselves and leave "the people" out of it – it made no difference to him whether Stalin or Hitler ruled the state. He surrendered to the enemy in September 1941 and became a POW, only to run away from camp, return home, and live until 1944 on occupied territory. In April 1944 he was drafted back into the Red Army, deserted in October of the same year, was caught and put into a penal unit, where he served until a wound took him out of action in January 1945.[182]

At the very least, the large numbers of prisoners imply a lack of combat incentive on a mass level, as Martin Malia has pointed out – "they could not have been taken prisoner in such numbers had they had any strong motivation to fight."[183] It might be misleading, however, to stress motivational and, hence, ideological factors when trying to explain existential choices on the battlefield. "Combat and soldiering," Merridale notes, "do not depend on a single emotional impulse."[184] There were many factors "pushing" Soviet soldiers to surrender in 1941 – including, for some, the lack of attraction of the Soviet system. All were affected by the hopeless battle situations, many mistrusted the propaganda of their own side about German brutality, and all were faced with the apparent military and technological superiority of the Germans. Most Soviet citizens had learned to arrange themselves somehow with the Soviet system – a system which allowed only few to "belong" in any uncomplicated way.[185] Why not assume that one would find an arrangement with another dictatorship as well? Such reasoning was well known to the regime and its propagandists – and they had a straightforward answer.[186] "I don't say it will be pleasant under the Nazis," states one potential collaborator in the 1943 movie *She Defends the Motherland*, "but *we're accustomed to that*.... Don't try to scare us.... Did you see them hang *everyone*? ... Oh, sure, maybe the Communists and the Jews.... Enough of this rotten Red paradise!" The movie's heroine shoots the traitor point blank: "While we live, we fight."[187]

---

[181] Quoted by Thurston, "Cauldrons of Loyalty and Betrayal," 242.

[182] Revision file on anti-Soviet agitation, GARF f. A-461, op. 1, d. 1820, l. 11.

[183] Malia, *The Soviet Tragedy*, 283–4.

[184] Merridale, "Culture, Ideology and Combat," 312.

[185] Sheila Fitzpatrick, *Stalin's Peasants*; id., *Everyday Stalinism*; Hellbeck, *Revolution on My Mind*.

[186] Brandenberger, *National Bolshevism*, 117.

[187] Quoted from Denise J. Youngblood, *Russian War Films: On the Cinema Front, 1914–2005* (Lawrence: University Press of Kansas, 2007), 63–4.

Surrender became less frequent already by late 1941 and even more so after the victories at Stalingrad and Kursk in 1943. One reason were the threats from the own side. Another was the recovery of the Red Army. But giving up also became a poor option because the German mistreatment of POWs soon became known to the troops through one of these peculiar processes of mass communication where rumor and the reports of escapees went hand in hand with official propaganda.[188] By "ill-treating and starving our prisoners to death," noted one commander in 1942, "the Germans are *helping us*."[189]

The Soviets added their own incentives. In 1941, the military press reported extensively on what Soviet soldiers could expect when becoming POWs, often based on the reports of those who had escaped from this hell.[190] More forcefully, commanders used "friendly fire" against "deserters" and "traitors" as a matter of course from the very start of the war.[191] Order No. 270 of 16 August 1941 further increased the pressure. Commanders and political workers who "gave themselves over to the enemy" were considered deserters, "whose families are liable to arrest as families of deserters, who have broken the [military] oath and betrayed their country." If recovered, these "traitors" were to be shot on the spot. All other soldiers were told to fight no matter what in encirclement and to demand the same from their commanders, if necessary by force of arms. The families of soldiers who "gave themselves over" were to be denied state aid and welfare payments.[192] Further legislation ruled that grown-up members of the families of those POWs who were sentenced to death should be deported for five years.[193]

Flight was another option used frequently. Soviet soldiers retreating through their home regions in the Don area took this opportunity to slip away and return to their villages or to major cities such as Khar'kov, Bogodukhov, or Belgorod.[194] Whenever a region was liberated by the Red Army, the NKVD got busy finding these people. In 1943, the agency temporarily arrested 582,515 soldiers, among them nearly 43,000 who had left the field of battle on their own, 158,585 who had gone AWOL, and 254,922 who did not hold proper

---

[188] Argyrios K. Pisiotis, "Images of Hate in the Art of War," in *Culture and Entertainment in Wartime Russia*, ed. Richard Stites (Bloomington and Indianapolis: Indiana University Press, 1995), 141–56; Mark Edele, "Paper Soldiers: The World of the Soldier Hero According to Soviet Wartime Posters," 89–108; Merridale, "Culture, Ideology and Combat," 319.

[189] Alexander Werth, *Russia at War, 1941–1945*, 2nd ed. (New York: Carroll & Graf, 2000), 422.

[190] Based on a systematic reading of the coverage in *Red Star* (*Krasnaia zvezda*) between June and the end of October 1941. This central newspaper, while not read by all soldiers, was often read to small groups by agitators, as Merridale points out in *Ivan's War*, 109.

[191] Glantz, *Colossus Reborn*, 580.

[192] "Prikaz Stavki Verkhovnogo Glavnogo Komandovaniia Krasnoi Armii No. 270 (16 August 1941)," *Voenno-istoricheskii zhurnal*, no. 9 (1988), 26–8.

[193] Ivashov and Emelin, "Nravstvennye i pravovye problemy plena v Otechestvennoi istorii," 47–8.

[194] Report of military correspondent A. Gutman to Agitprop department of Central Committee (undated, sometime in 1943), RGASPI f. 17, op. 125, d. 130, l. 33–6, here: 33.

documents. Another 23,418 were arrested as deserters.[195] During similar operations in the first three months of 1944, the NKVD arrested 8407 deserters,[196]
followed by 87823 in July and August.[197] The flood of desertion of the first
months of the war might have become a trickle of "a few hundred a month"
after Kursk, but they added up to sizable numbers nevertheless.[198]

Many of them had slipped away to German-held territory because their own
side had increased the cost for flight backward, behind the own lines, from the
first days of the war. In July 1941, the Main Administration of Political Propaganda of the Red Army directed commanders to "explain every day" to
their subordinates that "to abandon a position without order" was a "crime."
Officers should consider the use of "drastic measures" to enforce discipline –
a reiteration of the rights they had since 1940.[199] Two days later, the Special
Sections received the right to shoot deserters on the spot "if necessary."[200] Not
surprisingly, such signals led to physical and verbal abuse and "arbitary executions."[201] By October 1941, the NKVD alone had shot 10,201 deserters, 3,321
of them in front of their units.[202] At around the same time, Stalin pulled back,
blaming those instituting his directives for "the substitution of repression for
educational work."[203] It soon turned out, however, that "education" had little
impact on the tenacity of soldiers confronted with Wehrmacht attacks. A year
later, thus, the regime returned to violence as an encouragement. Disorderly
retreat without explicit order was now threatened by immediate execution
through the so-called blocking detachments, introduced by Stalin's Order No.
227 of 28 July 1942 ("Panic-mongers and cowards should be exterminated on
the spot!").[204] They were a resurrection of an institution from the Civil War;
that might explain why individual commanders had introduced them ad hoc

---

[195] Report to Stalin, 8 January 1944, Stalin's special files, GARF f. r-9541, op. 2, d. 64, l. 9–13,
here: 9–10.

[196] Report to Stalin, 19 April 1944, Stalin's special files, GARF f. r-9541, op. 2, d. 64, l. 289–90,
here: 289.

[197] Report to Stalin, Fall 1944, Stalin's special files, GARF f. r-9541, op. 2, d. 67, l. 381–2, here:
382.

[198] Cf. Merridale, "Culture, Ideology and Combat," 318.

[199] "Direktiva GUPP KA, no. 081," (15 July 1941), reprinted in *Glavnye politicheskie organy
vooruzhennykh sil SSSR*, 42–4, here: 43. See also the GKO resolution no. 169ss, 16 July 1941,
signed by Stalin, reprinted in *1941 god. Dokumenty*, vol. 2: 472–3.

[200] GKO resolution no. 187ss, 17 July 1941, signed by Stalin. Reprinted in *1941 god. Dokumenty*,
vol. 2, 473–4, here: 474.

[201] Zolotarev, ed., *Glavnye politicheskie organy vooruzhennykh sil SSSR*, 328 n. 28.

[202] Report to Beria, October 1941; reprinted in Khaustov et al, eds., *Lubianka: Stalin i NKVD-
NKGB-GUKP "Smersh,"* 317–18.

[203] Stalin's order No. 248, 4 October 1941. Reprinted in *Glavnye politicheskie organy vooruzhennykh sil SSSR*, 77.

[204] The order is reprinted in Stalin, *O Velikoi Otechestvennoi voine*, 51–4; quotation: 53. It is
described in detail in Glantz, *Colossus Reborn*, 571–2; and Erickson, "Red Army Battlefield
Performance," 244. On the blocking units see Merridale, *Ivan's War*, 55–6; Glantz, *Colossus
Reborn*, 570–82, discusses both blocking and penal units in detail. The blocking detachments
existed until October 1944 (Mawdsley, *Thunder*, 215).

even before this order – they were part of their military repertoire.[205] However, both the blocking units and the penal battalions introduced by the same order were also, and quite explicitly, modeled on a German invention, which Stalin found worth emulating because it made soldiers "fight better."[206]

The tactic of relentless counterattack also relied on violence against one's own. It was not unusual for young, inexperienced commanders overwhelmed by their responsibility to kick subordinates hiding in trenches savagely, trying to abuse them into action.[207] Others used the stronger argument of the handgun: "Right away, our company commander warned us that, if we lay down, he would shoot all of us, and he really did shoot some. After that, we never tried to lie down again."[208] Stalin and his deputy Lev Mekhlis, on their part, used the threat of violence to encourage the newly instituted commissars on 20 July 1941 charged with enforcing "with an iron fist...revolutionary order" against "panic-mongers, cowards, defeatists, deserters." "Remember that the war commissars and the commanders carry complete responsibility for instances of treason and betrayal in their unit."[209] A German summary of experience gained "in the East" reported on the results: "The attacking infantry leaves its positions in compact groups...shouting 'Hooray!' Officers and commissars follow, shooting at those who lag behind."[210] No wonder that the kill ratio between the opponents was so uneven – it took between two and four dead Soviets to kill one German.[211]

Combat motivation, however, went well beyond sheer coercion. Soviet soldiers fought for a variety of reasons paralleling the wide variety of people who made up the Red Army. These motivations often coexisted and reinforced each other, or soldiers shifted from the one to the other. Some of them are not specifically Soviet. The German army – and, following it later, the U.S. army as well – even made a tactical doctrine out of the knowledge that people kill more

---

[205] On the civil war origin, see Erickson, "Red Army Battlefield Performance," 242; A. A. Maslov, "How Were Soviet Blocking Detachments Employed?" *The Journal of Slavic Military Studies* 9, no. 2 (1996): 427–35, here: 427. On their use before Stalin's order see ibid., 428; Glantz, *Colossus Reborn,* 580–1; and Merridale, "Culture, Ideology and Combat," 318. The NKVD had used blocking detachments from the beginning of the war, too. See Khaustov et al, eds., *Lubianka: Stalin i NKVD-NKGB-GUKP "Smersh,"* 317.

[206] Stalin, O Velikoi Otechestvennoi voine, 53.

[207] Chukhrai, *Moia voina,* 50–1.

[208] Quoted in Glantz, *Colossus Reborn,* 585.

[209] "Direktiva Narkoma oborony SSSR i zam. Narkoma oborony – nachal'nika GLAVPU RKKA, no. 090," (20 July 1941), reprinted in *Glavnye politicheskie organy vooruzhennykh sil SSSR,* 48–51, here: 50.

[210] German report, 14 January 1942, reprinted in *Skrytaia pravda voiny,* 226–7.

[211] Compare "Personelle blutige Verluste des Feldheeres [im Osten] vom 22. Juni 1941 bis 20. März 1945," in *"Unternehmen Barbarossa:" Der deutsche Überfall auf die Sowjetunion 1941: Berichte, Analysen, Dokumente,* eds. Gerd R Ueberschär and Wolfram Wette (Paderborn: Ferdinand Schönigh, 1984), 402, with G. F. Krivosheev, *Soviet Casualties and Combat Losses in the Twentieth Century,* trans. Christine Barnard (London: Greenhill Books, 1997), 85; and Ellman and Maksudov, "Soviet Deaths in the Great Patriotic War: A Note."

readily if motivated by a concrete social unit – the famous "primary group."[212]
The Red Army was no exception and the affective bonds to comrades in battle
are a staple of memoirs, novels, films, and poetry written for and by *frontoviki*.
The Soviet replacement system – at least during the periods and the sections
of the army where rotation of forces was implemented – was favorable to the
development of such ties, which easily transformed into hate once the object
of affection was killed, maimed, or captured.[213]

Losses were horrendous. In 1941 much of the existing army was annihilated
on the frontiers – only 8 percent survived this ordeal. After mobilization and
horribly costly defense battles, the Red Army went on the offensive in the winter
of 1941–2, again producing heavy casualties, which were exacerbated by the
renewed defeats in the summer of 1942. A new buildup followed in 1943 which
created the army which would destroy – again with much blood – the German
Wehrmacht and fight its way to Berlin.[214] The focus on "irrecoverable losses"
(killed or missing in action, died of wounds or disease, POWs, noncombat
losses), moreover, obscures a much larger fluctuation of personnel in the armed
forces. While the years 1941 and 1942 account for nearly 57 percent of the
"irrecoverable" category, the vast majority of the "sick and wounded" (70
percent) fell into the years 1943, 1944, and 1945 – making for a rather equal
distribution of total losses during all of the full years of war (1942, 1943,
1944).[215] Soviet officers, in particular of rifle and penal units, report "that
their regiments routinely suffered about 50 percent casualties in each and every
penetration operation they participated in, regardless of the year of the war."[216]

The extraordinarily high casualty rates did not destroy emotional ties to
comrades, but – similarly to the German case – enhanced them. Under the conditions of life-and-death struggle, it did not take long to connect to a comrade
in arms, and his or her injury or death was traumatic and provoked anger and
grief. "Frontline life makes people close very quickly," as one soldier put it.
The constant destruction of people near and dear to the soldiers transformed

---

[212] On the German tradition, see Omer Bartov, *Hitler's Army: Soldiers, Nazis, and War in the
Third Reich* (New York and Oxford: Oxford University Press, 1992), 30–1; Thomas Kühne,
"Der Soldat," in *Der Mensch des 20. Jahrhunderts*, eds. Ute Frevert and Heinz-Gerhard
Haupt (Frankfurt am Main and New York: Campus, 1999), 344–83; Kühne, *Kameradschaft:
Die Soldaten des nationalsozialistischen Krieges und das 20. Jahrhundert*. See also Edward
A. Shils and Morris Janowitz, "Cohesion and Disintegration in the Wehrmacht in World
War II," *The Public Opinion Quarterly* 12, no. 2 (1948): 280–315; Omer Bartov, *The Eastern
Front 1941–45, German Troops and the Barbarization of Warfare*, 2nd ed. (London: Palgrave,
2001).

[213] Joshua A. Sanborn, "Brothers under Fire: The Development of a Front-Line Culture in the
Red Army 1941–1943" (M.A. thesis, The University of Chicago, 1993); and Seniavskaia,
Frontovoe pokolenie, 85–6. For a skeptical view about the importance of small group bonding
see Merridale, *Ivan's War*, 15–16, 78, 134. For movies, see Youngblood, *Russian War Films*.
On the replacement system see Erickson, "Red Army Battlefield Performance," 239.

[214] Erickson, "Red Army Battlefield Performance," 237; Seniavskaia, *Frontovoe pokolenie*, 77.

[215] Calculated from Krivosheev, *Soviet Casualties and Combat Losses*, 94.

[216] Glantz, *Colossus Reborn*, 621.

the primary group into a more extensive, "imagined" community of warriors–some of them still alive, the majority of them already dead, slaughtered by an inhuman enemy. Moments of intense bonding before battle – waiting for the morning, sharing food and drink, and preparing to fight – resembled quasi-religious experiences of collective effervescence among men and women, many of whom would soon be dead. But even if soldiers were killed, the memory of such hours lived on and gave the survivors a sense of belonging, purpose, and reason to fight, kill, and die. It was within this emotional conjuncture that the symbolic representation of the Homeland (*rodina*) unfolded.[217]

Rage was also a powerful incentive to kill – both on the field of battle and between engagements. Revenge for fallen comrades went hand in hand with vengeance for or on behalf of civilian loved ones. "You have asked me to bump off two Germans for you," wrote a soldier home. "Please be advised that your request has been fulfilled." Hate propaganda allowed such sentiments to shift from the concrete to the universal, from friends and loved ones to the country at large. "My soul is full of hatred against the fascist monsters, and I have pledged to take revenge for the atrocities they have committed against our people."[218] Such rage could lie dormant and break out suddenly when triggered by a confrontation with enemy atrocities. Vladimir Tendriakov relates a disturbing episode that illustrates how the benevolent feelings of soldiers toward a young German captive could suddenly shift to aggression and cruelty when his unit stumbled upon the remains of two of their scouts who had been covered with water and frozen to death. The same soldiers who had shared food and drink with the German the night before – in a scene reminiscent of the bonding between soldiers celebrated in much of wartime literature – now mete out the same punishment to this representative of the foreign "monsters."[219]

Under the influence of a constant barrage of hate propaganda – which distributed the news of German atrocities against civilians and linked it to the

---

[217] Rass, *Menschenmaterial: Deutsche Soldaten an Der Ostfront – Innenansichten einer Infanteriedivision 1939–1945*; Sanborn, "Brothers under Fire," 51–2; Seniavskaia, *Frontovoe pokolenie*, 85; Merridale, "Culture, Ideology and Combat," 322; id., *Ivan's War*, 134; Konstantin Simonov, "Dom v Viaz'me" (1943), www.simonov.co.uk/domvvyazme.htm, accessed 7 June 2007; for a translation which manages to keep some of the flavor of the original see www.simonov.co.uk/vyazma.htm. The poem is quoted and analyzed – from a slightly different perspective than the one chosen here – in Elena Shulman, "'That Night as We Prepared to Die': Frontline Journalists and Russian National Identity during WWII," paper presented at the *National Convention 2006 of the American Association for the Advancement of Slavic Studies* (Washington, DC: 2006).

[218] Sabine Rosemarie Arnold, "'Ich bin bisher noch lebendig und gesund': Briefe von den Fronten des sowjetischen 'Grossen Vaterländischen Krieges,'" in *Andere Helme – Andere Menschen? Heimaterfahrung und Frontalltag im Zweiten Weltkrieg, ein internationaler Vergleich*, eds. Detlef Vogel and Wolfram Wette (Essen: Klartext, 1995), 148–9.

[219] Vladimir Tendriakov, "Liudi ili neliudi," *Druzhba narodov*, no. 2 (1989): 114–44; Mark Edele, "Totalitarian War and Atrocity Process: Reconsidering Violence at the German-Soviet Front, 1941–1945," paper presented at the *Biannual Conference of the Australasian Association for European History (AAEH)* (Sydney: University of Sydney, 2007).

barbarous nature of a dehumanized enemy– such experiences of rage and grief for fallen comrades blended over into the impulse to defend the loved ones from the impending danger, which in turn gave way to a more generalized impulse to defend women and children, home and hearth.[220] These highly charged emotions were shared not only with a close circle of frontline friends, but also in organized meetings devoted to grieving atrocity and celebrating revenge.[221] This was not merely or entirely a "cultural" or "imaginary" affair, either, once soldiers could see with their own eyes what had happened on territory they liberated from German occupation. "However much they write in the papers about atrocities," wrote an officer to his wife, "the reality is much worse." Interactions with locals were crucial in motivating revenge. "They took a cow and a duck from me, took away my chickens, and cleaned out the trunks in my home. Damned robbers!" complained a sixty-six-year-old woman to the soldiers who had liberated her town and added, "Kill them, boys!"[222]

The result of this multifaceted process of learning about and from the enemy was that Soviet soldiers quickly realized "that we weren't dealing with human beings but with foul beasts, drunk with blood."[223] A former information officer remembers this intermingling of propaganda and reality during his own "learning curve." At first, he naively expected the German working class to rise up against fascism in order to "defend the first Worker- and Peasant-State." The small number of German deserters and POWs during this early phase came as a huge disappointment, followed by increasing rage in response to reports of German conduct in the occupied territories. Once the Red Army was on the offensive, this foundation of anger was massively reinforced as the real scale of barbarism and destruction became apparent. This officer remembered the deep impact of letters by *Ostarbeiter,* who asked for revenge.[224]

Other letters were read as well. Already in 1941, the relentless counterattacks of the Red Army sometimes led to temporary and small-scale victories,

---

[220] Argyrios K. Pisiotis, "Images of Hate in the Art of War," in *Culture and Entertainment in Wartime Russia,* ed. Richard Stites (Bloomington and Indianapolis: Indiana University Press, 1995), 141–56; Lisa A. Kirschenbaum, "'Our City, Our Hearths, Our Families': Local Loyalties and Private Life in Soviet World War II Propaganda," *Slavic Review* 59, no. 4 (2000): 825–47. On evidence for the defense of the own family as a primary motivating factor see Merridale, "Culture, Ideology and Combat," 312.

[221] "Direktiva GlavPU RKKA, no. 16," (30 March 1943), reprinted in *Glavnye politicheskie organy vooruzhennykh sil SSSR,* 211–12.

[222] Seniavskaia, *Frontovoe pokolenie,* 79, 86–7; Merridale, "Culture, Ideology and Combat," 319; I. Dzhenalaev, *Pod Gvardeiskim Znamenem* (Alma-Ata: Kazakhstan, 1970), 51, as quoted by Sanborn, "Brothers under Fire," 59.

[223] Mikhail Sholokhov, "Hate," in *We Carry On* (Moscow: Foreign Languages Publishing House, 1942), 24, as quoted in Sanborn, "Brothers under Fire," 16.

[224] Michail Semirjaga, "Die Rote Armee in Deutschland im Jahre 1945," in *Erobern und Vernichten: Der Krieg gegen die Sowjetunion 1941–1945,* eds. Peter Jahn and Reinhard Rürup (Berlin: Aragon, 1991), 202–4.

which yielded not only enemy corpses, but also their letters and diaries.[225] The propaganda apparatus selected some exemplars which displayed despair or reports about hunger and cold (showing the enemy as weak), or those with descriptions of war crimes and clear expressions of an arrogant, callous, and racist Nazi worldview.[226] This work continued throughout the conflict and was recognized as a major tool to "stir up the hatred of the troops and the population...towards the enemy."[227] It became an important means to fuse the diverse human beings who made up the Red Army into a violent collectivity. Wartime propaganda skillfully linked individual examples of victimized women (with all of their connotations in a patriarchal society) with more generalized images of "Mother Russia" (or, more literally, "Mother Homeland" – *Rodina mat'*) – symbols which resonated with nationalism as well as with religious iconography (the Holy Virgin, like Mother Russia, was traditionally dressed in red).[228] The similarities of this symbolic strategy to German wartime propaganda are striking – both tried to mobilize soldiers to fight with appeals to higher values and beliefs, civilization, and the defense of women and children.[229] Similar reasons might have been at work – the knowledge that the ideological commitment of rank-and-file soldiers to (National) Socialism was uneven and often sketchy. Stalin admitted as much to a Western diplomat: "The population won't fight for us Communists, but they will fight for Mother Russia."[230] Despite the massive recruitment effort at the front, the Party never drew the majority of soldiers into its ranks. Only about one-quarter of the personnel were "Communist" – that is, either a Party member or a candidate in 1944 – a share which might have risen to around 30 percent by war's end. The more specialized the branch of arms and the higher the rank, the higher the incidence of membership. As many as 80 percent of officers were Communists or Komsomol members; artillery, tank troops, engineers, and air force had up to 40 percent Communists in their ranks – with submariners topping the list with 56 percent. By contrast, the vast majority of the footsoldiers – 90 percent as of 1944 – were not in the Party.[231]

---

225 On the early interest of the propaganda apparatus in German personal documents see "Direktiva GUPP KA, no. 056" (24 June 1941) and no. 077 (14 July 1941), reprinted in *Glavnye politicheskie organy vooruzhennykh sil SSSR*, 26, 40.

226 For example: "Dokumenty o krovavozhadnosti fashistskikh merzavtsev," *Krasnaia zvezda*, 29 October 1941, 3.

227 "Direktiva GlavPU RKKA, no. 107" (12 July 1942), reprinted in *Glavnye politicheskie organy vooruzhennykh sil SSSR*, 151. On hate propaganda and its organization see also Poliakov, "Istoki narodnogo podviga," 15–18.

228 Edele, "Paper Soldiers," 89–108.

229 Streit, *Keine Kameraden*, 86–7.

230 Malia, *The Soviet Tragedy*, 288. See also Brandenberger, *National Bolshevism*.

231 T. H. Rigby, *Communist Party Membership in the USSR 1917–1967* (Princeton, NJ: Princeton University Press, 1968), 253–6; M. M. Minasian, ed., *Great Patriotic War of the Soviet Union 1941–1945: A General Outline*, trans. David Skvirsky and Vic Schneierson (Moscow: Progress, 1974), 464–5; Erickson, *Stalin's War with German*, vol. 2. *The Road to Berlin*, 401; G. G. Morekhina, *Partiinoe stroitel'stvo v period Velikoi Otechestvennoi voiny Sovetskogo*

Given the substitution of fighting capacity for "political maturity" in admissions during the war, the ideological commitment of many of these "young communists" was in doubt.[232] Even for self-professed ideological warriors in elite units Stalinism meant many things, most of them not connected to the Supreme Commander himself:

> The crucial point is that our multi-national motherland was dear to all of us, as were honor and dignity, ours and that of our parents, our girls, our friends, who did not wish to be slaves of the Germans. We knew how many sacrifices industrialization had cost our parents, and it hurt us when all of this was destroyed.[233]

But clear ideological commitment was secondary. After the initial confusion of 1941, fear and hate, anger and revenge, entangled as they were with a confused but potent mix of leader cult, socialism, nationalism, religion, and love for those near and dear, drew larger and larger sectors of Soviet society into the killing process. The cadres of totalitarian violence who had been ready for this war all along were no longer alone. During "deep war" (Ilya Ehrenburg), when – after the battle of Stalingrad – peace "had been put out of mind . . . and was . . . unimaginable," these emotions became widely shared.[234] Once Soviet forces entered enemy territory they became overwhelming. Attempts by the military leadership to channel the aggression away from civilians and onto the battlefield (largely in order to maintain discipline and operational order) were bound to fail. "To tell the truth," as one staff officer wrote, "many of our soldiers understand only with difficulty such a line, . . . especially those whose families had suffered from the Nazis during occupation." The determined resistance of the Wehrmacht only made things worse. Meetings with titles like "How I will take revenge on the German invaders" or "An eye for an eye, a tooth for a tooth" did their part to psyche up the troops further. In the resulting rampage, the resistance of a few could not stop the cruelty of the many.[235] And while Stalin played down and justified Soviet cruelty, it was clear enough to more far-sighted Soviet observers that these passions of war could only undermine the politics of victory.[236]

Soiuza 1941–1945 (Moscow: Izd-vo polit. lit-ry, 1986), 372–3; Katrin Boeckh, *Stalinismus in der Ukraine: Die Rekonstruktion des sowjetischen Systems nach dem Zweiten Weltkrieg* (Wiesbaden: Harrassowitz Verlag, 2007), 130, 179.

[232] "Direktiva GLavPU RKKK, no. 010," (7 September 1943), reprinted in *Glavnye politicheskie organy Vooruzhennykh sil SSSR*, 233–6, here: 234.

[233] Chukhrai, *Moia voina*, 281–2.

[234] Ilya Ehrenburg, *The War: 1941–1945* (Cleveland: World Publishing, 1964), 107, as quoted in Sanborn, "Brothers under Fire," 5.

[235] Seniavskaia, *Frontovoe pokolenie*, 197 (quotations) and 196–215; Zubov, "Pobeda, kotoruiu my poteriali," 388; Naimark, *The Russians in Germany*, 69–140; Manfred Zeidler, *Kriegsende im Osten: Die rote Armee und die Besetzung Deutschlands östlich von Oder und Neisse 1944/45* (Munich: Oldenbourg, 1996), 135–54; Antony Beevor, *The Fall of Berlin 1945*; Merridale, *Ivan's War*, 299–335; Mawdsley, *Thunder*, 215–17. On the futility of individual resistance see Kopelev, *No Jail for Thought*, 15–58.

[236] Naimark, *The Russians in Germany: A History of the Soviet Zone of Occupation, 1945–1949*.

STATES OF EXCEPTION

> One has to understand the soldier. The Red Army is not ideal. The important thing is that it fights Germans – and it is fighting them well, while the rest doesn't matter.[237]

The rest did matter, notwithstanding Stalin, because what Stalin leaves out tells us what kind of war the Wehrmacht and the Red Army were fighting. Hatred and revenge, a sense of invincibility and superiority, the dehumanization of the enemy – these emotions are common in war. But it is the exception that these passions of war take over – not a battle, but an entire war; not units of an army or even an army, but entire nations – and become the very reason for war. Explaining this exception became the main issue, and the main argument was that in both armies and in both regimes the exception was not some excess, but a state or a condition.

Throughout the essay, we were struggling with this very basic observation. We were grappling with the best way of describing and making sense of the phenomenon, because it seemed to us a more productive way to approach the conduct of war than the thick description of the "ideology" or, alternatively, the practice of war that prevails in historiography. In this context, we made a special effort to explore the different social roles and places of the passions of war. No doubt, more detail in describing these emotions and their respective vocabularies would have been useful. But it seemed to us more important to demonstrate that the passions of war made up very different military societies. Again a rather simple observation seems apt. The striking thing about the Red Army was the extraordinary energy of mobilizing ever new soldiers into ever new armies (and the propagandistic effort invested in generating this mobilization) – and the fervent, overbearing, death-defying appeals and the sheer relentlessness and recklessness and, not to forget, the terror that went into this effort. There was no lack of propaganda, no lack of indoctrination, no lack of terror on the German side. All this is well documented. But if the *Ostarmee* was driven by passions, it was the passion of "sticking together through thick and thin" as the proverb goes in victory and defeat. Also, their passion remained highly disciplined, "cold" if you wish, notwithstanding recurrent panics and acts of mindless hot-headed and sadistic cruelty. This discipline was one of the main reasons that German soldiers and the security apparatus were so extraordinarily lethal, and that they had a much greater chance of survival than their Soviet counterparts, and that, even in retreat and even in defeat (until they faced, or rather could not bear facing, their women at home), they thought they had an edge, were superior. What stands out is the sense of a "community of fate" that formed in victory in the face of a strange land and a society the soldiers had learned, and propaganda had taught them, to suspect, if not hate, and coalesced in retreat and defeat. The compact nature of the

---

[237] Milovan Djilas, *Conversations with Stalin*, trans. Michael B. Petrovich (New York: Harcourt, Brace & World, 1962), 110–11.

German military community and its self-centered emotional makeup stands in stunning contrast to the quicksand nature of Soviet mobilization and the ideological overdrive of its propagandists.

Both regimes had violent prehistories; both saw extralegal brutality as the normal state of affairs in a world of class war or the survival of the racially fittest, respectively; both were shaped by and shaped themselves in the projection of deadly enmities; both dictatorships, too, could not count on the cooperation of all of their subjects, who were neither completely Nazified nor thoroughly Bolshevized. War was the "space of experience" that radicalized soldiers. The unfettering of violence, however, was the prerequisite of this process and it was intimately tied to the understanding of war as a civil or, if you wish, societal war.[238] We see in this war what happens when legal and moral constraints are removed and, indeed, when unrestraint becomes the order of the day. Unrestraint liberates brutality, and in turn the rumor of cruelty, even if it is random rather than systematic, spreads like wildfire, setting in motion a spiral of violence that, once unleashed, is only stopped in utter defeat. Unrestraint, we discover, is a learning process – both in the sense that it is responsive to purported or real (but always mediated and rumored) actions of the enemy and that ways and means of unrestrained conduct themselves are worked up, picked up, and taught. Cruelty can be learned and, sadly, it can be improved on. And, yet again, the ways of mediation and the learning processes differ in the two regimes.

This way of approaching "barbarization" seems to us so productive because the process of mediation, the moments of innovation, and the ways of consolidating unrestraint into conduct differed between the Wehrmacht and the Red Army, possibly even from one army or front to another, and certainly between the military and security forces. It is common to all that unrestraint breaks the mold of experience and tradition – even in "traditionally" violent societies or political movements. What we see in the Nazi-Soviet war is a liberation of violence and, thus, a savage dynamic of cruelty – that even soldiers, observing themselves, noted with a great deal of astonishment.[239] But then we must account for the differences as well. The question is how to get at it. Is it good or bad intentions, deterioration of conditions, habitualization of hatred? The question of difference turns us back to the issue of the radicalization of war one last time.

The one element that channels this dynamic is the horizon of expectations – and here we disagree with all those who think that dictatorships or, as it were, totalitarianisms are all the same because they all are extremely violent. We

---

[238] Reinhart Koselleck, "'Erfahrungsraum' und 'Erwartungshorizont' – Zwei historische Begriffe," in *Vergangene Zukunft: Zur Semantik geschichtlicher Zeiten*, ed. Reinhart Koselleck (Frankfurt am Main: Suhrkamp, 1987), 349–75.

[239] For two particularly impressive memoirs in this respect see Willy Peter Reese, *Mir selber seltsam fremd: Die Unmenschlichkeit des Krieges: Russsland 1941–44*, 1st ed. (Berlin: List, 2004); and Paul Feyerabend: *Killing Time: The Autobiography of Paul Feyerabend* (Chicago and London: University of Chicago Press, 1995).

also part ways with those historians who think of genocide as a matter or military or war culture. In a state of exception the question is "who decides" – and what this decision might entail. In war this question amounts to asking what kind of peace the combatants thought feasible. The long and the short of it is that National Socialism never contemplated peace with and for its enemies, certainly not for Bolsheviks or Jews, but neither for Russians or Poles. The National Socialist regime pursued their subjection or extermination, quite literally radicalizing, returning to the roots, of war as life-and-death struggle. The alternative of extermination or self-destruction was there all along as a fatal worldpicture, but it became the key to the German war plan. This is why we think of the Holocaust as an integral part of the war the Third Reich fought and why we think it must not be artificially separated from the eradication of the social institutions of Stalinism and the spoliation of the Soviet Union or, for that matter, of destruction of the social fabric of Polish society. Holocaust and destructive war were not identical, but they fall into the same spectrum of radical violence. The Soviet Union also did not make peace with fascists before and after the war, although it was caught in odd compromises. But it was surely ready to make peace with Germany and the Germans. What Stalin and so many communists could not figure out – and this was the animus of much of their war making and surely the conundrum of their peacemaking – is why the Germans of all peoples were so resistant to (their) revolution. After all, it had been their idea in the first place.

Mutual Perceptions and Projections

*Stalin's Russia in Nazi Germany – Nazi Germany
in the Soviet Union*

Katerina Clark and Karl Schlögel

ENCOUNTER IN PARIS 1937

Without doubt, the centers of attention for visitors to the 1937 World's Fair in Paris were the German and Soviet pavilions, and to a lesser extent the Italian pavilion. They were perceived as they were projected: as well-designed symbolic constructions – true representations of their "systems."[1] Both represented different, even opposing and competing worldviews (*Weltanschauungen*), political orders, and systems. Yet, at the same time, the constructions were seen not only as rivals, but also as twins, deeply related to each other by virtue of their monumentalist and power-centered aesthetics. One Italian visitor even used the term "totalitarian." An observer from *Art Digest* wrote in his report from Paris:

> The finest pavilions are those of Japan and the smaller countries, those which aren't striving for prestige. In contrast, the German building with its frighteningly vast tower can only be seen as an expression of fascist brutality. Russia is represented by another construction in the same spirit and the Italian pavilion also produces a surprisingly similar effect, this time achieved by more contemporary means.[2]

It seemed that even the topographical location of the exhibition halls evoked a comparative view. Every visitor entering the World's Fair in Paris had to pass

---

[1] The exhibition is analyzed in detail in Igor Golomstok, *Totalitarian Art in the Soviet Union, the Third Reich, Fascist Italy and the People's Republic of China* (New York: HarperCollins, 1990), 132–8; Jürgen Harten, Hans-Werner Schmidt, and Marie Luise Syring, eds., *"Die Axt hat geblüht–": Europäische Konflikte der 30er Jahre in Erinnerung an die frühe Avantgarde* (Düsseldorf: Städtische Kunsthalle Düsseldorf, Düsseldorf 1987), especially Dieter Bartetzko, "Tödliches Lächeln: Der deutsche Ausstellungspavillon von Albert Speer," 336–43, and Maria Christina Zopff, "Ein Rundgang im sowjetischen Pavillon der Weltausstellung 1937 in Paris: Architektur, Bauplastik, Wandmalerei in ihrer Aussage und Bedeutung," 426–9; Suzanne Pagé et al., eds., *Années 30 en Europe: Le temps menacant 1929–1939* (Paris: Musée d'Art de la Ville de Paris, Flammarion, 1997).
[2] Quoted in Igor Golomstok, 135.

the buildings, which stood directly opposite each other along the avenue leading from the Eiffel Tower to the Champs de Mars. Both dominated their environment. The German pavilion was designed by Albert Speer, Hitler's master
planner and architect, responsible for the reconstruction of Berlin as Germania,
the Third Reich's capital. Boris Iofan, who had won the competition for the
470-meter-high Palace of the Soviets in the center of Moscow, designed the
Moscow pavilion. Both were educated in classic academic institutions of pre-
1917 Russia und pre-1933 Germany. Neither liked his modernist rivals of the
1920s. Speer's pavilion represented a direct response to Mies van der Rohe's
avant-gardist pavilion for the World's Fair in Barcelona in 1929. Iofan's pavilion ignored all the aesthetic principles of the functionalist and constructivist
schools in the Soviet Union. Both architects received gold medals for their Paris
pavilions. But the parallels between the symmetrically located constructions
went even further: at the gates of the German pavilion stood the monumentalist sculptures *Friendship* and *Family* by Josef Thorak, whereas on the top of the
Soviet pavilion stood a monumental sculpture depicting two figures, *Worker
and Collective Farm Woman*, by Vera Mukhina. Each nation's respective symbol of power was clearly visible – the imperial eagle with swastika on the
front of the German building, hammer and sickle on top of the Soviet pavilion.
The interiors of both exhibition halls combined elements of modernity and
neoclassicist pomp. The organizers of the exhibition wanted to demonstrate
the achievements of their modern and civilized countries. The Soviet pavilion,
for example, included an exhibit highlighting the Soviet constitution of 1936, a
five-meter-high plaster model of the Palace of Soviets, and walls decorated with
scenes from "a better and joyful Soviet life" (the painters were Deineka, Pakho-
mov and Samokhvalov). But attentive visitors and observers noted differences
and antagonisms, as well. The German pavilion was sometimes described as
"static," whereas the Soviet one was perceived as "dynamic." The symbolism
of the German sculptures was considered "traditional," whereas the Soviet
sculpture group was characterized as an "emancipation of class and gender."
From the memoirs of Albert Speer, we know that a "silent dialogue" existed
between the German and Soviet pavilions:

> While looking over the site in Paris, I by chance stumbled into a room containing
> the secret sketch of the Soviet pavilion. A sculpted pair of figures thirty-three feet
> tall, on a high platform, was striding triumphantly towards the German pavilion.
> I therefore designed a cubic mass, also elevated on stout pillars, which seemed to
> be checking this onslaught, while from the cornice of my tower an eagle with a
> swastika in its claws looked down on the Russian sculptures. I received a gold
> medal for the building; so did my Soviet colleague.[3]

The symbolism inherent in this encounter is perfectly clear, but the symbolic
representations of (and confrontation between) National Socialist Germany

---

[3] Albert Speer, *Inside the Third Reich: Memoirs*, trans. Richard Winston and Clara Winston
(New York: Macmillan, 1970), 130.

and the Soviet Union at the 1937 World's Fair hinted at a much more complex, multilayered reality. The year 1937 was the time of the "Great Terror" in Russia, of the great exhibition of "Degenerate Art" in Munich, and of the Spanish Civil War. It was also one year prior to the Munich conference and the dismemberment of Czechoslovakia. In retrospect, the similarities and differences between these two representative constructions appear as a prologue to the problems of mutual relations and mutual perceptions that are the subject of the following analysis.

When we started to write our joint chapter on German perceptions of Stalin's Russia and Russian perceptions of Hitler's Germany, it seemed quite easy to define our subject. The questions we asked were, How did Germany and Russia perceive each other during the Hitler and Stalin regimes? What were the main features of these images? What was the historical and cultural background of these images? Who generated and articulated these images? What impact did they have on German-Russian relations in the 1930s and 1940s?

However, as we submerged ourselves in the project, as a result of the independent course of our investigations we approached these questions from widely different angles. Schlögel focused upon the multiplicity of images and perceptions of the Soviet Union that coexisted within German society, their origins, and their evolution over the course of the Nazi regime. Clark, in turn, contrasted the text-based cultural forms privileged in the Soviet Union with the visual and oral cultural forms favored in Nazi Germany, highlighting the role of anti-Nazi German intellectuals and cosmopolitan Soviet intellectuals in the construction of Soviet images of Nazi Germany. In the end, rather than a comparative analysis of the representations of Nazi Germany in the Soviet Union and of the Soviet Union in Nazi Germany, the chapter offers two unique contributions, two different approaches to understanding German and Soviet history – and particularly that of representation – beyond the model of totalitarianism.

Walter Laqueur remarked forty years ago in his seminal book *Russia and Germany* (1965) that the mutual perceptions of Nazi Germany and Stalin's Russia have been a series of misunderstandings. This insight is still true today.[4] But it has become clear that "the titanic clash" between Germany and the Soviet Union, then the greatest military action in world history, would have been impossible without the mobilization and instrumentalization of an imagined "other" that had to be defeated and destroyed. In clashes of this kind and dimension, it is not only military forces that are engaged, but entire economies and societies – their industrial, organizational, and logistical potential and, of course, their passions, ideas, images, and visions. The central question today is probably not whether "ideas move the masses" but, rather, how images and visions are related to certain interests, and how politics is represented in the rhetoric and iconography of a given system.

---

[4] Walter Laqueur, *Deutschland und Russland* (Frankfurt am Main and Berlin: Propyläen Verlag, 1965), 10.

In the constructivist/deconstructivist discourse of the last decade, we have lost all naïveté in dealing with ideas and programs. We can no longer take them for granted; in each and every case, we have to analyze whether they are the reflection of a given reality or, rather, a tool for creating social reality. In this particular case, does Nazi propaganda against the Soviet Union and its counterpart, Soviet propaganda against Nazi Germany, at all reflect reality – that is, is there a "grain of truth" in these purely ideological constructs, or are they entirely a priori tools for "marking" and "making" the adversary, the enemy, the target? Obviously, images not only reflect given realities but also project desires and ambitions. To that extent, these images are much more indicative of the interests and ambitions of the "projector" *behind* them than of any supposed reality reflected *in* them.[5]

Recognizing the instrumental relationship between representation and reality, both of us emphasize, albeit in different ways, the diversity and complexity of representation: how it is produced and disseminated, its historical origins and ongoing evolution, its diverse authorship, its varied distribution, and the relationship between core and periphery, bureaucrat and citizen. Thus, while this essay does not provide a mirror-image comparison of representation in Nazi Germany and the Soviet Union, by shifting the matrix of analysis from traditional Cold War binaries to one that situates twentieth-century German and Russian history within the context of a broader crisis of European civilization, it illuminates the potential of these new directions in German and Soviet history.

THE COMPARATIVE APPROACH

From the outset of our research, it became clear to us that there was no *one* image of Stalin's Russia or Nazi Germany. In any historical period, there is always a process of evolution and transformation of ideas and images; images too have a history of rise and fall. Even in a controlled and censored public sphere, as that of Nazi Germany, many different, even opposing, views, perspectives, and images coexist.

When we reflect on the potential productivity of a comparative approach in coming to terms with Nazi Germany and Stalinist Russia, it is obvious that a study on mutual perceptions is complementary as well as comparative.[6] Certainly, there is no need to legitimate comparison as a method of analysis. We compare implicitly and *expressis verbis*. Nevertheless, discussions about comparative methods should focus more on the *historic* arguments that determine

---

[5] On the limits of constructivist approaches, cf. Richard J. Evans, *Fakten und Fiktionen: Über die Grundlagen historischer Erkenntnis* (Frankfurt/Main: Campus, 1998).

[6] Cf. the contributions in Ian Kershaw and Moshe Lewin, eds., *Stalinism and Nazism: Dictatorships in Comparison* (Cambridge: Cambridge University Press, 1997), especially "Introduction: The Regimes and Their Dictators: Perspectives of Comparison," 1–25. For an early comparative study in the form of parallel biographies, see Alan Bullock, *Hitler and Stalin: Parallel Lives* (London: HarperCollins, 1991).

why we decide to stress one subject and to ignore another. We compare
Germany and Russia in this particular period because Nazi Germany and Stalinist Russia have, from a certain point of view, striking similarities. Both were
contrary to what we call an "open society," a "liberal system," or "democratic
society" in terms of adequate institutions of freedom and representation. From
this point of view, there was a clash of political cultures in twentieth-century
Europe, a dividing line between open and closed societies, the history of which
began in 1917 and came to an end in 1989. Historiography has reflected this
opposition from the very beginning, although in different stages: from Bolshevism versus anti-Bolshevism to fascism versus the antifascist coalition to the
Cold War opposition between East and West.[7]

We also compare Germany and Russia because some nations, some peoples, and some segments of society experienced both regimes simultaneously or
successively. The nations and states "in between" experienced occupation and
great suffering – including occupation regimes, terror, expulsion, deportation,
forced migration, sometimes with genocide-like implications. This especially
typifies the experience of the nations "in between" – that is, eastern Central
Europe, Central Europe, and the western part of the USSR. Historiography on
twentieth-century Russia and Germany largely reflects this dual experience of
the imposition of power, violence, and "revolution from abroad."[8] We compare Germany and Russia because the societies are strikingly similar in the
amount of violence they experienced and unleashed. Not only are the numbers
of atrocities important, but also their specific form, their unprecedented ruthlessness, and the emancipation of such violence from the rules of "traditional"
war.[9] We compare Germany and Russia because both societies in that period
shared with other European societies the discourses of modernity and modernization, whether promodernist or antimodernist. The German and Soviet

---

[7] Of the huge literature on totalitarianism, one can mention here only Hannah Arendt, *Elemente
und Ursprünge totaler Herrschaft* (Munich and Zürich: Piper Verlag, 1986). For analysis of discourse see Abbott Gleason, *Totalitarianism: The Inner History of the Cold War* (New York and
Oxford: Oxford University Press, 1995); Alfons Söllner, Ralf Walkenhaus, and Karin Wieland,
eds., *Totalitarismus: Eine Ideengeschichte des 20. Jahrhunderts* (Berlin: Akademie Verlag, 1997).
See also the anthology of Bruno Seidel and Siegfried Jenkner, eds., *Wege der Totalitarismusforschung* (Darmstadt: Wissenschaftliche Buchgesellschaft, 1968). Opening the field beyond an
approach focused on total political rule, see Sheila Fitzpatrick, ed., *Stalinism: New Directions*
(London & New York: Routledge, 2000) esp., 1–14.

[8] Cf. Jan T. Gross's study on Soviet occupied eastern Poland, *Revolution from Abroad: The Soviet
Conquest of Poland's Western Ukraine and Western Belorussia* (Princeton, NJ: Princeton University Press, 1988). See also Pavel Polian, *Ne po svoei vole . . . : Istoriia i geografiia prinuditel'nykh
migratsii v SSSR* (Moscow: OGI-Memorial, 2001).

[9] There are studies on the specific form and function of violence and atrocities in Norman M.
Naimark, *Fires of Hatred: Ethnic Cleansing in Twentieth-Century Europe* (Cambridge, MA:
Harvard University Press, 2001); Nikolai Bougai, *The Deportation of Peoples in the Soviet
Union* (New York: Nova Science, 1996); Dittmar Dahlmann and Gerhard Hirschfeld, eds.,
*Lager, Zwangsarbeit, Vertreibung und Deportation: Dimensionen der Massenverbrechen in der
Sowjetunion und in Deutschland 1933 bis 1945* (Essen: Klartext, 1999).

discourses are part of a genuinely European intellectual landscape – from the New Man and *Lebensreform* to redesigning nature and nations.[10]

Yet, despite the indisputably positive results of comparative approaches, there remain some doubts about what comparisons may or may not achieve. The following offers some arguments for an, as it were, angular view of both "systems." The comparative perspective on Russia and Germany has traditionally been determined by historical and political constellations that allow some insights but simultaneously distract from more pertinent questions and approaches. This view on Germany and Russia is a view from outside, from a normative basis alien to what happened there. The parameters are the *universalia* of modern liberal society, the categories developed in one region of the world pretending to give a matrix for analysis and interpretation of cultures and traditions all over the world. This is an illusion.

We need to move two or three steps back to a different matrix of analysis. The matrix of open versus closed society does not allow for more basic questions such as empire versus nation-state; preindustrial versus industrial; preurban versus urbanized; semicolonial versus imperial; introverted and self-destructive violence versus extroverted and aggressive violence; weak and "failing" powers versus superstates; Russia on the move versus settled Germany; unmastered Russian space versus the well-ordered Third Reich police state; "Faust's metropolis" versus the "Peasant metropolis"; social revolution and upward mobility versus seizure of power by the "movement"; the *longue durée* of the Soviet Revolution versus the twelve-year episode of Nazi Germany; and so forth.[11] In other words, we have to resist the suggestive power of the kinds of comparisons that have been central for understanding the world during the Cold War period, but which are not so central for analysis beyond the divide. We should move toward designing different matrices for a *histoire événementielle*. Convincing arguments exist in favor of a shift in priorities: from comparing to reconstructing the contexts, the interactions, the transfers and interplays of "national" histories in the framework of European civilization. There is something artificial and overly ambitious in making the Nazism-Stalinism comparisons. There is a tendency toward symmetry and symmetrical

---

[10] There is a mass of new literature about discourses on modernity, aesthetics, sport, body, health, hygiene, reproductive medicine, leisure time, architecture, planning, nature, etc. For the early period see Kai Buchholz, ed., *Die Lebensreform: Entwürfe zur Neugestaltung von Leben und Kunst um 1900*, 2 vols. (Darmstadt: Häusser, 2001). For the later period, cf. the catalogues of the two exhibitions *Paris-Moscou 1900–1930* (Paris: Centre Georges Pompidou, 1979) and Irina Antonowa and Jörn Merkert, eds., *Berlin-Moskau, Ausstellungskatalog* (Munich and New York: Prestel, 1995). See also Nicola Lepp and Martin Roth, eds., *Der neue Mensch: Obsessionen des 20: Jahrhunderts: Katalog der Ausstellung im Deutschen Hygiene-Museum vom 2. August bis 8. August 1999* (Ostfildern-Ruit: Crantz, 1999).

[11] The terms are from Alexandra Richie, *Faust's Metropolis: A History of Berlin* (London: Harper Collins, 1998), and David L. Hoffmann, *Peasant Metropolis: Social Identities in Moscow, 1929–1941* (Ithaca, NY: Cornell University Press, 1994).

analysis, which does not coincide with the real asymmetry in the preconditions found in the two countries and societies.

STALINISM AND NAZISM IN A EUROPEAN CONTEXT

Of course, National Socialism is a German phenomenon and Stalinism is a Russian/Soviet phenomenon, and each is subject to its own national historiography. Yet, at the same time, they are an integral part of the crisis of European civilization and cross the boundaries of national historiography. The point is not to escape "national responsibility" for terror and violence, but to understand and explain it. Nazism and Stalinism may have been the most radical movements, but they articulated general European trends. One cannot talk about Soviet Russia and Nazi Germany, for example, without talking about fascist Italy.[12] The Paris World's Fair of 1937 encompassed not only the aesthetic encounter of Vera Mukhina's sculpture and Albert Speer's German pavilion, but also of Italy's pavilion.[13] It could be useful, in a certain way, to denationalize the framework of historiography and to Europeanize the site of events, to escape the bilateralism that is implicit in the German-Russian comparison. When we compare Germany and Russia, we are dealing not with static, independent entities, but with enemy and ally states in a life-and-death struggle, the most intense relationship imaginable. One can call it a "special relationship," as many historians and writers have done in the past: "a community of fate"; "incompatible allies"; "the Devil's alliance" (*Das Teufelsbündnis*); "the crusade for Europe against Bolshevism" (*Europäischer Kreuzzug gegen den Bolschewismus*); "an ideological war" (*Weltanschauungskrieg*); "a war of annihilation" (*Vernichtungskrieg*); or "the European civil war" (*der europäische Bürgerkrieg*). All of these notions reflect the fact that National Socialism and Stalinism were actors on the same stage.[14]

---

[12] Gerd Koenen, *Der Russland-Komplex: Die Deutschen und der Osten 1900–1945* (Munich: Beck Verlag, 2005); Cf. also Dawn Ades et al., eds., *Kunst und Macht im Europa der Diktatoren 1930 bis 1945: XXIII. Kunstausstellung des Europarates*, with an introduction by Eric Hobsbawm and an epilogue by Neal Ascherson, trans. Bram Opstelten and Magda Moses (London: Hayward Gallery, 1996).

[13] The sculpture of Giorgio Gori in front of the Italian pavilion was directly facing Albert Speer's German house and Vera Mukhina's sculpture. See *Kunst und Macht im Europa der Diktatoren 1930 bis 1945*. Very important for the European reception of German and Russian aesthetics in the 1930s are the reviews from the Paris Fair of 1937; see Zopf, 427–9; Bartetzko, 337–43.

[14] Some of these titles are taken from the main publications on the subject: Edward H. Carr, *German-Soviet Relations between the Two World Wars, 1919–1939* (Baltimore: John Hopkins University Press, 1951); Gerald Freund, *Unholy Alliance: Russian-German Relations from the Treaty of Brest-Litovsk to the Treaty of Berlin* (London: Harcourt, Brace, 1957); Sebastian Haffner, *Der Teufelspakt: Die deutsch-russischen Beziehungen vom Ersten zum Zweiten Weltkrieg* (Zürich: Manesse, 1988); Dietrich Goldschmidt, ed., *Frieden mit der Sowjetunion – eine unerledigte Aufgabe* (Gütersloh: Gütersloher Verlags-Haus Mohn, 1989); F. A. Krummacher and Helmut Lange, *Krieg und Frieden: Geschichte der deutsch-sowjetischen Beziehungen: Von Brest-Litowsk zum Unternehmen Barbarossa* (Munich-Esslingen: Bechtle, 1970);

We need to redesign the matrix of analysis: to go (1) from "rule and system" to civilizational spaces; (2) from national or individual states to a European frame of reference; (3) from static to dynamic relationships between European states and societies. The title for that enterprise could be "Russia and Germany in the Age of War and Revolution." Viewed from this broader perspective (the proper term would be history of civilization), the so-called *Historikerstreit* in 1980s Germany had relatively little to do with the empirical and material rewriting of German and Russian history or their mutual relationship. The *Historikerstreit* was more a symptom of the changes in the intellectual landscape in late postwar Germany than an elaboration of a new framework for understanding European history, especially the relationship between the two leading totalitarian powers. It tells us much more about the spiritual and intellectual climate in West Germany in the second half of the 1980s than about Stalin's Russia and Hitler's Germany.[15] Thus, the task of reintegrating the German and the Russian experience into a European history of war and revolution remains unfulfilled.

GERMAN PERCEPTIONS AND GERMAN IMAGES OF SOVIET RUSSIA IN THE 1930S

There was no single, coherent German perception or image of Soviet Russia in the 1930s. Rather, there were countless individual experiences and biographical peculiarities – after all, even in a police state like Nazi Germany, society has many layers and social strata. As any history of the Weimar Republic will show, the Russian revolution was part of inner-German discourse since 1917: a political and highly partisan struggle operating both at the level of semantics (for example, *Kulturbolschewismus*) and at the level of outright physical violence (for example, street warfare; civil war). Thus any reliable analysis or research on this topic has to examine different spheres and different epochs in which the "Russian question" evolved. The first striking observation to be made is that since Walter Laqueur's seminal book on German-Russian relations in the nineteenth and twentieth centuries, much research has been done, but only very little on images of Russia in Germany during the 1930s.

Nonetheless, an important gap has been filled by studies dealing with the images of Soviet Russia in National Socialist propaganda, in the German Wehrmacht, among diplomats and members of the foreign office, inside the

Ernst Nolte, *Der europäische Bürgerkrieg, 1917–1945: Nationalsozialismus und Bolschewismus* (Frankfurt am Main and Berlin: Propyläen, 1987).

[15] Rudolf Augstein, ed., *Der Historikerstreit: Die Dokumentation der Kontroverse um die Einzigartigkeit der nationalsozialistischen Judenvernichtung* (Munich and Zürich: Piper, 1987); Hans-Ulrich Wehler, *Entsorgung der deutschen Vergangenheit: Ein polemischer Essay zum "Historikerstreit"* (Munich: Beck, 1988); Helmut Fleischer, "Zu einer Historik für die Geschichte des 20. Jahrhunderts: Präliminarien, Perspektiven, Paradigmen" in *Das 20. Jahrhundert: Zeitalter der tragischen Verkehrungen: Forum zum 80. Geburtstag von Ernst Nolte*, eds Helmut Fleischer and Pierluca Azzaro (Munich: Herbig, 2003), 506–58.

leadership of the army as well as among the SS, among experts on Eastern Europe and Russia in scholarly institutions, among Protestants and Catholics, and even among schoolteachers, writers, and German physicians. These studies reconstruct a field that has been neglected for years, showing that even in "open societies," with open access to archives, it takes time to face the past.[16] This field of historiography is also interesting because there have been two German historiographies, parallel and competing with each other – one in East Germany and the other in West Germany. Especially in East Germany, the German-Russian, German-Soviet relationship had a privileged position. But even there, research focused primarily on the Weimar period, especially the Brest-Litovsk and Rapallo period,[17] meaning that the bulk of historiography deals with the pre-Nazi period.

A new wave of research on German perceptions of Stalinist Russia deals with World War II and German rule in the East. This research concerns the editing of correspondence and letters from the front, including a mass of photographs.[18] This means that research is quite uneven, fragmented, and dispersed.[19] There is no systematic analysis of the coverage of news from the USSR in German newspapers and journals.[20] Very important sources – not only for reconstructing the German view, but for getting insider materials for the study of Stalinist

[16] The main publication dealing with Nazi-period perceptions of Russia is, in my view, Hans-Erich Volkmann, ed., *Das Rußlandbild im Dritten Reich* (Cologne; Weimar; and Vienna: Böhlau, 1994).

[17] Günter Rosenfeld, *Sowjetrußland und Deutschland 1917–1922* (Berlin: Akademie Verlag, 1960); Günter Rosenfeld, *Sowjetunion und Deutschland, 1922–1933* (Berlin: Akademie Verlag, 1984); Gerd Voigt, *Rußland in der deutschen Geschichtsschreibung* (Berlin: Akademie Verlag, 1994); Bibliographies in Karin Borck, ed., *Sowjetische Forschungen (1917 bis 1991): Zur Geschichte der deutsch-russischen Beziehungen von den Anfängen bis 1949* (Berlin: Akademie, 1993). The most extensive and annotated bibliography can be found in *West-östliche Spiegelungen*. See also Gerd Koenen and Lew Kopelew, eds., *Deutschland und die Russische Revolution, 1917–1924* (Munich: W. Fink Verlag, 1998), bibliography, 827–934. More generally, see Deutsch-Russisches Museum Berlin-Karlshorst, ed. *Unsere Russen – Unsere Deutschen: Bilder vom Anderen 1800 bis 2000* (Berlin: Christoph Links Verlag, 2007); Stiftung Preußische Schlösser und Gärten Berlin-Brandenburg, ed. *Macht und Freundschaft 1800–1860* (Berlin: Koehler & Amelang, 2007).

[18] Manfred Zeidler, "Das Bild der Wehrmacht von Rußland und der Roten Armee zwischen 1933 und 1939," in *Das Russlandbild im Dritten Reich*, ed. Hans-Erich Volkmann (Cologne: Böhlau, 1994), 105–24; Ortwin Buchbender and Reinhold Sterz, *Das andere Gesicht des Krieges: Deutsche Feldpostbriefe 1939–1945* (Munich: Beck, 1982); Wolf Dieter Mohrmann, ed., *Der Krieg hier ist hart und grausam!: Feldpostbriefe an den Osnabrücker Regierungspräsidenten, 1941–1944* (Osnabrück: H. Th. Wenner, 1984); Anatoly Golovchansky et al., eds., *"Ich will raus aus diesem Wahnsinn": Deutsche Briefe von der Ostfront, 1941–1945: Aus sowjetischen Archiven*, with a preface by Willy Brandt (Wuppertal: P. Hammer, 1991).

[19] The main project is Gerd Koenen and Lew Kopelew, eds., *West-östliche Spiegelungen: Russen und Rußland aus deutscher Sicht und Deutsche und Deutschland aus russischer Sicht von den Anfängen bis zum 20. Jahrhundert: Wuppertaler Projekt zur Erforschung der Geschichte deutsch-russischer Fremdenbilder*. Series A: *Russen und Rußland aus deutscher Sicht*, 4 vols., Series B: *Deutsche und Deutschland aus russischer Sicht*, 2 vols. (Munich: Fink, 1985).

[20] Exceptions are Wolfram Wette, "Das Rußlandbild in der NS-Propaganda: Ein Problemaufriss," in *Das Russlandbild im Dritten Reich*, ed. Hans-Erich Volkmann (Cologne: Böhlau, 1994),

society – are still undiscovered or insufficiently used, such as reports by journalists, diplomats, and representatives of trade and commercial firms. GDR historiography has published materials, documents, and correspondence from German émigrés (rank-and-file-workers as well as engineers and technical experts) working in the USSR in the 1930s, which had some influence on the formation of the more positive image of a minority.[21]

The state of research is much better for the pre-Nazi period. In many ways, the perception of Russia in the 1930s was formed long before 1933 – especially during World War I and the Weimar Republic. Characteristic elements of the image of post-1917 Russia had been articulated by the 1920s. We have analyses of the images of Russia in the German conservative and right-wing press in the 1920s[22] and in the Social Democratic newspapers,[23] but not for the main National Socialist newspapers, journals, and other media, such as exhibitions, and atlases. There are studies about the perception of political parties and activists (SPD, Zentrum) and of intellectuals and fellow travelers.[24] We do have a series of studies on Russian émigrés in Germany[25] and German émigrés in Russia,[26] on political parties like the Mensheviks in Germany, and on

---

55–780; Bianka Pietrow-Ennker, "Das Feindbild im Wandel: Die Sowjetunion in den nationalsozialistischen Wochenschauen, 1935–1941," *Geschichte in Wissenschaft und Unterricht* 41 (1990): 337–51.

[21] About German engineers and architects in the USSR, see Christian Borngräber, "Ausländische Architekten in der UdSSR: Bruno Taut, die Brigaden Ernst May, Hannes Meyer und Hans Schmidt," in *Wem gehört die Welt: Kunst und Gesellschaft in der Weimarer Republik* (Berlin: Neue Gesellschaft für Bildende Kunst, 1977), 109–42.

[22] Kai-Uwe Merz, *Das Schreckbild: Deutschland und die Idee des Bolschewismus, 1917 bis 1921* (Berlin and Frankfurt am Main: Propyläen, 1995); Ute Döser, "Das bolschewistische Rußland in der deutschen Rechtspresse, 1918–1925" (diss., Free University Berlin, 1961).

[23] Jürgen Zarusky, *Die deutschen Sozialdemokraten und das sowjetische Modell: Ideologische Auseinandersetzung und außenpolitische Konzeptionen, 1917–1933* (Munich: R. Oldenbourg, 1992).

[24] On fellow travelers, see David Caute, *The Fellow-Travellers: Intellectual Friends of Communism* (New Haven, CT: Yale University Press, 1988); Bernhard Furler, *Augen-Schein: Deutschsprachige Reisereportagen über Sowjetrußland, 1917–1939* (Frankfurt am Main: Athenäum, 1987); Michael Rohrwasser, *Der Stalinismus und die Renegaten: Die Literatur der Exkommunisten* (Stuttgart: J. B, Metzler, 1991).

[25] Hans-Erich Volkmann, *Die russische Emigration in Deutschland 1919–1929* (Würzburg: Holzer, 1966); Robert Chadwell Williams, *Culture in Exile: Russian Émigrés in Germany, 1881–1941* (Ithaca, NY: Cornell University Press, 1972); Lazar' Fleishman, Robert P. Hughes, and O. Raevskaia-Kh'iuz, eds., *Russkii Berlin, 1921–1923: Po materialam arkhiva B. I. Nikolaevskogo v Guverovskom Institute* (Paris: YMCA-Press, 1983); Fritz Mierau, ed., *Russen in Berlin, 1918–1933: Eine kulturelle Begegnung* (Weinheim-Berlin: Quadriga, 1988); Karl Schlögel, ed., *Russische Emigration in Deutschland, 1918–194: Leben im europäischen Bürgerkrieg* (Berlin: Akademie Verlag, 1995); Karl Schlögel et al., eds., *Chronik russischen Lebens in Deutschland, 1918–1941* (Berlin: Akademie Verlag, 1999); Bettina Dodenhoeft, *"Laßt mich nach Rußland heim": Russische Emigranten in Deutschland von 1918 bis 1945* (Frankfurt am Main: P. Lang, 1993).

[26] On German émigrés in the USSR, cf. Reinhard Müller, *Die Akte Wehner* (Reinbek bei Hamburg: Rowohlt, 1993); Carola Tischler, *Flucht in die Verfolgung: Deutsche Emigranten im*

the cooperation and collaboration of the Russian and German right.[27] Works have been published on German expertise on Russia in the Ostausschuss der Deutschen Wirtschaft (Eastern Europe Committee of the German Economy)[28] and in the Russlandabteilung des Auswärtigen Amtes (Russian Division of the Foreign Office).[29] There have been several studies on Russian prisoners of war and slave labor in Germany; on military collaboration;[30] on the Baltic connection;[31] on *Russlandkunde* (Russian studies);[32] and on scholarly and academic relations and exchange. Also we have many works on cultural networks and

sowjetischen Exil, 1933 bis 1945 (Münster: Lit, 1996); David Pike, *German Writers in Soviet Exile, 1933–1945* (Chapel Hill: University of North Carolina Press, 1982).

[27] On Russian right-wing émigrés, cf. Walter Laqueur, *Deutschland und Rußland* (Berlin: Propyläen, 1965), and the articles by R. Ganelin, "Das Leben des Gregor Schwartz-Bostunitsch (Grigorij V. Švarc-Bostunič), Teil 1," and M. Hagemeister, "Das Leben des Gregor Schwartz-Bostunitsch (Grigorij V. Švarc-Bostunič), Teil 2" in *Russische Emigration in Deutschland 1918–1941*, ed. Karl Schlögel (Berlin: Akademie, 1995), 201–8, 209–18, respectively. On the Mensheviks in Germany see André Liebich, *From the Other Shore: Russian Social Democracy after 1921* (Cambridge, MA: Harvard University Press, 1997).

[28] Heinrich Schwendemann, *Die wirtschaftliche Zusammenarbeit zwischen dem Deutschen Reich und der Sowjetunion von 1939 bis 1941: Alternative zu Hitlers Ostprogramm?* (Berlin: Akademie Verlag, 1993); Hans-Jürgen Perrey, *Der Rußlandausschluß der Deutschen Wirtschaft: Die deutsch-sowjetischen Wirtschaftsbeziehungen der Zwischenkriegszeit: Ein Beitrag zur Geschichte des Ost-West-Handels* (Munich: Oldenbourg, 1985).

[29] Herbert Helbig, *Die Träger der Rapallo-Politik* (Göttingen: Vandenhoeck & Ruprecht, 1958); Ingmar Sütterlin, *Die "Russische Abteilung" des Auswärtigen Amtes in der Weimarer Republik* (Berlin: Duncker & Humblot, 1994): Günter Rosenfeld, *Sowjetrußland und Deutschland, 1918–1922* (Berlin: Akademie-Verlag, 1960); id., *Sowjetunion und Deutschland, 1922–1933* (Berlin: Akademie-Verlag, 1984); id., "Kultur und Wissenschaft in den Beziehungen zwischen Deutschland und der Sowjetunion von 1933 bis 1941," *Berliner Jahrbuch für osteuropäische Geschichte* no. 1 (1995): 99–129.

[30] Manfred Zeidler, *Reichswehr und Rote Armee 1920–1933: Wege und Stationen einer ungewöhnlichen Zusammenarbeit* (Munich: Oldenbourg, 1993); Bianka Pietrow-Ennker, "Die Sowjetunion in der Propaganda des Dritten Reiches: Das Beispiel der Wochenschauen" in *Militärgeschichtliche Mitteilungen*, no. 2 (1989): 79–120; Olaf Groehler, *Selbstmörderische Allianz: Deutsch-russische Militärbeziehungen, 1920–1941* (Berlin: Vision Verlag, 1992).

[31] Michael Garleff, *Deutschbalten, Weimarer Republik und Drittes Reich*, vols. 1–3 (Cologne: Böhlau, 2001).

[32] Martin Burkert, *Die Ostwissenschaften im Dritten Reich. Part I: Zwischen Verbot und Duldung: Die schwierige Gratwanderung der Ostwissenschaften zwischen 1933 und 1939* (Wiesbaden: Harrassowitz, 2000); Gabriele Camphausen, *Die wissenschaftliche historische Rußlandforschung im Dritten Reich, 1933–1935* (Frankfurt am Main: P. Lang, 1990); Gabriele Camphausen, "Das Rußlandbild in der deutschen Geschichtswissenschaft 1933 bis 1945," in *Das Rußlandbild im Dritten Reich*, ed. Hans-Erich Volkmann (Cologne: Böhlau, 1994), 257–83; Uwe Liszkowski, *Osteuropaforschung und Politik: Ein Beitrag zum historisch-politischen Denken und Wirken von Otto Hoetzsch*, 2 vols. (Berlin: Verlag A. Spitz, 1988); Gerd Voigt, *Otto Hoetzsch, 1876–1946: Wissenschaft und Politik im Leben eines deutschen Historikers* (Berlin: Akademie, 1978); Gerd Voigt, *Rußland in der deutschen Geschichtswissenschaft, 1843–1945* (Berlin: Akademie, 1994); Michael Burleigh, *Germany Turns Eastwards: A Study of Ostforschung* (Cambridge: Cambridge Univeristy Press, 1988); Erwin Oberländer, "Historische Osteuropaforschung im Dritten Reich," in Erwin Oberländer, ed., *Geschichte Osteuropas: Zur Entwicklung einer historischen Disziplin in Deutschland, Österreich und der Schweiz, 1945–1990* (Stuttgart: Franz Steiner, 1992), 12–30.

intellectual encounters such as Bauhaus, Vkhutemas, theater, cinema, and literary journals.[33]

There is insufficient research on the role played by the communities of the diplomatic corps and of journalists in both countries.[34] These groups held, in general, privileged positions for communication and observation, and thus they were in an almost exclusive position to fabricate the images of the foreign country. There are very few studies on the Nazi image of Russia or on one of the most central issues in Nazi propaganda – the complex of "Judaeo-Bolshevism."[35] It would require the study of a mass of materials: trivial literature; brochures in mass distribution; pamphlets; analyses of the Nazi experts on Russia and Bolshevism; the talks and public discussions organized by the Nazi Party; the many affiliations of the *Anti-Komintern*; schoolbooks; atlases; and so forth.[36] Surprisingly, we have no analysis of the central topics of Nazi propaganda concerning the Soviet Union. There is nothing like Edward Said's *Orientalism* in the good sense – a reconstruction of the "Images of the East" or "Images of Russia in 20th-Century Germany."[37] We have detailed studies

---

[33] On Bauhaus and Vkhutemas, see the catalogues to the exhibition "Berlin-Moscow" and Klaus Kändler and Helga Karolewski, eds., *Berliner Begegnungen: Ausländische Künstler in Berlin 1918 bis 1933: Aufsätze, Bilder, Dokumente* (Berlin: Dietz, 1987); Derek Müller, *Der Topos des Neuen Menschen in der russischen und sowjetrussischen Geistesgeschichte* (Bern: P. Lang, 1998).

[34] Hans von Herwarth, *Zwischen Hitler und Stalin, Erlebte Zeitgeschichte 1931 bis 1945* (Berlin and Frankfurt am Main: Propyläen, 1982); Gustav Hilger, *Wir und der Kreml: Deutsch-sowjetische Beziehungen, 1918–1941: Erinnerungen eines deutschen Diplomaten* (Frankfurt am Main: A. Metzner, 1955); Rudolf Nadolny, *Mein Beitrag: Erinnerungen eines Botschafters des Deutschen Reiches* (Cologne: DME Verlag, 1985); Peter Longerich, *Propagandisten im Krieg: Die Presseabteilung des Auswärtigen Amtes unter Ribbentrop* (Munich: R. Oldenbourg, 1987). On journalism, see Artur Just, *Die Sowjetunion: Staat, Wirtschaft, Heer* (Berlin: Junker and Dünnhaupt, 1940); id., *Rußland in Europa: Gedanken zum Ostproblem der abendländischen Welt* (Stuttgart: Union Deutsche Verlaggesellschaft, 1949).

[35] Johannes Rogalla von Bieberstein, *"Jüdischer Bolschewismus": Mythos und Realität*, with a preface by Ernst Nolte (Dresden: Edition Antaios, 2002).

[36] On Edwin-Erich Dwinger and his work, there is almost no literature. Cf. Karl Schlögel, "Die russische Obsession: Edwin Erich Dwinger," in *Traumland Osten. Deutsche Bilder vom östlichen Europa im 20. Jahrhundert*, ed. Gregor Thum (Göttingen: Vandenhoek & Ruprecht, 2006), 66–87. On Il'yin see Iu. T. Lisitsa, *Ivan Il'in i Rossiia* (Moscow: Russkaia kniga, 1999); Karl Albrecht, *Der verratene Sozialismus: Zehn Jahre als hoher Staatsbeamter in der Sowjetunion* (Berlin: Nibelungen-Verlag, 1939); Emilian Klinsky, *Vierzig Donkosaken erobern die Welt: S. Jaroff und seine Donkosakenchor* (Leipzig: Matthes-Verlag, 1933). On the connection between Russian émigrés and the Nazi Party cf. Michael Kellogg, *The Russian Roots of Nazism: White Émigrés and the Making of National Socialism 1917–1945* (Cambridge: Cambridge University Press 2005).

[37] Hans-Heinrich Nolte, *"Drang nach Osten": Sowjetische Geschichtsschreibung der deutschen Ostexpansion* (Stuttgart: Europäische Verlaganstalt, 1976); Rolf-Dieter Müller, "Von Brest-Litowsk bis zum 'Unternehmen Barbarossa' – Wandlungen und Kontinuität des deutschen 'Drangs nach Osten,'" in *Frieden mit der Sowjetunion*, ed. Dietrich Goldschmidt (Gütersloh: Gütersloher Verlaghaus G. Mohn, 1989), 70–86; Gregor Thum, ed., *Traumland Osten: Deutsche Bilder vom östlichen Europa im 20. Jahrhundert* (Göttingen: Vandenhoeck & Ruprecht, 2006).

(for example, Russia in the view of physicians or Catholic priests), but no general, comprehensive study on the question, Where was Russia or the Soviet Union positioned on the mental maps of Germans?

TOPOI AND TYPOLOGY OF "RUSSIANNESS"

The following is a small selection of the central images of Russia and Russianness. It is worthwhile to present the most important notions, even if it can be done here only in a very schematic and simple way.

RUSSIAN SPACE. There is an obsession with space in Germany for many reasons that cannot be discussed here.[38] Russian space as a cliché or idiosyncratic complex is, in general terms, endless, immeasurable, and grand. It has a strong impact on psychology, mentality, and character. It is unbelievably rich in natural resources, but the people living there are unable to exploit them appropriately. Russian space is "space without people"; in other words, it is contrary to the "overcrowded" German situation, "people without space." Russian space has no boundaries or contours; it is shapeless and formless. It is unexplored, unacquired, unmastered (*"nicht bewältigt"*). Russian space is a space of fear, of threat, but at the same time a space of immense technical and economic potential – "if there would be the right people" (*Völkischer Beobachter*).[39] This space is ambiguous, colonial space ("our India," as Hitler put it), and a space where you can get lost, as Charles XII and Napoleon Bonaparte did.[40] Russian space is the opposite of what Germans have. A naturalization of history takes place: German generals failing to conquer Moscow did not talk about Russian patriotic resistance or Soviet military power, but about their rival and counterpart "General Winter." A remarkable change in the perception of Russian space occurred after 22 June 1941 and again after Stalingrad. First it was perceived as vast, open space, inviting for cultivation and agriculture. Then, "after Stalingrad," it became the space of diseases, epidemics, and quarantines; of filth and lice. Colonial space, conquered in a few weeks or months in Blitzkrieg operations, had become a space of dissolution, getting lost, despair.[41]

---

[38] On the German obsession with space, cf. Guntram Henrik Herb, *Under the Map of Germany: Nationalism and Propaganda, 1918–1945* (London and New York: Routledge, 1997); Karl Schlögel, *Im Raume lesen wir die Zeit: Über Zivilisationsgeschichte und Geopolitik* (Munich: Carl Hanser, 2003), 52–60.

[39] Cf. Manfred Weißbecker, "'Wenn hier Deutsche wohnten...': Beharrung und Veränderung im Rußlandbild Hitlers und der NSDAP," in *Das Rußlandbild im Dritten Reich,* ed. Hans Erich Volkmann (Cologne: Böhlau, 1994), 9–54.

[40] Rolf-Dieter Müller, *Das Tor zur Weltmacht: Die Bedeutung der Sowjetunion für die deutsche Wirtschafts- und Rüstungspolitik zwischen den Kriegen* (Boppard am Rhein: H. Boldt, 1984); Rolf-Dieter Müller, *Hitlers Krieg im Osten, 1941–1945: Ein Forschungsbericht* (Darmstadt: Wissenschaftliche Buchgesellschaft, 2000).

[41] The ambiguous fascination with space is analyzed in Vejas Gabriel Liulevicius in *War Land on the Eastern Front: Culture, National Identity, and German Occupation in World War I* (Cambridge: Cambridge University Press, 2000).

"THE" RUSSIANS. There is a huge literature on the cliché of the "Russian soul," from the late nineteenth century up to 1945. The "Russian soul" is good-natured, calm, patient, warm, childlike, not deformed by education, but, at the same time, brutal, cruel, physically strong, and able to suffer without complaining. The opposite type to this image is, of course, the disciplined German or the smart Jew. This image of the Russian is ambiguous. On the one hand, he is close to Rousseau's "noble savage," a beautiful barbarian, the opposite of the corrupt man of the cities. He is the source for renewal and rebirth of culture. The Russian is good "human material" (*gutes Menschenmaterial*), as it was called in the Third Reich and before. "The" Russians love their homeland and are ready to sacrifice themselves in defense of their country. The Russian is a passionate patriot and, especially, a good soldier. Here we see a mixture of disdain and respect, of fear and admiration. The sentimental attitude toward Russia and the Russians had a long and well established tradition in Germany. This tradition starts with the national psychology (*Völkerpsychologie*) of the nineteenth century, if not with Leibniz's and Herder's admiration for the bright prospects of the young Slavic peoples. The tradition reached a high point around the turn of the century with the pilgrimages of Rilke and others to Russia, with a later echo in the Russophilia and Dostoyevsky cult of Thomas Mann and others.[42] This tradition was still alive in Nazi Germany, and it was only after the atrocities of the war in the East that the long tradition of empathy for Russia died, and probably for all time.[43]

RUSSIA BEYOND EUROPE. Russia is perceived as non-European, Asiatic or semi-Asiatic. Russian power and culture are excluded from certain European traditions. A wide range of positions exists. One finds the purely racist discrimination against Asia and Russia, as well as more sophisticated cultural theories by figures such as Chaadaev, Kireevskii, and the Eurasian ideologues. But there was a positive understanding of the "Russian soul" too, as in the then well-known anti-Nazi book *Europa und die Seele des Ostens* (1938) by Walter Schubarth.[44] Different positions were stressed in different periods. The "Asiatic" concept obviously prevailed during the period when Nazi Germany was pretending to "defend Europe in the final battle."[45] It is often overlooked that

---

[42] On the "Ex oriente lux" spirit in Germany, cf. the contributions in Gerd Koenen and Lew Kopelew, eds., *West-östliche Spiegelungen*. On the young Joseph Goebbels, his fascination for Russia and the Russian revolution, and his fascination with the "Ex oriente lux" idea, see Gerd Koenen, *Der Russland-Komplex: Die Deutschen und der Osten 1900–1945* (Munich: C. H. Beck Verlag, 2006), 398–401.

[43] Heinrich Stammler, "Wandlungen des deutschen Bildes vom russischen Menschen" in *Jahrbücher für Geschichte Osteuropas*, Neue Folge [new series] 5 (1957): 271–305.

[44] Walter Schubart, *Europa und die Seele des Ostens* (Luzern: Vita nova Verlag, 1938).

[45] On intra-Nazi controversies in dealing with Russia/Soviet Union, see Alexander Dallin, *Deutsche Herrschaft in Rußland, 1941–1945: Eine Studie über Besatzungspolitik* (Düsseldorf: Droste, 1958); Ekkehart Klug, "Das 'asiatische' Rußland: Über die Entstehung eines europäischen Vorurteils," in *Historische Zeitschrift* 245 (1987): 265–89; Leonid Luks, "'Eurasier' und 'Konservative Revolution': Zur antiwestlichen Versuchung in Rußland und in Deutschland," in *Deutschland und die russische Revolution*, 219–39.

the War in the East was accompanied by Europeanist rhetoric: The Wehrmacht defending the Occident against the barbarous hordes of Huns, Mongols, and Slavs.[46]

THE COLOSSUS MADE OF CLAY, THE SHAKY COLOSSUS. According to the German perception, Russia had immense resources, above all physical and human ones. But its might was based on physical power and on numbers, whereas the strength of Germany, Europe, and the West was seen as based on rational organization, intelligence, and cleverness. One could thus defeat the colossus with a quick, strategic strike, or "Blitz." The image of the weak colossus originated in the long period of occupation in the eastern lands (*Land Oberost*) during World War I. The use of this image, of course, depends on circumstances. Hitler finally recognized in his last days in the Reichskanzlei that "his people" proved to be inferior to other, "stronger peoples."[47]

"THE MASSES." In Nazi ideology, "the" Russian never has individual features, only collective ones. The Bolshevik revolution intensified these features by liquidating the old elites and uprooting millions of Russian peasants from their private allotments and farms. As an element of the proletarianized masses, the Russian became the victim of demagogy and manipulation. The Russians lost their leading stratum and were now, so to speak, decapitated. In the stereotyped image, Russians do not have their own will. "The masses" never acquired the distinct features of a nation, have lost any specific physiognomy, and are likely to be a *Völkergemisch*, that is, an amalgamation of different nations and races. Soviet Russia is perceived in many ways like the United States, as a melting pot, destroying a more or less ethnically homogeneous society. The Soviet New Man is a *mixtum compositum*.[48]

THE "JEWISH FACE" OF BOLSHEVIK RUSSIA. For Hitler and his entourage and in Nazi propaganda, Jews ruled postrevolutionary Russia. Nazi propagandists tried to demonstrate this in every way possible: "unveiling" the real names "behind" the Russian names (so they always referred to Litvinov as Finkelstein,[49] Trotsky as Bronstein, and so forth). They declared public figures to be of Jewish origin, or, if no relation to Jewishness existed, they declared Russians to be under Jewish influence. They had entire branches, institutes, experts who produced this kind of analysis.[50] In Nazi propaganda, the visualization of politics played an important role. They used every chance and any medium (cartoons, photography, exhibitions) to accuse Jews of infiltrating the

[46] The iconography of early anti-Bolshevik patterns was revived in the election campaigns in Cold War West Germany after 1945.

[47] Characteristic for this mixed attitude is a text by Karl Nötzel, *Die Grundlagen des geistigen Russland: Versuch einer Psychologie des russischen Geisteslebens* (Jena: Diederich, 1917).

[48] On represenative exhibitions for 1934 and 1943, see *Das Sowjetparadies: Ausstellung der Reichspropagandaleitung der NSDAP: Ein Bericht in Wort und Bild* (Berlin: Zentralverlag der NSDAP, Franz Eher Nachf., 1943).

[49] The Bolshevik leader and diplomat known as Maksim Maksimovich Litvinov (1876–1951) was born Meir Henoch Mojszewicz Wallach-Finkelstein.

[50] On the *Anti-Komintern* see Walter Laqueur, 209–36; Gabriele Camphausen, op. cit.

party, the state, and other organizations. Books and booklets in huge numbers were distributed in order to show a deep gap between the so-called Jewish ruling elite and the broad masses.[51] The classical gallery of *Stürmer* caricatures included Trotsky, Kamenev, Zinoviev, and again and again Kaganovich, "the man behind Stalin."[52] We are convinced that the mass circulation of these portraits and cartoons had an immense impact in forging the image of the "Jewishness of Bolshevism," the identification of Jews with revolution. Nazi propagandists used much Russian émigré material and the émigrés' own interpretations of the radical turnover of elites in Russia and the total difference in the "physiognomy" of power.[53] According to this rhetoric, even the Palace of Soviets, then under construction, represented a revival of King Solomon's temple.[54]

KULTURBOLSCHEWISMUS, GEFAHR FÜR EUROPA. The old regime in Russia had many links to elites in the West. Under the conditions of severe economic crisis and radical instability in the Weimar Republic, the Nazis utilized the traditional stereotypes of Russia to mobilize fear and resentment among portions of the German public, especially the middle class, by pointing to Soviet atrocities: the expropriation of and labor duty for members of the bourgeoisie, the closing or demolition of churches, the persecution of clergymen, the dissolution of libraries, the destruction of palaces, the atrocities of the Russian Civil War, and so on.[55] Many men in leading positions in the 1930s (in the party and in state administration) had been shaped by their experiences of brutal warfare in the eastern lands and by their experiences with the Freicorps in the immediate aftermath of World War I.[56]

None of these images were purely Nazi inventions, as their emergence can be traced further back in history. These clichés represented deeply rooted

[51] On Nazi perception of "Jewish rule" in Russia, see Johannes Baur, "Die Revolution und 'Die Weisen von Zion': Zur Entwicklung des Rußlandbildes in der frühen NSDAP," in Koenen and Kopelew, 165–90; Johannes Rogalla von Bieberstein, *"Jüdischer Bolschewismus": Mythos und Realität* (Dresden: Antaios, 2002); Gerd Koenen, "Hitlers Russland: Ambivalenzen im deutschen 'Drang nach Osten'" in *Kommune: Forum Politik, Ökonomie, Kultur*, no. 1 (2003): 65–79.

[52] Representative is Rudolf Kommoss, *Juden hinter Stalin: Die jüdische Vormachtstellung in der Sowjetunion auf Grund amtlicher sowjetischer Quellen dargestellt* (Berlin: Nibelungen, 1944).

[53] Bianka Pietrow-Ennker, "Das Feindbild im Wandel: Die Sowjetunion in den nationalsozialistischen Wochenschauen 1935–1941," *Geschichte in Wissenschaft und Unterricht* 41 (1990): 337–51.

[54] On the Palace of Soviets (*Dvorets sovetov*) under construction, seen as "temple of the international Jewry," see Rudolf Kommoss, *Juden hinter Stalin*, 135–7.

[55] On "Bolshevik danger," chaos, etc., see Donald O' Sullivan, *Furcht und Faszination: Deutsche und britische Rußlandbilder, 1921–1933* (Cologne and Weimar: Böhlau, 1996); on *Kulturbolschewismus* (cultural Bolshevism), see Eckhard John, *Musikbolschewismus: Die Politisierung der Musik in Deutschland, 1918–1938* (Stuttgart: J. B. Metzler, 1994); Karl Nötzel, *Gegen den Kultur-Bolschewismus* (Munich: Paul Müller, 1930).

[56] For instance, Rudolf Höss, the commander of Auschwitz, was a member of a Freikorps in the Baltic. See Ljulevicius, *Kriegsland im Osten*, 297.

layers and discourses. They bridged the gap between prejudices and perceptions of the petty bourgeoisie and aggressive racism. "Russian space" was a
fascination for many theoreticians and ideologues. However, some features
also fit into European discourses on America: American space, absence of class
restrictions and borders, absence of aristocratic elites. These notions had an
impact not only on minor and marginal intellectual communities, but also in a
broader sense. Some notions reflected a remarkable experience – and fear – of
modernization: the processes of proletarization, migration, urbanization, and
destruction of traditional bonds. Such fear was commonplace among experts
and émigrés and was not limited to right-wing or right-extremist views. "The
Russian" was an ambivalent and multidimensional figure: he or she represented "Holy Russia," the "common man," the "noble savage." The same
can be said about the topos of Russia as a country and culture "in between."
The ambiguity allowed everyone to identify and to construct his or her own
Russia, the "Other." Russia the "Other" was simultaneously the holy, the Asiatic, the barbarian, the simple, and the enigmatic. Nazi ideologues profited not
least from this overwhelming elasticity by exploiting the multiple commonplace
images of Russia. But these images were open to evolve, as they later did, in
a racist direction, open to degrees of brutalization and dehumanization that
were unthinkable before 1933, even within the most conservative of political
circles.

THE RUSSIAN-GERMAN CONNECTION: PREHISTORY, GENEALOGY, AND AGENTS

In order to understand how the ideological background for the perception and
production of images of Soviet Russia in the 1930s was shaped, it is necessary
to go back to the formative years – that is, to the time before 1914–1917 and,
certainly, before 1933.

Ilya Ehrenburg, commuting between Moscow and Berlin, coined the phrase
that Berlin and Moscow belonged to *eine Zeitheimat*: that is to say, Berliners
and Muscovites were embedded in the same and simultaneous experiences –
two different hometowns but the same "hometime."[57] This "common ground"
is the precondition for all further analysis. In order best to characterize the high
degree and intensity of cooperation and rivalry, however, an even stronger term
may be appropriate: "negative intimacy" in the European framework of "war
and revolution." The following is an abbreviated account of why German-
Russian relations were probably the most intense between any European powers in the period 1914–1945.

LINKS AND NETWORKS UNDER THE OLD REGIMES – THE PREHISTORY OF
1914–1917. For centuries, the "German connection" was an intensive one,
both culturally and economically, even in the last decades before the outbreak

---

[57] Ilya Ehrenburg in *Visum der Zeit* (Leipzig: P. List, 1929), 70.

of the Great War. Big German companies (Siemens, Schuckert, AEG, Orenstein, and Koppel, and others) very actively promoted the modernization and industrialization of the Russian empire.[58] Elements of *longue durée* include the impact of German language and culture in Russia. There was a clear and recognizable German element in certain occupation groups, such as pharmacists, engineers, craftsmen, brewers, and publishers. There were important communities of Germans as subjects of the tsar and large groups of German "expats." Many of these conducted their studies in Germany; others went for recreation to German spas. There were strong and influential German minorities along the Volga River, in the Black Sea region, on the Crimea, and in the Caucasus. There was a strong orientation of Russian democratic movements toward the German Social Democrats. This impressive network was disrupted by World War I and the Russian revolution. This physical, organizational, and mental network can be illustrated in many ways. (Lenin's enthusiasm for the German Post as an example of advanced modern organization and logistics is a good instance.) The result is that the image of Russia existing in the interwar period had been created in the prewar period, all images rooted in the prerevolutionary, imperial space. All actors of the interwar period – on the left or on the right – were products of this prehistory. This is a very important point. These old-line elites were challenged, in both postwar Germany and Russia, by the rising classes of the new "movements": by upwardly mobile groupings inspired by the national-revolutionary idea in Germany and by the new cohorts of the *vydvizhentsy* in the Soviet Union. In the 1930s, a turnover of elites in both countries took place in diplomacy, party politics, and academia.[59]

THE GREAT WAR – CHAOS AND REVOLUTION. Germany and Russia had a joint and parallel experience of war, revolution, and civil war. Millions of Russians and Germans fought in the eastern battlefields, some for months, and some for years. Millions came into contact with the other country and its people as occupation forces or in POW camps. Tens of thousands took part in the domestic struggles and civil war. World War I was called the German War; the occupied zone was called *Land Oberost*. *Land Oberost* is a kind of German *lieu de mémoire*. The war in the eastern lands was the central experience of an entire generation of young and not so young men. The war made thousands of young men pacifists and revolutionaries, not by theory but by disillusionment. An entire generation of leading central European communists developed in Russian POW camps – Karel Capek, Ernst Reuter (the mayor of West Berlin after World War II), Josip Broz Tito, Bela Kun, and many, many others. The Eastern Front and the Russian Civil War became a school of radicalization

---

[58] On German entrepreneurs and their privileged position in Russia, see the catalogue by Dittmar Dahlmann et al., eds., *"Eine grosse Zukunft": Deutsche in Russlands Wirtschaft* (Berlin: Reschke & Steffens, 2000).

[59] Karl Schlögel, "Nikolai Krestinski, and Graf von der Schulenburg: Diplomatie als Verrat," in *Berlin, Ostbahnhof Europas: Russen und Deutsche in ihrem Jahrhundert* (Berlin: Siedler, 1998), 177–99.

and military education on both sides: for communists and sympathizers with Soviet Russia and for the hard-core White Russian and Freicorps members, for the "Baltikumer" and others. For many Germans, the sites of events of the German civil war in 1918–23 were almost directly connected to Europe's most important site of revolutionary events in this period, Russia. The activists of the Russian October moved to the stage of the German October, and vice versa. An entire generation had been educated and shaped by war and revolution between 1914 and 1923. We can find the echo of this experience in a vast corpus of literature of the 1920s and 1930s.[60]

THE COMPLEX OF THE HUMILIATED AND EXCLUDED – ANTI-POLISH AND ANTI-WESTERN REVISIONISM. Both empires fell apart during World War I. This raises questions: How does one live with the collapse of a centuries-old order? How does one live with deep national humiliation, especially when accompanied by economic crisis and breakdown? Brest-Litovsk, Versailles, new borders, disintegration of the state, the collapse of the old elites, the question of responsibility and guilt, theories of conspiracy, phobias of encirclement, the fear of "fifth columns," international discrimination. How could Russia and Germany cope with this hopeless situation? There was, in the eyes of many of the interwar generation, one negative experience – Brest-Litovsk and Versailles – and there was one positive experience – Rapallo and the Molotov-Ribbentrop treaty of 23 August 1939. Both events were rooted in deeply anti-Western sentiments. Two different forms of *ressentiment* against the West, as embodied in the victorious alliance at the Paris peace conferences, coexisted: German "Kultur" against French and British "civilization," and Russian "revolutionary spirit" against the commercialized and pragmatic materialism of "the West."[61]

ROMANTICS AND NOSTALGIA FROM THE LEFT AND, ESPECIALLY, FROM THE RIGHT. The general perception is that only Germans of the extreme left were enthusiastic about the "fatherland of the working class." But it seems clear now that being pro-Russian and pro-Soviet was, if not the mainstream feeling, nevertheless widespread among German conservatives, even at the reactionary end of the political spectrum. Germany and Russia were "fortresses" against modernity, Westernism, and liberalism. The "leftists on the right" (Otto Ernst Schüddekopf), that is, the representatives of the conservative and national-Bolshevist revolution, were, in many respects, more pro-Soviet than their fellow political travelers on the left.[62] For people from the extreme left to the extreme right, from communists to national-Bolsheviks, Soviet Russia was, in many ways, a projection screen for fantasizing about a new Germany.[63]

---

[60] Norman Stone, *The Eastern Front, 1914–1917*; Vejas Gabriel Ljulevicius, op. cit.

[61] On "twofold revisionism," see Gerd Koenen, *Der Russland-Komplex: Die Deutschen und der Osten 1900–1945* (München: Beck, 2005), 277–300

[62] Otto Ernst Schüddekopf, *Linke Leute von rechts: Die national-revolutionären Minderheiten und der Kommunismus in der Weimarer Republik* (Stuttgart: Kohlhammer, 1960).

[63] Besides Schüddekopf, see Hans Hecker, *Die Tat und ihr Osteuropa-Bild, 1909–1939* (Cologne: Wissenschaft und Politik, 1974); Karl Nötzel, *Die Grundlagen des geistigen Rußland: Versuch einer Psychologie des russischen Geisteslebens* (Jena: E. Diederichs, 1917); Waldemar Gurian, *Der Bolschewismus* (Freiburg i. Br., Herder, 1931); Rolf Günter Renner, "Grundzüge und

BETWEEN MODERNITY AND ANTIMODERNISM, OPEN SPACES, TRANSITIONS. The period after World War I represented a time of transition, improvisation, dissolution, and, at the same time, invention of traditions. This experience concerns both countries, especially the urban centers and the metropolitan cultures. It was a time of radical acceleration of upward social mobility and, at the same time, of fragmentation of the old elites. It is true that despite all the differences between the two countries, there was an amazing degree of parallels. Weimar Germany and the Russia of the NEP were the staging grounds of a world in flux. There were great societal debates on initiating a new age and trying to find new paths out of decay and crisis: debates on the rational organization of the work process (Fordism and non-Fordism), on production and recreation, on work and housing, on new forms of urban life, on garden cities and deurbanization. There were the takeoff of sociology (mostly in the form of Marxism), new questions about organization as science, and the scientification of all questions. We find in both societies all the elements of a radicalized rationality: the idea of the New Man created by health, hygiene, and the rational organization of life; the notion of the trained and beautiful body; the idea of the death of belles lettres and the birth of *literatura fakta*, that is, factology and information instead of bourgeois novels; the rationalistic and functionalistic dream of "form follows function." In short, the collapse of the old order was followed by the impressive takeoff of a self-assertive and self-conscious modernity, mostly limited, of course, to very small circles, but not exclusively.[64] The path to this modernity had been paved long before the First World War, but modernity had now come to the surface thanks to the total collapse of the old order. The project of creating a new world had crossed national borders. There was a certain style – international, cosmopolitan, rationalistic, antitraditionalistic. Even the successors and enemies of this modernity – Fascism, National Socialism, and Stalinism – had to pay their tribute to this main trend if they wanted to succeed.

EUROPE AS A FIELD OF INTERFERENCE. We are not only talking about the sophisticated ideas of isolated intellectuals. There were very strong social groups identifying themselves with these experiences and experiments. There was a spirit, a style, a way of life, a "Zeitgeist."[65] The main actors of the interwar period were children of the prewar period – both revolutionaries and counterrevolutionaries. They include Germans from the former Russian empire; Baltic Germans as mediators and experts on Russian affairs; soldiers and military men; radicalized prisoners of war; members of the Freicorps; the large numbers of Russian agents in the domestic German clashes in the Ruhr region, Hamburg, and Berlin; the radicalized parts of the working class, especially among youths; and members of the prewar elite in diplomacy, politics, and

Voraussetzungen deutscher literarischer Rußlandbilder während des Dritten Reiches," in *Das Rußlandbild im Dritten Reich*, 387–419.

[64] See Marshall Berman's seminal book on modernity, *All That Is Solid Melts into Air: The Experience of Modernity* (New York: Penguin Books, 1988).

[65] Eckhard John, *Musikbolschewismus: Die Politisierung der Musik in Deutschland 1918–1938*.

culture. Domestic and international conflicts were interwoven. The rejection of Versailles's Europe, territorial revisionism, and class war established a link between Russia and Germany. All domestic parties were tied to external questions, supporters, and powers. This was important everywhere (there was the "Red Scare" in Great Britain and in the United States), but nowhere did it go as deeply as in Germany. For German communists, the Soviet Union functioned as a substitute for the revolution that had failed at home. The "Fatherland of the toiling masses" was a kind of hinterland for the "community of despair" (R. C. Williams). Unsurprisingly, the KPD was accused of being the vehicle of social upheaval, directed by a foreign power. German communists did not succeed in making their own revolution, though they played "German October" in 1923. There was much talk about the "Bolshevizing" of political parties and "Sovietization" of work; there was even the duplication of the conflicts and factions of the Soviet party. Germany had its "own" Trotsky, its own Bukharin, and its own Stalin. There was in fact a Stalinization of the German Communist Party, but it came mostly from inside and not from outside.[66] German communists nourished their hopes in analogies and parallels. The Papen government was to repeat the fate of Kerenskii's provisional government. The image of the Soviet Union was largely a function of internal clashes, and it was instrumental in the struggle against the internal class enemy. The pictures and newsreels of collectivization, from the Baltic-Belomor Canal, from Solovki, from activities of the OGPU, and so forth, had a firm place in the German mediascape. It would be interesting to know how, on the Soviet side, the German image became instrumental for Russian internal conflicts (for example, the dialogue between Vyshinskii and Bukharin at the Moscow trial on subtle details of the German language – the meaning of *sollen*).[67]

It is very important to keep in mind that all this took place in an extremely short period of, say, twenty to thirty years – less than a life span. That means that men who served in World War I went on duty a second time in World War II. (Dwinger's book on the invasion of 22 June 1941 is called *Wiedersehen mit Russland*.)[68]

FORGING THE IMAGES: THE BERLIN-RUSSIA CONNECTION

Berlin is the place where all of this comes together, where we can study the production process of the images that turned into lethal weapons in ideological

---

[66] Hermann Weber, *Die Wandlung des deutschen Kommunismus: Die Stalinisierung der KPD in der Weimarer Republik* (Frankfurt am Main: Europäische Verlagsanstalt, 1969).

[67] The semantics of the German word sollen were discussed at the 1938 Moscow show trial between Vyshinskii and Bukharin. See *Prozessbericht über die Strafsache des antisowjetischen "Blocks der Rechten und Trotzkisten," verhandelt vor dem Militärkollegium des Obersten Gerichtshofes der UdSSR vom 2. Bis 13. März 1938* (Moscow: Volkskommissariat für Justizwesen der UdSSR, 1938), 474.

[68] Edwin Erich Dwinger, *Wiedersehen mit Sowjetrußland: Tagebuch vom Ostfeldzug* (Jena: E. Diederichs, 1943).

and military warfare against Soviet Russia.[69] In the 1920s, much was still in the making, in flux, open-ended, not yet clear.

BERLIN – A PLACE OF HIGH-DENSITY CULTURAL EXCHANGE. All actors, activities, processes of concern took place and took shape here. The participants were diplomats, officers and rank and file, party leaders and party members, high culture, émigrés, undercover agents, intelligence people, experts on Russia, Baltic Germans, former *franctireurs*, Freicorps, ex-Red Guards, right-wing terrorists, party apparatchiki, institutions of persecution and repression, the entire urban fabric that weaves all this together.[70]

ALL TOPICS AND ASPECTS CONCERNED ARE MIXED UP. The image of Russia was present in all of its various dimensions: as a lost and inaccessible economic space; the other Russia of the exiled; the official representation of the USSR as a vanguard of the world revolution; the Russia of subversion and espionage; the Russia of Vladimir Nabokov and Prince Iusupov; Russia as a main power to help to fight the system of Versailles; the Russia of great economic prospects (*Russengeschäfte*, Russian deals); the Russia of the Jewish refugees; the Russia of the false princess and future Hollywood celebrity Anastasia; the Russia of serious scholars and of obsessive, even obscurantist experts on Russia, inundating Germany with a flood of anti-Soviet brochures and leaflets; Russia as a destination for innovative and talented artists and architects; Russia as a center and stimulus for urban planning, for reform of the penitentiary system, for new ways of organizing life and work, for the equality of men and women, for new theater, new education, and new aesthetics. Russia not only represented a source of inspiration for many talented intellectuals, but found a broader audience, especially among the young, and not just among communist youths (youth movements like *Wandervogel*, where the *Balalaika* and the *Russenbluse* were popular accessories). This "Russkii Berlin" was a place ranking among the most prominent and most contested sites of European culture in the first half of the twentieth century.

BERLIN AS THE SITE OF ANTAGONISM, POLARIZATION, AND CIVIL WAR. All antagonisms in Germany and especially in the German capital had a way of being pro- or anti-Soviet, pro- or anti-Russian, because Soviet Russia was not only a country among others, but the alternative, a different way of life, which provoked sympathy or opposition. Almost all crucial questions were discussed in reference or in opposition to Russia: right against left, Freicorps against communists, Russian émigrés against Soviet diplomats, and Russian monarchists against Russian Jews. (It would be interesting to compare this somewhat strange state of affairs to the situation in other countries like France, the United States,

[69] Irina Antonowa and Jörn Merkert, eds., *Berlin-Moskau 1900–1950, Ausstellungskatalog* (Munich and New York: Prestel, 1995).
[70] For studies on the Berlin-Russia connection see Karl Schlögel, *Berlin, Ostbahnhof Europas* (Berlin: Siedler, 1998), 2nd enlarged ed., *Das russische Berlin: Ostbahnhof Europas* (Munich: Hanser, 2007); Ulrich Fauré, *Im Knotenpunkt des Weltverkehrs: Herzfelde, Heartfield, Grosz und der Malik-Verlag, 1916–1947* (Berlin: Aufbau Verlag, 1992).

or England.) There were positions bridging these antagonisms: the Reichswehr, which cooperated with the Red Army; the émigrés who worked in the Soviet embassy; the monarchists, who supported their Soviet Russian ally in order to destroy the second Polish republic. It was Andrey Belyi who articulated his feeling in Berlin as "boom-boom" coming soon.[71] This was the sound of the anticipated civil war. But no one could seriously anticipate the images of 9 May 1945 in Berlin-Karlshorst, when German generals signed the surrender of German military power.

CONTINUITY AND DISCONTINUITY: THE NAZI IMAGE OF RUSSIA

The images of Russia in Nazi Germany reflected both the internal radicalization of the Nazi movement in Germany and developments inside Soviet Russia. The mass media covered Russia well. Before 1933 there were news reports on the trials against the engineers of Metro-Vickers, the Woltscht-Kinderman incident, the trials against the Mensheviks and Shakhty, and the repression of bourgeois specialists. A brilliant expertise existed among Menshevik émigrés (*Sotsialisticheskii vestnik*) writing for German newspapers and among German journalists (Arthur Feiler, Paul Scheffer, and others). There were eyewitnesses who had just returned from Russia, where they had worked. Their image was different from that of the KPD press or the media of the procommunist Münzenberg media complex. All major events found a large audience and readership:

• Forced collectivization was published in reports, even with pictures, and monitored by experts in the German embassy and consulates in the country, who at that time could move quite freely within the country.[72]
• Reports about the persecution of believers and religious groups, who suffered most from the militant campaigns of communist youths in the late 1920s and early 1930s, had a great impact on the German image of Russia. The religious media especially acted very politically and were full of news, eyewitness reports, and solidarity messages.[73]
• The persecution and repression of bourgeois scholars and experts were taken very seriously by their academic counterparts in Germany.[74]
• The great Moscow trials had significant impact, although difficulties existed in giving them a proper interpretation. Who was accusing whom of what?

[71] Andrej Belyj [Andrei Belyi], *Im Reich der Schatten: Berlin 1921 bis 1923* (Frankfurt am Main: Insel, 1987), 40.
[72] For reports with photographs on collectivization, see Ewald Ammende, *Muß Rußland hungern?: Menschen- und Völkerschicksale in der Sowjetunion* (Vienna: Braumüller, 1935); Hans von Herwarth, *Zwischen Hitler und Stalin, Erlebte Zeitgeschichte 1931 bis 1945*.
[73] Cf. Kurt Meier, "Sowjetrußland im Urteil der evangelischen Kirche (1917–1945)," and Herbert Smolinsky, "Das katholische Rußlandbild in Deutschland nach dem Ersten Weltkrieg und im Dritten Reich," in *Das Russlandbild im Dritten Reich*, 285–322, 323–56.
[74] On Hoetzsch, Platonov, Tarle, and others, see Zh. I. Alferov, V. P. Leonov, eds., *Akademicheskoe delo 1929–1931 gg.*, 2 vols. (St. Petersburg, Biblioteka Rossiiskoi akademiia nauk, 1998).

Yet, this difficulty was not confined to the German Nazi-controlled press. There was an atmosphere of irritation, intimidation, and enigma, especially concerning the execution of the military leadership in the summer of 1937. Many of these military officers, who had previously visited Germany, were accused of being German spies. The media coverage had multiple effects, among which were the disorientation and demoralization of the remaining communists and sympathizers with Soviet Russia.[75]

- One event that historians have had difficulty handling is the nonaggression treaty of August of 1939 between Germany and the Soviet Union, signed the week before the Wehrmacht invaded Poland. It requires separate, in-depth analysis beyond the well-known and spectacular quotations in which Stalin and the USSR were praised, and vice versa. Other memorable events include the theatrical production of *Ivan Susanin* in Berlin and Eisenstein's staging of Wagner's *Die Walkyrie* in Moscow. And for many – perhaps most – the treaty signaled the return to the rational and traditional pro-Russian policy that Bismarck had once pursued.

The Nazi-controlled press in Germany tended to interpret the great purges and general developments under Stalin's leadership as "healthy nationalism," directed against the "Jewish leadership" of early Bolshevism, whereas Trotskyites were accused of being agents of fascism by the Stalinist leadership. Many brochures intended for a mass audience as well as exhibitions were dedicated to the "Jewish question." These mass publications identified Jews among the leadership, referring to their Jewish family names (for example, "Litvinov-Wallach") and very often caricaturing them to demonstrate the "Jewish physiognomy of Russia's elite."[76]

It is less clear, however, how other aspects of Soviet life were perceived in Nazi Germany, especially aspects of the "great leap forward," such as large-scale construction sites, the grand designs of exploring and exploiting, the reconstruction of Moscow and other cities, and the redesigning of public spaces. And there are many other open questions, such as how Arno Brecker appreciated the sculptures of his colleague and rival Vera Mukhina, how Boris Iofan's project for the Palace of Soviets was perceived by Albert Speer, and what impact the example of the Palace of Soviets had for the planning of the Reichshauptstadt Germania.

A broader question is this: What is the relation between pre-1933 and post-1933 images of Soviet Russia? In other words, is there a direct path from typically *German* images and prejudices to the *Nazi* image of the "Slavic Subhuman" (*Untermensch*)? There is a striking continuity in the German rhetoric of *Kulturträgertum* with respect to Russia, but there is no direct path from German or European superiority discourses to the *Untermenschen* rhetoric of

---

[75] Manfred Zeidler, "Das Bild der Wehrmacht von Rußland und der Roten Armee zwischen 1933 und 1939," in Hans-Erich Volkmann, *Das Russlandbild im Dritten Reich*, 105–23.

[76] Rudolf Kommoss on Kaganovich's role, see Kommoss, 34.

the Nazi Party. There were stereotypes of Russians in Germany to which most Germans, even educated ones, adhered: Russians as *Naturmenschen*; Russians as *Kollektivwesen* and *vermasst*; the rhetoric about the radical replacement of the elites in the Russian revolution; and the disproportionately high contribution of non-Russian nationalities to the revolutionary movement and the establishment of power, and so forth.

But no direct path existed between the distinct sense of superiority and unconscious Eurocentrism (related to Western or Central Europe) of the German elites and, especially, of the petit bourgeois and working-class masses to the racist contempt for and hatred of all Russians during the Nazi period. There was a difference between the "usual" arrogance of Germans toward Russians and racist hatred, including dehumanizing rhetoric and genocidal practices against so-called *Untermenschen*. The Nazis exploited the deeply anti-Russian or anti-Slav sentiments of the wider population, but their racist idea of the inferiority of the Slavs was distinct. These racist ideas, combined with a tendency to regard human beings as mere "raw material" (*Rohmaterial*), provided the Nazis' legitimation for their extermination practices. This racial and racist doctrine played its role at the moment when Nazi Germany crossed the Bug River. Extermination war, starving to death of hundreds of thousands of POWs, the calculated death of millions in a very short time, and the systematic mass murder of the Soviet Jews should be understood as all of one piece.[77] The war that started on 22 June 1941 opened a new and unprecedented chapter not only in the history of modern warfare and crimes against humanity, but also in relations between Germany and Russia.[78]

---

[77] Relevant for the perception by army personnel is *Ich sah den Bolschewismus: Dokumente der Wahrheit gegen die bolschewistische Lüge: Thüringer Soldaten schreiben an ihren Gauleiter und Reichsstatthalter* (Weimar: Der Nationalsozialist, 1942); Hans Joachim Schröder, "Erfahrungen deutscher Mannschaftssoldaten während der ersten Phase des Rußlandkrieges," in Bernd Wegner, ed., *Zwei Wege nach Moskau: Vom Hitler-Stalin-Pakt zum "Unternehmen Barbarossa"* (Munich and Zürich: Piper, 1991), 309–25; Heinz Boberach, ed., *Meldungen aus dem Reich 1938–1945: Die geheimen Lageberichte des Sicherheitsdienstes der SS* (Herrsching: Pawlak, 1984); Peter Jahn and Reinhard Rürup, eds., *Erobern und Vernichten: Der Krieg gegen die Sowjetunion* (Berlin: Argon, 1991); Andreas Hillgruber, "Das Rußland-Bild der führenden deutschen Militärs vor Beginn des Angriffs auf die Sowjetunion," in *Das Rußlandbild im Dritten Reich*, 125–63; Jürgen Förster, "Zum Rußlandbild der Militärs 1941–1945," in *Das Rußlandbild im Dritten Reich*, 141–63; Peter P. Knoch, "Das Bild des russischen Feinds," in Wolfram Wette and Gerd R. Ueberschär, eds., *Stalingrad: Mythos und Wirklichkeit einer Schlacht* (Frankfurt am Main: Fischer Taschenbuch Verlag, 1992); Roland Foerster, ed., *"Unternehmen Barbarossa": Zum historischen Ort der deutsch-sowjetischen Beziehungen von 1933 bis Herbst 1941* (Paderborn: F. Schöningh, 1993); Ortwin Buchbender, *Das tönende Erz: Deutsche Propaganda gegen die Rote Armee im Zweiten Weltkrieg* (Stuttgart: Seewald Verlag, 1978); Ernst Klee Willi Dreßen, and Volker Rieß, eds., *"Gott mit uns": Der deutsche Vernichtungskrieg im Osten, 1939–1945* (Frankfurt am Main: S. Fischer, 1989); Wolfram Wette, "Die propagandistische Begleitmusik zum Überfall auf die Sowjetunion 1941," in Gerd R. Ueberschär and Wolfram Wette, eds., *Der deutsche Überfall auf die Sowjetunion: "Unternehmen Barbarossa" 1941* (Frankfurt am Main: Fischer Taschenbuch Verlag, 1991).

[78] Omer Bartov, *The Eastern Front, 1941–1945: German Troops and the Barbarisation of Warfare* (Basingstoke: Palgrave, 2001).

The more these practises developed, the more the idea of Russia the "Other" resurfaced – for example, in memoranda, protests, and interventions inside and outside the Wehrmacht – especially after the fierce resistance of the Red Army and the population became evident and the plans for Blitzkrieg in Russia had failed. Once again the sentimental cliché of the brave and patriotic private "Ivan" came into circulation. But, as we know, there were different plans for defeating Russia: with the support of the Russians themselves and with the support of non-Russian nationalities, getting support from collaborators, building up a military force (for example, the Vlasov army), and so forth.[79] Hitler's image of Russia was not only obsessive, racially motivated, and obscurantist. It was also, concurrently, a function of his struggle to keep power at any price. Extermination was not only a result of a cumulative radicalization but also a matter of deliberate policy to create a point of no return and to burn the bridges at one's back, with Europe in ruins and one's own nation as hostage.

THE GERMAN IMAGE OF RUSSIA

In Nazi Germany, the image of Russia was a *mixtum compositum*. This image was a function of German political struggles and, thus a construction, a very selective and instrumental perception of facts and experiences connected to Russian reality. The emergence of this image was highly dramatic because internal and external conflicts became intensively interwoven. Nowhere else was the network between Russia and the outside world as dense and intensive as in prewar Germany. The images of Russia in Nazi Germany were deeply rooted in the pre-1914 world and in the experience of the postwar and postrevolution chaos. There was a common ground for images of Russia and Germany: namely, the experience of war, revolution, and civil war. That means that further research and discussion should be placed in a European framework, the texture of which can be termed *Katastrophenzusammenhang Europa* (the conjuncture of European catastrophe). There are some sites where this can be studied more closely than elsewhere. One of these sites is Berlin; another one is certainly Moscow (or Budapest, or Vienna). And, of course, there is no Berlin-Moscow connection without Rome, and no Russian-German discourse without Italian fascism. These were the sites of synchronized historical experience of an entire epoch (*Synchronisierung von Epochenerfahrung*). The National Socialist image of Russia was not the logical result of nineteenth-century prejudices, but something new, aimed at the establishment of a new type of racial state.

For future analyses, it may be of value to leave aside, at least to some extent, comparisons between Russia and Germany, in order to move toward a genetic reconstruction of the interplay of all the actors of the European theater of war and revolution in the core period of 1914 to 1945. All of the aspects discussed have European dimensions and European implications.

---

[79] On the Vlasov army, see Catherine Andreyev, *Vlasov and the Russian Liberation Movement* (Cambridge: Cambridge University Press, 1987).

Although Germany and Russia, as the epicenters, may remain at the center of analysis, all aspects go beyond national historiography: the collapse of empires; the drawing of new borders; irredentism and revisionism; the instability of the newly established orders; the search for modernity or for an escape from modernity; social revolution; accelerated upward mobility; exile and forced migration; the globalization of class conflicts (*Komintern*); and ethnic struggles (the minority problems in the League of Nations). We should pay tribute to what nation-to-nation comparison can give us, but we should move ahead to a method of contextualization, of remapping the European landscape of war and revolution. That does not necessarily mean national comparison, but reconstruction of the European dimension of almost all relevant processes and projects, especially communism and fascism.

THE SOVIET IMAGE OF NAZI GERMANY

To a marked degree both Soviet Russia and Nazi Germany viewed each other and composed their image of each other in terms of their putative roles in an epic struggle for "Europe." However, Soviet analyses of Nazi Germany generally avoided ethnic essentialism, largely preferring to attribute contemporary Germany's ills to Nazism, although in other key respects, its image of Nazi Germany was comparable to the Nazi image of the Soviet Union.

Soviet rhetoric characteristically dealt in Manichaean binaries (us/them) with a hyperbolically positive account of "us" and a hyperbolically negative account of "them," and the Nazi regime gave politicians and journalists ample material for this. During the 1930s in almost every Soviet account of Nazi Germany, it figured implicitly or explicitly as the opposite of their country. But in this instance the two sides of the us/them binary (Soviet/Nazi) corresponded roughly to a key Nazi contrast between the Bolsheviks and *themselves*, though, needless to say, the positive and negative colorations of the two poles of the Nazi binary have been reversed. In effect, each country developed a model for the other which was virtually a mirror image of that of its rival; that which was represented as positive in one side's account of the contrast between themselves and the other was presented in hyperbolically negative terms in the other, and vice versa. Each of these regimes thereby dismissed the other's country as primitive and backward, even "barbaric,"[80] thereby claiming superiority for themselves as more rational and organized. In other words, the debate over which country had the right to lead in Europe was partly about which one was the more modernized, but only partly. The specific way each regime articulated its backward/progressive binary is telling. In deploying these binaries, spokesmen for the two regimes pinpointed critical differences in their respective value systems and cultural practices.

---

[80] Goebbels, for example, spoke of the "furchtbarste Barbarei" of the Bolshevik "Untermensch" ("Die Rede von Goebbels in Nürnberg," in *Ausgewählte Reden des Führers und seiner Mitarbeiten, 1937* [Munich and Berlin: Zentralverlag der NSDAP, 1937], 122).

Here it must be quickly noted that not all coverage of Nazi Germany in the Soviet press and culture was structured by this binary. Moreover, the binaries do not of course necessarily have much to do with actualities; they were simply useful heuristic devices deployed by the two regimes for purposes of agitation. Nevertheless, the Soviet binary I am adducing here was fundamental to its image of Nazi Germany. In most of the Soviet press of the 1930s, Nazi Germany was not a major preoccupation (in terms of editorials, lead articles, etc.) until shortly before the Second World War. The central press was somewhat parochial and preoccupied largely with such topics as sowing and harvesting crops, production heroes, and construction projects, as well as the trials and purges. To be sure there were foreign news bulletins and some commentary on foreign affairs, both of which provided readers with a sense of the rising menace of fascism, and that topic became a standard item in speeches by the Bolshevik leaders. Also, at the show trials, the accused were generally alleged to be involved in a conspiracy with fascist agents, but most of that was presented in very general and formulaic terms.

In the press, there were three main kinds of treatment of Nazi Germany. Firstly, there were news items that tended to minimize Nazism's rising power and significance, recurrently reporting some economic crisis dooming the Nazi regime and widespread worker dissatisfaction there.[81] An even more common topic was the repressive character of the Nazi regime under such recurring rubrics as "The Atrocities [*zverstva*] in Germany" or "Fascist Terror in Germany." Item after item reported mass arrests, confiscation of the property of leftists, beatings, torture, and imprisonment of dissidents in concentration camps (particularly of communists),[82] implicitly dissociating the Soviet Union from such practices. Such reports periodically proclaimed triumphantly that the Communist Party of Germany was, despite all, thriving in the underground.[83] As in the West, however, much of the venom for representing the Nazis was reserved for a second category of representation, caricatures, published especially in *Krokodil*, but also in places like *Pravda*. A typical one from *Pravda* shows a bloated Nazi in jackboots, with hair protruding through his uniform over his rear end, suggesting a bestiality that could not be covered up entirely.[84]

The caricature of the Nazi, that depicted him as sinister or more likely as subhuman, presents somewhat predictable images. Consequently, our coverage here does not deal with crude representations of the Nazis such as are found in *Krokodil*, but rather with serious, theoretically informed analyses of the Nazi regime that appeared in the Soviet press and in cultural products. The press critiques of German fascism that most prominently and thoroughly contest its

---

[81] E.g., "Golod i nishcheta v fashistskoi Germanii," *Pravda*, July 6, 1935.

[82] These two rubrics were actually in *Izvestiia*. Note: As early as 1933, the Soviet Union published Hans Beimler, *V lagere smerti – Dakhau: Chetyre nedeli v rukakh korichnevykh banditov* (Moscow: Kooperativnoe izdatel'stvo inostrannykh rabochikh v SSSR, 1933).

[83] E.g., "'Govorit Krasnaia volna' . . . Epizod iz germanskogo podpol'ia," *Vecherniaia Moskva*, 27 July 1935.

[84] Bor. Efimov, "Chto napisano perom, to mozhno vyrubit' toporom!," *Pravda*, March 4, 1935.

right to claim leadership in Europe were largely written by a fairly small number of highly cultivated Bolshevik and fellow-traveler intellectuals, most with
some association with the Comintern, a knowledge of German, and familiarity
with German culture – Karl Radek, at one time head of propaganda in the
Comintern, who frequently published in *Pravda* or *Izvestiia* on the subject;
Mikhail Koltsov, the *Pravda* journalist, Soviet publishing magnate, head of the
Foreign Commission of the Writers Union (after it was founded in 1935),[85]
and Soviet emissary to the international antifascist movement; the Paris-based
writer Ilya Ehrenburg, likewise a Soviet emissary to the international antifascist
movement and special correspondent for *Izvestiia*; and Nikolai Bukharin, the
Party leader and from 1934 editor of *Izvestiia*. As one will recognize, all but
Ehrenburg in this group were purged some time between 1936 and 1938. After
approximately 1937–8 when the Soviet Union became decidedly less internationalist, the coverage shifted and became less sophisticated (factors bearing on
this shift include the demise of the Popular Front and of the Republican side in
the Spanish Civil War).

Soviet spokesmen were not however the main sources on Nazi Germany in
the press. That role was fulfilled by Germanophone intellectual refugees from
fascism, some of whom had moved to Soviet Russia while others had relocated
to France, Switzerland, America, and other sites of the diaspora. After March
1933 a (largely pro-Soviet) selection of these exiles contributed many articles
and literary works to such central organs as *Pravda*, *Izvestiia*, *Literaturnaia
gazeta*, and Koltsov's *Ogonek*. These exiles also had outlets in Moscow-based
German language periodicals, the newspaper *Deutsche Zentral-Zeitung*, and
the journals *Internationale Literatur* (*Deutsche Blätter*) and *Das Wort* (founded
1936), where they published a greater number of critiques and descriptions
of Nazi Germany. Generally the articles that appeared in Russian language
periodicals were translations of this material, often in abbreviated form.[86]
Additionally, many literary or publicity books by Germanophone authors were
published in translation, in some instances with huge print runs; several of these
texts became very popular with the Soviet reader.

Not surprisingly then, a great deal of overlap existed between the images
of the Soviet Union in the texts of the German and Soviet contributors. The
German texts generally included more specific material on Nazi Germany, but
a relatively common line can be found in both sources.

The Soviet image of Nazi Germany was in large measure created both by
anti-Nazi German intellectuals and by highly sophisticated and cosmopolitan
Soviet intellectuals who associated with them. In that, then, both used a similar
catalogue of clichés, making it difficult to ascertain what is specifically Soviet

---

[85] It is to be noted that the Foreign Commission's predecessor, MORP (the International Society
of Revolutionary Writers), reported to the Comintern.
[86] *Internationale Literatur* had a Russian-language version, as well as editions in French, English,
and, later, Spanish and Chinese.

about any image presented. The two categories of authors cannot in any case be seen as absolutely distinct in that almost every German refugee in Soviet Russia was a Communist (only Party members were granted entry, and then not all). Moreover, before the Nazi takeover German leftist intellectuals were to a large extent participating in the same field of discourse as their Soviet counterparts, particularly those associated with the Comintern. Germans after all invented Marxism, and German and Russian Marxists had always considered themselves part of, or rival claimants for, *the* international Marxist movement. In the late Weimar period, this Soviet-German discursive field provided the context for some of the major Soviet statements on ideology and culture, right down to Stalin's canonical letter to *Proletarskaia revoliutsiia* of December 1931.[87] Many leftist intellectuals in both countries did not at that time regard Soviet culture as a separate entity and saw themselves as part of a transnational, cosmopolitan, and leftist culture. Also, as Karl Schlögel has shown in *Berlin, Ostbahnhof Europas*, by the early thirties "Red Berlin" was essentially a city within a city, a complete Communist world with even its own schools, and a world whose citizens frequently shuttled back and forth to Moscow.[88] Karl Radek, one of the leading Bolshevik commentators on the Nazis, was fluent in German and had spent time in Berlin in the early twenties.

The image of Nazi Germany was not, however, created exclusively within the Communist-cum-Comintern world; several non-Communist German intellectuals who lived in exile outside the Soviet Union were also influential formulators of the image of Nazi Germany presented in Soviet Russia. To some extent, then, the "Soviet" image of Nazi Germany came from the German antifascist intellectual milieu, though in Soviet versions this image had a marked Bolshevik inflection.

FROM CLASS WAR TO CULTURE WAR: IMAGINING GERMANY AFTER THE NAZI TAKEOVER OF POWER

An initial response of the Soviet Communists and their German sympathizers to the Nazi takeover had been to write it off as a new phase in the development of the class war. Nazism was represented as the inevitable outcome of capitalism; by this account, as the bourgeoisie found itself ever more threatened by the rising proletariat it had to resort to nationalist demagoguery and ever more repressive means (send in the thugs).[89] The Nazis, then, were the agents of big capital. The underlying motive for their accession to power was seen as a desire for class revenge against an increasingly uppity proletariat. This position was

---

[87] I. V. Stalin, *O nekotorykh voprosakh istorii bol'shevizma: Pis'mo v redaktsiiu zhurnala "Proletarskaia revoliutsiia"* (Moscow: Moskovskii rabochii, 1931).

[88] Karl Schloegel, *Berlin, Ostbahnhof Europas*.

[89] E.g., Frits Gekkert, "Chlen TsK kommunisticheskoi partii Germanii, "Chto proiskhodit v Germanii?" *Pravda*, 12 April 1933.

recurrently advanced in Party rhetoric and sources such as *Pravda*, but more elaborated versions were in fact produced by German Communists.[90]

This analysis in class terms was largely abandoned in the era of the Popular Front (from approximately 1935), when there was an attempt to set up a transnational, transclass, and trans-Party bloc of opposition to the fascists. Increasingly, another of the existing critiques of Nazi Germany, our subject here, was foregrounded to provide the dominant image both in the literature of the German exiles and in the official rhetoric and culture of the Soviet Union. Ironically, however, this clichéd contrast between Nazi Germany and the Soviet Union that informed most Soviet accounts as well as that of the antifascist émigrés could be seen as having been derived from Nazi accounts of themselves, as well as from their actual practices. In particular, it could be seen as taking off from points Hitler made in *Mein Kampf* and the many speeches he gave both before and after acceding to power.

In both these sources Hitler obsessively identified the main impediment to "the spirit of Germany" as what he called "Jewish Bolshevik internationalists." As if to confirm this, almost all the Soviet spokesmen used in the press to provide intellectually respectable rejoinders to the Nazis were Jewish, as is true of the ones listed above, and most of them were also Party members, an exception being Ehrenburg. A large number of the antifascist German intellectuals who published in Soviet-sponsored periodicals were also Jewish and, as mentioned, many were also Communist.

When Hitler condemned "Jewish Bolshevik internationalists," he typically did so in the context of their, in his view, disastrous effect on the press and in publishing. By his account, all too many intellectuals in general, and among them writers most particularly, were themselves Jews and leftists, had been published by Jews and leftists, or had been corrupted by the cosmopolitan outlook of Jews and leftists. As a consequence, the German spirit was stifled. Hitler argued that German culture had to become more "healthy" and even "primitive," and for this reason this entire sphere – the world of written texts – needed purification.

But Hitler's diatribes against written texts were not only on the grounds of their "Jewish Bolshevik internationalist" bias. In *Mein Kampf* and elsewhere, Hitler argued against the written text as the potential embodiment of the German spirit, contending that oral utterances were always purer and more effective than the written.[91]

Besides oral utterances, Hitler favored visual cultural forms (principally architecture, and to a lesser extent sculpture, painting, and film)[92] over a

---

[90] For example, Georg Lukacs, *Die Zerstörung der Vernunft. Der Weg des Irrationalismus von Schelling zu Hitler* (Berlin: Aufbau Verlag, 1954); Hans Günther, *Der Herren eigener Geist: Die Ideologie des Nationalsozialismus* (Moscow, Leningrad: Verlagsgenossenschaft ausländischer Arbeiter in der UdSSR, 1935).

[91] E.g., Adolf Hitler, *Mein Kampf*, 525–34.

[92] A qualification has to be made here. As two recent studies have shown (Linda Schulte-Sasse's *Entertaining the Third Reich: Illusions of Wholeness in Nazi Cinema* [Durham, NC: Duke

text-based verbal culture. In, for example, his "Kultur-Tagung" speech in Nuremberg of 6 September 1938, he singled out architecture as the form that most clearly shows how a work of art can "express the general will of the period." He pointed to "German architecture, sculpture, painting, drama and the rest" as "documentary proof of a creative period in art," "a new awakening of our cultural life," and contrasted them with what he dismissed as mere "literary phrases."[93] Hitler repeatedly juxtaposed the culture of the true German spirit (to be found in architecture, sculpture, and so forth) with textual culture that he saw as not only currently corrupted but in any case somewhat jejune. In consequence, perhaps, written texts assumed not even a remotely comparable importance in Nazi culture to that which they enjoyed in the Stalinist 1930s.

Hitler saw culture as a subfunction of ethnicity, or what he called "blood," a position Bukharin was particularly fond of belittling in his writings on Nazi Germany. Blood was pronounced higher than the word, especially than the printed word. Good (German) blood gave a person "inner value," which in turn "spoke" through music and the visual.[94] Furthermore, Hitler insisted in a speech in March 1935 in Saarbrücken, "Blood is stronger than all the paper documents. What ink wrote will one day be blotted out by blood."[95] This is, of course, an implicit reference to the various international treaties that Hitler intended to flout, but its message applied as a general principle.

Hitler also defined Germanness in terms of German blood, or in other words putative ethnic identity. The anti-Nazi émigrés, by contrast – and this was also the Soviet position – reckoned Germanness by command of German language and culture, especially its written culture. This radically opposed stance on written texts and literature was defining for the Soviet image of Nazi Germany.

In the 1930s, both Germany and the Soviet Union laid claim to representing a higher-order civilization as a mandate for their respective bids for world domination, but the "world" they sought to dominate was distinctly Eurocentric. It could be said that the rivalry between the two powers was played out via the soft underbelly of culture. But, actually, for them culture was not such a soft underbelly. Both needed to claim legitimacy for their regimes, and hence culture acquired greater prominence in both than is generally the case for modern states. As the archives of the former Soviet Union have become more open to scholars in recent years, one of the most striking discoveries has been the

University Press, 1996] and Eric Rentschler's *The Ministry of Illusion: Nazi Cinema and Its Afterlife* [Cambridge, MA: Harvard University Press, 1996]), little Nazi cinema, other than the well-known films of Leni Riefenstahl, was directly propagandistic, and most of it was essentially light entertainment.

[93] "Die grosse Kulturrede des Führers: Die grosse Kulturtagung," *Völkischer Beobachter* 7 September 1938. See also Hitler's Kulturtagung speech of 1935, in which he foregrounds opera and architecture ("Der Führer stiftet die Ehrenpreise der Bewegung für Kunst und Wissenschaft," *Völkischer Beobachter*, 13 September 1935).

[94] Hitler's speech of 27 January 1932 to the Düsseldorf Industry Club.

[95] "Schenkt Eure Treue dem neuen Reich! Die grosse Rede des Führers an die Deutschen der Saar," *Völkischer Beobachter*, 3–4 March 1935.

extent to which in the 1930s the Politburo were engaged in legislating cultural matters – especially Stalin, who, when the Politburo divided up stewardship of the various branches of government, took the area of culture for himself.[96]

Since the Soviet Union could not claim to be technologically or militarily more advanced, it emphasized instead as the grounds of its preeminence a superior ideology and culture. It was *the* "country of world culture" while Nazi Germany was falling far behind in that critical criterion; indeed culture was, as it were, withering away there.[97] Soviet spokesmen belittled the way Nazi Germany, for all its technological and military advances, failed to use an advanced science of society (read Marxism-Leninism) and hence, as Bukharin put it, failed to read "the book of history" and were hurtling their country backward into the dark ages rather than forward.[98] Since history was on the Soviet side, Bolsheviks could proceed with confidence while Nazis would always be plagued by the fear that their program would fail and their party fall apart.[99]

Nazi Germany, represented as the land of "medieval barbarism and terror,"[100] provided a convenient villain for a country that was stepping up its own terror and also entering the period of the show trials. But the accusation that the Nazis were barbaric was not just a matter of name calling. Though they were seen as barbaric in the more literal sense of violently repressive, "barbaric" also pinpointed their position on the Bolshevik map of historical progress. The indicator of their position was less their violence than their attitude to textual culture. To the Soviets, culture meant above all written texts and among written texts (other than classics of Marxism-Leninism-Stalinism) literature especially.

In Soviet rhetoric "culture," or as it was also represented, "humanism" (an "ism" particularly associated with a textual culture), provided one side of an overarching binary (the other side being "barbarism") that structured most representations of the contrast between Nazi Germany and, variously, the Soviet Union, true Europe, or a true representative of humankind (these three categories were in their sense of things closely linked). The binary was presented primarily in terms of the relative command and commitment to language and culture (after all, we call substandard locutions "barbarisms"). This master binary subsumed several others which structured most representations of "them" (Nazis) in Soviet rhetoric of the thirties and the contrast with "us" (Soviets/Europeans/human beings): unreason/reason, irrational (sadistic, hysterical)/rational (calm), destroyers of culture/champions and rescuers of culture, the Dark Ages/the Enlightenment. At the center of all these binaries was

---

[96] Leonid Maksimenkov, *Sumbur vmesto muzyki: Stalinskaia kul'turnaia revoliutsiia, 1936–1938* (Moscow: Iuridicheskaia kniga, 1997), esp. 52–3.

[97] E.g., G. Ryklin, "Zdrastvuite, tridtsat' piatyi," *Ogonek*, no. 1 (1935): 4–5.

[98] N. Bukharin, "Pochemu my pobedim?" *Izvestiia*, 1 May 1934.

[99] Karl Radek, "Kuda idet Germaniia?" *Izvestiia*, 22 March 1933.

[100] *Pravda*, 3 March 1935.

a concern for the written word, for what "humanism" was deemed ipso facto to be most committed to foster and preserve.

That this binary was not entirely generated by the Bolsheviks problematizes the question of the provenance of the basic image of Nazi Germany. One of its most explicit and pointed formulations is to be found in Lion Feuchtwanger's novel *The Oppermanns* (originally: *Die Geschwister Oppenheim*; after revisions in exile: *Die Geschwister Oppermann*),[101] which was first published in 1933 and was thus a trendsetter in representation of the Nazi regime. Feuchtwanger was not a Communist. Though somewhat Moscow-leaning,[102] he went into exile in southern France and later the United States. As Feuchtwanger makes clear in his preface, the novel is essentially a fictional rejoinder to Nazi theory and practice and especially draws, in representing them, on such Hitler sources as *Mein Kampf*. *The Oppermanns* became one of the most popular novels in the Soviet Union after it was subsequently released in Russian translation in hundreds of thousands of copies; it was also made into a film.[103] Thus it was an important text in establishing the Soviet image of Nazi Germany.

The Oppermanns could be approximately characterized as a Jewish version of Thomas Mann's *Buddenbrooks* in that the novel chronicles the decline and fall of a prosperous merchant family (in this case Berlin-based Jews who own a chain of furniture stores) culminating in the death of a particularly sensitive and cultivated male heir. Feuchtwanger's novel, however, rather than following his family over a long expanse of time, as does Mann's, shows a rapid decline over the period 1932 to 1933. As these dates suggest, a further difference is that the main reason for this decline is the rise of the Nazis and the persecution of the Jews; the young scion of the dynasty, Berthold, for example, does not die of natural causes as in the case of his counterpart in *Buddenbrooks* but commits suicide because he cannot take Nazi persecution.[104]

The novel provides a sociological study of the fate of Germany's Jews, the various family members each representing a different occupation and often a different political orientation as well. Its primary purpose, however, is to establish how the Nazi "barbarians," as Feuchtwanger calls them,[105] are destroying

---

[101] The title for the first edition (Amsterdam: Querido Verlag, 1933) was *Die Geschwister Oppenheim*.

[102] Later in the thirties Feuchtwanger was more closely identified with the Soviet cultural front. He became an editor of *Das Wort*, which ran from 1936 to 1939, and in 1937 he published *Moscow 1937*, a commissioned rejoinder to Gide's attack on the country, *Back from the U.S.S.R.*

[103] *Sem'ia Oppenheim*, adapted for the screen by Serafima Roshal' and directed by Grigorii Roshal', Mosfilm, January 1939; Viktor Fink, "Sem'ia Oppengeim na ekrane," *Literaturnaia gazeta*, 1 December 1938.

[104] A similar account of the situation of the educated Jews in Nazi Germany and Nazi disregard for intellectual values is presented in Friedrich Wolf's play *Dr. Mamlock*, also of 1933, which was widely reproduced in Russian in the Soviet Union.

[105] Lion Feuchtwanger, *Die Geschwister Oppenheim* (Amsterdam: Querido Verlag, 1933), 144. Lion Feuchtwanger, *The Oppermanns*, trans. Jane Cleugh (London: Martin Secker, 1933), 180–1.

true culture and professionalism. Here the central account is provided in a confrontation between Berthold and his new, Nazi teacher at the gymnasium, Dr. Vogelsang. Berthold had intended to prepare a class paper "Humanism in the Twentieth Century" but was required by Vogelsang to write instead about the alleged triumphs of Arminius against the Romans. Berthold's failure to present a sufficiently heroic account of Arminius as the victorious German warrior (together with his Jewish identity) makes him a marked man for Vogelsang.

The Nazi/humanist clash is also played out in a series of hypocritically polite exchanges between Vogelsang and the cultivated gymnasium rector, an anti-Nazi friend of the Oppermann family. The rector reproaches Vogelsang for the abominable grammar and general desecration of the German language that he finds in Hitler's *Mein Kampf*. Vogelsang, who has recognized these deficiencies to himself and is embarrassed by them, rather than admit this retorts that Hitler himself made the point in *Mein Kampf* that oral speech is higher than the written.[106] Berthold's suicide occurs in the middle of the novel, but when the work was adapted for film, the suicide was made the film's climax. And the novel's end, when an uncle returns to Nazi Germany to join the Communist underground and perishes, a narrative one might have expected to be foregrounded, was cut from the film.

That Soviet spokesmen foregrounded written texts in their account of true culture while the Nazis, and Hitler in particular, insisted that oral culture was more authentic could be explained in terms of the fact that Hitler was more successful as an orator (several German contemporaries remarked that they came away from his speeches convinced, but if they subsequently had occasion to read the same speeches, they were totally unimpressed) than Stalin, who unlike Lenin or Trotsky was not a gifted orator. His speeches were often not heard at all by the populace but only read in *Pravda* or some such print source.

Arguably, however, this difference did not just have to do with the respective strengths and weaknesses of the two national leaders but pinpoints a fundamental difference in values. Nazis regarded written culture with suspicion, the Soviets with extraordinary veneration.[107]

NARRATING NAZI GERMANY: SCENES AND SITES OF CONTENTION

The contrast between the two rival regimes to be found in Soviet sources of the 1930s was framed by a narrative developed in response to two conflagrations of the initial year of Nazi rule, 1933: the burning of the books and the Reichstag fire. This narrative was highlighted in a series of public events with great international visibility which included the Leipzig trial of Dimitrov

---

[106] Lion Feuchtwanger, *Die Geschwister Oppenheim*, 111–13. Lion Feuchtwanger, *The Oppermanns*, 112–14.

[107] Clearly this opposition was far from absolute *in practice* inasmuch as Hitler's *Mein Kampf* functioned in Nazi culture as the highest authority. Also, as Peter Fritzsche and Jochen Hellbeck bring out in their essay in this volume, Nazis were, like Soviet citizens, encouraged to write their "autobiographies."

and others accused of burning down the Reichstag (1933), the Paris Congress for the Defense of Culture (1935), its sequel in Madrid and Valencia (1937), and the International Exposition in Paris the same year where the Soviet and German pavilions were most pointedly set up opposite one another for direct comparison.

The books were burned in an infamous moment on 10 May 1933, in a bonfire on a square opposite the University of Berlin (many of its students participated), a fact that was particularly poignant given the role of its founder, Alexander von Humboldt, in fostering a humanist education in German universities (something Radek was quick to point out in his commentary when he also alluded to Fichte's addresses from Berlin to the German nation).[108] This event was just the most dramatic in a systematic campaign by the Nazis to eradicate the kinds of literature and culture they found threatening, whether by actual physical destruction, as in this case, or by banning or bowdlerizing a text. Many of the big names in literature and culture had already emigrated from Germany, but this gesture alienated them further. The Soviet Union took up their cause and acted as patrons of a transnational fellowship of what the Soviet writer Sergei Tretiakov called, in the title of his book that contains chapters on many of them, *Liudi odnogo kostra* (People of the one bonfire). Among many antifascists, it became a point of pride to have had one's books burned. The writer Oskar Maria Graf was distressed to find that only some of his books had been burned, and in an open letter titled "Burn Me," he begged the Nazis to consign the rest to the flames.[109] Tretiakov's title is ambiguous. On the one hand, it suggests a fraternity attracted to the light/heat/fire of the great cause, possibly the revolutionary cause, but on the other hand, it also suggests the willful destruction wreaked by the Nazis, that is, versions of the two poles of possibility that structured the main Soviet narrative on the Nazis: culture/barbarism.

This dichotomy received its most prominent airing at the great international antifascist meeting in Paris of June 1935, the Congress for the Defense of Culture. By "culture" its title primarily meant literature – mostly writers attended – and at the conference literature was characterized as the bearer of "humanism," "civilization," and other such transcendent values which the Nazis trampled on in their "barbarism" and the burning of books.

Among the antifascists, literature played a central role in cementing a sense of common cause among politicians and intellectuals of widely differing political and class backgrounds who were to unite as a "popular front." The Soviet Union, which largely bankrolled and organized the event (here Ehrenburg and Koltsov were particularly active), was using it to enhance its stature in the world arena.[110] However, in order to unite such disparate factions it was

---

[108] Karl Radek, "Vysshe znamia sotsialisticheskoi kul'tury," *Izvestiia*, 13 May 1933.
[109] David Caute, 53.
[110] Boris Frezinskii, "Velikaia illiuziia – Parizh, 1935 (Materialy k istorii Mezhdunarodnogo kongressa pisatelei v zashchitu kul'tury)," *Minuvshee: Istoricheskii al'manakh*, no 24 (1998): 166–239.

decided that the fact that it was a Soviet initiative with Soviet backing should not be evident, and even that there should be no explicit resolutions of support for the Soviet Union[111] and that in the speeches and resolutions due respect should be paid to the "bourgeois" as well as the proletarian and revolutionary cultural tradition.[112] Consequently, for the congress such slogans as "culture," "humanism," and "world literature" were chosen – slogans that were suitably grandiose but equally suitably vague.

A later, highly visible confrontation between the two came in 1937 at the International Exposition in Paris. The Nazi-Soviet rivalry there is generally discussed in terms of architecture, that is, in terms of their two juxtaposed pavilions, each with a conspicuously high tower. Unfortunately, the Nazi tower was taller. However, Soviet officials were not overly downcast, because they could claim that *their* pavilion contained a better collection of German books than could be found in the pavilion of the Third Reich. The world could see that they were the better champions of German culture: since 1933 Soviet publishing houses had put out scores of German books, some in German, and others in Russian or Ukrainian translation.[113] They also prided themselves on publishing versions of the German classics that were free of the bowdlerization to which the Nazis subjected them.

In effect, the Soviets were challenging the Nazis to a battle over texts, a battle over who has the right to claim the title of guardian of *true* culture, over which texts represent that "true" culture and which the "false," and over who has the right to decide. Their regime won thereby the right to lead Europe.

The Soviet challenge was not, however, bound to deter the Nazis unduly since they held book culture in relatively low regard, seeing it as an impediment to a virile and victorious nation. An eyewitness report on the Berlin book burning from the special correspondent of *Izvestiia* describes how a professor of "political education" in addressing the crowds drew a comparison between the "intellectual" brought up on hitherto existing philosophies and the "type of a simple soldier" who was previously considered "uncultured." "It was not idealist-humanist philosophy that won battles in the world war," he continued, "but the silent philosophy of the simple soldier."[114]

---

[111] Symptomatically, Johannes Becher reported to a meeting of the secretariat of MORP (the Comintern-sponsored International Society of Revolutionary Writers) that some proposed for the Paris conference the slogans "Defense of the Soviet Union," "Struggle against Capitalist War," and "Struggle with Fascism," but these slogans were like the ones proposed at the Kharkov writers' conference in 1930, so he opposed them. After a long discussion it was decided to make the conference for the defense of culture (Doklad tov. I. Bekhera. Sekretariat MORPa," Rossiiskii gosudarstvennyi arkhiv sotsial'noi i politicheskoi istorii (RGASPI) f .495, op. 30, d .1076, l. 12, l. 15).

[112] "Stellungnahme zu einigen Frage der Schriftsteller Arbeit in Paris," RGASPI, f 495, op 30, d 1076, l. 77.

[113] Simone Barck et al., ed., *Exil in der UdSSR*, Band I/I (Leipzig: Phillipp Reclam jun., 1989), 274–302.

[114] L. Kait, "Publichnoe sozhzhenie knig. Germanskoe srednevekov'e," *Izvestiia*, 12 May 1933.

Soviet commentators, by no means averse to militarism, nevertheless weighted the contrast differently.[115] Radek, for example, in a *Pravda* article of 21 November1935, "Conversation with a Foreigner" (*Razgovor s inostrantsem*), compares German military commanders unfavorably with their Soviet counterparts and, to establish this, makes the point that Germans are incredulous to learn that Soviet military commanders are trained in philosophy. He further contends that German military commanders have long been captivated by the notion of intuition, partly derived from a distorted appropriation of Bergson, and more recently they have abandoned even that and regressed to an infatuation with Wotan of German mythology, "a dated god," something Radek calls "hard to reconcile with a belief in tanks which, by the way," he adds optimistically, "will not help them."[116]

This charge represents a variant on the notion of the Nazi as essentially irrational and premodern in his outlook – backward (as Nazis for their part often labeled the Russians, too). But Radek also adduces as an indicator of German decline the fact that Clausewitz based his theories of military strategy on the French Revolution. This is typical of Soviet commentary on the Nazis during the years of the Popular Front. Rather than advance the Russian Revolution as a model for an enlightened society, they emphasized the French, which was conveniently not only the first great milestone in the canonical progression to October (the French Revolution – the Paris Commune – the Russian Revolution of 1905–17), but also central to the narratives of the Popular Front. In a similar vein, Koltsov compared those attending the Paris Congress for the Defense of Culture with the French encyclopedists.[117]

At the sequel to the Paris Congress of 1935, the one that took place in Madrid and Valencia in 1937, the theme implicit in Radek's article of the necessity of combining the sword with the book was further underlined. Those meeting in Madrid, with fascist shells bursting about them as they conferred, declared somewhat quixotically that "the most dangerous weapon for fascism is not soldiers or weapons but the written *Word*."[118] As Koltsov put it, "What should a writer do in the Civil War in Spain? He has to fight with his weapon – the word. Byron with his work did more for freeing all of mankind than he did with his death for freeing a single land."[119]

The second conflagration of 1933, the Reichstag fire and the subsequent trial of Dimitrov and company, played a much more prominent role in the

---

[115] See also Radek's characterization of Nazi Germany in his speech to the First Writers Congress of August 1934.

[116] Karl Radek, "*Razgovor s inostrantsem*," *Pravda*, 21 November 1935.

[117] Mikhail Kol'tsov, "Otchet sovetskoi delegatsii na kongresse zashchity kul'tury v Parizhe. Rasshirennoe zasedanie pravleniia SP SSSR ot 21 iunia 1935 g.," Rossiiskii gosudarstvennyi arkhiv literatury i iskusstva (RGALI) f 631, op. 15, d. 47, l. 24.

[118] This is actually a quotation from Gorky and the emphasis is his. Quoted in Willi Bredel, "Vorwort," *Das Wort* no. 9 (1937): 6.

[119] Mikhail Kol'tsov, [address to] "Zweiter internationaler Schriftsteller Kongress," *Das Wort* no. 10 (1937): 70.

development of a Soviet (as opposed to a German antifascist) countermytho-
logy – even more so than the burning of books – as did no doubt the fact that
Dimitrov, a leader of the Comintern in Berlin, and most of the accused (two
other Bulgarians and van der Lubbe, a member of a Dutch splinter communist
organization) were not Germans and hence their conduct there could not be
construed as exemplifying Germanness.

The Reichstag fire burned on 27 February 1933, not long after the Nazis
came to power, but the accused did not come to trial until late September 1933.
By then many international intellectuals had taken up the cause of the accused,
issuing a *Brown Book* (from Paris and London), which exposed the weaknesses
in the case for the prosecution,[120] and staging a counter trial in London.[121]
The *Brown Book* was released the day before the trial and undermined its
credibility.

Throughout the trial, *Pravda* published several items on it daily, generally
on page 1. Koltsov, active in the international effort on behalf of Dimitrov
and his alleged co-conspirators, contributed many of these. In the articles the
trial was often represented as mere "theater" (a charge, incidentally, that has
commonly been leveled against the Soviet show trials of 1936-8), farce, or
comedy.[122] Later, the impending Nazi trial of the German Communist leader
Ernst Thälman was represented in similar terms.[123]

The Nazis in their conduct of the trial contributed to this characterization.
At times the trial verged on farcical melodrama, especially in the famous confrontation between Dimitrov and Göring, who had sought to turn the trial into
a crusade against the Communists. Most of Göring's venom, and indeed the
focus of the trial, was directed at Dimitrov. On 4 November he appeared there
in person dressed in a brown tunic, riding breeches, and polished jackboots. In
the exchange with Göring, and indeed throughout the trial, Dimitrov emerged
as calm, reasoned, and confident of his cause. Göring, by contrast, became
increasingly hysterical as their confrontation continued, turning beet red and
screaming threats at him. The trial ended with an acquittal for the Communists
(other than van Lubbe, who was executed in January 1934). Dimitrov was not
released until he was made a Soviet citizen in February 1934; he made a tri-
umphal return to the Soviet Union and was elevated to head the Comintern. In
narratives published in the Soviet press, many extravagant claims were made
for the significance of the victory in the Dimitrov trial, which was often proclaimed a turning point for the Nazis, a "fiasco" that was the impetus for their
(alleged) decline in power.[124] Some claimed that the Popular Front emerged
out of Dimitrov's defense at his trial.[125] Certainly it was a propaganda coup

[120] For some details on Soviet involvement in the activities of the committee for the defense of
    those accused of burning down the Reichstag see RGASPI f. 538, op 3, d 154.
[121] Kond., "Pokazaniia svidetelei na londonskom protsesse," *Pravda*, 17 September 1933.
[122] E.g., Mikh. Kol'tsov, "Besprimernoe zrelishche," *Pravda*, 24 September 1933.
[123] *Pravda*, 28 November 1935.
[124] Rudolf Braun, "Rot Front, tovarishch Tel'man," *Pravda*, 3 March 1935.
[125] Wilhelm Pieck, "Leiptsigskii signal," *Pravda*, 10 December 1936.

for the Soviet Union. A Soviet-made film about resistance in Germany, Gustav von Wangenheim's *Fighters* (*Kämpfer*), that featured Dimitrov's defense at the trial, was shown all over the world to alleged great success, especially in New York.[126]

The conduct of Dimitrov at the trial became in Soviet rhetoric a paradigm for the true Bolshevik, one that was often alluded to in the press and in speeches, marked in ceremonies, and used pedagogically. Central to the account was the contrast between Dimitrov's calmness and the Nazi (Göring) as the irrational and weak hysteric. The photographer John Heartfield (then in exile in Prague) generated a special photomontage (published in *Pravda*) in which a small Göring (shot from behind) confronts a giant figure of Dimitrov (facing the reader), as it was a synecdoche for the confrontation between the giant Soviet Union and puny Nazi Germany.[127] The German Nazi as hysteric became a standard moment in Soviet cultural production seen most paradigmatically in Grigorii Aleksandrov's hit musical film *The Circus* (*Tsirk*, 1936), that uses a pointed symbolic contrast of dark and light (black and white). Here the villain, the German boss of an American circus performer, plays the clichéd Nazi – sadist, paranoid, racist, and hysteric.[128]

Typically Dimitrov was represented as a man of letters writing against the Nazis like a Christian who keeps his faith in the catacombs. When a Comintern envoy visited Dimitrov in Moabit prison, Berlin, on May Day 1933 as Dimitrov was awaiting trial, he reported that in his cell he was surrounded by books and writing a diary, determined that ill health and a gloomy outlook would not deter him.[129] After his release, Dimitrov testified in a speech to antifascist writers in Moscow in 1935 to literature's "extraordinary role in the formation of a generation of revolutionaries." "Don Quixote was the strongest weapon of the bourgeois writer in his struggle against feudalism and autocracy," he maintained, adding that Nikolai Chernyshevsky's novel *What Is To Be Done?* sustained him earlier through his trials when imprisoned in Bulgaria, but particularly as he was awaiting the Leipzig trial.[130]

POWER OVER THE PEN: THE SOVIET UNION AS A CULTURE OF LETTERS

Why so much emphasis on letters in Soviet coverage of the Nazis and their iconic opponents? This is more understandable in the case of the German exiles

---

[126] "Erfolg des Dimitrov Films in New York," *Deutsche Zentral-Zeitung*, 3 October 1936.

[127] Dzhon Khartfil'd, "Gering i Dimitov – klass protiv klassa," *Pravda*, 13 December 1933.

[128] In this respect he provides a total contrast with the German prisoner-of-war hero of Boris Barnet's earlier film *Outskirts* (*Okraina*) of 1933. Note, also, the Nazi as hysteric was far from unique to Soviet culture and can be seen in many Western examples, including Charlie Chaplin's *The Great Dictator* (1940).

[129] RGASPI f.538, op.3, d. 163, l. 139.

[130] Georgi Dimitroff, "Die revolutionäre Literatur im Kampfe gegen den Faschismus," *Internationale Literatur*, no. 5 (1935): 10–11.

who sought to realize a diaspora nation. They no longer had economic, political, or military power and were scattered over several countries. Thus, to put it bluntly, all they had was language and culture. One is reminded of the Russian émigrés from the Soviet Union who in 1925, after the border was closed and emigration became a finality, pronounced themselves the only true guardians of the Russian cultural heritage and rallied together under the sign of Pushkin.[131] But Soviet Russians were not in that position.

The privileging of lettered culture in the Soviet account of themselves and their dismissal of the Nazis as unlettered "barbarians" is not just borrowed from writers like Feuchtwanger but also has to do with defining Soviet values of the 1930s, which inflected their own representations of the Nazis. The rise to power in Nazi Germany happened to coincide roughly with a significant shift in Soviet political culture.

Over the years 1932–4, but most particularly in 1933, the year of the Nazi takeover, the book burning, and the Leipzig trial, lettered culture acquired enormous importance in the Soviet polity. Arguably, the 1930s were in Soviet history a decade when written texts played a critical role in the culture system. Rather as, in the Reformation, there was a turn to the fundamental texts of Christianity and a spate of new exegeses, the 1930s became a time of textual obsession and anxiety with rival claimants to exegetical authority. They were in some senses launched with a spate of publications by the Marx-Engels-Lenin Institute (IMEL) of texts by Marx and Lenin and commentaries on them (several German intellectuals who would subsequently play significant roles in the antifascist movement had worked on this project). The year 1933, the time of the Nazi accession and the book burning, was also an anniversary year for Marx and the high point in publicizing these endeavors with frequent articles in *Pravda* and *Izvestiia* on IMEL and its latest publications.

Within the country a hierarchy evolved, structured in terms of power over texts. It was orchestrated in terms of who had and who did not have *access* to written documents, in terms of the *right* to control their content (ranging from mere scribes at the lowest levels through ever higher degrees of authorship and also of "editorship," including censorship). Stalin had begun to spend an inordinate amount of time vetting novels, films, and plays; he was the ultimate censor. But in looking at each work Stalin's main concern was the text (for an opera, the libretto; for a film or play, the script).[132]

It was not only Marxist texts and Party documents that enjoyed a special status in both Party and state culture of the 1930s. Literature, as the branch of culture most concerned with texts, was propelled to prominence. Starting from at least April–May 1932, when the Writers Union was founded to function

---

[131] Greta Slobin, "The Homecoming of the First Wave: Diaspora and Its Cultural Legacy," *Slavic Review* 60, no. 3 (2001): 515–16.

[132] Andrei Artizov and Oleg Naumov, compilers, *Vlast' i khudozhestvennaia intelligentsia: Dokumenty TsK RKP (b) – VKP (b), VChK – OGPU – NKVD o kul'turnoi politike 1917–1953 gg.* (Moscow: Mezhdunarodnoi fond "Demokratiia," 1999).

as the flagship of Soviet culture and the term "socialist realism" announced as *the* method for Soviet culture, literature provided both the organizational (the single writers' union) and the textual models for Soviet culture. Writers became extremely privileged members of Soviet society, but the state also began to promote literature in a major way. Within the Party, the Komsomol, and the military, reading circles were set up that included literary texts in their reading lists. Other art forms, such as painting and even architecture, became more discursive in this period, more tied to illustrating narratives that were to be found in political or literary texts.

This privileging of literature did not just amount to harnessing writers to turn out propaganda tracts. Both the leadership *and* the populace at large did not have a purely instrumentalist attitude to literature. They revered it to such an extent that one could talk in terms of a cult of literature.

In the 1930s literature enjoyed a semisacral status among a broad spectrum of the population, regime stalwarts, and dissidents alike. We might recall here that most famous line from Mikhail Bulgakov's novel *The Master and Margarita* (written over the course of the thirties), "Manuscripts don't burn" (compare Hitler's dictum that what is on paper blood can blot out). As we have become particularly aware since the KGB files have become more open, manuscripts often did "burn" (were destroyed), but a faith in the immortality of texts is very defining for Soviet culture of the 1930s.

In the 1930s literary models became particularly important for people in a wide range of positions on the sociological spectrum in forming their sense of identity. Evidence from recently published diaries of the period shows that many Russians of the 1930s in their struggle to find an identity for themselves at this difficult time modeled themselves on characters or utterances from literature.[133]

This extraordinary veneration of literature was actually quite widespread throughout Europe at this time (though generally not of the same cult proportions as one saw in the Soviet Union).[134] This faith intensified with the formation in 1934–5 of the antifascist alliance known as the Popular Front. Thus to a marked degree the cult of literature was in the Soviet Union at its most intense during the years when a cult of "Europe" as bulwark against a "barbaric" fascism was also at its height. In the mid- to late 1930s it was widely felt that any educated person should have a thorough knowledge of European literature, both classical and contemporary works. European literature was stressed in the high school curriculum and an impressive number of literary

---

[133] One can find several examples of this in the anthology *Intimacy and Terror: Soviet Diaries of the 1930s*, eds. Veronique Garros, Natalia Korenevskaia, and Thomas Lahusen (New York: The New Press, 1995).

[134] Note, for example, Paul Fussell's work on British soldiers in the Great War that establishes how "fiercely literary" they were (*The Great War and Modern Memory* [London and New York: Oxford University Press, 1975], esp. 157–8). See also Marc Fumaroli, "La Coupole" in *Realms of Memory: Rethinking the French Past*. Vol. 2, *Traditions* (New York: Columbia University, 1997), 300–4.

works appeared in Russian translation, principally French and German works, but also works of English, Italian, and Spanish literature.

This emphasis on the French and German occurred in part because a new European cultural axis was in effect promoted in the antifascist movement, one that transcended old antagonisms. Hence two novels in particular, the French writer Romain Rolland's *Jean Christophe* (a ten-book epic novel that appeared between 1904 and 1912), in which the protagonist, a German musician, moves back and forth from Germany to France, and the German writer Heinrich Mann's *Henri Quatre* (Part I 1935, Part II 1938), which extols the virtues of a sixteenth-century French king, who championed humanist values, were promoted for Soviet readers and used by writers as models in their own work (perhaps not coincidentally, both authors were also prominent in the antifascist movement). Another factor was that the antifascist movement and the Germanophone émigré intellectual community were centered in Paris. But there was also a distinct element of Eurocentrism abroad observed, for example, in accounts of the Spanish Civil War where authors tended less to foreground as the enemy actual Spanish Falangists than the non-European troops from Africa deployed by Franco and Mussolini, and the "barbaric" German bomber pilots.

The pattern that we have been adducing here was, however, less strongly felt in the late 1930s. For a start, as mentioned, the majority of the prominent Soviet formulators of the image of Nazism perished in the purges and show trials (e.g., Karl Radek, Nikolai Bukharin, and Mikhail Koltsov). Thereafter, cruder and more caricatured images of Nazi Germany appeared in the Soviet press. Additionally, well before Republican Spain fell at the end of March 1939 (an event anticipated for some months), the Popular Front fell apart, and the Soviet government became progressively less invested in "Europe." Already the volume of translated literature by European authors had significantly diminished, and such journals as *Arkhitektura za rubezhom* (Architecture Abroad), that reviewed the latest developments in the West, ceased publication in 1937-8. By the end of the 1930s, also, most of the intellectual leaders of the antifascist emigration had moved on from Europe to New York or Hollywood. In the Soviet press there was a corresponding increased emphasis on American affairs and a deemphasis on European ones.

SOVIET NAZI IMAGERY AFTER THE MOLOTOV-RIBBENTROP PACT OF 1939

The Molotov-Ribbentrop pact was signed in August 1939, and thereafter the negative portraits of Nazi Germany essentially disappeared in the press. One is struck, however, by the virtual absence of positive portraits, and also by a lingering nostalgia among Soviet intellectuals for the ethos of the Republican cause in the Spanish Civil War. This nostalgia was particularly felt in annual commemorations of the death of Mate Zalka, the Hungarian writer who, as General Lukacs, was a military commander of an International Brigade and was killed in combat. But also a new, young generation of writers emerged (e.g., Pavel Kogan and Konstantin Simonov) who effectively became bards of Soviet expansionism in the wake of the pact but identified the military engagements against the Japanese in the Far East, and in Western Ukraine, the Baltic countries, and above all Finland, with carrying the ethos of the Republican cause in the Spanish war forward into new engagements.

Until the late 1930s, however, the theme of territorial expansion was one of the principal areas where there was an asymmetry between the Soviet image of Nazi Germany and the Nazi account of the Soviet Union. As Karl Schlögel brings out above, "space" was a central preoccupation of the Nazis in writing about the Soviet Union. Evident already in *Mein Kampf*, the Nazis consistently emphasized Soviet/Russian topography (the great expanses with their potential as *Lebensraum*) and the country's climate, while the physical reality of Nazi Germany played almost no role in Soviet accounts of it, which, as mentioned previously, focused on terror, oppression, the class basis of support, and above all the Nazi threat to "culture" and "Europe" (but Europe conceived less as a physical reality than as an entity defined by its ethos and the culture it generated).

This pattern became less marked in Soviet rhetoric of the late 1930s, particularly after the German invasion on 22 June 1941. Then the Nazi hunger for territorial conquest was represented as their defining attribute, and they were now recurrently referred to as "cannibals" (*liudoedy, kanibaly*), a term that both conveyed how the Nazis were rapaciously devouring (Soviet) territory and referred to what would be called today their ethnic cleansing of "the Slavs" (the Nazis' racist policy toward the Jews was less emphasized).[135] Already by 1938 in such texts as Sergei Eisenstein's film *Alexander Nevsky*, released that year to mark the 7 November anniversary, Germans (as in this case represented in the Teutonic Knights who under the eponymous Alexander had in the thirteenth century been thwarted in their attempt to capture territory in northeast Russia) were seen as would-be ravagers and conquerors of Russian lands. In Eisenstein's film, their distorted bodies and their brutal murder of blond Russian babies testify to a warped and pathological inner self. The film's implied message of centuries-old German hunger for Russian territory and of ethnic abuse was frequently reiterated in Soviet articles published after the invasion, often by reference to this historical precedent.[136]

Not all accounts of Nazi Germany and its people reflect this increasing Russocentrism, which many have remarked on in Soviet culture of the late 1930s. Lingering in intellectuals' responses to the invasion, and especially those

[135] E.g., Aleksei Tol'stoi, "Kto takoi Gitler i chego on dobivaetsia," *Izvestiia*, 7 July 1941; V. Grossman, "Korichnevye klopy," *Izvestiia*, 13 July 1941; Mikh. Osipov, "Fashistskie vyrodki – zakliatye vragi russkogo naroda," *Izvestiia*, 18 July 1941; I. Bachelis, "Kanibaly," *Izvestiia*, 19 July 1941; D. Gustinich, "Fashistskie izvergi istrebliaiut slavianskie narody," *Izvestiia*, 30 July 1941.

[136] E.g., K. Demidov, "Germanskii fashizm – v strakhe pered slavianstvom," *Izvestiia*, 15 July 1941.

of Ilya Ehrenburg, one of the few early formulators of the Soviet image of Nazi
Germany to have survived the purges and who during the war emerged as the
leading provider of anti-Nazi missives for the Soviet press, were a nostalgia for
the dream of "Europe" and an outrage at the rape of Europe at the hands of the
Nazis. A central obsession of his essays (and fiction) from these years was the
fall of Paris, the putative cultural center of Europe and cradle of revolutionary
values, to the jackbooted (cultural) infidel.[137]

CONCLUSION

At first glance, the juxtaposition at the Paris International Exposition of the
two pavilions, one from Nazi Germany and the other from Stalin's Russia, each
with its marked aesthetics of power, would suggest a kind of symmetry between
the two projects, and by extension between their respective countries' culture
systems. But features common to the two pavilions – especially monumentalism
and propaganda – are shared by the architecture of other nations from that
time, including that of their hosts, Popular Front France. Taking the symmetry
of the iconography of power to be seen in these two pavilions as a point of
departure for analyzing each country's image of its own system and that of its
rival is, as we hope we have shown, inadequate to account for these images'
complexity and even asymmetry. For a start, each country's culture generated a
multiplicity of images or interpretations – from sentimental and nostalgic ideas
of Russia and Germany, respectively, to radicalized and primitivized images
that are based on an ideology of cultural and even racist supremacy. Some
of them were contradictory, such as the obsessive image of the other state
as an enemy system coupled with the more romantic idea of "the other" –
"Russian soul" and "German culture" – as allegedly oppressed in the enemy
state. Another striking feature is the impact that émigré communities had (by
providing information and interpretations) on the images of their own countries
formed by those countries' "enemies." Clearly, however, the Nazi German and
Stalinist Russian images of each other were based to a large extent on cultural
patterns and clichés generated long before the Nazis took power, long before
"Stalin's time," and are deeply rooted in pre-Nazi German and pre-Stalinist
Russian culture. The traditional images were, however, refracted through some
of the defining features of Nazism and Stalinism, respectively. One sees this
in the obvious difference between the nationalistic and racist ideology and
rhetoric of Nazi Germany concerning Russia, and the universalistic rhetoric of
Stalin's Russia about Nazi Germany, the one more expressed in an ideology
of race and blood, the other more in a rhetoric of (book-centered) culture. But
both purport to be fighting not just for their own systems, but in defense of the
Occident (*Abendland*) and European civilization: Nazi Germany with its vision
of a racially defined Europe pent against Bolshevism, Stalin's Russia presenting

---

[137] E.g., I. Erenburg, "Chas natsi," *Trud*, 25 April 1941. See also his novel, *The Fall of Paris*
(Padenie Parizha), begun in 1940 and completed in 1941.

itself as a defender of civilization against Nazi barbarism. Both systems were engaged in a struggle for hegemony over Europe – cultural and military. But a productive course for further analysis might be not the differences or the contrasts between the two culture systems and their images of each other but rather the exchange and transfer of culture and ideas that took place in a context defined by the crisis of interwar Europe.

Works Cited

Archives

Archive of the Ludwig Boltzmann Institute for Research on War Consequences, Vienna
Bundesarchiv Berlin (BA-B)
Bundesarchiv (Militärisches Zwischenarchiv) Potsdam
Bundesarchiv-Militärarchiv, Freiburg (BAMA)
Gosudarstvennyi arkhiv noveishei istorii Azerbaidzhanskoi Respubliki (GANI)
Gosudarstvennyi arkhiv Rossiiskoi Federatsii (GARF)
Harvard Interview Project on the Soviet Social System, Cambridge, MA
Hoover Institution Archive, Stanford, CA
Landesarchiv Berlin (LAB)
National Archive, Washington, DC
Public Record Office, London (PRO)
Rossiiskii gosudarstvennyi arkhiv literatury i iskusstva (RGALI)
Rossiiskii gosudarstvennyi arkhiv sotsial'noi i politicheskoi istorii (RGASPI)
Rossiiskii gosudarstvennyj arkhiv ekonomiki (RGAE)
Rossiiskii gosudarstvennyi istoricheskii arkhiv (RGIA)
Tsentral'nyj arkhiv goroda Moskvy (TsMAM)

Newspapers and Periodicals

AGfV Mitteilungen
Berliner Morgenpost
Berliner Tageblatt
Deutsche Zentral-Zeitung
Front nauki i tekhniki
Gigiena i zdorov'e
Illustrierter Beobachter
Internationale Literatur
Istochnik
Izvestiia
Krasnaia zvezda
Martenovka

Die Mode
Neues Volk
Ogonek
Pravda
Das Reich
Rabotnitsa i krest'ianka
Rodina
Schwarzes Korps
Sobranie zakonov i rasporiazhenii raboche-krest'ianskogo pravitel'stva SSSR
Sovetskaia iustitsiia
SS Leithefte
Trud
Vecherniaia Moskva
Völkischer Beobachter
Volk und Rasse
Vossische Zeitung
Das Wort

Comparative, International, and Transnational Studies: Totalitarianism, Fascism

Ades, Dawn et al., eds. *Kunst und Macht im Europa der Diktatoren 1930 bis 1945*. Stuttgart: Oktagon, 1996.

Adorno, Theodor W. et al. *The Authoritarian Personality*. New York: Harper & Row, 1950.

Antonowa, Irina and Jörn Merkert, eds., *Berlin-Moskau 1900–1950*, Ausstellungskatalog. Munich and New York: Prestel, 1995.

Arendt, Hannah. *Elemente und Ursprünge totaler Herrschaft*. Munich: Piper, 1986.

———. *The Origins of Totalitarianism*. New York: Harcourt, Brace, and World, 1966

———. "Understanding and Politics (the Difficulties of Understanding)," In *Essays in Understanding 1930–1954*, edited by Hannah Arendt. New York: Harcourt, Brace, 1994), 307–27.

Armanski, Gerhard. *Maschinen des Terrors: Das Lager (KZ und GULAG) in der Moderne*. Münster: Westfälisches Dampfboot, 1993.

Aron, Raymond. "L'avenir des religions séculières." *Commentaire* 8, no. 28–29 (1985): 369–83.

Aschheim, Steven E. *Hannah Arendt in Jerusalem*. Berkeley and Los Angeles: University of California Press, 2001.

Baberowski, Jörg, and Anselm Doering-Manteuffel. *Ordnung durch Terror: Gewaltexzesse und Vernichtung im nationalsozialistischen und im stalinistischen Imperium*. Bonn: Dietz, 2006.

Baehr, Peter, and Melvin Richter, eds. *Dictatorships in History and Theory: Bonapartism, Caesarism, and Totalitarianism*. Cambridge and New York: Cambridge University Press and German Historical Institute, Washington, DC, 2004.

Barber, Benjamin. *Fear's Empire: War, Terrorism and Democracy*. New York and London: W. W. Norton, 2003.

Bartov, Omer. *Mirrors of Destruction: War, Genocide and Modern Identity*. Oxford and New York: Oxford University Press, 2000.

Bauman, Zygmunt. *Moderne und Ambivalenz: Das Ende der Eindeutigkeit*. Translated by Martin Suhr. Frankfurt am Main: Fischer-Taschenbuch-Verl., 1995.

———. *Modernity and the Holocaust*. Ithaca, NY: Cornell University Press, 1989.

————. "Utopie und Gewalt: Neugeburt und Vernichtung des Menschen." In *Wege in die Gewalt: Die modernen politischen Religionen*, edited by Bronislaw Baczko and Hans Maier, 92–120. Frankfurt am Main: Fischer Taschenbuch Verlag, 2000.

Beimler, Hans. *V lagere smerti – Chetyre nedeli v rukakh korichnevykh*. Moscow: Kooperativnoe izzdatel'stvo inostrannykh rabochikh v SSSR, 1933.

Bell, David A. *The First Total War: Napoleon's Europe and the Birth of Warfare as We Know It*. Boston: Houghton Mifflin, 2007.

Berman, Marshall. *All That Is Solid Melts into Air: The Experience of Modernity*. New York: Penguin Books, 1988.

Berman, Paul. *Terror and Liberalism*. New York and London: W. W. Norton, 2003.

Beyrau, Dietrich, ed. *Im Dschungel der Macht: Intellektuelle Professionen unter Stalin und Hitler*. Göttingen: Vandenhoeck & Ruprecht, 2000.

————. "Nationalsozialistisches Regime und Stalin System: Ein riskanter Vergleich." *Osteuropa: Zeitschrift für Gegenwartsfragen des Ostens* 50, no. 6 (2000): 709–20.

Blank, Margot, ed. *Beutestücke: Kriegsgefangene in der deutschen und sowjetischen Fotografie 1941–1945*. Berlin: Ch. Links, 2003.

Bloch, Marc. "Toward a Comparative History of European Societies." In *Enterprise and Secular Change: Readings in Economic History*, edited by Frederic C. Lane and Jelle C. Rimersma, 494–521. Homewood, IL: R. D. Irwin, 1953.

Böll, Heinrich, Lev Kopelev, and Klaus Bednarz. *Warum haben wir aufeinander geschossen?* Bornheim-Merten: Lamuv-Verlag, 1981.

Borck, Karin, ed. *Sowjetische Forschungen (1917 bis 1991) zur Geschichte der deutsch-russischen Beziehungen von den Anfängen bis 1949: Bibliographie*, Publikationen der Historischen Kommission zu Berlin. Berlin: Akademie Verlag, 1993.

Borejsza, Jerzy W., Klaus Ziemer, and Magdalena Hulas, eds. *Totalitarian and Authoritarian Regimes in Europe: Legacies and Lessons from the Twentieth Century*. New York: Berghahn Books, 2006.

Borngräber, Christian. "Ausländische Architekten in der UdSSR: Bruno Taut, die Brigaden Ernst May, Hannes Meyer und Hans Schmidt." In *Wem gehört die Welt: Kunst und Gesellschaft in der Weimarer Republik*, edited by Jürgen Kleindienst, 109–42. Berlin: Neue Gesellschaft für Bildende Kunst, 1977.

Bracher, Karl Dietrich. *The Age of Ideologies: A History of Political Thought in the Twentieth Century*. Translated by Ewald Osers. New York: St. Martin's Press, 1984.

Brubaker, Rogers, and Frederick Cooper. "Beyond 'Identity'." *Theory and Society* 29, no. 1 (2000): 1–47.

Brzezinski, Zbigniew. *The Permanent Purge: Politics in Soviet Totalitarianism*, Russian Research Center Studies. Cambridge, MA: Harvard University Press, 1956.

Buchloh, Benjamin. "From Faktura to Factography." *October* 30 (Fall 1984): 83–118.

Bullock, Alan. *Hitler and Stalin: Parallel Lives*. London: HarperCollins, 1991.

Burleigh, Michael. *Sacred Causes: The Clash of Religion and Politics, from the Great War to the War on Terror*. New York: HarperCollins, 2007.

Burrin, Philippe. "Totalitäre Gewalt als historische Möglichkeit." In *Utopie und Gewalt: Neugeburt und Vernichtung des Menschen*, edited by Bronislaw Baczko and Hans Maier, 83–201. Frankfurt am Main: Fischer, 2000.

Canovan, Margaret. *Hannah Arendt: A Reinterpretation of Her Political Thought*. Cambridge: Cambridge University Press, 1992.

Carr, Edward Hallett. *German-Soviet Relations between the Two World Wars, 1919–1939*, The Albert Shaw Lectures on Diplomatic History. Baltimore: Johns Hopkins Press, 1951.

Castoriadis, Cornelius. *The Castoriadis Reader*. Oxford and Malden, MA: Blackwell, 1997.

Caute, David. *The Fellow-Travellers: Intellectual Friends of Communism*. Rev. ed. New Haven, CT: Yale University Press, 1988.

Chalk, Frank Robert, and Kurt Jonassohn. *The History and Sociology of Genocide: Analyses and Case Studies*. New Haven, CT: Yale University Press in cooperation with the Institut montréalais des Études sur le Génocide, 1990.

Chaumont, Jean-Michel. *Autour d'Auschwitz: De la critique de la modernité à l'assomption de la responsabilité historique: Une lecture de Hannah Arendt*, Mémoires de la classe des lettres. Brussels: Academie Royale des sciences, des lettres et des beaux-arts, 1991.

Christofferson, Michael Scott. *French Intellectuals against the Left: The Antitotalitarian Moment of the 1970's*, Berghahn Monographs in French Studies. New York: Berghahn Books, 2004.

Churchill, Winston *The Second World War*. 2 vols. Vol. 2. London, 1949.

Clermont, Pierre. *De Lénine à Ben Laden: La grande révolte antimoderniste du XXe siècle*, Démocratie ou totalitarisme. Monaco: Rocher, 2004.

Cohen, Deborah. "Comparative History: Buyer Beware." *Bulletin of the German Historical Institute Washington* 29 (Fall 2001): 23–34.

Cohen, Deborah, and Maura O'Connor, eds. *Comparison and History: Europe in Cross-National Perspective*. New York: Routledge, 2004.

Colombijn, Freek, and J. Thomas Lindblad, eds. *Roots of Violence in Indonesia: Contemporary Violence in Historical Perspective*, Verhandelingen van het Koninklijk Instituut voor Taal-, Land- en Volkenkunde. Leiden: KITLV, 2002.

Conrad, Sebastian. *Globalisierung und Nation im deutschen Kaiserreich*. Munich: Beck, 2006.

Courtois, Stéphane, ed. *Les logiques totalitaires en Europe*. Monaco: Rocher, 2006.

———. *Quand tombe la nuit: Origines et émergence des régimes totalitaires en Europe, 1900–1934*, Mobiles géopolitiques. Lausanne, Switzerland: L'Age d'homme, 2001.

———. *The Black Book of Communism: Crime, Terror, Repression*, trans. Jonathan Murphy and Mark Kramer. Cambridge, MA: Harvard University Press, 1999.

———. *Une si longue nuit: L'apogée des régimes totalitaires en Europe, 1935–1953*, Démocratie ou totalitarisme. Monaco: Rocher, 2003.

Dahlmann, Dittmar, and Gerhard Hirschfeld, eds. *Lager, Zwangsarbeit, Vertreibung und Deportation: Dimensionen der Massenverbrechen in der Sowjetunion und in Deutschland 1933 bis 1945*, Schriften der Bibliothek für Zeitgeschichte. Essen: Klartext, 1999.

Davies, Norman *No Simple Victory: World War II in Europe, 1939–1945*. New York: Viking, 2007.

Deutsch-Russisches Museum Berlin-Karlshorst, ed. *Unsere Russen – Unsere Deutschen: Bilder vom Anderen 1800 bis 2000*. Berlin: Christoph Links Verlag, 2007.

Dickinson, Edward Ross. "Biopolitics, Fascism, Democracy: Some Reflections on Our Discourse about 'Modernity.'" *Central European History* 37, no. 1 (2004): 1–48.

Diner, Dan. *Das Jahrhundert verstehen: Eine universalhistorische Deutung*. Munich: Luchterhand, 1999.

Dlugoborski, Waclaw. "Das Problem des Vergleichs von Nationalsozialismus und Stalinismus." In *Lager, Zwangsarbeit, Vertreibung und Deportation: Dimensionen der Massenverbrechen in der Sowjetunion und in Deutschland 1933 bis 1945*, edited by Dittmar Dahlmann and Gerhard Hirschfeld, 19–29. Essen: Klartext, 1999.

Dodenhoeft, Bettina. *Lasst mich nach Russland heim: Russische Emigranten in Deutschland von 1918 bis 1945*, Studien zur Technik-, Wirtschafts- und Sozialgeschichte. Frankfurt am Main: P. Lang, 1993.

Doering-Manteuffel, Anselm. "Mensch, Maschine, Zeit: Fortschrittsbewusstsein und Kulturkritik im ersten Drittel des 20. Jahrhunderts'." In *Jahrbuch des Historischen Kollegs 2003*, 91–119. Munich: Oldenbourg, 2004.

Döser, Ute. "Das bolschewistische Russland in der deutschen Rechtspresse, 1918–1925: Eine Studie zum publizistischen Kampf in der Weimarer Republik." Diss., Freie Universität, Berlin, 1961.

Durkheim, Emile *The Elementary Forms of Religious Life*. Translated by Karen E. Fields. New York: Free Press, 1995.

Edele, Mark. "Totalitarian War and Atrocity Process: Reconsidering Violence at the German-Soviet Front, 1941–1945." In *Biannual Conference of the Australasian Association for European History (AAEH)*. University of Sydney, 2007.

Eimermacher, Karl, and Astrid Volpert, eds. *Verführungen der Gewalt: Russen und Deutsche im Ersten und Zweiten Weltkrieg*, West-östliche Spiegelungen. Munich: Fink, 2005.

Eimermacher, Karl, Astrid Volpert, and G. A. Bordiugov, eds. *Stürmische Aufbrüche und enttäuschte Hoffnungen: Russen und Deutsche in der Zwischenkriegszeit*, West-östliche Spiegelungen. Munich: W. Fink, 2006.

Espagne, Michel. *Russie, France, Allemagne, Italie: Transferts quadrangulaires du néoclassicisme aux avant-gardes*, Transferts. Tusson: Du Lérot, 2005.

Evans, Richard J. *Fakten und Fiktionen: Über die Grundlagen historischer Erkenntnis*. Translated by Ulrich Speck. Frankfurt Campus, 1998.

Evtuhov, Catherine, and Stephen Kotkin, eds. *The Cultural Gradient: The Transmission of Ideas in Europe, 1789–1991*. Lanham, MD: Rowman & Littlefield, 2003.

Fehér, Ferenc, and Agnes Heller. *Eastern Left, Western Left: Totalitarianism, Freedom, and Democracy*. Atlantic Highlands, NJ: Humanities Press International, 1987.

Ferguson, Niall. *The War of the World: History's Age of Hatred*. London and New York: Allen Lane, 2006.

Fildes, Valerie A., Lara Marks, and Hilary Marland, eds. *Women and Children First: International Maternal and Infant Welfare, 1870–1945*, The Wellcome Institute Series in the History of Medicine. London and New York: Routledge, 1992.

Fitzpatrick, Sheila, and Robert Gellately, eds. *Accusatory Practices: Denunciation in Modern European History, 1789–1989*, Studies in European History from the Journal of Modern History. Chicago: University of Chicago Press, 1997.

Fleischer, Helmut. "Zur einer Historik für die Geschichte des 20. Jahrhunderts: Präliminarien, Perspektiven, Paradigmen." In *Das 20. Jahrhundert: Zeitalter der tragischen Verkehrungen: Forum zum 80. Geburtstag von Ernst Nolte*, edited by Helmut Fleischer and Pierluca Azzaro, 506–58. Munich: F. A. Herbig, 2003.

Fraenkel, Ernst et al. *The Dual State: A Contribution to the Theory of Dictatorship*. New York and London: Oxford University Press, 1941.

Frank, Bajohr, Werner Johe, and Uwe Lohalm, eds. *Zivilisation und Barbarei: Die widersprüchlichen Potentiale der Moderne*, Hamburger Beiträge zur Sozial- und Zeitgeschichte. Hamburg: Christians, 1991.

Freund, Gerald. *Unholy Alliance: Russian-German Relations from the Treaty of Brest-Litovsk to the Treaty of Berlin*. New York: Harcourt, Brace, 1957.

Friedrich, Carl J. and Zbigniew Brzezinski. *Totalitarian Dictatorship and Autocracy.* Cambridge, MA: Harvard University Press, 1956.

Funke, Manfred, ed. *Totalitarismus: Ein Studien-Reader zur Herrschaftsanalyse moderner Diktaturen*, Bonner Schriften zur Politik und Zeitgeschichte. Düsseldorf: Droste, 1978.

Furet, François. *Le passé d'une illusion: Essai sur l'idée communiste au XXe siècle.* Paris: R. Laffont: Calmann-Lévy, 1995.

_____. *The Passing of an Illusion: The Idea of Communism in the Twentieth Century.* Translated by Deborah Furet. Chicago: University of Chicago Press, 1999.

Furet, François, and Ernst Nolte. *Fascism and Communism.* Translated by Katherine Golsan, European Horizons. Lincoln: University of Nebraska Press, 2001.

_____. *"Feindliche Nähe": Kommunismus und Faschismus im 20. Jahrhundert: Ein Briefwechsel.* Translated by Klaus Jöken and Konrad Dietzfelbinger. Munich: Herbig, 1998.

Furler, Bernhard. *Augen-Schein: Deutschsprachige Reportagen über Sowjetrussland, 1917–1939.* Frankfurt am Main: Athenäum, 1987.

Fussell, Paul. *The Great War and Modern Memory.* New York: Oxford University Press, 1975.

Galtung, Johan. *Hitlerismus, Stalinismus, Reaganismus: Drei Variationen zu einem Thema von Orwell*, Militär, Rüstung, Sicherheit. Baden-Baden: Nomos, 1987.

Gellately, Robert. *Lenin, Stalin, and Hitler: The Age of Social Catastrophe.* New York: Alfred A. Knopf, 2007.

Gellately, Robert, and Ben Kiernan, eds. *The Specter of Genocide: Mass Murder in Historical Perspective.* Cambridge: Cambridge University Press, 2003.

Gerlach, Christian. "Extremely Violent Societies: An Alternative to the Concept of Genocide." *Journal of Genocide* 8, no. 4 (2006): 455–71.

_____. "Nationsbildung im Krieg: Wirtschaftliche Faktoren bei der Vernichtung der Armenier und beim Mord an den ungarischen Juden." In *Der Völkermord an den Armeniern und die Shoah = The Armenian Genocide and the Shoah*, edited by Hans-Lukas Kieser and Dominik J. Schaller, 347–422. Zürich: Chronos, 2002.

Gleason, Abbott. *Totalitarianism: The Inner History of the Cold War.* New York: Oxford University Press, 1995.

Goldschmidt, Dietrich, ed. *Frieden mit der Sowjetunion – eine unerledigte Aufgabe.* Gütersloh: Gütersloher Verlags-Haus Mohn, 1989.

Golomshtok, Igor. *Totalitarian Art in the Soviet Union, the Third Reich, Fascist Italy and the People's Republic of China.* Translated by Robert Chandler. New York: IconEditions, 1990.

Gourevitch, Peter. "The Second Image Reversed: The International Sources of Domestic Politics." *International Organization* 32 (1978): 881–912.

Graham, Loren R. "Science and Values: The Eugenics Movement in Germany and Russia in the 1920s." *American Historical Review* 82, no. 5 (1977): 1113–64.

Griffin, Roger. *Modernism and Fascism: The Sense of a Beginning under Mussolini and Hitler.* Basingstoke and New York: Palgrave Macmillan, 2007.

Griffin, Roger, Werner Loh, and Andreas Umland, eds. *Fascism Past and Present, West and East: An International Debate on Concepts and Cases in the Comparative Study of the Extreme Right*, Soviet and Post-Soviet Politics and Society. Stuttgart: Ibidem-Verlag, 2006.

Groehler, Olaf. *Selbstmörderische Allianz: Deutsch-Russische Militärbeziehungen 1920–1941.* Berlin: Vision Verlag, 1992.

Groh, Dieter. "Cäsarismus, Napoleonismus, Bonapartismus: Führer, Chef, Imperialismus." In *Geschichtliche Grundbegriffe*, edited by Otto Brunner, Conze Werner and Reinhart Koselleck, 726–71, Stuttgart: Ernst Klett, 1972.

Grossman, Dave. *On Killing: The Psychological Cost of Learning to Kill in War and Society*. Boston: Little, Brown, 1995.

Guardini, Romano. *Der Heilbringer in Mythos, Offenbarung und Politik: Eine theologisch-politische Besinnung*, Der Deutschenspiegel, Schriften zur Erkenntnis und Erneuerung. Stuttgart: Deutsche Verlags-Anstalt, 1946.

Günther, Hans F. K. *Der Herren eigner Geist: Die Ideologie des Nationalsozialismus*. Moscow, Leningrad: Verlagsgenossenschaft ausländischer Arbeiter in der UdSSR, 1935.

Gurian, Waldemar. *Der Bolschewismus*. Freiburg i. Br., Herder 1931.

Haffner, Sebastian. *Die Teufelspakt: Die deutsch-russischen Beziehungen vom Ersten zum Zweiten Weltkrieg*. 3rd ed., Manesse Bücherei. Zürich: Manesse, 1988.

Hagemeister, Michael. "Das Leben des Gregor-Schwartz-Botunitsch (Grigorij V. Švarc-Bostunič)." In *Russische Emigration in Deutschland 1918 bis 1941*, edited by Karl Schlögel, 209–18. Berlin: Akademie Verlag, 1995.

Halberstam, Michael. *Totalitarianism and the Modern Conception of Politics*. New Haven, CT: Yale University Press, 1999.

Halfin, Igal, ed. *Language and Revolution: Making of Modern Political Identities*, The Cummings Center Series. London and Porland, OR: F. Cass, 2002.

Harrison, Mark. "The Economics of World War II: An Overview." In *The Economics of World War II: Six Great Powers in International Comparison*, edited by Mark Harrison, 1–42. Cambridge: Cambridge University Press, 1998.

Harten, Jürgen, Hans-Werner Schmidt, and Marie Luise Syring, eds. *"Die Axt hat geblüht–": Europäische Konflikte der 30er Jahre in Erinnerung an die frühe Avantgarde*. Düsseldorf: Städtische Kunsthalle Düsseldorf, 1987.

Haupt, Heinz-Gerhard, and Jürgen Kocka. "Historischer Vergleich: Methoden, Aufgaben, Probleme." In *Geschichte und Vergleich: Ansätze und Ergebnisse international vergleichender Geschichtsschreibung*, edited by Heinz-Gerhard Haupt and Jürgen Kocka, 9–45. Frankfurt and New York: Campus, 1996.

Helbig, Herbert. *Die Träger der Rapallo-Politik*, Veröffentlichungen des Max-Planck-Instituts für Geschichte. Göttingen: Vandenhoeck & Ruprecht, 1958.

Hermet, Guy, Pierre Hassner, and Jacques Rupnik, eds. *Totalitarismes*. Paris: Economics, 1984.

Herwarth, Hans von. *Zwischen Hitler und Stalin: Erlebte Zeitgeschichte 1931 bis 1945*. Frankfurt am Main and Berlin: Propyläen, 1982.

Heydemann, Günther, and Eckhard Jesse, eds. *Diktaturvergleich als Herausforderung: Theorie und Praxis*, Schriftenreihe der Gesellschaft für Deutschlandforschung. Berlin: Duncker & Humblot, 1998.

Hilger, Gustav. *Wir und der Kreml: Deutsch-Sowjetische Beziehungen 1918–1941: Erinnerungen eines deutschen Diplomaten*. Translated by Roland Schacht. Frankfurt am Main: A. Metzner, 1955.

Hobsbawm, E. J. *The Age of Extremes: A History of the World, 1914–1991*. New York: Pantheon Books, 1994.

Horkheimer, Max, and Theodor W. Adorno. *Dialectic of Enlightenment: Philosophic Fragments*. Translated by John Cumming. New York: Continuum, 2002.

Horn, David G. *Social Bodies: Science, Reproduction and Italian Modernity*, Princeton Studies in Culture/Power/History. Princeton, NJ: Princeton University Press, 1994.

Institut für Zeitgeschichte, ed. *Totalitarismus und Faschismus: Eine wissenschaftliche und politische Begriffskontroverse: Kolloquium im Institut für Zeitgeschichte am 24. November 1978*. Munich and Vienna: Oldenbourg, 1980.

International Military Tribunal. *Trial of the Major War Criminals before the International Military Tribunal, Nuremberg, 14 November 1945–1 October 1946*. 42 vols. Vol. 38. Nuremberg, Germany: Secretariat of the Tribunal, 1947.

Jarvie, I. C., and Sandra Pralong. *Popper's Open Society after Fifty Years: The Continuing Relevance of Karl Popper*. London: Routledge, 1999.

Jesse, Eckhard, Christiane Schröder, and Thomas Grosse-Gehling, eds. *Totalitarismus im 20. Jahrhundert: Eine Bilanz der internationalen Forschung*. 2nd enlarged ed. Baden-Baden: Nomos, 1999.

Jones, William David. *The Lost Debate: German Socialist Intellectuals and Totalitarianism*. Urbana: University of Illinois Press, 1999.

Juergensmeyer, Mark, ed. *Violence and the Sacred in the Modern World*. London: Frank Cass, 1991.

Kämpfer, Frank. *Der rote Keil: Das politische Plakat: Theorie und Geschichte*, Gebr. Mann Studio-Reihe. Berlin: Mann, 1985.

Kaplan, E. Ann. *Trauma Culture: The Politics of Violence and Loss in Media and Literature*. New Brunswick, NJ: Rutgers University Press, 2005.

Kara-Murza, A. A. and A. K. Voskresenskii, eds. *Totalitarizm kak istoricheskii fenomen*. Moscow: Filosofskoe ob-vo SSSR, Vses. assotsiatsiia molodykh filosofov, 1989.

Karner, Stefan. "Konzentrations- und Kriegsgefangenenlager in Deutschland und in der Sowjetunion: Ansätze zu einem Vergleich von Lagern in totalitäten Regimen." In *In der Hand des Feindes: Kriegsgefangenschaft von der Antike bis zum Zweiten Weltkrieg*, edited by Rüdiger Overmans, 387–411. Cologne: Böhlau, 1999.

Kassimeris, George, ed. *The Barbarization of Warfare*. New York: New York University Press, 2006.

Katznelson, Ira. *Desolation and Enlightenment: Political Knowledge after Total War, Totalitarianism, and the Holocaust*, Leonard Hastings Schoff Memorial Lectures. New York: Columbia University Press, 2003.

Kershaw, Ian. *Fateful Choices: Ten Decisions that Changed the World, 1940–1941*. New York: Penguin Press, 2007.

———. "Totalitarianism Revisited: Nazism and Stalinism in Comparative Perspective." *Tel Aviver Jahrbuch für deutsche Geschichte* 33 (1994): 23–40.

Kershaw, Ian, and Moshe Lewin, eds. *Stalinism and Nazism: Dictatorships in Comparison*. Cambridge: Cambridge University Press, 1997.

Kiernan, Ben. *The Pol Pot Regime: Race, Power, and Genocide in Cambodia under the Khmer Rouge, 1975–79*. New Haven, CT: Yale University Press, 1996.

Kieser, Hans-Lukas, and Dominik J. Schaller, eds. *Der Völkermord an den Armeniern und die Shoah = The Armenian Genocide and the Shoah*. Zürich: Chronos, 2002.

Kocka, Jürgen. "Asymmetrical Historical Comparison: The Case of the German Sonderweg." *History and Thoery* 38, no. 1 (1999): 40–50.

Koenen, Gerd. *Utopie der Säuberung: Was war der Kommunismus?* Berlin: A. Fast, 1998.

Koenen, Gerd, and Lew Kopelew, eds. *Deutschland und die Russische Revolution, 1917–1924*, West-östliche Spiegelungen, vol 5. Munich: W. Fink Verlag, 1998.

Koenen, Gerd, and Lew Kopelew, eds. *West-östliche Spiegelungen: Russen und Rußland aus deutscher Sicht und Deutsche und Deutschland aus russischer Sicht von den Anfängen bis zum 20. Jahrhundert*. Wuppertaler Projekt zur Erforschung der

Geschichte deutsch-russischer Fremdenbilder. Series A: Russen und Rußland aus deutscher Sicht, 4 vols., Series B: Deutsche und Deutschland aus russischer Sicht, 2 vols. Munich: Fink, 1985–.

Koestler, Arthur. *Darkness at Noon*. New York: Random House, 1941.

Koselleck, Reinhart. "'Erfahrungsraum und 'Erwartungshorizont' – Zwei Historische Begriffe." In *Vergangene Zukunft: Zur Semantik geschichtlicher Zeiten*, edited by Reinhart Koselleck, 349–75. Frankfurt am Main: Suhrkamp, 1987.

Kramer, Alan. *Dynamic of Destruction: Culture and Mass Killing in the First World War*. Oxford and New York: Oxford University Press, 2007.

Kraushaar, Wolfgang. "Sich aufs Eis wagen: Plädoyer für eine Auseinandersetzung mit der Totalitarismustheorie." *Mittelweg 36*, no. 2 (1993): 6–29.

Kroll, Frank-Lothar. "Endzeitvorstellungen im Kommunismus und im Nationalsozialismus." In *Der Engel und die siebte Posaune... Endzeitvorstellungen in Geschichte und Literatur*, edited by Stefan Krimm and Ursula Triller, 186–204. Munich: Bayerischer Schulbuch Verlag, 2000.

Krummacher, F. A., and Helmut Lange. *Krieg und Frieden: Geschichte der deutsch-sowjetischen Beziehungen*. Munich: Bechtle, 1970.

Kurilo, O. V., ed. *Der Zweite Weltkrieg im deutschen und russischen Gedächtnis*. Berlin: Avinus, 2006.

Laqueur, Walter. *Deutschland und Russland*. Translated by K. H. Abshagen. Berlin: Propyläen, 1965. (The original English edition is *Russia and Germany: A Century of Conflict*. London: Weidenfeld and Nicolson, 1965.)

Lefort, Claude. *Complications: Communism and the Dilemmas of Democracy*. Translated by Julian Bourg, Columbia Studies in Political Thought/Political History. New York: Columbia University Press, 2007.

————. *The Political Forms of Modern Society: Bureaucracy, Democracy, Totalitarianism*. Cambridge, MA: MIT Press, 1986.

Lepp, Nicola, and Martin Roth, eds. *Der Neue Mensch: Obsessionen des 20. Jahrhunderts*. Ostfildern-Ruit: Cantz, 1999.

Levene, Mark. "Creating a Modern 'Zone of Genocide': The Impact of Nation- and State Formation on Anatolia, 1878–1923." *Holocaust and Genocide Studies* 12, no. 3 (1998): 393–433.

Lietzmann, Hans J. *Politikwissenschaft im "Zeitalter der Diktaturen": Die Entwicklung der Totalitarismustheorie Carl Joachim Friedrichs*. Opladen: Leske + Budrich, 1999.

Linz, Juan. "Some Notes Toward a Comparative Study of Fascism in Sociological Historical Perspective." In *Fascism: A Reader's Guide: Analyses, Interpretations, Bibliography*, edited by Walter Laqueur, 3–121. Harmondsworth, England: Penguin Books, 1979.

Lukács, Georg. *Die Zerstörung der Vernunft: Der Weg des Irrationalismus von Schelling zu Hitler*. Berlin: Aufbau-Verlag, 1955.

Linz, Juan J., and Alfred C. Stepan. *Problems of Democratic Transition and Consolidation: Southern Europe, South America, and Post-Communist Europe*. Baltimore: Johns Hopkins University Press, 1996.

Lübbe, Hermann, and Wladyslaw Bartoszewski, eds. *Heilserwartung und Terror: Politische Religionen des 20. Jahrhunderts*. Schriften der Katholischen Akademie in Bayern. Düsseldorf: Patmos, 1995.

Luks, Leonid. "Bolschewismus, Faschismus, Nationalsozialismus – Verwandte Gegner." *Geschichte und Gesellschaft* 14, no. 2 (1988): 96–115.

————. "'Eurasier' und 'Konservative Revolution': Zur antiwestlichen Versuchung in Russland und in Deutschland." In *Deutschland und die russische Revolution*, 219–39. Munich: W. Fink Verlag, 1998.

Maier, Hans. *Politische Religionen: Die totalitären Regime und das Christentum*, Herder Spektrum. Freiburg im Breisgau: Herder, 1995.

————, ed. *Totalitarismus und politische Religionen: Konzepte des Diktaturvergleichs.* 3 vols, Politik- und kommunikationswissenschaftliche Veröffentlichungen der Görres-Gesellschaft. Paderborn: Ferdinand Schöningh, 1996.

————. *Totalitarianism and Political Religions: Concepts for the Comparison of Dictatorships.* Translated by Jodi Bruhn. London and New York: Routledge, 2004.

Mandt, Hella. "Cäsarismus, Napoleonismus, Bonapartismus: Führer, Chef, Imperialismus." In *Geschichtliche Grundbegriffe*, edited by Otto Brunner, Werner Conze and Reinhart Koselleck, 651–706. Stuttgart: Ernst Klett, 1990.

Mann, Michael. "The Contradiction of Continuous Revolution." In *Stalinism and Nazism: Dictatorship in Comparison*, edited by Ian Kershaw and Moshe Lewin, 135–57. Cambridge: Cambridge University Press, 1997.

————. *The Dark Side of Democracy: Explaining Ethnic Cleansing.* Cambridge and New York: Cambridge University Press, 2005.

Mannheim, Karl. *Man and Society in the Age of Reconstruction: Studies in Modern Social Structure.* London: Routledge and Kegan Paul, 1951.

Marcuse, Herbert, ed. *Feindanalyse: Über die Deutschen*, edited by Jansen Peter-Erwin. Lüneburg: zu Klampen, 1998.

————. *One Dimensional Man: Studies in the Ideology of Advanced Society.* Boston: Beacon Press, 1964.

Marx, Karl. *Historisch-kritische Gesamtausgabe.* 8 vols. Vol. 3. Frankfurt am Main: Marx-Engels-Archiv, Verl.-Ges., 1932.

Matard-Bonucci, and Marie-Anne Milza Pierre, eds. *L'homme nouveau dans l'Europe fasciste (1922–1945): Entre dictature et totalitarisme*, Nouvelles études contemporaines. Paris: Fayard, 2004.

Mawdsley, Evan. *Thunder in the East: The Nazi-Soviet War, 1941–1945.* London: Hodder Arnold, 2005.

Mayer, Arno J. *The Furies: Violence and Terror in the French and Russian Revolutions.* Princeton, NJ: Princeton University Press, 2000.

Mazower, Mark. *Dark Continent: Europe's Twentieth Century.* New York: Vintage Books, 2000.

Middell, Matthias. "Kulturtransfer und Historische Komparatistik – Thesen zur ihren Verhältnis." *Comparativ* 10 (2000): 7–41.

Möll, Marc-Pierre. *Gesellschaft und totalitäre Ordnung: Eine theoriegeschichtliche Auseinandersetzung mit dem Totalitarismus*, Nomos Universitätsschriften, Politik. Baden-Baden: Nomos, 1998.

Möller, Horst. *Der rote Holocaust und die Deutschen: Die Debatte um das "Schwarzbuch des Kommunismus."* Munich: Piper, 1999.

Mommsen, Hans. "The Concept of Totalitarian Dictatorship vs. the Comparative Theory of Fascism." In *Totalitarianism Reconsidered*, edited by Ernest A. Menze, 146–66. Port Washington, NY: Kennikat Press, 1981.

————. "Das Ressentiment als Wissenschaft: Anmerkungen zu Ernst Noltes 'Der europäische Bürgerkrieg.'" *Geschichte und Gesellschaft* 14, no. 4 (1988): 495–512.

Mommsen, Wolfgang J. "Die Anfänge des Ethnic Cleansing und die Umsiedlungspolitik im Ersten Weltkrieg." In *Mentalitäten – Nationen – Spannungsfelder: Studien zu*

Mittel- und Osteuropa im 19. und 20. Jahrhundert: Beiträge eines Kolloquiums zum 65. Geburtstag von Hans Lemburg, edited by Edward Lemberg and Hans Mühle, 147–62. Marburg: Verlag Herder-Institut, 2001.

Mosse, George L. *Nationalism and Sexuality: Respectability and Abnormal Sexuality in Modern Europe*. New York: H. Fertig, 1985.

Moyn, Samuel. "Of Savagery and Civil Society: Pierre Clastres and the Transformation of French Political Thought." *Modern Intellectual History* 1, no. 1 (2004): 55–80.

Müller, Jan-Werner. *A Dangerous Mind: Carl Schmitt in Post-War European Thought*. New Haven, CT: Yale University Press, 2003.

Müller, Klaus-Dieter, Konstantin Nikischkin, and Günther Wagenlehner, eds. *Die Tragödie der Gefangenschaft in Deutschland und in der Sowjetunion 1941–1956*. Köln: Böhlau, 1998.

Naimark, Norman M. *Fires of Hatred: Ethnic Cleansing in Twentieth-Century Europe*. Cambridge, MA: Harvard University Press, 2001.

Nelles, Dieter. "Jan Valtins 'Tagebuch der Hölle': Legende und Wirklichkeit eines Schlüsselromans der Totalitarismustheorie." *1999: Zeitschrift für Sozialgeschichte des 20. und 21. Jahrhunderts* 9, no. 1 (1994): 11–45.

Nelson, Daniel. "Political Convergence." *World Politics* 30, no. 3 (1978): 411–32.

Neumann, Franz L. *Behemoth: The Structure and Practice of National Socialism*. Toronto and New York: Oxford University Press, 1942.

Nolte, Ernst. "Die historisch-genetische Version der Totalitarismustheorie: Ärgernis oder Einsicht?" *Zeitschrift für Politik* 43, no. 2 (1996): 111–22.

———. *Der europäische Bürgerkrieg, 1917–1945: Nationalsozialismus und Bolschewismus*. Berlin: Propyläen Verlag, 1987.

———. *Marxism, Fascism, Cold War*. Atlantic Highlands, NJ: Humanities Press, 1982.

———. "Marxismus und Nationalsozialismus." *Vierteljahrshefte für Zeitgeschichte* 31 (1983): 389–417.

O'Donnell, Guillermo A., Philippe C. Schmitter, and Laurence Whitehead, eds. *Transitions from Authoritarian Rule: Comparative Perspectives*. Baltimore: Johns Hopkins University Press, 1986.

Orwell, George. *1984: A Novel*. London: Secker & Warburg, 1949.

Osterhammel, Jürgen. "Die Wiederkehr des Raumes: Geopolitik, Geohistorie und historische Geographie." *Neue politische Literatur* 43 (1998): 374–97.

O'Sullivan, Donald. *Furcht und Faszination: Deutsche und britische Rußlandbilder, 1921–1933*. Cologne and Weimar: Böhlau, 1996.

Overmans, Rüdiger, ed. *In der Hand des Feindes: Kriegsgefangenschaft von der Antike bis zum Zweiten Weltkrieg*. Cologne: Böhlau, 1999.

Overy, Richard. *The Dictators: Hitler's Germany and Stalin's Russia*. London: Penguin Books, 2005.

Pagé, Suzanne, ed. *Années 30 en Europe: Le Temps menaçant 1929–1939: Exposition du 20 février au 25 mai 1997, Musée d'art moderne de la ville de Paris*. Paris: Flammarion, 1997.

Petersen, Roger Dale. *Understanding Ethnic Violence: Fear, Hatred, and Resentment in Twentieth-Century Eastern Europe*, Cambridge Studies in Comparative Politics. Cambridge: Cambridge University Press, 2002.

Pietrow-Ennker, Bianca "Das Feindbild im Wandel: Die Sowjetunion in den national-sozialistischen Wochenschauen 1935–1941," *Geschichte in Wissenschaft und Unterricht* 41 (1990): 337–51.

Pike, David. *German Writers in Soviet Exile, 1933–1945.* Chapel Hill: University of North Carolina Press, 1982.

Pipes, Richard. *Vixi: Memoirs of a Non-Belonger.* New Haven, CT: Yale University Press, 2003.

Poliakov, Léon, and Jean-Pierre Cabestan. *Les totalitarismes du XXe siècle: Un phénomène historique dépassé?* Paris: Fayard, 1987.

Pompidou, Centre National d'Art et de Culture Georges. *Paris-Moscow, 1900–1930: Catalogue de l'exposition Paris-Moscow.* 2nd ed. Paris: The Centre, 1979.

Popper, Karl Raimund *The Open Society and Its Enemies.* 2 vols. London: G. Routledge & Sons, 1945.

Postone, Moishe, and Eric L. Santner, eds. *Catastrophe and Meaning: The Holocaust and the Twentieth Century.* Chicago: University of Chicago Press, 2003.

Quine, Maria Sophia. *Population Politics in Twentieth-Century Europe: Fascist Dictatorships and Liberal Democracies*, Historical Connections. London and New York: Routledge, 1996.

Rabinbach, Anson. "Moments of Totalitarianism." *History and Theory* 45 (2006): 72–100.

Reichardt, Sven. "Was mit dem Faschismus passiert ist: Ein Literaturbericht zur internationalen Faschismusforschung seit 1990, Teil I." *Neue Politische Literatur* 49, no. 3 (2004): 385–406.

Reichardt, Sven, and Armin Nolzen, eds. *Faschismus in Italien und Deutschland: Studien zu Transfer und Vergleich*, Beiträge zur Geschichte des Nationalsozialismus. Göttingen: Wallstein, 2005.

Roberts, David D. *The Totalitarian Experiment in Twentieth-Century Europe: Understanding the Poverty of Great Politics.* London and New York: Routledge, 2006.

Rosanvallon, Pierre. *Democracy Past and Future*, Columbia Studies in Political Thought/Political History. New York: Columbia University Press, 2006.

Rosenfeld, Günter. "Kultur und Wissenschaft in den Beziehungen zwischen Deutschland und der Sowjetunion von 1933 bis 1941." *Berliner Jahrbuch für osteuropäische Geschichte* no. 1 (1995): 99–129.

———. *Sowjetrussland und Deutschland, 1917–1922.* 2nd ed. Cologne: Pahl-Rugenstein, 1984.

———. *Sowjetunion und Deutschland, 1922–1933.* Berlin: Akademie, 1984.

Rousso, Henry, and Richard Joseph Golsan, eds. *Stalinism and Nazism: History and Memory Compared*, European Horizons. Lincoln: University of Nebraska Press, 2004.

Rousso, Henry, and Nicolas Werth, eds. *Stalinisme et Nazisme: Histoire et mémoire comparées*, Collection "Histoire du temps présent." Brussels: Complexe, 1999.

Royster, Charles. *The Destructive War: William Tecumseh Sherman, Stonewall Jackson, and the Americans.* New York: Random House, 1991.

Ryklin, Michail K. *Räume des Jubels: Totalitarismus und Differenz: Essays.* Translated by Dirk Uffelmann, Edition Suhrkamp. Frankfurt am Main: Suhrkamp, 2003.

Schieder, Wolfgang. "Der Nationalsozialismus im Fehlurteil philosophischer Geschichtsschreibung: Zur Methode von Ernst Noltes 'Europäische Bürgerkrieg.'" *Geschichte und Gesellschaft* 15, no. 1 (1989): 69–114.

Schivelbusch, Wolfgang. *Three New Deals: Reflections on Roosevelt's America, Mussolini's Italy, and Hitler's Germany, 1933–1939.* Translated by Jefferson Chase. New York: Metropolitan Books, 2006.

Schlögel, Karl. *Im Raume lesen wir die Zeit: Über Zivilisationsgeschichte und Geopolitik*. Munich: Carl Hanser, 2003.

Schmeitzner, Mike, ed. *Totalitarismuskritik von links: Deutsche Diskurse im 20. Jahrhundert*, Schriften des Hannah-Arendt-Instituts für Totalitarismusforschung. Göttingen: Vandenhoeck & Ruprecht, 2007.

Schmitt, Carl. *Die Diktatur: Von den Anfängen des modernen Souveränitätsgedankens bis zum proletarischen Klassenkampf*. 2nd ed. Munich and Leipzig: Duncker & Humblot, 1928.

Schmuhl, Hans-Walter. "Rassenhygiene in Deutschland – Eugenik in der Sowjetunion: Ein Vergleich." In *Im Dschungel der Macht: Intellektuelle Professionen unter Stalin und Hitler*, edited by Dietrich Beyrau, 360–77. Göttingen: Vandenhoeck & Ruprecht, 2000.

Schöler, Uli. "Frühe totalitarismustheoretische Ansätze der Menschewiki im Exil." *Beiträge zur Geschichte der Arbeiterbewegung* 38, no. 2 (1996): 32–47.

Schönpflug, Daniel. "Histoires Croisées: Francois Furet, Ernst Nolte and a Comparative History of Totalitarian Movements." *European History Quarterly* 37, no. 2 (2007): 265–90.

Schöttler, Peter. "Henri Pirennes Kritik an der deutschen Geschichtwissenschaft und seine Neubegründung des Komparatismus im Ersten Weltkrieg." *SozialGeschichte* 19, no. 2 (2004): 53–81.

Schubart, Walter. *Europa und die Seele des Ostens*. Lucerne: Vita nova Verlag, 1938.

Schulin, Ernst. "Der Erste Weltkrieg und das Ende des alten Europas." In *Jahrhundertwende: Der Aufbruch in die Moderne 1880–1930*, edited by August Nitschke et al., 369–403. Reinbek: Rowolt, 1990.

Schwendemann, Heinrich. *Die wirtschaftliche Zusammenarbeit zwischen dem Deutschen Reich und der Sowjetunion von 1939 bis 1941: Alternative zu Hitlers Ostprogramm?* Quellen und Studien zur Geschichte Osteuropas. Berlin: Akademie Verlag, 1993.

Seidel, Bruno, and Siegfried Jenkner, eds. *Wege der Totalitarismus-Forschung*, Wege der Forschung. Darmstadt: Wissenschaftliche Buchgesellschaft, 1968.

Seidler, Franz Wilhelm. *Die Kollaboration, 1939–1945*. Munich: Herbig, 1995.

Semelin, Jacques. "Analysis of a Mass Crime: Ethnic Cleansing in the Former Yugoslavia, 1991–1999." In *The Specters of Genocide: Mass Murder in Historical Perspective*, edited by Ben Kiernan and Robert Gellately, 353–73. Cambridge: Cambridge University Press, 2003.

Shaw, Martin. *War and Genocide: Organized Killing in Modern Society*. Cambridge: Polity Press in Association with Blackwell, 2003.

Shlapentokh, Vladimir. "American Sovietology from 1917–1991: An Attempt at Diagnosis." *Russian History* 22, no. 4 (1995): 406–32.

Shorten, Richard. "Europe's Twentieth Century in Retrospect? A Cautious Note on the Furet/Nolte Debate." *European Legacy* 9, no. 3 (2004): 285–304.

Siegel, Achim, ed. *The Totalitarian Paradigm after the End of Communism: Towards a Theoretical Reassessment*, Poznan Studies in the Philosophy of the Sciences and the Humanities. Amsterdam: Allen Lane, 1998.

———. *Totalitarismustheorien nach dem Ende des Kommunismus*, Schriften des Hannah-Arendt-Instituts für Totalitarismusforschung. Cologne: Böhlau, 1998.

Slezkine, Yuri. *The Jewish Century*. Princeton, NJ: Princeton University Press, 2004.

Smith, Roger. "Human Destructiveness and Politics: The Twentieth Century as an Age of Genocide." In *Genocide and the Modern Age: Etiology and Case Studies of Mass*

Death, edited by Isidor Wallimann and Michael N. Dobkowski, 21–40. New York: Greenwood Press, 1987.

———. "Pluralismus und Humanismus in der Genozidforschung." In *Genozid und Moderne*, edited by Mihran Dabag and Kristin Platt, 309–19. Opladen: Leske + Budrich, 1998.

Söllner, Alfons. "Totalitarismus: Eine notwendige Denkfigur des 20. Jahrhunderts." *Mittelweg 36*, no. 2 (1993): 83–8.

Söllner, Alfons, Ralf Walkenhaus, and Karin Wieland, eds. *Totalitarismus, eine Ideengeschichte des 20. Jahrhunderts*. Berlin: Akademie Verlag, 1997.

Spies, S. B. *Methods of Barbarism?: Roberts and Kitchener and Civilians in the Boer Republics, January 1900–May 1902*. Cape Town: Human & Rousseau, 1977.

Stiftung Preußische Schlösser und Gärten Berlin-Brandenburg, ed. *Macht und Freundschaft 1800–1860*. Berlin: Koehler & Amelang, 2007.

Strauss, Leo, and Eric Voegelin. *Faith and Political Philosophy: The Correspondence between Leo Strauss and Eric Voegelin, 1934–1964*. Translated by Peter Emberley and Barry Cooper. University Park: Pennsylvania State University Press, 1993.

Streit, Christian. "Deutsche und sowjetische Kriegsgefangene." In *Kriegsverbrechen im 20. Jahrhundert*, edited by Wolfram Wette and Gerd R. Ueberschär, 178–92. Darmstadt: Wissenschaft Buchgesellschaft, 2001.

Szporluk, Roman. *Communism and Nationalism: Karl Marx versus Friedrich List*. New York: Oxford University Press, 1988.

Tischler, Carola. *Flucht in die Verfolgung: Deutsche Emigranten im sowjetischen Exil, 1933 bis 1945*, Arbeiten zur Geschichte Osteuropas. Münster: Lit, 1996.

Tucker, Robert C. *Philosophy and Myth in Karl Marx*. 2nd ed. Cambridge: Cambridge University Press, 1972.

Vahlefeld, Hans Wilhelm. *Deutschlands totalitäre Tradition: Nationalsozialismus und SED-Sozialismus als politische Religionen*. Stuttgart: Klett-Cotta, 2002.

van Der Linden, Marcel. "Socialisme ou Barbarie: A French Revolutionary Group (1949–65)." *Left History* 5, no. 1 (1997): 7–37.

Voegelin, Eric. *Die politischen Religionen*, Schriftenreihe "Ausblicke." Stockholm: Bermann-Fischer Verlag, 1939.

Voegelin, Eric et al., eds. *Politische Religion?: Politik, Religion und Anthropologie im Werk von Eric Voegelin*, Periagoge. Munich: Fink, 2003.

Wasserstein, Bernard. *Barbarism and Civilization: A History of Europe in Our Time*. Oxford and New York: Oxford University Press, 2007.

Weinberg, Gerhard L. *A World at Arms: A Global History of World War II*. New York: Cambridge University Press, 1994.

Weindling, Paul. *Epidemics and Genocide in Eastern Europe, 1890–1945*. Oxford: Oxford University Press, 2000.

Weisbrod, Bernd. "Fundamental Violence: Political Violence and Political Religion in Modern Conflict." *International Social Science Journal* 174 (2002): 499–508.

Weitz, Eric D. *A Century of Genocide: Utopias of Race and Nation*. Princeton, NJ: Princeton University Press, 2003.

Wells, H. G. *The Outline of History: Being a Plain History of Life and Mankind*. 2 vols. New York: Macmillan Co., 1920.

Welskopp, T. "Stolpersteine auf dem Königsweg: Methodenkritische Anmerkung zum internationalen Vergleich in der Gesellschaftsgeschichte." *Archiv für Sozialgeschichte* 35 (1995): 339–67.

Wette, Wolfram, and Gerd R. Ueberschär, eds. *Kriegsverbrechen im 20. Jahrhundert.* Darmstadt: Wissenschaftliche Buchgesellschaft, 2001.

Wheatcroft, Stephen. "Ausmass und Wesen der deutschen und sowjetischen Massentötungen und Repressionen." In *Lager, Zwangsarbeit, Vertreibung und Deportation: Dimensionen der Massenverbrechen in der Sowjetunion und in Deutschland 1933 bis 1945,* edited by Dittmar Dahlmann and Gerhard Hirschfeld, 67–109. Essen: Klartext, 1999.

Wippermann, Wolfgang. *Faschismustheorien: Zum Stand der gegenwärtigen Diskussion.* 5th rev. ed, Erträge der Forschung. Darmstadt: Wissenschaftliche Buchgesellschaft, 1976.

———. *Totalitarismustheorien: Die Entwicklung der Diskussion von den Anfängen bis heute.* Darmstadt: Primus, 1997.

Wolff, Robert Paul, Barrington Moore Jr., and Herbert Marcuse. *A Critique of Pure Tolerance.* Boston: Beacon Press, 1965.

Young-Bruehl, Elisabeth. *Hannah Arendt: For Love of the World.* New Haven, CT: Yale University Press, 1982.

Zeidler, Manfred. *Reichswehr und Rote Armee, 1920–1933: Wege und Stationen einer ungewöhnlichen Zusammenarbeit,* Beiträge zur Militärgeschichte. Munich: R. Oldenbourg, 1993.

Zernack, Klaus. *Polen und Russland: Zwei Wege in der europäischen Geschichte.* Berlin: Propyläen Verlag, 1994.

Zimmerer, Jürgen. "Die Geburt des 'Ostlandes' aus dem Geiste des Kolonialismus: Die nationalsozialistische Eroberungs- und Beherrschungspolitik in (post)kolonialer Perspektive." *SozialGeschichte: Zeitschrift für historische Analyse des 20. und 21. Jahrhunderts* 19, no. 1 (2004): 19–43.

———. "Holocaust und Kolonialismus: Beitrag zu einer Archäologie des genozidalen Gedankens." *Zeitschrift für Geschichtswissenschaft* 51, no. 12 (2003): 1098–119.

Zimmermann, Bénédicte, Claude Didry, and Peter Wagner, eds. *Le travail et la nation: Histoire croisée de la France et de l'Allemagne.* Paris: Maison des sciences de l'homme, 1999.

Žižek, Slavoj. *Did Somebody Say Totalitarianism?* London and New York: Verso, 2001.

Europe

Bednarski, Waldemar. "Das Gesicht des Krieges in der Gemeinde Kotlice (Kreis Zamosc) 1939–1945." In *Die polnische Heimatarmee: Geschichte und Mythos der Armia Krajowa seit dem Zweiten Weltkrieg,* edited by Bernhard Chiari, 411–30. Munich: Oldenbourg, 2003.

Benecke, Werner. *Die Ostgebiete der Zweiten Polnischen Republik: Staatsmacht und öffentliche Ordnung in einer Minderheitenregion 1918–1939,* Beiträge zur Geschichte Osteuropas. Cologne: Böhlau, 1999.

Berezen, Mabel. "Political Belonging: Emotion, Nation, and Identity in Fascist Italy." In *State/Culture: State Formation after the Cultural Turn,* edited by George Steinmetz, 355–77. Ithaca, NY: Cornell University Press, 1999.

Biuletyn Głównej Komisji Badania Zbrodni Hitlerowskich w Polsce. Vol. 21. Kraków: Wydawn. Ministerstwa Sprawiedliwosci, 1970.

Bourg, Julian, ed. *After the Deluge: New Perspectives on the Intellectual and Cultural History of Postwar France,* After the Empire. Lanham, MD: Lexington Books, 2004.

Bucur, Maria. *Eugenics and Modernization in Interwar Romania*, Pitt Series in Russian and East European Studies. Pittsburgh, PA: University of Pittsburgh Press, 2002.

Chodakiewicz, Marek Jan. *Between Nazis and Soviets: A Case Study of Occupation Politics in Poland, 1939–1947*. Lanham, MD: Lexington Books, 2004.

Coeuré, Sophie. *La grande lueur à l'Est: Les Français et l'Union soviétique, 1917–1939*, Archives du communisme. Paris: Seuil, 1999.

Comacchio, Cynthia R. "'The Infant Soldier': Early Child Welfare Efforts in Ontario." In *Women and Children First: International Maternal and Infant Welfare, 1870–1945*, edited by Valerie Fildes et al. New York: Routledge, 1993.

Dlugoborski, Waclaw, ed. *Polozenie ludnosci w Rejencji Katowickiej w latach 1939–1945*. Vol. 1, Documenta occupationis. Poznan: Instytut Zachodni, 1983.

Falasca-Zamponi, Simonetta. *Fascist Spectacle: The Aesthetics of Power in Mussolini's Italy*, Studies on the History of Society and Culture. Berkeley: University of California Press, 1997.

Fumaroli, Marc. "La Coupole." In *Realms of Memory: Rethinking the French Past*, edited by Pierre Nora, 249–306. New York: Columbia University Press, 1997.

Golczewski, Frank. "Die Heimatarmee und die Juden." In *Die polnische Heimatarmee: Geschichte und Mythos der Armia Krajowa seit dem Zweiten Weltkrieg*, edited by Bernhard Chiari, 635–76. Munich: Oldenbourg, 2003.

Gross, Jan Tomasz. *Polish Society under German Occupation: The Generalgouvernement, 1939–1944*. Princeton, NJ: Princeton University Press, 1979.

Havel, Václav, and John Keane. *The Power of the Powerless: Citizens against the State in Central-Eastern Europe*, Contemporary Politics. London: Hutchinson, 1985.

Hunt, Lynn Avery. *Politics, Culture, and Class in the French Revolution*, Studies on the History of Society and Culture. Berkeley: University of California Press, 1984.

Ipsen, Carl. *Dictating Demography: The Problem of Population in Fascist Italy*. New York: Cambridge University Press, 1996.

Johannisson, Karin. "The People's Health: Public Health Policies in Sweden." In *The History of Public Health and the Modern State*, edited by Dorothy Porter, 165–82. Amsterdam: Editions Rodopi B. V., 1994.

Judt, Tony. *Past Perfect: French Intellectuals, 1944–1956*. Berkeley: University of California Press, 1992.

Laasi, E. "Der Untergrundkrieg in Estland, 1945–1953." In *Auch wir sind Europa: Zur jüngeren Geschichte und aktuellen Entwicklung des Baltikums: Baltische Pressestimmen und Dokumente*, edited by Ruth Kibelka, 70–82. Berlin: Aufbau Taschenbuch Verlag, 1991.

Luczak, Czeslaw, ed. *Polozenie ludnosci polskiej w tzw. Kraju Warty w okresie hitlerowskiej okupacji*, Documenta occupationis. Poznan: Instytut Zachodni, 1990.

———, ed. *Wysiedlenia ludnosci polskiej na tzw. ziemiach wcielonych do Rzeszy 1939–1945*, Documenta Occupationis. Poznan: Instytut Zachodni, 1969.

Michnik, Adam, and Zinaïda Erard. *Penser la Pologne: Morale et politique de la résistance*, Cahiers libres. Paris: Découverte/Maspero, 1983.

Motyka, Grzegorz. "Der polnisch-ukrainische Gegensatz in Wolhynien und Ostgalizien." In *Die polnische Heimatarmee: Geschichte und Mythos der Armia Krajowa seit dem Zweiten Weltkrieg*, edited by Bernhard Chiari, 531–47. Munich: Oldenbourg, 2003.

Nash, Mary. "Protonatalism and Motherhood in Franco's Spain." In *Maternity and Gender Policies: Women and the Rise of the European Welfare States, 1880s–1950s*, edited by Gisela Bock and Pat Thane, 160–77. London: Routledge, 1991.

Niwinski, Piotr. "Die nationale Frage im Wilnagebiet." In *Die polnische Heimatarmee: Geschichte und Mythos der Armia Krajowa seit dem Zweiten Weltkrieg*, edited by Bernhard Chiari, 617–64. Munich: Oldenbourg, 2003.

Oberländer, Erwin, ed. *Geschichte Osteuropas: Zur Entwicklung einer historischen Disziplin in Deutschland, Österreich und der Schweiz 1945–1990*, Quellen und Studien zur Geschichte des östlichen Europa. Stuttgart: Franz Steiner, 1992.

Oberländer, Erwin, and Rolf Ahmann, eds. *Autoritäre Regime in Ostmittel- und Südosteuropa, 1919–1944*. Paderborn: F. Schöningh, 2001.

Raun, Toivo U. *Estonia and the Estonians*. 2nd ed., Studies of Nationalities in the USSR. Stanford, CA: Hoover Institution Press, Stanford University, 1991.

Rowe, Michael. *Collaboration and Resistance in Napoleonic Europe: State Formation in an Age of Upheaval, c. 1800–1815*. Basingstoke and New York: Palgrave Macmillan, 2003.

Schivelbusch, Wolfgang. *Die Bibliothek von Löwen: Eine Episode aus der Zeit der Weltkriege*. Munich: C. Hanser, 1988.

Szonert, M. B. *World War II through Polish Eyes: In the Nazi-Soviet Grip*, East European Monographs. Boulder, CO and New York: Columbia University Press, 2002.

Thane, Pat. "Visions of Gender in the Making of the British Welfare State: The Case of Women in the British Labour Party and Social Policy, 1906–1945." In *Maternity and Gender Policies: Women and the Rise of the European Welfare States 1880s–1950s*, edited by Gisela Bock and Pat Thane. London: Routledge, 1991.

National Socialism, Third Reich, Germany

Ausgewählte Reden des Führers und seiner Mitarbeiter, 1937. Sonderausgabe für die Wehrmacht. ed. Munich: Zentralverlag der NSDAP, 1937.

Das Sowjetparadies: Ausstellung der Reichspropagandaleitung der NSDAP: Ein Bericht in Wort und Bild. Berlin: Zentralverlag der NSDAP, Franz Eher Nachf., 1942.

Ich sah den Bolschewismus: Dokumente der Wahrheit gegen die bolschewistische Lüge: Thüringer Soldaten schreiben an ihren Gauleiter und Reichsstatthalter (Weimar: Der Nationalsozialist, 1942).

Forever in the Shadow of Hitler?: Original Documents of the Historikerstreit, the Controversy concerning the Singularity of the Holocaust. Atlantic Highlands, NJ: Humanities Press, 1993.

"Kluften der Erinnerung: Rußland und Deutschland sechzig Jahre nach dem Krieg." *Osteuropa* 55, no. 4–6 (2005).

Abel, Theodore Fred. *The Nazi Movement: Why Hitler Came to Power*. New York: Atherton Press, 1966.

Abelshauser, Werner. "Germany: Guns, Butter and Economic Miracles." In *The Economics of World War II: Six Great Powers in International Comparison*, edited by Mark Harrison, 122–76. Cambridge: Cambridge University Press, 1998.

Adam, Uwe Dietrich. *Judenpolitik im Dritten Reich*, Tübinger Schriften zur Sozial-und Zeitgeschichte. Düsseldorf: Droste Verlag, 1972.

Allen, William Sheridan. *The Nazi Seizure of Power: The Experience of a Single German Town, 1922–1945*. Rev. ed. New York: F. Watts, 1984.

Aly, Götz. *Endlösung: Völkerverschiebung und der Mord an den europäischen Juden*. Frankfurt am Main: S. Fischer, 1995.

————. *'Final solution': Nazi Population Policy and the Murder of the European Jews.* Translated by Belinda Cooper and Allison Brown. London and New York: Oxford University Press, 1999.

————. *Hitler's Beneficiaries: Plunder, Racial War, and the Nazi Welfare State.* Translated by Jefferson Chase. New York: Metropolitan, 2007.

————. "'Judenumsiedlung': Überlegungen zur politischen Vorgeschichte des Holocaust." In *Nationalsozialistische Vernichtungspolitik, 1939–1945: Neue Forschungen und Kontroversen*, 67–97. Frankfurt am Main: Fischer, 1998.

————, ed. *Aussonderung und Tod: Die klinische Hinrichtung der Unbrauchbaren.* 2nd ed. Vol. 1, Beiträge zur nationalsozialistischen Gesundheits- und Sozialpolitik. Berlin: Rotbuch, 1987.

Aly, Götz, and Susanne Heim. *Vordenker der Vernichtung: Auschwitz und die deutschen Pläne für eine neue europäische Ordnung.* Hamburg: Hoffmann und Campe, 1991.

Aly, Götz, and Karl Heinz Roth. *Die restlose Erfassung: Volkszählen, Identifizieren, Aussondern im Nationalsozialismus.* Berlin: Rotbuch Verlag, 1984.

Angrick, Andrej. *Besatzungspolitik und Massenmord: Die Einsatzgruppe D in der südlichen Sowjetunion 1941–1943.* Hamburg: Hamburger, 2003.

Arnold, Klaus Jochen. "Das Beispiel Charkow: Massenmord unter deutscher Besatzung." In *Verbrechen der Wehrmacht: Bilanz einer Debatte*, edited by Christian Hartmann, Johannes Hürter, and Ulrike Jureit, 17–24. Munich: Beck, 2002.

————. "Die Eroberung und Behandlung der Stadt Kiew durch die Wehrmacht im September 1941: Zur Radikalisierung der Besatzungspolitik." *Militärgeschichtliche Mitteilungen* 58, no. 1 (1999): 23–63.

————. *Die Wehrmacht und die Besatzungspolitik in den besetzten Gebieten der Sowjetunion: Kriegführung und Radikalisierung im "Unternehmen Barbarossa,"* Zeitgeschichtliche Forschungen. Berlin: Duncker & Humblot, 2005.

————. "Hitlers Wandel im August 1941: Ein Kommentar zu den Thesen Tobias Jersaks." *Zeitschrift für Geschichtswissenschaft* 48, no. 3 (2000): 239–50.

Arnold, Sabine R., and Gerd R. Ueberschär. *Das Nationalkommittee "Freies Deutschland" und der Bund Deutscher Offiziere*, Die Zeit des Nationalsozialismus,Geschichte Fischer. Frankfurt am Main: Fischer Taschenbuch Verlag, 1995.

Aschheim, Steven E. *Brothers and Strangers: The East European Jew in German and German Jewish Consciousness, 1800–1923.* Madison: University of Wisconsin Press, 1982.

Augstein, Rudolf, ed. *Historikerstreit: Die Dokumentation der Kontroverse um die Einzigartigkeit der nationalsozialistischen Judenvernichtung.* Munich: R. Piper, 1987.

Ayass, Wolfgang. "'Asoziale': Die verachteten Verfolgten." In *Verfolgung als Gruppenschicksal*, edited by Wolfgang Benz and Barbara Distel, 50–66. Dachau: Verlag Dachauer Hefte, 1998.

————. *"Asoziale" im Nationalsozialismus.* Stuttgart: Klett-Cotta, 1995.

Ayass, Wolfgang et al., eds. *Feindererklärung und Prävention: Kriminalbiologie, Zigeunerforschung und Asozialenpolitik*, Beiträge zur Nationalsozialistischen Gesundheits- und Sozialpolitik. Berlin: Rotbuch Verlag, 1988.

Backes, Uwe, and Eckhard Jesse. *Totalitarismus, Extremismus, Terrorismus: Ein Literaturführer und Wegweiser zur Extremismusforschung in der Bundesrepublik Deutschland.* 2nd rev. and expanded ed., Analysen. Opladen: Leske + Budrich, 1985.

Backes, Uwe, Eckhard Jesse, and Rainer Zitelmann, eds. *Die Schatten der Vergangenheit: Impulse zur Historisierung des Nationalsozialismus.* Berlin: Propyläen, 1990.

Balke, Friedrich, *Der Staat nach seinem Ende: Die Versuchung Carl Schmitts.* Munich: W. Fink, 1996.

Banach, Jens. *Heydrichs Elite: Das Führerkorps der Sicherheitspolizei und des SD 1936–1945*, Sammlung Schöningh zur Geschichte und Gegenwart. Paderborn: F. Schöningh, 1998.

Bankier, David. *The Germans and the Final Solution: Public Opinion under Nazism, Jewish Society and Culture.* New York: Oxford University Press, 1992.

Banse, Ewald. *Raum und Volk im Weltkriege: Gedanken über eine nationale Wehrlehre.* Oldenburg: G. Stalling, 1932.

Barkai, Avraham. *Das Wirtschaftssystem des Nationalsozialismus: Ideologie, Theorie, Politik, 1933–1945.* 2nd ed. Frankfurt am Main: Fischer Taschenbuch, 1988.

―――. *From Boycott to Annihilation: The Economic Struggle of German Jews, 1933–1943.* Translated by William Templer, The Tauber Institute for the Study of European Jewry Series. Hanover, NH: University Press of New England, 1989.

Bartov, Omer. *Eastern Front, 1941–1945: German Troops and the Barbarisation of Warfare.* 2nd ed., St Antony's Series. Basingstoke: Palgrave, 2001.

―――. "Defining Enemies, Making Victims: Germans, Jews, and the Holocaust." *American Historical Review* 103, no. 3 (1998): 258–71.

―――. "From Blitzkrieg to Total War: Controversial Links between Image and Reality." In *Stalinism and Nazism: Dictatorships in Comparison*, edited by Ian Kershaw and Moshe Levin, 158–84. Cambridge and New York: Cambridge University Press, 1997.

―――. *Hitler's Army: Soldiers, Nazis, and War in the Third Reich.* New York: Oxford University Press, 1991.

―――. "The Missing Years: German Workers, German Soldiers." *German History* 8 (1990): 46–65.

―――. "Von unten betrachtet: Überleben, Zusammenhalt und Brutalität an der Ostfront." In *Zwei Wege nach Moskau: Vom Hitler-Stalin-Pakt zum "Unternehmen Barbarossa*, edited by Bernd Wegner, 326–44. Munich and Zurich: Piper, 1991.

Basler, Werner. *Deutschlands Annexionspolitik in Polen und im Baltikum, 1914–1918*, Veröffentlichungen des Instituts für Geschichte der Völker der UdSSR an der Martin-Luther-Universität Halle-Wittenberg. Berlin: Rütten & Loening, 1962.

Baur, Johannes. "Die Revolution und 'Die Weisen von Zion': Zur Entwicklung des Russlandbildes in der frühen NSDAP." In *Jüdischer Bolschewismus: Mythos und Realität*, edited by Johannes Rogalla von Bieberstein, 165–90. Dresden: Antaios, 2002.

Beck, Birgit. *Wehrmacht und sexuelle Gewalt: Sexualverbrechen vor deutschen Militärgerichten 1939–1945*, Krieg in der Geschichte. Paderborn: Schöningh, 2004.

Beevor, Antony. *The Fall of Berlin, 1945.* New York: Viking, 2002.

Bely, Andrey, and Karl Schlögel. *Im Reich der Schatten: Berlin 1921 bis 1923.* Frankfurt am Main: Insel, 1987.

Berendse, Gerrit-Jan. *Schreiben im Terrordrom: Gewaltkodierung, kulturelle Erinnerung und das Bedingungsverhältnis zwischen Literatur und RAF-Terrorismus.* Munich: text + kritik, 2005.

Bergen, Doris L. *Twisted Cross: The German Christian Movement in the Third Reich.* Chapel Hill: University of North Carolina Press, 1966.

Bergerson, Andrew Stuart. "Listening to the Radio in Hildesheim, 1923–53." *German Studies Review* 24 (2001): 83–113.

Berghoff, Hartmut. "Methoden der Verbrauchslenkung im Nationalsozialismus." In *Wirtschaftskontrolle und Recht in der nationalsozialistischen Diktatur*, edited by Dieter Gosewinkel, 281–316. Frankfurt am Main: Klostermann, 2005.

Berkhoff, Karel C. *Harvest of Despair: Life and Death in Ukraine under Nazi Rule.* Cambridge, MA: Belknap Press of Harvard University Press, 2004.

Berlitz, Erich. *Ehestandsdarlehen*, Bücherei des Steuerrechts. Berlin and Vienna: Industrieverlag Spaeth und Linde, 1940.

Bernbaum, S. John A. "The New Elite: Nazi Leadership in Austria, 1938–1945." *Austrian History Yearbook* 14 (1978): 145–60.

Berthold, Eva, ed. *Kriegsgefangene im Osten: Bilder, Briefe, Berichte.* Königstein: Athenäum, 1981.

Bessel, Richard. *Nazism and War*, Modern Library Chronicles. New York: Modern Library, 2004.

———. *Germany after the First World War.* Oxford: Clarendon Press, 1993.

———. *Political Violence and the Rise of Nazism: The Storm Troopers in Eastern Germany, 1925–1934.* New Haven, CT: Yale University Press, 1984.

Biess, Frank. *Homecomings: Returning POWs and the Legacies of Defeat in Postwar Germany.* Princeton, NJ: Princeton University Press, 2006.

Birn, Ruth Bettina. "'Zaunkönig' an 'Uhrmacher': Grosse Partisanenaktionen 1942/43 am Beispiel des 'Unternehmens Winterzauber.'" *Militärgeschichtliche Zeitschrift* 60, no. 1 (2001): 99–118.

———. *Die höheren SS- und Polizeiführer: Himmlers Vertreter im Reich und in den besetzten Gebieten.* Düsseldorf: Droste, 1986.

Bleuel, Hans Peter. *Sex and Society in Nazi Germany.* Translated by J. Maxwell Brownjohn. Philadelphia: Lippincott, 1973.

Boberach, Heinz, ed. *Meldungen aus dem Reich, 1938–1945: Die geheimen Lageberichte des Sicherheitsdienstes der SS.* Herrsching: Pawlak, 1984.

Bock, Gisela. *Zwangssterilisation im Nationalsozialismus: Studien zur Rassenpolitik und Frauenpolitik*, Schriften des Zentralinstituts für Sozialwissenschaftliche Forschung der Freien Universität Berlin. Opladen: Westdeutscher Verlag, 1986.

Böhme, K. W. *Die deutschen Kriegsgefangenen in sowjetischer Hand: Eine Bilanz*, edited by Erich von Maschke, Zur Geschichte der deutschen Kriegsgefangenen des Zweiten Weltkrieges. Bielefeld: E. und W. Gieseking, 1966.

Boll, Bernd, and Hans Safrian. "On the Way to Stalingrad: The 6th Army in 1941–42." In *War of Extermination: The German Military in World War II, 1941–1944*, edited by Hannes Heer and Klaus Naumann, 237–71. New York and Oxford: Berghahn Books, 2000.

Bosma, Koos. "Verbindungen zwischen Ost- und Westkolonisation." In *Der "Generalplan Ost": Hauptlinien der nationalsozialistischen Planungs- und Vernichtungspolitik*, edited by Mechtild Rössler, Sabine Schleiermacher, and Cordula Tollmien, 198–214. Berlin: Akademie Verlag, 1993.

Bracher, Karl Dietrich. *The German Dictatorship: The Origins, Structure, and Effects of National Socialism.* Translated by Jan Steinberg. New York: Praeger Publishers, 1970.

———. *Zeitgeschichtliche Kontroversen: Um Faschismus, Totalitarismus, Demokratie*, Serie Piper. Munich: Piper, 1976.

Bracher, Karl Dietrich, Wolfgang Sauer, and Gerhard Schulz. *Die nationalsozialistische Machtergreifung: Studien zur Errichtung des totalitären Herrschaftssystems in*

Deutschland 1933/34, Schriften des Instituts für Politische Wissenschaft. Cologne and Opladen: Westdeutscher Verlag, 1960.

Brecht, Bertolt, ed. *Gesammelte Werke*. 20 vols. Vol. 12, Werkausgabe Edition Suhrkamp. Frankfurt am Main: Suhrkamp, 1967.

———, ed. *Gesammelte Werke*. 20 vols. Vol. 9, Werkausgabe Edition Suhrkamp. Frankfurt am Main: Suhrkamp, 1967.

Brechtken, Magnus. *Madagaskar für die Juden: Antisemitische Idee und politische Praxis 1885–1945*, Studien zur Zeitgeschichte. Munich: Oldenbourg, 1997.

Breuer, Stefan. *Ordnungen der Ungleichheit: Die deutsche Rechte im Widerstreit ihrer Ideen 1871–1945*. Darmstadt: Wissenschaftliche Buchgesellschaft, 2001.

Broszat, Martin. *Der Nationalsozialismus: Weltanschauung, Programm und Wirklichkeit*. Stuttgart: Deutsche Verlags-Anstalt, 1960.

———. *Der Staat Hitlers: Grundlegung und Entwicklung seiner inneren Verfassung*, DTV-Weltgeschichte des 20. Jahrhunderts. Munich: Deutscher Taschenbuch Verlag, 1969.

———. "Konzentrationslager." In *Anatomie des SS-Staates*, 9–135. Munich: Deutschen Taschenbuch Verlag, 1984.

———. "Soziale Motivation und Führerbindung des National Sozialismus." *Vierteljahrshefte für Zeitgeschichte* 18 (1970): 395–409.

———. *The Hitler State: The Foundation and Development of the Internal Structure of the Third Reich*. Translated by John W. Hiden. London and New York: Longman, 1981.

Browning, Christopher R. *Fateful Months: Essays on the Emergence of the Final Solution*. Rev. ed. New York: Holmes & Meier, 1991.

———. "German Killers: Behavior and Motivation in the Light of New Evidence." In *Nazi Policies, Jewish Workers, German Killers*, edited by Christopher R. Browning, 143–69. Cambridge and New York: Cambridge University Press, 2000.

———. "Ideology, Culture, Situation, and Disposition: Holocaust Perpetrators and the Group Dynamic of Mass Killing," *NS-Gewaltherrschaft: Beiträge zur historischen Forschung und juristischen Aufarbeitung*, eds. Alfred Gottwaldt, Norbert Kampe, and Peter Klein Berlin: Edition Hentrich, 2005, 66–76.

———. *Ordinary Men: Reserve Police Battalion 101 and the Final Solution in Poland*. New York: HarperCollins, 1992.

———. "The Euphoria of Victory and the Final Solution: Summer-Fall 1941." *German Studies Review* 17, no. 3 (1994): 473–81.

———. *The Path to Genocide: Essays on Launching the Final Solution*. Cambridge and New York: Cambridge University Press, 1992.

Browning, Christopher R., and Jürgen Matthäus. *Die Entfesselung der "Endlösung": Nationalsozialistische Judenpolitik 1939–1942*. Translated by Klaus-Dieter Schmidt. Berlin: Propyläen, 2003.

———. *The Origins of the Final Solution: The Evolution of Nazi Jewish Policy*. Lincoln, NE and Jerusalem: The University of Nebraska Press and Yad Vashem, 2004.

Bruendel, Steffen. *Volksgemeinschaft oder Volksstaat: Die "Ideen von 1914" und die Neuordnung Deutschlands im Ersten Weltkrieg*. Berlin: Akademie Verlag, 2003.

Brunner, Claudia. *Frauenarbeit im Männerstaat: Wohlfahrtspflegerinnen im Spannungsfeld kommunaler Sozialpolitik in München 1918–1938*, Forum Frauengeschichte. Pfaffenweiler: Centaurus, 1994.

————. "Fürsorgeempfänger wurden ausgemerzt: Die Sozialpolitik des Münchner Wohlfahrtsamtes am Ende der Weimarer Republik und in der frühen NS-Zeit." In *Durchschnittstäter: Handeln und Motivation*, edited by Christian Gerlach, 53–72. Berlin: Verlag der Buchläden, 2000.

Buchbender, Ortwin. *Das tönende Erz: Deutsche Propaganda gegen die Rote Armee in zweiten Weltkrieg*, Militärpolitische Schriftenreihe. Stuttgart: Seewald Verlag, 1978.

Buchbender, Ortwin, and Reinhold Sterz, eds. *Das andere Gesicht des Krieges: Deutsche Feldpostbriefe, 1939–1945*. Munich: Beck, 1982.

Buchheim, Hans. "Die SS – Das Herrschaftsimperium." In *Anatomie des SS-Staates*, 30–40. Munich: Deutscher Taschenbuch Verlag, 1999.

Buchholz, Kai, ed. *Die Lebensreform: Entwürfe zur Neugestaltung von Leben und Kunst um 1900*. Darmstadt: Institut Mathildenhöhe; Häusser, 2001.

Burkert, Martin. *Die Ostwissenschaften im Dritten Reich: Zwischen Verbot und Duldung: Die schwierige Gratwanderung der Ostwissenschaften zwischen 1933 und 1939*. Wiesbaden: Harrassowitz, 2000.

Burleigh, Michael. *Death and Deliverance: "Euthanasia" in Germany c. 1900–1945*. Cambridge: Cambridge University Press, 1994.

————. *Germany Turns Eastwards: A Study of Ostforschung in the Third Reich*. Cambridge: Cambridge University Press, 1988.

————. *The Third Reich: A New History*. New York: Hill & Wang, 2001.

Burleigh, Michael, and Wolfgang Wippermann. *The Racial State: Germany, 1933–1945*. Cambridge and New York: Cambridge University Press, 1991.

Camphausen, Gabriele. "Das Russlandbild in der deutschen Geschichtswissenschaft 1933 bis 1945." In *Das Russlandbild im Dritten Reich*, edited by Hans Erich Volkmann, 257–83. Cologne: Böhlau, 1994.

————. *Die wissenschaftliche historische Russlandforschung im Dritten Reich 1933–1945*, Europäische Hochschulschriften, Series III, Geschichte und ihre Hilfswissenschaften. Frankfurt am Main: P. Lang, 1990.

Caplan, Jane. *Government without Administration: State and Civil Service in Weimar and Nazi Germany*, Oxford Historical Monographs. Oxford: Clarendon Press, 1988.

Cesarani, David. *Eichmann: His Life, Crimes and Legacy*. London: Heinemann, 2003.

Chiari, Bernhard. "Grenzen deutscher Herrschaft: Voraussetzungen und Folgen der Besatzung der Sowjetunion." In *Das Deutsche Reich und der Zweite Weltkrieg. Vol. 9/2, Ausbeutung, Deutungen, Ausgrenzungen*, edited by Militärgeschichtliches Forschungsamt, 877–976. Munich: Deutsche Verlagsanstalt, 2005.

Connelly, John. "The Uses of Volksgemeinschaft: Letters to the NSDAP Kreisleitung Eisenach, 1939–1940." *Journal of Modern History* 68, no. 4 (1996): 899–930.

Czarnowski, Gabriele. "Frauen – Staat – Medizin: Aspekte der Körperpolitik im Nationalsozialismus." *Beiträge zur feministischen Theorie und Praxis* 8 (1985), 79–98.

————. *Das kontrollierte Paar: Ehe- und Sexualpolitik im Nationalsozialismus*, Ergebnisse der Frauenforschung. Weinheim: Deutscher Studien Verlag, 1991.

Dallin, Alexander. *Deutsche Herrschaft in Russland, 1941–1945*. Düsseldorf: Droste, 1958.

Dean, Martin. *Collaboration in the Holocaust: Crimes of the Local Police in Belorussia and Ukraine, 1941–44*. New York: St. Martin's Press published in association with the United States Holocaust Memorial Museum, 2000.

_____. "The German Gendarmerie, the Ukrainian Schutzmannschaft and the 'Second Wave' of Jewish Killings in Occupied Ukraine: German Policing at the Local Level in the Zhitomir Region, 1941–1944." *German History* 14, no. 2 (1996): 168–92.

Dedering, Tilman. "'A Certain Rigorous Treatment of All Parts of the Nation': The Annihilation of the Herero in German South-West Africa 1904." In *The Massacre in History*, edited by Mark Levene and Penny Roberts, 205–22. New York: Berghahn Books, 1999.

Didier, Friedrich. *Ich sah den Bolschewismus: Dokumente der Wahrheit gegen die bolschewistische Lüge [Thüringer Soldaten schreiben an ihren Gauleiter und Reichsstatthalter].* 2nd ed. Weimar: Der Nationalsozialist, 1942.

Dieckmann, Christoph. "Der Krieg und die Ermordung der litauischen Juden." In *Nationalsozialistische Vernichtungspolitik: Neue Forschungen und Kontroversen*, edited by Ulrich Herbert, 240–75. Frankfurt am Main: Fischer Taschenbuch Verlag, 2001.

_____. "Deutsche Besatzungspolitik und Massenverbrechen in Litauen 1941–1944: Täter, Zuschauer, Opfer." Ph.D. thesis, University of Freiburg, 2003.

Diehl-Thiele, Peter. *Partei und Staat im Dritten Reich: Untersuchungen zum Verhältnis von NSDAP und allgemeiner innerer Staatsverwaltung 1933–1945*, Münchener Studien zur Politik. Munich: Beck, 1969.

Dietrich, Otto. *12 Jahre mit Hitler.* Munich: Isar Verlag, 1955.

Diewald-Kerkmann, Gisela. *Politische Denunziation im NS-Regime oder die kleine Macht der "Volksgenossen."* Bonn: Dietz, 1995.

Diner, Dan. "Rassistisches Völkerrecht: Elemente der nationalsozialistischen Weltordnung." *Vierteljahrshefte für Zeitgeschichte* 37 (1989): 23–56.

Dördelmann, Katrin. *Die Macht der Worte: Denunziationen im nationalsozialistischen Köln*, Schriften des NS-Dokumentationszentrums der Stadt Köln. Cologne: Emons Verlag, 1997.

Dörner, Bernward. *"Heimtücke": Das Gesetz als Waffe: Kontrolle, Abschreckung und Verfolgung in Deutschland 1933–1945*, Sammlung Schöningh zur Geschichte und Gegenwart. Paderborn: Schöningh, 1998.

Domarus Max, ed. *Hitler: Reden und Proklamationen 1932–1945: Kommentiert von einem deutschen Zeitgenossen.* 2 vols. Vol. 1. Würzburg: Domarus [self-published], 1963.

Dwinger, Edwin Erich. *Wiedersehen mit Sowjetrussland: Tagebuch vom Ostfeldzug.* Jena: E. Diederichs, 1943.

Dwork, Debórah, and R. J. van Pelt. *Auschwitz, 1270 to the Present.* New York: Norton, 1996.

Eichholtz, Dietrich. "Der 'Generalplan Ost': Über eine Ausgeburt imperialistischer Denkart und Politik." *Jahrbuch für Geschichte* 26 (1982): 217–74.

Esch, Michael G. *Gesunde Verhältnisse: Deutsche und polnische Bevölkerungspolitik in Ostmitteleuropa 1939–1950*, Materialien und Studien zur Ostmitteleuropa-Forschung. Marburg: Herder-Institut, 1998.

Fahlbusch, Michael. *"Wo der deutsche... ist, ist Deutschland": Die Stiftung für Deutsche Volks- und Kulturbodenforschung in Leipzig 1920–1933*, Abhandlungen zur Geschichte der Geowissenschaften und Religion/Umwelt-Forschung. Bochum: Universitätsverlag Dr. N. Brockmeyer, 1994.

Falter, Jürgen. *Hitlers Wähler.* Munich: Beck, 1991.

_____. "Kontinuität und Neubeginn: Die Bundestagswahl 1949 zwischen Weimar und Bonn." *Politische Vierteljahresschrift* 22, no. 3 (1981): 236–63.

———. "The National Socialist Mobilization of New Voters, 1928–1933." In *The Formation of the Nazi Constituency, 1919–1933*, edited by Thomas Childers, 202–31. Totowa, NJ: Barnes & Noble, 1986.

———. "The Young Membership of the NSDAP between 1925 and 1933: A Demographic and Social Profile." In *The Rise of National Socialism and the Working Classes in Weimar Germany*, edited by Conan Fischer, 117–36. Providence, RI: Berghahn Books, 1996.

———. "War die NSDAP die erste deutsche Volkspartei?" In *Nationalsozialismus und Modernisierung*, edited by Michael Prinz and Rainer Zitelmann, 21–47. Darmstadt: Wissenschaftliche Buchgesellschaft, 1994.

Faure, Ulrich. *Im Knotenpunkt des Weltverkehrs: Herzfelde, Heartfield, Grosz und der Malik-Verlag, 1916–1947*, Aufbau Sachbuch. Berlin: Aufbau-Verlag, 1992.

Fenske, Hans. "Die Verwaltung im Ersten Weltkrieg "In *Deutsche Verwaltungsgeschichte*, edited by Kurt G. A. Jeserich, Dieter Pohl, and Georg-Christoph von Unruh, 866–908. Stuttgart: Deutsche Verlags-Anstalt, 1983.

Feuchtwanger, Lion. *Die Geschwister Oppenheim: Roman*, Gesammelte Werke. Amsterdam: Querido Verlag, 1933.

———. *The Oppermanns: A Novel*. Translated by Jane Cleugh. London: M. Secker, 1933.

Fischer, Conan. *The Rise of the Nazis*. 2nd ed., New Frontiers in History. Manchester and New York: Manchester University Press and Palgrave, 2002.

Fleischhacker, Hedwig, ed. *Die deutschen Kriegsgefangen in der Sowjetunion: Der Faktor Hunger*, Zur Geschichte der deutschen Kriegsgefangenen des Zweiten Weltkrieges. Munich: Kommission für deutsche Kriegsgefangenengeschichte, 1965.

Föllmer, Moritz, ed. *Sehnsucht nach Nähe: Interpersonale Kommunikation in Deutschland seit dem 19. Jahrhundert*. Stuttgart: Steiner, 2004.

Förster, Jürgen. "Die Sicherung des 'Lebensraumes.'" In *Der Angriff auf die Sowjetunion. Vol. 4, Das Deutsche Reich und der Zweite Weltkrieg*, edited by Horst Boog et al. 1227–87. Stuttgart: Deutsche Verlags-Anstalt, 1983.

———. "From 'Blitzkrieg' to 'Total War': Germany's War in Europe." In *A World at Total War: Global Conflict and the Politics of Destruction, 1937–1945*, edited by Roger Chickering, Stig Förster, and Bernd Greiner, 89–108. Washington, DC, and Cambridge: German Historical Institute and Cambridge University Press, 2005.

———. "Hitlers Entscheidung für den Krieg gegen die Sowjetunion." In *Der Angriff auf die Sowjetunion. Vol. 4, Das Deutsche Reich und der Zweite Weltkrieg*, edited by Horst Boog et al., 27–68. Stuttgart: Deutsche Verlags-Anstalt, 1983.

———. "Hitlers Wendung nach Osten: Die deutsche Kriegspolitik, 1940–1941." In *Zwei Wege nach Moskau: Vom Hitler-Stalin-Pakt zum "Unternehmen Barbarossa,"* edited by Bernd Wegner, 113–32. Munich and Zurich: Piper, 1991.

———. "Unternehmen 'Barbarossa' als Eroberungs- und Vernichtungskrieg." In *Der Angriff auf die Sowjetunion. Vol. 4, Das Deutsche Reich und der Zweite Weltkrieg*, edited by Horst Boog et al. 498–538. Stuttgart: Deutsche Verlags-Anstalt, 1983.

———. "'Verbrecherische Befehle." In *Kriegsverbrechen im 20. Jahrhundert*, edited by Wolfram Wette and Gerd R. Ueberschär, 137–51. Darmstadt: Wissenschaftliche Buchgesellschaft, 2001.

———. "Wehrmacht, Krieg und Holocaust." In *Die Wehrmacht: Mythos und Realität*, edited by Rolf-Dieter Müller and Hans Erich Volkmann, 948–63. Munich: Beck, 1999.

————. "Zum Russlandbild der Militärs 1941–1945." In *Das Russlandbild im Dritten Reich*, edited by Hans Erich Volkmann, 141–63. Cologne: Böhlau, 1994.

Foerster, Roland, ed. *"Unternehmen Barbarossa": Zum historischen Ort der deutsch-sowjetischen Beziehungen von 1933 bis Herbst 1941*. Paderborn: F. Schöningh, 1993.

Frame, Lynne-Marie Hoskins. "Forming and Reforming the New Woman in Weimar Germany." Ph.D. diss., University of California, Berkeley, 1997.

Frank, Bajohr. *"Aryanisation" in Hamburg: The Economic Exclusion of Jews and the Confiscation of their Property in Nazi Germany*, Monographs in German History. New York: Berghahn Books, 2002.

Frei, Norbert, ed. *Medizin und Gesundheitspolitik in der NS-Zeit*, Schriftenreihe der Vierteljahrshefte für Zeitgeschichte. Munich: R. Oldenbourg, 1991.

Frevert, Ute. *Die kasernierte Nation: Militärdienst und Zivilgesellschaft in Deutschland*. Munich: C. H. Beck, 2001.

————. *Women in German History: From Bourgeois Emancipation to Sexual Liberation*. Translated by Stuart McKinnon-Evans, Terry Bond and Barbara Norden. New York and Oxford: Berg, 1989.

Friedlander, Henry. *The Origins of Nazi Genocide: From Euthanasia to the Final Solution*. Chapel Hill: University of North Carolina Press, 1995.

Friedländer, Saul. *Nazi Germany and the Jews: The Years of Extermination, 1939–45*. 2 vols. Vol. 2. New York: HarperCollins, 2007.

————. *Nazi Germany and the Jews: The Years of Persecution, 1933–1939*. 2 vols. Vol. 1. New York: HarperCollins, 1997.

Friedrich, Jörg. *Das Gesetz des Krieges: Das deutsche Heer in Russland, 1941 bis 1945: der Prozess gegen das Oberkommando der Wehrmacht*. Munich: Piper, 1993.

Frieser, Karl-Heinz. "Die deutschen Blitzkriege: Operativer Triumph – Strategische Tragödie." In *Erster Weltkrieg – Zweiter Weltkrieg: Krieg, Kriegserlebnis, Kriegserfahrung in Deutschland*, edited by Bruno Thoss and Hans Erich Volkmann, 182–96. Paderborn: Ferdinand Schöningh, 2002.

Fritz, Stephen G. *Frontsoldaten: The German Soldier in World War II*. Lexington: University Press of Kentucky, 1995.

Fritzsche, Peter. *A Nation of Fliers: German Aviation and the Popular Imagination*. Cambridge, MA: Harvard University Press, 1992.

————. *Germans into Nazis*. Cambridge, MA: Harvard University Press, 1998.

————. *Life and Death in the Third Reich*. Cambridge, MA: The Belknap Press of Harvard University Press, 2008.

Fuhrmann, Martin. *Volksvermehrung als Staatsaufgabe?: Bevölkerungs- und Ehepolitik in der deutschen politischen und ökonomischen Theorie des 18. und 19. Jahrhunderts*, Rechts- und staatswissenschaftliche Veröffentlichungen der Görres-Gesellschaft. Paderborn: Schöningh, 2002.

Gailus, Manfred. *Protestantismus und Nationalsozialismus: Studien zur nationalsozialistischen Durchdringung des protestantischen Sozialmilieus in Berlin*, Industrielle Welt. Cologne: Böhlau, 2001.

Gansel, Carsten, ed. *Der gespaltene Dichter: Johannes R. Becher: Gedichte, Briefe, Dokumente 1945–1958*, ATV Dokument und Essay. Berlin: Aufbau Taschenbuch Verlag, 1991.

Garleff, Michael, ed. *Deutschbalten, Weimarer Republik und Drittes Reich*. 3 vols. Vol. 1, Das Baltikum in Geschichte und Gegenwart. Cologne: Böhlau, 2001.

Gellately, Robert. *Backing Hitler: Consent and Coercion in Nazi Germany*. New York: Oxford University Press, 2001.

———. "Denunciations in Twentieth-Century Germany: Aspects of Self-Policing in the Third Reich and in the German Democratic Republic." In *Accusatory Practices: Denunciation in Modern Eureopean History, 1889–1989*, edited by Sheila Fitzpatrick and Robert Gellately, 129–58. Chicago and London: University of Chicago Press, 1997.

———. *Hingeschaut und weggesehen: Hitler und sein Volk*. Translated by Holger Fliessbach. Stuttgart: Deutsche Verlags-Anstalt, 2002.

———. *The Gestapo and German Society: Enforcing Racial Policy, 1933–1945*. Oxford: Clarendon Press, 1990.

Genschel, Helmut. *Die Verdrängung der Juden aus der Wirtschaft im Dritten Reich*, Göttinger Bausteine zur Geschichtswissenschaft. Göttingen: Musterschmidt-Verlag, 1966.

Gerlach, Christian. *Kalkulierte Morde: Die deutsche Wirtschafts- und Vernichtungspolitik in Weissrussland 1941 bis 1944*. Hamburg: Hamburger Edition, 1999.

———. "La Wehrmacht et la radicalisation de la lutte contre les partisans en Union Soviétique." In *Occupation et répression militaire allemandes: La politique de "maintien de l'ordre" en Europe occupée, 1939–1945*, edited by Gaël Eismann and Martens Stefan, 71–88. Paris: Institut historique allemand, 2007.

———. *Krieg, Ernährung, Völkermord: Forschungen zur deutschen Vernichtungspolitik im Zweiten Weltkrieg*. Hamburg: Hamburger, 1998.

———. "The Wannsee Conference, the Fate of German Jews, and Hitler's Decision in Principle to Exterminate All European Jews." *Journal of Modern History* 70, no. 4 (1998): 759–812.

———. "Umsiedlungen und gelenkte Bevölkerungsbewegung in Weißrußland 1941–1944." In *Lager, Zwangsarbeit, Vertreibung und Deportation: Dimensionen der Massenverbrechen in der Sowjetunion und in Deutschland 1933 bis 1945*, edited by Dittmar Dahlmann and Gerhard Hirschfeld, 553–65. Essen: Klartext, 1999.

———. "Verbrechen deutscher Fronttruppen in Weissrussland 1941–1944: Eine Annäherung." In *Vernichtungspolitik: Militär im nationalsozialistischen System*, Karl Heinrich Pohl, 89–114. Göttingen: Vandenhoeck & Ruprecht, 1999.

———, ed. *Besatzung und Bündnis: Deutsche Herrschaftsstrategien in Ost- und Südosteuropa*, Beiträge zur nationalsozialistischen Gesundheits- und Sozialpolitik. Berlin: Verlag der Buchläden, 1995.

———, ed. *Durchschnittstäter: Handeln und Motivation*, Beiträge zur Geschichte des Nationalsozialismus. Berlin: Verlag der Buchläden, 2000.

Geyer, Michael. "Endkampf 1918 and 1945." In *No Man's Land of Violence: Extreme Wars in the 20th Century*, edited by Alf Lüdtke and Bernd Weisbrod, 35–68. Göttingen: Wallstein, 2006.

———. "German Strategy in the Age of Machine Warfare, 1914–1945." In *Makers of Modern Strategy from Machiavelli to the Nuclear Age*, edited by Peter Paret, 527–97. Princeton, NJ: Princeton University Press, 1985.

———. "Restaurative Elites, German Society and the Nazi Pursuit of War." In *Fascist Italy and Nazi Germany: Comparison and Contrast*, edited by Richard Bessel, 134–64. Cambridge: Cambridge University Press, 1996.

———. "Vom massenhaften Tötungshandeln, oder: Wie die Deutschen das Krieg-Machen lernten." In *Massenhaftes Töten: Krieg und Genozide im 20. Jahrhundert*, edited by Peter Gleichmann and Thomas Kühne, 105–42. Essen: Klartext Verlag, 2004.

Giles, Geoffrey. "Männerbund mit Homo-Panik: Die Angst der Nazis vor der Rolle der Erotik." In *Nationalsozialistischer Terror gegen Homosexuelle: Verdrängt und ungesühnt*, edited by Burkhard Jellonnek and Rüdiger Lautmann, 105–18. Paderborn: Schöningh, 2002.

———. "The Denial of Homosexuality: Same-Sex Incidents in Himmler's SS and Police." *Journal of the History of Sexuality* 11, no. 1–2 (2002): 256–90.

———. "The Institutionalization of Homosexual Panic in the Third Reich." In *Social Outsiders in Nazi Germany*, edited by Robert Gellately and Nathan Stoltzfuss, 233–55. Princeton, NJ: Princeton University Press, 2001.

———. "'The Most Unkindest Cut of all': Castration, Homosexuality, and Nazi Justice." *Journal of Contemporary History* 27, no. 1 (1992): 41–61.

Giordano, Ralph. *Wenn Hitler den Krieg gewonnen hätte: Die Pläne der Nazis nach dem Endsieg*. Hamburg: Rasch & Röhring, 1989.

Goebbels, Joseph. *Michael: A Novel*. Translated by Joachim Neugroschel. New York: Amok Press, 1987.

Golovchansky, Anatoly, ed. *"Ich will raus aus diesem Wahnsinn": Deutsche Briefe von der Ostfront 1941–1945: Aus sowjetischen Archiven*. Wuppertal P. Hammer, 1991.

Grell, Ursula. "Aufgaben der Gesundheitsämter im Dritten Reich." In *Totgeschwiegen, 1933–1945: Zur Geschichte der Wittenauer Heilstätten, seit 1957 Karl-Bonhoeffer-Nervenklinik*, edited by Arbeitsgruppe zur Erforschung der Geschichte der Karl-Bonhoeffer-Nervenklinik, 77–92. Berlin: Hentrich, 1989.

Grode, Walter. *Die "Sonderbehandlung 14f13" in den Konzentrationslagern des Dritten Reiches: Ein Beitrag zur Dynamik faschistischer Vernichtungspolitik*, Europäische Hochschulschriften, Politikwissenschaft. Frankfurt am Main: P. Lang, 1987.

Grossmann, Atina. *Reforming Sex: The German Movement for Birth Control and Abortion Reform, 1920–1950*. New York: Oxford University Press, 1995.

———. "The Debate That Will Not End: The Politics of Abortion in Germany from Weimar to National Socialism and the Postwar Period." In *Medicine and Modernity: Public Health and Medical Care in Nineteenth- and Twentieth-Century Germany*, edited by Manfred Berg and Geoffrey Cocks, 193–212. Washington, DC, and Cambridge: German Historical Institute and Cambridge University Press, 1997.

Grotjahn, Alfred. "Differential Birth Rate in Germany." In *Proceedings of the World Population Conference* held at the Salle Centrale, Geneva, August 29th to September 3rd, 1927, edited by Margaret Sanger, 149–57. London: E. Arnold, 1927.

Gruchmann, Lothar. "Die 'Reichsregierung' im Führerstaat: Stellung und Funktion des Kabinetts im nationalsozialistischen Herrschaftssystem." In *Klassenjustiz und Pluralismus: Festschrift für Ernst Fraenkels 75. Geburtstag am 26. Dezember 1978*, edited by Winfried Steffani and Falk Esche, 187–223. Hamburg: Hoffmann und Campe, 1973.

Gründel, E. Günther. *Die Sendung der jungen Generation: Versuch einer umfassenden revolutionären Sinndeutung der Krise*. Munich: Beck, 1932.

Gumz, Jonathan E. "Wehrmacht Perceptions of Mass Violence in Croatia, 1941–1942." *Historical Journal* 44, no. 4 (2001): 1015–38.

Gütt, Arthur. *Bevölkerungs- und Rassenpolitik*. Berlin: Industrieverlag Spaeth & Linde, 1936.

———. *Der Aufbau des Gesundheitswesens im Dritten Reich*. 4th rev. ed, Schriften der Deutschen Hochschule für Politik. Berlin: Junker und Dünnhaupt, 1938.

―――. *Die Rassenpflege im Dritten Reich*, Schriften des Reichsinstituts für Geschichte des neuen Deutschlands. Hamburg: Hanseatische Verlagsanstalt, 1940.

―――. *Gesetz zur Verhütung erbkranken Nachwuchses vom 14. Juli 1933: Mit Auszug aus dem Gesetz gegen gefährliche Gewohnheitsverbrecher und über Massregeln der Sicherung und Besserung vom 24. Nov. 1933*. Munich: J. F. Lehmanns Verlag, 1934.

Haar, Ingo, and Michael Fahlbusch, eds. *German Scholars and Ethnic Cleansing, 1919–1945*. New York: Berghahn Books, 2005.

Hachtmann, Rüdiger. *Industriearbeit im "Dritten Reich": Untersuchungen zu den Lohn- und Arbeitsbedingungen in Deutschland, 1933–1945*, Kritische Studien zur Geschichtswissenschaft. Göttingen: Vandenhoeck & Ruprecht, 1989.

Haeberle, Erwin J. "Swastika, Pink Triangle, and Yellow Star: The Destruction of Sexology and the Persecution of Homosexuals in Nazi Germany." In *Hidden from History: Reclaiming the Gay and Lesbian Past*, edited by Martin Duberman et al., 365–79. New York: New American Library, 1989.

Haffner, Sebastian. *Anmerkungen zu Hitler*. Munich: Kindler, 1978.

―――. *Geschichte eines Deutschen: Die Erinnerungen 1914–1933*. Stuttgart: Deutsche Verlags-Anstalt, 2000.

Hagemann, Karen. "Men's Demonstrations and Women's Protest: Gender in Collective Action in the Urban Working-Class Milieu during the Weimar Republic." *Gender & History* 5, no. 1 (1993): 101–20.

Hamburger Institut für Sozialforschung, ed. *Verbrechen der Wehrmacht: Dimensionen des Vernichtungskrieges 1941–1944: Ausstellungskatalog*. Hamburg: Hamburger Edition, 2002.

Hammerschmidt, Peter. *Die Wohlfahrtsverbände im NS-Staat: Die NSV und die konfessionellen Verbände Caritas und innere Mission im Gefüge der Wohlfahrtspflege des Nationalsozialismus*. Opladen: Leske + Budrich, 1999.

Hancock, Eleanor. "'Only the Real, the True, the Masculine Held Its Value': Ernst Röhn, Masculinity, and Male Homosexuality." *Journal of the History of Sexuality* 8, no. 4 (1998): 616–41.

Hardtwig, Wolfgang. "Der Krise des Geschichtsbewusstseins in Kaiserreich und Weimarer Republik und der Aufstieg des Nationalsozialismus." In *Jahrbuch des Historischen Kollegs 2001*, 47–75. Munich: Oldenbourg, 2002.

―――, ed. *Politische Kulturgeschichte der Zwischenkriegszeit 1918–1939*, Geschichte und Gesellschaft: Zeitschrift für historische Sozialwissenschaft. Göttingen: Vandenhoeck & Ruprecht, 2005.

Hartmann, Christian. *Halder, Generalstabschef Hitlers, 1938–1942*, Sammlung Schöningh zur Geschichte und Gegenwart. Paderborn: F. Schöningh, 1991.

―――. "Massensterben oder Massenvernichtung? Sowjetische Kriegsgefangene im Unternehmen Barbarossa' – Aus dem Tagebuch eines Lagerkommandanten." *Vierteljahrshefte für Zeitgeschichte* 49 (2001): 97–158.

―――. "Verbrecherischer Krieg – Verbrecherische Wehrmacht? Überlegungen zur Struktur des deutschen Ostheeres 1941–1944." *Vierteljahrshefte für Zeitgeschichte* 52, no. 1 (2004): 1–75.

Hartmann, Christian, Johannes Hürter, and Ulrike Jureit, eds. *Verbrechen der Wehrmacht: Bilanz einer Debatte*. Munich: Beck, 2005.

Harvey, Elizabeth. "'Die deutsche Frau im Osten': 'Rasse,' Geschlecht, und öffentlicher Raum im besetzten Polen 1940-1944." *Archiv für Sozialgeschichte* 38 (1998): 191–214.

———. *Women and the Nazi East: Agents and Witnesses of Germanization.* New Haven, CT: Yale University Press, 2003.

Havemann, Nils. *Fussball unterm Hakenkreuz: Der DFB zwischen Sport, Politik und Kommerz.* Frankfurt: Campus, 2005.

Hecker, Hans. *Die Tat und ihr Osteuropa-Bild, 1909–1939.* Cologne: Wissenschaft und Politik, 1974.

Heer, Hannes. "How Amorality Became Normality: Reflections on the Mentality of German Soldiers on the Eastern Front." In *War of Extermination: The German Military in World War II, 1941–44,* edited by Hannes Heer and Klaus Naumann, 329–44. New York: *Berghahn Books,* 2000.

———. "The Logic of War Extermination: The Wehrmacht and the Anti-Partisan War." In *War of Extermination: The German Military in World War II, 1941–1944,* edited by Hannes Heer and Klaus Naumann, 92–126. New York and Oxford: Berghahn Books, 2000.

———. *Tote Zonen: die deutsche Wehrmacht an der Ostfront.* Hamburg: Hamburger Edition, 1999.

———. *Vom Verschwinden der Täter: Der Vernichtungskrieg fand statt, aber keiner war dabei.* 2nd ed. Berlin: Aufbau-Verlag, 2004.

Heer, Hannes, and Klaus Naumann, eds. *War of Extermination: The German Military in World War II, 1941–1944,* Studies on War and Genocide. New York: Berghahn Books, 1999.

Heiber, Helmut. "Der Generalplan Ost." *Vierteljahrshefte für Zeitgeschichte* 3 (1958): 283–325.

Heinemann, Isabel. *Rasse, Siedlung, deutsches Blut: Das Rasse- und Siedlungshauptamt der SS und die rassenpolitische Neuordnung Europas,* Moderne Zeit. Göttingen: Wallstein, 2003.

Henke, Josef. *England in Hitlers politischem Kalkül 1935–1939,* Schriften des Bundes-archivs. Boppard am Rhein: H. Boldt, 1973.

Hepp, Michael. "'Die Durchdringung des Ostens in Rohstoff- und Landwirtschaft': Vorschläge des Arbeitswissenschaftlichen Instituts der Deutschen Arbeitsfront zur Ausbeutung der UdSSR aus dem Jahre 1941." *SozialGeschichte* 2, no. 4 (1987): 96–134.

Herb, Guntram Henrik. *Under the Map of Germany: Nationalism and Propaganda, 1918–1945.* London and New York: Routledge, 1997.

Herbert, Ulrich. *Arbeit, Volkstum, Weltanschauung: Über Fremde und Deutsche im 20. Jahrhundert,* Geschichte Fischer. Frankfurt am Main: Fischer Taschenbuch, 1995.

———. *Best: Biographische Studien über Radikalismus, Weltanschauung und Vernunft, 1903–1989.* Bonn: J. H. W. Dietz, 1996.

———. "'Generation der Sachlichkeit': Die völkische Studentenbewegung der frühen zwanziger Jahre in Deutschland." In *Zivilisation und Barbarei: Die widersprüchlichen Potentiale der Moderne,* edited by Frank Bajohr et al., 115–44. Hamburg: Christians 1991.

———. "Good Times, Bad Times: Memories of the Third Reich." In *Life in the Third Reich,* edited by Richard Bessel, 97–113. Oxford: Oxford University Press, 1987.

———. *Hitler's Foreign Workers: Enforced Foreign Labor in Germany under the Third Reich.* Translated by William Templer. Cambridge and New York: Cambridge University Press, 1997.

———. "Von der Gegnerbekämpfung zur rassischen Generalprävention: 'Schutzhaft' und Konzentrationslager in der Konzeption der Gestapo-Führung 1933–1939." In

Die nationalsozialistischen Konzentrationslager: Entwicklung und Struktur, edited by Ulrich Herbert, Karin Orth, and Christoph Dieckmann, 397–407. Göttingen: Wallstein, 1998.

Herbst, Ludolf. *Das nationalsozialistische Deutschland 1933–1945: Die Entfesselung der Gewalt–Rassimus und Krieg*, Neue historische Bibliothek. Frankfurt am Main: Suhrkamp, 1996.

Herf, Jeffrey. *The Jewish Enemy: Nazi Propaganda during World War II and the Holocaust*. Cambridge, MA: Belknap Press of Harvard University Press, 2006.

Hering, Rainer. *Konstruierte Nation: Der Alldeutsche Verband, 1890 bis 1939*, Hamburger Beiträge zur Sozial- und Zeitgeschichte Darstellungen. Hamburg: Christians, 2003.

Herzog, Dagmar. "'Pleasure, Sex and Politics Belong Together': Post-Holocaust Memory and the Sexual Revolution in West Germany." *Critical Inquiry* 24, no. 2 (1998): 393–444.

———, *Sex After Fascism: Memory and Morality in Twentieth-Century Germany*. Princeton, NJ and Oxford: Princeton University Press, 2005.

———, ed. *Sexuality and German Fascism*. New York: Berghahn Books, 2004.

Herzog, Markwart. *Der "Betze" unterm Hakenkreuz: Der 1. FC Kaiserslautern in der Zeit des Nationalsozialismus*. Göttingen: Werkstatt, 2006.

Hilberg, Raul. *The Destruction of the European Jews*. Chicago: Quadrangle Press, 1961.

Hildebrand, Klaus. *Deutsche Aussenpolitik, 1933–1945: Kalkül oder Dogma?* 4th ed. Stuttgart [u.a.]: Kohlhammer, 1980.

Hilger, Andreas. *Deutsche Kriegsgefangene in der Sowjetunion, 1941–1956: Kriegsgefangenenpolitik, Lageralltag und Erinnerung*, Schriften der Bibliothek für Zeitgeschichte. Essen: Klartext, 2000.

Hillgruber, Andreas. "Das Russland-Bild der führenden deutschen Militärs vor Beginn des Angriffs auf die Sowjetunion." In *Das Russlandbild im Dritten Reich*, edited by Hans Erich Volkmann, 125–63. Cologne: Böhlau, 1994.

———. "Die 'Endlösung' und das Deutsche Ostimperium als Kernstück des rassenideologischen Programms des Nationalsozialismus." *Vierteljahrshefte für Zeitgeschichte* 20 (1972): 133–53.

———. *Hitlers Strategie: Politik und Kriegführung, 1940–1941*. Frankfurt am Main: Bernard & Graefe Verlag für Wehrwesen, 1965.

———. "'Revisionismus': Kontinuität und Wandel in der Aussenpolitik der Weimarer Republik." *Historische Zeitschrift* 237 (1983): 597–621.

Hoeschen, Hans. *Zwischen Weichsel und Wolga*. Gütersloh: C. Bertelsmann, 1943.

Höhne, Heinz. *Der Orden unter dem Totenkopf: Die Geschichte der SS*. Munich: C. Bertelsmann, 1983.

———. *Mordsache Röhm: Hitlers Durchbruch zur Alleinherrschaft, 1933–1934*. Hamburg: Rowohlt, 1984.

Horne, John N., and Alan Kramer. *German Atrocities, 1914: A History of Denial*. New Haven, CT: Yale University Press, 2001.

Hubatsch, Walther, ed. *Hitlers Weisungen für die Kriegführung, 1939–1945: Dokumente des Oberkommandos der Wehrmacht*. Unabridged ed. Munich: Deutscher Taschenbuch Verlag, 1965.

Hull, Isabel V. *Absolute Destruction: Military Culture and the Practice of War in Imperial Germany*. Ithaca, NY and London: Cornell University Press, 2005.

———. *Sexuality, State, and Civil Society in Germany, 1700–1815*. Ithaca, NY: Cornell University Press, 1996.

Humburg, Martin. *Das Gesicht des Krieges: Feldpostbriefe von Wehrmachtssoldaten aus der Sowjetunion 1941–1944*, Kulturwissenschaftliche Studien zur deutschen Literatur. Opladen: Westdeutscher, 1998.

Hüppauf, Bernd. "Langemarck, Verdun, and the Myth of a New Man in Germany after the First World War." *War and Society* 6 (1988): 70–103.

Hürter, Johannes. "Auf dem Weg zur Militäropposition: Treskow, Gersdorff, der Vernichtungskrieg und der Judenmord: Neue Dokumente über das Verhältnis der Heeresgruppe Mitte zur Einsatzgruppe B im Jahre 1941." *Vierteljahrshefte für Zeitgeschichte* 52, no. 3 (2004): 527–62.

———. "Die Wehrmacht vor Leningrad: Krieg und Besatzungspolitik der 18. Armee im Herbst und Winter 1941/42." *Vierteljahrshefte für Zeitgeschichte* 49, no. 3 (2001): 377–440.

———. *Hitlers Heerführer: Die deutschen Oberbefehlshaber im Krieg gegen die Sowjetunion 1941/42*, Quellen und Darstellungen zur Zeitgeschichte. Munich: Oldenbourg, 2006.

Hüttenberger, Peter. *Die Gauleiter: Studie zum Wandel des Machtgefüges in der NSDAP*. 3rd ed., Schriftenreihe der Vierteljahrshefte für Zeitgeschichte. Stuttgart: Deutsche Verlags-Anstalt, 1969.

Jäckel, Eberhard. *Hitler's Weltanschauung: A Blueprint for Power*. Translated by Herbert Arnold. Middletown, CT: Wesleyan University Press, 1972.

Jacobsen, Hans-Adolf. "Komissarbefehl und Massenexekutionen sowjetischer Kriegsgefangener." In *Anatomie des SS-Staates: Gutachten des Instituts für Zeitgeschichte*, edited by Hans Buchheim, 161–278. Olten: Walter-Verlag, 1965.

———. "Zur Struktur der NS – Aussenpolitik, 1933–45." In *Hitler, Deutschland und die Mächte: Materialien zur Aussenpolitik des Dritten Reiches*, edited by Manfred Funke, 169–75. Düsseldorf: Droste, 1978.

Jahn, Peter, and Reinhard Rürup, eds. *Erobern und Vernichten: Der Krieg gegen die Sowjetunion 1941–1945: Essays*. Berlin: Argon, 1991.

Jander, Martin. *Theo Pirker über "Pirker": Ein Gespräch*. Marburg: SP-Verlag N. Schüren, 1988.

Jansen, Christian, and Arno Weckbecker. *Der "Volksdeutsche Selbstschutz" in Polen 1939/40*, Schriftenreihe der Vierteljahrshefte für Zeitgeschichte. Munich: Oldenbourg, 1992.

Janssen, Karl-Heinz, and Fritz Tobias. *Der Sturz der Generäle: Hitler und die Blomberg-Fritsch-Krise 1938*. Munich: Beck, 1994.

Jarausch, Konrad H., and Michael Geyer. *Shattered Past: Reconstructing German Histories*. Princeton, NJ: Princeton University Press, 2003.

Jersak, Tobias. "Die Interaktion von Kriegsverlauf und Judenvernichtung: Ein Blick auf Hitlers Strategie im Spätsommer 1941." *Historische Zeitschrift* 268, no. 2 (1999): 311–74.

John, Eckhard. *Musikbolschewismus: Die Politisierung der Musik in Deutschland, 1918–1938*, Metzler Musik. Stuttgart: J. B. Metzler, 1994.

Johnson, Eric. *Nazi Terror: The Gestapo, Jews, and Ordinary Germans*. New York: Basic Books, 1999.

Jones, Larry Eugene. *German Liberalism and the Dissolution of the Weimar Party System, 1918–1933*. Chapel Hill: University of North Carolina Press, 1988.

Joshi, Vandana. *Gender and Power in the Third Reich: Female Denouncers and the Gestapo (1933–45)*. Basingstoke: Palgrave Macmillan, 2003.

Jünger, Ernst. *Copse 125: A Chronicle from the Trench Warfare of 1918*. New York: Howard Fertig, 1988.

Kahrs, Horst. "Die ordnende Hand der Arbeitsamter: Zur deutschen Arbeitsverwaltung 1933 bis 1939." In *Arbeitsmarkt und Sondererlass: Menschenverwertung, Rassenpolitik und Arbeitsamt*, edited by Wolf Gruner, 9–61. Berlin: Rotbuch Verlag, 1990.

———. *Modelle für ein deutsches Europa: Ökonomie und Herrschaft im Grosswirtschaftsraum*, Beiträge zur nationalsozialistischen Gesundheits- und Sozialpolitik. Berlin: Rotbuch, 1992.

Kändler, Klaus, Helga Karolewski, and Ilse Siebert, eds. *Berliner Begegnungen: Ausländische Künstler in Berlin 1918 bis 1933: Aufsätze, Bilder, Dokumente*, Veröffentlichung der Nationalen Forschungs- und Gedenkstätten der DDR für Deutsche Kunst und Literatur des 20. Jahrhunderts. Berlin: Dietz, 1987.

Kansteiner, Wulf. *In Pursuit of German Memory: History, Television, and Politics after Auschwitz*. Athens: Ohio University Press, 2006.

Kaplan, Marion. *Between Dignity and Despair: Jewish Women in the Aftermath of November 1938*. New York: Leo Baeck Institute, 1996.

Kappeler, Manfred. *Der schreckliche Traum vom vollkommenen Menschen: Rassenhygiene und Eugenik in der Sozialen Arbeit*. Marburg: Schüren, 2000.

Kater, Michael H. *The Nazi Party: A Social Profile of Members and Leaders, 1919–1945*. Cambridge, MA: Harvard University Press, 1983.

———. "The Work Student: A Socio-Economic Phenomenon of Early Weimar Germany." *Journal of Contemporary History* 10 (1975): 71–94.

Keiderling, Gerhard. "'Als Befreier unsere Herzen brachen': Zu den Übergriffen der Sowjetarmee in Berlin 1945." *Deutschland Archiv* 28 (1995): 234–43.

Keller, Rolf, and Reinhard Otto. "Das Massensterben der sowjetischen Kriegsgefangenen und die Wehrmachtbürokratie: Unterlagen zur Registrierung der sowjetischen Kriegsgefangenen 1941–1945 in deutschen und russischen Institutionen." *Militärgeschichtliche Mitteilungen* 57 (1998): 49–80.

Kellogg, Michael. *The Russian Roots of Nazism: White Émigrés and the Making of National Socialism, 1917–1945*, New Studies in European History. Cambridge and New York: Cambridge University Press, 2004.

Kempowski, Walter. *Das Echolot: Barbarossa '41: Ein kollektives Tagebuch*. Munich: Knaus, 2002.

———. *Das Echolot: Fuga furiosa: Ein kollektives Tagebuch, Winter 1945*. 4 vols. Munich: A. Knaus, 1999.

Kenkmann, Alfons. *Wilde Jugend: Lebenswelt grossstädtischer Jugendlicher zwischen Weltwirtschaftskrise, Nationalsozialismus, und Währungsreform*, Düsseldorfer Schriften zur neueren Landesgeschichte und zur Geschichte Nordrhein-Westfalens. Essen: Klartext, 1996.

Kenkmann, Alfons, and Bernd- A. Rusinek, eds. *Verfolgung und Verwaltung: Die wirtschaftliche Ausplünderung der Juden und die westfälischen Finanzbehörden*. Münster: Oberfinanzdirektion Münster, 1999.

Kershaw, Ian. "Adolf Hitler und die Realisierung der nationalsozialistischen Rassenutopie." In *Utopie und politische Herrschaft im Europa der Zwischenkriegszeit*, edited by Wolfgang Hardtwig, 133–44. Munich: Oldenbourg, 2003.

———. *Der Hitler-Mythos: Volksmeinung und Propaganda im Dritten Reich*, Schriftenreihe der Vierteljahrshefte für Zeitgeschichte. Stuttgart: Deutsche Verlags-Anstalt, 1980.

———. *Hitler, 1936–1945: Nemesis*. 2 vols. Vol. 2. New York: W. W. Norton, 2000.

———. *Hitler, 1889–1936: Hubris*. 2 vols. Vol. 1. New York: W. W. Norton, 1999.

―――. *Popular Opinion and Political Dissent in the Third Reich, Bavaria 1933–1945*. Oxford: Clarendon Press 1983.

―――. *The " Hitler Myth": Image and Reality in the Third Reich*. Oxford: Oxford University Press, 1987.

―――. *The Nazi Dictatorship: Problems and Perspectives of Interpretation*. 4th ed. London: Arnold, 2000.

―――. "The Persecution of the Jews and German Popular Opinion in the Third Reich." *Leo Baeck Institute Yearbook* 26 (1981): 261–89.

Klee, Ernst. *"Euthanasie" im NS-Staat: die "Vernichtung lebensunwerten Lebens."* Frankfurt am Main: Fischer, 1985.

Klee, Ernst, and Willi Dressen, eds. *"Gott mit uns": Der deutsche Vernichtungskrieg im Osten 1939–1945*. Frankfurt am Main: S. Fischer, 1989.

Klemperer, Victor. *LTI: Notizbuch eines Philologen*. 3rd ed. Halle/Saale: M. Niemeyer, 1957.

Kletzin, Birgit. *Europa aus Rasse und Raum: Die nationalsozialistische Idee der Neuen Ordnung*, Region, Nation, Europa. Münster: Lit, 2000.

Knoch, Peter P. "Das Bild des russischen Feindes." In *Stalingrad: Mythos und Wirklichkeit einer Schlacht*, edited by Wolfram Wette, Gerd R. Ueberschär, and Sabine R. Arnold, 143–63. Frankfurt am Main: Fischer Taschenbuch Verlag, 1992.

Knox, MacGregor. "1 October 1942: Adolf Hitler, Wehrmacht Officer Policy and Social Revolution." *The Historical Journal* 43, no. 3 (2000): 801–25.

Koehl, Robert Lewis. *The Black Corps: The Structure and Power Struggles of the Nazi SS*. Madison: University of Wisconsin Press, 1983.

―――. *RKFDV: German Resettlement and Population Policy, 1939–1945: A History of the Reich Commission for the Strengthening of Germandom*, Harvard Historical Monographs. Cambridge, MA: Harvard University Press, 1957.

Koenen, Gerd. *Der Russland-Komplex: Die Deutschen und der Osten, 1900–1945*. Munich: Beck, 2005.

―――. "Hitlers Russland: Ambivalenzen im deutschen 'Drang nach Osten'." *Kommune: Forum Politik, Ökonomie, Kultur*, no. 1 (2003): 65–79.

―――. "Zwischen Antibolschewismus und 'Ostorientierung': Kontinuitäten and Diskontinuitäten." In *Strukturmerkmale der deutschen Geschichte des 20. Jahrhunderts*, edited by Anselm Doering-Manteuffel, 241–52. Munich: R. Oldenbourg Verlag, 2006.

Kohtz, Kerstin. "Väter und Mütter im Dialog mit der Berliner Jugendfürsorge in den 1920er Jahren." *SOWI Sozialwissenschaftliche Informationen* 27 (1998): 113–18.

Koonz, Claudia. *Mothers in the Fatherland: Woman, the Family, and Nazi Politics*. New York: St. Martin's Press, 1981.

―――. *The Nazi Conscience*. Cambridge, MA: Belknap Press of Harvard University Press, 2003.

Köster, Werner. *Die Rede über den "Raum": Zur semantischen Karriere eines deutschen Konzepts*, Studien zur Wissenschafts- und Universitätsgeschichte. Heidelberg: Synchron Wissenschaftsverlag der Autoren, 2002.

Kranig, Andreas. *Lockung und Zwang: zur Arbeitsverfassung im Dritten Reich*, Schriftenreihe der Vierteljahrshefte für Zeitgeschichte. Stuttgart: Deutsche Verlags-Anstalt, 1983.

Kraushaar, Wolfgang. *Linke Geisterfahrer: Denkanstösse für eine antitotalitäre Linke*. Frankfurt am Main: Verlag Neue Kritik, 2001.

Krausnick, Helmut. "Judenverfolgung." In *Anatomie des SS-Staates*, 233–366. Munich: Taschenbuch Verlag, 1999.

Krausnick, Helmut, and Hans-Heinrich Wilhelm. *Die Truppe des Weltanschauungskrieges: Die Einsatzgruppen der Sicherheitspolizei und des SD 1938–1942*, Quellen und Darstellungen zur Zeitgeschichte. Stuttgart: Deutsche Verlags-Anstalt, 1981.

Kroener, Bernard R. "Auf dem Weg zu einer 'nationalsozialistischen Volksarmee': Die soziale Ordnung des Heeresoffizierkorps im Zweiten Weltkrieg." In *Von Stalingrad zur Währungsreform: Zur Sozialgeschichte des Umbruchs in Deutschland*, edited by Martin Broszat, 651–82. Munich: Oldenbourg, 1988.

———. "Der 'Erfrorene Blitzkrieg': Strategische Planungen der Deutsche Führung geggen die Sowjetunion und die Ursachen ihres Scheiterns." In *Zwei Wege nach Moskau: Vom Hitler-Stalin-Pakt zum "Unternehmen Barbarossa*, edited by Bernd Wegner, 133–48. Munich and Zurich: Piper, 1991.

———. "'Menschenbewirtschaftung,' Bevölkerungsverteilung und personelle Rüstung in der zweiten Kriegshälfte (1941–1944)." In *Das Deutsche Reich und der Zweite Weltkrieg. Vol. 5/2, Kriegsverwaltung, Wirtschaft und personelle Ressourcen 1942–1944/45*, edited by Militärgeschichtliches Forschungsamt, 777–995. Munich: Deutsche Verlagsanstalt, 1999.

Kroll, Frank-Lothar. *Utopie als Ideologie: Geschichtsdenken und politische Handeln im Dritten Reich*. Paderborn: Schöningh, 1998.

Krüger, Gerd. "Straffreie Selbstjustiz: Öffentliche Denunzierungen im Ruhrgebiet 1923–1926." *SOWI Sozialwissenschaftliche Informationen* 27 (1998): 119–25.

Krüger, Gesine. *Kriegsbewältigung und Geschichtsbewusstsein: Realität, Deutung und Verarbeitung des deutschen Kolonialkriegs in Namibia 1904 bis 1907*, Kritische Studien zur Geschichtswissenschaft. Göttingen: Vandenhoeck & Ruprecht, 1999.

Kühne, Thomas. "'Aus diesem Krieg werden nicht nur harte Männer heimkehren': Kriegskameradschaft und Männlichkeit im 20. Jahrhundert." In *Männergeschichte, Geschlechtergeschichte: Männlichkeit im Wandel der Moderne*, edited by Thomas Kühne, 174–92. Frankfurt am Main: Campus, 1996.

———. "Der Soldat." In *Der Mensch des 20. Jahrhunderts*, edited by Ute Frevert and Heinz-Gerhard Haupt, 344–83. Frankfurt am Main and New York: Campus, 1999.

———. "Kameradschaft – 'das Beste im Leben des Mannes': Die deutschen Soldaten des Zweiten Weltkriegs in erfahrungs- und geschlechtlicher Perspektive." *Geschichte und Gesellschaft* 22 (1996): 504–29.

———. *Kameradschaft: Die Soldaten des nationalsozialistischen Krieges und das 20. Jahrhundert*, Kritische Studien zur Geschichtswissenschaft. Göttingen: Vandenhoeck & Ruprecht, 2006.

———. "Zwischen Männerbund und Volksgemeinschaft: Hitlers Soldaten und der Mythos der Kameradschaft." *Archiv für Sozialgeschichte* 38 (1998): 165–89.

Labisch, Alfons, and Florian Tennstedt. *Der Weg zum "Gesetz über die Vereinheitlichung des Gesundheitswesens vom 3. Juli 1934: Entwicklungslinien und -momente des staatlichen und kommunalen Gesundheitswesens" in Deutschland*. 2 vols, Schriftenreihe der Akademie für öffentliches Gesundheitswesen in Düsseldorf. Düsseldorf: Akademie für öffentliches Gesundheitswesen, 1985.

Länderrat des Amerikanischen Besatzungsgebiets, ed. *Statistisches Handbuch von Deutschland, 1928–1944*. Munich: F. Ehrenwirth, 1949.

Latzel, Klaus. *Deutsche Soldaten – Nationalsozialistischer Krieg?: Kriegserlebnis, Kriegserfahrung 1939–1945*, Krieg in der Geschichte. Paderborn: Schöningh, 1998.

Leibfried, Stephan, and Florian Tennstedt. "Health-Insurance Policy and Berufsverbote in the Nazi Takeover." In *Political Values and Health Care: The German Experience*, edited by Donald Light and Alexander Schuller, 127–84. Cambridge, MA: MIT Press, 1986.

Leonhard, Wolfgang. *Die Revolution entlässt ihre Kinder*. Cologne: Kiepenheuer & Witsch, 1990.

Lewy, Guenter. *The Nazi Persecution of the Gypsies*. New York: Oxford University Press, 2000.

Lieb, Peter. "Täter aus Überzeugung? Oberst Carl von Andrian und die Judenmorde der 707. Infanteriedivision 1941/42." *Vierteljahrshefte für Zeitgeschichte* 50, no. 3 (2002): 523–57.

Light, Donald W. "State, Profession, and Political Values." In *Political Values and Health Care: The German Experience*, edited by Donald W. Light and Alexander Schuller, 1–23. Cambridge, MA and London: MIT University Press, 1986.

Lilienthal, Georg. *Der "Lebensborn e.V.": Ein Instrument nationalsozialistischer Rassenpolitik*, Forschungen zur neueren Medizin- und Biologiegeschichte. Stuttgart: Fischer, 1985.

Liszkowski, Uwe. *Osteuropaforschung und Politik: Ein Beitrag zum historisch-politischen Denken und Wirken von Otto Hoetzsch*, Osteuropaforschung Berlin. Berlin: Verlag A. Spitz, 1988.

Liulevicius, Vejas G. *War Land on the Eastern Front: Culture, National Identity and German Occupation in World War I*, Studies in the Social and Cultural History of Modern Warfare. Cambridge and New York: Cambridge University Press, 2000.

Löffler, Klara. *Aufgehoben: Soldatenbriefe aus dem Zweiten Weltkrieg: Eine Studie zur subjektiven Wirklichkeit des Krieges*, Regensburger Schriften zur Volkskunde. Bamberg: WVB, 1992.

Longerich, Peter. *Die braunen Bataillone: Geschichte der SA*. Munich: Beck, 1989.

———. *Hitlers Stellvertreter: Führung der Partei und Kontrolle des Staatsapparates durch den Stab Hess und die Partei-Kanzlei Bormann*. Munich: K. G. Saur, 1992.

———. *Politik der Vernichtung: Eine Gesamtdarstellung der nationalsozialistischen Judenverfolgung*. Munich: Piper, 1998.

———. *Propagandisten im Krieg: Die Presseabteilung des Auswärtigen Amtes unter Ribbentrop*, Studien zur Zeitgeschichte. Munich: R. Oldenbourg, 1987.

———. *The Unwritten Order: Hitler's Role in the Final Solution*. Stroud and Charleston, SC: Tempus, 2001.

Lotfi, Gabriele. *KZ der Gestapo: Arbeitserziehungslager im Dritten Reich*. Stuttgart: Deutsche Verlags-Anstalt, 2000.

Lower, Wendy. "A New Ordering of Space and Race: Nazi Colonial Dreams in Zhytomir, Ukraine, 1941–1944," *German Studies Review* 25 (2002): 227–54.

———. *Nazi Empire-Building and the Holocaust in Ukraine*. Chapel Hill: University of North Carolina Press, 2005.

Ludendorff, Erich. *The General Staff and Its Problems: The History of the Relations between the High Command and the German Imperial Government as Revealed by Official Documents*. Translated by F. A. Holt. 2 vols. New York: E. P. Dutton, 1920.

Lüdtke, Alf. "'Deutsche Qualitätsarbeit,' 'Spielereien' am Arbeitsplatz und 'Fliehen' aus der Fabrik: Industrielle Arbeitsprozesse und Arbeiterverhalten in den 1920er Jahren." In *Arbeiterkulturen zwischen Alltag und Politik: Beiträge zum europäischen Vergleich in der Zwischenkriegszeit*, edited by Friedhelm Boll, 155–97. Vienna: Europa-Verlag, 1986.

————. "Hunger in der Grossen Depression: Hungererfahrungen und Hungerpolitik am Ende der Weimarer Republik." *Archiv für Sozialgeschichte* 27 (1987): 145–76.

————. "People Working: Everyday Life and German Fascism." *History Workshop Journal*, no. 50 (2000): 74–92.

Madajczyk, Czeslaw. "Generalplan Ost." *Polish Western Affairs* 3, no. 2 (1962): 391–442.

Madajczyk, Czeslaw, and Stanislaw Biernacki, eds. *Vom Generalplan Ost zum Generalsiedlungsplan*, Einzelveröffentlichungen der Historischen Kommission zu Berlin. Munich: Saur, 1994.

Madajczyk, Czeslaw, and Franciszek Cieselak, eds. *Zamojszczyzna – Sonderlaboratorium SS: Zbiór dokumentów polskich i niemieckich z okresu okupacji hitlerowskiej.* 2 vols. Warsaw: Ludowa Spóldzielnia Wydawnicza, DSP, 1977.

Madajczyk, Czeslaw, and Berthold Puchert. *Die Okkupationspolitik Nazideutschlands in Polen 1939–1945.* Translated by Berthold Puchert. Cologne: Pahl-Rugenstein, 1988.

Maschmann, Melita. *Fazit: Mein Weg in der Hitler-Jugend.* München: DTV, 1963.

Mason, Timothy W. "Intention and Explanation: A Current Controversy about the Interpretation of National Socialism." In *Der "Führerstaat," Mythos und Realität: Studien zur Struktur und Politik des Dritten Reiches = The "Führerstaat," Myth and Reality: Studies on the Structure and Politics of the Third Reich*, edited by Lothar Kettenacker and Gerhard Hirschfeld, 23–72. Stuttgard: Klett-Cotta, 1981.

————. *Social Policy in the Third Reich: The Working Class and the National Community.* Translated by John Broadwin. Providence, RI: Berg, 1993.

Matzerath, Horst. *Nationalsozialismus und kommunale Selbstverwaltung*, Schriftenreihe des Vereins für Kommunalwissenschaften e. V. Berlin. Stuttgart [u.a.]: Kohlhammer, 1970.

Meier, Kurt. "Sowjetrussland im Urteil der evangelischen Kirche." In *Das Russlandbild im Dritten Reich*, edited by Hans Erich Volkmann, 285–322. Cologne: Böhlau, 1994.

Merkl, Peter H. *Political Violence under the Swastika: 581 Early Nazis.* Princeton, NJ: Princeton University Press, 1975.

Merz, Kai-Uwe. *Das Schreckbild: Deutschland und der Bolschewismus, 1917–1921.* Berlin: Propyläen, 1995.

Michalka, Wolfgang. *Ribbentrop und die deutsche Weltpolitik, 1933–1940: Aussenpolitische Konzeptionen und Entscheidungsprozesse im Dritten Reich*, Veröffentlichungen des Historischen Instituts der Universität Mannheim. Munich: W. Fink, 1980.

Mierau, Fritz, ed. *Russen in Berlin 1918–1933: Eine kulturelle Begegnung*, Reclams Universal-Bibliothek. Weinheim: Quadriga, 1988.

Militärgeschichtlichen Forschungsamt, ed. *Das Deutsche Reich und der Zweite Weltkrieg.* 10 vols, Beiträge zur Militär- und Kriegsgeschichte. Stuttgart: Deutsche Verlags-Anstalt, 1979–2008.

Milton, Sybil. "'Gypsies' as Social Outsiders in Germany." In *Social Outsiders in Nazi Germany*, edited by Robert Gellately and Nathan Stoltzfuss, 212–32. Princeton, NJ: Princeton University Press, 2001.

Möding, Nori. "Ich muss irgendwo engagiert sein – fragen Sie mich bloss nicht, warum," Überlegungen zu Sozialisationserfahrungen von Mädchen im NS-Organisationen." In *"'Wir kriegen jetzt andere Zeiten': Auf der Suche nach der Erfahrung des Volkes in nachfaschistischen Ländern,"* edited by Lutz Niethammer and Alexander von Plato, 256–304. Berlin: J. H. W. Dietz, 1985.

Moeller, Robert G. *Protecting Motherhood: Women and the Family in the Politics of Postwar West Germany.* Berkeley: University of California Press, 1993.

———. *War Stories: The Search for a Usable Past in the Federal Republic of Germany.* Berkeley: University of California Press, 2001.

Mohrmann, Wolf-Dieter, ed. *Der Krieg hier ist hart und grausam!: Feldpostbriefe an den Osnabrücker Regierungspräsidenten, 1941–1944.* Osnabrück: H. Th. Wenner, 1984.

Mommsen, Hans. "Die Realisierung des Utopischen: Die 'Endlösung im Dritten Reich." *Geschichte und Gesellschaft* 9 (1983): 381–420.

———. *From Weimar to Auschwitz: Essays in German History.* Translated by Philip O'Connor. Cambridge: Polity, 1991.

———. "[Introduction] Hannah Arendt und der Prozess gegen Adolf Eichmann." In *Eichmann in Jerusalem: Ein Bericht von der Banalität der Böse,* edited by Hannah Arendt, I–XXXVII. Munich and Zurich: Piper, 1986.

———. "The Dissolution of the Third Reich: Crisis, Management and Collapse, 1943–1945." *Bulletin of the German Historical Institute,* no. 27 (Fall 2000): 9–24.

———. *Von Weimar nach Auschwitz: Zur Geschichte Deutschlands in der Weltkriegsepoche: ausgewählte Aufsätze.* Stuttgart: Deutsche Verlags-Anstalt, 1999.

Mühl-Benninghaus, Sigrun. *Das Beamtentum in der NS-Diktatur bis zum Ausbruch des Zweiten Weitkrieges: Zu Entstehung, Inhalt und Durchführung der einschlägigen Beamtengesetze,* Schriften des Bundesarchivs. Düsseldorf: Droste, 1996.

Mühlberger, Detlef. *Hitler's Followers: Studies in the Sociology of the Nazi Movement.* London and New York: Routledge, 1991.

Müller, Jan-Werner. *German Ideologies since 1945: Studies in the Political Thought and Culture of the Bonn Republic.* New York: Palgrave Macmillan, 2003.

Müller, Klaus Jürgen. *Das Heer und Hitler: Armee und nationalsozialistisches Regime 1933–1940,* Beiträge zur Militär- und Kriegsgeschichte. Stuttgart: Deutsche Verlags-Anstalt, 1969.

Müller, Klaus Jürgen, and Ernst Willi Hansen, eds. *Armee und Drittes Reich, 1933–1939: Darstellung und Dokumentation,* Sammlung Schöningh zur Geschichte und Gegenwart. Paderborn: F. Schöningh, 1987.

Müller, Rolf-Dieter. *Das Tor zur Weltmacht: Die Bedeutung der Sowjetunion für die deutsche Wirtschafts- und Rüstungspolitik zwischen den Weltkriegen,* Wehrwissenschaftliche Forschungen, Abteilung Militärgeschichtliche Studien. Boppard am Rhein: H. Boldt, 1984.

———. *Hitlers Ostkrieg und die deutsche Siedlungspolitik: Die Zusammenarbeit von Wehrmacht, Wirtschaft und SS,* Geschichte Fischer. Frankfurt am Main: Fischer Taschenbuch Verlag, 1991.

———. "Von Brest-Litowsk bis zum 'Unternehmen Barbarossa' – Wandlungen und Kontinuität des deutschen 'Drangs nach Ostland.'" In *Frieden mit der Sowjetunion: Eine unerledigte Aufgabe,* edited by Dietrich Goldschmidt, 70–86. Gütersloh: Gütersloher Verlagshaus G. Mohn, 1989.

Müller, Rolf-Dieter, and Gerd R. Ueberschär. *Hitlers Krieg im Osten 1941–1945: Ein Forschungsbericht.* Darmstadt: Wissenschaftliche Buchgesellschaft, 2000.

Müller, Rolf-Dieter, and Hans Erich Volkmann, eds. *Die Wehrmacht: Mythos und Realität.* Munich: Oldenbourg, 1999.

Murphy, David Thomas. *The Heroic Earth: Geopolitical Thought in Weimar Germany, 1918–1933*. Kent, OH: Kent State University Press, 1997.

Nadolny, Rudolf. *Mein Beitrag: Erinnerungen eines Botschafters des Deutschen Reiches*. Cologne: DME-Verlag, 1985.

Neliba, Günter. *Wilhelm Frick: Der Legalist des Unrechtsstaates: Eine politische Biographie*, Sammlung Schöningh zur Geschichte und Gegenwart. Paderborn: Schöningh, 1992.

Neulen, Hans Werner. *An deutscher Seite: Internationale Freiwillige von Wehrmacht und Waffen-SS*. Munich: Universitas, 1985.

Niemiecki Instytut Historyczny w Warszawie, ed. *"Grösste Härte–": Verbrechen der Wehrmacht in Polen September-Oktober 1939: Ausstellungskatalog*. Osnabrück: Fibre, 2005.

Niethammer, Lutz et al., eds. *Der "gesäuberte" Antifaschismus: Die SED und die roten Kapos von Buchenwald: Dokumente*. Berlin: Akademie Verlag, 1994.

———. *"Die Jahre weiss man nicht, wo man die heute hinsetzen soll": Faschismuserfahrungen im Ruhrgebiet: Lebensgeschichte und Sozialkultur im Ruhrgebiet 1930 bis 1960*. Berlin: Dietz, 1983.

Nitschke, Asmus. *Die "Erbpolizei" im Nationalsozialismus: Zur Alltagsgeschichte der Gesundheitsämter im Dritten Reich: Das Beispiel Bremen*. Wiesbaden: Westdeutscher Verlag, 1999.

Noakes, Jeremy, and Geoffrey Pridham, eds. *Nazism, 1919–1945: A Documentary Reader: State, Economy and Society, 1933–1939*. Rev. ed. 2 vols, Exeter Studies in History. Exeter: University of Exeter Press, 2000.

Nötzel, Karl. *Gegen den Kultur-Bolschewismus*, Christliche Wehrkraft. Munich: Paul Müller, 1930.

Nyomarkay, Joseph. *Charisma and Factionalism in the Nazi Party*. Minneapolis: University of Minnesota Press, 1967.

Oberländer, Erwin. "Historische Osteuropaforschung im Dritten Reich." In *Geschichte Osteuropas: Zur Entwicklung einer historischen Disziplin in Deutschland, Österreich und der Schweiz, 1945–1990*, edited by Erwin Oberländer, 12–30. Stuttgart: Franz Steiner, 1992.

Oldenburg, Manfred. *Ideologie und militärisches Kalkül: Die Besatzungspolitik der Wehrmacht in der Sowjetunion 1942*. Cologne: Böhlau, 2004.

O'Neill, Robert John. *The German Army and the Nazi Party, 1933–1939*. New York: J. H. Heineman, 1967.

Orlow, Dietrich. *The History of the Nazi Party: 1933–1945*. 2 vols. Vol. 2. Pittsburgh: University of Pittsburgh Press, 1973.

Orth, Karin. *Das System der nationalsozialistischen Konzentrationslager: Eine politische Organisationsgeschichte*. Hamburg: Hamburger Edition, 1999.

Oswald, Rudolf. "'Ein Gift, mit echt jüdischer Geschicklichkeit ins Volk gespritzt': Nationalsozialistische Judenverfolgung und das Ende des mitteleuropäischen Profifussballs, 1938–1941." In *Emanzipation durch Muskelkraft: Juden und Sport in Europa*, edited by Michael Brenner and Gideon Reuveni, 159–72. Göttingen: Vandenhoeck & Ruprecht, 2006.

Otto, Reinhard. *Wehrmacht, Gestapo und sowjetische Kriegsgefangene im deutschen Reichsgebiet 1941/42*, Schriftenreihe der Vierteljahrshefte für Zeitgeschichte. Munich: Oldenbourg, 1998.

Overmans, Rüdiger. *Deutsche militärische Verluste im Zweiten Weltkrieg*, Beiträge zur Militärgeschichte. Munich: R. Oldenbourg, 1999.

Overy, Richard J. *The Nazi Economic Recovery, 1932–1938*. Reprinted ed., Studies in Economic and Social History. London [u.a.]: Macmillan, 1984.

Patel, Kiran Klaus. *"Soldaten der Arbeit": Arbeitsdienste in Deutschland und den USA 1933–1945*, Kritische Studien zur Geschichtswissenschaft. Göttingen: Vandenhoeck & Ruprecht, 2003.

Paul, Christa. *Zwangsprostitution: Staatlich errichtete Bordelle im Nationalsozialismus*, Reihe deutsche Vergangenheit. Berlin: Edition Hentrich, 1994.

Paul, Gerhard, ed. *Die Täter der Shoah: Fanatische Nationalsozialisten oder ganz normale Deutsche?* Dachauer Symposien zur Zeitgeschichte. Göttingen: Wallstein, 2002.

Penter, Tanja. "Die lokale Gesellschaft im Donbass unter deutscher Okkupation 1941–1943." In *Kooperation und Verbrechen: Formen der "Kollaboration" im östlichen Europa 1939–1945*, edited by Christoph Dieckmann, 183–223. Göttingen: Wallstein, 2003.

Perrey, Hans-Jürgen. *Der Russlandausschuss der deutschen Wirtschaft: Die deutsch-sowjetischen Wirtschaftsbeziehungen der Zwischenkriegszeit: Ein Beitrag zur Geschichte des Ost-West-Handels*, Studien zur modernen Geschichte. Munich: Oldenbourg, 1985.

Petö, Andrea. "Stimmen des Schweigens: Erinnerungen an Vergewaltigungen in den Hauptstädten des 'ersten Opfers' (Wien) und des 'letzten Verbündeten Hitlers' (Budapest) 1945." *Zeitschrift für Geschichtswissenschaft* 47 (1999): 892–913.

Petzina, Dietmar. *Autarkiepolitik im Dritten Reich*, Schriftenreihe der Vierteljahrshefte für Zeitgeschichte. Stuttgart: Deutsche Verlagsanstalt, 1968.

Peukert, Detlev. *Die Weimarer Republik: Krisenjahre der klassischen Moderne*. Frankfurt am Main: Suhrkamp, 1987.

———. *Inside Nazi Germany: Conformity, Opposition, and Racism in Everyday Life*. Translated by Richard Deveson. New Haven, CT and London: Yale University Press, 1987.

———. "The Genesis of the 'Final Solution' from the Spirit of Science." In *Reevaluating the Third Reich*, edited by Thomas Childers and Jane Caplan, 234–52. New York and London: Homes & Meier, 1993.

———. *The Weimar Republic: The Crisis of Classical Modernity*. Translated by Richard Deveson. New York: Hill & Wang, 2002.

———. *Volksgenossen und Gemeinschaftsfremde: Anpassung, Ausmerze und Aufbegehren unter dem Nationalsozialismus*. Cologne: Bund-Verlag, 1982.

Peukert, Detlev et al., eds. *Die Reihen fast geschlossen: Beiträge zur Geschichte des Alltags unterm Nationalsozialismus*. Wuppertal: Hammer, 1981.

Pietrow-Ennker, Bianca. "Das Feindbild im Wandel: Die Sowjetunion in den nationalsozialistischen Wochenschauen, 1935–1941." *Geschichte in Wissenschaft und Unterricht* 41 (1990): 337–51.

———. "Die Sowjetunion in der Propaganda des Dritten Reiches." *Militärgeschichtliche Mitteilungen*, no. 2 (1989): 79–120.

Pine, Lisa. *Nazi Family Policy, 1933–1945*. Oxford and New York: Berg, 1997.

Pleyer, Kleo. *Volk im Feld*. 2nd ed, Schriften des Reichsinstituts für Geschichte des neuen Deutschlands. Hamburg: Hanseatische Verlagsanstalt, 1943.

Pohl, Dieter. *Nationalsozialistische Judenverfolgung in Ostgalizien 1941–1944: Organisation und Durchführung eines staatlichen Massenverbrechens*. 2nd ed, Studien zur Zeitgeschichte. Munich: Oldenbourg, 1997.

———. "Russian, Ukrainians, and German Occupational Policy, 1941–1943." In *Culture, Nation, and Identity: The Ukrainian-Russian Encounter, 1600–1945*, edited by

Andreas Kappeler, 277–97. Toronto: Canadian Institute of Ukrainian Studies Press, 2003.

———. *Verfolgung und Massenmord in der NS-Zeit 1933–1945*, Geschichte kompakt, Neuzeit. Darmstadt: Wissenschaftliche Buchgesellschaft, 2003.

———. *Von der "Judenpolitik" zum Judenmord: Der Distrikt Lublin des General-gouvernements, 1934–1944*, Münchner Studien zur neueren und neuesten Geschichte. Frankfurt am Main: P. Lang, 1993.

Pommerin, Reiner. *Sterilisierung der Rheinlandbastarde: Das Schicksal einer farbigen deutschen Minderheit 1918–1937*. Düsseldorf: Droste, 1979.

Proctor, Robert. *Racial Hygiene: Medicine under the Nazis*. Cambridge, MA: Harvard University Press, 1988.

———. *The Nazi War on Cancer*. Princeton, NJ: Princeton University Press, 1999.

Przyrembel, Alexandra. *Rassenschande: Reinheitsmythos und Vernichtungslegitimation im Nationalsozialismus*, Veröffentlichungen des Max-Planck-Instituts für Geschichte. Göttingen: Vandenhoeck & Ruprecht, 2003.

Puschner, Uwe. *Die völkische Bewegung im wilhelminischen Kaiserreich: Sprache-Rasse-Religion*. Darmstadt: Wissenschaftliche Buchgesellschaft, 2001.

Quinkert, Babette, ed. *"Wir sind die Herren dieses Landes": Ursachen, Verlauf und Folgen des deutschen Überfalls auf die Sowjetunion*. Hamburg: VSA-Verlag, 2002.

Rabinbach, Anson. *In the Shadow of Catastrophe: German Intellectuals between Apoc-alypse and Enlightenment*. Berkeley and Los Angeles: University of California Press, 1997.

Raphael, Lutz. "Sozialexperten in Deutschland zwischen konservativem Ordnungs-denken und rassistischer Utopie (1918–1945)." In *Utopie als Notstandsdenken – Einige Überlegunge zur Diskussion über Utopie und Sowjetkommunismus*, edited by Wolfgang Hardtwig, 327–46. Munich: Oldenbourg, 2003.

Rass, Christoph. *"Menschenmaterial": Deutsche Soldaten an der Ostfront: Innenan-sichten einer Infanteriedivision, 1939–1945*, Krieg in der Geschichte. Paderborn: Schöningh, 2003.

Ratza, Werner. *Die deutschen Kriegsgefangenen in der Sowjetunion: Der Faktor Arbeit*, Zur Geschichte der deutschen Kriegsgefangenen des Zweiten Weltkrieges. Bielefeld: Gieseking, 1973.

Reagin, Nancy Ruth. *A German Women's Movement: Class and Gender in Hanover, 1880–1933*. Chapel Hill: University of North Carolina Press, 1995.

Rebentisch, Dieter. *Führerstaat und Verwaltung im Zweiten Weltkrieg: Verfassungsent-wicklung und Verwaltungspolitik 1939–1945*, Frankfurter historische Abhandlun-gen. Stuttgart: F. Steiner Verlag Wiesbaden, 1989.

Reese, Willy Peter. *Mir selber seltsam fremd: Die Unmenschlichkeit des Krieges, Russ-land 1941–44*. Berlin: List, 2004.

Reibel, Carl-Wilhelm. *Das Fundament der Diktatur: Die NSDAP-Ortsgruppen 1932–1945*. Paderborn, Schöningh, 2002

Renner, Günter Rolf. "Grundzüge und Voraussetzungen deutscher literarischer Russ-landbilder während des Dritten Reiches." In *Das Russlandbild im Dritten Reich*, edited by Hans Erich Volkmann, 387–419. Cologne: Böhlau, 1994.

Rentschler, Eric. *The Ministry of Illusion: Nazi Cinema and Its Afterlife*. Cambridge, MA: Harvard University Press, 1996.

Richie, Alexandra. *Faust's Metropolis: A History of Berlin*. London: HarperCollins, 1998.

Richter, Timm C. "Die Wehrmacht und der Partisanenkrieg in den besetzten Gebieten der Sowjetunion." In *Erster Weltkrieg – Zweiter Weltkrieg: Krieg, Kriegserlebnis, Kriegserfahrung in Deutschland*, edited by Bruno Thoss and Hans Erich Volkmann, 837–57. Paderborn: Ferdinand Schöningh, 2002.

_____. "Handlungsspielräume am Beispiel der 6. Armee." In *Verbrechen der Wehrmacht: Bilanz einer Debatte*, edited by Christian Hartmann, Johannes Hürter, and Ulrike Jureit, 60–68. Munich: Beck, 2005.

_____. *Krieg und Verbrechen: Situation und Intention: Fallbeispiele*, Villa Ten Hompel Aktuell; 9. Munich: Meidenbauer, 2006.

Riess, Volker. *Die Anfänge der Vernichtung "lebensunwerten Lebens" in den Reichsgauen Danzig-Westpreussen und Wartheland, 1939/40*. Frankfurt am Main: P. Lang, 1995.

Robel, Gert. *Die deutschen Kriegsgefangenen in der Sowjetunion: Antifa*. Zur Geschichte der deutschen Kriegsgefangenen des Zweiten Weltkrieges, vol. 8. Munich, Gieseking: 1974.

Röhm, Ernst. *Die Geschichte eines Hochverräters*. Munich: F. Eher Nachf., 1928.

Rosenberg, Peter. "The Origin and the Development of Compulsory Health Insurance in Germany." In *Political Values and Health Care: The German Experience*, edited by Donald W. Light and Alexander Schuller, 105–26. Cambridge, MA and London: MIT University Press, 1986.

Rossino, Alexander B. *Hitler Strikes Poland: Blitzkrieg, Ideology, and Atrocity*, Modern Warfare Series. Lawrence: University Press of Kansas, 2003.

Rössler, Mechtild, Sabine Schleiermacher, and Cordula Tollmien, eds. *Der "Generalplan Ost": Hauptlinien der nationalsozialistischen Planungs- und Vernichtungspolitik*. Berlin: Akademie Verlag, 1993.

Roth, Karl Heinz. "'Generalplan Ost' – 'Gesamtplan Ost': Forschungsstand, Quellenprobleme, neue Ergebnisse." In *Der "Generalplan Ost": Hauptlinien der nationalsozialistischen Planungs- und Vernichtungspolitik*, edited by Mechtild Rössler, Sabine Schleiermacher, and Cordula Tollmien, 25–95. Berlin: Akademie Verlag, 1993.

_____. "Scheinalternativen im Gesundheitswesen: Alfred Grotjahn (1869–1931) – Integrationsfigur etablierter Sozialmedizin und nationalsozialistischer Rassenhygiene." In *Erfassung zur Vernichtung: Von der Sozialhygiene zum "Gesetz über Sterbehilfe,"* edited by Karl Heinz Roth, 31–56. Berlin: Verlagsgesellschaft Gesundheit, 1984.

Ruck, Michael. *Die freien Gewerkschaften im Ruhrkampf 1923*. Cologne: Bund Verlag, 1986.

Sachse, Carola. *Angst, Belohnung, Zucht und Ordnung: Herrschaftsmechanismus im Nationalsozialismus*. Opladen: Westdeutscher Verlag, 1982.

_____. *Siemens, der Nationalsozialismus und die moderne Familie: Eine Untersuchung zur sozialen Rationalisierung in Deutschland im 20. Jahrhundert*. Hamburg: Rasch und Röhring, 1990.

Saldern, Adelheid von. "Sozialmilieus und der Aufstieg des Nationalsozialismus in Norddeutschland." In *Norddeutschland im Nationalsozialismus*, edited by Frank Bajohr, 20–53. Hamburg: Ergebnisse Verlag, 1993.

_____. *The Challenge of Modernity: German Social and Cultural Studies, 1890–1960*. Translated by Bruce Little, Social History, Popular Culture, and Politics in Germany. Ann Arbor: University of Michigan Press, 2002.

Sandkühler, Thomas. *"Endlösung" in Galizien: Der Judenmord in Ostpolen und die Rettungsinitiativen von Berthold Beitz, 1941–1944*. Bonn: Dietz, 1996.

Schäfer, Wolfgang. *Die Fabrik auf dem Dorf: Studien zum betrieblichen Sozialverhalten ländlicher Industriearbeiter*, Andere Perspektiven. Göttingen: Davids Drucke, 1991.

Schenk, Dieter. *Hitlers Mann in Danzig: Albert Forster und die NS-Verbrechen in Danzig-Westpreussen*. Bonn: J. H. W. Dietz, 2000.

Scherer, Klaus. *"Asozial" im Dritten Reich: Die vergessenen Verfolgten*. Münster: VOTUM Verlag, 1990.

Schiedeck, Jürgen, and Martin Stahlmann. "Die Inzenierung 'totalen Erlebens': Lagererziehung im Nationalsozialismus." In *Politische Formierung und soziale Erziehung im Nationalsozialismus*, edited by Hans-Uwe Otto and Heinz Sünker, 167–202. Frankfurt am Main: Suhrkamp, 1991.

Schleunes, Karl. *The Twisted Road to Auschwitz*. Urbana: University of Illinois Press, 1970.

Schlögel, Karl. "Archäologie totaler Herrschaft." In *Deutschland und die Russische Revolution, 1917–1924*, edited by Gerd Koenen and Lev Kopelev, 780–804. Munich: W. Fink Verlag, 1998.

———. *Berlin, Ostbahnhof Europas: Russen und Deutsche in ihrem Jahrhundert*. Berlin: Siedler, 1998.

———. *Das russische Berlin: Ostbahnhof Europas*. Munich: Hanser, 2007.

———. "Die russische Obsession: Edwin Erich Dwinger." In *Traumland Osten: Deutsche Bilder vom östlichen Europa im 20. Jahrhundert*, edited by Gregor Thum, 66–87. Göttingen: Vandenhoeck & Ruprecht, 2006.

———, ed. *Russische Emigration in Deutschland 1918 bis 1941: Leben im europäischen Bürgerkrieg*. Berlin: Akademie Verlag, 1995.

Schlögel, Karl et al., eds. *Chronik russischen Lebens in Deutschland 1918–1941*. Berlin: Akademie Verlag, 1999.

Schmiechen-Ackermann, Detelf. "Der 'Blockwart.'" *Vierteljahrshefte für Zeitgeschichte* 48 (2000): 575–602.

Schmölders, Claudia, and Sander L. Gilman, eds. *Gesichter der Weimarer Republik: Eine physiognomische Kulturgeschichte*. Cologne: DuMont, 2000.

Schnurr, Stefan. "Die nationalsozialistische Funktionalisierung sozialer Arbeit: Zur Kontinuität und Diskontinuität der Praxis sozialer Berufe." In *Politische Formierung und soziale Erziehung im Nationalsozialismus*, edited by Hans-Uwe Otto and Heinz Sünker, 106–40. Frankfurt: Suhrkamp, 1991.

Schöttler, Peter. "Eine Art 'Generalplan West': Die Stuckart-Denkschrift vom 14. Juni 1940 und die Planungen für eine neue deutsch-französische Grenze im Zweiten Weltkrieg." *Sozial Geschichte* 18 (2003): 83–131.

Schröder, Hans Joachim. *Die gestohlenen Jahre: Erzählgeschichten und Geschichtserzählung im Interview: Der Zweite Weltkrieg aus der Sicht ehemaliger Mannschaftssoldaten*, Studien und Texte zur Sozialgeschichte der Literatur. Tübingen: Niemeyer, 1992.

———. "Erfahrungen deutscher Mannschaftssoldaten während der ersten Phase des Russlandkrieges." In *Zwei Wege nach Moskau: Vom Hitler-Stalin-Pakt zum 'Unternehmen Barbarossa*, edited by Bernd Wegner, 309–25. Munich: Piper, 1991.

Schüddekopf, Carl. *Krieg: Erzählungen aus dem Schweigen: Deutsche Soldaten über den Zweiten Weltkrieg*. Hamburg: Rowohlt, 1997.

Schüddekopf, Otto Ernst. *Linke Leute von rechts: Die national-revolutionären Minderheiten und der Kommunismus in der Weimarer Republik*. Stuttgart: Kohlhammer, 1960.

Schulte, Theo J. *The German Army and Nazi Policies in Occupied Russia.* Oxford and New York: Berg, 1989.

Schulte-Sasse, Linda. *Entertaining the Third Reich: Illusions of Wholeness in Nazi Cinema*, Post-Contemporary Interventions. Durham, NC: Duke University Press, 1996.

Schulze, Hagen. *Freikorps und Republik, 1918–1920*, Wehrwissenschaftliche Forschungen, Abteilung Militärgeschichtliche Studien. Boppard am Rhein: H. Boldt, 1969.

Schumann, Dirk. *Politische Gewalt in der Weimarer Republik 1918–1933: Kampf um die Strasse und Furcht vor dem Bürgerkrieg*, Geschichte und Gesellschaft, Zeitschrift für historische Sozialwissenschaft. Essen: Klartext, 2001.

Schwartz, Michael. *Sozialistische Eugenik: Eugenische Sozialtechnologien in Debatten und Politik der deutschen Sozialdemokratie 1890–1933*, Reihe Politik- und Gesellschaftsgeschichte. Bonn: J. H. W. Dietz, 1995.

Schwarz, Gudrun. *Eine Frau an seiner Seite: Ehefrauen in der "SS-Sippengemeinschaft."* Hamburg: Hamburger Edition, 1997.

Seidler, Franz Wilhelm. *Die Organisation Todt: Bauen für Staat und Wehrmacht, 1938–1945.* Koblenz: Bernard & Graefe, 1987.

Sereny, Gitta. *The German Trauma: Experiences and Reflections, 1938–2001.* London: Penguin, 2001.

Shepherd, Ben. "Hawks, Doves and Tote Zonen: A Wehrmacht Security Division in Central Russia 1943." *Journal of Contemporary History* 37, no. 3 (2002): 349–69.

———. *War in the Wild East: The German Army and Soviet Partisans.* Cambridge, MA: Harvard University Press, 2004.

Shils, Edward, and Morris Janowitz. "Cohesion and Disintegration in the Wehrmacht in World War II." *The Public Opinion Quarterly* 12, no. 2 (1948): 280–315.

Siegel, Tilla. *Leistung und Lohn in der nationalsozialistischen "Ordnung der Arbeit,"* Schriften des Zentralinstituts für Sozialwissenschaftliche Forschung der Freien Universität Berlin. Opladen: Westdeutscher Verlag, 1989.

Smelser, Ronald M. *Robert Ley: Hitler's Labor Front Leader.* New York: St. Martin's Press, 1988.

———. *Robert Ley: Hitlers Mann an der "Arbeitsfront": Eine Biographie.* Translated by Karl Nicolai and Heidi Nicolai, Sammlung Schöningh zur Geschichte und Gegenwart. Paderborn: Ferdinand Schöningh, 1989.

Smith, Arthur Lee. *Die "vermisste Million": Zum Schicksal deutscher Kriegsgefangener nach dem Zweiten Weltkrieg*, Schriftenreihe der Vierteljahrshefte für Zeitgeschichte. Munich: Oldenbourg, 1992.

Smith, Woodruff D. *Politics and the Sciences of Culture in Germany, 1840–1920.* New York: Oxford University Press, 1991.

Smolinsky, Herbert. "Das katholische Russlandbild in Deutschland nach dem Ersten Weltkrieg und im Dritten Reich." In *Das Russlandbild im Dritten Reich*, edited by Hans Erich Volkmann, 323–56. Cologne: Böhlau, 1994.

Sonnenberger, Franz. "'Der neue Kulturkampf': Die Gemeinschaftsschule und ihre historischen Voraussetzungen." In *Bayern in der NS-Zeit*, edited by Martin Broszat, 235–324. Munich: Oldenbourg, 1981.

Speer, Albert. *Inside the Third Reich: Memoirs.* Translated by Richard Winston and Clara Winston. New York: Macmillan, 1970.

Spicer, Kevin P. *Resisting the Third Reich: The Catholic Clergy in Hitler's Berlin.* Dekalb: Northern Illinois University Press, 2004.

Spiethoff, Bodo. *Die Geschlechtskrankheiten im Lichte der Bevölkerungspolitik, Erbgesundheits- und Rassenpflege.* Berlin, 1934.

Stachura, Peter D. "'Der Fall Strasser': Gregor Strasser, Hitler and National Socialism." In *The Shaping of the Nazi State*, edited by Peter D. Stachura, 88–130. London: Croom Helm, 1978.

Stammler, Heinrich. "Wandlungen des deutschen Bildes vom russischen Menschen." *Jahrbücher für Geschichte Osteuropas* 5 (1957): 271–305.

Statistisches Bundesamt, ed., *Bevölkerung und Wirtschaft 1872–1972* (Stuttgart, Kohlhammer, 1972.

Stein, George H. *The Waffen SS: Hitler's Elite Guard at War, 1939–1945*. Ithaca, NY: Cornell University Press, 1966.

Steinbacher, Sybille. *"Musterstadt" Auschwitz: Germanisierungspolitik und Judenmord in Ostoberschlesien*, Darstellungen und Quellen zur Geschichte von Auschwitz. Munich: Saur, 2000.

Steiniger, P. A., ed. *Der Nürnberger Prozess: Aus den Protokollen, Dokumenten und Materialien des Prozesses gegen die Hauptkriegsverbrecher vor dem Internationalen Militärgerichtshof*. 4 ed. Berlin: Rütten & Loening, 1960.

Stenzel, Thilo. *Das Russlandbild des "kleinen Mannes": Gesellschaftliche Prägung und Fremdwahrnehmung in Feldpostbriefen aus dem Ostfeldzug, 1941–1944/45*. Munich: Mitteilungen Osteuropa-Institut, 1998.

Stieff, Hellmuth. *Briefe*. Horst Mühleisen ed. Berlin: Siedler, 1991.

Stokes, Patricia R. "Contested Conceptions: Experiences and Discourses of Pregnancy and Childbirth in Germany, 1914–1933." Ph.D. diss., Cornell University, 2003.

Stöver, Bernd. *Volksgemeinschaft im Dritten Reich: Die Konsensbereitschaft der Deutschen aus der Sicht sozialistischer Exilberichte*. Düsseldorf: Droste, 1993.

Strachan, Hew. "Time, Space and Barbarisation: The German Army and the Eastern Front in Two World Wars." In *The Barbarization of Warfare*, edited by George Kassimeris, 58–82. New York: New York University Press, 2006.

Strazhas, Abba, *Deutsche Ostpolitik im Ersten Weltkrieg: der Fall Ober Ost 1915–1917*, Veröffentlichungen des Osteuropa-Institutes München. Wiesbaden: Harrassowitz, 1993.

Streim, Alfred. *Die Behandlung sowjetischer Kriegsgefangener im "Fall Barbarossa": Eine Dokumentation unter Berücksichtigung der Unterlagen deutscher Strafverfolgungsbehörden und der Materialien der Zentralen Stelle der Landesjustizverwaltungen zur Aufklärung von NS-Verbrechen*, Motive, Texte, Materialien. Heidelberg and Karlruhe: Müller, Juristischer Verlag, 1981.

Streit, Christian. *Keine Kameraden: Die Wehrmacht und die sowjetischen Kriegsgefangenen 1941–1945*. Bonn: Verlag J. H. W. Dietz Nachf., 1991.

———. "Ostkrieg, Antibolschewismus und 'Endlösung.'" *Geschichte und Gesellschaft* 17 (1991): 242–55.

Süss, Winfried. "Gesundheitspolitik." In *Drei Wege deutscher Sozialstaatlichkeit*, edited by Hans Günter Hockerts, 55–100. Munich: R. Oldenbourg, 1998.

Sütterlin, Ingmar. *Die "Russische Abteilung" des Auswärtigen Amtes in der Weimarer Republik*, Historische Forschungen. Berlin: Duncker & Humblot, 1994.

Swett, Pamela E. *Neighbors and Enemies: The Culture of Radicalism in Berlin, 1929–1933*. Cambridge and New York: Cambridge University Press, 2004.

Szejnmann, Claus-Christian W. *Nazism in Central Germany: The Brownshirts in "Red" Saxony*, Monographs in German History. New York: Berghahn Books, 1999.

Talos, Emmerich, Ernst Hanisch, and Wolfgang Neugebauer, eds. *NS – Herrschaft in Österreich, 1938–1945*, Österreichische Texte zur Gesellschaftskritik. Vienna: Verlag für Gesellschaftskritik, 1988.

Thoss, Bruno, and Hans Erich Volkmann, eds. *Erster Weltkrieg, Zweiter Weltkrieg, Ein Vergleich: Krieg, Kriegserlebnis, Kriegserfahrung in Deutschland.* Paderborn: F. Schöningh, 2002.

Thum, Gregor, ed. *Traumland Osten: Deutsche Bilder vom östlichen Europa im 20. Jahrhundert.* Göttingen: Vandenhoeck & Ruprecht, 2006.

Timm, Annette F. "Sex with a Purpose: Prostitution, Venereal Disease and Militarized Masculinity in the Third Reich." *Journal of the History of Sexuality* 11, no. 1/2 (2002): 223–55.

———. "The Politics of Fertility: Population Politics and Health Care in Berlin, 1919–1972." Ph.D. diss., University of Chicago, 1999.

Tooze, Adam. *The Wages of Destruction: The Making and Breaking of the Nazi Economy.* New York: Viking, 2006.

Trevor-Roper, Hugh, ed. *Hitler's Secret Conversations, 1941–1944.* New York: Farrar, Straus and Young, 1953.

Ueberschär, Gerd R., and Wolfram Wette, eds. *"Unternehmen Barbarossa": Der deutsche Überfall auf die Sowjetunion, 1941: Berichte, Analysen, Dokumente,* Sammlung Schöningh zur Geschichte und Gegenwart. Paderborn: F. Schöningh, 1984.

Uhlig, Heinrich. *Die Warenhäuser im Dritten Reich.* Cologne: Westdeutscher Verlag, 1956.

Umbreit, Hans. "Auf dem Weg zur Kontinentalherrschaft." In *Das Deutsche Reich und der Zweite Weltkrieg V/1,* 3–328. Stuttgart: Deutsche Verlags-Anstalt, 1988.

Usborne, Cornelie. *The Politics of Body in Weimar Germany: Women's Reproductive Rights and Duties,* Studies in Gender History. Basingstoke: Macmillan, 1992.

Verhey, Jeffrey. *The Spirit of 1914: Militarism, Myth and Mobilization in Germany,* Studies in the Social and Cultural History of Modern Warfare. Cambridge: Cambridge University Press, 2000.

Voigt, Gerd. *Otto Hoetzsch, 1876–1946: Wissenschaft und Politik im Leben eines deutschen Historikers,* Quellen und Studien zur Geschichte Osteuropas. Berlin: Akademie-Verlag, 1978.

———. *Russland in der deutschen Geschichtsschreibung 1843–1945,* Quellen und Studien zur Geschichte Osteuropas. Berlin: Akademie Verlag, 1994.

Volkmann, Hans Erich, ed. *Das Russlandbild im Dritten Reich.* Cologne: Böhlau, 1994.

———. *Die russische Emigration in Deutschland 1919–1929,* Marburger Ostforschungen, Johann Gottfried Herder Forschungsrat. Würzburg: Holzner, 1966.

Vorländer, Herwart. *Die NSV: Darstellung und Dokumentation einer nationalsozialistischen Organisation,* Schriften des Bundesarchivs. Boppard am Rhein: H. Boldt, 1988.

Wachsmann, Nikolaus. "'Annihilation through Labor': The Killing of State Prisoners in the Third Reich." *Journal of Modern History* 71, no. 3 (1999): 624–59.

———. "From Indefinite Confinement to Extermination: 'Habitual Criminals' in the Third Reich." In *Social Outsiders in Nazi Germany,* edited by Robert Gellately and Nathan Stoltzfuss, 165–91. Princeton, NJ: Princeton University Press, 2001.

Wagner, Patrick. *Volksgemeinschaft ohne Verbrecher: Konzeptionen und Praxis der Kriminalpolizei in der Zeit der Weimarer Republik und des Nationalsozialismus,* Hamburger Beiträge zur Sozial- und Zeitgeschichte. Hamburg: Christians, 1996.

Waite, Robert G. L. "Kollaboration und deutsche Besatzungspolitik in Lettland 1941 bis 1945." In *Okkupation und Kollaboration (1938–1945): Beiträge zu Konzepten und Praxis der Kollaboration in der deutschen Okkupationspolitik*, edited by Werner Röhr, 217–37. Berlin: Hüthig, 1994.

————. "Teenage Sexuality in Nazi Germany." *Journal of the History of Sexuality* 8, no. 3 (1998): 434–76.

————. *Vanguard of Nazism: The Free Corps Movement in Post-War Germany, 1918–1923*, Harvard Historical Studies. Cambridge, MA: Harvard University Press, 1952.

Wasser, Bruno. *Himmlers Raumplanung im Osten: Der Generalplan Ost in Polen, 1940–1944*, Stadt, Planung, Geschichte. Basel and Boston: Birkhauser, 1993.

Weber, Hermann. *Die Wandlung des deutschen Kommunismus: Die Stalinisierung der KPD in der Weimarer Republik*. 2 vols. Frankfurt am Main: Europäische Verlagsanstalt, 1969.

Wegner, Bernd. "Die Aporie des Krieges." In *Das Deutsche Reich und der Zweite Weltkrieg*, Vol. 8: *Die Ostfront 1943/44*, edited by Militärgeschichtliches Forschungsamt, 211–76. Munich: Deutsche Verlagsanstalt, 2007.

————. *Hitlers politische Soldaten, die Waffen-SS 1933–1945: Leitbild, Struktur und Funktion einer nationalsozialistischen Elite*. 4 ed., Sammlung Schöningh zur Geschichte und Gegenwart. Paderborn: F. Schöningh, 1990.

Wehler, Hans Ulrich. *Deutsche Gesellschaftsgeschichte*, Vol. 4: *Vom Beginn des Ersten Weltkriegs bis zur Gründung der beiden deutschen Staaten*. Munich: C. H. Beck, 2003.

————. *Entsorgung der deutschen Vergangenheit?: Ein polemischer Essay zum "Historikerstreit,"* Beck'sche Reihe. Munich: Beck, 1988.

Weinberg, Gerhard L. *The Foreign Policy of Hitler's Germany: Diplomatic Revolution in Europe, 1933–36*. Chicago: University of Chicago Press, 1970.

Weindling, Paul. *Health, Race, and German Politics between National Unification and Nazism, 1870–1945*, Cambridge History of Medicine. Cambridge and New York: Cambridge University Press, 1989.

Weingart, Peter; Jürgen Kroll, and Kurt Bayertz. *Rasse, Blut und Gene: Geschichte der Eugenik und Rassenhygiene in Deutschland*. Frankfurt am Main: Suhrkamp, 1988.

Weiss, Sheila Faith. "The Race Hygiene Movement in Germany 1904–1945." In *The Wellborn Science: Eugenics in Germany, France, Brazil, and Russia*, edited by Mark B. Adams, 3–68. New York: Oxford University Press, 1990.

Weissbecker, Manfred. "'Wenn hier Deutsche wohnten...': Beharrung und Veränderung im Russlandbild Hitlers und der NSDAP." In *Das Russlandbild im Dritten Reich*, edited by Hans Erich Volkmann, 9–54. Cologne: Böhlau, 1994.

Welch, David. "Nazi Propaganda and the Volksgemeinschaft: Constructing a People's Community." *Journal of Contemporary History* 39, no. 2 (2004): 213–38.

Wenzel, Eike. *Gedächtnisraum Film: Die Arbeit an der deutschen Geschichte in Filmen seit den 60er Jahren*, M & P Schriftenreihe für Wissenschaft und Forschung. Stuttgart: Metzler, 2000.

Werner, Wolfgang Franz. *"Bleib übrig!": Deutsche Arbeiter in der nationalsozialistischen Kriegswirtschaft*. Düsseldorfer Schriften zur Neueren Landesgeschichte und zur Geschichte Nordrhein-Westfalens. Düsseldorf: Schwann, 1983.

Wette, Wolfram. "Das Russlandbild in der NS-Propaganda: Ein Problemaufriss." In *Das Russlandbild im Dritten Reich*, edited by Hans-Erich Volkmann, 55–78. Cologne: Böhlau, 1994.

_____. "Die propagandistische Begleitmusik zum Überfall auf die Sowjetunion 1941." In *Der Deutsche Überfall auf die Sowjetunion: "Unternehmen Barbarossa" 1941*, edited by Gerd R. Ueberschär and Wolfram Wette, 111–29. Frankfurt am Main: Fischer Taschenbuch Verlag, 1991.

Weyrather, Irmgard. *Muttertag und Mutterkreuz: Der Kult um die "deutsche Mutter" im Nationalsozialismus*, Die Zeit des Nationalsozialismus. Frankfurt am Main: Fischer Taschenbuch Verlag, 1993.

Wiedemann, Fritz. *Der Mann, der Feldherr werden wollte: Erlebnisse und Erfahrungen des Vorgesetzten Hitlers im 1. Weltkrieg und seines späteren persönlichen Adjutanten*: Velbert: Kettwig, 1964.

Wiedmann, Hanns. *Landser, Tod und Teufel: Aufzeichngn aus dem Feldzug im Osten.* Munich: Piper, 1943.

Wildt, Michael. *Generation des Unbedingten: Das Führungskorps des Reichssicherheitshauptamtes.* Hamburg: Hamburger Edition, 2002.

_____. "Gewalt gegen Juden in Deutschland 1933 bis 1939." *WerkstattGeschichte* 8, no. 18 (1997): 59–80.

_____. *Judenpolitik des SD 1935 bis 1938: Eine Dokumentation*, Schriftenreihe der Vierteljahrshefte für Zeitgeschichte. Munich: Oldenbourg, 1995.

_____. "'Volksgemeinschaft' als politischer Topos in der Weimar." In *NS-Gewaltherrschaft: Beiträge zur historischen Forschung und juristischen Aufarbeitung*, edited by Alfred Bernd Gottwaldt, Norbert Kampe and Peter Klein, 23–39. Berlin: Edition Hentrich, 2005.

Williams, Robert Chadwell. *Culture in Exile: Russian Émigrés in Germany, 1881–1941.* Ithaca, NY: Cornell University Press, 1972.

Wippermann, Wolfgang. *"Wie Die Zigeuner": Antisemitismus und Antiziganismus im Vergleich.* Berlin: Elefanten Press, 1997.

Wirsching, Andreas. "'Man kann nur Boden germanisieren': Eine neue Quelle zu Hitlers Rede vor den Spitzen der Reichswehr am 3. Februar 1933." *Vierteljahrshefte für Zeitgeschichte* 49 (2001): 517–50.

Witte, Peter, ed. *Der Dienstkalender Heinrich Himmlers 1941/42*, Hamburger Beiträge zur Sozial- und Zeitgeschichte, Quellen. Hamburg: Christians, 1999.

Woltereck, Heinz, ed., *Erbkunde, Rassenpflege, Bevölkerungspolitik: Schicksals Fragen des deutschen Volkes.* 2nd ed. Leipzig: Quelle & Meyer, 1935.

Wolters, Rita. *Verrat für die Volkswirtschaft [i.e. Volksgemeinschaft]: Denunziantinnen im Dritten Reich*, Forum Frauengeschichte. Pfaffenweiler: Centaurus, 1996.

Zarusky, Jürgen. *Die deutschen Sozialdemokraten und das sowjetische Modell: Ideologische Auseinandersetzung und aussenpolitische Konzeptionen, 1917–1933*, Studien zur Zeitgeschichte. Munich: R. Oldenbourg, 1992.

Zeidler, Manfred. "Das Bild der Wehrmacht von Russland und der Roten Armee zwischen 1933 und 1939." In *Das Russlandbild im Dritten Rreich*, edited by Hans-Erich Volkmann, 105–24. Cologne: Böhlau, 1994.

Ziemke, Earl Frederick. *Stalingrad to Berlin: The German Defeat in the East*, Army Historical Series. Washington D.C.: Office of the Chief of Military History, U.S. Army, 1968.

Zimmermann, Michael. *Rassenutopie und Genozid: Die nationalsozialistische "Lösung der Zigeunerfrage,"* Hamburger Beiträge zur Sozial- und Zeitgeschichte. Hamburg: Christians, 1996.

Stalinism, Soviet Union, Russia

Adams, Mark B. "Eugenics as Social Medicine in Revolutionary Russia: Prophets, Patrons, and the Dialectics of Discipline-Building." In *Health and Society in Revolutionary Russia*, edited by Susan Gross Solomon and John F. Hutchinson, 200–23. Bloomington: Indiana University Press, 1981.

———. "Eugenics in Russia, 1900–1940." In *The Wellborn Sciences: Eugenics in Germany, France, Brazil and Russia*, edited by Mark B. Adams, 153–216. Oxford: Oxford University Press, 1989.

Albrecht, Karl I. *Der verratene Sozialismus: Zehn Jahre als hoher Staatsbeamter in der Sowjetunion*. Berlin: Nibelungen-Verlag, 1939.

Aleksievich, Svetlana. *U voiny ne zhenskoe litso*. Moscow: Sov. pisatel', 1988.

———. *War's Unwomanly Face*. Moscow: Progress Publishers, 1988.

Alexijewitsch, Swetlana. *Der Krieg hat kein weibliches Gesicht*. Translated by Johann Warkentin, Dialog. Berlin: Henschelverl. Kunst u. Gesellschaft, 1987.

Alexopoulos, Golfo. *Stalin's Outcasts: Aliens, Citizens, and the Soviet State, 1926–1936*. Ithaca, NY: Cornell University Press, 2003.

———. "The Ritual Lament: A Narrative of Appeal in the 1920s and 1930s." *Russian History/Histoire Russe* 24, nos. 1–2 (1997): 117–30.

Alferov, Zh. I. and V. P. Leonov, eds. *Akademicheskoe delo 1929–1931 gg.*, 2 vols. St. Petersburg: Biblioteka Rossiiskoi akademiia nauk, 1998.

Alieva, Svetlana, ed. *Tak eto bylo: Natsional'nye repressii v SSSR 1919–1952 gody: v 3-kh tomakh*. 3 vols. Vol. 2. Moscow: Rossiiskii mezhdunar. fond kul'tury: "Insan," 1993.

Ammende, Ewald, and Alexander Wienerberger. *Muss Russland hungern?: Menschen- und Völkerschicksale in der Sowjetunion*. Vienna: W. Braumüller Universitäts-Verlagsbuchhandlung, 1935.

Andreyev, Catherine. *Vlasov and the Russian Liberation Movement: Soviet Reality and Émigré Theories*, Soviet and East European Studies. Cambridge: Cambridge University Press, 1987.

Andrle, Vladimir. *A Social History of Twentieth-Century Russia*. London: Edward Arnold, 1994.

Annette, Michelson, ed. *Kino-Eye: The Writings of Dziga Vertov*. Berkeley: University Of California Press, 1984.

Arnold, Sabine R. "'Ich bin bisher noch lebendig und gesund': Briefe von den Fronten des sowjetischen 'Grossen VaterländischeKrieges.'" In *Andere Helme – Andere Menschen? Heimaterfahrung und Frontalltag im Zweiten Weltkrieg, ein internationaler Vergleich*, edited by Detlef Vogel and Wolfram Wette, 135–56. Essen: Klartext, 1995.

Artizov, Andrei, and Oleg Naumov, compilers, *Vlast' i khudozhestvennaia intelligentsia: Dokumenty TsK RKP (b) – VKP (b), VChK – OGPU – NKVD o kul'turnoi politike 1917–1953 gg.* (Moscow: Mezhdunarodnoi fond "Demokratiia," 1999).

Attwood, Lynnne, and Catriona Kelly. "Programmmes for Identity: The 'New Man' and the 'New Woman.'" In *Constructing Russian Culture in the Age of Revolution, 1881–1940*, edited by Catriona Kelly and David Shepherd, 256–90. New York and Oxford: Oxford University Press, 1998.

Avaramov, Vl. "Zhertvy imperialisticheskoi voiny v Rossii." *Izvestiia narodnogo komissariata zdravookhraneniia* 3, no. 1–2 (1920): 39–42.

Avdeichik, I. P. and G. K. Iukhnovich, eds. *Plakaty pervykh let Sovetskoi vlasti i sotsialisticheskogo sotrudnichestva (1918–1941): Katalog*, Minsk: "Polymia," 1985.

Avtorkhanov, Abdurakhman. "The Chechens and Ingush during the Soviet Period and Its Antecedents." In *The North Caucasus Barrier: The Russian Advance towards the Muslim World*, edited by Abdurakhman Avtorkhanov and Marie Broxup, 157–66. New York: St. Martin's Press, 1992.

Baberowski, Jörg. *Der Feind ist überall: Stalinismus im Kaukasus*. Munich: Deutsche Verlags-Anstalt, 2003.

_____. *Der rote Terror: Die Geschichte des Stalinismus*. Munich: Deutsche Verlags-Anstalt, 2003.

_____. "Stalinismus an der Peripherie: Das Beispiel Azerbaidzhan 1920–1941." In *Stalinismus vor dem Zweiten Weltkrieg: Neue Wege der Forschung*, edited by Manfred Hildermeier and Elisabeth Müller-Luckner, 307–35. Munich: Oldenbourg, 1998.

_____. "Stalinismus 'von oben': Kulakendeportationen in der Sowjetunion 1929–1933." *Jahrbücher für Geschichte Osteuropas* 46 (1998): 572–95.

Bagotzky, Serge. "Les perts de la Russie pendant la guerre mondiale." *Revue internationale de la Croix Rouge* 61 (1924): 16–21.

Baikov, B. "Vospominaniia o Revoliutsii v Zakavkaz'e 1917–1920 g.g." *Arkhiv Russkoi Revoliutsii* 9 (1923): 120–36.

Barber, John, and Mark Harrison. *The Soviet Home Front, 1941–1945: A Social and Economic History of the USSR in World War II*. London: New York, 1991.

Barck, Simone. *Exil in der UdSSR*. 2nd rev. ed. 2 vols., Kunst und Literatur im antifaschistischen Exil 1933–1945. Leipzig: Reclam, 1989.

Bauer, Raymond A. *The New Man in Soviet Psychology*. Cambridge, MA: Harvard University Press, 1952.

Bauer, Raymond A., Alex Inkeles, and Clyde Kluckhohn. *How the Soviet System Works: Cultural, Psychological, and Social Themes*, Russian Research Center Study. Cambridge, MA: Harvard University Press, 1956.

Belinsky, Vissarion Grigor'evich. *Polnoe sobranie sochinenii*. 13 vols. Moscow: Akademiia Nauk, 1953.

Bellamy, Chris. *Absolute War: Soviet Russia in the Second World War: A Modern History*. London: Macmillan, 2007.

Bennigsen, Alexandre, and Chantal Lemercier-Quelquejay *Les Mouvements nationaux chez les Musulmans de Russie*, Société et idéologie. Paris: Mouton, 1960.

Bennigsen, Alexandre, and Samuel E. *Wimbush. Muslim National Communism in the Soviet Union: A Revolutionary Strategy for the Colonial World*, Publications of the Center for Middle Eastern Studies. Chicago: University of Chicago Press, 1979.

Berelowitch, Alexis, and V. A. Danilov, eds. *Sovetskaia derevnia glazami VChK-OGPU-NKVD, 1918–1939: Dokumenty i materialy v 4 tomakh*. 3 vols. Moscow: ROSSPEN, 1988 -.

Berkhin, I. B. "K istorii razrabotki konstitutsii SSSR v 1936 g." In *Stroitel'stvo sovetskogo gosudarstva: Sbornik Statei: K 70 – letiiu doktora istoricheskikh nauk, prof E. B. Genkinoi*, edited by Iurii Aleksandrovich Poliakov. Moscow: "Nauka," 1972.

Bernstein, Frances Lee. *The Dictatorship of Sex: Lifestyle Advice for the Soviet Masses*, Studies of the Harriman Institute. Dekalb: Northern Illinois University Press, 2007.

Berzhe, A. P. "Vyselenie gortsev s Kavkaza." *Russkaia starina*, no. 1 (1882): 161–76; 337–63.

Beyrau, Dietrich. "Der Erste Weltkrieg als Bewährungsprobe: Bolschewistische Lernprozesse aus dem 'imperialistischen' Krieg." *Journal of Modern History* 1, no. 1 (2003): 96–204.

Binner, Rolf, and Marc Junge. "'S etoj publikoj ceremonit'sja ne sleduet': Die Ziel-gruppen des Befehls Nr. 00447 und der Grosse Terror aus der Sicht des Befehls Nr. 00447." *Cahiers du Monde russe* 43 (2002): 43–8.

———. "Wie der Terror 'gross' wurde: Massenmord und Lagerhaft nach Befehl 00447." *Cahiers du Monde russe* 42, no. 2–4 (2001): 557–614.

Bonnell, Victoria E. *Iconography of Power: Soviet Political Posters under Lenin and Stalin*, Studies on the History of Society and Culture. Berkeley: University of California Press, 1997.

Borshchagovskii, Aleksandr. *Orden für einen Mord: Die Judenverfolgung unter Stalin*. Translated by Alfred Frank. Berlin: Propyläen, 1997.

Brandenberger, David. *National Bolshevism: Stalinist Mass Culture and the Formation of Modern Russian National Identity, 1931–1956*. Cambridge, MA: Harvard University Press, 2002.

Brent, Jonathan, and Vladimir Pavlovich Naumov. *Stalin's Last Crime: The Plot against the Jewish Doctors, 1948–1953*. New York: HarperCollins, 2003.

Broido, G. I. "Materialy k istorii vosstaniia kirgiz v 1916 godu." *Novyi Vostok* 6 (1924): 407–34.

Brooks, Jeffrey. *Thank You, Comrade Stalin! Soviet Public Culture from Revolution to Cold War*. Princeton, NJ: Princeton University Press, 2000.

Brower, Daniel. "Kyrgyz Nomads and Russian Pioneers: Colonization and Ethnic Conflict in the 'Turkestan Revolt of 1916.'" *Jahrbücher für Geschichte Osteuropas* 44 (1996): 41–53.

Brusilov, Aleksei Alekseevich. *Moi vospominaniia*. Moscow: ROSSPEN, 2001.

Bucher, Greta Louise. "The Impact of World War II on Moscow Women: Gender Consciousness and Relationships in the Immediate Postwar Period, 1945–1953." Ph.D. diss., Ohio State University, 1995.

Bougai, Nikloai [Bugai, Nikolai F.]. *The Deportation of Peoples in the Soviet Union*. New York: Nova Science, 1996.

Bugai, N.F. *Iosif Stalin–Lavrentiiu Berii: "Ikh nado deportirovat'": Dokumenty, fakty, kommentarii*. Moscow: "Druzhba narodov," 1992.

———. "K voprosu o deportatsii narody SSSR v 30–40-kh godakh." *Istoriia SSSR* 6 (1989): 135–44

———. *L. Beriia–I. Stalinu: "Soglasno Vashemu ukazaniiu–."* Moscow: AIRO XX, 1995.

———. "Vyselenie sovetskikh koreitsev s Dal'nego Vostoka." *Voprosy istorii* 5 (1994): 141–8.

Bugai, N. F., and A. M. Gonov. *Kavkaz–narody v eshelonakh: 20–60-e gody*. Moscow: INSAN, 1998.

Bukharin, Nikolai, and Genrikh Iagoda. *Prozessbericht über die Strafsache des antisowjetischen "Blocks der Rechten und Trotzkisten," verhandelt vor dem Militärkollegium des Obersten Gerichtshofes der UdSSR vom 2.-13.* Moscow: Volkskommissariat für Justizwesen der UdSSR, 1938.

Bukharin, Nikolai Ivanovich *Tiuremnye rukopisi N. I. Bukharina*. 2 vols., Seriia "Pervaia publikatsiia." Moscow: AIRO-XX, 1996.

Burton, Chris. "Medical Welfare during Late Stalinism: A Study of Doctors and the Soviet Health System, 1945–53." Ph.D. diss., University of Chicago, 2000.

Carr, Edward Hallett. *Socialism in One Country, 1924–1926*. 3 vols. Vol. 2. New York: Macmillan, 1960.

Chase, William J. *Workers, Society and the Soviet State: Labor and Life in Moscow, 1918–1929*. Urbana and Chicago: University of Illinois Press, 1987.

Chekalov, Vasilii. *Voennyi dnevnik, 1941, 1942, 1943*, Biblioteka zhurnala "Zdravyi smysl." Moscow: Rossiiskoe gumanisticheskoe ob-vo, 2003.

Chiari, Bernhard. *Alltag hinter der Front: Besatzung, Kollaboration und Widerstand in Weissrussland 1941–1944*, Schriften des Bundesarchivs. Düsseldorf: Droste Verlag, 1998.

———. "Geschichte als Gewalttat: Weissrussland als Kind zweier Weltkriege." In *Wehrmacht, Verbrechen, Widerstand: Vier Beiträge zum nationalsozialistischen Weltanschauungskrieg*, edited by Clemens Vollnhals, 27–44. Dresden: Hannah Arendt Institut für Totalitarismusforschung, 2003.

Chor'kov, Anatoli. "The Red Army during the Initial Phase of the Great Patriotic War." In *From Peace to War: Germany, Soviet Russia and the World, 1939–1941*, edited by Bernd Wegner, 415–30. Oxford: Berghahn Books, 1997.

Chuev, Feliks,. *Sto sorok besed s Molotovym: Iz dnevnika F. Chueva*. Moscow: Terra, 1991.

Chukhrai, Grigorii Naumovich. *Moia voina*, Biblioteka "O vremeni i o sebe." Moscow: Algoritm, 2001.

Chukovskaia, Lydia. *Sofia Petrovna*. Translated by Aline Worth. Evanston, IL: Northwestern University Press, 1988.

Chumachenko, Tatiana. *Church and State in Soviet Russia: Russian Orthodoxy from World War II to the Khrushchev Years*. Translated by Edward E. Roslof, The New Russian History. Armonk, NY: M. E. Sharpe, 2002.

Clark, Katerina. *Petersburg, Crucible of Cultural Revolution*. Cambridge, MA: Harvard University Press, 1995.

Clark, Toby. "The 'New Man's' Body: A Motif in Early Soviet Culture." In *Art of the Soviets: Painting, Sculpture, and Archictecture in a One-Party State, 1917–1992*, edited by Matthew Cullerne Bown and Brandon Taylor, 33–50. Manchester: Manchester University Press, 1993.

Coale, Ansley J., Barbara A. Anderson, and Erna Härm. *Human Fertility in Russia since the Nineteenth Century*. Princeton, NJ: Princeton University Press, 1979.

Conquest, Robert. *Stalins Völkermord Wolgadeutsche, Krimtataren, Kaukasier*. Vienna: Europaverlag, 1970.

Dahlmann, Dittmar, ed. *"Eine große Zukunft": Deutsche in Russlands Wirtschaft: Begleitband zur Ausstellung "Eine große Zukunft. Deutsche in Russlands Wirtschaft."* Berlin: Reschke & Steffens, 2000.

Daniels, Robert V. "The Secretariat and the Local Organizations in the Russian Communist Party, 1921–1923." *American Slavic and East European Review* 16, no. 1 (1957): 32–49.

Danilov, Viktor et al., eds. *Tragediia sovetskoi derevni: Kollektivizatsiia i raskulachivanie: Dokumenty i materialy v 5 tomakh, 1927–1939*. 5 vols. Moscow: ROSSPEN, 1999.

Danilov, V. P., and S. A. Krasil'nikov, eds. *Spetspereselentsy v Zapadnoi Sibiri, 1933–1938*. 4 vols. Vol. 3. Novosibirsk: "EKOR," 1994.

Danilov, V. P., and L. V. Milov, eds. *Mentalitet i agrarnoe razvitie Rossii, XIX-XX vv.: Materialy mezhdunarodnoi konferentsii, Moskva, 14–15 iiunia 1994 g.* Moscow: ROSSPEN, 1996.

Danilov, V. P. et al., eds. *Kak lomali NEP: Stenogrammy plenumov TSK VKP(b) 1928–1929 gg.* 5 vols, Rossiia XX vek, Dokumenty. Moscow: MFD, 2000.

Davies, R. W. *Soviet History in the Yeltsin Era*, Studies in Russian and East European History and Society. New York: St. Martin's Press in association with Centre for Russian and East European Studies, University of Birmingham, 1997.

Davies, Sarah. *Popular Opinion in Stalin's Russia: Terror, Propaganda, and Dissent, 1934–1941*. Cambridge: Cambridge University Press, 1997.

Deker-Novak, N. K., ed. *Soviet Youth: Twelve Komsomol Histories*. Vol. 51, Issledovaniia i materialy (Institut zur Erforschung der UdSSR), Series 1. Munich: Institut zur Erforschung der UdSSR, 1959.

Deni, V., and N. Dolgorukov. "Fashizm – eto voina (1936)." In *Simvoly epokhi v sovetskom plakate*, edited by T. G. Koloskova. Moscow: Gos. istoricheskii muzei, 2001.

Dickerman, Leah. "The Propagandizing of Things." In *Aleksandr Rodchenko*, edited by Magdalena Dabrowski, Leah Dickerman, and Peter Galassi, 62–99. New York: Museum of Modern Art, 1998.

Dimanshtein, S. "Stalin – tvorets sovetskoi gosudarstvennosti narodov SSSR." *Revoliutsiia i natsional'nosti*, no. 1 (1937): 15–24.

Djilas, Milovan. *Conversations with Stalin*. Translated by Michael B. Petrovich. New York: Harcourt, Brace & World, 1962.

Dolgopolov, I., and Iu. Uzbekov. "Doloi fashistskikh pogzhigatelei voiny! (1938)." In *Plakaty pervykh let Sovetskoi vlasti i sotsialisticheskogo stroitel'stva, 1918–1941: Katalog*, edited by I. P. Avdeichik and G. K. Iukhnovich, 112. Minsk: "Polymia," 1985.

Dönninghaus, Victor. *Die Deutschen in der Moskauer Gesellschaft: Symbiose und Konflikte (1494–1941)*, Schriften des Bundesinstituts für Kultur und Geschichte der Deutschen im östlichen Europa. Munich: R. Oldenbourg, 2002.

Drobizhev, V. Z. *U istokov sovetskoi demografii*. Moscow: "Mysl'," 1987.

Dunlop, John B. *Russia Confronts Chechnya: Roots of a Separatist Conflict*. Cambridge: Cambridge University Press, 1998.

Dzagurov, G. A. *Pereselenie gortsev v Turtsiiu: materialy po istorii gorskikh narodov*. Rostov-Don: Sevkavkniga, 1925.

Edele, Mark. "Paper Soldiers: The World of the Soldier Hero According to Soviet Wartime Posters." *Jahrbuch für Geschichte Osteuropas* 47, no. 1 (1999): 89–108.

———. "Soviet Veterans as an Entitlement Group." *Slavic Review* 65, no. 1 (2006): 111–37.

Ehrenburg, Ilya. *Cent lettres*. Translated by A. Roudnikov. Moscow: Éditions en langues étrangères, 1944.

———. *The Fall of Paris*. Translated by Gerard Shelley. London: Hutchinson, 1942.

———. *Visum der Zeit*. Translated by Hans Ruoff. Leipzig: P. List, 1929.

Ellman, Michael, and S. Maksudov. "Soviet Deaths in the Great Patriotic War: A Note." *Europe-Asia Studies* 46, no. 4 (1994): 671–80.

Engel, Barbara Alpern, and Anastasia Posadskaya-Vanderbeck, eds. *A Revolution of Their Own: Voices of Women in Soviet History*. Boulder, CO: Westview Press, 1998.

Engelstein, Laura. "Soviet Policy toward Male Homosexuality: Its Origins and Historical Roots." *Journal of Homosexuality* 29, no. 2–3 (1994): 155–78.

Erickson, John. "Red Army Battlefield Performance, 1941–1945: The System and the Soldier." In *Time to Kill: The Soldier's Experience of War in the West, 1939–1945*, edited by Paul Addison and Angue Calder, 233–48. London: Pimlico, 1997.

———. *Stalin's War with Germany*. 2 vols. 1. *The Road to Stalingrad*. 2. *The Road to Berlin*. New Haven, CT and London: Yale University Press, 1999.

Etinger, Iakov. "The Doctors' Plot: Stalin's Solution to the Jewish Question." In *Jews and Jewish Life in Russia and the Soviet Union*, edited by Yaacov Ro'i, 103–24. Ilford, England: Frank Cass, 1995.

Fadeev, Aleksandr. *Molodaia gvardiia: Roman.* Moscow: TsK VLKSM, 1946.

Fainsod, Merle. *Smolensk under Soviet Rule.* Cambridge, MA: Harvard University Press, 1958.

Feyerabend, Paul. *Killing Time: The Autobiography of Paul Feyerabend.* Chicago and London: University of Chicago Press, 1995.

Filippov, S. G. "Deiatel'nost' organov VKP(b) v zapadnykh oblastiakh Ukrainy i Belorussii v 1939–1941 gg." In *Repressii protiv poliakov i pol 'skikh grazhdan,* edited by A. E. Gur'ianov, 1–12. Moscow: Zven 'ia, 1997.

Filtzer, Donald. *Soviet Workers and Stalinist Industrialization: The Formation of Modern Soviet Production Relations, 1928–1941.* Armonk, NY: M. E. Sharpe, 1986.

Fink, Victor. "Sem'ia Oppengeim na ekrane." *Literaturnaia gazeta,* 1 December 1938.

Fitzpatrick, Sheila. "Ascribing Class: The Construction of Social Identity in Soviet Russia." *Journal of Modern History* 65, no. 4 (1993): 745–68. Reprinted in *Stalinism: New Directions,* edited by Sheila Fitzpatrick, 20–46. London and New York: Routledge, 2000.

_____. "Cultural Revolution as Class War." In *Cultural Revolution in Russia, 1928–1931,* edited by Sheila Fitzpatrick, Bloomington: Indiana University Press, 1978. 8–40.

_____. *Education and Social Mobility in the Soviet Union, 1921–1934.* Cambridge: Cambridge University Press, 1979.

_____. *Everyday Stalinism: Ordinary Life in Extraordinary Times: Soviet Russia in the 1930s.* New York: Oxford University Press, 1999.

_____. "Postwar Soviet Society: The 'Return to Normalcy,' 1945–1953." In *The Impact of World War II on the Soviet Union,* edited by Susan J. Linz, 129–56. Totowa, NJ: Rowman & Allanheld, 1985.

_____. "Signals from Below: Soviet Letters of Denunciation in the 1930s." In *Accusatory Practices: Denunciation in Modern European History, 1789–1989,* edited by Robert Gellately and Sheila Fitzpatrick, 85–120. Chicago and London: University of Chicago Press, 1997.

_____. *Stalin's Peasants: Resistance and Survival in the Russian Village after Collectivizaton.* New York: Oxford University Press, 1994.

_____. *Tear off the Masks! Identity and Imposture in Twentieth-Century Russia.* Princeton, NJ: Princeton University Press, 2005.

_____. "The Bolsheviks' Dilemma: Class, Culture and Politics in the Early Soviet Years." *Slavic Review* 47, no. 4 (1988): 599–613.

_____. "The Civil War as a Formative Experience." In *Bolshevik Culture,* edited by Abbott Gleason, Peter Kenez, and Richard Stites, 57–76. Bloomington: Indiana University Press, 1985.

_____. *The Cultural Front: Power and Culture in Revolutionary Russia,* Studies in Soviet History and Society. Ithaca, NY: Cornell University Press, 1992.

_____. "The Problem of Class Identity in NEP Society." In *Russia in the Era of NEP: Explorations in Soviet Society and Culture,* edited by Sheila Fitzpatrick, Alexander Rabinowitch, and Richard Stites, 12–33. Bloomington: Indiana University Press, 1991.

_____. "The Legacy of the Civil War." In *Party, State, and Society in the Russian Civil War: Explorations in Social History,* edited by William G. Rosenberg, Diane Koenker and Ronald Grigor Suny, 385–98. Bloomington and Indianapolis: Indiana University Press, 1989.

————. "War and Society in Soviet Context: Soviet Labor before, durirng, and after World War II." *International Labor and Working Class History* 35 (Spring 1989): 37–52.

————, ed. *Cultural Revolution in Russia, 1928–1931*. Bloomington, IN: Indiana University Press, 1978.

————. *Stalinism: New Directions*, New York and London: Routledge, 2000.

Fitzpatrick, Sheila, Alexander Rabinowitch, and Richard Stites, eds. *Russian in the Era of NEP: Explorations in Soviet Society and Culture*, Bloomington, IN: Indiana University Press, 1991.

Fleishman, Lazar', Robert P. Hughes, and O. Raevskaia-Kh'iuz, eds. *Russkii Berlin 1921–1923: Po materialam arkhiva B. I. Nikolaevskogo v Guverovskom institute*, Literaturnoe nasledstvo russkoi emigratsii. Paris: YMCA-Press, 1983.

Frezinskii, Boris. "Velikaia illiuziia – Parizh 1935 (Materialy k istorii Mezhunarodnogo kongressa pisatelei v zashchitu kul'tury)." *Minuvshee: Istoricheskii al'manakh*, no. 24 (1998): 166–239.

Frolov, I. T., and A. V. Ado, eds. *Filosofskii slovar'*. Izd. 6., perer. i dop. ed. Moscow: Izd-vo polit. lit-ry, 1991.

Gaidar, Arkadii. *Timur i ego komanda*. Moscow: TSK VLKSM, Izd-vo detskoi lit-ry, 1941.

Ganelin, Rafail. "Das Leben des Gregor-Schwartz-Botunitsch (Grigorij V. Švarc-Bostunič) Teil 1." In *Russische Emigration in Deutschland 1918 bis 1941*, edited by Karl Schlögel, 201–8. Berlin: Akademie Verlag, 1995.

Ganzenmüller, Jörg. *Das belagerte Leningrad 1941–1942: Die Stadt in den Strategien von Angreifern und Verteidigern*. Paderborn: Schöningh, 2005.

Garros, Véronique, Natalia Korenevskaya, and Thomas Lahusen, eds. *Intimacy and Terror: Soviet Diaries of the 1930s*. New York: New Press, 1995.

Gatrell, Peter. *A Whole Empire Walking: Refugees in Russia during World War I*, Indiana-Michigan Series in Russian and East European Studies. Bloomington: Indiana University Press, 1999.

Geiger, Kurt. *The Family in Soviet Russia*. Cambridge, MA: Harvard University Press, 1968.

Gelb, Michael. "An Early Soviet Ethnic Deportation: The Far-Eastern Koreans." *Russian Review* 54 (1995): 389–411.

————. "Ethnicity during the Ezhovshchina: A Historiography." In *Ethnic and National Issues in Russian and Eastern European History: Selected Papers from the Fifth World Congress of Central and Eastern European Studies, Warsaw, 1995*, edited by John Morison, 192–213. New York: St. Martin's Press, 2000.

————. "The Western Finnic Minorities and the Origins of the Stalinist Nationalities Deportations." *Nationalities Papers* 24 (1996): 237–68.

Getty, J. Arch, and Oleg Naumov. *The Road to Terror: Stalin and the Self-Destruction of the Bolsheviks, 1932–1939*. New Haven, CT: Yale University Press, 1999.

Getty, J. A., G. T. Rittersporn, and V. Zemskov. "Les victimes de la répression pénale dans l'USSR d'Avant-Guerre." *Revue des Etudes Slaves* 65, no. 4 (1993): 631–70.

Gibadulin, Ia. N., ed. *Tainy natsional'noi politiki TSK RKP: Chetvertoe Soveshchanie TSK RKP s otvetstvennymi rabotnikami natsional'nykh respublik i oblastei v g. Moskve, 9–12 iiunia 1923 g.: Stenograficheski otchet*. Moscow: INSAN, 1992.

Glantz, David M. *Barbarossa: Hitler's Invasion of Russia, 1941*, Battles & Campaigns. Stroud and Gloucestershire: Tempus, 2001.

———. *Colossus Reborn: The Red Army at War: 1941–1943*, Modern War Studies. Lawrence: University Press of Kansas, 2005.

———. *The Battle for Leningrad, 1941–1944*, Modern War Studies. Lawrence: University Press of Kansas, 2002.

———. "The Red Army's Lublin-Brest Offensive and Advance on Warsaw (18 July-30 September 1944)." *Journal of Slavic Military Studies* 19, no. 2 (2006): 401–44.

Glantz, David M., and Jonathan M. House. *When Titans Clashed: How the Red Army Stopped Hitler*, Modern War Studies. Lawrence: University Press of Kansas, 1995.

Golczewski, Frank, ed. *Die Ukraine im Zweiten Weltkrieg*, Geschichte der Ukraine. Göttingen: Vandenhoeck & Ruprecht, 1993.

———. "Ukraine – Bürgerkrieg und Resowjetisierung." In *Kriegsende in Europa: Vom Beginn des deutschen Machtzerfalls bis zur Stabilisierung der Nachkriegsordnung 1944–1948*, edited by Ulrich Herbert and Axel Schildt, 89–99. Essen: Klartext, 1998.

Goldman, Wendy Z. *Women at the Gates: Gender and Industry in Stalin's Russia.* Cambridge: Cambridge University Press, 2002.

———. *Women, the State, and Revolution: Soviet Family Policy and Social Life, 1917–1936*, Cambridge Russian, Soviet, and Post-Soviet Studies. Cambridge and New York: Cambridge University Press, 1993.

Gorbunov, A. V. "Vliianie mirovoi voiny na dvizhenie naseleniia Evropy." *Russkii evgenicheskii zhurnal*, no. 1 (1922).

Gor'kii, Maksim. *Gor'kii i sovetskie pisateli: Neizdannaia perepiska*, Literaturnoe nasledstvo. Moscow: Izd-vo Akademii nauk SSSR, 1963.

———. *Sobranie sochinenii v tridtsati tomakh.* 30 vols. Vol. 26. Moscow: Gos. izd.-vo khudozh lit-ry, 1953.

Gor'kii, M., L. L. Averbakh, and S. G. Firin, eds. *Belomorsko-Baltiiskii kanal imeni Stalina: istoriia stroitel'stva.* Moscow: Gosudarstvennoe izdatel'stvo "Istoriia fabrik i zavodov," 1934.

Gor'kov, Iu. A. *Gosudarstvennyi komitet oborony postanovliaet: 1941–1945: Tsifry, dokumenty.* Moscow: OLMA-Press, 2002.

Gorlizki, Yoram. "Ordinary Stalinism: The Council of Ministers and the Soviet Neo-Patrimonial State, 1945–1953." *Journal of Modern History* 74, no. 4 (2002): 699–736.

Gorlizki, Yoram, and Oleg Khlevniuk. *Cold Peace: Stalin and the Soviet Ruling Circle, 1945–1953.* Oxford: Oxford University Press, 2004.

———. "Stalin and His Circle." In *The Cambridge History of Russia*, Vol. 3, edited by Ronald Grigor Suny, 243–67. Cambridge: Cambridge University Press, 2006.

Gorsuch, Anne E. *Youth in Revolutionary Russia: Enthusiasts, Bohemians, Delinquents*, Indiana-Michigan Series in Russian and East European Studies. Bloomington: Indiana University Press, 2000.

Graham, Loren. *Between Science and Values.* New York: Columbia University Press, 1981.

Graziosi, Andrea. "Collectivisation, révoltes paysanne et politiques gouvernementales à travers les rapports du GPU d'Ukraine de février-mars 1930." *Cahiers du Monde russe* 35, no. 3 (1994): 437–632.

Gross, Jan Tomasz. *Revolution from Abroad: The Soviet Conquest of Poland's Western Ukraine and Western Belorussia.* Expanded ed. with a new preface by the author. Princeton, NJ: Princeton University Press, 2002.

Grossman, Vasilii Semenovich *The Years of War (1941–1945).* Translated by Elizabeth Donnelly and Rose Prokofiev. Moscow: Foreign Languages Publishing House, 1946.

Gudov, I. I. *Sud'ba rabochego, O zhizni i o sebe.* Moscow: Politizdat, 1970.

Günther, Hans. *Der sozialistische Übermensch: M. Gor'kij und der sowjetische Helden-mythos.* Stuttgart: J. B. Metzler, 1993.

Gur'ianov, A. E. "Masshtaby deportatsii naseleniia v glub SSR v mae-june 1941g." In *Repressii protiv poliakov i pol 'skikh grazhdan,* edited by A. E. Gur' ianov, 137–75. Moscow: Zven 'ia, 1997.

Gutkin, Irina. *The Cultural Origins of the Socialist Realist Aesthetic, 1890–1934,* Studies in Russian Literature and Theory. Evanston, IL: Northwestern University Press, 1999.

Habeck, R. Mary. *Storm of Steel: The Development of Armor Doctrine in Germany and the Soviet Union, 1919–1939.* Ithaca, NY: Cornell University Press, 2003.

Hachten, P. Charles. "Property Relations and the Economic Organization of Soviet Russia: 1941–1948." Ph.D. diss., University of Chicago, 2005.

Hagen, Mark von. *Soldiers in the Proletarian Dictatorship: The Red Army and the Soviet Socialist State, 1917–1930,* Studies in Soviet History and Society. Ithaca, NY: Cornell University Press, 1990.

———. "Soviet Soldiers and Officers on the Eve of the German Invasion: Toward a Description of Social Psychology and Political Attitudes." In *The People's War: Responses to World War II in the Soviet Union,* edited by Robert W. Thurston and Bernd Bonwetsch, 186–210. Urbana and Chicago: University of Illinois Press, 2000.

———. "The Great War and the Mobilization of Ethnicity in the Russian Empire." In *Post-Soviet political Order: Conflict and State Building,* edited by Barnett R. Rubin and Jack L. Synder, 34–57. London and New York: Routledge, 1998.

Hagenloh, Paul. "'Socially Harmful Elements' and the Great Terror." In *Stalinism: New Directions,* edited by Sheila Fitzpatrick, 286–308. New York and London: Routledge, 2000.

Halfin, Igal. *From Darkness to Light: Class, Consciousness, and Salvation in Revolutionary Russia,* Pitt Series in Russian and Eastern European Studies. Pittsburgh: University of Pittsburgh Press, 2000.

———. *Terror in My Soul: Communist Autobiographies on Trial.* Cambridge, MA: Harvard University Press, 2003.

Harris, James. "Stalin as General Secretary: The Appointment Process and the Nature of Stalin's Power." In *Stalin: A New History,* edited by Sarah Davies and James Harris, 63–82. Cambridge: Cambridge University Press, 2005.

Harrison, Mark. "The Soviet Union: The Defeated Victor." In *The Economics of World War II: Six Great Powers in International Comparison,* edited by Mark Harrison, 268–301. Cambridge: Cambridge University Press, 1998.

———. "The USSR and Total War: Why Didn't the Soviet Economy Collapse in 1942?" In *A World at Total War: Global Conflict and the Politics of Destruction, 1937–1945,* edited by Roger Chickering, Stig Förster, and Bernd Greiner, 137–56. Washington D.C. and Cambridge: German Historical Institute and Cambridge University Press, 2005.

Hatch, John. "Labor Conflict in Moscow, 1921–25." In *Russian in the Era of NEP: Explorations in Soviet Society and Culture,* edited by Sheila Fitzpatrick, Alexander Rabinowitch, and Richard Stites, 58–71. Bloomington: Indiana University Press, 1991.

Hauslohner, Peter. "Politics before Gorbachev: Destalinization and the Roots of Reform." In *Politics, Society, and Nationality inside Gorbachev's Russia*, edited by Seweryn Bialer, 41–90. Boulder, CO: Westview Press, 1989.

Healey, Dan. *Homosexual Desire in Revolutionary Russia: The Regulation of Sexual and Gender Dissent*. Chicago: University of Chicago Press, 2001.

Hellbeck, Jochen. "Fashioning the Stalinist Soul: The Diary of Stepan Podlubnvi (1931–1939)." *Jahrbücher für Geschichte Osteuropas* 44 (1996): 344–73; also in Fitzpatrick, ed., *Stalinism: New Directions*.

———. *Revolution on My Mind: Writing a Diary under Stalin*. Cambridge, MA: Harvard University Press, 2006.

Hellebust, Rolf. *Flesh to Metal: Soviet Literature and the Alchemy of Revolution*. Ithaca, NY: Cornell University Press, 2003.

Hessler, Julie. *A Social History of Soviet Trade: Trade Policy, Retail Practices and Consumption, 1917–1953*. Princeton, NJ: Princeton University Press, 2004.

———. "Culture of Shortages: A Social History of Soviet Trade." Ph.D. diss., University of Chicago, 1996.

Hiden, John, and Patrick Salmon. *The Baltic Nations and Europe: Estonia, Latvia and Lithuania in the Twentieth Century*. Rev. ed. London: Longman, 1994.

Hill, Alexander. *The War Behind the Eastern Front: The Soviet Partisan Movement in North-West Russia, 1941–1944*, Cass Series on the Soviet (Russian) Study of War. London and New York: Frank Cass, 2005.

Hindus, Maurice Gerschon. *Red Bread*. New York: J. Cape & H. Smith, 1931.

Hirsch, Francine. "Empire of Nations: Colonial Technologies and the Making of the Soviet Union, 1917–1939." Ph.D. diss., Princeton University, 1998.

———. "Race without the Practice of Racial Politics." *Slavic Review* 61, no. 1 (2002): 30–43.

———. "The Soviet Union as a Work-in-Progress. Ethnographers and the Category Nationality in the 1926, 1937, and 1939 Censuses." *Slavic Review* 57 (1997): 251–78.

———. "Toward an Empire of Nations: Border-Making and the Formation of Soviet National Identities." *Russian Review* 59 (2000): 201–26.

Hoffmann, David L. *Peasant Metropolis: Social Identities in Moscow, 1929–1941*, Studies of the Harriman Institute. Ithaca, NY: Cornell University Press, 1994.

———. *Stalinist Values: The Cultural Norms of Soviet Modernity, 1917–1941*. Ithaca, NY: Cornell University Press, 2003.

———, ed. *Stalinism: The Essential Readings*, Blackwell Essential Readings in History. Malden, MA: Blackwell, 2003.

Hoffmann, Joachim. *Stalins Vernichtungskrieg 1941–1945*. 3rd rev. ed. Munich: Verlag für Wehrwissenschaften, 1996.

Holquist, Peter. "To Count, to Extract, and to Exterminate: Population Statistics and Population Politics in Late Imperial and Soviet Russia." In *A State of Nations: Empire and Nation-Making in the Age of Lenin and Stalin*, edited by Ronald G. Suny and Terry Martin, 111–41. New York and Oxford: Oxford University Press, 2001.

———. *Making War, Forging Revolution: Russia's Continuum of Crisis, 1914–1921*. Cambridge, MA: Harvard University Press, 2002.

Hooper, Cynthia. "Shifting Stalinism: The 'Normalization' of Repression, 1939–41." In *BASEES Annual Conference*. Cambridge, England, 2004.

_____. "Terror From Within: Participation and Coercion in Soviet Power, 1924–1964." Ph.D. diss., Princeton University, 2003.

_____. "Terror of Intimacy: Family Politics in the 1930s Soviet Union." In *Everyday Life in Early Soviet Russia: Taking the Revolution Inside*, edited by Christina Kiaer and Eric Naiman, 61–91. Bloomington: Indiana University Press, 2006.

Hosking, Geoffrey. *A History of the Soviet Union, 1917–1991*. London: Fontana Press, 1992.

Hough, Jerry F. *The Soviet Union and Social Science Theory*. Russian Research Center Studies. Cambridge, MA: Harvard University Press, 1977.

Hughes, James. "Patrimonialism and the Stalinist System: The Case of S. I. Syrtsov." *Europe-Asia Studies* 48, no. 4 (1996): 551–68.

Hutchinson, John F. *Politics and Public Health in Revolutionary Russia, 1890–1918*, Henry E. Sigerist Series in the History of Medicine. Baltimore: Johns Hopkins University Press, 1990.

_____. "Who Killed Cock Robin? An Inquiry into the Death of Zemstvo Medicine." In *Health and Society in Revolutionary Russia*, edited by Susan Gross Solomon and John F. Hutchinson, 3–26. Bloomington: Indiana University Press, 1990.

Hyer, Janet. "Managing the Female Organism: Doctors and the Medicalization of Women's Paid Work in Soviet Russia during the 1920s." In *Women in Russia and Ukraine*, edited by Rosalind J. Marsh, 111–20. New York: Cambridge University Press, 1996.

Iakushevskii, A. S. "Rasstrel v klevernom pole." *Novoe vremia* 25 (1993): 40–2.

Ilic, Melanie. *Women Workers in the Soviet Interwar Economy: From "Protection" to "Equality,"* Studies in Russian and East European History and Society. New York: St. Martin's Press in association with the Centre for Russian and East European Studies, University of Birmingham, 1999.

Inkeles, Alex, and Raymond Bauer. *The Soviet Citizen: Daily Life in a Totalitarian Society*, Russian Research Center Studies. New York: Athenaeum, 1968.

Iunge (Junge), Marc, and Rolf Binner. *Kak terror stal "bolshim": Sekretnyi prikaz no. 00447 i tekhnologiia ego ispolneniia*, Seriia "AIRO-XX–Pervaia publikatsiia v Rossii." Moscow: AIRO-XX, 2003.

Ivashov, L. G., and A. S. Emelin, "Nravstvennye i pravovye problemy plena v Otechestvennoi istorii," *Voenno-istoricheskii zhurnal*, no. 1 (1992): 44–9.

Ivnitskii, Nikolai A. "Stalinskaia revoliutsiia 'sverkhu' i krest'ianstvo." In *Mentalitet i agrarnoe razvitie Rossii (XIX–XX vv.)*, edited by V. P. Danilov and L. V. Milov, 247–59. Moscow: ROSSPEN, 1996.

Iwanou, Mikola. "Terror, Deportation, Genozid, Demographische Veränderungen Weissrussland im 20. Jahrhundert." In *Handbuch der Geschichte Weissrusslands*, edited by Dietrich Beyrau and Rainer Lindner, 426–36. Göttingen: Vandenhoeck & Ruprecht, 2001.

Jahn, Hubertus. *Patriotic Culture in Russia during World War I*. Ithaca, NY: Cornell University Press, 1995.

Jansen, Marc, and N. V. Petrov. *Stalin's Loyal Executioner: People's Commissar Nikolai Ezhov, 1895–1940*. Stanford, CA: Hoover Institution Press, 2002.

Jowitt, Kenneth. *New World Disorder: The Leninist Extinction*. Berkeley: University of California Press, 1992.

Just, Artur W. *Die Sowjetunion, Staat, Wirtschaft, Heer*. Berlin: Junker und Dünnhaupt, 1940.

_____. *Russland in Europa: Gedanken zum Ostproblem der abendländischen Welt.* Stuttgart: Union Deutsche Verlagsgesellschaft, 1949.

Kabo, V. R. *The Road to Australia: Memoirs.* Translated by Rosh Ireland and Kevin Windle. Canberra: Aboriginal Studies Press, 1998.

Kaganovich, Lazar M. *Pamiatnye zapiski.* Moscow: Vagrius, 1997.

Kaganovsky, Lilya. "How the Soviet Man Was (Un)Made." *Slavic Review* 63, no. 3 (2004): 557–96.

Kamp, Marianne Ruth. "Unveiling Uzbek Women: Liberation, Representation and Discourse, 1906–1929." Ph.D. diss., University of Chicago, 1997.

Karner, Stefan. *Im Archipel GUPVI: Kriegsgefangenschaft und Internierung in der Sowjetunion 1941–1956*, Kriegsfolgen-Forschung. Vienna and Munich: R. Oldenbourg, 1995.

_____. "GUPVI: The Soviet Main Administration for Prisoners of War and Internees during World War II." *Bulletin du Comité international d'histoire de la deuxième guerre mondiale* no. 27/28 (1995).

Karner, Stefan, and B. Marx. "World War II Prisoners of War in the Soviet Economy." *Bulletin du Comité international d'histoire de la deuxième guerre mondiale*, no. 27/28 (1995): 191–201.

Kelly, Catriona. *Comrade Pavlik: The Rise and Fall of a Soviet Boy Hero.* London: Granta Books, 2005.

Kessler, G. "The Passport System and State Control over Population Flows in the Soviet Union, 1932–1940." *Cahiers du Monde russe* 42, no. 2–4 (2001): 477–503.

Khaled, Adib "Nationalizing the Revolution in Central Asia: The Transformation of Jadidism 1917–1920," in Suny and Martin, 145–62; Alexandre Bennigsen and Samuel E. Wimbush, *Muslim National Communism in the Soviet Union: A Revolutionary Strategy for the Colonial World* (Chicago: University of Chicago Press, 1979), 8–19.

Khaustov, V. N., V. P. Naumov, and N. S. Plotnikova, eds. *Lubianka: Stalin i Glavnoe upravlenie gosbezopasnosti NKVD, 1937–1938*, Rossiia XX vek., Dokumenty. Moscow: Mezhdunarodnyi fond "Demokratiia," 2004.

_____. *Lubianka: Stalin i NKVD-NKGB-GUKR "Smersh," 1939 – mart 1946.* Rossiia XX vek., Dokumenty. Moscow: Mezhdunarodnyi fond "Demokratiia," 2006.

Khlevniuk, Oleg V. *In Stalin's Shadow: The Career of "Sergo" Ordzhonikidze.* Edited with an introduction by Donald J. Raleigh. Translated by David J. Nordlander, The New Russian History. Armonk, NY: M. E. Sharpe, 1995.

_____. "Party and NKVD: Power Relationships in the Years of the Great Terror." In *Stalin's Terror: High Politics and Mass Repression in the Soviet Union*, edited by Barry McLoughlin and Kevin McDermott, 21–33. New York: Palgrave Macmillan, 2003.

_____. *Politbiuro: Mekhanizmy politicheskoi vlasti v 1930-e gody.* Moscow: ROSSPEN, 1996. (in English as *Master of the House: Stalin and His Inner Circle*, trans. By Nora Seligman Favorov (New Haven: Yale University Press, 2008).

_____. "Sistema tsentr-regionv v 1930–1950e gody: Predposylki politizatsii 'nomenklatury." *Cahiers du Monde russe* 44, no. 2–3 (2003): 253–68.

_____. "The First Generation of Stalinist 'Party Generals.'" In *Centre-Local Relations in the Stalinist State 1928–1941*, edited by E. A. Rees, 37–64. Basingstoke: Palgrave, 2002.

———, "The Objectives of the Great Terror, 1937–1938." In *Soviet History, 1917–53: Essays in Honour of R. W. Davies*, edited by Julian Cooper, Maureen Perrie, and E. A. Rees, 158–76. New York: St. Martin's Press, 1995.

———. "The Reasons for the Great Terror: The Foreign Political Aspects." In *Russia in the Age of Wars, 1914–1945*, edited by Silvio Pons and Andrea Romano, 159–70. Milan: Feltrinelli, 2000.

———, ed. *Stalinskoe Politbiuro v 30-e gody: Sbornik dokumentov*, Seriia "Dokumenty sovetskoi istorii." Moscow: AIRO – XX, 1995.

Khlevniuk, Oleg V. et al., eds. *Stalin i Kaganovich: Perepiska 1931–1936 gg.*, Annaly kommunizma. Moscow: ROSSPEN, 2001. [in English as *The Stalin-Kaganovich Correspondence 1931–36*, compiled and edited by R. W. Davies, Oleg V. Khlevniuk, E. A. Rees et al., translated by Steven Shabad. Annals of Communism. New Haven & London, Yale University Press, 2003.]

Kiaer, Christina and Eric Naiman, eds. *Everyday Life in Early Soviet Russia: Taking the Revolution Inside*, Bloomington, IN: Indiana University Press, 2006.

Kirschenbaum, Lisa A. "'Our City, Our Hearths, Our Families': Local Loyalties and Private Life in Soviet World War II Propaganda." *Slavic Review* 59, no. 4 (2000): 825–47.

Klinsky, Emilian, ed. *Vierzig Donkosaken erobern die Welt: S. Jaroff und sein Donkosakenchor*. Leipzig: Matthes-Verlag, 1933.

Klug, Ekkehart. "Das 'asiatische' Russland: Über die Entstehung eines europäischen Vorurteils." *Historische Zeitschrift* 245 (1987): 265–89.

Koenen, Gerd. "Alte Reiche, neue Reiche: Der Maoismus auf der Folie des Stalinismus – eine Gedankenskizze." In *Moderne Zeiten?: Krieg, Revolution, und Gewalt im 20. Jahrhundert*, edited by Jörg Baberowski, 174–201. Göttingen: Vandenhoeck & Ruprecht, 2006.

Kokurin, A.I, N. V. Petrov, and R. G. Pikhoia, eds. *Lubianka: VChK-OGPU-NKVD-NKGB-MGB-MVD-KGB: 1917–1960: Spravochnik*, Rossiia XX vek: Dokumenty. Moscow: Mezhdunarodnyi fond "Demokratiia," 1997.

Kommoss, Rudolf. *Juden hinter Stalin: Die jüdische Vormachtstellung in der Sowjetunion, auf Grund amtlicher Sowjetquellen dargestellt*. 4th rev. ed. Berlin-Leipzig: Nibelungen-verlag, 1944.

Kon, Igor "Sexual Minorities." In *Sex and Russian Society*, edited by I. Kon and James Riordan. Bloomington: Indiana University Press, 1993.

Konasov, V. B. *Sud'by nemetskikh voennoplennykh v SSSR: Diplomaticheskie, pravovye i politicheskie aspekty problemy: Ocherki i dokumenty*. Vologda: Izd-vo Vologodskogo in-ta povysheniia kvalifikatsii i perepodgotovki pedagogicheskikh kadrov, 1996.

Konstitutsiia (Osnovnoi zakon) Soiuza Sovetskikh Sotsialisticheskikh Respublik. Moscow: Gos. izd-vo iurid. lit-ry, 1963.

Kopelev, Lev. *No Jail for Thought*. Translated by Anthony Austin. London: Secker & Warburg, 1977.

———. *The Education of a True Believer*. Translated by Gary Kern. London: Wildwood House, 1981.

Kosheleva, L. P., O. V. Naumov, and L. A. Rogova, eds., "Materialy fevral'sko-martovskogo plenuma TsK VKP(b) 1937 goda." *Voprosy istorii*, no. 5 (1993): 14–15; no. 6 (1993): 5–6, 21–5.

Kostyrchenko, Gennadii. *Out of the Red Shadows: Anti-Semitism in Stalin's Russia*, Russian Studies Series. Amherst, NY: Prometheus Books, 1995.

———. *Tainaia politika Stalina: Vlast' i antisemitism.* Moscow: Mezhdunarodnye ostosheniia, 2001.

Kotkin, Stephen. *Magnetic Mountain: Stalinism as a Civilization.* Berkeley: University of California Press, 1997.

Kozlov, Vladimir A. "Denunciation and its Functitons in Soviet Governance: A Study of Denunciations and their Bureaucratic Handling from Soviet Archives, 1944–1953." In *Accusatory Practices: Denunciation in Modern European History, 1789–1989,* edited by Sheila Fitzpatrick and Robert Gellately, 121–52. Chicago and London: University of Chicago Press, 1997.

KPSS v rezoliutsiiakh i resheniiakh s"ezdov, konferentsii i plenumov TsK. 9th ed. 15 vols. Moscow: Politizdat, 1982–1989.

Krasil'nikov, S. A. *Na izlomakh sotsial'noi struktury: Marginaly v poslerevoliutsionnom rossiiskom obshchestve (1917-konets 1930-kh godov).* Novosibirsk: Novosibirskii gos. universitet, 1998.

Krivosheev, G. F. *Soviet Casualties and Combat Losses in the Twentieth Century.* Translated by Christine Barnard. London: Greenhill Books, 1997.

———, ed. *Grif sekretnosti sniat: Poteri vooruzhennykh Sil SSSR v voinakh, boevykh deistviiakh i voennykh konfliktakh.* Moscow: Voennoe izd-vo, 1993.

Krivosheev, G. F. and M. F. Filimoshin, "Poteri vooruzhennykh sil SSSR v Velikoi Otechestvennoi voine," in *Naselenie Rossii v xx veke: Istoricheskie ocherki, 1940–1959,* Vol 2, eds. Iu. A. Poliakov and V. B. Zhiromskaia (Moscow: Rosspen, 2001), 19–39.

Khrushchev, Nikita S. *Khrushchev Remembers: The Glasnost Tapes,* translated and edited by Jerrold L. Schechter with Vyacheslav V. Luchkov. Boston: Little, Brown, 1990.

Krylova, Anna. "The Tenacious Liberal Subject in Soviet Studies." *Kritika: Explorations in Russian and Eurasian History* 1, no. 1 (2000): 119–46.

Kumanev, G. *Govoriat stalinskie narkomy.* Smolensk: Rusich, 2005.

Kumykov, T. Kh., ed. *Vyselenie adygov v Turtsiiu–posledstvie Kavkazskoi voiny.* Nal'chik: "El'brus," 1994.

Kuromiya, Hiroaki. "Accounting for the Great Terror." *Jahrbücher für Geschichte Osteuropas* 53, no. 1 (2005): 86–101.

———. *Freedom and Terror in the Donbas: A Ukrainian-Russian Borderland, 1870s-1990s.* Cambridge: Cambridge University Press, 2002.

———. *Stalin's Industrial Revolution: Politics and Workers, 1928–1932,* Soviet and East European Studies. Cambridge: Cambridge University Press, 1988.

———. "The Crisis of Proletarian Identity in the Soviet Factory, 1928–1929." *Slavic Review* 44, no. 2 (1985): 280–97.

———. "Workers' Artels and Soviet Production Relations." In *Russia in the Era of NEP: Explorations in Soviet Society and Culture,* edited by Sheila Fitzpatrick, Alexander Rabinowitch, and Richard Stites, 72–88. Bloomington: Indiana University Press, 1991.

Kvashonkin, A. V. et al., eds. *Bol'shevistskoe rukovodstvo: Perepiska 1912–1927,* Seriia "Dokumenty sovetskoi istorii." Moscow: ROSSPEN, 1996.

———. *Sovetskoe rukovodstvo: Perepiska, 1928–1941,* Seriia "Dokumenty sovetskoi istorii." Moscow: ROSSPEN, 1999.

Lahusen, Thomas. *How Life Writes the Book: Real Socialism and Socialist Realism in Stalin's Russia.* Ithaca, NY: Cornell University Press, 1997.

Lebina, Natalia. *Povsednevnaia zhizn' sovetskogo goroda: Normy i anomalii, 1920–1930 gody.* St. Petersburg: Zhurnal "Neva," 1999.

Lemon, Alaina. "Without a 'Concept'? Race as Discursive Practice." *Slavic Review* 61, no. 1 (2002): 54–61.

"Lenin i vospitanie novogo cheloveka." *Revoliutsiia i kul'tura*, no. 1 (1928): 5–10.

Lenin, Vladimir I. *Ausgewählte Werke*. Vol. 1. East Berlin: Dietz, 1978.

———. *Collected Works*. 55 vols. Vol. 26. London: Lawrence and Wishart, 1964.

———. *Polnoe sobranie sochinenii*. 5th ed. 55 vols. Vol. 34. Moscow: Partizdat, 1959–1965.

———. *The Years of Reaction and of the New Revival (1908–1914)*, edited by J. Fineberg. 4 vols. Vol. 4, Selected works (Vladimir Ilich Lenin). London: Lawrence and Wishart, 1936.

Leonov, Valerii P., ed. *Akademicheskoe delo: 1929–1931 gg.: Dokumenty i materialy sledstvennogo dela, sfabrikovannogo OGPU. Vyp. 2: Delo po obvinenii akademika E. V. Tarle*. St. Petersburg, 1998.

Lewin, Moshe. "Concluding Remarks." In *Making Workers Soviet: Power, Class and Identity*, edited by Lewis H. Siegelbaum and Ronald Grigor Suny, 376–90. Ithaca, NY: Cornell University Press, 1994.

———. *Russia – USSR – Russia: The Drive and Drift of a Superstate*. New York: New Press 1995.

———. *Russian Peasants and Soviet Power: A Study of Collectivization*. Translated by Irene Nove and John Biggart. London: Allen & Unwin, 1968.

———. "The Civil War: Dynamics and Legacy." In *Party, State, and Society in the Russian Civil War: Explorations in Social History*, edited by Diane Koenker, William G. Rosenberg, and Ronald Grigor Suny, 399–423. Bloomington: Indiana University Press, 1989.

———. *The Making of the Soviet System: Essays in the Social History of Interwar Russia*. New York: Pantheon Books, 1985.

Lieberman, Sanford R. "Crisis Management in the USSR: Wartime System of Administrations and Control." In *The Impact of World War II on the Soviet Union*, edited by Susan J. Linz. Totowa, NJ: Rowman & Allanheld, 1985.

———. "The Re-Sovietization of Formerly Occupied Areas of the USSR during WWII." In *The Soviet Empire Reconsidered: Essays in Honor of Adam B. Ulam*, edited by Sanford R. Lieberman et al., 49–67. Boulder, CO: Westview Press, 1994.

Liebich, André. *From the Other Shore: Russian Social Democracy after 1921*, Harvard Historical Studies. Cambridge, MA: Harvard University Press, 1997.

Lih, Lars T., et al., eds. *Stalin's Letters to Molotov, 1925–1936*, Annals of Communism. New Haven, CT: Yale University Press, 1995.

Lisitsa, Iu T. *Ivan Il'in i Rossiia: Neopublikovannye fotografii i arkhivnye materialy*. Moscow: Russkaia kniga, 1999.

Livshin, A. Ia., and I. B. Orlov. *Vlast' i obshchestvo: Dialog v pis'makh*, Seriia "Sotsial'naia istoriia Rossii XX veka." Moscow: ROSSPEN, 2002.

Lohr, Eric. *Nationalizing the Russian Empire: The Campaign against Enemy Aliens during World War I*, Russian Research Center Studies. Cambridge, MA: Harvard University Press, 2003.

———. "The Russian Army and the Jews: Mass Deportations, Hostages, and Violence during World War I." *Russian Review* 60 (2001): 404–19.

Lokshin, Aleksander. "The Doctors' Plot: The Non-Jewish Response." In *Jews and Jewish Life in Russia and the Soviet Union*, edited by Yaacov Ro'i, 157–67. Ilford, England: F. Cass, 1995.

Lomakin, Ark. "Lenin o Chernyvshevskom." *Revoliutsiia i kul'tura*, no. 22 (1928): 5–12.

Lorimer, Frank. *The Population of the Soviet Union: History and Prospects*, Series of League of Nations Publications. Geneva: League of Nations, 1946.

Lustiger, Arno. *Rotbuch: Stalin und die Juden: Die tragische Geschichte des Jüdischen Antifaschistischen Komitees und der sowjetischen Juden*. Berlin: Aufbau-Verlag, 1998.

Maier, Robert. *Die Stachanov-Bewegung 1935–1938: Der Stachanovismus als tragendes und verschärfendes Moment der Stalinisierung der sowjetischen Gesellschaft*, Quellen und Studien zur Geschichte des östlichen Europa. Stuttgart: F. Steiner, 1990.

Makarenko, A. S. *Pedagogicheskaia poema*, Biblioteka sovetskoi prozy. Moscow: Khudozh. literatura, 1964.

Maksimenkov, Leonid. *Sumbur vmesto muzyki: Stalinskaia kul'turnaia revoliutsiia 1936–1938*. Moscow: Iuridicheskaia kniga," 1997.

Malia, Martin E. *The Soviet Tragedy: A History of Socialism in Russia, 1917–1991*. New York: Free Press, 1996.

Mal'kov, V. L., ed. *Pervaia mirovaia voina: prolog XX veka*. Moscow: "Nauka," 1998.

Mally, Lynn. *Culture of the Future: The Proletkult Movement in Revolutionary Russia*, Studies on the History and Society of Culture. Berkeley: University of California Press, 1990.

——. *Revolutionary Acts: Amateur Theater and the Soviet State, 1917–1938*. Ithaca, NY: Cornell University Press, 2000.

Manley, Rebecca "The Evacuation and Survival of Soviet Civilians, 1941–1946." Ph.D. diss., University of California, Berkeley, 2004.

Manning, Roberta T. "Massovaia operatsiia kulakov i prestupnykh elementov." In *Stalinizm v rossiiskoi provintsii: Smolenskie arkhivnye dokumenty v prochtenii zarubezhnykh i rossiiskikh istorikov*, edited by E. V. Kodina, 230–54. Smolensk: SGPU, 1999.

——. "Women in the Soviet Countryside on the Eve of World War II, 1935–1940." In *Russian Peasant Women*, edited by Beatrice Farnsworth and Lynne Viola, 206–35. New York: Oxford University Press, 1992.

Martin, Terry. "Modernization or Neo-Traditionalism? Ascribed Nationality and Soviet Primordialism." In *Stalinism: New Directions*, edited by Sheila Fitzpatrick, 348–67. London and New York: Routledge, 2000.

——. "Origins of Soviet Ethnic Cleansing." *Journal of Modern History* 70 (1998): 813–61.

——. *The Affirmative Action Empire: Nations and Nationalism in the Soviet Union, 1923–1939*, The Wilder House Series in Politics, History, and Culture. Ithaca, NY: Cornell University Press, 2001.

Maslov, A. A. "How Were Soviet Blocking Detachments Employed?" *The Journal of Slavic Military Studies* 9, no. 2 (1996): 427–35.

Mawdsley, Evan. *Thunder in the East: The Nazi-Soviet War, 1941–1945*. London; New York: Hodder Arnold; Oxford University Press, 2005.

McDermott, Kevin. *Stalin: Revolutionary in an Era of War*. Basingstoke and New York: Palgrave Macmillian, 2006.

McLoughlin, Barry. "Die Massenoperationen des NKVD: Dynamik des Terrors 1937/1938." In *Stalinscher Terror 1934–41: Eine Forschungsbilanz*, edited by Wladislaw Hedeler, 33–50. Berlin: BasisDruck, 2002.

_____. "Mass Operations of the NKVD: A Survey." In *Stalin's Terror: High Politics and Mass Repression in the Soviet Union*, edited by Barry McLoughlin and Kevin McDermott, 118–52. New York: Palgrave McMillan, 2003.

Medvedev, Zhores A. "Stalin i 'delo vrachei': Novye materialy." *Voprosy istorii* 1 (2003): 78–103.

Megargee, Geoffrey P. *War of Annihilation: Combat and Genocide on the Eastern Front, 1941*, Total War. Lanham, MD: Rowman & Littlefield, 2006.

Mehnert, Klaus. *Youth in Soviet Russia*. Translated by Michael Davidson. New York: Harcourt, Brace, 1933.

Merridale, Catherine. "Culture, Ideology and Combat in the Red Army, 1939–45." *Journal of Contemporary History* 41, no. 2 (2006): 305–24.

_____. *Ivan's War: Life and Death in the Red Army, 1939–1945*. New York: Henry Holt, 2006.

Meyer, Alfred G. "Theories of Convergence." In *Change in Communist Systems*, edited by Chalmers Johnson, 36–42. Stanford, CA: Stanford University Press, 1970.

Mikoian, Anastas. *Tak bylo*. Moscow: Vagrius, 1999.

Miliutin, Dmitrii. *Vospominaniia general-fel'dmarshala grafa Dmitriia Alekseevicha Miliutina. 1816–1843*. Moscow: Studiia "TRITE" Nikity Mikhalkova: Rossiiskii arkhiv, 1997.

Minasian, M. M., ed. *Great Patriotic War of the Soviet Union, 1941–1945: A General Outline* [abridged translation of *Velikaia Otechestvennaia voina Sovetskogo Soiuza, 1941–1945*]. Translated by David Skvirsky and Vic Schneierson. Moscow: Progress, 1974.

Morekhina, G. G. *Partiinoe stroitel'stvo v period Velikoi Otechestvennoi voiny Sovetskogo Soiuza, 1941–1945*. Moscow: Izd-vo polit. lit-ry, 1986.

Moskoff, William. *The Bread of Affliction: The Food Supply in the USSR during World War II*, Soviet and East European Studies. Cambridge: Cambridge University Press, 1990.

Müller, Derek. *Der Topos des neuen Menschen in der russischen und sowjetrussischen Geistesgeschichte*, Geist und Werk der Zeiten. Bern: P. Lang, 1998.

Müller, Reinhard. *Die Akte Wehner: Moskau 1937 bis 1941*. Hamburg: Rowohlt, 1994.

Musial, Bogdan. *"Konterrevolutionäre Elemente sind zu erschiessen": Die Brutalisierung des deutsch-sowjetischen Krieges im Sommer 1941*. Berlin and Munich: Propyläen, 2000.

Nagel, Jens, and Jörg Osterloh. "Wachmannschaften in Lagern für sowjetischen Kriegsgefangene: Eine Annäherung." In *Durchschnittstäter: Handeln und Motivation*, edited by Christian Gerlach, 73–93. Berlin: Verlag der Büchladen, 2000.

Naiman, Eric. *Sex in Public: The Incarnation of Early Soviet Ideology*. Princeton, NJ: Princeton University Press, 1997.

Naimark, Norman M. *The Russians in Germany: A History of the Soviet Zone of Occupation, 1945–1949*. Cambridge, MA: Belknap Press of Harvard University Press, 1995.

Naumov, Oleg, and Andrei Artizov, eds. *Vlast' i khudozhestvennaia intelligentsiia: dokumenty TSK RKP(b)-VKP(b), VChK-OGPU-NKVD o kul'turnoi politike, 1917–1953 gg, Rossiia*. Moscow: Mezhdunarodnyi fond "Demokratiia," 1999.

Naumov, Vladimir P. "Die Vernichtung des Jüdischen Antifaschistischen Komitees." In *Der Spätstalinismus und die "jüdische Frage": Zur antisemitischen Wendung des Kommunismus*, edited by Leonid Luks, 117–42. Cologne: Böhlau Verlag, 1998.

————. "Sud'ba voennoplennykh i deportirovannykh grazhdan SSSR. Materialy komissii po reabilitatsii zhertv politicheskikh repressii," *Novaia i noveishaia istoriia* no. 2 (1996): 91–112.

————, ed. *1941 god: v dvukh knigakh*. 2 vols. Vol. 2, Rossiia., XX vek. Moscow: Mezhdunarodnyi fond "Demokratiia," 1998.

Naumov, V. P., A. A. Kraiushkin, and N. V. Teptsov, eds. *Nepravednyi sud: Poslednii stalinskii rasstrel: stenogramma sudebnogo protsessa nad chlenami Evreiskogo antifashistskogo komiteta*. Moscow: Nauka, 1994.

Naumov, V. P., and Iu. Sigachev, eds. *Lavrentii Beriia, 1953: Stenogramma iiul'skogo plenuma TsK KPSS i drugie dokumenty*, Rossiia: XX vek. Moscow: Mezhdunarodnyi fond "Demokratiia," 1999.

Nekrich, Aleksandr M. *1941, 22 iiunia*. 2nd rev. ed. Moscow: Pamiatniki istoricheskoi mysli, 1995.

————. *The Punished Peoples: The Deportation and Fate of Soviet Minorities at the End of the Second World War*. Translated by George Saunders. New York: Norton, 1978.

Nelipovich, S. G. "Nemetskuiu pakost' uvolit', i bez nezhnostei." *Voenno-istoricheskii zhurnal*, no. 1 (1997): 42–52.

Nolte, Hans-Heinrich. *"Drang nach Osten": Sowjetische Geschichtsschreibung der deutschen Ostexpansion*, Studien zur Gesellschaftstheorie. Cologne: Europäische Verlagsanstalt, 1976.

Norris, Stephen M. *A War of Images: Russian Popular Prints, Wartime Culture and National Identity, 1812–1945*. Dekalb: Northern Illinois University Press, 2006.

Northrop, Douglas. "Nationalizing Backwardness: Gender, Empire, and Uzbek Identity." In *A State of Nations: Empire and Nation-Making in the Age of Lenin and Stalin*, edited by Ronald G. Suny and Terry Martin, 125–81. New York and Oxford: Oxford University Press, 2001.

————. "Nationalizing the Revolution in Central Asia: The Transformation of Jadidism 1917–1920." In *A State of Nations: Empire and Nation-Making in the Age of Lenin and Stalin*, edited by Ronald Grigor Suny and Terry Martin, 191–220. New York and Oxford: Oxford University Press, 2001.

————. "Subaltern Dialogues: Subversion and Resistance in Soviet Uzbek Family Law." *Slavic Review* 60, no. 1 (2001): 115–39.

————. *Veiled Empire: Gender and Power in Stalinist Central Asia*. Ithaca, NY: Cornell University Press, 2004.

Nötzel, Karl. *Die Grundlagen des geistigen Russlands: Versuch einer Psychologie des russischen Geisteslebens*, Politische Bibliothek. Jena: E. Diederichs, 1917.

Oberbefehlshaber Ost, ed. *Völker-Verteilung in West-Russland*. 2 ed. Hamburg: Friederichsen, 1917.

Ochotin, Nikita, and Arseni Roginski. "Zur Geschichte der 'Deutschen Operation' des NKWD 1937–1938." *Jahrbuch für Historische Kommunismusforschung* (2000/2001): 89–125.

Oja, Matt F. *From Krestianka to Udarnitsa: Rural Women and the Vydvizhenie Campaign, 1933–1941*, Carl Beck Papers in Russian & East European Studies. Pittsburgh, PA: Center for Russian and East European Studies, University of Pittsburgh, 1996.

Ol'shevskii, M. "Kavkaz i pokorenie vostochnoi ego chasti, 1858–1861." *Russkaia starina*, no. 9 (1894): 22–43.

Orlova, R. D. *Memoirs* [*Vospominaniia o neproshedshem vremeni*]. Translated by Samuel Cioran. New York: Random House, 1983.

Orlovsky, Daniel T. "State Building in the Civil War Era: The Role of the Lower–Middle Strata." In *Party, State, and Society in the Russian Civil War: Explorations in Social History*, edited by Diane P. Koenker, William G. Rosenberg, and Ronald Grigor Suny, 180–209. Bloomington: Indiana University Press, 1989.

Osokina, E. A. *Ierarkhiia potrebleniia: O zhizni liudei v usloviiakh stalinskogo snabzheniia, 1928–1935 gg.* Moscow: Izd-vo MGOU, 1993.

———. *Za fasadom "stalinskogo izobiliia": Raspredelenie i rynok v snabzhenii naseleniia v gody industrializatsii, 1927–1941*, Seriia "Sotsial'naia istoriia Rossii XX veka." Moscow: ROSSPEN, 1998. [In English as *Our Daily Bread. Socialist Distribution and the Art of Survival in Stalin's Russia, 1927–1941*, trans. and ed. Kate Transchel and Greta Bucher. Armonk, NY: M. E. Sharpe, 2001.]

Otto, Reinhard. "Sowjetische Kriegsgefangene: Neue Quellen und Erkenntnisse." In *"Wir sind die Herren dieses Landes": Ursachen, Verlauf und Folgen des deutschen Überfalls auf die Sowjetunion*, edited by Babette Quinkert, 124–35. Hamburg: VSA Verlag, 2002.

Overy, Richard. *Russia's War: A History of the Soviet War Effort: 1941–1945*. New York: Penguin, 1997.

Papazian, Elizabeth A. "Reconstructing the (Authentic Proletarian) Reader: Mikhail Zoschenko's Changing Model of Authorship, 1929–1934." *Kritika: : Explorations in Russian and Eurasian History* 4, no. 4 (2003): 816–48.

Paperno, Irina. *Chernyshevsky and the Age of Realism: A Study in the Semiotics of Behavior*. Stanford, CA: Stanford University Press, 1988.

Papkov, S. A., and V. A. Isupov. *Stalinskii terror v Sibiri: 1928–1941*. Novosibirsk: Izd-vo Sibirskogo otd-nie Rossiiskoi akademii nauk, 1997.

Parsadanov, V. "Deportatsiia naseleniia iz Zapadnoi Ukrainy i Zapadnoi Belorussii." *Novaia i noveishaia istoriia* 2 (1989): 26–44.

Pavliuchenkov, S. A. *Rossiia Nepovskaia*. Moscow: Novyi khronograf, 2002.

Pechenkin. A. A. "Gosudarstvennyi Komitet Oborony v 1941 godu." *Otechestvennaia istoriia*, no. 3–5 (1994): 126–42.

Peris, Daniel. "'God Is Now on Our Side': The Religious Revival on Unoccupied Soviet Territory during World War II." *Kritika: Explorations in Russian and Eurasian History* 1, no. 1 (2000): 97–118.

———. *Storming the Heavens: The Soviet League of the Militant Godless*. Ithaca, NY: Cornell University Press, 1998.

Pethybridge, Roger William. *The Social Prelude to Stalinism*. London and Basingstoke: Macmillan, 1974.

Petrone, Karen. *"Life Has Become More Joyous, Comrades": Celebrations in the Time of Stalin*, Indiana-Michigan Series in Russian and East European Studies. Bloomington: Indiana University Press, 2000.

Petrov, Nikita V., and Arseni B. Roginskii. "'Pol'skaia operatsiia' NKVD 1937–1938 gg." In *Repressii protiv poliakov i pol'skikh grazhdan*, edited by A. E. Gur'ianov, 22–43. Moskva: "Zven'ia," 1997.

Petrov, P. "KPSS – Organizator i rukovoditel' pobedy sovetskogo naroda v velikoi otechestvennoi voine." *Voprosy istorii*, no. 5 (1970): 3–27.

Phillips, Laura J. *Bolsheviks and the Bottle: Drink and Worker Culture in St Petersburg, 1900–1929*. Dekalb: Northern Illinois Press, 2000.

Piaskovskii, A. V., and S. G. Agadzhanov, eds. *Vosstanie 1916 goda v Srednei Azii i Kazakhstane: Sbornik dokumentov*. Moscow: Izdatel'stvo Akademii nauk SSSR, 1960.

Piatnitskii, V. I. *Zagovor protiv Stalina*, Zhestokii vek, Kremlevskie tainy. Moscow: Sovremennik, 1998.

Pietrow-Ennker, Bianka. *Russlands "neue Menschen": Die Entwicklung der Frauenbewegung von den Anfängen bis zur Oktoberrevolution*, Reihe "Geschichte und Geschlechter." Frankfurt: Campus, 1999.

Pikhoia, R. G., and Aleksandr Geishtor. *Katyn': Plenniki neob"iavlennoi voiny* Rossiia, XX vek. Moscow: Mezhdunarodnyi Fond "Demokratiia," 1997.

Pinkus, Benjamin. "Die Deportation der deutschen Minderheit in der Sowjetunion 1941–1945." In *Zwei Wege nach Moskau: Vom Hitler-Stalin-Pakt bis zum "Unternehmen Barbarossa,"* edited by Bernd Wegner, 464–79. Munich: Piper, 1991.

Pisiotis, Argyrios K. "Images of Hate in the Art of War." In *Culture and Entertainment in Wartime Russia*, edited by Richard Stites, 141–56. Bloomington and Indianapolis: Indiana University Press, 1995.

Plaggenborg, Stefan. "Gewalt und Militanz in Sowjetrussland." *Jahrbuch für Geschichte Osteuropas* 44, no. 3 (1996): 409–30.

———. *Revolutionskultur: Menschenbilder und kulturelle Praxis in Sowjetrussland zwischen Oktoberrevolution und Stalinismus*, Beiträge zur Geschichte Osteuropas. Cologne: Böhlau, 1996.

———. "Weltkrieg, Bürgerkrieg, Klassenkrieg, Mentalitätsgeschichtliche Versuch über die Gewalt in Sowjetrussland." *Historische Anthropologie* 3 (1995): 493–505.

Platonov, Andrei. *Schastlivaia Moskva*, Grand libris. Moscow: "Gud'ial-Press," 1999.

Pogonii, Ia. F., ed. *Stalingradskaia epopeia: Vpervye publikuemye dokumenty, rassekrechennye FSB RF*. Moscow: "Zvonnitsa-MG," 2000.

Pohl, Dieter. "Die Ukraine im Zweiten Weltkrieg." In *Ukraine: Geographie, ethnische Struktur, Geschichte, Sprache und Literatur, Kultur, Politik, Bildung, Wirtschaft, Recht*, edited by Peter Jordan, 339–62. Frankfurt am Main: Lang, 2001.

Poliakov, Iu. A., ed. *Stroitel'stvo Sovetskogo gosudarstva: sbornik statei: K 70-letiiu doktora istoricheskikh nauk, prof. E. B. Genkinoi*. Moscow: "Nauka," 1972.

———. *Vsesoiuznaia perepis' naseleniia, 1937 g.: Kratkie itogi*. Moscow: Akademiia nauk SSSR, In-t istorii SSSR, 1991.

———. *Vsesoiuznaia perepis' naseleniia 1939 goda: Osnovnye itogi*. Moscow: Nauka, 1992.

Poliakov, Iu. A., and V. B. Zhiromskaia, eds. *Naselenie Rossii v XX veke: Istoricheskie ocherki*. 3 vols. Moscow: ROSSPEN, 2000.

———. "Poteri vooruzhennykh sil SSSR v Velikoi Otechestvennoi voine." In *Naselenie Rossii v XX veke: Istoricheskie ocherki, 1939*. Moscow: ROSSPEN, 2001.

Polian, Pavel. M. *Ne po svoei vole–: istoriia i geografiia prinuditel'nykh migratsii v SSSR*. Moscow: O. G. I.: Memorial, 2001.

———. *Zhertvy drukh diktatur: Ostarbaitery i voennoplennye v tret'em reikhe i ikh repatriatsiia* Moscow: Vash Vybor TsIPZ, 1996.

Profsoiuznaia perepis' 1932–1933 g. Moscow: Profizdat, 1934.

Prut, Iosif. *Nepoddaiushchiisia: O mnogikh drugikh i koe-chto o sebe*, Moi 20. vek. Moscow: "Vagrius," 2000.

Rapoport, Ia. L. *The Doctors' Plot*. London: Fourth Estate, 1991.

Redlich, Shimon, Anderson K. M., and I. Al'tman, eds. *War, Holocaust, and Stalinism: A Documented Study of the Jewish Anti-Fascist Committee in the USSR*, New History of Russia. Luxembourg: Harwood Academic, 1995.

Rees, E. A. "The Changing Nature of Centre-Local Relations in the USSR, 1928–36." In *Centre-Local Relations in the Stalinist State 1928–1941*, edited by E. A. Rees, 9–36. Basingstoke: Palgrave, 2002.

_____. "The Great Purges and the XVIII Party Congress of 1939." In *Centre-Local Relations in the Stalinist State 1928–1941*, edited by E. A. Rees, 191–211. Basingstoke: Palgrave, 2002.

Reese, Roger R. *Red Commanders: A Social History of the Soviet Army Officer Corps, 1918–1991*, Modern War Series. Lawrence: University Press of Kansas, 2005.

_____. *Stalin's Reluctant Soldiers: A Social History of the Red Army, 1925–1941*, Modern War Series. Lawrence: University Press of Kansas, 1996.

Reshin, L.E. comp. *1941 god. Dokumenty v 2-kh knigakh*, 2 vols. Moscow: Demokratiia, 1998.

Rieber, Alfred J. "Stalin, Man of the Borderlands." *The American Historical Review* 106, no. 5 (2001): 1651–91.

Rigby, T. H. *Communist Party Membership in the U.S.S.R., 1917–1967*, Studies of the Russian Institute, Columbia University. Princeton, NJ: Princeton University Press, 1968.

_____. *Political Elites in the USSR: Central Leaders and Local Cadres from Lenin to Gorbachev*. Aldershot: Elgar, 1990.

Riordan, James. "Sexual Minorities: The Status of Gay and Lesbians in Russian-Soviet-Russian Society." In *Women in Russia and Ukraine*, edited by Rosalind J. Marsh, 156–72. New York: Cambridge University Press, 1996.

Rodin, Aleksandr. *Tri tysiachi kilometrov v sedle* (Moscow: IPO Profizdat, 2000).

Rohrwasser, Michael. *Der Stalinismus und die Renegaten: die Literatur der Exkommunisten*, Metzler Studienausgabe. Stuttgart: J. B. Metzler, 1991.

Roman, Wanda K. "Die sowjetische Okkupation der polnischen Ostgebiete 1939 bis 1941." In *Die polnische Heimatarmee: Geschichte und Mythos der Armia Krajowa seit dem Zweiten Weltkrieg*, edited by Bernhard Chiari, 87–110. Munich: R. Oldenbourg, 2003.

Ronen, O. "'Inzhenery chelovecheskikh dush': K istorii izrecheniia." *Lotmanovskii sbornik* 2 (1997): 393–400.

Rorlich, Azade-Ayse. "Sultangaliev and Islam." In *Ethnic and National Issues in Russian and East European History: Selected Papers from the Fifth World Congress of Central and East European Studies, Warsaw, 1995*, edited by John Morison, 64–73. New York: St. Martin's Press, 2000.

Rosenthal, Bernice Glatzer. *New Myth, New World: From Nietzsche to Stalinism*. University Park: Pennsylvania State University Press, 2002.

Roslof, Edward E. *Red Priests: Renovationism, Russian Orthodoxy, and Revolution, 1905–1946*, Indiana-Michigan Series in Russian and East European Studies. Bloomington, IN: Indiana University Press, 2002.

Rossman, Jeffrey J. *Worker Resistance under Stalin: Class and Revolution on the Shop Floor*, Russian Research Center Studies. Cambridge, MA: Harvard University Press, 2005.

Rubenstein, Joshua. *Tangled Loyalties: The Life and Times of Ilya Ehrenburg*. New York: Basic Books, 1996.

Ryklin, G. "Zdrastvuite, tridtsat' piatyi." *Ogonek*, no. 1 (1935): 4–5.

Sadvokasova, E. A. *Sotsial'no-gigienicheskie aspekty regulirovaniia razmerov sem'i*. Moscow: Meditsina, 1969.

_____, ed. *Obshchestvo i vlast': Rossiiskaia provintsiia, 1917–1980-e gody: v trekh tomakh*. 3 vols. Vol. 2. Moscow: Institut rossiiskoi istorii RAN, 2002.

Sakharov, Andrei N. *Mein Leben*. Translated by Annelore Nitschke, Anton Manzella and Wilhelm von Timroth. 2nd ed. Munich: Piper, 1991.

Sanborn, Joshua A. "Brothers under Fire: The Development of A Front-Line Culture in the Red Army 1941–1943." M.A. thesis, University of Chicago, 1993.

————. *Drafting the Russian Nation: Military Conscription, Total War, and Mass Politics, 1905–1925*. Dekalb: Northern Illinois University Press, 2003.

Schlögel, Karl. *Jenseits des grossen Oktober: Das Laboratorium der Moderne, Petersburg 1909–1921*. Berlin: Siedler, 1988.

————. "Utopie als Notstandsdenken: Einige Überlegunge zur Diskussion über Utopie und Sowjetkommunismus." In *Utopie und politische Herrschaft im Europa der Zwischenkriegszeit*, edited by Wolfgang Hardtwig, 77–96. Munich: Oldenbourg, 2003.

Schrand, Thomas Gregory. "Industrialization and the Stalinist Gender System: Women Workers in the Soviet Economy, 1928–1941." Ph.D. diss., University of Michigan, 1994.

Schulman, Elena. "'That Night as We Prepared to Die': Frontline Journalists and Russian National Identity during WWII." In *National Convention 2006 of the American Association for the Advancement of Slavic Studies*. Washington, DC, 2006.

Scott, John. *Behind the Urals: An American Worker in Russia's City of Steel*. Bloomington: Indiana University Press, 1989.

Semirjaga, Michail. "Die Rote Armee in Deutschland im Jahre 1945." In *Erobern und Vernichten: Der Krieg gegen die Sowjetunion 1941–1945*, edited by Peter Jahn and Reinhard Rürup, 200–10. Berlin: Aragon, 1991.

Seniavskaia, E. S. *Frontovoe pokolenie, 1941–1945. Istoriko-psikhologicheskoe issledovanie* (Moscow: RAN institut Rossiiskoi istorii, 1995).

————. *Protivniki Rossii v voinakh XX veka: evoliutsiia "obraza vraga" v soznanii armii i obshchestva*, Chelovek i voina. Moscow: ROSSPEN, 2006.

————. *Psikhologiia voiny v XX veke: Istoricheskii opyt Rossii*, Seriia "Sotsial'naia istoriia Rossii XX veka." Moscow: ROSSPEN, 1999.

Service, Robert. *Comrades!: A History of World Communism*. Cambridge, MA: Harvard University Press, 2007.

————. *Stalin: A Biography*. Cambridge, MA: Belknap Press of Harvard University Press, 2005.

————. *The Bolshevik Party in Revolution: A Study in Organisational Change, 1917–1923*. London: New York, 1979.

Shanin, Teodor. *The Awkward Class: Political Sociology of Peasantry in a Developing Society: Russia 1910–1925*. Oxford: Clarendon Press, 1972.

Shapoval, Yuri. "The GPU-NKVD as an Instrument of Counter-Ukrainization in the 1920s and 1930s." In *Culture, Nation, and Identity: The Ukrainian-Russian Encounter, 1600–1945*, edited by Andreas Kappeler, 325–44. Toronto: Canadian Institute of Ukrainian Studies Press, 2003.

Shearer, David. "Crime and Social Disorder in Stalin's Russia: A Reassessment of the Great Retreat and the Origins of Mass Repression." *Cahiers du Monde russe* 39 (1998): 119–48.

————. "Modernity and Backwardness on the Soviet Frontier: Western Siberia in the 1930s." In *Provincial Landscapes: Local Dimensions of Soviet Power, 1917–1953*, edited by Donald J. Raleigh, 194–216. Pittsburgh: University of Pittsburgh Press, 2001.

————. "Policing the Soviet Frontier: Social Disorder and Repression in Western Siberia during the 1930s." In *Annual Convention of the American Association for the Advancement of Slavic Studies*. Boca Raton, FL, 1997.

————. "Social Disorder, Mass Repression and the NKVD during the 1930s." *Cahiers du Monde russe* 42, no. 2–4 (2001): 505–34. Also in *Stalin's Terror: High Politics and Mass Repression in the Soviet Union*, edited by Barry McLoughlin and Kevin McDermott, 85–117. New York: Palgrave Macmillan, 2003.

————. "To Count and Cleanse: Passportization and the Reconstruction of the Soviet Population during the 1930s." In *Annual Convention of the American Association for the Advancement of Slavic Studies*. Crystal City (Arlington), VA, 2001.

Shneer, A. *Plen: Sovetskie voennoplennye v Germanii, 1941–1945*. Moscow: Mosty kul'tury, 2005.

Siegelbaum, Lewis H. *Soviet State and Society between Revolutions, 1918–1929*, Cambridge Soviet Paperbacks. Cambridge and New York: Cambridge University Press, 1992.

————. *Stakhanovism and the Politics of Productivity in the USSR, 1935–1941*. Cambridge: Cambridge University Press, 1988.

Siegelbaum, Lewis H., and Ronald Grigor Suny, eds. *Making Workers Soviet: Power, Class, and Identity*. Ithaca, NY: Cornell University Press, 1994.

Simonov, Konstantin M. *Glazami cheloveka moego pokoleniia: Razmyshleniia o I. V. Staline*, Vremia, sobytiia, liudi. Moscow: Novosti, 1989.

Skrytaia pravda voiny: 1941 god. Neizvestnye dokumenty Moscow: Russkaia kniga, 1992).

Slavko, T. I. *Kulatskaia ssylka na Urale 1930–1936*. Moscow: Mosgorarkhiv, 1995.

Slepyan, Kenneth. *Stalin's Guerrillas: Soviet Partisans in World War II*, Modern War Studies. Lawrence: University Press of Kansas, 2006.

Slezkine, Yuri. "N. Ia. Marr and the National Origins of Ethnogenesis." *Slavic Review* 55 (1996): 826–62.

————. "The USSR as a Communal Apartment or How a Socialist State Promoted Ethnic Particularism." *Slavic Review* 51, no. 1 (1992): 414–52.

Slobin, Greta. "The Homecoming of the First Wave: Diaspora and Its Cultural Legacy." *Slavic Review* 60, no. 3 (2001): 513–29.

Slowes, Salomon W., ed. *Der Weg nach Katyn: Bericht eines polnischen Offiziers*. Hamburg: Europäische Verlagsanstalt, 2000.

"'Sluzhit' rodine prikhoditsia kostiami...' Dnevnik N. V. Ustrialova 1935–1937 gg." *Istochnik*, no. 5–6 (1998): 3–1000.

Smirnova, T. M. *"Byvshie liudi" Sovetskoi Rossii: Strategii vyzhivaniia i puti integratsii, 1917–1936 gody*. Moscow: "Mir istorii" izdatel'skii dom, 2003.

Smith, Jeremy. *The Bolsheviks and the National Question, 1917–23*, Studies in Russia and East Europe. Basingstoke: MacMillan in association with the School of Slavonic and East European Studies, University of London, 1999.

Smith, Walter Bedell. *Meine drei Jahre in Moskau*. Translated by Werner G. Krug. Hamburg: Hoffmann und Campe, 1950.

Sokol, Edward Dennis. *The Revolt of 1916 in Russian Central Asia*. Baltimore: Johns Hopkins Press, 1954.

Sokolov, Andrei, ed. *Golos naroda: Pis'ma otkliki riadovykh sovetskikh grazhdan o sobytiiakh 1918–1932 gg*. Moscow: ROSSPEN, 1998.

Sokolov, Andrei, and Lewis H. Siegelbaum, eds. *Stalinism as a Way of Life: A Narrative in Documents*. New Haven, CT and London: Yale University Press, 2001.

Solomon, Peter H. *Soviet Criminal Justice under Stalin*, Cambridge Russian, Soviet and Post-Soviet Studies. New York: Cambridge University Press, 1996.

Solomon, Susan Gross. "The Demographic Argument in Soviet Debates over the Legalization of Abortion in the 1920s." *Cahiers du Monde russe et soviétique* 33 (1992): 59–82.

———. "The Soviet Legalization of Abortion in German Medical Discourse: A Study of the Use of Selective Perceptions in Cross-Cultural Scientific Relations." *Social Studies of Science* 22 (1992): 455–85.

Solzhenitsyn, Aleksandr Isaevich, Edward E. Ericson, and Daniel J. Mahoney. *The Solzhenitsyn Reader: New and Essential Writings, 1947–2005*. Wilmington, DE: ISI Books, 2006.

Stakhanov, A. G. *Rasskaz o moei zhizni*. Moscow: Gos. sots-ekon izd-vo, 1937.

Stalin, I.V. (Joseph). *O nekotorykh voprosakh istorii bol'shevizma: Pis'mo v redaktsiiu zhurnala "Proletarskaia revoliutsiia."* Moscow: "Moskovskii rabochii," 1931.

———. *O proekte konstitutsii Soiuza SSR: Doklad na chrezvychainom VIII vsesoiuznom s"ezde Sovetov, 25 noiabria 1936 g.* Moscow: Partizdat TSK VKP(b), 1936.

———. *O Velikoi Otechestvennoi voine Sovetskogo Soiuza*. Moscow: Izd-vo "Kraft," 2002.

———. *Sochineniia*. 13 vols. Moscow: Gos. izd-vo polit. lit-ry, 1946.

———. *Sochineniia*, ed. Robert H. McNeal. 3 vols (1/14-3/16). Hoover Institution Foreign Language Publications. Stanford, CA: The Hoover Institution on War, Revolution, and Peace, Stanford University, 1967.

Steinberg, Mark D. *Proletarian Imagination: Self, Modernity, and the Sacred in Russia, 1910–1925*. Ithaca, NY: Cornell University Press, 2002.

Steinwedel, Charles. "To Make a Difference: The Category of Ethnicity in Late Imperial Russian Politics 1861–1917." In *Russian Modernity: Politics, Knowledge, Practices*, edited by David L. Hoffmann and Yanni Kotsonis, 67–86. New York: St. Martin's Press, 2000.

Stites, Richard. *Revolutionary Dreams: Utopian Vision and Experimental Life in the Russian Revolution*. New York: Oxford University Press, 1989.

Stites, Richard, ed. *Culture and Entertainment in Wartime Russia*. Bloomington: Indiana University Press, 1995.

Stone, Norman. *The Eastern Front, 1914–1917*. London: Penguin, 1998.

Streim, Alfred. *Sowjetische Gefangene in Hitlers Vernichtungskrieg: Berichte und Dokumente, 1941–1945*, Recht, Justiz, Zeitgeschehen. Heidelberg: Müller, 1982.

Strumilin, S. G. *Problemy ekonomiki truda*. Moscow: Gos. izd-vo polit. lit-ry, 1957.

Sword, Keith. *Deportation and Exile: Poles in the Soviet Union, 1939–48*, Studies in Russia & East Europe. London: Macmillan Press, 1994.

Temkin, Gabriel. *My Just War: The Memoir of a Jewish Red Army Soldier in World War II*. Novato, CA: Presidio, 1998.

Tendriakov, Vladimir. "Liudi ili neliudi." *Druzhba narodov*, no. 2 (1989): 114–44.

Thurston, Robert W. "Cauldrons of Loyalty and Betrayal: Soviet Soldiers' Behavior, 1941 and 1945." In *The People's War: Responses to World War II in the Soviet Union*, edited by Robert Thurston and Bernd Bonwetsch, 235–57. Urbana and Chicago: University of Illinois Press, 2000.

Thurston, Robert W. and Bernd Bonwetsch, eds. *The People's War: Responses to World War II in the Soviet Union*. Urbana and Chicago: University of Illinois Press, 2000.

Todes, Daniel Philip. *Darwin without Malthus: The Struggle for Existence in Russian Evolutionary Thought*, Monographs on the History and Philosophy of Biology. Oxford: Oxford University Press, 1989.

Todorov, Vladislav. *Red Square, Black Square: Organon for Revolutionary Imagination*, SUNY Series, The Margins of Literature. Albany, NY: State University of New York Press, 1995.

Tolz, Vera. "New Information about the Deportation of Ethnic Groups in the USSR during World War 2." In *World War 2 and the Soviet People*, edited by John Gordon Garrard and Carol Garrard, 161–79. New York: St. Martin's Press, 1993.

Torchinov, V. A., and Leontiuk A. M. *Vokrug Stalina: Istoriko-biograficheskii spravochnik*. Sankt-Peterburg: Filologicheskii fakul'tet Sankt-Peterburgskogo gos. universitet, 2000.

Trud v SSSR: statisticheskii sbornik. Moscow: "Statistika," 1968.

Tsfasman, A. B. "Pervaia mirovaia voina i evrei Rossii 1914–1917." In *Chelovek i voina: Voina kak iavlenie kul'tury*, edited by I. V. Narskii and O. Iu. Nikonova, 171–80. Moscow: AIRO-XX, 2001.

Tucker, Robert C. *The Soviet Political Mind: Stalinism and Post-Stalin Change*. Rev. ed. New York: Norton, 1971.

———. "Stalinism as Revolution from Above." In *Stalinism: Essays in Historical Interpretation*, edited by Robert C. Tucker, 77–108. New York: Norton, 1977.

Usenbaev, Kushbek, ed. *Vosstanie 1916 goda v Kirgizii*. Frunze: "Ilim," 1967.

Ustinkin, S.V. "Apparat vlasti i mekhanizm upravleniia obschestva." In *Obschestvo i vlast': Rossiiskaia provintsiia: 1930 g. - iun' 1941 g.*, vol. 2, edited by A. N. Sakharov et al. Moscow: Institut rossiiskoi istorii RAN, 2002.

Ustrialov, N. *Pod znakom revoliutsii*. 2nd rev. ed. Kharbin: Poligraf, 1927.

Vasil'iev, Valery. "Vinnitsa Oblast." In *Centre-Local Relations in the Stalinist State 1928–1941*, edited by E. A. Rees, 65–91. Basingstoke: Palgrave, 2002.

Velikaia Otechestvennaia voina 1941–1945, Kniga 4: Narod i voina. Moscow: Nauka, 1999.

Venediktov, Anatolii Vasil'evich. *Organizatsiia gosudarstvennoi promyslennosti v SSSR*. 2 vols. 2. *1921–1934*. Leningrad: Izdat. Leningrads. Univ., 1961.

Vert [Werth] N., and S. V. Mironenko, eds. *Massovye repressii v SSSR*. Vol. 1, Istoriia stalinskogo GULAGa. Moscow: ROSSPEN, 2004.

Viola, Lynne. *The Best Sons of the Fatherland: Workers in the Vanguard of Soviet Collectivization*. New York: Oxford University Press, 1987.

———. *The Unknown Gulag: The Lost World of Stalin's Special Settlements*. Oxford and New York: Oxford University Press, 2007.

Vishnevskii, Vsevolod. *Sobranie sochinenii v 5-ti tomakh (dopolnitel'nyi): Vystupleniia i radiorechi: Zapisnye knizhki, Pis'ma*. 6 vols. Vol. 6. Moscow: Gos. izd-vo khudozh. lit-ry, 1961.

Vitukhovskaia, M., ed. *Na korme vremeni: Interv'iu s leningradtsami 1930-kh godov*. St. Petersburg: Zhurnal "Neva," 2000.

Volkov, Vadim. "The Concept of Kul'turnost': Notes on the Stalinist Civilizing Process." In Fitzpatrick, ed., *Stalinism: New Directions*, 210–30. London: Routledge, 2000.

Von Geldern, James, and Richard Stites, eds. *Mass Culture in Soviet Russia: Tales, Poems, Songs, Movies, Plays, and Folklore, 1917–1953*. Bloomington: Indiana University Press, 1995.

Wade, Rex A., ed. *The Triumph of Bolshevism, 1917–1919*, Vol. 1, Documents of Soviet History. Gulf Breeze, FL: Academic International Press, 1991.

Weiner, Amir. "In the Long Shadow of War: The Second World War and the Soviet and Post-Soviet World." *Diplomatic History* 25, no. 3 (2001): 443–56.

_____. *Making Sense of War: The Second World War and the Fate of the Bolshevik Revolution*. Princeton, NJ: Princeton University Press, 2001.

_____. "Nature, Nurture, and Memory in a Socialist Utopia: Delineating the Soviet Socio-Ethnic Body in the Age of Socialism." *American Historical Review* 104, no. 4 (1999): 1114–55.

_____. "Nothing by Certainty." *Slavic Review* 61, no. 1 (2002): 44–53.

_____. "Saving Private Ivan: From What, Why, and How?" *Kritika: Explorations in Russian and Eurasian History* 1, no. 2 (2000): 305–36.

_____. "Something to Die for, A Lot to Kill for: The Soviet System and the Brutalization of Warfarre." In *The Barbarization of Warfare*, edited by George Kassimeris, 101–25. New York: New York University Press, 2004.

Weinerman, Eli "Racism, Racial Prejudice and the Jews in Late Imperial Russia." *Ethnic and Racial Studies* 17 (1994): 442–95.

Weisenberg, Alexander. *Hexensabbat: Russland im Schmelztiegel der Säuberungern*. Frankfurt am Main: Verlag der Frankfurter Hefte, 1951.

Weitz, Eric D. "Racial Politics without the Concept of Race." *Slavic Review* 61, no. 1 (2002): 1–29.

Werth, Alexander. *Russia at War, 1941–1945*. 2nd ed. New York: Carroll & Graf, 2000.

Werth, Nicolas. "A State against Its People: Violence, Repression, and Terror in the Soviet Union." In *The Black Book of Communism: Crime, Terror, Repression*, edited by Stéphane Courtois, trans. Jonathan Murphy and Mark Kramer, Cambridge, MA: Harvard University Press, 1999, 33–269.

_____. *Cannibal Island: Death in a Siberian Gulag*. Translated by Steven Rendall, Human Rights and Crimes against Humanity. Princeton, NJ: Princeton University Press, 2007.

_____. "Déplacés spéciaux et colons de travail dans la société stalinienne." *XXème Siècle. Revue d'Histoire* 54 (2001): 34–50.

_____. *Ein Staat gegen sein Volk: Das Schwarzbuch des Kommunismus – Sowjetunion*. Translated by Bertold Galli, Serie Piper. Munich: Piper, 2002.

_____. "Repenser la Grande Terreur." *Le Débat* 122 (2002): 116–43.

Willerton, John. *Patronage and Politics in the USSR*, Soviet and East European Studies. Cambridge: Cambridge University Press, 1992.

Wood, Elizabeth A. *The Baba and the Comrade: Gender and Politics in Revolutionary Russia*, Indiana-Michigan Series in Russian and East European Studies. Bloomington: Indiana University Press, 1997.

Yekelchyk, Serhy. *Stalin's Empire of Memory: Russian-Ukrainian Relations in the Soviet Historical Imagination*. Toronto: University of Toronto Press, 2004.

_____. "Stalinist Patriotism as Imperial Discourse: Reconciling the Ukrainian and Russian 'Heroic' Pasts,' 1939–1945." Paper to Midwest Russian History Workshop, University of Chicago, 2000.

Youngblood, Denise J. *Russian War Films: On the Cinema Front, 1914–2005*, Modern War Series. Lawrence: University Press of Kansas, 2007.

Zagorul'ko, Maksim Matveevich, ed. *Voennoplennye v SSSR 1939–1956: Dokumenty i materialy*. Moscow: Logos, 2000.

Zakir, A. "Zemel'naia politika v kolkhoznom dvizhenii sredi koreitsev." *Revoliutsiia i natsional'nosti* 2–3 (1931): 76–81.

Zarubinsky, Oleg A. "The 'Red' Partisan Movement in Ukraine during World War II: A Contemporary Assessment." *Journal of Slavic Military Studies* 9 (1996): 399–416.

Zeidler, Manfred. *Kriegsende im Osten: Die Rote Armee und die Besetzung Deutschlands östlich von Oder und Neisse 1944/45*. Munich: Oldenbourg, 1996.

Zemskov, V. N. "Spetsposelentsy (po dokumentatsii NKVD-MVD SSSR)." *Sotsiologicheskie issledovaniia* 11 (1990): 3–17.

———. *Spetsposelentsy v SSSR, 1930–1960*. Moscow: "Nauka," 2003.

———. "Zakliuchennye, spetsposelentsy, ssyl'noposelentsy, ssyl'nye i vyslannye: Statistiko-geograficheskii aspekt." *Istoriia SSSR*, no. 5 (1991): 151–65.

Zhiromskaia, V. B., I. N. Kiselev, and Iu. A. Poliakov. *Polveka pod grifom "sekretno": Vsesoiuznaia perepis' naseleniia 1937 goda*. Moscow: "Nauka," 1996.

Zhukov, Innokenty. "Voyage of the Red Star Pioneer Troop to Wonderland (1924)." In *Mass Culture in Soviet Russia: Tales, Poems, Songs, Movies, Plays, and Folklore, 1917–53*, edited by James von Geldern and Richard Stites, 90–112. Bloomington and Indianapolis: Indiana University Press, 1995.

Zima, V. F. *Golod v SSSR 1946–1947 godov: Proiskhozhdenie i posledstviia*. Moscow: In-t rossiiskoi istorii, 1996.

Zolotarev, V. A., ed., *Glavnye politicheskie organy vooruzhennykh sil SSSR v Velikoi Otechestvennoi voine 1941–1945 gg. Dokumenty i materialy*. Vol. 17–6, Russkii Arkhiv. Velikaia Otechestvennaia Moscow: Terra, 1996.

Filmography

The Great Dictator. Chaplin, Charlie, Paulette Goddard, Jack Oakie, Reginald Gardiner, and Henry Daniell. (126 min.) VHS. New York: CBS Fox Video, 1992.

Okraina (The Outskirts). Directed by Petr Lutsik. Performances by Aleksei Samoriadov, Iurii Dubrovin, Nikolai Olialin, and Aleksei Vanin. (95 min.), DVD. Chicago: Facets Video, 2004.

The Russian Front. Directed by John Erikson and Michael Leighton. (182 min.) 4 videocassettes. Lamancha and Cromwell Productions, 1998.

Sem'ia Oppengeim [The Oppenheim Family]. Based on the novel by Lion Feuchtwanger, adapted for the screen by Serafima Roshal'. Directed by Grigorii Roshal'. (99 min.) VHS. Moscow: Mosfilm, 2002.

Shtrafbat [Penal Battalion]. Directed by Nikolaj Dostal'. Performances by Aleksei Serebriakov, Iurii Stepanov and Aleksandr Bashirov. (525 min.). Russia: Kachestvo DVD, 2004.

Svoi [Our Own], Directed by Dmitrii Meskhiev. Performances by Valentin Chernykh, Bohdan Stupka, Konstantin Khabenskii, Sergei Garmash, and Mikhail Mikhalkova, Anna Kurashov and Sviatoslav Evlanov. (105 min.), DVD. Moscow: ORT Video, 2004.

Index

4953096R00320

Printed in Germany
by Amazon Distribution
GmbH, Leipzig